THE ARDEN SHAKESPEARE

THIRD SERIES
General Editors: Richard Proudfoot, Ann Thompson,
David Scott Kastan and H.R. Woudhuysen

THE WINTER'S TALE

THE ARDEN SHAKESPEARE

* Second series

THE
WINTER'S TALE

Edited by
JOHN PITCHER

Arden Shakespeare

1 3 5 7 9 10 8 6 4 2

This edition of *The Winter's Tale* by John Pitcher first published
2010 by the Arden Shakespeare

Editorial matter copyright © 2010 John Pitcher

Arden Shakespeare is an imprint of Methuen Drama

Methuen Drama
A & C Black Publishers Ltd
36 Soho Square
London W1D 3QY
www.methuendrama.com
www.ardenshakespeare.com

A CIP catalogue record for this book is available from the British
Library
ISBN: 9781903436349 (hbk)
ISBN: 9781903436356 (pbk)

The general editors of the Arden Shakespeare have been
W.J. Craig and R.H. Case (first series 1899-1944)
Una Ellis-Fermor, Harold F. Brooks, Harold Jenkins and
Brian Morris (second series 1946-82)

Present general editors (third series)
Richard Proudfoot, Ann Thompson, David Scott Kastan and
H.R. Woudhuysen

Typeset by DC Graphic Design Ltd

Printed by Zrinski, Croatia

The Editor

John Pitcher is an Official Fellow of St John's College, Oxford, and University Lecturer in English at Oxford University. His research interests are in early modern poetry and drama. His publications include editions of Francis Bacon's *Essays* for Penguin Classics and *Cymbeline* for the Penguin Shakespeare. He is finishing a four-volume Oxford English Texts edition of the Elizabethan poet Samuel Daniel.

For love is strong as death; jealousy is cruel as the grave: the coals thereof are fiery coals, and a most vehement flame.

Song of Solomon

And such, as yet once more I trust to have
Full sight of her in heaven without restraint,
Came vested all in white, pure as her mind.

John Milton

These are not things transformed.
Yet we are shaken by them as if they were.
We reason about them with a later reason.

Wallace Stevens

CONTENTS

Contents

ILLUSTRATIONS

GENERAL EDITORS'
PREFACE

The earliest volume in the first Arden series, Edward Dowden's *Hamlet*, was published in 1899. Since then the Arden Shakespeare has been widely acknowledged as the pre-eminent Shakespeare edition, valued by scholars, students, actors and 'the great variety of readers' alike for its clearly presented and reliable texts, its full annotation and its richly informative introductions.

In the third Arden series we seek to maintain these well-established qualities and general characteristics, preserving our predecessors' commitment to presenting the play as it has been shaped in history. Each volume necessarily has its own particular emphasis which reflects the unique possibilities and problems posed by the work in question, and the series as a whole seeks to maintain the highest standards of scholarship, combined with attractive and accessible presentation.

Newly edited from the original Quarto and Folio editions, texts are presented in fully modernized form, with a textual apparatus that records all substantial divergences from those early printings. The notes and introductions focus on the conditions and possibilities of meaning that editors, critics and performers (on stage and screen) have discovered in the play. While building upon the rich history of scholarly activity that has long shaped our understanding of Shakespeare's works, this third series of the Arden Shakespeare is enlivened by a new generation's encounter with Shakespeare.

THE TEXT

On each page of the play itself, readers will find a passage of text supported by commentary and textual notes. Act and scene divisions (seldom present in the early editions and often the product of eighteenth-century or later scholarship) have been retained for ease of reference, but have been given less prominence than in previous series. Editorial indications of location of the action have been removed to the textual notes or commentary.

In the text itself, unfamiliar typographic conventions have been avoided in order to minimize obstacles to the reader. Elided forms in the early texts are spelt out in full in verse lines wherever they indicate a usual twenty-first century pronunciation that requires no special indication and wherever they occur in prose (except where they indicate non-standard pronunciation). In verse speeches, marks of elision are retained where they are necessary guides to the scansion and pronunciation of the line. Final -ed in past tense and participial forms of verbs is always printed as -ed, without accent, never as -'d, but wherever the required pronunciation diverges from modern usage a note in the commentary draws attention to the fact. Where the final -ed should be given syllabic value contrary to modern usage, e.g.

> Doth Silvia know that I am banished?
> (*TGV* 3.1.214)

the note will take the form

    214 **banished** banishèd

Conventional lineation of divided verse lines shared by two or more speakers has been reconsidered and sometimes rearranged. Except for the familiar *Exit* and *Exeunt*, Latin forms in stage directions and speech prefixes have been translated into English and the original Latin forms recorded in the textual notes.

COMMENTARY AND TEXTUAL NOTES

Notes in the commentary, for which a major source will be the *Oxford English Dictionary*, offer glossarial and other explication of verbal difficulties; they may also include discussion of points of interpretation and, in relevant cases, substantial extracts from Shakespeare's source material. Editors will not usually offer glossarial notes for words adequately defined in the latest edition of *The Concise Oxford Dictionary* or *Merriam-Webster's Collegiate Dictionary*, but in cases of doubt they will include notes. Attention, however, will be drawn to places where more than one likely interpretation can be proposed and to significant verbal and syntactic complexity. Notes preceded by * discuss editorial emendations or variant readings from the early edition(s) on which the text is based.

Headnotes to acts or scenes discuss, where appropriate, questions of scene location, Shakespeare's handling of his source materials, and major difficulties of staging. The list of roles (so headed to emphasize the play's status as a text for performance) is also considered in the commentary notes. These may include comment on plausible patterns of casting with the resources of an Elizabethan or Jacobean acting company and also on any variation in the description of roles in their speech prefixes in the early editions.

The textual notes are designed to let readers know when the edited text diverges from the early edition(s) or manuscript sources on which it is based. Wherever this happens the note will record the rejected reading of the early edition(s), in original spelling, and the source of the reading adopted in this edition. Other forms from the early edition(s) recorded in these notes will include some spellings of particular interest or significance and original forms of translated stage directions. Where two or more early editions are involved, for instance with *Othello*, the notes also record all important differences between them. The textual notes take a form that has been in use since the nineteenth century. This comprises, first: line reference, reading adopted in the text and closing square bracket; then: abbreviated reference, in italic, to the earliest edition to adopt the accepted reading, italic semicolon and noteworthy alternative reading(s), each with abbreviated italic reference to its source.

Conventions used in these textual notes include the following. The solidus / is used, in notes quoting verse or discussing verse lining, to indicate line endings. Distinctive spellings of the basic text (Q or F) follow the square bracket without indication of source and are enclosed in italic brackets. Names enclosed in italic brackets indicate originators of conjectural emendations when these did not originate in an edition of the text, or when the named edition records a conjecture not accepted into its text. Stage directions (SDs) are referred to by the number of the line within or immediately after which they are placed. Line numbers with a decimal point relate to centred entry SDs not falling within a verse line and to SDs more than one line long, with the number after the point indicating the line within the SD: e.g. 78.4 refers to the fourth line of the SD following line 78. Lines of SDs at the start of a scene are numbered 0.1, 0.2, etc. Where only a line number precedes a square bracket, e.g. 128], the note relates to the whole line; where SD is added to the number, it relates to the whole of a SD within or immediately following the line. Speech prefixes (SPs) follow similar conventions, 203 SP] referring to the speaker's name for line 203. Where a SP reference takes the form e.g. 38+ SP, it relates to all subsequent speeches assigned to that speaker in the scene in question.

Where, as with *King Henry V*, one of the early editions is a so-called 'bad quarto' (that is, a text either heavily adapted, or reconstructed from memory, or both), the divergences from the present edition are too great to be recorded in full in the notes. In these cases, with the exception of *Hamlet*, which prints an edited text of the quarto of 1603, the editions will include a reduced photographic facsimile of the 'bad quarto' in an appendix.

INTRODUCTION

Both the introduction and the commentary are designed to present the plays as texts for performance, and make appropriate reference to stage, film and television versions, as well as introducing the reader to the range of critical approaches to the plays. They discuss the history of the reception of the texts within the theatre and scholarship and beyond, investigating the interdependency of the literary text and the surrounding 'cultural text' both at the time of the original production of Shakespeare's works and during their long and rich afterlife.

PREFACE

I am sure I am not the first editor to have a mix of feelings as they complete an Arden edition – glad to see it gone, but regretful as it goes, or as Shakespeare put it, looking with one eye auspicious, the other dropping. Some of the regret, which every editor feels, is that there is more I might have done, glossing this line more succinctly, explaining that idea more carefully. What I have missed or misunderstood is entirely my fault, because I've had the best examples before me. The modern editions of *The Winter's Tale* I have drawn on – especially Arden, Cambridge and Oxford – are full of learning and good judgement, and the 2005 New Variorum edition is a hugely impressive work of scholarship. I am indebted to all the earlier editions of the play.

I owe individuals just as much. Richard Proudfoot invited me to edit *The Winter's Tale*, and he has forgiven my ignorance and dilatoriness more times than I care to remember. His guidance on the commentary in particular was invaluable. I trust he knows how important his support has been. Ann Thompson made tactful, decisive interventions about the shape of the Introduction; whatever clarity it has now is in large part due to her. Henry Woudhuysen read everything here in many drafts, with unnerving perspicacity and attention to detail. There were times when he asked for more and yet more from me (be clearer, be consistent, make the argument tauter) and I could cheerfully have wrung his neck. But he has been an exemplary general editor and an outstanding friend: he has made the edition much, much better than it would have been without him.

This is equally true of Hannah Hyam, who has copy-edited the edition. I don't exaggerate when I say that in places Hannah has become my co-editor, quizzing, correcting and gently nudging me towards what she's sure I meant to say. I am deeply grateful to her. Lizzy Emerson, at an earlier stage, read the whole edition in draft. Her improvements and encouragement helped no end. My debt to the Arden commissioning editors is considerable – first to Jane Armstrong, then to Jessica Hodge and latterly to Margaret Bartley. I hope they will think their persistence with me has been worth it.

Special thanks are due to Christopher Wilson, who transformed what I had said about the music into something far more convincing. He has generously provided the scores, assisted by his colleague Michael Fletcher in the Salmon Grove Studios in the University of Hull. Other friends and colleagues have assisted, with help and advice of various kinds: Margaret Berrill, Tony Boyce, Anna Brewer, Terence Cave, Susan Cerasano, David Cunnington, Malcolm Davies, Sarah Dewar-Watson, Jason Lawrence, Michael Leslie, Charlotte Loveridge, John Montgomery, Matthew Nichols, Pat Parker, Mike Purcell, Frank Romany, Linden Stafford and Francis Warner.

Bob Welch – poet, novelist and critic – has been a star I've set my course by for many years, and in the work for this edition too. I am grateful for his friendship. The person to whom I owe most is Alexandra; in Mandelshtam's words, 'the sea and Homer – all is moved by love'.

John Pitcher
St John's College, Oxford

INTRODUCTION

Shakespeare wrote *The Winter's Tale* at the end of his career, in late 1610. He had already written more than thirty plays, which had made him well known to theatre-goers and at court. In his first ten years, until about 1599, he wrote mainly comedies and histories, but then, for another decade, from *Hamlet* onwards, he turned to tragedy. He became particularly interested in mixing genres, so that his later comedies have darker, potentially tragic themes and their endings are less and less happy. In this period, in part because of his plays, the status and sophistication of public stage drama rose considerably. It was no longer unthinkable that a common player like Shakespeare might write about themes and debate questions that had long been reserved for court poetry and for the social elite. In his last five years as a writer, Shakespeare enlarged still further what the public might see, in a series of philosophical romance plays, at the centre of which was the group *Cymbeline*, *The Winter's Tale* and *The Tempest*.

To understand *The Winter's Tale* we need to look first at its generic and intellectual framework. From this we can see at once how intriguing a play it is. Everyone knows it ends with a statue that comes to life, but Shakespeare won't let us be fully sure what we have seen. Did Hermione die, and this is her reanimation? Or was she just hidden, waiting, numbed and dead to the world? This is the question which this Introduction begins with (in 'Death and art'), and from which everything else flows. The play has a daring generic shape (a tragedy and a comedy held together at mid-point), which Shakespeare developed out of *King Lear* and out of Greek tragedy – but so transformed that it was no longer tragedy, where a wronged queen must die, but had become romance, in which she is able to die and not die ('Tragedy into romance').

The Winter's Tale is alive with such romance impossibilities. They are the stuff of childhood dreaming and wish fulfilment;

in a more sinister form they supply the fantasies we see in adult males who refuse to grow out of controlling everyone and knowing everything (discussed in 'Childhood'). Shakespeare leads us from the obsession and self-infantilizing in this – Leontes' condition – into the biggest of Renaissance philosophical questions. What can be known? Is there truly a reality outside the mind that is Nature ('Knowledge')? And what *is* Nature? Simply the physical matter that God gave humankind, irretrievably ruined by sin? Or the space that the human mind, through art, might reshape triumphantly in its own image ('Pastorals' and 'Nature and art')?

These are the big questions behind everything that happens in *The Winter's Tale*. Of special importance, because it is a drama, is the psychological state known in the Renaissance as 'Wonder', by which the mind, according to philosophers and critics, understood what was around it. The function of wonder in art, and Shakespeare's reflections on his own dramatic art, are considered in general terms in 'Rules and types in drama' and more specifically in 'Disguising'. This part of the Introduction concludes with 'Time', and its place in the scheme of things.

DEATH AND ART

In the past hundred years human beings have learnt how to postpone death. Drugs and surgery slow the progress of illness and decay, and resuscitation can return people to life even after their heart stops. However, the point when the body actually dies is still our horizon, whatever medical research may make possible in the future.

In Shakespeare's England, there were no antibiotics or anaesthetics and men and women often died early, messily and in pain – in childbirth or from a gangrenous wound or the plague. The Church said that there was eternal life in the next world, but getting through the door to it, in the final moment, wasn't always easy. One response was to say that how you died showed who you were: a calm, courageous end could complete a well-lived life, or put right a misguided one. 'Nothing in his life became him like the leaving it' is said of a traitor facing execution in *Macbeth*. Thinking and talking about death was a national pastime. Not to do so was undutiful, suggesting that you were too much in love with the world's transient pleasures. Despite Protestant teaching, however, Elizabethans couldn't stop thinking about the other possibility, that they might live on as ghosts, neither in heaven nor in hell. The orthodox view was that this was a remnant of unreformed Catholic England – only superstitious papists believed it – but no one in the lower orders paid any attention. Ghosts had bodies, albeit spectral ones, that had survived death.

This outlook gave Shakespeare an opportunity. His first ghosts, eleven people murdered by Richard III, came onstage and cursed the king as he slept. Next it was Caesar's ghost (appearing to Brutus not in a dream but as he sat wide awake), and after that, Old Hamlet, and Banquo in *Macbeth*, spectres who sometimes couldn't be seen by anyone but the tormented hero. Ghosts thrilled audiences. They were revengers, unreal but substantial enough to be played by real actors. Equally enthralling were Shakespeare's other survivors of death, the women who only seemed dead, or who came back to life, unaccountably. Juliet, and Imogen (*Cymbeline*), take mysterious drugs that show them dead, and Thaisa (*Pericles*) is placed in a coffin, her life functions gone, yet they all wake up. Othello stifles Desdemona to death, yet she returns, for a moment, struggling for breath, in part absolving her murderer. Hero in *Much Ado About Nothing* swoons at the altar, but her death, which had convinced her detractors, turns out to be feigned.

For twenty years Shakespeare kept the ghosts separate from the women who wouldn't die. Then at the end of his career he brought them together in *The Winter's Tale*, in the same person, the queen Hermione. In Act 3, when she hears her son is dead, Hermione collapses and is carried offstage, where, according to Paulina, she dies (3.2.200; see Fig. 1). In the next scene her death

1 'Thou canst not speak too much. I have deserved / All tongues to talk their bitterest' (3.2.212–13). Eileen Atkins as Paulina and Tim Piggott-Smith as Leontes, at the news that his wife and son are dead, in the 1988 National Theatre production, directed by Peter Hall. The designer, Alison Chitty, modelled Sicilia on the neoclassical English court of the 1630s, with Van Dyck settings, lace and silk costumes, and statues on pedestals (as here): a place where a miracle of art might, in the end, outdo Nature

is confirmed for the audience by Antigonus' description of the figure that appeared to him in a dream – or was he awake and visited by the spirit of the dead queen, a revenant (3.3.15–18, 36–8)? The spectre of Hermione, all in white, bowed to him, wept and gasped before it spoke. He must take her baby to Bohemia, it said, and give her the name Perdita, since the child was 'counted lost for ever' (32; see List of Roles, 8n.). For his part in the crime against Perdita, it prophesied that Antigonus would never see his wife again.

This is as far as Shakespeare would go. Spirits of dead women were rarely shown on the Elizabethan stage, and female wraiths and revengers were rarer still (Dolan, 219–26). By describing but not showing it, he kept the spectre's secret. Was it an unholy apparition, or a figment of Antigonus' guilty mind, or an instrument of Apollo and providence, protecting the child? Or was there a woman's murderous resentment and 'fury' beneath its sorrow and beauty (3.3.20–5)? Whatever it is, this offstage dream spectre is as real and necessary as any ghost in Shakespeare, and it proves, almost certainly we say, that Hermione is dead.

Yet despite this, at the end of the play, a marvellous statue of the queen comes to life in Paulina's chapel (5.3.99–103). Common sense tells us that this is impossible. A woman can't literally die, reappear as a spirit and then be alive again. This is even more implausible than a statue becoming a living person. Surely we know the truth. Hermione, aided by Paulina, went into hiding in 3.2, to wait, preserving herself, she says, for her daughter's return (5.3.125–8). In a play full of deceptions – Autolycus' disguises, the Shepherd concealing how Perdita was found – Hermione's death is the final grand illusion that audiences need to believe in, up to the point of un-enchantment in 5.3, when the statue moves.

But if Hermione isn't dead, where did that creature in white come from, directing Antigonus, naming Perdita, and foretelling his death? Ghosts by convention could do such things, but only when the person was dead and buried. We may say the plot requires the apparition to intervene, and the oracle too (*'the king shall live without an heir if that which is lost be not found'*, 3.2.132–3). What matters is Shakespeare's art – his completion of the story – rather than death or ghosts. Yet the feeling remains that he wanted this perplexing contradiction to stay with us, particularly at certain moments: in Act 5, for instance, when Leontes imagines how, were he to remarry, Hermione's spirit would assume her dead body and stalk the stage, telling him, horribly, to murder his new wife (5.1.56–62).

Some critics try to explain away the contradiction because they see it is irrational and intractable. They speculate that in the first version of the play (a guess, for which there is no solid evidence) Hermione really did die; when Shakespeare revised it to bring her back to life he failed to rewrite Antigonus' dream (see pp. 90–1). Others see in the contradiction – Hermione surpassing the deadness of the spectre and the statue, her life outdoing un-life – the grounds for a redemptive miracle, modelled on the Christian mystery of resurrection.

Romance is the literary form in which contradictions like these thrive, and we should take our cue from it with *The Winter's Tale*. In romance a green knight can be beheaded, ride away with the head under his arm and reappear a bit later, his head back on, as an impish magical lord. Romance lets us have it both ways: in modern terms the counterfactuals (the what if) persist alongside the facts (the what happened). Hermione, in romance, is and isn't dead; she exists as a factual woman but also a counterfactual spectre and statue.

Romance is the place for delusion, too, when it is hard to bear the difference between what is and what you want there to be. After the trial in Act 3 Leontes believes he has killed all his family, so in romance terms what might his best 'counterfactual' dream be? That he might see his dead wife again in the pagan hereafter, where she might return, gentle and unvengeful, to pardon his polluting and murdering her? Shakespeare's spectre isn't like this, however, and it isn't Leontes that dreams or sees it. According to romance logic, the creature that Antigonus encounters – a Fury from Greek tragedy as much as a Kindly One – is the displaced, distorted version of the forgiving Hermione that Leontes wished for.

A full response to *The Winter's Tale*, not just to rich strands of it in isolation (spectral emanations from a guilty mind or the indestructibility of Nature), requires that we look again at what can and can't be, this side of death and beyond, and what human hearts and minds are capable of. In *All's Well That Ends Well*, a play Shakespeare wrote six or seven years before *The Winter's Tale*, the heroine Helena is a wise healer. The king she wants to heal won't believe she can cure his fatal sickness, because every rational treatment has been attempted, so she tells him to start trusting in the miraculous sixth sense her art can wake inside him. He does what she says and he is healed. This is the art of recuperation, in the face of impossibility, that audiences are urged to experience in *The Winter's Tale*. As Helena puts it, in a cunning woman's riddle,

> what impossibility would slay
> In common sense, sense saves another way.
> (*AW* 2.1.176–7)

*

At the date of *The Winter's Tale*, there was another sense in which art might triumph over death. Critics and philosophers, following the ancients, claimed that a really great artist – poet, painter or sculptor – if he were true to Nature, could create works of art that would live on after his own death. In his *Sonnets* Shakespeare shows that he was acutely aware of this claim. When he died, contemporaries praised him in these very terms. Ben Jonson, in his memorial poem prefacing the First Folio of 1623, said of Shakespeare that he had matched everything in Greek and Roman drama; he was 'not of an age, but for all time'.

For Renaissance writers, fame after death came from outdoing predecessors. The classical poet Virgil wrote pastorals about shepherds and the country life, so Elizabethan writers, if they wanted to be as famous as Virgil and to live as long in people's memory – conquering Time as he had – must also write pastorals, to better him if they could. Getting literary fame was competitive and involved theft as well as obligation. The most impressive way of achieving immortality was to create something that earlier artists had attempted but failed in. This is what Giulio Romano in *The Winter's Tale* is said to have done. His statue of Hermione is so lifelike that 'they say one would speak to her and stand in hope of answer' (5.2.98–9).

Shakespeare appears to have invested aspects of his own identity in these themes of creativity, theft and life-giving in *The Winter's Tale*. He was forty-six when he wrote the play, very likely the same age as the protagonist Leontes when it ends (see List of Roles, 1 and 2nn.). This doesn't mean that Shakespeare thought of himself as Leontes, but it does emphasize the unsettling parallel between the king's perverse imaginings, whereby he denies everything that is real, and the artist's impulse to outdo Nature. Shakespeare's desire for fame, by writing something never accomplished before, is also visible in *The Winter's Tale*; indeed his ambition gives the play its novel tragicomic shape. It begins as a tragedy of manners – jealousy and pathology inside a love triangle – which turns, with a comic step-change, into a philosophical romance, an enquiry into what in *King Lear* is called the 'mystery of things' (5.3.16), which only discloses itself because of tragedy.

It is in his choice of materials for this hybrid that Shakespeare the writer shows himself most openly. The plot in the first half of the play he took from a romance novel by his contemporary, Robert Greene (1558–92). The philosophical and high aesthetic elements in the second half (the fertility princess, the statue that breathes, the wife back from the dead) he borrowed from the Greek dramatist Euripides and the Roman poet Ovid. These writers provided Shakespeare with storylines and characters, but other elements too, their reputations and associations, which

8

he gathered into a personal mythology. Euripides was present as the father of tragicomedy, the form every Renaissance dramatist dreamed of mastering. Greene was there because early in the 1590s he – or rather the Greene persona someone else created after his death – had attacked Shakespeare as a money-grubbing plagiarist, an uneducated imitator who stole lines from more original writers. At the heart of the mythology was Ovid, from whom Shakespeare learnt that the gods gave immortality to artists who had enough skill to trust in their own genius.

We don't know how private Shakespeare's personal mythology was. Early audiences may have recognized more easily than we do the interconnections between writers and works. Autolycus, for instance, is from Ovid's *Metamorphoses*, but he looks suspiciously like Shakespeare's alter ego, a personification of the disreputable, greedy thief in Greene's slander – the same Greene from whom Shakespeare 'borrowed' another couple of works for *The Winter's Tale*. Perhaps the resemblance was obvious in 1611, or perhaps it was just a personal stimulus, or even a private joke Shakespeare used to breathe life into his fictions (Pitcher, 'Autolycus', 252–5, 265; Greenblatt, 371).

There is one area, however, where the mythology is more public. Ovid's story of Pygmalion, the sculptor who made a statue of a woman and fell in love with it, was ubiquitous in the Renaissance. It combined scandalous wish-fulfilment with piety: the perfect artist Pygmalion prayed to Venus for a perfect wife but she gave him his true desire, the statue brought to life. Shakespeare invokes Pygmalion in 5.3 of *The Winter's Tale* – incomparable art, a statue, a perfect wife and an appeal to faith – but there are differences. Pygmalion's statue is real marble until Venus transforms it, and Ovid says nothing of a wife restored to life. If Hermione never actually died, and her death and statue were just faked, probably the most we can say is that the pretence was humane and benign (a distant recollection of Ovid), because it insisted that faith, channelled through art, is vital to us even when we don't believe in miracles.

This is the prevailing modern view of the final scene of *The Winter's Tale*. No miracle happened, unless we think Hermione forgiving Leontes would be close to miraculous. Inside his personal mythology, however, Shakespeare may have had other ideas. The Pygmalion story was a comedy (the sculptor shaped the girl he wanted and a god blessed him with marriage), but the person who told the story in Ovid was the arch-poet Orpheus, whose own famous story was utterly tragic. When his wife Eurydice died, Orpheus went into hell to rescue her. The gods, moved by his singing, let her return with him, on condition he didn't look back as he led her up into life. His moment of weakness, turning to check she was there, then seeing her fall back into hell, brings him unending grief and regret. Not even a supreme artist can restore the dead to life unless he has complete faith in something. Orpheus, when he told the story of Pygmalion, the sculptor who never once doubted Venus, was compensating for his own tragedy with a comedy of new life or, as recent critics have seen it, with a life-giving romance (Crider, 155–62).

Orpheus' failure to overcome death is compensated for in *The Winter's Tale* as well. For this, Shakespeare, in a masterstroke, turned to another ancient romance about a wife who died, but who was brought back to life through a struggle and a profound ritual. This romance was Euripides' 'tragedy' *Alcestis*, in which death did indeed give way to art.

TRAGEDY INTO ROMANCE

The cycle of human life, from birth to death, has been a preoccupation in Western art for thirty centuries at least. In literature, writers from antiquity to the Renaissance examined this cycle, and attempts to evade or cheat it, through the different genres, or species of writing. In Greek tragedy, the cycle of life was shown as a dangerous riddle. 'What is it', the Sphinx asked Oedipus, 'that goes on four legs in the morning, two at noon, and three at the end of the day?' To us now, the answer is easy, 'a man' – crawling baby, an adult walking on two legs, old age leaning on a stick – but to the ancient Greeks such a riddle could only be solved by uncovering the mysterious continuity of human consciousness.

Beneath the puzzle about stages of self-awareness in a man's life was another mystery, about fate, the gods, and biology. Oedipus, unknowingly, murdered his father and slept with his mother, impregnating the womb he had come from (Sophocles, *Oedipus*, 242). Was it the gods who tricked him with their oracle, enjoying his painful realizations, or was there something in him that led ineluctably to his crimes? The shock of tragedy was that it mattered less which of these was true than that there was no escape from either. It was inevitable that Oedipus would be an incestuous parricide, a perversion of the life cycle, just as it was inevitable that Agamemnon, conqueror of Troy, would be murdered on the bathroom floor by his wife Clytemnestra, in revenge for his sacrificing his daughter Iphigenia (Aeschylus, *Agamemnon*, 160–6).

Agamemnon's sacrifice of Iphigenia, appeasing a dark goddess by cutting the girl's throat so that the Greeks might sail for Troy, was stubbornly tragic until Euripides drew out of the episode an astonishing new genre, which we now know as romance. Euripides wrote the story twice, refusing to let the girl die. In his first version, as the sword fell, the goddess Artemis snatched Iphigenia from death and hid her in Tauris, among the barbarous peoples of the Black Sea. There Iphigenia became a grisly priestess, forced to sacrifice foreigners landing on the shore, until one day her brother Orestes and cousin Pylades arrived, though she had no idea who they were. The first tragedy was averted, but it seemed that a yet more terrible one was about to close on the family: the rescued daughter would unwittingly murder her brother.

Escaping this seems impossible, yet Euripides makes it happen, by the most unbelievable chance. Iphigenia, trying to send a message to Orestes (standing beside her, though she doesn't know it), repeats aloud what she wants Pylades to memorize and to take to him. When she discloses who she is, in this provocatively roundabout way, a recognition scene begins between her and her brother, and the play changes direction completely. Iphigenia, suddenly a bold and clever liar (like all women, Orestes says), uses an elaborate ruse to carry off the holy statue of Artemis and get everyone home safely. The final part of the play, all narrated, is pure romance: tricking the barbarian king and his soldiers and scrambling on board a ship, only to have the waves draw them back, bit by bit, to their enemies on the beach. At last they are saved by Athene, who brings them the official view from Olympus – but who by now believes it or cares? – that everything that happened was ordained by Necessity (Euripides, *Tauris*, 176–8).

Euripides' great discovery was that tragedy, tested to destruction, did not necessarily become hyper-tragic but might develop into romance. His genres of tragedy and romance were not alternatives (one delving into painful mysteries about men and gods, the other encouraging escapes into fairy tales); rather they were successive stages in human feelings. Euripides was not the first Greek poet to make romance emerge out of another literary form (Homer had done it centuries earlier with epic and romance in the *Odyssey*), but his was the breakthrough in drama that helped free it from its roots in religious festival, and nearly freed it from the gods themselves.

Perhaps this is why, when Euripides wrote the Iphigenia story again, he treated it as an ethical problem, placing the sacrifice at the close of the play. This time, in Aulis, just as the priest struck at Iphigenia, she vanished and was replaced by an animal sacrifice, a mountain deer spattering the altar with its blood. It was said that the girl was with the gods, but no one knew for sure whether this meant she was dead (Euripides, *Aulis*, 425–6). It is possible that Euripides simply lost his nerve about what he had shown the gods to be. Romance, with its emphasis on impossible reversals, capriciousness, and the restorative function of fantasy and ceremony, threatened to make the gods of tragedy just one among many forces; it even made Necessity seem less inescapable.

Years earlier, long before Iphigenia, Euripides had looked at another part of the life cycle in his treatment of Alcestis, the wife and mother who agreed to die in place of her husband, Admetus. Much of *Alcestis* deals with preparations for her approaching death, and the guilt Admetus feels at her sacrifice, but the conclusion, once again, is high romance. When all seems lost, and Alcestis has died, the buffoon hero Hercules, half-god half-man, intervenes to save her; offstage he wrestles with Death at the funeral and snatches her back into life. The way she is returned to her husband is one of the most intriguing moments in ancient literature. Hercules leads her in, not as Alcestis, but as a veiled lady, another wife to replace the irreplaceable one. Admetus is horrified, insisting he'll never marry again, but Hercules persists. Be bold, he says, 'take her hand in yours', and then for Admetus comes recognition:

> O gods! O gods! What marvel is this? Is it true?
> I see my wife, her very self! – Or is this joy
> Some mockery sent by the gods to drive me mad?
> (Euripides, *Alcestis*, 78)

Throughout, Alcestis stays utterly silent: she says nothing about her husband's effort to believe that even death can be overcome.

Two thousand years after Euripides, in an open-air wooden theatre on the south bank of the Thames in London, the story of Alcestis surfaced again, in Shakespeare's plays, first in *Much Ado About Nothing* around 1600 (via an Italian novel), and then more openly a decade later, in *The Winter's Tale*. Hero, the heroine in *Much Ado*, appears to die from shock at being slandered by her husband-to-be on their wedding day. When she is returned to him, at the altar, Hero comes back not as herself, but disguised as her cousin, an exact double, whose face, like Alcestis', is hidden (*MA* 5.4.51.2). In *The Winter's Tale*, the slandered dead wife Hermione doesn't reappear as a living double; rather, as a statue that looks as she would have looked much older, that suddenly comes to life. In this version, a curtain concealing the statue replaces the veil, and Alcestis' silence in her reunion with Admetus is transformed into Hermione's mysteriously saying nothing to her husband when they are reunited, though she speaks to her daughter.

The Alcestis story reached Shakespeare through novels and poems and through Euripides' original play. It used to be said that because Shakespeare's Latin was limited, and his Greek even more so, he was unlikely to have read *Alcestis* in the original, or in a Latin translation. This is no longer tenable. His Greek probably wasn't good enough but *Alcestis*, like Euripides' other plays, was published in readable Latin versions several times in the sixteenth century. Shakespeare, educated in an Elizabethan grammar school (a school for teaching Latin to adolescents by drilling them in grammar and translation), would have been able to read these (Schleiner, 36–45, argues that Latin versions of Euripides' *Oresteia* were shaping influences in the writing of *Hamlet*).

One indication that Shakespeare knew *Alcestis* comes from early in Euripides' play when Admetus, watching his wife in her dying moments, promises to grieve as long as he lives, and never again to have feasts or music in their home. 'I shall order a cunning sculptor (*dextera . . . ficta*) to carve your image in stone, and lay it in our bed', he says, and continues (in George Buchanan's Latin translation of 1556, reproduced more fully on p. 446):

> *amplectar illam manibus, illi procidens*
> *tuum vocabo nomen; ulnis coniugem*
> *caram tenere, non tenens, fingam tamen.*
> *est ea voluptas frigida . . .*
> (ll. 361–4; Buchanan, 222)

14

'And I shall prostrate myself before it (*illi procidens*), and throw my arms round it, and speak your name', Admetus tells Alcestis, 'and I shall imagine that I'm holding my dear wife in my embrace, even though I am not (*non tenens*); it will be a pleasure with no warmth in it.' Shakespeare revisited some of this material in Act 5 of *The Winter's Tale* – an imaginary statue, a sculptor with a commission, and a husband's painful awareness that her image will be stone cold (5.3.35–6) – but only after he had combined it with the story of Pygmalion (see pp. 9–10, 93–4, 97–9).

Euripides' discovery that tragedy and romance were not independent, unchanging kinds of drama, but might evolve one out of the other, even within a single play, confirmed for Shakespeare something he himself had been working towards. Dramatists, academics and courtiers around him in London at the same date were excited by the possibility of fresh creation and movement within and between the dramatic genres. The first wave of excitement had started half a century earlier in Italy, when poets and philosophers read (in Greek and in Latin) the newly published *Poetics*, Aristotle's account of tragedy, unknown in Renaissance Europe before 1500.

The *Poetics* introduced Aristotle's ideas of how tragedy came into being, how it affected audiences, through catharsis and wonder, and how it might be compared with epic. Along with these went his perplexing notion of satisfactory plots in tragedy: in the events of a play, he declared, a probable impossibility was to be preferred to an improbable possibility; and the concession, it appeared, that a tragedy might properly have a happy ending, or at least not an unfortunate one (see Aristotle, 123–4, 135–9). This stimulated a question: might it be possible to create a new mixed genre that combined tragedy and comedy?

Because Aristotle had not said much directly about comedy, some Italian critics felt freer to invent 'Aristotelian' ideas about mixed genre. The poet and academic Guarini went further and claimed that in his play *Il Pastor Fido* ('The Faithful Shepherd'), acted at Italian courts in the 1580s, he had achieved a synthesis of the genres, which he called tragicomedy. This new genre, he acknowledged, was anticipated in part by Euripides, but he (Guarini) was the first writer to create it according to precise rules and give it proper status (though he didn't add that the term 'tragicomedy' was mocked in antiquity by the Roman dramatist Plautus).

Guarini's was a grand claim, outrageous and arrogant to some, and much disputed across Europe. By the time *Il Pastor Fido* arrived in England, around 1600, the concept of tragicomedy was avant-garde, but suspiciously foreign. To some, it was compelling, to others a literary mongrel. But in Protestant London, far removed from counter-Reformation courts and culture, how useful could 'tragicomedy' be to Shakespeare and other professional dramatists, writing, not for erudite aristocrats as Guarini had, but for the general public in the commercial theatres? Elizabethans were used to rumbustious plays that mixed moods, events and outcomes (e.g. Thomas Preston's *Cambyses*, described on its title-page as a 'lamentable tragedy, mixed full of pleasant mirth'). In such plays, certain death might suddenly be averted by the appearance of a magician, a big-hearted king, or even a god. Wasn't there an unbridgeable gap between Guarini's highbrow neoclassical tragicomedy and this native English drama that for half a century had subsumed tragedy and comedy into romance plots, daft confusions of the kind found in love comedies, allegorical moralities, melodrama and fairytale happy endings?

The Winter's Tale is Shakespeare's masterclass in bridging this gap between high and low art. His contemporaries weren't entirely sure what to make of the play, and four centuries later we have still not settled what generic name to give it (romance, late comedy, tragicomedy, romantic or pastoral tragicomedy have all been used). One recent solution has been to define the first three acts as tragedy – a mini-tragedy which concludes, in neatly Aristotelian terms, with death and recognition when the husband at last realizes that his wife and son have died because of his jealousy – followed by an unusual kind of two-act comedy.

Shakespeare may indeed have been thinking along these lines. The third act doesn't conclude in Sicily, with Leontes vowing penitence for his fatal jealousy, but a thousand miles north on the coast of Bohemia, with the Shepherd finding Perdita, and the Clown describing how the Bear ate Antigonus and the ship went down in the storm. 'Now bless thyself', the Shepherd tells the Clown, 'thou met'st with things dying, I with things newborn' (3.3.110–11).

This is the turning point in the play, when the themes of rebirth and regeneration are announced. But the line is even more significant in terms of genre, because Shakespeare appears to have in mind a famous definition in Latin by Evanthius, a grammarian of late antiquity (it was printed in editions of Terence's comedies studied at school), of how comedy and tragedy differed (Hardman, 229–31). In comedy, it was said, 'the beginning is turbulent, the end tranquil, while in tragedy the opposite holds true. Tragedy depicts life as something to be fled, comedy, as something to be seized' (Miola, 329). This modern translation is accurate, but it doesn't make visible all the meanings in the Latin. The phrase in the original, '*prima turbulenta, tranquilla ultima*' ('the beginning is turbulent, the end tranquil'), can mean 'comedy begins with a tempest, and ends with peace', and the words '*fugienda vita*' ('life as something to be fled') have other meanings too, of dying or of shunning a kind of life, or even of the fleetingness of life.

Shakespeare joined the two genres together in *The Winter's Tale*. At the join ('thou met'st with things dying, I with things newborn') he confirms what he has done, alluding to the familiar definition. The play's miniature tragedy begins with peace and

17

harmony (*'tranquilla'*) between the brother princes, followed by more and more turbulence until Act 3 when there is literally a tempest (*'turbulenta'*) that wrecks the ship and kills the crew, and in which Antigonus dies fleeing the Bear (*'fugienda'*). At the close of Act 3, according to this argument, the comedy begins with the same tempest in Bohemia, but it ends in Sicily with reconciliation, joy and new marriages. There are similar patterns in Shakespeare's other plays of 1610–11. *The Tempest* opens in a storm, and *Cymbeline* concludes with repeated references to peace after a battle. In *The Winter's Tale*, the comic life to be 'seized' is shown in the festival in 4.4: young people, passionate and in love, bring their parents – an older generation grieving, resentful and dead to one another – back to life.

Shakespeare's direction to us – look how newborn things have come out of these commonplaces about tragedy and comedy – is completed by the entry of the Bear. The Roman poet and critic Horace thought very little of popular drama, that it was mere crowd-pleasing, not much better than baiting animals and watching gladiators fight to the death. On occasions, Horace complained, right in the middle of a play, irrespective of the plot and just to keep the mob happy, a couple of boxers would be sent onstage, or perhaps a bear or two (Randall, 91). Shakespeare's response to this in the middle of *The Winter's Tale* was to send on the Bear, one that could resolve a complication in the plot by eating Antigonus since he mustn't get home and reveal where he had abandoned the baby princess. Shakespeare uses the Bear to seal Antigonus' fate, but also to seal up the join in the play where the genres have been put together abruptly, and where apparently incompatible upper- and lower-class tastes in drama meet. As modern productions confirm, the Bear is terrible and ridiculously funny, its explosive entry nearly unstageable but the best pantomime around.

To these ideas about the genres, we might add other shaping influences, especially those from Roman writers: the comic formula of Plautus' New Comedy, for instance, where children outwit and replace obstructive parents in the way spring replaces winter, or the macabre union of speechifying, dilemma and murderousness the Elizabethans delighted in finding in Seneca's tragedies. Shakespeare had drawn on all this inheritance since his earliest plays. The models and theories that came later in his career, such as Euripides' mixed tragedies, may have encouraged him to be more groundbreaking and startling.

Looking at genre as something external, that Shakespeare used or adapted, only tells us part of the story. His innovations in genre were achieved most often inside his plays, and between earlier plays and later ones. It is generally agreed that for *The Winter's Tale* the key influence was *King Lear*, written about five years earlier in 1605. There is visible flow between the plays – a reference in *King Lear* to being caught between a bear and a raging sea (3.4.9–11) is made real in *The Winter's Tale* – but there are deeper points of connection too. The most unsettling one is in the harrowing final lines in *King Lear*, where the old king holds first a mirror then a feather to his daughter Cordelia's mouth, searching for breath from her lifeless body. One moment Lear says she'll 'come no more' but the next, his own dying moment, he asks, as he sees something no one else can,

> Do you see this? Look on her: look, her lips,
> Look there, look there!

(5.3.309–10)

In his delirium Lear believes that Cordelia's lips have life in them. In the final scene of *The Winter's Tale*, when Leontes faces what he thinks is the inanimate statue of his dead wife, he sees (in words someone else has to express for him) that 'The very life seems warm upon her lip', and in his heightened state, painful but as sweet as 'any cordial comfort', he thinks Hermione is breathing and tries to kiss her (5.3.66, 76–7). This time, though, the man who wrongs a woman gets her back. The attention in the life cycle shifts from daughter to mother, or rather to a mother who returns to life for her daughter.

Shakespeare's audacity, daring to go beyond his own earlier tragedy, with the same motif and words (especially the half-hidden, bitter-sweet pun passing from 'Cordelia' to 'cordial'), is not to be underestimated. He did it in *Cymbeline* as well, when Arviragus carries onstage the body of his sister, Imogen, apparently lifeless. In fact Imogen isn't dead but in a drugged trance (4.2.195 SD). This is a deliberate reversal, romance for tragedy, of Lear's coming from the prison, holding in his arms Cordelia, who really has died (5.3.254.1). In the interval between these plays and *King Lear* Shakespeare, like Euripides before him, took another of the steps in drama leading from tragedy to romance.

Even in *King Lear* itself, so overwhelmingly tragic, tragedy seems to open naturally into romance. An old, blinded nobleman is brought – he believes – to the edge of a cliff at Dover by a crazed beggar, in reality the loyal son he has wronged. The father plans to kill himself by jumping, but the son deceives him, first with a made-up description of the great height of the cliff (fishermen walking on the beach below look as small as mice) and second, after his father thinks he has stepped off the edge, with an astonished exclamation, in another put-on voice, that the old man's survival is a miracle, he must have fallen like a feather. Then Edgar the son asks Gloucester the father what thing it was that stood with him at the precipice. 'A poor unfortunate beggar', Gloucester replies, but Edgar says no,

> As I stood here below methought his eyes
> Were two full moons. He had a thousand noses,
> Horns whelked and waved like the enraged sea.
> It was some fiend.

> (4.6.69–72)

This episode (borrowed from Sidney's romance *The Arcadia*) is, as one recent critic puts it, an invitation to us to participate in romance. Gloucester's attempt at suicide produces for us 'the beneficent illusion of a death which proves to be none, but rather a kind of redemption or new birth' (F. Parker, 112–13). So his fall from the cliff proves to be no fall at all, but a means of rising. The non-existent thing that concealed itself from Gloucester (an imaginary devil of bits and pieces, with two white, blinded eyes) turns out to be one of the nightmare monsters that disappear when we wake (see pp. 30, 133–4).

The cliff at Dover is an illusion, but it is more real for us than any real place could be. Romance has many definitions, but this aspect of it, the truth of an illusion, is what matters most. In this it resembles folk tales and fairy tales. When we are told that a princess has slept for a hundred years, waiting for a prince to wake her with a kiss, we aren't troubled that this is literally impossible. As children, we know that an envious witch would want to put a princess to sleep; as adults, that children must sleep long in adolescence to prepare them for maturity.

Shakespeare knew the truth of folk and fairy tales (*King Lear* begins with a version of Cinderella and her sisters), and he knew that the illusion most important in romance, which we long to believe, is that the dead don't die. In tragedy, we are robbed of this illusion and it hurts; in comedy, we are shown that other illusions matter more (death comes to everyone, so why not just laugh, especially at marriage, greed and pomposity?). Only in romance is the illusion of overcoming death treated with the respect it deserves. Romance acknowledges that tragedy is right: there is no escape from destiny and biology; but it shows that this isn't the full truth about us. The need to believe in the truly impossible (life after death) and to take consolation and even pleasure from it, is part of our humanity.

Romance has other forms – heroic adventures or quests for enlightenment and spiritual wholeness – but in Shakespeare it has a distinctive mode of expression. In *King Lear*, it appears in the exquisitely stylized description of Cordelia weeping when she heard how her sisters had mistreated their father. Then, says a gentleman,

> patience and sorrow strove
> Who should express her goodliest. You have seen
> Sunshine and rain at once, her smiles and tears
> Were like a better way. Those happy smilets
> That played on her ripe lip seemed not to know
> What guests were in her eyes, which parted thence
> As pearls from diamonds dropped.
>
> (4.3.16–22)

When we least expect it, Shakespeare presents Cordelia to us as if she were one of his romance heroines, like Marina in *Pericles* or Imogen in *Cymbeline*. What was Shakespeare thinking of here, we ask, confusing romance and tragedy like this? And he may well have asked himself the same question, because this passage and the scene around it, although they are present in one text of *King Lear* (the 1608 Quarto), aren't in the other (the 1623 Folio: see Weis, 228–33).

Many scholars now believe that Shakespeare revised his first version of *King Lear* – to speed up the action, to emphasize different themes, to change our perception of characters (e.g. the Fool: see Kerrigan, 218–30). One argument advanced recently about this Cordelia scene is that Shakespeare took it out, along with similar passages, to extrude the romance element: to make *King Lear* more definitely a tragedy and less of a proto-romance (see Jones, 208–15). If this is indeed what happened, the revision could have been stimulated, around 1610, by the writing of *Cymbeline*, *The Winter's Tale* and *The Tempest*; alternatively, Shakespeare's drive to purify *King Lear* of romance may have led him towards plays in which tragic beginnings have romance endings. Of course the revision might not be all one way, and it might not be consistent. Lear's final, 'Look on her: look' lines, quoted above, are in the 1623 Folio (said to be the theatrical version) but not in 1608, printed, it is said, from Shakespeare's papers.

This explanation rests on circumstantial evidence and a still-contested hypothesis that it was Shakespeare himself who altered *King Lear*, rather than an actor or functionary in the playhouse. Nevertheless, when we look beyond 1610, to the very last plays Shakespeare wrote, collaborations with John Fletcher in 1613–14, we find that all three are romance dramas. One of them, *The Two Noble Kinsmen*, is a chivalric story borrowed from Chaucer's *The Knight's Tale*, another is *Cardenio*, from Cervantes' *Don Quixote*, and the third is a fantasy history of Henry VIII entitled *All Is True*. Significantly, in the story from Chaucer, a serio-comic subplot has been added, in which a lower-class girl falls in love with a knight. When she can't have him, she goes mad and behaves like a parody of another of Shakespeare's tragic young heroines, the distraught Ophelia in *Hamlet*. In her lovesick lunacy this lower-class girl certainly inhabits romance, albeit a distorted, burlesque version of it.

In many places after *King Lear*, Shakespeare signals that romance is his goal. The creative practice that led him from comedy to romance is well understood by modern critics; indeed this evolution has become the chief way we look at his comedies from the early 1590s forward. Perhaps we may refine this, however, by arguing that throughout his career, in tragedy as in comedy, Shakespeare had always been heading towards romance. A small but telling illustration is in the 'comedy' he wrote around 1597, *The Merchant of Venice*, at the point when half-blind Old Gobbo comes to visit his son, Lancelot Gobbo. The first thing young Gobbo does, with no motive but to raise a laugh, is to put on a voice and pretend he is someone else, to baffle his father. He tells the old man his son is dead, just to make him weep (2.2.45–62).

To modern tastes the scene is funnier than it ought to be (is it right to laugh at a blind man goaded by his son?), but we can see in it, with hindsight, that Shakespeare had already started on the path of romance leading to blind Gloucester and his seeing son on the imaginary cliff at Dover. Even Lancelot's name points the way: he is a stock figure out of English comedy, a cheeky, unreliable servant stumbling from one malapropism to another, but he bears the name of the most famous knight in all romance.

So after all this what shall we call *The Winter's Tale*? A romance that flows out of *King Lear*, with the catastrophe reversed and part of the harm mysteriously undone, or a tragicomedy, in which tragedy is joined halfway through by comedy? Happily, these are not rival categories. For Shakespeare's making and thinking about the play, the term tragicomedy is indispensable; this is what *The Winter's Tale* is. For the spirit of the play, however, and the intellectual and emotional goals it urges audiences towards, romance is the only proper word.

CHILDHOOD

To Elizabethans, romances were instructive stories about upper-class people, chiefly knights and ladies. The stories might have implausible or unbelievable aspects – a flying horse or a magician that changed shape – but these were justified so long as there was a didactic purpose, especially if it was a warning against the destructive effects of love. When a story was too unbelievable or didn't have a clear moral aim, it was said to be 'a tale'. The phrases 'the tale of a tub' and 'the tale of a roasted horse' (Tilley, T45 and T44) were used of yarns and falsehoods. An 'old wives' tale' (Tilley, W388) was a silly, made-up story that only old women or witless men would listen to or bother to repeat. The phrase 'a winter's tale' referred to gossip, outright lies, or to the kind of trivial fairy story that no one but nursemaids and children would find entertaining. The ghost story Mamillius starts telling his mother is of this kind: 'A sad tale's best for winter', he says, 'I have one / Of sprites and goblins' (2.1.25–6).

Shakespeare used the title *The Winter's Tale* to challenge the audience, as he had with earlier plays (for example 'what you will', the alternative title for *Twelfth Night*). Calling the play '*the* winter's tale' distinguished it from the commonplace saying. This is it, the title declares, this is the ultimate fanciful story: how much of it will you believe? And the title also reminded the audience that Shakespeare had taken the play from a well-known but ageing romance, *Pandosto*, by Robert Greene: see how Greene's winter's tale, old and hoary, has been deepened and given new life, made green again (Shakespeare couldn't resist playing on Greene's name, linking it to revivification: see Everett, 12–13).

The biggest challenge in the title, however, was to the kind of watching (or reading) that the play would require. The Elizabethans weren't supposed to prize childhood or the condition of being a child, so it was highly unusual to offer them a story or a play into which childlike and childish sentiments and thinking had been woven, and in which they too were invited to be like a child. This is what Shakespeare did in *The Winter's Tale*. The hard thing for Elizabethan audiences – and this is true in the modern theatre – is that they needed to have childlike trust and openness about what they were shown, but they had to be very sophisticated in interpreting it.

We don't know whether early audiences thought about *The Winter's Tale* like this. The modern emphasis on children and childhood in the play didn't appear explicitly until the 1810s. This was when the German Romantic critic Friedrich von Schlegel declared that *The Winter's Tale* recovered in us the child's power to imagine. It is one of those tales, Schlegel wrote, that are

> peculiarly calculated to beguile the dreary leisure of
> a long winter evening, and are even attractive and
> intelligible to childhood, while animated by fervent
> truth in the delineation of character and passion, and
> invested with the embellishments of poetry lowering
> itself, as it were to the simplicity of the subject, they

transport even manhood back to the golden age of imagination.

(Bate, *Romantics*, 558)

Here the Elizabethan commonplace that a 'winter's tale' was childish and trivial is turned on its head. As adults (according to this Romantic idea) we lose the experience of Nature and beauty we had as children. A work of art like *The Winter's Tale* returns us to the experience of childlike wonder (the startling appearance of the Bear, the statue moving). Schlegel's was the first step in the post-Enlightenment revaluation of childhood in the play, but his notion had little impact in the theatre or lecture-hall. It was Freud, another German Romantic, with a darker version of childhood, whose views reshaped the understanding of *The Winter's Tale* on stage and in the study. Freud claimed that childhood was not innocent: it left adults mentally scarred by fantasies and fetish because they repressed their feelings, or tried to forget some awful sexual incident. Therapy, the cure of talking about their infancy, was one way for guilty grown-ups to free themselves from their past. This caricatures Freud, of course, but modern directors in particular have tried to represent *The Winter's Tale* as a Freudian sexual fable of childhood.

On stage in the twentieth century, Freudian 'caricatures' of *The Winter's Tale* have enlarged immeasurably how we understand aspects of the play that seemed, to earlier generations, inexplicable or false. The most celebrated production to do this was directed by Trevor Nunn in 1969 for the Royal Shakespeare Company (see Tatspaugh, 33–9). This was the year after the mix of harmonies and dissonance in the Beatles' famous *White Album*, the moment when everyone in public life and the arts was supposed to be young, 'with it' and high on drugs. Nunn himself wasn't thirty – he had just been made the youngest director ever at the RSC – and he took his cue from the mood in Britain and the United States, fostered by rock lyrics, newspapers and television, that a sexual revolution was sweeping away old moral and political verities: no one should want or need to grow up.

Nunn made his production open in a nursery where everything was creamy white, from the set and faux Regency costumes to the familiar childhood toys, some oddly oversized, including a rocking horse. The chic royal couple (Barry Ingham as Leontes, Judi Dench as Hermione) seemed adult enough at first, though a bit puppyish, clambering on and off the rocking horse with Mamillius. This was how an elite 1960s couple should be: young, fashionable, and indulgent with their young son. Polixenes wasn't dressed in white, however, but in what appeared to be, in the glow, a russet-red version of Leontes' outfit.

The difference in colour soon made sense. 'The mellow light turns abruptly white and cold', one reviewer wrote, 'the actors freeze, and then glide in slow motion',

> Hermione's voice becomes salacious, inviting, and Polixenes wolfishly strokes her pregnant stomach. We are being shown Leontes's hallucinations: the sickness has struck and, after a few more lucid intervals, it overwhelms him. He remains certifiably mad until the shock, some might say the trauma, of Apollo's vindication of Hermione. Even then the illness isn't over. He is left with a psychosomatic symptom, the slight dragging of a foot.
>
> (Nightingale, 746)

Polixenes' suit changed, in the white glare, to blood red, then back to russet in the brief intervals when Leontes returned to sanity, and the light softened. In Nunn's production, white was first the colour of the nursery, then the symbol of the asylum, and red stood for Leontes' incandescent jealousy. The key was Autolycus' enigmatic line 'the red blood reigns in the winter's pale' (4.3.4), which for Nunn contained encrypted knowledge about the pathology of boy-men who couldn't mature.

Nunn's approach shocked the critics: if Leontes' crimes were explained away as a Peter Pan syndrome, how could there be high tragedy in the play? Even more shocking was Nunn's treatment of the festival in Act 4, which he populated with lazy urban hippies, not working rustics taking a holiday. The reviewers didn't doubt Nunn's intelligence and inventiveness. The quarrel was about the kind of fable Shakespeare had written, and whether the play should be driven by actors – Eric Porter's many-sided portrayal of Leontes for the RSC in 1960, for instance, which led audiences to feel for the man even though they hated what he had done – or instead by a director's Big Idea, in Nunn's case about male sexual development.

Productions of *The Winter's Tale* after 1969 have broadly accepted Nunn's childhood interpretation. Even in the 1992 'alternative' version mounted at the Lyric Theatre in Hammersmith by Théâtre de Complicité under the direction of Annabel Arden, the premise was the same. This was a troupe of improvisers and clowns, whose production began with the court tumbling through an overlarge wardrobe, the kings in clothes too big for them, like children dressed up as adults. The party games, balloons, the characters' jumble-sale clothes, the magic tricks, the giant white tablecloth – which became, in later scenes, snow covering Sicily and then, astonishingly, an amorphous, monstrous, fanged bear (Fig. 2) – were all made to tell the same story, in the manner of a circus, that too prolonged a childhood was the root of Leontes' jealous condition.

Théâtre de Complicité added for the audience the capacity to see things as a child, watching with delight how the actors morphed into new roles, sometimes with a sly wink (not just doubling parts but quadrupling them or more: see p. 120). At the end of 4.4, when Perdita and Florizel sailed from Bohemia, the actors moved around the stage carrying above their heads a toy ship, a prop from Mamillius' box in Act 1. Soon they were followed by Polixenes and Camillo, carrying a larger toy ship; as the actors circled slowly in a wheel, pursuers and pursued, they

2 'This is the chase' (3.3.56). Dhobi Oparei as a bedsheet-demon Bear in the Théâtre de Complicité production, directed by Annabel Arden, on tour in the UK in 1992

and the rest of the cast, with Autolycus spinning at the centre, peeled away clothes and hats and false moustaches and dressed themselves anew, as they walked, in black veils and sheets, entering Act 5 as a procession of mourners in Sicily following Leontes.

Shakespeare looked at being like a child from different angles in *The Winter's Tale*, and he didn't hesitate to show how crude it might be. In Act 3, for instance, he has the Clown rush onstage, half-stupefied after seeing the mariners drowning in the sea and the Bear eating Antigonus. 'But I am not to say it is a sea, for it is now the sky', the Clown says, 'betwixt the firmament and it you cannot thrust a bodkin's point' (3.3.82–4). Sometimes he could see the mariners, sometimes not, 'now the ship boring the moon with her mainmast, and anon swallowed with yeast and froth, as you'd thrust a cork into a hogshead' (89–92), and then

for the land-service, to see how the bear tore out his
shoulder-bone, how he cried to me for help, and said
his name was Antigonus, a nobleman! But to make an
end of the ship – to see how the sea flapdragoned it!

(92–6)

This speech shifts the mood of the play, partly because of the
way the Clown says it (either as a child, wide-eyed, or as a slow-
speaking country hick), but mostly because of his images and
analogies, all of them about the mouth and fingers at work, cutting, gobbling, jabbing, drinking, gorging oneself and, mouth
open, swallowing whole (see 82–96nn.). The Clown saw the
storm and Bear as an ungrown mind would, in terms of appetite
and gratification.

The Clown has no false civility or adult repression, and his
descriptions always make audiences laugh. They are relieved that
their first guess was right; everything horrible here, including
the Bear, will turn out to be, in Elizabethan idiom, a terror of the
night, a 'bugbear' from a child's nightmare (see pp. 133–4). Even
the shoreline isn't real. Bohemia was a real place on the map, but,
as Shakespeare and his contemporaries knew full well, it was
land-locked, hundreds of miles from the sea (see pp. 100–2). In
the world of folktale and children's stories, however, Bohemia
must have a coast, because how else could a ship sail there and the
mariners drown, and where else could the Bear eat Antigonus?
This is fairytale logic, where reality moulds itself around wish-
fulfilment, as in *Cinderella*, for instance, where the slipper will
only fit one princess.

Children's fairy tales, like romance, deal with events and
behaviour not as they are real but as they are true. Antigonus
doesn't die because he is evil but because he is Leontes'
surrogate: *someone* has to die for the crime against Perdita, and it
can't be the king. The mariners die for plot reasons because they
mustn't get home and because – and this is where grown-ups are
more squeamish than children – the prospect of them all, lost in

gigantic waves, shouting and desperate, brings an audience just enough vicarious excitement, without overly upsetting them.

The Clown in this world has stopped in his development; he is permanently a child. This would have chimed with the upper-class view that everyone in the countryside beneath a certain rank (almost all the population) was childish: irresponsible, dirty and uncivilized. Real children in early modern England weren't to be seen or heard. Boys were controlled strictly and beaten. Children's minds and bodies were weak, and the best thing, according to even charitable critics, was to get childhood over as soon as possible (Marcus, 25). But people in the country, other than gentry and landowners, were stuck in childishness for good. For the Elizabethan elite, the commonplace that children were just small adults was in this case reversible: most country adults were just small children.

But being a child did have the advantage of not having to behave like a grown-up. In literary terms this childhood fantasy was the genre known as pastoral (from *pastor*, Latin for shepherd). Escaping to an imaginary countryside and playing at being shepherds was a regular feature of entertainments for the social elite. In literary pastorals, aristocrats, soldiers and even kings unburdened themselves for a while: by taking a holiday among their inferiors, they could play at being childlike again. There were conventions in pastorals (singing contests, disguised princes in love with shepherdesses who turned out to be princesses), but the key element was that adults of superior rank were allowed to enjoy simple things again without inhibition, and behave like adolescents. Unsurprisingly, this included sex with people they weren't married to, and sometimes even with people of the same sex.

Shakespeare had written a pastoral comedy a decade before *The Winter's Tale*, giving it the throwaway title 'as you like it' (telling citizen audiences, 'you enjoy seeing court folk out of place in the country, don't you'). In *As You Like It* Shakespeare included the opposite of the pastoral ideal, i.e. satirical 'anti-pastoral'. This was the usual way of undercutting idealizations of the countryside and mocking the soppiness of shepherd-courtiers. In real life, anti-pastoral insisted, the weather was foul, country people were stupid, and no young man ever died of unrequited love. In *The Winter's Tale* this anti-pastoral strain is lessened. The rustics are coarse, dirty-minded and gullible (4.4.10–12, 55–62, 194–202, 260–84; and see Fig. 3), but still there is the feeling that inside their boozy, clodhopping dances and preoccupations with sex and money, there is the music of 'great creating Nature' (4.4.88), as vigorously at work in them as in the seeds and animals around them. Shakespeare knew that the underclass was as ridiculous and greedy as its social

3 'Our feasts / In every mess have folly, and the feeders / Digest it with a custom' (4.4.10–12). Engraving by Peter van der Heyden of Pieter Brueghel the Elder's 1570 painting *The Peasant Wedding Dance*, showing vigorous but coarse rural dancing; the mood is explicitly sexual (a bagpipe, associated with the male genitals, is visible on the left)

betters; even so, he has Perdita see beneath the brutish rural life, glimpsing, on our behalf, the profound ceremonies enacted by Nature (see pp. 49–53).

Shakespeare also examined the connections between childhood and adult regression. This is seen first in Polixenes, when he recalls his childhood with Leontes. 'We were as twinned lambs', he tells Hermione, who has been teasing him playfully (see Fig. 4), mixing banter with a touch of sexual openness,

> that did frisk i'th' sun
> And bleat the one at th'other: what we changed
> Was innocence for innocence
>
> (1.2.67–9)

4 'When you were boys. / You were pretty lordings then?' (1.2.61–2). Ray Jewers (left) as Polixenes, Gemma Jones as Hermione and Patrick Stewart as Leontes in the Royal Shakespeare Company production at the Barbican in 1982, directed by Richard Eyre. Hermione's crown is reminiscent of a garland, and the print on her dress is of flowers, stalks and leaves, which all anticipate her daughter's appearance in 4.4 as a floral goddess

As boys we were oblivious to anything but ourselves, he says, not born as twins but twined into each other (see 1.2.67n.). We weren't aware of sin, neither in the abstract, theological sense (original sin) nor in the temptations of the flesh. The sun was shining, and we played, eternal boys, bleating harmlessly. For Polixenes to go back like this to when he was a child needn't be dangerous: people do it all the time. He knows this is a perfected reminiscence, a pastoral pre-pubertal idyll, not real at all (in fact Elizabethan farmers thought twin lambs were better for breeding because they would turn out to be far keener on sex: see Tusser, 127).

Polixenes' temporary slipping back to childhood has no consequences for him. Shortly afterwards, something different happens with Leontes. At 1.2.65–86 he watches Polixenes and Hermione talking frankly about sex; then at 108–46 he is overcome with jealousy, which he splutters out with his little son beside him. Leontes' expression alters when he thinks of the couple as adulterers, so much so that they see his distress. 'You look', Hermione says, 'As if you held a brow of much distraction' (148–9), alluding inadvertently to the one part of his face he is sure has changed for ever, his brow, which now (he thinks) has a cuckold's 'invisible' horns growing out of it (see 185 and nn., and Fig. 5). 'Are you moved, my lord?' she asks, to which he replies, concealing what he has been thinking, 'No, in good earnest' (150),

> . . . Looking on the lines
> Of my boy's face, methoughts I did recoil
> Twenty-three years, and saw myself unbreeched,
> In my green velvet coat; my dagger muzzled,
> Lest it should bite its master

(153–7)

Leontes means this as a screen to cover his jealousy. The innocence in Mamillius' face, he says, reminded him of his puny condition when a little boy. But this memory of childhood isn't what he was thinking at all, it's a fake, or he intends it to be.

5   'To the infection of my brains / And hard'ning of my brows' (1.2.145–6).
Print from *English Customs* of 1628 showing wives of different ranks with the
husbands they have cuckolded: the antlers and bobbins on the men represent
the cuckold's invisible horns

As often in *The Winter's Tale*, the fake turns out to be real;
here because Leontes outsmarts himself. His lie – that he had
gone back involuntarily to his own pre-pubertal moment (green
coat, muzzled dagger) – was supposed to hide his ugly thoughts.
But that image of himself as a powerless little boy is what this
grown-up man has indeed made himself. The 'lines' of 'my
boy's face' should mean 'the 'features of my young son's face',
but what he actually says (and sees) is '*my* face when I was a
boy'. Gazing on his own and his son's face – the same and as
inseparable as Polixenes said he and Leontes were as boys –
caused him to 'recoil' in time, to when he was 'unbreeched',
dressed in the garment children wore until boys put on breeches
at seven (see List of Roles, 2n., and Fig. 6). At his waist, in this
reverie, was a little knife, its blade sheathed and point tipped, to
stop it hurting him.

6 'Methoughts I did recoil / Twenty-three years, and saw myself unbreeched'
(1.2.154–5). Portrait of Henry Stewart, Lord Darnley, and his brother
Charles Stewart, later fifth Earl of Lennox, attributed to Hans Eworth
(*c.* 1562). Elizabethan upper-class males wore different clothes at different
stages in their lives: the 'coat' (a long dress to the floor) for boys up to seven
or eight, breeches for older boys and adults

It has been said that Leontes' way of speaking in the first act is so fevered and clogged with passion (or just mad) as to be unintelligible. In this case, his language is exact and inexact. Twenty-three years is almost over-specific, and so too are the colour and material of the 'green velvet coat'. But there are ambiguities in 'recoil' and 'unbreeched'. At this date, to 'recoil' meant to spring or shrink back, hurt or in disgust, or to withdraw from an enemy, and it was used too of the recoil of a gun when fired. To be 'unbreeched' was to be without breeches, but also to have one's breeches removed or taken down, and it could refer to the breech of an unloaded or fired gun; and the pun 'unbreached' also allowed the meaning 'intact, unwounded'.

How we read this and the speeches around it will determine the kind of play we take *The Winter's Tale* to be. Leontes confesses to fear, disgust and resentment (shrinking from the enemy, Hermione and Polixenes, protecting himself with a little knife and gun). Watching the couple, he is a small boy, vulnerable, pre-sexual, unguilty, while they are the mature sinful betrayers. But he isn't really a boy; he is a man-boy, in whom what he was and is have fused. The fusions are pitifully obvious. His penis-gun lacks bullets but has been fired; his penis-dagger is a toy that needs muzzling.

If this is a failure of progression (the way Nunn treated Leontes in 1969), we are seeing the pathology of an immature male, an unavoidable mental condition. But if we see Leontes' fantasy as a *deliberate* regression, we have the beginnings of tragedy. Viewed like this, as following from his choice to become a chimera of power and powerlessness, a monstrous fake, Leontes' behaviour makes sense. His mood swings – from adult despair and despondency to childish glee at how clever he is – and his sudden, wholly unexpected release from delusion the moment Mamillius is dead (3.2.141–4) all point to one conclusion. Leontes objectifies his fears and frustration, making a false man-boy image of them (the Elizabethans called such images idols). He doesn't get free of this image until the real boy, Mamillius, has been sacrificed to it, his death killing off the fake 'boy' element in his mind.

This is a cruel fable of childhood, in which the father sacrifices the son. If Leontes does this because he is insane or weak, then he is no tragic hero, and *The Winter's Tale* is the melodrama some critics think it is. But Leontes knows how readily the mind fabricates things even as he fixates on the imaginary amalgam of himself as adult and child. Similarly, he imagines that Hermione is 'slippery' (1.2.271), a 'hobby horse' Polixenes has been riding (274), even when he knows he may have dreamt up these lewd images out of absolutely 'nothing' (139–42; see pp. 40–2). To be so aware that his imagination might delude him, and yet still persist in believing what it showed him, makes Leontes wicked, not feeble-minded or mad. He doesn't have the defence of diminished responsibility that can be made for Othello. From this perspective Leontes is a tragic figure: he chooses to believe he can make truth whatever he says it is, irrespective of what it costs others.

KNOWLEDGE

In the first half of *The Winter's Tale*, Leontes says he knows for certain that his wife has been unfaithful. To the other characters and the audience, this 'knowledge' of his is manifestly absurd. Modern critics sometimes suggest that Hermione is too familiar with Polixenes, giving her husband cause to doubt her. But this view misses the point, because Leontes doesn't need a reason to be jealous. Critics and directors may feel they have to give him one (he is neurotic or repressed or doesn't understand his feelings), but Leontes' conviction that Hermione has had sex with Polixenes and is pregnant by him is entirely solipsistic. No one but he, Leontes insists, can see what the adulterers have been doing. His courtiers are deaf, dumb and blind, or are only guessing the truth (he is a cuckold), and even Apollo's oracle, when it contradicts him, is lying. Alas, if only I could know less, he declares, 'how accursed' I am in 'being so blest' with a gift of special knowledge (2.1.38–9).

This knowledge comes not from observation of the world but from within Leontes' imagination, freed of reason. To know what is true, he must doubt everything, and believe that the truth is the opposite of common sense. 'All's true that is mistrusted', he announces triumphantly (48), by which he thinks he is saying 'my mistrust has turned out to be completely right', when he is actually saying, 'everyone I distrust is loyal, my doubts are completely unfounded'. The action moves quickly beyond the sexual starting-point – jealous fantasies of the 'adulterers' kissing – to delusions where truth is untrue, huge things are tiny, and dreams replace reality.

Leontes supposes he has this knowledge because he has the symptoms of brain fever. The condition that afflicts him, which he calls 'affection' (1.2.138), has given him superhuman mental powers. Everyone else is sane but deceived by the adulterers. Only he, inside his frantic hallucinatory state, which no ordinary person would dare trust, has grasped that reality is a lie and unreality the truth.

The word 'affection' today means gentle feeling or liking. It meant this at the date of *The Winter's Tale*, but it also had other meanings that are now obsolete: irrational behaviour, over-whelming passion, lust and animosity. The word was also used in quasi-technical senses, to mean a person's predisposition (e.g. to be hurtful or generous), and to account for how the mind functioned. In 1624 it was defined as 'the lively representment of any passion whatsoever, as if the figures stood not upon a cloth or board, but as if they were acting upon a stage' (quoted in *OED* affection *n.*[1] 1c).[1] This was part of the word's larger meaning, of emotional or mental states produced by internal or external influences (e.g. memories or particular tastes and smells). As the

---

1 Quotations from contemporary sources, whether in original or modern editions, are presented in modernized form throughout this edition.

Tudor scholar Roger Ascham put it, man 'is subject to immeasurable affections' (quoted in *n.*[1] 1a).

There are seven instances of 'affection' in *The Winter's Tale* (see 1.1.24n.). The special technical meaning it has, of brain fever and delusion, is at the heart of Leontes' opaque and troubled speech at 1.2.136–46. Standing beside him is Mamillius, whom he asks, half in play half in earnest, 'Art thou my boy?' (120). For all his perverse 'knowledge' about Hermione and the child she is pregnant with, even he doesn't doubt that his son is his. 'Look on me with your welkin eye', he says,

>   Sweet villain,
> Most dearest, my collop! Can thy dam? May't be
> Affection? – Thy intention stabs the centre,
> Thou dost make possible things not so held,
> Communicat'st with dreams – how can this be? –
> With what's unreal thou coactive art,
> And fellow'st nothing. Then 'tis very credent
> Thou mayst co-join with something, and thou dost,
> And that beyond commission, and I find it,
> And that to the infection of my brains
> And hard'ning of my brows.
>
>   (136–46)

These have been called the most obscure lines in Shakespeare.[1] In many modern productions, they are either heavily cut or omitted altogether, or the actor splutters over them, speaking like a madman. There is madness here, or something like it, but the speech isn't as unintelligible as people say. 'Affection' can mean different things (see above), but here only its 'brain fever' meaning fits the whole passage. Several critics have argued this – that Leontes is raging against his own mind or, more exactly, the illusion of power in his *disturbed* mind – but their insights haven't made it into the lecture hall, let alone to the stage, largely

---

1   See the commentary for a detailed explication of the lines.

because this technical meaning of 'affection' is so lost from modern English.

The recovery of the specialized psycho–medical meaning of 'affection', derived from the Latin *affectio*, makes sense of the raving. In Tudor reference books, *affectio* was used of deranged minds. In 1582 Cooper defined it as 'a disposition or mutation happening to body or mind', or simply 'trouble of mind' (H. Smith, '*Affectio*', 163). It was a kind of severe mental sickness, a seizure with recognizable physical symptoms: agitation followed by palpitations, feverish sleeplessness and exhaustion, all of which Leontes experiences (e.g. 1.2.110–11; 2.3.1–2, 8-9, 30–8). The condition produced delusions because reason lost control of the imagination. The senses (sight, touch) communicated impressions to the mind in the normal way but memory and judgement failed to interpret them correctly. People with this complaint might believe they saw monsters or impossible events.

Leontes persuades himself that he has this condition. Addressing 'affection' by way of self-diagnosis, he tells it 'Thou dost make possible things not so held', and 'With what's unreal thou coactive art, / And fellow'st nothing.' This is followed by a sudden acceptance that 'affection' might very well 'co-join with something' which he has found out ('I find it'). The key phrase is 'fellow'st nothing', which means that affection produces 'nothing' – i.e. unreal imaginings – from out of itself, impossibly self-coupling and begetting ('coactive', 'fellow'st') since it is uncontrolled by reason. However, saying these words, with their powerful sexual meanings, makes Leontes think of the adulterers having sex ('nothing' and 'something' could be used as vulgar words for the vulva and penis respectively). Merely mentioning 'nothing' drives him, suddenly, to the non-sequitur, ''tis very credent [believable]' that 'Thou [affection] may'st co-join with something', i.e. the delusions might attach themselves to real things, and reveal Hermione and Polixenes attached as lovers.

Whether Leontes really is suffering from this illness is debatable: because he thinks he is mad doesn't mean he is. He can pretend to be perfectly sane (as he does to cover his thoughts at 1.2.153–60), so there is no way of knowing for sure if he is psychotic or schizophrenic – or just a very clever self-deceiver. Incidentally, his skill at lying means that disputes about when he first became jealous aren't likely to settle anything definitively. Some critics think he wasn't jealous until he saw Hermione taking Polixenes' hand (1.2.108 SD; see Fig. 7), others that his jealousy was aroused before then and he is furious at her, though slyly concealing it, from the moment we see him. But what conclusive evidence is there either way except what he says? And we have seen how easy he finds it to conflate past and present, and true and untrue memories.

Other commentators find more arcane technical meanings in the 'affection' speech – for example that 'intention' and 'Communicat'st' were exclusively philosophical terms inherited from Aquinas (Hankins, 98–101) – but these redefinitions risk clouding the choice the king has made. He knows he is probably hallucinating, but chooses to believe the delusions, and from this convinces himself that only he knows what truth is. Shakespeare certainly did not write this crucial speech just to show that Leontes is mad. Rather he is a character who believes his mental breakdown leads him to divine the truth of things, because his unsettled mind is a stronger source of truth than anything outside him.

Leontes tells himself to trust nothing in the real world. Instead he must rely on the images (or idols) he has created in his imagination. The immediate context is his private jealousy, but Shakespeare uses the perversity of Leontes' decision to open *The Winter's Tale* into bigger, public questions: namely, how do we know what we know, and what things shouldn't we imagine?

The modern world has confidence in measurement and verification. In Shakespeare's lifetime there was, among educated people, a new enthusiasm for exact calculation and accuracy, though most of the population were unaffected by it and couldn't do the simplest sums in their head. There are signs of the new

7 'And clap thyself my love' (1.2.104). Emblem by George Wither (1635) which, together with its motto, 'manus manum lauat' (one hand washes another), signified harmonious give and take between well-matched husbands and wives. The gesture was also a reminder of how couples took hands in betrothal and friends gave hands in friendship – a key gesture in *The Winter's Tale*.

and old ways in *The Winter's Tale*. Money on a balance sheet at court is *increased* by adding noughts (1.2.6–9; see n.), which in common sense seems impossible. Time is calibrated precisely in years, months, weeks and days, even hours and minutes. This is the modern measure of reality, observing the clock instead of the phases of the moon (Crosby, 81–6). Older ways of measuring are used in the country (Autolycus and the Clown say 'millions' when they mean 'very large numbers', 4.3.58–9), and even the upper class use traditional phrases for indefinite periods of time, for instance 'seven years' and 'twenty years' (see 4.4.583, 5.3.71, 84 and nn.).

The Elizabethans were interested in greater precision and in manipulating numbers as part of a general movement to turn empirical observation into abstraction. Mental arithmetic was still new (the Clown can't do it and has to use counters, 4.3.36), and most people still believed that the sun went round the earth. In 1610, the mathematician Galileo constructed a telescope and detected Jupiter's moons, from which he concluded that the opposite was true, the 'universe' was heliocentric. It appears Shakespeare knew what Galileo had seen and what it meant – the end of the old cosmology. He alluded to it in *Cymbeline*, written a few months before *The Winter's Tale* (see Maisano, 402–3, 406, 416, 429–30).

Shakespeare wasn't concerned with contemporary science for itself; it was abstract thought resting on certitude that attracted him. If he invested this abstraction in the character of a loving husband, perhaps he might develop further the study of jealousy he had begun in *Othello*. The Moor had wanted ocular proof of his wife's infidelity: let me see her doing it (*Oth* 3.3.363, 367). But what if, using Greene's old story of jealousy, Shakespeare could create a new kind of husband who would *never* be convinced his wife was faithful, because he could never be certain – demonstrably, with proof beyond doubt – that she wasn't *un*faithful?

The private question 'how can I be sure my wife is faithful?' was only a short step from the larger philosophical question 'how can I be sure of anything?' This was a question the sceptics had been asking for centuries before *The Winter's Tale*, but it coincided with what Renaissance scientists and theologians also wanted to know. What limits are there to our knowledge of reality; does God wish us to know more, and if so, how – from within our minds, or in the physical world? Some of these questions led to abstruse, bookish problems, separated from day-to-day life, but the practical limits of what people should know mattered in ordinary circumstances too. There were, for

example, correct ways of thinking about God, set out by law in
sermons in church every Sunday.

It is likely that Shakespeare wanted Leontes' denial of reality
to have wider application to the general epistemological crisis
occurring at this date (see Cavell, 197–8, 201–3). As critics have
pointed out, however, the king's catastrophic doubts don't last
beyond Act 3, and they are not the sum of the play (Altieri, 276–
83). Just as important is the recuperation from doubt – through,
for instance, Perdita's mythologizing response to the real world
around her (see pp. 50–3). And Leontes himself is shown to
recover, in Act 5, from having gone too far in his idolizing of
Hermione, beyond the proper limit of human imagination.

At the date of *The Winter's Tale* a man was expected to control the love he felt for his wife. Centuries of misogyny gave a
husband every reason to distrust women in general and his own
wife in particular. It wasn't just her infidelity he should be careful of. A greater danger was that he might love her to excess.
Love, wrote Francis Bacon in 1612, was a fit subject for the
stage, but in life it did 'much mischief; sometimes like a syren,
sometimes like a fury'. By love Bacon meant the sexual passion
that could overwhelm a man. There were many reasons for not
surrendering to it. You would never be rich, your wife or lover
would despise you, and you would never accomplish anything
important in the world. It was degrading that a man

> made for contemplation of heaven and all noble
> objects, should do nothing but kneel before a little
> idol, and make himself a subject, though not of the
> mouth (as beasts are), yet of the eye; which was given
> him for higher purposes.

> (Bacon, 358)

Much of what Bacon says is from classical writers and the Bible,
so it is the same sour stuff he and educated contemporaries can
often be found saying.

A man kneeling 'before a little idol' was provocative. If we now say 'he idolized that woman', or 'she's a Hollywood idol', we don't mean 'idol' literally, i.e. a physical object. For the Elizabethans, however, this is what an idol was: an object wrongly given the worship owed to God alone. Idols, to the Reformation mind, were statues of the Virgin, effigies of Christ, or images in stained-glass windows. Protestant theology taught that kneeling to idols or praying for miracles from them was popish idolatry. True knowledge of God came from *not* imagining him or giving him human form in sculpture or paintings.

In *The Winter's Tale*, Hermione's image returns twice after her apparent death, first as the spectre seen by Antigonus (see pp. 3, 5–6), then as the statue. The image in Paulina's house is secular, commemorating a dead wife, but the setting could hardly be more inflammatory in Protestant London. The statue is curtained off, as effigies were in Roman Catholic churches, and the sculptor is said to be Giulio Romano, an Italian artist associated with Rome, papal politics and pornography. Everything about Hermione's image is intoxicating and taboo. There is magic in it, it conjures, and it looks as if it is just about to come to life, so much so that Perdita, alarmingly, kneels to implore a blessing and kiss its hand (5.3.42–6). Though she pleads 'do not say 'tis superstition' (unrestrained idolatry), the audience in the Globe would have thought it was.

And idolatry delighted them. In the theatres, actors pretended to be people they weren't – princes, moors, magicians – which made them seductive idols whom it was tempting to take pleasure in. Even worse, though they were men, on stage the actors pretended to be women, wearing wigs, dresses and make-up. The theatres broke every religious and social rule about who you were – man or woman, king or thief, true or fake – which is why audiences paid to get into them. The thrill of idolatry was irresistible. Little wonder the theatre was a special target for Puritan iconoclasts.

Hermione's image in 5.3 is every kind of false idol in one. It is not a statue but a living person, not a woman but a male actor in drag, not a queen but a lowborn player. It is inanimate, but by petition and 'faith' it can be made to move and speak. The idol appears first as a mental picture without matter (as the spectre in 3.3), then it acquires a body, dressed perhaps in white as Antigonus saw it. Above all, it arouses love and intense feeling in those who look at it, particularly Leontes, which is a sign that he has long been guilty of a special kind of idolatry, uxoriousness – placing the love of one's wife above God, what Bacon meant by kneeling 'before a little idol'.

The statue is the key to what happened in Leontes' mind. It had always been there, as an image, long before it appeared in the chapel scene. The king had created a simulacrum of Hermione in his imagination, an idol of an unyielding stony lady elevated above him. Part of the idolization was sexual – her beauty, like her hand, seemed unattainable (1.2.101–4) – but he had wanted something even more forbidden, that the image would replace the real woman, hence his telling her, in the trial scene, 'Your actions are my dreams. / You had a bastard by Polixenes, / And I but dreamed it' (3.2.80–2). The idols of Hermione (either on a pedestal or as a lewd unfaithful wife) must be seen for what they are, and the static images shattered as the real woman steps down and speaks, before the grip they have on Leontes' mind can be loosened.

Making images of women isn't confined to the statue in the chapel. When Florizel praises Perdita, he describes her like an artist recasting a perfect living woman, in movement certainly, but still confusing art and worship. 'What you do', he says,

> Still betters what is done. When you speak, sweet,
> I'd have you do it ever; when you sing,
> I'd have you buy and sell so, so give alms,
> Pray so, and for the ordering your affairs,
> To sing them too. When you do dance, I wish you

> A wave o'th' sea, that you might ever do
> Nothing but that, move still, still so,
> And own no other function.

(4.4.135–43)

This is much admired by modern critics, for its poise and authenticity, but it is nevertheless risky stuff, as Perdita realizes Florizel's desire to exaggerate, catching every moment of her beauty, makes her deeply uneasy (4.4.147–51). His devotion to her as an idol, his eyes fixed on everything she does, is in its way as intense and controlling as what Leontes felt for Hermione. Perhaps Shakespeare was saying that men risk idolizing women by transforming them into never-changing objects (a dance step like 'A wave o'th' sea' repeated over and over, with no other 'function'), but the message may be different: that even in ordinary, unexceptional things (talking or singing), the beauty of Nature's working is manifest when seen through the eyes of love.

PASTORALS

To know what 'Nature's working' means in *The Winter's Tale*, we need to return to the subject of pastoral. We saw earlier that one strand of pastoral was associated with loss of childhood and regression. But pastoral marked loss in the real world too, as the Bible and pagan mythology explained.

According to the Old Testament, Adam and Eve ate the fruit of the forbidden tree of knowledge in the Garden of Eden, and 'the eyes of them both were opened, and they knew that they were naked' (Genesis, 3.7). They had disobeyed God and lost their sexual innocence, and their sin had to be paid for. No longer immortal, they would die and they would have to work. This was the Fall, or the loss of Paradise. Their descendants, inheriting 'original' sin, would be punished too. In Eden it had been perpetual spring and everything lived for ever, but Nature too went into terminal decline. Later, Christ's redemption of mankind from eternal death saved their souls but it didn't reverse the physical degeneration.

This was still the explanation in Shakespeare's lifetime of why people died, and why there were seasons, wars and work. The connection between sex and sin was commonplace – a serious matter but sophisticated people could joke about it, as Hermione and Polixenes do in *The Winter's Tale* (1.2.69–86). Leontes, jealous that they 'know' one another (have had sex), also alludes to the Eden story, slyly and bitterly. They tell him they are going for a stroll, but he can find them if he wants. 'We are yours i'th' garden', they say (177), to which he replies, like God in Eden discovering sin, 'You'll be found, / Be you beneath the sky' (178–9; see n.).

There was a parallel story of loss in pagan mythology. Classical writers said that the first men and women lived in a Golden World, without seafaring, trade or war. The land didn't need cultivating, and human beings lived at peace with animals, not killing and eating them. This world changed, not abruptly as in Eden, but in stages, from golden to silver to bronze, and finally to an iron age – the present – when human beings were greedy and bloodthirsty. Traces of the Golden World survived, however, far from cities, among humble shepherds. Their pastoral life was hard, tending flocks, milking and shearing, and it had unrequited loves, jealousies and deaths, but it gave a glimpse of what Nature and humanity had once been.

The mythologies of Eden and the Golden World merged long before Shakespeare. Pagan literary pastorals combined easily with the New Testament theology of Christ the shepherd (rescuing lost sheep, sacrificing himself as the Lamb of God). In *The Winter's Tale*, Shakespeare puts together Christian and classical pastorals but in an intriguing way. At the festival, Perdita is Mistress of the Feast. She thinks she is only a common shepherdess, but the 'robe' Florizel has persuaded her to wear makes her feel, for all her modesty, that there may be something more to her. 'Methinks I play', she says,

> as I have seen them do
> In Whitsun pastorals; sure this robe of mine
> Does change my disposition.
>
> (4.4.133–5)

This is real and unreal. Perdita is supposed to be lowborn but she is really a princess; she is a pagan living in far-off Bohemia but she likens herself to the Whitepot Queen who presided over the celebrations in rural England at Whitsun, one of the holiest days in the Christian calendar. Whitsun country games were indeed called 'pastorals' but were a far cry from highbrow literary pastorals.

The pastoral scene in *The Winter's Tale*, 4.4, is one of Shakespeare's major additions to the source, *Pandosto*. Unusually, he wrote the scene around Perdita, with men as her foils. Renaissance pastorals always had women in them, but usually as objects of devotion or figures in a spiritual vision. Looking at 'a troupe of ladies' dancing (as in Edmund Spenser's *The Faerie Queene*, 6.10.10), a knight in pastoral disguise might suddenly see in them the Graces, who in classical mythology ruled over everything good in Nature (Spenser, *FQ*, 990–2). This is how Florizel sees Perdita. His love gives him insight into the real nature of things. He means it when he says she is Flora, the goddess of flowers and spring, embodying beauty and fruitfulness.

Perdita thinks this is extravagant – something a man might say to seduce a woman – but she does have a special gift, of seeing beneath the surface, as her flower-giving at the feast shows. At first she keeps to the usual ceremony of presenting flowers to match people's ages or the season. She regrets that because it is late summer she doesn't have spring flowers to give the young girls who are still unmarried, which in turn leads her to the deeper story the flowers have to tell:

> O Proserpina,
> For the flowers now that, frighted, thou let'st fall
> From Dis's wagon! Daffodils,

That come before the swallow dares, and take
The winds of March with beauty; violets, dim,
But sweeter than the lids of Juno's eyes
Or Cytherea's breath . . .

(4.4.116–22)

Onstage these lines are sometimes treated as if they are just ornamental, which misses a vital point, that this is an epiphany, normally reserved in pastorals for men.

What Perdita describes in her reverie of flowers – and we need to remember she is just sixteen – is the commonplace mystery of how girls pass from puberty to womanhood. There is nothing sentimental in this. Perdita doesn't think first of Flora's fecundity or grace, as Florizel does, but of the ravishing of another deity of springtime, Proserpina, the virgin daughter of the goddess Ceres. Proserpina (Persephone in Roman mythology) was collecting flowers at the fountain of Arethusa in Sicily when the god Dis (Pluto) carried her off on a chariot to Hades, the land of the dead, where he made her his queen (see Fig. 8). Her mother Ceres, the goddess of harvests, searched everywhere but couldn't find her, and in angry desperation cursed Sicily, blighting everything that grew there. To appease Ceres, Dis freed Proserpina each year for the spring and summer.

Proserpina thus became a fertility goddess who symbolized the cycle of life, death and rebirth in Nature. Shakespeare makes Perdita speak specifically of the flowers the goddess dropped as she was abducted: spring daffodils, violets and primroses, all female here; and their male counterparts, the 'bold' oxlip, crown imperial, and 'lilies of all kinds', including the flower-de-luce (fleur-de-lis), the prince's flower (122, 125–7). This is a miniature mythology of sexual attraction and mating – pale daffodils braving the cold to meet spring before it has properly arrived – which begins with the acknowledgement that virginity

8 'O Proserpina, / For the flowers now that, frighted, thou let'st fall / From Dis's wagon' (4.4.116–18). Detail from Hans von Aachen's 1589 painting *The Rape of Proserpina*, showing Pluto (Dis) carrying off Proserpina (Persephone) to Hades, kingdom of the dead. In classical mythology this abduction was said to be the reason for winter and spring

is lost by a 'fall' from innocence. To get a husband, daughters have to leave their mothers behind.

Perdita sees all this but she doesn't see that the myth of Proserpina applies more personally to her, not just as an archetypal rite of spring and sexual maturity, but because of who she really is. Like Proserpina, Perdita is a young girl from Sicily, another lost daughter whom everyone except Hermione believes is dead; while latter-day Sicily, where Perdita was wronged, has a curse of winter and death on it until the lost girl is restored to her mother.

Shakespeare is careful not to make this cumbersomely allegorical, or to romanticize Perdita's character. She sees what she does because she is her father's daughter and has his penetrating intelligence – except that she has turned his fatal way of thinking on its head. Leontes convinced himself that he could see the essence of things by looking into his mind, and shutting out natural truths. Perdita by contrast looks deep into the natural world around her, and finds there the true scope and reality of her mind.

NATURE AND ART

The chief product of the mind was art. This led artists and writers to wonder (not unlike Leontes in a way) how much they needed Nature. Their materials (paint, marble, pens and paper) came from Nature, but what about their minds and what they imagined, were they Nature too? Had God created Adam and Eve with minds that were separate from the physical world in Eden, or was this the true fruit of the tree of knowledge – that the Fall happened when the mind broke free of Nature?

Renaissance writers approached this question in different ways. In 'The Garden', for instance, written a generation after Shakespeare, the poet Andrew Marvell famously described the 'luscious' sensations of the body, but said that these were 'pleasure less' than those of the mind,

> that ocean where each kind
> Does straight its own resemblance find,
> Yet it creates, transcending these,
> Far other worlds, and other seas.
> (Marvell, 'The Garden', 43–6)

The mind, an unfathomable ocean, is Nature's double: everything ('each kind') inside mirrors what is outside, so there is nothing in Nature that isn't already in the mind – and it is superior to Nature because it can make many copies of itself ('other seas').

In *The Winter's Tale* the mind and art are not as independent of Nature as they later become in Marvell, but things are heading that way. Recounting what he knows about the statue, the Steward tells the Gentlemen it is

> newly performed by that rare Italian master Giulio
> Romano, who, had he himself eternity and could put
> breath into his work, would beguile Nature of her
> custom, so perfectly he is her ape.

> (5.2.94–7)

Art isn't yet Nature's double, not even in Romano's hands. The copy of Hermione doesn't have life ('breath') in it, nor does its creator possess eternal life. The statue nevertheless is powerfully lifelike in the way Shakespeare's contemporaries thought representational art should be (see Barkan, 653-4, 658-62).

The debate about art and Nature was very old indeed. Most thinkers had concluded that the two weren't separate. Plato in the *Laws* said a good legislator 'ought to support the law and also art, and acknowledge that both alike exist by nature, and no less than nature'. Aristotle went further, arguing that when we claim art perfects Nature, what we are really saying is that Nature perfects herself: 'a doctor doctoring himself: nature is like that' (quoted in Tayler, 135–6). This view lasted well beyond the date of *The Winter's Tale*.

Art, it was claimed, could repair as well as 'perfect' Nature. Man and the world had decayed, but human inventiveness might improve things, which is the subject of the famous exchange – 'art itself is Nature' – between Perdita and Polixenes at the feast. This begins with Perdita handing flowers to Polixenes and Camillo, 'rosemary and rue' – evergreen shrubs that keep their appearance, she says, and smell 'all the winter long' (4.4.74–5).

She has none of the most beautiful flowers of the summer season to give them,

> our carnations and streaked gillyvors,
> Which some call Nature's bastards; of that kind
> Our rustic garden's barren, and I care not
> To get slips of them.
>
> (82–5)

Polixenes asks why she won't plant gillyflowers and she replies that 'piedness' – streaks of colours on white petals – shows they are not entirely natural. Art (in this case cross-fertilization) has produced an adulterated hybrid with Nature. Polixenes responds with the old explanation that Nature is made better by this art, and that the art is only Nature anyway because everything comes from Nature. By grafting cuttings on to uncultivated trees, gardeners fertilize their barks with higher-grade strains. Grafting strengthens plants and flowers, thus changing Nature for the better. There is nothing wrong in this: 'make your garden rich in gillyvors', he tells Perdita, and 'do not call them bastards' (98–9).

To early audiences this would have been a set-piece dialogue, straight from the schoolroom ('Art is Nature. Discuss'), but with some unexpected twists. A king condescending to debate with a woman was odd and amusing enough, but even more so if she were a shepherdess who turned into a princess who then became the king's daughter-in-law. It was even more of a surprise that the shepherdess appeared to accept, in principle, that 'art itself is Nature', but still wouldn't plant the gillyflowers. She likens them to women wearing make-up ('painted'), which a man would only want for sex ('to breed') because of their alluring appearance (99–103).

Critics often underestimate this exchange because Polixenes' view is so well worn, and he prevails so easily. But just around the date of *The Winter's Tale*, the art and Nature debate had come alive again, and it seemed possible that art might give back to Nature some of its former fecundity. Francis Bacon argued that experimental science, still a fledgling, might eventually do this. Nature, because of the Fall, could only deliver a single harvest a year, but art – by which Bacon meant natural science, in particular manipulating seeds – might discover how to grow two or three crops annually. So too with human bodies: new drugs might alleviate suffering and infirmity, and surgical experiments show what medicine could do for 'the body of man' (Bacon, 482).

It was Elizabethan gardeners who led the way in 'improving' Nature, and it was the gillyflower that illustrated what horticulture might do. The flower appeared to be a degenerate, its over-pale petals showing it was sickly, but after grafting it could be reinvigorated and the petals given new splashes of colour. Moreover, for reasons no one understood, in certain soils white gillyflowers would spontaneously acquire coloured streaks. Did this show that art was doing what Nature struggled to do? And that God wanted mankind to experiment with Nature, to ease the debilitating effects of sin?

These are the reasons Perdita is suspicious of gillyflowers. Polixenes treats her unease about them as uneducated naivety, but he is wrong. As she sees, what is at stake with such hybrids is the damage art may do to Nature when it forces it to become what the mind desires. In this exchange it is Polixenes – with his platitudes and patronizing response, 'don't worry dear, everything is Nature' – who is naive and un-grown-up.

But there is another reason Perdita won't plant them: she fears that she too is one of 'Nature's bastards'. Whenever she looked at her dim-witted 'brother' and her illiterate, gnarled old peasant 'father', she could hardly avoid thinking, 'who on earth are my real parents?' Her 'mother' had been bustling and coarse whereas she is reserved and gracious. Everyone in Bohemia has heard that this shepherdess is inexplicably beautiful and intelligent. Is she one of Nature's wonderful freaks (like the gillyflower with its spontaneous streaks), or just another village foundling, an illegitimate child of parents who couldn't keep her? This is what the Shepherd thought she was, and Perdita had every reason to think the same.

Academics and directors often ignore this aspect of her exchange with Polixenes. This diminishes the emotional charge of the whole scene, and leaves the social and philosophical elements in Bohemia not quite fitted together. The idea that Perdita is a bastard had maddened Leontes. Within the moral framework of the play – very different from a modern outlook – it is vital that Perdita be cleansed of the stain of illegitimacy, and released from her conviction that she was conceived in sin.

One stain not wiped away in the play sticks on art itself. In Shakespeare, artistic imitation is always worthless, suspect or deceptive (e.g. *LLL* 4.2.125–7), but in *The Winter's Tale* even more so, as is evident in the speech where the Steward describes what he has heard about the statue (5.3.92–9). He says that art (Romano's genius) would like to steal Nature's customers, by giving them copies of her creations (i.e. living beings), but these imitations can't be any more than dead fakes. In this view, there is nothing pure in art: it mimics and competes (wanting to outdo Nature), and it looks for a profit (getting customers).

In Paulina's chapel when Leontes looks at the statue, he thinks art is mocking him with a lifeless replica of Hermione. We saw earlier that the statue is there to remind him how lifeless his mental images of her had been, but there is a comment in this too from Shakespeare, about mimicry and the money drive in art. The statue breathes, moves and speaks, so for a moment art appears to have outdone Nature, and in a sense it has. A male actor in a dress, wearing greasepaint, pretends to be the painted stone image of a dead queen, which turns into a living woman, whose role is then played by the same male actor. How terribly smart and self-referential of the theatre, and how exciting!

And there is money in it too, because the actors' dressing up and mimicking real people like apes is the reason audiences pay the admission price, a few pence each to watch clever art competing with great creating Nature. It's not hard to see in what

Autolycus says about money the author's own outlook: money is a meddler that gets into everything, messing it up (4.4.327–8 and n.), especially into the art of the theatre he makes a living from. The mix of triumph, disgust and self-disgust in Autolycus, when he describes how he entertained the crowd (4.4.605–18), may well be what Shakespeare felt about audiences at the Globe.

Yet for all this, the lasting impression of the statue scene isn't one of impersonation or moneymaking. Instead it is of a confused interflow of feelings that leaves us wanting more. Shakespeare plans an enchantment where the characters and the audience, when they see art at the top of its power (the statue), aping life but not able to give it, inevitably want to go to the next stage – that Nature overwhelm its imitator and perform the impossible, make stone into flesh.

RULES AND TYPES IN DRAMA

Art and Nature was the theme of the most famous critical essay of Shakespeare's lifetime, *The Defence of Poesy* by Sir Philip Sidney. Poetry, Sidney wrote, was the 'highest point of man's wit', and with it a poet might bring 'things forth surpassing' what Nature could do (Sidney, *Defence*, 217). Sidney conceded that in England – he was writing in the late 1570s – neither poetry nor the newly built London theatres had accomplished much; indeed most public stage plays were ridiculous. In them, a prince and princess would first fall in love and then, after many troubles,

> she is got with child, delivered of a fair boy; he is
> lost, groweth a man, falls in love, and is ready to get
> another child; and all this in two hours' space: which,
> how absurd it is in sense, even sense may imagine, and
> art hath taught, and all ancient examples justified.
>
> (243)

Even more absurd was the way such plays mingled 'kings and clowns' (244), not because the plot required it, but because the actors didn't understand the inner laws of comedy and tragedy, and the distinctions between them. 'So falleth it out', Sidney concludes, that 'having indeed no right [proper] comedy, in that comical part of our tragedy', the theatres give their audiences

> nothing but scurrility, unworthy of any chaste ears, or some extreme show of doltishness, indeed fit to lift up a loud laughter, and nothing else: where the whole tract of a comedy should be full of delight, as the tragedy should be still maintained in a well-raised admiration.

> (244)

Lacking 'sense' and ignorant of classical drama ('ancient examples'), the theatres didn't offer anything but bawdiness, inane jokes and skits – in them there was neither the 'delight' of comedy nor the heightened wonder ('admiration') of tragedy.

Sidney's *Defence* was more sophisticated and informed than anything earlier in England. He drew on Aristotle's *Poetics*, and the Italian neoclassical critics who wrote commentaries on it. They said Aristotle's rules were clear. Writers of stage plays must observe the unities of time, place and action. A play must have one main action, preferably without a subplot; the stage shouldn't be used to represent more than one place; and events should take place over no more than twenty-four hours.

Sidney didn't live to see the arrival of Marlowe and Shakespeare, who used dumb-shows, stage armies and spectacular effects, the outlandish things neoclassical critics abhorred. The excesses and errors of the public stage grew ever more outrageous. This was the view – this time from inside the theatre – of the dramatist Ben Jonson, Sidney's heir as the leading English neoclassical critic. Jonson set out to reform the stage by writing comedies that observed the neo-Aristotelian rules, mixed with those of another ancient critic, the poet Horace. Jonson thought that Shakespeare in particular had pandered to and ruined popular taste, and around 1600 he began a debate with him about the proper way to write plays.

It used to be thought that Shakespeare hadn't participated in this debate, but critics now think he did express his views, not in an essay but through the plays, especially those of 1610–11 (Honigmann, *Impact*, 109–20). In *The Tempest*, for instance, he keeps to the unities exactly – one story, one island, and one duration of time, in the action and its depiction onstage. He may even have had in mind a general notion of catharsis in the same play (Briggs, 115–30), and he was fully aware of another of Aristotle's ideas – that drama, in moments of intense surprise and recognition, could induce 'wonder' (here a technical word, what Sidney meant by 'a well-raised admiration': see Bishop, 26–41, and below, pp. 69–70, 72).

Where Sidney found faults, Shakespeare saw opportunities. Indeed, the mistakes in construction, verisimilitude and taste castigated in the *Defence* appear to be alluded to, in one way or another, in *The Winter's Tale*. In this ludicrous kind of play, Sidney said,

> you shall have Asia of the one side, and Afric of the other, and so many other under-kingdoms, that the player when he cometh in, must ever begin with telling where he is, or else the tale will not be conceived [understood]. Now you shall have three ladies walk to gather flowers: and then we must believe the stage to be a garden. By and by we hear news of shipwreck in the same place: and then we are to blame if we accept it not for a rock.

> (Sidney, *Defence*, 243)

Shakespeare's 'tale' happens in kingdoms hundreds of miles apart, spanning sixteen years, from a 'garden' in the first act (1.2.177) to 'news of a shipwreck' in the last (5.2.68–9). The play has 'scurrility' and 'doltishness' (Autolycus and the Shepherd), and it mingles 'kings and clowns' at the feast and at court. It even has a scene in which a king and a shepherdess argue about art and Nature. Some of these 'errors' are in *Pandosto*, but Shakespeare added most of them, provocatively, to make the action even more implausible.

Jonson responded by saying that Shakespeare's plays were absurdly unnatural. In his own writing, he protested, he was 'loath to make Nature afraid', unlike Shakespeare who had created 'tales, tempests and suchlike drolleries' (Jonson, 6.16; see p. 86). To Jonson's neoclassical mind, the unnaturalness was not so much in Shakespeare's characters – though he didn't think much of the monster Caliban in *The Tempest* – but in the 'fable', what he called the 'soul' of poems and plays, the writer's controlling idea of the whole fiction. Jonson followed Aristotle in believing that the fable was expressed chiefly through the plot. In Shakespeare's 'tales' and 'tempests', as Jonson saw it, the plots were contrived turns of fate, accidents and pretended magic (6.16).

The Winter's Tale has two plots. The first ends with Hermione's death, while the second begins, after the storm and Bear, with the Shepherd and Clown. Shakespeare didn't believe that unity in the fable required a unified sequence of action. Instead, he connected the plots through a form of literary typology, or corresponding 'types'.

Typology began in antiquity as a method for interpreting the interconnectedness of events in the Bible. The 'type' anticipated the 'antitype'. Some event, the significance of which wasn't understood at the time, would come to make sense when fulfilled by a later event (see Auerbach, 28–49, 53–4). This was how the Church read the Old Testament against the New. In Exodus, Moses struck a rock with his staff and water flowed out. Theologians said this was a miraculous real event, but explained its significance as an allegorical foreshadowing of Christ's side pierced by a spear at the Crucifixion.

Typology was later adapted for secular writing as well. Shakespeare in earlier plays used repeated figures of speech and verbal parallels to elucidate elements of the story (e.g. 'honest' in *Othello*), but in *The Winter's Tale* he went much further. To see the 'wonder' in the unity of the fiction, audiences must recognize the typologies he had invented or modified. Superficially, the action of the play might seem disjointed, but at a deeper level, where types and antitypes, large and small, were articulated between the plots, the fiction would show itself as a pleasing whole.

Some types are visible at once. Towards the end of 3.3, the Clown describes how the Bear tore out Antigonus' 'shoulder-bone' (93). Sixteen years later, the Clown encounters another stranger, the swindler Autolycus (see Fig. 9), who claims to have been set upon and beaten. As the Clown helps him up, Autolycus says 'O, good sir, softly, good sir! I fear, sir, my shoulder-blade is out' (4.3.72–3). Autolycus' injuries are so obviously imaginary that only the Clown could think them real. His gullibility carries us back to the unintentionally hilarious account he gave of the Bear gobbling Antigonus. Just how 'real' was that grisly scene, we wonder? Was it just comic knockabout where no one was really eaten, or only in the way that animals eat people in fairy tales? In other words, does the antitype compromise the 'reality' or 'believability' of the type?

Critics often say that the routine between Autolycus and the Clown in 4.3 is a lighthearted parody of Jesus' parable of the Good Samaritan, which establishes a carnival and comic mood in 4.4 (see 4.3.49–125 and n.). But the typological link through the shoulder-bone/blade, merely funny at first, also reminds us of the difference between the Bear's savagery – eating according to Nature's law because it is famished – and the greedy, wolfish Autolycus' preying on victims according to no law at all.

The key types and antitypes are – like so much else in the play – concerned with Leontes' mind. The deaths of his son and wife in 3.2 shock him out of his 'diseased opinion' (1.2.295),

9 'Having flown over many knavish professions, he settled only in rogue' (4.3.96–7). Richard McCabe as Autolycus, supported by balloons, coming down from the heavens to surprise Graham Turner as the Clown, in the 1992 Royal Shakespeare Company production at Stratford-upon-Avon, directed by Adrian Noble

but the perversions he has imagined can't be simply forgotten or atoned for without effort – they must be made literal, acted out and mocked. The best way to drive out the Devil, Luther said, was to laugh at him and be disrespectful, because in his pride he couldn't bear the scorn. The therapeutic side of the feast works like this, to provide the holiday state of mind that cleanses the play of the old, diseased Leontes before Hermione returns.

The images that most need to be scorned or turned into play are in Acts 1 and 2 – for instance when Leontes says his wife is a 'hobby-horse', straddled for pleasure, who

> deserves a name
> As rank as any flax-wench that puts to
> Before her troth-plight.

(1.2.274–6)

'My wife's a slut everyone rides', he declares, 'who deserves as foul a reputation as any low-bred girl who has sex with her fiancé before she marries in church.'

When Leontes imagines Hermione's unfaithfulness, his mind doesn't stay in court, civil and restrained, but moves out into the country, where the rustics have their uninhibited holiday games – a 'hobby-horse' was the wickerwork outfit worn in bawdy morris dances (see 1.2.274n.) – and women, with nothing but work in their dreary lives (making clothes from linen), can't wait to get into bed with anyone. The fantasy is social as well as sexual. The lower orders are lascivious, careless of reputation, and they stink; but Leontes is drawn down the social ladder to the unrepressed lives he imagines them living.

This libidinous mental image, of Hermione as loose and lower class, is laughed out of the play because of Mopsa and Dorcas. These are straightforward country girls who work for a living, and get excited by sex and snigger about it. They wouldn't mind marrying someone with money, even the dim Clown, and they might well sleep with a stranger (a disguised king or a flashy pedlar), but they are nothing like the sex-crazed flax-wench Leontes imagines. Whether they are gossiping, squabbling, singing with Autolycus or receiving flowers from Perdita, they make Leontes' unpleasant sex fantasy look ridiculous. The social travesty looks just as absurd, because of Perdita. In romance, an elite lady could never be confused for long with an inferior. The social degradation of Hermione in Leontes' mind is expelled when her daughter's beauty and quality shine through her humble clothes and circumstances.

Parody cleans up after Leontes' grotesque imaginings. In 1.2, he describes himself as shaggy and animal-like, with a cuckold's horns (128; see Fig. 10). In 4.4, a dozen rustics, 'all men of hair' (331) and dressed in satyr skins with horns, leap about frantically ('a gallimaufry of gambols', 333). Their dance externalizes and ridicules the fits and starts of his jealousy, and the over-sexed

10   'Thou want'st a rough pash and the shoots that I have / To be full like me' (1.2.128–9). Engraving in Giambattista della Porta, *De humana physio-gnomonia* (1586), a series of juxtaposed human and animal heads, which illustrates the Renaissance commonplace that the face proclaimed the mind. Leontes in a jealous fit imagines his head is like a bull's, but also like a cuck-old's with horns (see Fig. 5)

65

man and horned beast he had imagined himself. Leontes' pervasive mental tyrannies in the first half of the play are dealt with, along similar lines, through the figure of Autolycus. Where the king demands 'lawfulness' and absolute control, his antitype – a rogue, liar and cheat, but no hypocrite – refuses to obey laws and morality of any kind (see Hartwig, 98–101).

Leontes tramples on the dignity of his subjects, as well as the laws and obligations that bind him. He humiliates his wife and calls his unborn child a bastard. He plans to have his closest friend poisoned, and incites his chief counsellor to do it. He attacks Antigonus and calls Paulina a liar and a bawd. He imprisons his wife, though she is nine months pregnant, and won't allow her time to recover before bringing her to trial, most likely in an open cart like a prostitute (see 3.2.103n., and Fig. 11 for the layout of state trials at this date). When Apollo's judgement is read out, he dismisses it, even though he had sworn to be guided by the god.

This is why the report of the religious rite in Apollo's temple is crucial, placed in contrast – antitype to type – to the disregard of ceremony in Sicily. On Delphos (see Fig. 12), the offering to Apollo is 'solemn and unearthly' (3.1.7), but when the god speaks through his oracle the thunderous sound briefly stuns Cleomenes and Dion (8–11). Apollo's worshippers need an established rite (3.1.4–8) to protect their senses from the god's overwhelming raw power. In Sicilia, by ignoring all proper ceremony, Leontes uses his power to overwhelm his subjects.

Audiences understand that in the statue scene the earlier failure of ritual in Sicily is being put right. The ritual of bringing Hermione to life, with petitions, music and Paulina's supposed magic, is improvised from religious liturgy. Nothing else will do, when so much must be believed and forgiven, but an extemporary rite. This is why the moment is anxious and tentative – the ritual might not work. Leontes' shame and contrition, the astonishment at how lifelike the statue is, the sight of the princess kneeling to an image like a papist – all these might come to nothing, and

11 'Thou art here accused and arraigned of high treason' (3.2.13–14). Drawing of the trial of Mary Queen of Scots, done in 1587, soon after Mary's trial and execution. In 1612, around the date of *The Winter's Tale*, Mary's son James I had her remains exhumed and reinterred in Westminster Abbey, beneath a marble effigy and tomb. Early audiences may have recognized parallels between Hermione's trial and Mary's, and the statue and the effigy (and also perhaps between Hermione and another queen, Anne Boleyn, famously tried for adultery and treason by Henry VIII)

12   'The climate's delicate, the air most sweet, / Fertile the isle, the temple
     much surpassing / The common praise it bears' (3.1.1–3). Claude Lorrain's
     Landscape with Aeneas at Delos (1682), showing a neoclassical view of
     Apollo's temple at Delphos. The setting is based on the same passage in
     Virgil's *Aeneid* that Shakespeare used for *The Winter's Tale*

the statue not move, unless the different elements can be fitted
together in a new rite of secular faith and forgiveness.

The replacement of traditional public ceremonies with more
private, impromptu rituals has been noticed in other literature
of the late Renaissance – in Cervantes' *Don Quixote*, for instance.
Some historians think that this may be part of a shift in the
collective psyche, as older ceremonies (saints' days and coronations)
spoke less to people's religious and emotional needs. Certainly at
this date the idea of ceremony was identified with show and
speciousness, not least in Shakespeare's histories and tragedies

(see T. Greene, 283–90). In *The Winter's Tale*, however, especially in the statue scene, the ritual isn't at all empty or merely outward form. This is because the characters, and in turn the audience, participate in the wonder Shakespeare creates for them.

WONDER

The starting point of *The Winter's Tale* is Leontes' irrational jealousy. The play concludes in Paulina's chapel with a different kind of irrationality, the temporary and contrived delirium that Renaissance critics, following Aristotle, called wonder.

Aristotle said that wonder, by which he meant an astounding experience, was essential for tragedy. 'The marvellous gives pleasure', he wrote, 'this can be seen from the way in which everyone exaggerates in order to gratify when recounting events' (Aristotle, 60). His academic disciples in sixteenth-century Italy went on to apply the concept of wonder to all kinds of drama. They argued that a play must present events that seemed impossible or unpredictable and show characters mistaking the strange things happening to them. It must stun the senses and overwhelm the rational mind, by using spectacular stage effects if need be (a flat contradiction of Aristotle). The pleasure came first when the mind was engulfed with new and unexpected sensations. When the wonder subsided, and reason regained control, pleasure was renewed – in the form of knowledge – because what had seemed absurd and inexplicable (twists in the plot, misrecognitions) was accounted for.

The critics thought that wonder would work best at court. Cost was unimportant there, so expensive stage machinery could be used to create apparently impossible illusions, and the fictions could be written, acted, sung and danced by the very best artists. Wonder was what Ben Jonson and Inigo Jones were seeking in the masques they devised for the English court at the date of *The Winter's Tale*. In their masques the wonder lay in the transformation of disorder – symbolized by unruly or ugly figures, such as witches or baboons – into order, represented by queens or knights who danced or walked gracefully in harmony. Scenes and sounds changed too. In one masque, the pit of hell, filled with smoke and infernal music, gave way in a flash to the House of Fame, with a pyramid all circled in light (Jonson, 7.300–2).

Shakespeare was one of the King's Men, regularly putting on plays at court, so he saw the masques at first hand, and was intrigued by the form (he put masques into *The Tempest* and *Cymbeline*). He drew on one masque in particular for *The Winter's Tale*. This was Jonson's *Oberon, the Fairy Prince*, performed at court on 1 January 1611, in honour of Henry, Prince of Wales. Early in *Oberon* there was a dance of satyrs. Shakespeare lifted the satyrs and their dance wholesale into *The Winter's Tale*, along with the music (see Fig. 13, and pp. 92–3, 394–6, 402–4), but he was interested in this masque for another reason too.

Oberon was the epitome of Renaissance stage wonder. It had three full sets. The first showed mountains, with the satyrs in front of them; then the mountains opened to disclose a gothic palace with translucent towers and walls; and finally the palace itself opened and out came Prince Henry as Oberon on a chariot drawn by two real polar-bear cubs, guarded by bear-wards dressed as sylvans (see Ravelhofer, 287, 305–8). The message was that Henry/Oberon, emerging from Wales (the mountains), would shock men out of their disordered, lascivious urges (the satyrs) when he became prince of Britain.

But Oberon was also Shakespeare's name for the larger-than-life fairy prince in *A Midsummer Night's Dream*. Shakespeare's Oberon, as Jonson would have known, was the antithesis of Henry – troublesome, big and sexy, and jealous of his wife Titania, an equally difficult immortal. Jonson turned Oberon into a chaste overgrown child, denying his own sexual urges and everyone else's: the old comic jealous Oberon had been neutered. Moreover, in the play, Oberon's enchantments were inside the fiction (Puck's magic potions), but in the masque, the spells were technical effects to intoxicate the audience, with the mountain

13 'They call themselves saultiers' (4.4.331–2). Sketch by Inigo Jones of satyrs dancing, from Ben Jonson's *The Masque of Oberon* (1611). The satyr in classical mythology was a monster of the woods and mountains, half-man, half-goat, with horns and hooves. In Jonson's masque the arrival of a chaste prince tames an unruly troop of satyrs. In *The Winter's Tale* Shakespeare shows this same troop, but turns them into rustics ('saultiers' misnamed for 'satyrs') dressed up in animal skins

breaking open, light spilling out and loud bursts of orchestral music (Jonson, 7.351).

It is not hard to see in the two Oberons – child and man-god – the germ of the conflated sexual image Leontes made of himself in *The Winter's Tale* (see pp. 34–5, 37–8). Perhaps Shakespeare intended this as a conscious response to what Jonson was doing in the masque. *Oberon* fed Henry the illusion that he could transform things – restore sexual purity – with a fantasy of power. This was the theme, of a king's private transforming of the real world, with which *The Winter's Tale* began. Jonson's satyrs too were turned to different ends. In the masque they were figures of licentiousness needing to be curbed. In the play they became figures of fun, bumpkins dressed up in hair suits – but their dance helped drive out the memory of Leontes' grossness (see pp. 65–6, 395).

Masques showed symbolic transformations from the outside, with the wonder in the poetry and in the astonishing technical changes of scenery. In *The Winter's Tale*, in Paulina's chapel, we are never certain that the statue is transformed into Hermione – or that it isn't. The wonder is in the characters' wanting it, and the audience's wanting it too, so intensely that it isn't (as the Aristotelians claimed) reason that is overwhelmed, but corrosive doubt. This is the transformation – in the mind – that the play brings about.

DISGUISING

In *The Winter's Tale* Shakespeare also writes about another kind of transformation, that of disguising. Most of this happens at or before the feast in 4.4. This is a very long scene – at 847 lines the second longest in Shakespeare, only sixty shorter than the final scene of *Love's Labour's Lost*. The disguising is one reason for the length. At the Globe, the time needed for the whole of 4.4, delivering verse at eighteen to twenty lines per minute (see MacIntyre, xiii–xiv) would have been more than forty-five minutes, with no allowance for the comic routines (changing clothes and hats) or the two dances, of shepherds and satyrs. Even in the modern theatre, where speeches are cut and things omitted altogether (often the satyrs), the playing time is upwards of forty minutes.

The challenge Shakespeare set himself in this scene is comparable to what movie directors do when they film a sequence in a single 'take', without breaks or second cameras. There is bravura in such a tour de force, but risk too – will audiences pay attention for so long where the setting doesn't change but the stage is filled with wave after wave of characters entering, exiting, singing, dancing, courting and shouting at each other, and where the moods range from light opera (Perdita and Florizel) to vaudeville (Autolycus and the Clown) and melodrama (Polixenes)?

The disguising ensures that there is variety and thematic continuity in the scene. Some of the disguises are commonplace in Elizabethan drama – Florizel pretends to be a shepherd to conceal his rank, Polixenes assumes a disguise to spy on his subjects (as the Duke does in *Measure for Measure*). But there are some surprises. The heroine Perdita doesn't get dressed as a boy, for example, though she does end up wearing Florizel's hat. Camillo tells her to pull the hat over her brows, muffle her face and 'Dismantle' herself (4.4.654–6), but she is still wearing a dress, perhaps covered by a cloak. This is a departure from the convention of 'a boy actor playing a girl who dresses as a boy who later reveals herself as a girl' which Shakespeare made distinctively his own in comedies up to *Twelfth Night* (even as late as *Cymbeline* he was still using the convention – the heroine travels incognito, in a man's shirt and breeches, to find her husband).

Perdita doesn't get dressed up as a boy because in this play gender games are replaced by confusions of rank. Shakespeare hadn't pushed social disguising as far as this before (though the maid Margaret does dress as her mistress Hero in *Much Ado About Nothing*). At this date people were supposed to stay in the place assigned them at birth. A shopkeeper might make money, even become mayor, but he was forbidden to dress above his rank. Sumptuary legislation set out the fabrics and styles permitted: silk for a nobleman, coarse yarns for a labourer.

The laws were flouted, of course, especially in London, and professional actors, playing kings or men of state, broke the rules every day. They got away with it because the laws couldn't be fully enforced. This left people excited about social cross-dressing, and even more attracted to the theatres, where there were all kinds of transgression.

Perdita's disguising isn't truly subversive even though, as a 'shepherdess', she thinks it is. When the scene begins she talks uneasily about her 'unusual weeds' and 'borrowed flaunts' (1, 23). Florizel, she says, has pranked her up, 'Most goddess-like', and she would swoon if she saw herself in a mirror (10, 13–14). She is unhappy too with the way he has dressed down. He is 'Vilely bound up' as a 'swain' she says (22, 9) – in a shepherd's sheepskin jacket – but this is the same outfit, with the scent of the court on it, that Autolycus later wears when he is fooling the rustics (4.4.651 SD, 735–40). This doesn't sound like working clothes, but some fancy-dress version a prince might wear in a court entertainment.

Later, when Perdita gives out the flowers, she declares, unselfconsciously, 'sure this robe of mine / Does change my disposition' (134–5): looking like a princess, she feels she is becoming one. Audiences know of course that her 'disguise' is only transforming her into the princess she truly is. For the Elizabethans, this actually reaffirmed the rules about clothes: everyone would know who they were if they wore what they were supposed to.

But there is an important side issue about the dress she is wearing. In modern productions, because of the phrase 'unusual weeds', Perdita often appears with a garland of flowers in her hair. On the early stage, it probably meant that her clothes ('weeds') were utterly extraordinary ('unusual'). The borrowed robe Perdita is wearing has most likely come from court (like Florizel's), a special dress for the vows they are about to make (4.4.49–51). It is well known that the players used to acquire out-of-date court dresses for the company's costume box (Jones

& Stallybrass, 176–91, esp. 189–91). Onstage at the Globe, the costume worn by the male actor playing Perdita may even have been a real court dress worn by a real lady for a role in a real masque. This substitution of fake for real certainly *was* subversive.

Autolycus has four disguises in the play: a destitute beggar (4.3), a pedlar, then a pseudo-courtier dressed in Florizel's outfit (4.4), and finally what he passes himself off as when he speaks to the three gentleman at court in Sicily (5.2). This kind of disguising wasn't uncommon on the Elizabethan stage. Autolycus is a descendant of the Vice figures in Tudor morality plays who duped people, one after another, and got away with it.

Autolycus is more unusual in his attempt to dupe the audience. Vice figures – Iago in *Othello* is one – confided in audiences and told them what they were up to. Autolycus lets them into some but not all of his secrets. He has pretended to be a tinker, he says, and other times has gone from fair to fair, being paid to show a performing bear with a monkey on its back, he has run a catchpenny game with balls and hoops, and he has even served as a low-grade bailiff (4.3.86, 93–4; see nn.). But his most daring pretence – to the audience – is that he has fallen from the high position he enjoyed with Florizel (4.3.13–14, 86–8). This deception has taken in the critics, even Coleridge, who in 1818 declared that Autolycus had 'lived and been reared in the best society' (Bate, *Romantics*, 561) – in other words, he was a sort of Regency rake who had fallen from the heights of the beau monde, or one of the shameless middle-class prodigals in Hogarth.

Autolycus had indeed been Florizel's servant, but a very lowly one. He tries to suggest that he is a gentleman prodigal who has known grand days, but this is a barefaced lie. Dressed in Florizel's outfit, he can't even convince the Shepherd that he wears it properly (4.4.753–4). In a roundabout way, he confesses he was a footman (4.3.61–7), which at this date, before the coach arrived in high society, was a servant who ran alongside his master's horse. Autolycus' outrageous claim that he had been forced down the social ladder was probably greeted with catcalls at the Globe, and court audiences must have been amused by a menial – a lackey who ought to be blacking their boots – trying to pass himself off as a gentleman.

Autolycus lives on the margins – literally under hedges and keeping to the back roads, and in his associations, as a pedlar, with popish relics and superstition (see Fig. 14). In him there are all the delights of low life and feckless freedom that Elizabethan males fantasized about (for Leontes' fantasy, see p. 64). He might wear rags, but he could have sex without marriage, he didn't work or worry about the seasons, and he could give his word lightly and falsely (4.3.2, 11–12, 62–3; 4.4.800–17). His indifference to reward or punishment in the afterlife was scandalous (4.3.29–30), but wonderfully unburdened. In *The Alchemist*, performed at the Globe a few months before *The Winter's Tale*, Jonson showed the comedy of a butler, in cahoots with a rogue and a prostitute, taking over his master's London house and tricking people out of money. Autolycus by contrast – one that Shakespeare probably intended – is a rogue out of doors, cast off by his master; but the excitement of watching the underclass unashamedly lying, stealing and impersonating people of higher rank is the same.

The pleasure of seeing the Shepherd and Clown transformed into 'gentlemen born' at the end of the play (5.2.122–60) is different. Autolycus wears a variety of clothes but never actually changes. Perdita puts on her proper dress and is restored to the princess she is. Only the rustics are made into something new, and this is because Time intervenes.

TIME

Time appears in person at the beginning of Act 4. He has his traditional hourglass with him, which he turns over mid-way

14 'The pedlar's silken treasury' (4.4.355). Woodcut by Jost Amman (1568) of
a hawker selling trinkets and gloves from a tray, while another pedlar (left)
carries a pack on his shoulders

through his speech. This means that the first half of the play
is over and the second can begin (see 4.1.16n.). The gesture,
conventional enough to modern eyes, alerted early audiences
to something unusual. In the second 'hour' of the play, they
would see the social order turned upside down – a prince would
become a shepherd, a rogue a courtier, a clown a gentleman –

and human reason itself overthrown (the statue come to life). It was proverbial that the world might be made topsy-turvy in an hour (Tilley, W903) – Time says he can make it happen (8–9) – and the phrase 'the world turned upside down' was a byword for disorder and misrule (T165).

The word for this inversion in *The Winter's Tale*, and elsewhere in Shakespeare, is 'preposterous', which means literally 'upside down' or 'back to front'. Significantly, it is the Clown who uses the word – wrongly – when he congratulates himself and his father on their being made 'gentlemen born' by Polixenes. They are, he says, in a 'preposterous estate' – which is his malapropism for a *prosperous* estate or condition (5.2.145: see n., and P. Parker, *Margins*, 20–2, 52–3). The rustics have been elevated preposterously above their rank, a truth the Clown blunders into, though by mistake.

Time tells audiences that a period of play and preposterous misrule can begin, so long as everyone is tolerant about the liberties he is taking (4.1.15; see n.) – they must imagine they are waking after a long sleep (17), and not worry whether they are using time to their best advantage (29–32). The topsy-turviness might extend to the citizen audience themselves, making them too, for an hour, gentlemen born and ladies ('Gentle spectators', 20). Time – the Chorus outside the fiction – cajoles audiences, flattering and tempting them with their own power, saying that 'what the actors can do depends on your co-operation and tolerance'. Shakespeare used a similar choric figure in *Pericles* when he made the medieval English poet Gower present a stage version of his own romance. The story of *Pericles*, Gower says, was one that ancient 'lords and ladies in their lives' had 'read . . . for restoratives' (1.0.7–8). Time like Gower urges audiences to associate themselves with upper-class tastes.

But the rustics get their reward because Time is actually indifferent to status. Reporting how Leontes and Perdita were reunited, the Steward says that the Shepherd stood beside them with tears pouring down his worn old face, 'like a weather-bitten conduit of many kings' reigns' (5.2.54–5). Compressed in that phrase is Time on two levels: big public history (kings' reigns), and humbler, barely visible lives. A rain pipe (conduit) with a gargoyle gushing out water – what the old Shepherd looks like – has carried 'rains' off buildings through all those 'reigns'. Like the conduit, the Shepherd is unnoticed, but he and it have worn out the coming and going of kings. This is what the Fool sings about at the close of *Twelfth Night*, that 'the rain it raineth every day' (5.1.385). Time, like rain, wears down everything: buildings, lead pipes, and all human flesh, whatever its rank.

Overturning things was only one of Time's iconographic roles in the Renaissance. Time was the subject of some sixty English proverbs at this date (Tilley, T290–T343), and it had special associations with Death and Fortune (see Chew, 'Time', esp. 103–13). A phrase from Ovid – *'Tempus edax rerum'* ('Time the Devourer of Things') – was made into mottos and into pictures of an old man with iron teeth gnawing at books and buildings, smashing arches, slashing with a scythe and beating down everything with his wings (see Fig. 15). This was the winged figure Shakespeare had in mind when he wrote of 'cormorant devouring Time' (*LLL* 1.1.4) – images of greedy eating, wings and flight fused into a predator swallowing victims whole (in extreme versions Time was the grandfather god Saturn, who ate his own children: see Panofsky, 73–9).

Time was also the revealer of truth and lies (Dent, T324, T333; cf. *Luc* 940), the judge of wrongdoers (T336; cf. *AYL* 4.1.187–8), and sometimes a thief taking flight. Often it was a father rescuing his daughter. 'Truth is Time's daughter', the proverb said (T580), and it was Truth's protector too, especially in Reformation iconography. In a pageant at Queen Elizabeth's coronation in 1559, the figure of Time came out of a 'hollow place or cave', leading another person dressed in white silk – his daughter Truth, who had a book in her hand. The book was the Bible in English, and the figures represented the Protestant religion, brought to light at the death of the Catholic Queen Mary (*Progresses*, 1.16). The Latin

Marque du *Temps* nº 1

15 'I, that please some, try all; both joy and terror / Of good and bad' (4.1.1–2).
Sixteenth-century device, a printer's mark of Simon de Colines, showing
Time ('Tempus') with his scythe and goat-hooves, often a mark of the devil.
The ribbon from his mouth, '*hanc aciem sola retundit virtus*', means 'only
virtue blunts this blade', i.e. Time never stops cutting down the living, but
goodness can slow it and make death less sharp

version of 'Truth is Time's daughter' – '*Temporis filia veritas*' – was the motto on the title-pages of Robert Greene's stories, including *Pandosto*, the source of *The Winter's Tale* (see pp. 94–7, 405–6).

Londoners saw Time in their street pageants at holiday time or special anniversaries, when they had a day off work. The pageants were often in simple, doggerel verse, and audiences at the Globe would have seen Shakespeare's Time as a kind of pageant figure, with his out-of-date manners and stale old story (13–15), his rhyming couplets – one for each of the sixteen years gone by – and his half-apologetic encouragement that they treat the second half of the play as a holiday from using time over-diligently (29–32).

Shakespeare's Time has a few of the traditional attributes – he is a judge who examines and lays out truth (1–2), and he has an hourglass, and wings to fly swiftly (4–5). When he refers to 'news' to be 'brought forth', however, he doesn't refer to Truth, his traditional daughter, but to another daughter, Perdita, hidden in obscurity in rural Bohemia (26–7). And there is no sign that he is the slow devourer or violent destroyer (no scythe or iron teeth). This Time says he is a 'witness' to the way people have been tested by earlier 'times' (11–12), and that he can overthrow man-made rules and 'custom' (7–9) – a general claim, but applying specifically to Shakespeare's flouting of neoclassical rules about time (see pp. 59–61).

On the modern stage Time has been played as a wizard, with planets and stars on his robe, as a stately octogenarian (a svelte version of the Shepherd), and as a traditional Father Time, the stooping figure on weather vanes. Time's lines have been spoken by actors whose main role was Antigonus, or Leontes, or Autolycus, or even Mamillius. On one occasion the whole cast spoke them. But the most startling treatment of Time was in the St Petersburg Maly Theatre production that toured the United Kingdom in 1999.

This production, directed by Declan Donnellan, was in Russian with English surtitles, as in the opera house. One effect of the audience's not knowing the language was that it made them concentrate on repeated gestures and actions. At the close of each scene in the first three acts, as other characters exited, a frail babushka would come on, hooded and wrapped up like a bag lady, slowly sweeping dust. When, after the interval, the old lady entered at the beginning of 4.1, once more sweeping, the audience sat waiting for Time. Suddenly the babushka stood up straight, threw back her worn cape and revealed that *she* was Time, not some crusty old man but a stunning young sweetheart with a beautiful smile and masses of blonde curls. This was Time the Disguiser, who had outwitted expectation. The surprise and delight of the audience – that Time was so genial, young and sexy – prepared them, though they didn't know it, for her return at the end of the final scene.

In this production, the sixteen years that had passed had made Leontes and Hermione two very old, bowed people. When the queen at last moved and stepped down, she and he shuffled slowly towards each other. Just as they were about to embrace, they froze, centre stage, and so did all the characters watching them. Ten, perhaps twenty seconds passed, and then, still smiling beautifully, Time entered, but not alone. She was hand in hand with Mamillius, whom she guided towards each frozen character in turn. The little boy looked at each of them, smiling as happily as Time, and then approached his father. He raised his hands above Leontes' head, as if to give a blessing, whereupon the stage went suddenly black, and the production finished. The audience couldn't believe it, and wept. This was neither tragicomedy nor romance, just tragedy – the Maly Theatre's deliberate and brilliant misinterpretation. Time alone can give joy.

This coup de théâtre – Time as protector not devourer – leads us back to the opposing kinds of time in *The Winter's Tale* – time used up and wasted, as against time stored up and impossible to lose. From one angle, the 'triumph of Time' (the subtitle of *Pandosto*) is that it makes men count what they lose each moment. Sworn brothers lose their friendship, a husband and wife lose sixteen years, their son is 'gone' for ever (see 1.2.184n.), and their daughter is given the name Perdita, 'the one lost to us' (see List of Roles, 8n.). This is official 'lost' time; but there is another triumph of Time, hidden in the shepherds' feast, in serious play. This is time that Nature stores up, in flowers, seeds and the womb, making them indestructible and eternal – even if males go crazy and try to harm them. The figure of Time, who has witnessed the coming and going of men through history, and is outside time, never himself changing, invites the audience, playfully, to encounter Nature's time.

MAKING AND REMAKING THE PLAY

By altering the end of Act 5 the Maly Theatre recast *The Winter's Tale* as a tragedy. This wasn't the first time the play had been completely reinterpreted on stage. In the eighteenth century it was turned into an abbreviated *opéra comique*, in the nineteenth century into a pastiche of ancient Greek society in Sicily (see pp. 103, 110–11).

How and when Shakespeare made the play, and how others have remade it in the theatre, are the subjects of the remainder of this Introduction. After the first performance – most probably in the spring of 1611 – did Shakespeare revise the play to introduce the statue and bring Hermione back to life? How did he reshape his sources in the first place, and did he keep a balance between their claims on our attention? Have actors and directors over the centuries chosen to emphasize particular features of the play – psychology over mythology, perhaps, or the reverse? Modern experiments with doubling roles – common practice in Shakespeare's theatre – bring these questions into sharp focus. If actors play two or three or more roles, and we are aware that they are doing it, does this shift the effect of the play too much towards story at the expense of individual identity? The Introduction concludes with the sounds of *The Winter's Tale* – in the verse and word-play – and how these communicate meanings to audiences and readers. Can the sounds too be remade?

The date and circumstances of composition

The first we hear of *The Winter's Tale* is of a performance at the Globe seen by Simon Forman in spring 1611. Forman was a scholar and scientist, but also a charlatan who had lived a colourful life in London since the 1590s. He visited the playhouses regularly, and kept notes on performances at the Theatre and the Rose as well as the Globe (Cerasano, 145–50, 157–8). In April and May 1611 he was at the Globe at least four times, probably to catch the new season – the theatres had been shut for most of the previous three years (see p. 89). Forman saw *Macbeth* on 20 April, *Cymbeline* in late April, a play about Richard II (not Shakespeare's) on 30 April and *The Winter's Tale* on Wednesday 15 May. He wrote notes on these in his manuscript 'Book of Plays', compiled for what he called 'common policy', i.e. practical use.

In his 'Book' Forman reminds himself to note this or that detail, and to remember it. Of *The Winter's Tale* he wrote:

> Observe there how Leontes the King of Sicilia was overcome with jealousy of his wife with the King of Bohemia, his friend that came to see him, and how he contrived his death and would have had his cupbearer to have poisoned, who gave the King of Bohemia warning thereof and fled with him to Bohemia.
>
> Remember also how he sent to the oracle of Apollo, and the answer of Apollo, that she was guiltless and that the King was jealous, etc., and how except the child was found again that was lost the King should die without issue, for the child was carried into Bohemia and there laid in a forest and brought up by a shepherd. And the King of Bohemia his son married that wench, and how they fled into Sicilia to

Leontes, and the shepherd having showed the letter of the nobleman by whom Leontes sent away that child, and the jewels found about her, she was known to be Leontes' daughter, and was then sixteen years old.

Remember also the rogue that came in all tattered like colt-pixie [a shape-changer in folklore] and how he feigned him sick and to have been robbed of all that he had, and how he cozened the poor man of all his money, and after came to the sheep-shear with a peddler's pack and there cozened them again of all their money, and how he changed apparel with the King of Bohemia his son, and then how he turned courtier, etc. Beware of trusting feigned beggars or fawning fellows.

(Chambers, 2.340–1)

Forman's notes are fuller than other eyewitness accounts of plays at this date. When the lawyer John Manningham saw *Twelfth Night* in 1602, he wrote less than a hundred words about it in his diary. He recognized that the play was modelled on Roman and Italian comedies, but what interested him was Malvolio's ridiculousness (Chambers, 2.327–8). In this Manningham was like Forman, who was intrigued most by Autolycus' tricks. The fullness of Forman's descriptions makes some scholars suspect that they are forgeries, but the handwriting is genuine and the provenance of the 'Book' confirms that it is authentic (Warren, 4, n. 2).

Other people who saw *The Winter's Tale* in 1611 were the dramatists Thomas Middleton and Thomas Heywood. In his comedy *No Wit, No Help Like a Woman's*, written for the Fortune theatre in the first half of 1611, Middleton has a character say

Even when my lip touched the contracting cup
Even then to see the spider

(2.1.388–9)

This sounds very much like an echo of Leontes' 'I have drunk, and seen the spider', 2.1.45 (Eccles, 297). Heywood's debt is less certain, but there appear to be recollections of *The Winter's Tale* and *The Tempest* in his plays *The Golden Age* and *The Silver Age*, performed at the Red Bull Inn. Heywood may have written them in 1611 soon after seeing Shakespeare's plays (Schanzer, '*Ages*', 21–3).

Ben Jonson probably saw *The Winter's Tale* in 1611 too, though he didn't refer to it in public for a couple of years. In the Induction to *Bartholomew Fair*, performed in 1614, Jonson, speaking about himself in the third person, tells the audience, that 'If there be never a servant-monster i' the Fair', nor 'a nest of antiques', there is nothing he can do about it. The author 'is loath to make Nature afraid in his plays, like those that beget tales, tempests and such like drolleries, to mix his head with other men's heels' (Jonson, 6.16). Shakespeare's plays – *The Winter's Tale* and *The Tempest* – appal Nature because they overturn the artistic and social orders. By 'drolleries' Jonson means lower-class entertainment, and the 'servant-monster' is Caliban in *The Tempest*. Jonson couldn't be bothered to name *Cymbeline*, but the 'nest of antiques' is probably a jibe at the scene where Jupiter hovers on his eagle over a family of ancient ghosts (Pitcher, *Cymbeline*, xxii–xxiii). Jonson's reaction suggests that by 1614 he (and perhaps others) already thought of these three Shakespeare plays as a group.

The Winter's Tale was on stage by May 1611, but how much earlier was it written? The pace Shakespeare could write at makes it possible that he started on it only a few months earlier, perhaps in November 1610.

Shakespeare was famous for his pace. When the actors praised him, the thing they singled out was his speed of execution. Shakespeare 'never blotted out' a line, they said – he didn't pause or correct himself much. This infuriated Jonson, who had been ridiculed as a plodder. Shakespeare had a torrent of words in him, Jonson conceded, but he couldn't control himself. Would that Shakespeare had blotted a thousand lines, was Jonson's retort (*Timber or Discoveries*, Jonson, 8.583).

We don't know what this speed means in lines per day, nor how much time Shakespeare found for writing amid a busy life in the theatre. To compose *The Winter's Tale*, a play of 3,000 lines, at 600 lines per week, would take five weeks. This is the amount of time Jonson said it took him to write his comedy, *Volpone*, which was 3,000 lines long (Prologue, 16: Jonson, 5.24). Jonson was smarting at jibes about his only writing one play a year, so he probably meant that five weeks was exceptional. He also knew that this was Shakespeare's pace.

In *Volpone* Jonson also claimed that the whole process, writing the play and getting it ready for its first performance, took him and the actors two months (Prologue, 13–14). If Jonson, not known for fluency, could achieve this, then Shakespeare certainly could. At Jonson's rate, Shakespeare could make ready for the stage a total of 9,000 lines – the sum of *Cymbeline*, *The Winter's Tale* and *The Tempest* – in six months. For this he would have needed to write the plays back to back, which is probably unrealistic, but it does look as though Shakespeare and the actors had it in them to create and stage all three plays within, say, a year or fifteen months.

This would be a modification of the current, conventional chronology, in which Shakespeare, it is claimed (*TxC*, 131–2), wrote these plays, one per year, in 1609, 1610 and 1611, in the sequence *The Winter's Tale*, *Cymbeline* and *The Tempest*. The difference is more than just a few months (24 or 30 months as opposed to 12 or 15). Implicit in the 'one play a year' chronology is the idea that Shakespeare returned to subjects (lost children, storms, reunions, forgiveness and reconciliation) from one play to the next, making them into a group as he went along. The 'all three in one year' model, by contrast, would allow us to argue that he conceived and wrote the plays as a group.

We saw above (p. 70) that Shakespeare borrowed the dance of the satyrs at the feast from Jonson's masque *Oberon*. At 4.4.347, the Servant announces that a dozen rustics are waiting outside. Three of them 'by their own report', the Servant tells Polixenes, have 'danced before the king' (342–3) – a joke, because it was Polixenes, here in disguise, for whom they had danced at court. The 'king' also refers to King James, before whom *Oberon* was performed on 1 January 1611.

From this, many scholars conclude that Shakespeare wrote *The Winter's Tale* between 1 January and the Globe performance on 15 May (but see pp. 92–3). We might reasonably push the earlier date back a few months, however, because preparations for the masque – costuming, building painted screens and teaching courtiers how to dance their parts – must have taken several weeks. The King's Men, providing the professional dancers, would have had an outline of the masque by, say, mid-November. Jonson would certainly have told Shakespeare well ahead just how good *Oberon* was going to be (poetry, polar bears, and a palace inside a rock). Shakespeare probably started *The Winter's Tale* six weeks or more before the end of 1610, and completed it by early May 1611. It is not impossible that the title meant something to him personally (perhaps a reminder of winter 1610–11 when he wrote it, or a working title that was never replaced).

Most scholars think that Shakespeare wrote *Cymbeline* in summer or early autumn 1610, and *The Tempest* some while later, perhaps summer 1611 (Warren, 64–7; Pitcher, *Cymbeline*, 156–7; Orgel, 62-4). This year of writing is remarkable when we set it against the rest of Shakespeare's later career. In 1608 he wrote *Coriolanus*, and in 1613–14, in collaboration with John Fletcher, he wrote his very last plays. Within the five years 1609–1614, apart from revisions to *King Lear* (see pp. 22–3), it appears that Shakespeare's only sustained writing was the group *Cymbeline*, *The Winter's Tale* and *The Tempest* in 1610–11. There is no indication that he shared the writing of these, as he did *Pericles* in 1607 and the collaborations of 1613–14. If this is correct, we are bound to ask why Shakespeare wrote so much in a single year 1610–11 after what may have been a gap of eighteen months or more from 1608.

The main reason may have been money. The plague cost the King's Men dearly in lost revenue in the three years to spring 1611, when the theatres were shut for thirty out of thirty-six months (Barroll, 173, 178–86). The actors wouldn't miss an opportunity, plague permitting, to attract audiences back for the season in 1611 with newly written and revised plays by Shakespeare and others. Some performances that Forman saw may have been premieres. The demand for drama at court was strong enough for the King's Men to be confident that their plays would appear there sooner or later – and they needed a good number of them: twenty at court in a short spell in spring 1613, at least eight of which were new (Chambers, 2.343).

There may be another reason why Shakespeare didn't begin *The Winter's Tale* earlier than 1610. In 1608 Fletcher wrote *The Faithful Shepherdess*, an attempt to adapt for the public theatre the material and conventions of highbrow Italian tragicomedy (see p. 16). The play flopped, and Fletcher blamed his audience at the Globe for being stuck in their ways. The play, he insisted in 1609, 'is a pastoral tragicomedy', which the audience,

> having ever had a singular gift in defining, concluded
> it to be a play of country hired shepherds in grey
> cloaks, with curtailed dogs in string [i.e. with docked
> tails, and tied on a leash of string], sometimes
> laughing together, and sometimes killing one another;
> and missing Whitsun ales, cream, wassail and morris
> dances, began to be angry.

> (Fletcher, 15)

Shakespeare may have taken the failure of *The Faithful Shepherdess* as a challenge – he could write a popular tragicomedy even if Fletcher couldn't – or a warning not to follow Guarini and the Italians too closely. The King's Men had just acquired the Blackfriars, an upmarket indoor playhouse, where it might be possible to cultivate a taste for English tragicomedy among more refined audiences (Gurr, *Playgoing*, 162–9). Whatever he made of *The Faithful Shepherdess*, Shakespeare didn't rush to write a tragicomedy of any kind. Better to let Fletcher fume, and to prepare his own take on the genre, in three separate but linked plays, one of them *The Winter's Tale*.

Was the play revised?

Most scholars think that Shakespeare revised parts of some of his plays. The revisions aren't extensive, sometimes only a few words or lines. The early texts of *Hamlet* differ in important ways, as do the Quarto and Folio versions of *King Lear* (see above, pp. 22–3), but the differences don't amount to a full redirection of the plot or a new denouement. Lear and Cordelia die in both texts of *King Lear* – by contrast with the outcome in the anonymous *King Leir*, in which they survive and are reunited.

With *The Winter's Tale*, according to some critics, Shakespeare undertook a much larger revision. On the strength of Forman's notes on the May 1611 performance – in which he doesn't mention the statue – they propose that what he saw was an earlier version of the play where Hermione died in 3.2 and didn't come back to life (as in the source *Pandosto*). In the May performance, the argument runs, the reunion of Leontes and Perdita was shown onstage and the play ended at that point. Shakespeare subsequently added the statue scene (5.3), perhaps for the performance at court on 5 November 1611 (Chambers, 2.342), and he turned the reunion of Leontes and Perdita into a narrative (now 5.2). He altered other parts of the play as well, but he forgot or couldn't be bothered to rewrite Antigonus' description of the spectre in 3.3, which had seemed to confirm Hermione's death.

No known Shakespeare revision is of this magnitude – an entirely different ending – so the burden of proof is high. The only evidence, however, is in Forman – the rest of the case is conjecture and the critics' dissatisfaction with how Shakespeare wrote the play.

Forman is not a reliable witness. He misremembered and neglected what he saw in performances of other plays, and often he didn't retell the story so much as reorganize it, in terms of what interested him – hierarchies of rank, for example, and coincidences (see Pitcher, *Cymbeline*, xxvii–xxix). He may have left out things he couldn't see the point of, the Bear and the satyrs for example – the bear he saw in another play was an avenging devil, which made sense to him as a figure of retribution (Pitcher, 'Bear', 48–50). Also, like other playgoers, Forman probably didn't concentrate all the time in the theatre, and he may not have stayed to the end of the performance. If the prospect of Hermione's statue, promised in 5.2, didn't interest him, perhaps he left early (like a crowd leaving a football match before a goal in the final minute), never expecting the statue to come to life.

Without Forman's testimony, the theory is just guesswork. Its advocates maintain that the play as we have it doesn't prepare us for Hermione's return (it isn't referred to in the oracle, for example), but there are clear hints and anticipations that she will (e.g. 5.1.56–60, 73–5, 76–81; 5.2.102–5; and see Cam², 63–6, especially the list on 65). Other parts of the theory require special pleading, in particular that Shakespeare wrote a striking new ending but couldn't be bothered to revise earlier scenes to fit it. Furthermore, that it wasn't until he saw his 'first version' on stage that it occurred to him to bring the wronged wife back to life. But if he could imagine this daring alternative after he had seen the performance in May, why not before? One is left with the suspicion that some critics think *The Winter's Tale* would be a more credible play if Shakespeare hadn't ruined it with the spectre, the Bear and the statue.

Another claim continues to surface – that the play was revised for the royal family – but this is even more mistaken. *The Winter's Tale* was performed at court on some occasion between 16 February 1613 and 20 May 1613, as one of the celebrations of the wedding of Elizabeth, daughter of King James, to Frederick, Elector Palatine of Bohemia (Chambers, 2.342–3). It is argued that in Shakespeare's 'first version', Bohemia and Sicilia were as they are in the source *Pandosto* – the King of Sicily visits the King of Bohemia – but the names and places were swapped in 1613, to avoid offending Frederick of Bohemia. However, when Forman saw the play, at least twenty-one months before the wedding, the kings and counties had already been transposed (see pp. 84–5).

One argument for revision has a bearing on the date of the play. The contention above is that a starting date for composition (*c*. November 1610) can be established by the allusion to the satyrs that danced in the masque *Oberon*. This hasn't convinced everyone. It is accepted that Shakespeare wrote the speeches that introduce the satyrs (4.4.329–47), and that the passage contains a reference to the dance in *Oberon*. What is not proven, to some minds, is that the passage was present when the play was first written.

According to this view, the speeches and satyr dance were a topical interpolation. It is pointed out that the whole passage could be omitted without disturbing the dialogue around it. The transition from the end of Autolycus' song (money 'doth utter all men's ware-a', 328) to Polixenes' remark to the Shepherd ('you'll know more of that hereafter', 348) is more natural, it is said, without the passage. The interpolation must date from January 1611 or later, but the rest of *The Winter's Tale* may have been written months or even years earlier, for example in 1609 (Nicoll, 56–7; Oxf, 601).

The idea of interpolation isn't easy to accept in a scene as big as 4.4. Even without the satyrs, it is nearly 850 lines, needing more than forty minutes to play (see p. 72). Shakespeare, it is claimed, made this huge scene even longer by adding speeches and a second dance. Moreover, if the satyrs passage is so readily attachable, it must be equally detachable. Shakespeare knew that the actors would perform *The Winter's Tale* at court and on tour as well as in their London theatres. Writing a full text in 1610–11, from which speeches might be cut easily and dancers and extras dropped, according to the venue, would be expected of an experienced in-house dramatist. Viewed like this, the satyrs passage looks like an allusion from 1610–11, written so that it could be removed seamlessly when *Oberon* was no longer topical.

Shakespeare's reshaping of the sources

The revision theories in various ways underestimate how Shakespeare conceived of *The Winter's Tale* through its sources – conceived of it not as one source added to another (a narrative to which a statue was added), but as a whole from the outset.

This whole is made up of three strands of Greek writing and mythology. The first strand, familiar to us from Ovid's *Metamorphoses*, is the story of Pygmalion. In Ovid, the sculptor Pygmalion makes a statue of a woman whom Venus brings to life. In the much older Greek myth, however, Pygmalion isn't an artist who ends up making love to his creation but a king besotted with a statue of Aphrodite (Venus), which he tries to have sex with. There is no transformation, and the king is depicted as mad and disgusting. The myth was connected with a pagan cult of Aphrodite on Cyprus, where kings were high priests, but to modern eyes this is a dark story of pathological obsession, which Ovid domesticated and gave a happy end to.

The second strand, from the fifth century BC, is in Euripides' tragedy of Alcestis, the wife who gave her life so that her husband could live. The darkness this time is in the destructive obligation Apollo has to Alcestis' husband, Admetus. The god helps him to live beyond his allotted years but only by having another die in his place. This brings Admetus shame and self-loathing, made all the more agonizing when no one but Alcestis, not even his elderly parents, will sacrifice themselves for him. Euripides answers this old myth of powerlessness with the irreverent strength of the demigod Hercules, who literally fights and overcomes Death at Alcestis' funeral and brings her back to her husband (see further pp. 447–8).

The third strand, from the second century AD, isn't from a myth or a particular work, but from a genre, the ancient novel, often known as Greek romance. All the genres of antiquity (epic, tragedy, comedy, pastoral) flow confusedly into Greek romance, so it has a variety of styles, moods and plots, as well as different preoccupations – unrequited pastoral love in one, a mysterious heroine outsmarting pirates in another. In all these novels the darker element is at the edges of the story, perhaps because they were written when Christianity was replacing the pagan gods. The threat of incest in them, for instance, is only ever a threat, not the reality it is in Sophocles' *Oedipus the King*.

The Greek romances and Latinized novels that followed them were of immense appeal in the Renaissance. Shakespeare knew them in translation (he used *Apollonius of Tyre* for *Pericles*), and he read widely in the imitations of Greek romance (see Gesner, 116–25, for examples), including Sidney's *Arcadia*, from which he drew the Gloucester plot in *King Lear*. Robert Greene imitated the Greek romances and the *Arcadia* in several of his romances, among them *Pandosto*, which was Shakespeare's chief source for *The Winter's Tale*.[1]

Pandosto was an Elizabethan bestseller. Published in 1588 with two titles – *Pandosto or the Triumph of Time* and *The History of Dorastus and Fawnia* – it was reprinted more than a dozen times before 1642. There were a further dozen reprints by 1700 and twenty more by the early nineteenth century (Newcombe, 262). Only the flowering of the epistolary novel finished off the taste

---

1 Four of the play's sources are reproduced on pp. 405–52.

for it among the middle class, after which its readers were less sophisticated. In one comic episode in Samuel Richardson's *Clarissa* (1747–8), everyone in the house is nearly burnt to death because of the carelessness of a cook-maid who 'having sat up to read the simple history of Dorastus and Faunia when she should have been in bed', set fire to a pair of curtains (723). In its first fifty years *Pandosto* was imitated, abridged, turned into verse, twice translated into French, and twice adapted for the French stage. By the time Shakespeare used it, the story of Pandosto was familiar everywhere.

Greene's romance has two overlapping plots, hence the separate titles. The first deals with Pandosto, King of Bohemia, the second with his daughter Fawnia and her lover Dorastus. The action of *The Winter's Tale* is mostly the same as in the first plot, up to the trial scene 3.2. Pandosto believes that his wife Bellaria and his friend Egistus, King of Sicily, are lovers, and he orders a servant to poison Egistus. The servant informs Egistus and they flee, and Pandosto puts his wife in prison. She finds she is pregnant and gives birth to a daughter, Fawnia, whom the king declares illegitimate, the child of Egistus. The baby is cast out in a small boat in a storm. When Pandosto and his noblemen question the queen, she asks them to seek Apollo's judgement from his oracle at Delphos. The god's verdict, read out at her trial, is that she is chaste, Egistus blameless, her daughter innocent, and that 'the King shall live without an heir if that which is lost be not found'. Pandosto says at once that he has wronged his wife and promises to make amends, but news of the sudden death of their young son Garinter causes the queen to collapse and die. The king tries to kill himself, but is persuaded to live for the sake of his kingdom. He buries his queen and son in a magnificent tomb, where each day he mourns their deaths.

The second plot begins with the baby in the boat coming to shore in Sicily, Egistus' kingdom. Porrus, a poor shepherd, finds Fawnia, and takes her home to his wife. They adopt her, passing her off as their own child. Sixteen years go by and Fawnia grows into a beautiful shepherdess. At court Egistus wants his son Dorastus to marry a foreign princess but Dorastus prevaricates, to his father's annoyance. Out hawking one day, Dorastus sees Fawnia acting as mistress in a country feast. Despite himself, he is smitten. She also falls in love with him, but their difference in rank makes them struggle against their desires. Dorastus eventually convinces Fawnia that he wants to marry her, not just have sex, and they make plans to elope to Italy. Porrus gets wind of their love and fears Egistus' anger. He decides to tell Egistus how he found Fawnia, but on the way to the palace he encounters Capnio, Dorastus' servant, who forces him on board the lovers' ship just as it is leaving. When Egistus finds out about their marrying, the thought of it nearly kills him.

Dorastus and Fawnia, driven off course by a tempest, arrive in Pandosto's kingdom. When the couple appear at court, the prince makes up an unconvincing story about who they are. Pandosto puts him in prison, and tries to seduce Fawnia. Hearing that Dorastus is imprisoned, Egistus sends ambassadors to request his release and the immediate execution of Fawnia, the shepherd and Capnio. Pandosto agrees, but they are saved by the shepherd's account of how he found Fawnia, from which Pandosto recognizes that this is his daughter. There is great rejoicing and everyone travels to the court of Egistus, who is happy for the couple to be married at once. When the celebrations are finished, Pandosto becomes desperate and kills himself at the thought of his wickedness, including lust for his own daughter. His body is returned to Bohemia and placed in the tomb with his wife and son. Dorastus rules in his place.

Shakespeare's changes to the story show that he found a meaning in it that Greene never sought. The two halves of *Pandosto* are held together by chance and by 'the triumph of Time'. Fawnia survives the open seas, and a childhood later, as predicted by the oracle, she comes home, again by chance because of a storm. No questions are posed for readers about why she survived, or why Pandosto, after all his awfulness, should live to see her again. In Greene, circumstances change – a mother dies, her daughter grows up to marry a prince – but people don't. At the end Pandosto is the same impetuous, intemperate and irascible tyrant he was at the beginning. This appears to be Greene's point. His characters are unknowing captives in Time's triumph over them: they don't understand what happens to them, so when events unfold they learn nothing.

In *The Winter's Tale*, by contrast, the central characters are always on the verge of seeing larger patterns in their lives. Perdita glimpses the ancient daughter–mother myth of Proserpina and Ceres in a provincial country festival, and then she and Hermione unconsciously act it out in the statue scene. Autolycus, the selfish trickster, sees that he will end up doing good even when he doesn't want to. In Act 4 the play moves from day-to-day 'real' time into mythic timelessness. Shakespeare changes the end of the Pandosto plot, so that the queen doesn't die for ever, and he replaces Greene's Time with his own – a new Time who unfolds Nature and shows the art that human beings have to put into life to preserve what is natural.

Shakespeare's first attempt at a dead-wife and living-daughter myth was in *Pericles*, written in 1607. In this the daughter Marina is reunited onstage with her father Pericles, after being lost to him for sixteen years. In the final scene, when Marina and Pericles visit the shrine of Diana, they are by chance reunited with Thaisa, Marina's mother. Pericles had thought that Thaisa was dead, but she had survived – as the audience knew – and become one of Diana's priestesses.

In *The Winter's Tale* Shakespeare went further with the mythology of the dead wife. For this he combined two classical stories, one about giving life, the other restoring it – the first Pygmalion and the living statue in Ovid, the second Alcestis back from the dead in Euripides (see pp. 9–10, 14–15 and 446–8).

With Alcestis, Shakespeare drew on intermediaries as well as the story in Euripides. Critics have shown that the Latin translation he used was the one by the humanist George Buchanan (Dewar-Watson, 79–80). In some cases, Buchanan's small additions to the Greek original would have given hints. When, for instance, Admetus imagines his wife after her death visiting him while he sleeps, he says, in Buchanan (222), *'umbra me per somnia / utinam reversa oblectet'* ('would that your ghost might delight me, returning in my dreams') (ll. 365–6). There is no equivalent for *'umbra'* ('ghost') in Euripides, which Buchanan inferred from the context and added (Wilson, 349). From this Shakespeare probably got the idea for the Hermione spectre in Antigonus' dream.

Another intermediary – an adaptation of Euripides – was the Elizabethan short story *Admetus and Alcest*. This was by George Pettie, from whom Shakespeare borrowed details in other stories for *Cymbeline* and earlier plays. In *Admetus and Alcest* it isn't Hercules but Proserpina, goddess of the underworld, who restores Alcestis. Hearing of Admetus' grief, and 'pitying the parting of this loving couple (for that she herself knew the pain of parting from friends, being by Dis stolen from her mother Ceres)', Proserpina 'put life into his wife again, and with speed sent her unto him' (Pettie, 145). In Pettie there is neither a veiled lady nor Admetus' joyful recognition. The dead wife is returned simply because the goddess recalls how she lost her mother.

The Proserpina myth was famous everywhere – it is in the *Metamorphoses* – but this aspect of it has a particular place in *The Winter's Tale*. In the statue scene Hermione is restored to life and to her husband through the intervention of Perdita, her lost daughter, who alludes wistfully to Proserpina and Dis as she gives out flowers at the feast (see pp. 50–3). Pettie's version probably showed Shakespeare how to remake the Alcestis story as a reunion, not of a husband and wife alone, but of a family.

Euripides' play, read through the lens of *Admetus and Alcest*, gave something the Pygmalion story couldn't. Ovid portrayed a mind inflamed by its own power: if it imagined something vehemently enough, even a marble body would obey it. Venus is the immediate reason for the statue coming to life, but she is a mask for Pygmalion's wish-fulfilment. Shakespeare uses this story to show how, in Leontes' case, far from giving life to physical objects around him, he turns real bodies into figments of his imagination: 'Your actions are my dreams', he tells his wife at one point (3.2.80), not realizing what he has said (see p. 47).

The Alcestis story, by contrast, is about the ceremonies human beings use in the face of death. Apollo, to thank Admetus, gives him the gift of another life. Admetus isn't unusually greedy or selfish; he just wants to stay alive. The moment he accepts another gift, from Alcestis, and she begins to die for him, the play turns into a duet between the couple, who recount the love and happiness they have had together, as it slips away. What drew Shakespeare to them was their insistence on ceremony, including new personal ceremonies they had to make up to face the final farewell.

Of course the farewell isn't for ever, and is replaced by Admetus' recognizing his wife in the double she isn't, uneasy, tentative and full of wonder (see pp. 13, 447–8). This is what we see in the statue scene, in the acts of contrition, the humbleness and petitions, the tears and smiles, and the uncertainty of what lies next. Pygmalion was about control and fixation. *Alcestis* showed a couple facing one another after a disaster – rewarded, despite expecting nothing, with the gift of life together.

Some smaller changes that Shakespeare made to Greene's story have puzzled the critics. In *Pandosto* the action begins in Bohemia, moves to Sicilia and ends back in Bohemia: the jealous host is the King of Bohemia, the visitor the King of Sicilia. In the play, the countries and kings are swapped round, and the direction of the story is inverted, starting in Sicilia, moving to Bohemia, and then back to Sicilia.

Why would Shakespeare do this? There is not much specificity about either of the countries – no mention of the capitals or other locale, for instance, except an odd reference to a particular tuft of trees on the way to the coast in Sicilia (2.1.34). The setting for the feast in Bohemia is particularly unforeign. It is pure Warwickshire, in fact. The price of wool and holiday food and games are straight from Shakespeare's Stratford.

This shouldn't lead us to think that Shakespeare had no sense of geography. Certainly, his countries are nothing like the real countries in the sixteenth century. Shakespeare follows Greene in making Sicilia and Bohemia independent monarchies whose subjects worship the pagan gods. In reality they were subordinate nations, dominated by the Spanish and Austrian Habsburgs. In religion, Sicily was Catholic and Bohemia Protestant. Sicily was at the heart of the Mediterranean empire of Philip II of Spain, while Bohemia was famous for its imperial court in Prague, which attracted artists and scientists from all over Europe (Bate, 'Islands', 298–301).

Greene knew all this, and so did Shakespeare. They also knew where the countries were (Gillies, 34–6, 45–51). A glance at the maps drawn by Ortelius and Mercator would have shown them that Sicilia and Bohemia were on the exact same south–north axis, and that Bohemia was landlocked in middle Europe, ringed by mountains (see Fig. 16).

Perhaps Shakespeare's motive for transposing the countries was, yet again, serious play. By redirecting the flow of Greene's story upwards on the map from bottom to top – south to north rather than north to south – Shakespeare turned his source upside down. He made it another of the play's 'preposterous' inversions (where the world is turned upside down: see p. 78). Perhaps renaming the characters was part of this. The national symbol of real Bohemia was a lion, but in Shakespeare it is the King of Sicily who is called Leontes (*Leo*, Latin for 'lion'), while the King of Bohemia has a Greek name, Polixenes, thus associated with Sicily and the Mediterranean.

One detail in *Pandosto* that Shakespeare didn't change was Bohemia's coastline. This 'mistake' soon became a byword

16 'Our ship hath touched upon / The deserts of Bohemia' (3.3.1–2). The Renaissance map of Europe (detail): from Abraham Ortelius' world atlas of 1606 (which Shakespeare and his contemporaries were familiar with), showing Bohemia ringed by mountains and landlocked in central Europe (in the modern Czech republic), due north of Sicily and the Adriatic

for ignorance. In 1619 Jonson said that 'Shakespeare in a play brought in a number of men saying they had suffered shipwreck in Bohemia, where there is no sea near by some 100 miles' (Chambers, 2.207). This doesn't happen in any scene in *The Winter's Tale* as we have it, but the charge of gross error has stuck. To save Shakespeare's blushes, in the eighteenth century the editor Thomas Hanmer went so far as to replace 'Bohemia' throughout the play with 'Bithynia', a country that did have a coastline.

Believing that Bohemia had a coastline was widely taken as a sign of ignorance and stupidity. While in France in about 1620, Edward, Lord Herbert of Cherbury, saw the French king doting on a foolish favourite. How 'unfit this man was for the credit he had with the King', Herbert wrote, 'may be argued by this; that when there was question made about some business in Bohemia', the favourite demanded 'whether it was an inland country, or lay upon the sea?' (Herbert, 104–5). Around the same date, a fictitious but comparably ignorant alderman, 'Gregory Gandergoose' (i.e. a bumpkin), asked the poet John Taylor, who had just returned from Prague, if Bohemia was a large town, and whether the latest fleet of ships had arrived there yet (Taylor, sig. 3H4^v, p. 90).

This clearly wasn't Shakespeare's mistake, but a joke. Alluding to Bohemia's coastline would raise a laugh, as do modern jokes about the Jamaican ice hockey team or the Swiss Navy. A shipwreck off Bohemia in Act 3 would alert early audiences to the unreality and make-believe that was to follow in the remainder of *The Winter's Tale*. But if the joke was so familiar why didn't Jonson get it? Was he out of humour, or was there something that for once he simply didn't know he ought to laugh at?

The play on stage

As with Shakespeare's other plays, *The Winter's Tale* has two histories. The first history describes how it has been staged in the theatre and latterly on film, the second how readers, writers and painters have drawn on or alluded to it, or created it anew. The stage history is fairly complete from the eighteenth century onwards (see Bartholomeusz; Tatspaugh; and Turner, 798–851), but the wider, cultural history of the play remains unwritten. Milton borrowed from the play, as discussed below, and George Eliot made it one of the theatricals planned in *Daniel Deronda* (see Fig. 19, p. 106). The Romantic painter Joseph Wright showed the storm as a glimpse of the Sublime, with Antigonus and the Bear tiny figures dwarfed by crashing waves and a darkened sky. Henry Fuseli, famous for his version of the witches in *Macbeth*, transformed the Shepherd's discovery of Perdita into a moment of pure William Blake (Fig. 17), while his contemporary John Opie painted the Bear as from a nightmare (Fig. 22, p. 134). In 1865, John Tenniel drew Queen Victoria as Hermione fixed as a statue (Fig. 18).

The most intriguing overlap between the histories occurred in the nineteenth century. *The Winter's Tale* begins and ends in Sicily, and Perdita alludes to the Proserpina myth associated with the island. It seems likely that Shakespeare intended Sicily to have a special meaning in the play. In the Victorian theatre, however, Sicily's antiquity, or classical aspect, was exaggerated absurdly – to the point where Leontes' court was an amphitheatre, filled with hundreds of extras, and the feast in Bohemia a reconstruction of a Dionysian revel (see pp. 110–11).

In 1866 this impulse to classicize the play spilt out of the theatre into a book called *Scenes from the Winter's Tale*, a collection of twenty-three chromolithographic plates by the Welsh designer Owen Jones with Henry Warren. The plates rendered scenes from the play as coloured and gilt figures in relief, as if on ancient Greek vases and wall paintings. The implication was that Shakespeare was a classic, and that *The Winter's Tale* found truest expression in classical form. It also suggested that the play, an ancient artefact, recorded profound myths and tragic episodes.

17 'Methought I heard the shepherd say he found the child' (5.2.6–7).
Engraving by J. Neagle of a drawing by Henry Fuseli (1803) depicting the
Shepherd as muscular and strong, a Blake-like figure of fate in a cloak and
corselet

18   'Tis time; descend; be stone no more' (5.3.99). Cartoon by John Tenniel
      in *Punch* magazine (1865) showing Britannia (Paulina) drawing a curtain to
      reveal Victoria (Hermione), i.e. the British Empire urges its queen to come
      out of her overlong retirement following the death of Prince Albert

19 'You perceive she stirs' (5.3.103). Print showing Alexander Pope (d. 1835) as Leontes and Mary Ann Powell as Hermione in an unknown London production *c.* 1804, i.e. at the height of fears that the French were about to invade England. Leontes is made up to look like Napoleon in imperial robes, taken aback as a very English lady (or Britannia herself) wakes up to the threat of French tyranny. George Eliot may have remembered similar engravings for the description in Chapter 6 of *Daniel Deronda* (1876) of the private theatricals and choice of *The Winter's Tale*. 'It will be more Shakespearian and romantic', one character says, 'if Leontes looks like Napoleon' (90)

But the Warren figures showed nothing of the other side of the play, its scrutiny of Leontes' wickedness. In the theatre over the centuries actors and directors have also found it hard to hold together the two elements in *The Winter's Tale*, of psychology and myth. Sometimes they have emphasized one at the expense of the other, or simply cut out one altogether, deciding that it was impossible to reconcile the contradiction. The history of the play in the theatre tells us what choices have been made, and will continue to be made in the future.

It is not known how *The Winter's Tale* was played in the seventeenth century. It seems to have been successful at court, where it was performed several times (Chambers, 2.341–3, 346–7, 352). The play may have been popular with upper-crust people, like the group of amateurs in the 1630s who started preparing it for a private performance (Taylor & Jowett, 6). One person who surely saw it in the 1620s was the poet John Milton. In the early poem 'L'Allegro', Milton says that a man in good spirits may go to the theatre to enjoy either a Jonson comedy or a play by Shakespeare, warbling 'his native woodnotes wild' (ll. 131–4; Milton, 25). By this he meant watching Shakespeare's plays in general, but around the same date (1630) he wrote a poem of sixteen lines, 'On Shakespeare', that appeared among pieces prefacing the 1632 Second Folio. In this – his first poem in print – Milton says that Shakespeare has built himself a 'livelong monument' in the 'wonder and astonishment' of audiences (Milton, 20). His 'Delphic lines' bereave them of their 'fancy' and make them 'marble with too much conceiving'. The word-play here – in which Shakespeare frees himself from a marble tomb by transforming readers into marble statues (punning on 'marble' and 'marvel') – probably alludes to the statue in *The Winter's Tale* and to Apollo's oracle in Act 3. The sixteen lines may allude to the gap of time between Acts 3 and 4, and the words 'wonder and astonishment' to the end of the play.

In the decades that followed, Milton continued to draw on *The Winter's Tale* – the flowers in *Paradise Lost*, Book 9, are from 4.4.118–27 – but he shows no recollection of its transforming wonder on stage. He wasn't alone in this. Memories of the play in the theatre died out within a generation. The last time it was played in the seventeenth century was at court in 1634. After that, it wasn't on the stage for over a century. No one even bothered to rewrite it, as happened after the Restoration with *The Tempest* and *Cymbeline*.

It wasn't that the Leontes story was uninteresting – the popularity of *Pandosto*, which Shakespeare had used for the plot, continued well into the eighteenth century (see pp. 94–5). The difficulty was that audiences, newly neoclassical in their tastes, wouldn't accept the play's two-part structure. When at last the impresario Henry Giffard mounted a production at Covent Garden in 1741, it folded quickly. There was a good cast – the famous Hannah Pritchard was Paulina – but *The Winter's Tale*, played as a whole, was unacceptable in Georgian London.

The solution was to cut away half of the play. Macnamara Morgan attempted it first, in an adaptation called *The Sheep-Shearing: or, Florizel and Perdita*, which excluded everything but the feast in Act 4. *The Sheep-Shearing* was played first at Covent Garden in 1754, and was successful enough for a series of revivals before the end of the century. More importantly, it prompted David Garrick, the leading actor-manager of his day, to attempt another abbreviation, with the same title *Florizel and Perdita*. Like Morgan, Garrick did away with the first three Acts, opening his version at the feast in Bohemia, but he had the good sense to retain the heart of Act 5, the statue scene. He had to alter things to do it – Leontes and Paulina had to travel to Bohemia, for example – but it gave him a wonderful set-piece ending, between himself as Leontes and Hannah Pritchard as Hermione. The attention in Garrick's version was on the impossible victory of love over rank, and love over death.

Garrick's *Florizel and Perdita* opened at Drury Lane in 1756, with Susannah Cibber as Perdita and Richard Yates as Autolycus (a role Garrick expanded to show off Yates's comic talents). But it was Hannah Pritchard as the statue, and Garrick's reaction to her, that audiences wanted to see. The engraving of Pritchard, an elegant figure leaning gracefully against a classical plinth, became famous, as did Garrick's way of delivering his first line when the statue moved, retreating from it in a startled, exaggerated manner (a piece of stage business that soon became traditional: see Fig. 19). *Florizel and Perdita* was a vehicle for stars to perform duets and arias, full of sweetness, passion and sorrow, which brought the experience very close to opera. It was no accident that Susannah

Cibber was praised for the way she performed a song Garrick had added to Act 4, 'Come, come, my good shepherds, our flocks let us shear'. Mrs Cibber as Perdita, it was said, 'was the delight of the audience', singing with the same 'musical powers' Handel had admired 'when he produced her in his Oratorio of the *Messiah*' (Murphy, 1.286).

Garrick gave his audiences wonder and sentiment, but none of Leontes' perverse misunderstandings, nor any sense of irreparable loss. *Florizel and Perdita* was a fragment, with the unpalatable bits of the play left out. It was swept off the stage at the end of the century by a younger generation that wanted to know why Leontes thought and did such horrible things, and why Shakespeare had set the actors such a large and daunting task of binding the play together.

The Winter's Tale returned to the stage, complete in essentials, in 1802, in a production at Drury Lane directed by John Philip Kemble, another of the great actor-managers. Kemble did two bold things. He made Leontes' psychology the focus of the play, acting the part himself, and he turned the action and settings into a sequence of stage pictures. The first gained him praise from audiences and critics. When William Hazlitt wrote of Leontes' reasoning 'on his own jealousy, beset with doubts and fears, and entangled more and more in the thorny labyrinth', it was Kemble he recalled, who had, Hazlitt said, 'worked himself up into a very fine classical frenzy' (Hazlitt, 278, 281). But the stage designs and costumes were less admired. Kemble was attacked for putting together a jumble of historical reconstructions – pseudo-antiquities, medieval court furniture, buildings from Piranesi – that added nothing to the play. However, the production survived, because once again there was an actress on top form, Sarah Siddons, playing the queen. According to the poet and critic Thomas Campbell, Shakespeare's genius 'was at its zenith' when he wrote the statue scene in *The Winter's Tale*, 'but it was only a Siddons that could do justice to its romantic perfection' (Campbell, 2.265).

Kemble's playing of Leontes, as a sober, dignified man struggling gravely with jealousy, was soon replaced, but after Kemble no one in the nineteenth century theatre doubted that the key to the play was the king's mental state. William Charles Macready played him as a mercurial figure, volatile in the opening scenes, full of joy and contrition at the end. For Samuel Phelps, who took the part from the 1840s to the 1860s, Leontes was naturally predisposed to jealousy, as Coleridge believed. Phelps made the king less sympathetic but more convincing; audiences were gripped by his moodiness, truculence and morbid fear of being ridiculed. There was less innovation in the way Hermione was played, but the role continued to attract first-rank actresses, among them Helena Faucit – who corresponded with Tennyson about it – and Mary Amelia Warner.

The Kemble innovation of period-piece reconstructions, although the critics hated it, was taken up by his successors. The charge that Kemble had confused historical periods made them determined to be accurate. In the Phelps production at Sadler's Wells in 1845, the *Times* of 28 November noted 'felicitous representations of classical interiors, decorated in the polychromatic style'. No expense was spared on architraves, columns and friezes, with costumes based on what the Victorians thought the upper class had worn in ancient Greece and Rome.

In later productions, especially Charles Kean's in 1856, the spectacle became even more lavish and archaeologically correct; 'a sort of classical museum' was how one contemporary praised the *mise en scène* (*Times*, 29 April). There was a Pyrrhic dance in Act 1, and the feast in was 'heightened into a Dionysiac orgie' with two hundred dancers. The figure of Time in 4.1 was replaced with a classical Kronos who spoke his lines as part of a stellar pageant of the flight of time, with Luna in her car and Phoebus in his chariot. It is no surprise that Kean was lampooned in *Punch* for allowing the actors and Shakespeare's poetry to be buried under carpentry, dances and misused learning ('Mr Punch', 190, 198–9).

The Winter's Tale wasn't the only Shakespeare play given a historical makeover at this date, but the effect of misapplied scholarship was more harmful to it than to other plays, distracting audiences from the play's imaginative coherence – how the jealous palace, the idyll of the hidden princess and the chapel of mysterious life might be related to each other. The theatre for the rest of the nineteenth century did nothing to connect these. Indeed, the only new thing that happened on stage with *The Winter's Tale* was in the late 1880s when the beautiful American celebrity actress Mary Anderson staged a production, first in London then in New York, in which she played both Hermione and Perdita.

This was the first time this doubling had been attempted on the modern stage and it brought Anderson a great deal of attention. The critics liked her as Perdita, and she was praised for the static pose she struck as the statue, but there was severe criticism on both sides of the Atlantic for her sloppy diction and speaking of the verse (e.g. Archer, 214–19). The trick necessary in the statue scene, with an actor standing in for her as Perdita, was received very coolly. The 'confusion of identity between mother and daughter', one reviewer wrote, 'detracts from the spectator's enjoyment of the play as a whole' (*Times*, 12 September 1887). There is no sign that Anderson was making some deeper point about Hermione being given new life through her daughter (the aim of doublings of Hermione and Perdita in more recent times, as discussed on pp. 120–1). Anderson's production was a star vehicle, in which her costumes complemented more than a dozen sumptuous stage sets.

By 1900, the extravagance of the fictions in *The Winter's Tale* had given way entirely to theatrical profligacy. Impresarios spent big money on props, sets and shows, convinced that these enhanced the poetic effect of the play. As late as 1906, Herbert Beerbohm Tree put on a production from which he cut half the text to accommodate the spectacular sets (including, for the feast, a real donkey and a full-scale running brook). This had a good cast, with Ellen Terry as Hermione, but nothing could save it from the critics.

The inevitable reaction came in 1912 at the Savoy Theatre with Harley Granville-Barker's production. He created intimacy between actors and audience by building a completely new stage – a platform thrust over the orchestra pit with no footlights – and he did everything to quicken the pace of the playing and delivery of verse. The sets were abstract, with no pretence at realism, and drop curtains were used frequently to maintain continuous action. Costumes and furniture were just as revolutionary: Beardsley mixed eclectically with Hottentots, the Russian Ballet and art nouveau, and the rustics dressed out of Thomas Hardy. The cast was very talented (Henry Ainley as Leontes, Lillah McCarthy as Hermione and Cathleen Nesbitt as Perdita), but Granville-Barker shifted the emphasis away from stars to quality ensemble playing. He removed next to nothing of Shakespeare's text, and worked hard with the actors to perfect their lines.

Some reviewers loved the 1912 production, dubbing it post-impressionist Shakespeare. One headline read 'Startling discovery at the Savoy: Shakespeare alive!' Others hated it, and audiences weren't convinced either. It closed after six weeks, but it was perhaps the most exceptional version of *The Winter's Tale* in the twentieth century (Kennedy, 123–36). Its innovations and exuberance weren't seen again until Nunn's production in 1969 (see above, pp. 26–8). Only Peter Brook's production at the Phoenix Theatre in 1951, with John Gielgud in astonishing form as Leontes, can bear comparison with it.

Brook's was the most popular, longest-running production ever staged – 167 performances. It was criticized for its pseudo-Elizabethan staging, with scenery still placed within the proscenium, but no one doubted its cast. Diana Wynyard as Hermione was the epitome of beauty, sweet temper and patience, while Flora Robson, everyone agreed, was surely the best Paulina they would ever see, not a comic scold but a great court lady.

Playgoers recalled how, as Perdita left the stage at the end of 5.1, Robson gazed in silence at her, half knowing, before everyone else did, who this princess must be (Venezky, 338).

Gielgud's Leontes was the opposite of what Ainley made the role in 1912. For Ainley, Leontes was manic and black-hearted. The mischief in him – what Coleridge called his trivial hatred (Bate, *Romantics*, 160) – wasn't caused by anything external; it was simply looking for its outlet in jealousy and tyranny. Gielgud, by contrast, played the king as a good man trying to hold within himself his private nightmares, and only failing after a monumental struggle. His instinct always was to behave with dignity and to look deep into things. When in the statue scene (see Fig. 20) Paulina told him and the others, 'It is required / You do awake your faith' (5.3.94–5), he knelt at once, aware that this was a sacred moment. Theatre historians who saw Gielgud play the role with such gravity and sober grandeur thought they could hear echoes of Macready and the great actors of earlier centuries (Sprague, 164–5).

The divide between Ainley and Gielgud, and Granville-Barker and Brook, was more than just settings and style. Granville-Barker viewed *The Winter's Tale* as a modern, absurdist fiction. The human heart had cruel irrational things in it, including a desire to triumph over others; only Nature and capricious fate could overturn such unprepared-for evil. Granville-Barker came at the play through his earlier productions of Greek tragedy, Euripides in particular, and for him Shakespeare's theatre wasn't a temple of psychology but a place of myth, ritual, and ceremonial undoing of what seemed vile and unalterable in the world. For Brook, by contrast, Shakespeare had written *The Winter's Tale* around Leontes. The moral chaos inside the king had to be released through his own actions and those of the people around him. Hermione and Perdita would suffer, but not in vain if Leontes was a great enough human being, and truly penitent. Brook's underlying notion was that events and human motives are always intelligible even if unpleasant and painful.

20 'Methinks / There is an air comes from her. What fine chisel / Could ever yet cut breath?' (5.3.77–9). Flora Robson as Paulina and John Gielgud as Leontes, at the moment Diana Wynyard as Hermione is revealed (5.3.20 SD), in Peter Brook's production at the Phoenix Theatre, London, in 1951. Hermione, in 'shining, visionary white, a statue that with eyes lowered, open hands, arms slightly bent was strikingly beautiful, both sacred and human', as if Brook had taken 'his poetic vision of this scene from the dream of Antigonus' (Bartholomeusz, 173)

Since Brook, Leontes' moral character has become of less interest in the theatre, and the poetic fable linking his wife and daughter harder to believe in. In 1969 Nunn turned Leontes into an overgrown boy in need of therapy, and in 1992 the mythic, 'bigger truths than we can understand' element was presented by Théâtre de Complicité as another aspect of the child and childishness in Leontes (see p. 28). Making *The Winter's Tale* a coherent whole is still the prize in the theatre. To help achieve this, modern directors have gone back to the roots of Elizabethan drama and to the practice of actors doubling roles.

Doubling roles

Before the public theatres were built in the 1570s, dramatists wrote plays to be acted in different venues (halls, courtyards of inns) by groups of touring players. Doubling, where a single actor played two or more roles, allowed them to put on plays with a dozen parts performed by as few as four actors. The simplest model was to have an actor onstage in one role (the Vice in a morality play, for instance), while the other actors played different roles, exiting as one character and re-entering, after a change of costume, as another (the Vice's various dupes). Costume changes were minimal – a new hat or a false beard signalled a new character – even for female roles, played by men and older boys.

When the playing companies settled in the theatres, the number of actors available increased. By the 1590s the core of a company was its 'sharers', eight or so actors sharing the work and profits. When the plague forced the London theatres to shut, actors toured the provinces to make a living. Only the core toured, so doubling roles remained essential. No doubt leading actors – Edward Alleyn or Richard Burbage – attempted conspicuous doubling, where an audience could see their favourite player tackling two roles. The appeal would lie in their skill in moving between parts, from hero to villain, say, and quick costume changes carried off effortlessly. This may well have happened with two roles in *Cymbeline* if, as scholars suspect, Burbage played the romantic lead Posthumus as well as the gross villain Cloten (Booth, 'Doubling', 121–5). Some modern productions of *The Winter's Tale* have experimented in a parallel way by making Leontes and Polixenes almost identical (see Fig. 21). The roles are impossible to double onstage, but the

21 'You have mistook, my lady, / Polixenes for Leontes' (2.1.81–2). Charles
   Balsar as Polixenes sitting with Edith Wynne Matthison as Hermione,
   watched by Henry Kolker as Leontes and John Tansey as Mamillius, in the
   1910 New Theatre production in New York, directed by Winthrop Ames,
   where the kings were nearly indistinguishable

suggestion that the kings are twin manifestations of one identity
can be truly disturbing.

In *The Winter's Tale* the limit to doubling roles is fixed by the
statue scene. The characters listed in the First Folio to appear in
the scene are Leontes, Polixenes, Florizel, Perdita, Camillo and
Paulina, with Hermione '*like a Statue*'. The list ends with '*Lords,
&c.*', taken in many modern productions to mean Cleomenes
and Dion, along with the Shepherd, the Clown and Autolycus.
This requires a minimum of twelve actors throughout 5.3,
which makes doubling major roles impossible in the rest of the
play – except for Antigonus, 'gone for ever' halfway into 3.3,
and Time (the boy playing Mamillius was probably too young to

double other roles). Bringing the elite and non-elite together like this creates on the modern stage a mood of reconciliation – the royal houses are no longer divided, nor are court and country – but it probably wasn't what Shakespeare intended or early audiences would expect. Crossing the huge social divide to the extent that the Shepherd, the Clown and Autolycus could be invited to Paulina's private chapel may have been inconceivable, even in the heady, upside-down world of 5.2 and 5.3.

If these three characters weren't in 5.3 in early performances, many more parts could be doubled, as the following table shows. The actors playing Hermione, Antigonus or Paulina could double as the Shepherd or Clown, and the doubling of Hermione and Autolycus or Antigonus and Autolycus was also feasible. Cleomenes and Dion could play the Shepherd and Clown, combined with any number of smaller parts. The length of roles and particular talents – a good singing voice and a gift for clowning – mattered. There is reason to think that Burbage played Leontes, a medium-sized part (670 lines) compared with his earlier roles, Hamlet, Othello and Lear.

It is tempting to assign Autolycus to Burbage as well because of the thematic counterpoint – Leontes has nothing but author-ity, the rogue nothing but contempt for it – but the roles taken together are large (960 lines), and the routines with the Clown in 4.3 would need an experienced comic. (The prospect of Anthony Sher doubling the roles was touted by the RSC for its 1999 production, but it didn't happen: see P. Taylor.) Shakespeare probably wrote Autolycus for Robert Armin, the actor who played the Fool in *Twelfth Night* and in *King Lear*. One piece of doubling almost certainly took place in early performances. In 4.4 there are two dances, the first of shepherds, the second of countrymen dressed as satyrs. The interval between the dances, 190 lines, would have allowed time for six adult actors playing shepherds and six boys playing shepherdesses to change costume and return as the twelve satyrs (King, 93).

DISTRIBUTION OF ROLES

	1.1	1.2	2.1	2.2	2.3	3.1	3.2	3.3	4.1	4.2	4.3	4.4	5.1	5.2	5.3	Lines
Archidamus	x															20
Camillo	x	x								x		x			x	290
Polixenes		x								x		x			x	270
Leontes		x	x		x		x						x		x	670
Hermione		x	x				x								x	200
Mamillius		x	x													20
Antigonus			x		x			x								100
Paulina				x	x		x						x		x	320
Gaoler				x												10
Emilia				x												20
Cleomenes						x	x						x		x	20
Dion						x	x						x		x	30
Officer							x									20
Mariner								x								10
Shepherd								x				x		x		110
Clown								x			x	x		x		160

	1.1	1.2	2.1	2.2	2.3	3.1	3.2	3.3	4.1	4.2	4.3	4.4	5.1	5.2	5.3	Lines
Time									x							30
Autolycus											x	x		x		290
Florizel												x	x		x	200
Perdita												x	x		x	120
Mopsa												x				20
Dorcas												x				10
Gentleman													x	x		40
Rogero														x		10
Steward														x		60
																3,050

The table shows 25 roles, identified by name or function (with minor exclusions, e.g. Hermione's Ladies in 2.1), listed in order of first appearance. Actors don't always speak in the scene in which they appear (e.g. Florizel in 5.3, and perhaps the gentlemen who plan at 5.2.92–110 to see the statue). Cleomenes and Dion are included in 5.3, although not named in the entry SD, as probably among the 'Lords and others'. The table shows the extent of roles but it isn't an exact measure. Many lines are shared between characters, and verse and prose are counted together, with totals rounded to the nearest ten. This makes the line count here, 3,050, exceed the total for the whole play, 3,000. Totals for Autolycus, Mopsa and Dorcas include their songs.

Doubling ended when the playhouses were shut in 1642. We see it in modern plays and films, but when it is used for Shakespeare it is often a historical reconstruction, like playing Bach on original instruments. The most radical doubling of roles in *The Winter's Tale* was attempted in 1992 by Théâtre de Complicité (see p. 28). This certainly wasn't a museum piece. Nine actors performed twenty-two roles, about the same number of actors as on the early stage. The text was changed, as in most modern productions, and played in less than three hours, including an interval. Two actors played four parts each, the others two parts apiece. The roles doubled included Leontes and the Clown, Antigonus and Florizel, and Hermione and Dorcas. There was no attempt to conceal the doubling, quite the opposite. When the Clown found he was still wearing Leontes' ring, he took it off, telling the audience 'that's from my last part'.

This much doubling didn't confuse the audience – they knew that Kathryn Hunter, before she became Time, and then the Shepherd, had earlier been Paulina, and before that Mamillius – but it did unsettle them. Doubling Leontes with the Clown didn't produce insights into their characters, but the alarmingly easy shift from one identity to another made character seem subordinate to plot and action, something more often associated with literary romance than romance on stage. In this production, it was the story that mattered. Psychological portrayals of individuals were subsidiary.

Roles have been doubled in other productions. Perhaps the weakest of Nunn's innovations in 1969 (see pp. 26–8) was to have Hermione and Perdita played by the same actress, Judi Dench. The portrayal of Hermione was well received by reviewers, and some thought highly of Dench as Perdita, but the doubling damaged the effect of the statue scene. Instead of concentrating on the wonder of the statue moving, and the astonished onstage reactions, the audience watched to see how the actors would manage the substitution of another actress to play Perdita – using a trick box in this instance – as Dench resumed the role of Hermione (Roberts, 32; Roach, 127–8). The swap distracted attention from how an actor playing a statue was to turn into a woman.

Doubling Hermione and Perdita was tried again by the RSC at Stratford in Terry Hands's 1986 production, but with no greater success (Roach, 128–9). More recent doublings of Perdita with Mamillius – meant to match the preservation of one with the loss of the other – have been technically implausible and peripheral. They have also been untrue to the text. At seven or eight Mamillius is too young to be acted convincingly by even the youngest of teenagers playing Perdita. Gregory Doran's solution for the RSC in 1999, not a happy one, was to make Mamillius an invalid, scrunched up in a wheelchair, so that the petite female actor doubling the roles could later stand up straight to play Perdita. It was a mistake in an otherwise impressive production, which earned special praise for the way the verse was spoken (P. Taylor) – i.e. for the management of the sounds in the play.

Sounds, lines and ends

Our perception of the world through our senses is nowadays an epistemological or neurological question. In the Renaissance, by contrast, theories about the senses were focused on moral or spiritual matters. The interconnections between the senses and memory and imagination were of great importance, increasingly so in the seventeenth century. The key issue for artists was which of the organs of perception mattered most. Leonardo da Vinci claimed that the eye was superior. 'Though the poet is as free as the painter in the invention of his fictions', da Vinci wrote, 'his creations do not give as great a satisfaction to men as paintings do.' Poets serve the understanding by way of the ear, but painters by way of the eye, 'the nobler sense' (da Vinci, 190, 188).

The eye and ear were equally in competition in the Elizabethan theatre. Audiences attended Shakespeare's plays as 'spectators' but also as 'auditors', i.e. listeners or hearers (cf. *MND* 3.1.74). As spectators they accepted that male actors were dressed as women, feigning female movements and gestures, but as auditors they expected them to have plausible, higher-pitched voices. The eye had advantages – fights could be seen close up, and young lovers kissing for the first time – but some things just couldn't be shown on stage realistically, shipwrecks for instance. The ear could be fed by dialogue and soliloquy, especially where the sound approximated to everyday speech rhythms shaped into lines of verse, or by narration, providing pictures in words. Many Elizabethans wouldn't have agreed with da Vinci. They believed that sound had more direct access to the mind than sight. An actor describing something to an audience attracted attention through his expressions and demeanour, but what they understood from him most deeply was what they heard (Smith, *Acoustic*, 283–4).

Seeing and hearing are often juxtaposed in *The Winter's Tale*. Leontes has merely to see Hermione talking to Polixenes to 'know' they are cuckolding him, and he wouldn't trust what he heard them saying anyway. The Clown's description of the ship being destroyed and the Bear eating Antigonus is unintentionally absurd: he makes the bizarre things he had seen offstage into an even more bizarre fairy tale (see pp. 29–30). We might have expected Shakespeare to show us the reunion of Leontes and Perdita, as he does the father–daughter reunion in *Pericles*, but instead it is narrated, complete with swoons and ahs, by bystanders. Then, in the final scene, when we wouldn't think he would dare let us see a miracle – Hermione's statue moving – Shakespeare does precisely that. Everyone is stunned into silence, and suddenly what the characters and we are hearing doesn't really matter any more, only what we see – a believable but impossible illusion.

Nevertheless, in the course of the play sound is as indispensable as what we see. When an actor speaks Leontes' lines, we hear a sequence of phonemes, or small units of sound:

> Physic for't there's none:
> It is a bawdy planet, that will strike
> Where 'tis predominant; and 'tis powerful, think it,
> From east, west, north and south; be it concluded,
> No barricado for a belly. Know't,
> It will let in and out the enemy
> With bag and baggage.

(1.2.199–205)

The alliteration catches our ear first, along with the clusters of plosives – *ba*rrricado, *be*lly, *ba*g, *ba*ggage; *n*one, *N*o, *Kn*ow't; *ba*wdy, *p*owerful – but it is the tut, tut, tut sound, the phoneme /t/, that the speech rests on. Leontes simply can't get 'i*t*' (and related sounds in Physi*c*, stri*k*e, thin*k*) out of his jealous mind or his mouth: for'*t*, I*t* is, plane*t*, tha*t*, '*t*is predominan*t*, '*t*is, think i*t*, eas*t*, wes*t*, be i*t*, Know'*t*, I*t* will, le*t*, ou*t*. The sounds force the question, what is *it*? Of course *it* is female lust – there's no remedy (*Physic*) that can cure *it* – but other meanings come with *it*, of being certain (think *it*, be *it* concluded, Know'*t*), and of the vagina (*It* will let in), and perhaps, in a disturbing metamorphosis, the penis too (striking at the belly from every compass point). Leontes turns the libidinous unreliability of women, because of *it*, into something abstract he can rely on, an *it* that is conclusive beyond doubt. The 'meaning' here – part of Leontes' fantasy that he alone knows the truth of things (see pp. 38–42) – isn't 'supported' or 'assisted' by sound, but made out of sound.

The effects of other sounds are harder to define. One largely unexplored feature of Shakespeare's poetry is his use of rhyme or half-rhyme within and between lines of blank verse. Often this happens in the middle of a line, at or close to the caesura (the pause which breaks up the flow of sound in a verse). Examples of it are in *Othello*:

> As I have to be *hurt*. O gull, O dolt,
> As ignorant as *dirt*!
>
> (5.2.159–60)

and in *Hamlet*:

> till he that died to*day*,
> 'This must be *so*.' We *pray* you thr*ow* to earth
> This unprevailing w*oe* . . .
>
> (1.2.105–7)

The incidence of internal rhymes increases in the late plays, most markedly in *The Winter's Tale* (Muir, 'Trick of style', 307–9). In Act 4 Camillo tells Florizel, in lines connected by rhyme as well as assonance and alliteration,

> *M*ethinks I *see*
> *Le*ontes opening his *free* arms and *wee*ping
> His *w*elcomes forth; asks *thee* . . .
>
> (4.4.552–4)

and a little earlier, Polixenes, recalling how he used to court country girls, says

> I was wont
> To load my she with kn*ack*s. I would have rans*ack*ed
> The pedlar's silken treasury . . .
>
> (4.4.353–5)

The rhymes aren't confined to particular characters, or to any one part of the play (e.g. Leontes: issue/hiss, 1.2.187–8; Hermione: fright/sprites, 2.1.28; Paulina: sleep/creep, 2.3.32–3; Florizel: Peering/sheep-shearing, 4.4.3; Perdita: true/subdue, 4.4.580–1). Vowels in Elizabethan English didn't always sound the same as modern ones – for instance, Elizabethans pronounced the words 'meet' and 'meat' as 'mate' – so we can't always say whether a rhyme was perfect or imperfect. Even less certain is what this increase in rhyming tells us. We are taught to expect repeated sounds like these at the ends of couplets, not in the middle of lines of blank verse.

When we look elsewhere in Shakespeare's blank verse we see something equally intriguing, a progressive shift in the degree of metrical stress on the final syllable in a line. The proportion of unstressed-syllable ('feminine') endings, as opposed to stressed ('masculine') ones, increases substantially from his early plays until a high point in the late ones. In the first twelve plays, the average is three unstressed endings per play; in *Cymbeline*, *The Winter's Tale* and *The Tempest* the average is one hundred per play (Muir, 'Pentameter', 147–8; cf. Tarlinskaja, 335–6). This change is an aspect of Shakespeare's gradual refashioning of blank verse, giving it more and more the rhythm and gradations of living speech. In *The Two Gentlemen of Verona*, one of his earliest plays, we find a young woman, Julia, praising the man she loves like this:

> His words are bonds, his oaths are oracles,
> His love sincere, his thoughts immaculate,
> His tears pure messengers sent from his heart,
> His heart as far from fraud as heaven from earth.
>
> (2.7.75–8)

The metrical pattern here is of the simplest kind (five iambic feet, unstressed followed by stressed syllables: x / x / x / x / x /), and so too the shape of the line: Julia's small, balanced clauses are confined within single lines of verse.

This differs greatly from the verse in *The Winter's Tale*. When Florizel speaks, impassioned by love, the metre is far less regular:

>   x / x
>   Camillo,
>
> / x   x / (x) x / x   /   x   x
> Not for Bohemia, nor the pomp that may

```
   x   /  x     /    x / x  /  /  x
   Be thereat gleaned; for all the sun sees, or

   x    /    /    /     x  x  x  /    /    /
   The close earth wombs, or the profound seas hides

   x  x   /    / x    x  x  /   x  /
   In unknown fathoms, will I break my oath

   x  x   x   /  x  /
   To this my fair beloved.
```

(4.4.492–7)

Like Julia, Florizel sets one thing against another, in a complete sentence: Bohemia and pomp; sun, earth and seas. His lines, like hers, have ten syllables in them, which is the notional amount of stage speech our ear can take in, as a single unit, without losing the sense of a basic, recurring pattern of sound. There the resemblances end. Florizel's clauses are stretched across the lines, and in every case there is enjambment (i.e. the meaning runs over the end of one line into the next). Two lines end with unstressed syllables, 'may' and 'or'. Another two lines have only four stressed syllables in them while yet another has six ('earth wombs' and 'seas hides' are spondees, / /). The irregularity won't let our ear settle on a steadier rhythm, even as we recognize the repeated rhetorical pattern ('Not . . . nor . . . or . . . or'). All this makes Florizel sound defiant, never thwarted before and a touch self-regarding. By contrast, Julia's lines don't tell us much about her, except that she is naive (no man could be *that* perfect).

Something else happens to Shakespeare's lines in his later plays. He makes more of them hypermetrical, with eleven, twelve or even thirteen syllables instead of the pentameter norm of ten. He also elides vowels more readily, in effect squeezing more words in per line. Examples in *The Winter's Tale* are:

```
   x    / (x) x   /   x   /     x  /    /   /  x x
   My prisoner? Or my guest? By your dread 'verily'
```

/   x x   x   /   /
One of them you shall be.

(1.2.55–6)

and (in thirteen monosyllables):

/   x x / x x   /   / x   /   /   x
Give me the boy. I am glad you did not nurse him.

(2.1.56)

and, from the passage quoted above showing Leontes' preoccupation with *it*:

x   / x   / x /   x   /   /   x   / /
Where 'tis predominant; and 'tis powerful, think it,

x   /   /   /   x   /
From east, west, north and south . . .

(1.2.201–2)

Most times, the syllables can only be stressed or unstressed in line with the meaning. It would sound unnatural to our ear if the actor playing Florizel accentuated the words wrongly (e.g. 4.4.493–4 as 'nor *the* pomp that *may* / *Be* there*at* gleaned', x / x x / / x / x).

Shakespeare's general direction in his later plays is clear. He stretches the pentameter norm to give it more variety and expressiveness, and more of the tangles, pauses and stopping and starting of real English speech, and therefore real people. The verse becomes looser, the rhythm more heterogeneous, the stressed syllables less fixed in the same positions in the line and more varied in the degree of emphasis (Tarlinskaja, 334, 345–7). Moreover, probably as a corollary to the longer and looser lines, he also writes much shorter irregular ones, some with as few as six syllables. In *The Winter's Tale*, these are often used for conclusions of scenes (e.g. 'And think upon my bidding', 2.3.205; 'And gracious be the issue', 3.1.22), in direct address ('So please you, madam', 2.2.12), or to create moments of extended silence, as in the trial scene when Hermione wishes her dead father were alive to look upon her misery:

> yet with eyes
> Of pity, not revenge.
>
> (3.2.120–1)

There are also short lines to show other effects – intense, insistent anger, for instance, as when Leontes says that for him the stain of adultery on his sheets

> x /   /   /   x   /   x   /
> Is goads, thorns, nettles, tails of wasps
>
> (1.2.327)

This is almost entirely monosyllabic, a line of 'extraordinary expressive force' that appears 'to have gone beyond iambic pentameter' and become an accentual five-stress line (Wright, 178). Elsewhere there are pentameters that contain nothing but monosyllables. The effects of these vary greatly, from, for instance, dignified precision (Hermione saying she has to defend her honour):

> 'fore
> Who please to come and hear. For life, I prize it
> As I weigh grief, which I would spare . . .
>
> (3.2.40–2)

to withering reproach (Paulina scolding Leontes about a second wife):

> I'd bid you mark
> Her eye, and tell me for what dull part in't
> You chose her.
>
> (5.1.63–5)

Notably, there are few short monosyllabic lines, except ones shared between speakers (e.g. 2.3.112), and still fewer that are long.

In *The Winter's Tale*, the frequent enjambment, elisions, spondees and unstressed final syllables are connected to a general 'lengthening' of the pentameter, i.e. Shakespeare pushes small but perceptible amounts of extra sound into the line and beyond it, into the following line. It is possible that the mid-line rhymes referred to above are also connected to this lengthening. At her trial, Leontes tells Hermione 'You had a bastard by Polixenes' (3.2.81),

> And I but dreamed it. As you were *past* all shame –
> Those of your fact are so – so *past* all truth;
> Which to deny concerns more than avails; for as
> Thy brat hath been *cast* out . . .

> (82–5)

In thirty-six words, only three are disyllabic; all of them in line 84, which contains twelve syllables, the last of which is probably unstressed:

> /   x   x /   x   /   /   x   x /   x   x
> Which to deny concerns more than avails; for as

Perhaps the *past*/*cast* rhyme occurred because Shakespeare had taken line 84 well beyond its normal acoustic limit, and a rhyme at the next pause (close to the caesura at 'out, like' in 85), was his unconscious way of containing the overflow of sound.

One tangle in real speech happens sometimes when different words have the same pronunciation, i.e. they are homonyms. An example in *The Winter's Tale* occurs in the lines quoted above where Florizel declares he wouldn't break his vow to Perdita

> for all the sun *sees*, or
> The close earth wombs, or the profound *seas* hides
> (4.4.494–5)

The verb 'sees' and the noun 'seas' are the same sound. The syntax and context keep the meanings of the words separate, but another small overflow of sound between the words presents our ear with an unexpected compound: 'sun sees' bleeds across the line into 'seas hides', to leave in our minds a trace of something else, '*sees* hides'. This isn't a phrase or even a grammatical possibility, and Shakespeare certainly didn't consciously intend it, though the compound is curiously apposite because seeing and hiding are central at this point in the play (Polixenes sees Florizel in hiding).

Normally we filter out sounds that accidentally stick together like this, dismissing them as unavoidable background noise. Recently, however, critics have suggested that in Shakespeare, although such sounds may be non-significant they are not always insignificant. One sound in particular has attracted attention, a ubiquitous sound, the argument runs, in *Julius Caesar*, *Hamlet*, *Macbeth* and *Antony and Cleopatra*, but of greatest importance in *The Winter's Tale* (Booth, 'Exit', 51–64). This is the sound we hear in 'bear', i.e. the word for the animal, the action of giving birth or of carrying or enduring something. There are twenty-four instances of 'bear' in *The Winter's Tale*, used in various ways in ten of the play's fifteen scenes, e.g. 'Bear the boy hence' (2.1.59), 'the bear mocked him' (3.3.98) and 'bear no credit' (5.1.178).

Some critics listen beyond the sound 'bear' by itself, to cognates and imperfect homonyms. In Act 3, for instance, the *bear* (3.3.57 SD) appears just before the baby, a *bairn* (68), is found wrapped in a *bear*ing-cloth (112). The savage animal and harmless infant, it is said, 'give body to a sound vital to the play, a sound equivalent to, but more fluid' than the modern pronunciation of 'bear'; and in 'one of its myriad senses, the sound signals the most urgent concern of the play', the *bearing* of legitimate heirs (de Grazia, 'Homonyms', 144). Interpreted like this, the 'bear' sounds are not marginal or accidental ('sees' and 'seas'), but intentional and persistent word-play. The stage spectacle of the Bear generates puns on and homonymic variants of 'bear' throughout *The Winter's Tale* to give it 'the kind of coherence' we look for 'from character plot, imagery and theme' (de Grazia, 'Response', 299).

Word-play on 'bear', in this analysis, extends even to 'borne' (past tense of 'bear') and thus to 'gentleman born', the phrase the Clown mistakenly uses in Act 5, when he confuses the title conferred on him with a social rank only possible through birth (see 5.2.125n.). Thus 'bearing' – Hermione's being pregnant with a real 'bairn' and giving birth in Act 3 – is linked, in a cluster of puns on 'bear', to palpably impossible births (the Clown *wasn't* born a gentleman, and the usurer's wife in childbirth *didn't* bear 'twenty money-bags at a burden', 4.4.263–4). Other commentators go further, finding a yet more complex kinship of 'bear' sounds and meanings. Antigonus, for example, whose name means 'anti-birth' (see List of Roles, 4n.), is compelled to 'bear' the 'bairn' to a 'remote and desert place' (2.3.174), where he is eaten by the Bear; and there is a similar subterranean connection, it is said, between 'bearing' and Mistress Tale-Porter, the midwife referred to at 4.4.269–70, a helper at births but also a bawd or whore who bears men's 'tails' (penises) in sex (P. Parker, 'Polymorphic', 173–5).

Not everyone is convinced by the connections between the 'bear' sounds and what they mean. It has been pointed out, for instance, that the pronunciation of 'bear' and 'Barne' (F's spelling of *bairn*, 3.3.68) has *never* been the same, though the words are etymologically related. According to objectors, there is not even an etymological justification for the claim that gentleman *born* is an echo of *bear* (Hanowell, 295). Nonetheless, the more closely we examine this extended family of puns the more purposeful it seems. Puns are not the only patterned sounds in *The Winter's Tale*, however, nor necessarily the most inventive.

Take for example the phrase Leontes uses as he watches Hermione and Polixenes smiling at each other, and imagines them as lovers sighing, 'as 'twere / The mort o'th' deer' (1.2.117–18). This phrase was a technical term from hunting, for the moment when a dying stag let out its final breath. Leontes thinks that the couple have been doing more than sighing. The word 'mort', from the French for 'death', was commonly used for an orgasm (i.e. 'petit mort'; see Williams, 373–4), but in underworld slang it also meant a whore or lewd woman (Williams, 910–11); 'deer', as often in Elizabethan poetry, was a quibble on 'dear' or beloved. In Leontes' jealous mind, the whorish adulterers pant as they reach a sexual climax, sighing 'oh my darling' – while he, a cuckold with horns like a stag, gasps as they murder his love for them.

The packed phrase 'mort o'th' deer' shows just how much Leontes sees himself as a cheated and abandoned husband, a victim of love. Much later, in Act 4, when Autolycus first comes onstage, the phrase returns, a little distorted but still recognizable. 'I am out of service', Autolycus says (4.3.14), and continues in song:

> But shall I go *mourn for that, my dear*?
> The pale moon shines by night,
> And when I wander here and there
> I then do most go right.

> (15–18)

Autolycus means that he hasn't got a job, but it doesn't bother him; he goes where he likes by night, doing what he wants, i.e. thieving. But 'shall I go mourn for that, my dear' is like a refrain from a song where a lover defies a lady who has discarded him, perhaps telling her he'll be wandering out at night with women that suit him better and will have sex with him ('most go right'). Autolycus is Leontes' antitype in all respects, but especially in his feckless, untroubled, unjealous womanizing, the very opposite of the furious, hurt, self-regarding husband (see pp. 65–6). The repetitions and modulations of 'mort o'th' deer' in 'mourn for that, my dear' once again show Shakespeare working with sounds to unite characters and themes across the play.

Clearly *mourn* isn't a pun on *mort*; rather, it is a rounding out of the potential within a sound. Shakespeare does something comparable with the sounds *full* and *filled*. There are the references to fullness and being *full* (1.2.129; 4.4.351, 438, 769; 5.1.53) and to people and things being *filled*, as in time 'filled up' (1.2.4), Camillo 'filled with honour' (3.2.163), the spectre of Hermione 'filled and so becoming' (3.3.21), and the filling up of graves (4.4.459 and 5.3.101). In Act 5 the words come together – when things have been *filled full*, i.e. completed or made sense of. Paulina says the gods 'Will have *fulfilled* their secret purposes' (5.1.36), and when this happens, the 'oracle is *fulfilled*' (5.2.22, 74).

Was this a new union or a reunion of sounds, we wonder? Did Shakespeare divide *fulfilled* in two so that he could join its halves back together at the end of the play, like strands of the plot? The question is pertinent to an unexamined aspect of the word-play on *bear*. Critics who think of *bear* as the 'presiding word' in *The Winter's Tale* don't seem to have noticed that sometimes it too is part of a compound, which Shakespeare gives us a clue to in the trial scene in Act 3. Leontes tries to frighten Hermione with the prospect of torture and death, but she replies:

> Sir, spare your threats.
> The bug which you would fright me with I seek.
> (3.2.89–90)

The word *bug* was from Middle English 'bugge', a bogy or hobgoblin, which joined in the sixteenth century with *bear* to form 'bugbear', a word *OED* defines as 'a sort of hobgoblin (presumably in the shape of a bear) supposed to devour naughty children' (*n.* 1), and 'an object of dread esp. needless dread; an imaginary terror' (*n.* 2). The compound *bugbear* didn't settle down straightaway ('bear bugs' are referred to in the 1560s), but the meaning did. Elizabethan proverbs tell the same story: *bugs*, *bugbears* and *bear bugs* were scary, but only to children (Tilley, B703, K142).

133

At her trial, Hermione tells Leontes, 'I'm not a child you can frighten with stories of some demon waiting to catch me' (a reminder that, in play, she had earlier prompted Mamillius to tell his scariest story of 'sprites and goblins', 2.1.25–8). The *bug* having been spoken of, it is only a matter of time before the full *bugbear* appears, as the Bear chasing Antigonus to his tragicomic death (3.3.57 SD; see Fig. 22).

22 'The poor gentleman roared, and the bear mocked him' (3.3.97–8). Engraving of Antigonus and the Bear, published in 1794 from a painting by John Opie, showing Antigonus' horror as he protects Perdita from a terrifying bugbear

The *bugbear* is displaced into Bohemia, but it belongs to Leontes, as another bit of *bear* word-play confirms. By 1600, the colloquial phrase 'to play the bear' had entered Standard English, meaning 'to behave rudely and roughly' or to inflict great damage (Partridge, *Slang*, 56). The earliest citation in *OED* (bear *n.*[1] 2) is from 1579: 'when we have so turned all order upside down, there is nothing but playing the bear amongst us'. In Acts 1–3, Leontes bullies and manhandles people around him and breaks his nation's laws, i.e. he plays the bear. Once he stops this, at the end of 3.2, the *bug* leaves him to return as the Bear in Bohemia.

Listening to what was inside sounds, Shakespeare heard new meanings, and reversals of meanings. One might have thought that the play's title, *The Winter's Tale*, already had a cornucopia of meaning, but there was yet more to be uncovered. This time the clue is at the end of the play when Paulina tells the reunited families

> Go together,
> You precious winners all . . .
>
> (5.3.130–1)

We can't be certain, but there is every likelihood that inside 'winters' in Standard English, Elizabethan playgoers would have heard 'winners' (i.e. with the *t* lost: Kökeritz, 301; Cercignani, 315–16; cf. F's 'Currence' (currants) at 4.3.38). It appears that Shakespeare found in the *winter's* tale, of loss, separation and grief, its complete opposite, a tale of *winners* all.

THE
WINTER'S
TALE

LIST OF ROLES

THE NAMES OF THE ACTORS

[SICILIA]

LEONTES	*King of Sicilia*	
MAMILLIUS	*young prince of Sicilia*	
CAMILLO		
ANTIGONUS		
CLEOMENES	*four lords of Sicilia*	
DION		5
HERMIONE	*queen to Leontes*	
PERDITA	*daughter to Leontes and Hermione*	
PAULINA	*wife to Antigonus*	
EMILIA	*a lady-in-waiting to Hermione*	10
[GAOLER]		
[GENTLEMAN]		
[ROGERO	*a gentleman*]	
[STEWARD	*servant to Paulina*]	
[MARINER]		15
[OFFICERS	*at Hermione's trial*]	
[SERVANT	*to Mamillius*]	
[LORDS]		
[LADIES]		

[BOHEMIA]

POLIXENES	*King of Bohemia*	20
FLORIZEL	*prince of Bohemia [at first under the assumed name of Doricles]*	
SHEPHERD	*reputed father of Perdita*	
CLOWN	*his son*	
AUTOLYCUS	*a rogue*	
ARCHIDAMUS	*a lord of Bohemia*	25
[SERVANT]		

[MOPSA]⎱
[DORCAS]⎰ [*shepherdesses*]

[TIME   *as Chorus*]

Other Lords, [Ladies] and Gentlemen, and Servants   30
[Attendants]
Shepherds and Shepherdesses
[Twelve rustic Dancers dressed as satyrs]
[Bear]

0.1 THE . . . ACTORS] *two columns in F at the end of the play, concluding with* FINIS.   0.2
SICILIA] *this edn*   2 MAMILLIUS] *(Mamillus)*   5 CLEOMENES] *(Cleomines)*   10 *a . . . Hermione*]
Rowe subst.; a Lady F   11 GAOLER] *Rowe*   12 GENTLEMAN] *this edn*   13 ROGERO *a gentleman*]
Theobald subst.   14 STEWARD . . . *Paulina*] *this edn*   15 MARINER] *Theobald*   16 OFFICERS . . . *trial*]
Theobald subst.   17 SERVANT *to Mamillius*] *Theobald subst.*   18 LORDS] *this edn*   19 LADIES] *Theobald
subst.*   19.1 BOHEMIA] *this edn*   21 *at . . . Doricles*] *this edn*   22 SHEPHERD] *(Old Shepheard)*
24 AUTOLYCUS] *(Autolicus)*   26 SERVANT] *this edn*   27–8 MOPSA, DORCAS *shepherdesses*] *Rowe*
29 TIME *as Chorus*] *Theobald*   30 Ladies] *Theobald subst.*   31 Attendants] *Hanmer subst.*
33 Twelve . . . satyrs] *Theobald subst.*   34 Bear] *this edn*

LIST OF ROLES The 'Names of the Actors' in F, probably compiled by the scribe Ralph Crane (see p. 354), is in two parallel columns, mid-page, below the text. Roles are listed in terms of nation, rank and sex: Sicilians to the left, Bohemians right, men above women This order may hint at concerns with hierarchy and divisions between the sexes (Snyder, 6–7). Autolycus' position, beneath the Clown, perhaps indicates that his claim to be a disgraced court servant is untrue (see pp. 75–6). Shakespeare disposed of characters and names in *Pandosto* (see pp. 95–7). For new names he turned to Plutarch's *Lives*, the Bible, classical poets and Tudor dictionaries (e.g. Cooper, which lists a people in Sicily called the Leontini, possibly a hint for Leontes of Sicilia: see 1n.; Turner, 5). Most names are mythological or historical, or are patronyms, 'label names', with etymological pointers to a character's identity, e.g. Mamillius (see 2n.) (see Leimberg, 'Hermione', 133–9). The general effect, of a pagan-Christian world with Greek, Latin and Italian names, is sometimes more specific, e.g. Paulina (see 9n.).

0.1 SICILIA As with BOHEMIA (19.1), used of the country (as well as its king: see 1.1.4n., 5–6, 21–2 and n.; 1.2.146). In the play, Sicily (the English form at 1.2.174) and Bohemia are independent kingdoms, unlike the real countries at the date of *WT*: see p. 100.

1 LEONTES Leontes of Sicilia, resembles 'Sicilius Leonatus', the hero's father in *Cym*, and 'Leonato', Governor of Messina in Sicily, in *MA*: all are fathers whose names suggest hot, insular savagery (volcanic Sicily, fierceness through 'Leo', Latin for lion). Leontes is probably 30 in Acts 1–3, 46 in Act 5 (see 2n.). The name (pronounced 'lee-òn-teez') is first spoken at 1.2.42.

2 MAMILLIUS Coined from the heroine of Robert Greene's novel *Mamillia* (1583, 1593), the name, first spoken at 1.1.34, calls attention to the boy's dependency on his mother (Latin

mamilla, female breast). In modern productions, Mamillius is often 10 or 11 or even a teenager, but the social signals show that he is no more than 7. Until then upper-class children of both sexes wore a long petticoat (see 1.2.156 and n.), but at around 7 boys replaced the petticoat with breeches (plumped-out trousers to the knee), which was an important rite of passage that took them away from their mothers and nursemaids (Mack, 11; Snyder, 2–4; see Fig. 6). Mamillius isn't in breeches, and he is still looked after by Hermione's ladies (see 1.2.155 and n.; 2.1.1–32). He is most probably *exactly* 7, given the emphasis on characters' ages in *WT* (Bateson, 68), particularly 23 and 16. In *WT*, 23 is associated, as in *Ham*, *TC* and *Cym*, with fathers and sons (e.g. the trip to Delphos is to seek judgement from a divine father: see 2.3.196 and n.; cf. 1.2.154–5, 3.3.59–60 and nn.), and with males coming of age. In *Ham* 5.1.174–84 the 30-year-old prince recalls the times when he played with the jester Yorick, who has been dead 23 years (134–71). If Mamillius is 7, the configuration of ages, of father and son, is the same; indeed 23 in *WT* is more evocative, since it points forward in time as well as back. It would make Leontes 23 when Mamillius was born, 30 in Acts 1–3, 46 in Act 5. Florizel, born within a month of Mamillius (5.1.117–18), is 23 when, 16 years later, he woos Perdita.

3 CAMILLO Italian form of Latin 'Camillus', associated especially with Marcus Furius Camillus, a fifth-century BC statesman who forgave Rome for exiling him and rescued the city from the Gauls (his life is in Plutarch's *Lives*). Camillo, like Camillus, forgives his exile and saves the nation. The name is first spoken at 1.1.1.

4 ANTIGONUS Shakespeare's invention. The name ('an-tig-on-us'), first spoken at 2.3.41, is from Plutarch's *Lives*, which has several generals and kings called Antigonus (most connected to Alexander the Great: see 5.1.47–8n.), or

from Josephus' *Antiquities of the Jews*. Perhaps a male version of the female 'Antigone', Greek for 'against birth', possibly linked to Antigonus' threat to geld his daughters (2.1.147; see n.).

5–6 CLEOMENES, DION Greek names from Plutarch's *Lives*. Cleomenes was the name of three kings of ancient Sparta, Dion a fourth-century BC ruler of Sicily. Both names are first spoken at 2.1.184.

7 HERMIONE The most famous Hermione was the daughter of Helen of Troy, who notoriously cuckolded her husband Menelaus with a visiting prince, Paris. In Shakespeare's day, the first vowel in 'Hermione' rhymed with 'star' rather than modern English 'stir'. This allowed her to be identified with Harmonia, goddess of concord (Duncan-Jones), and associated with Aphrodite Pandemos, 'love that unites everyone', personification of civic unity. Scholars in the Renaissance took Hermione/ Harmonia to refer to universal harmony (Fowler, 39; cf. 'Philharmonus', 'lover of harmony' in *Cym*). Hermione was also linked to Hermes (Mercury), messenger of the gods, and Shakespeare may have derived his Hermione from 'herm', a Greek word from Sir Thomas North's translation of Plutarch's *Lives*, used of images of Mercury (Gasper & Williams). Latin *herma* was used of statues of saints, but this usage was probably confined to Roman Catholics. John Ruskin thought 'Hermione' meant 'herma', 'pillar-like', in keeping with her return as a statue (Levith, 109). Such links in 'Hermione' are intriguing but esoteric, and this is true for other names too (see Leimberg, 'Hermione', 139–49; Leimberg, 'Names', 135–55; Muir, 'Naming', 287–8; Leimberg, 'Answer', 291–3). The name, first spoken at 1.2.33, was used of men as well as women: in *The Rare Triumphs of Love and Fortune* (*c*. 1580, a source for *Cym*), the hero is Hermione.

8 PERDITA feminine of the Latin adjective *perditus*, past participle of *perdere*, 'lost'. 'Perdita' is a translation of the phrase in Apollo's prophecy, borrowed verbatim

from *Pandosto*, i.e. the king would live without an heir unless '*that which is lost*' was found (3.2.133). She is named by the dream-spectre that appears to Antigonus (3.3.31–3). In classical Latin *perditus* also meant 'desperate' or 'abandoned'; *OED* says that at this date the English adjective 'perdite' meant abandoned or debauched, i.e. cast away or morally lost (the adverb 'perditly' had similar meanings). 'Perdita' and 'perdite' sound similar enough for Antigonus to believe the baby 'lost' in both senses: left to perish, and illegitimate, the outcome of adultery. Cf. Marina in *Per*, 'born at sea' (3.3.13), and Miranda in *Tem*, whose name means 'she is to be wondered at' (see 3.1.37–9); the name is usually stressed on the first syllable, but perhaps on the second at 4.4.589. No one in *WT* asks why she is called Perdita.

9 PAULINA Shakespeare's invention. The name ('paul-eȳe-na'), first spoken at 3.3.35, is from Tacitus or Josephus (see 4n.). The Roman Paulina, wife of the philosopher Seneca, attempted suicide when he was ordered to kill himself. Shakespeare's Paulina views death differently, leading critics to connect her, through her name, to St Paul the Apostle (warning Leontes not to waver in devotion to Hermione's memory, insisting on faith to wake the queen from death, 5.1.63–7, 5.3.94–5). Traces of pagan and Christian in Paulina may be related to the belief that Seneca and St Paul had been in correspondence. Shakespeare may have taken aspects of Paulina, especially her shrewish forthrightness, from the shepherd's wife Mopsa in *Pandosto* (omitted from the play, except for the name: see 27n.).

10 EMILIA perhaps one of two Ladies in 2.1 and 2.2 who wait on Hermione, go with her to prison (2.2.19–64), and help at the birth of Perdita. In *Oth*, Emilia is Iago's wife and Desdemona's maid.

11 GAOLER not an aristocrat, nevertheless one of the elite: in Shakespeare's day, the Keeper of the Tower of London, a comparable office, was often held by a

knight. Paulina addresses him with the formal *you*, not 'thou', at 2.2.6.

12 GENTLEMAN In F the Gentlemen in SPs in 5.2 are '*Gent.*1', '*Gent.*2' and '*Gent.*3'. The dialogue shows that Rogero is '2' (see 13n.) and the Steward '3' (see 14n.). In 5.1 the character that announces the arrival of Florizel and Perdita is called '*Servant*' in F's SPs, which most editors emend to 'Gentleman' or 'Gentleman-poet', because he is a courtier who has written poetry praising Hermione (see 5.1.98–103 and nn.), and 'Servant' doesn't adequately reflect his social status at court. In this edition, this character is called Gentleman (5.1.85 SP), and it is assumed he is also '*Gent.*1.' in 5.2.

13 ROGERO '*Gent.*2' in F; see 12n. The name, spoken at 5.2.21, is partly anglicized from Italian 'Ruggiero', the form adopted by Oxf; English 'Roger' was used on stage of menial servants (e.g. in John Marston's *The Dutch Courtesan*). Early audiences may have been familiar with the tune called 'Rogero': one ballad sung to it was the 'Tragicall and true historye' of a jealous husband.

14 STEWARD '*Gent.*3' in F; see 12n. Called Paulina's steward at 5.2.26, his job was to manage her household and estate (cf. Malvolio, Olivia's steward in *TN*).

16 OFFICERS One officer is a sergeant-at-arms, who kept order in law courts and served as the sovereign's bodyguard, responsible for guarding traitors (see 3.2.10n.); another is the clerk of the court, who swore in witnesses and kept records of judgments.

19.1 BOHEMIA See 0.1n.

20 POLIXENES in *TC* (5.5.11), from 'Polyxinus', a Greek prince at the siege of Troy, mentioned in Homer's *Iliad*, 2.716. Levith (109) sees a link with 'polyxenos', Greek for 'hospitable', 'much visited'. The name ('po-lix-en-eez', stressed on the last syllable) is first spoken at 1.2.350.

21 FLORIZEL . . . *Doricles* 'Florizel', first spoken at 4.1.22, is from Latin *flos*, 'flower', or perhaps 'florise' (see *OED* flourish *v.*). 'Doricles', the name he assumes to woo Perdita (first spoken at 4.4.146), is probably from 'Doryclus', a Trojan prince in *Iliad*, 11.577; Virgil, *Aeneid*, 5.620. The root, 'doric', is from the Greek for 'oldest', 'plainest'.

22 SHEPHERD aged 83 in Acts 4–5 (see 4.4.458), older even than Lear.

23 CLOWN Clown was a Tudor word for a countryman or rustic, often a boorish, rude one. By 1600 it also meant a stage fool or professional fool at court or in great houses (e.g. Feste in *TN*). Autolycus refers to the character as 'My clown' at 4.4.609. The Clown is in his late teens or early twenties when he first appears (implied at 3.3.58–64).

24 AUTOLYCUS pronounced 'or-tòh-lee-kus', Greek for 'lone wolf' or 'the wolf himself', the name is spoken first at 4.3.24, where Autolycus says his father, a petty thief, named him. In Homer he was a celebrated thief (*Odyssey*, 19.447–9), son of the mortal Chione and god Mercury, patron of thieves and cheats (see 4.3.26n.). Ovid turned him into a fabulous, impossible twin. Mercury and Apollo made Chione pregnant simultaneously and a boy was born to each, the thief Autolycus to Mercury, the musician Philammon to Apollo, patron of music and art (*Met.*, 1.303–17). Autolycus in *WT* claims he was once a superior servant (4.3.13–14) but this is probably bogus (see pp. 75–6). The name in English, 'wolf', links him to lust and pimping (Williams, 1542–4): see 4.3.13–14n., 23n.

25 ARCHIDAMUS Shakespeare's invention. The name ('ar-kiy-dar-mus'), not spoken onstage, is in Plutarch's *Lives* (e.g. in life of Cleomenes; see 5–6n.). Archidamus appears only in 1.1.

27 MOPSA like Dorcas, Shakespeare's invention; the name is first spoken at 4.4.163. 'Mopsy' was a pet name for a lower-class girl (*OED* 1). Mopsa is the Shepherd's wife in *Pandosto* (see 9n.), and the name of a stupid country girl mocked by superiors in Sir Philip Sidney's *New Arcadia*.

28 DORCAS See 27n. The name, spoken once at 4.4.73, is from Acts, 9.36–42, in which Tabitha, Greek 'Dorcas', is the 'woman full of good deeds' whom St Peter restores to life (possibly a hint for Hermione's return in 5.3). Dorcas is first mentioned in the chapter about the conversion of St Paul, with whom Paulina may be associated (see 9n.).

29 TIME See pp. 76–83.

33 **Twelve . . . satyrs** In classical mythology, satyrs were half-men, half-goats. In Act 4 the dance of countrymen in satyr skins was reprised from the masque *Oberon* performed at court in 1611. See pp. 70, 71, 72; 4.4.329–36, 330–1n., 343n., 347.1–2. For the satyr costumes, see Fig. 13.

34 **Bear** The role of pursuing Antigonus offstage (3.3.57 SD) would have been played in early performances by an actor in a bear costume, possibly a white one. In 1610 the hit of the year for the King's Men was *Mucedorus*, an anonymous romantic play from *c.* 1590, to which new scenes had been added. In one added scene Mouse, a comically fearful clown, is in the middle of telling the audience how he has been followed by a white she-bear when the bear itself enters, and as '*he goes backwards the Beare comes in, and he tumbles over her, and runnes away*'

(*Mucedorus*, 107). The success of the white bear's entry evidently prompted Shakespeare a few months later to turn it into a comically serious moment in *WT*. He left out the tumbling-about routine, but carried over some of Mouse's wide-eyed dimwittedness into the Clown's account of how the Bear ate Antigonus (see pp. 29–30). It is also possible that there was something more frightening about these bears than animal savagery. Mouse says of the one he saw, 'A Beare? nay, sure it cannot be a Beare, but some Divell in a Beares Doublet: for a Beare could never have had that agilitie to have frighted me' (*Mucedorus*, 107). This probably means that the bear moved too much like a human being to be real, but also that there might be a devil, not an actor, in the bearskin, similar perhaps to the strange sprite 'in likeness of a bear' that took revenge in the anonymous 1600 murder play *Cox of Cullompton* (see Pitcher, 'Bear', 48–50). Older theories that the bear in early performances of *WT* was a real animal are unconvincing, in spite of recent attempts to revive them (Turner, 274–7; Ravelhofer, 297–318). Real bears were just too dangerous to have risked letting one run free across the stage.

THE WINTER'S TALE

1.1   *Enter* CAMILLO *and* ARCHIDAMUS.

ARCHIDAMUS   If you shall chance, Camillo, to visit
Bohemia on the like occasion whereon my services
are now on foot, you shall see, as I have said, great
difference betwixt our Bohemia and your Sicilia.

CAMILLO   I think this coming summer the King of Sicilia   5
means to pay Bohemia the visitation which he justly
owes him.

ARCHIDAMUS   Wherein our entertainment shall shame
us, we will be justified in our loves; for indeed –

TITLE See pp. 24–5, 88, 135.

1.1 F has no scene locations. Theobald,
near enough historically to know
court protocol, placed 1.1 in an
antechamber in Leontes' palace, i.e. a
private room outside the chamber for
official guests. The dialogue reflects
the speakers' rank: ambassadorial
manners, perhaps a little competitive.
Camillo answers Archidamus' exaggerations with elegant hyperbole
(21–31, 37–41, 43–4; cf. his courtly
speech, 4.4.526–30), until 1.1 closes
with some foreboding (45–6; see n.).

1   **shall** should (Abbott, 348)

2–3 **on . . . foot** on similar business to
this, i.e. attending the king

4   **difference** i.e. of culture as well as
terrain and climate (*difference* also
means row or disagreement, perhaps
prefiguring the coming conflict
between the Kings of Bohemia and
Sicilia; see List of Roles, 1n.). The
countries are on a north–south axis
with *opposed winds* (30–1) blowing hot
and cold (1.2.13): see p. 100.

5   **this coming summer** perhaps
indicating that Acts 1–3 are in winter
(see 2.1.25 and n.); Acts 4–5 are in

summer (see 4.3n., 4.3.4n.)

6   **visitation** social or state visit (*OED*
5a; see also 4.4.560, 5.1.91–2), but
also inspection, e.g. into heraldic
pedigrees (*OED* 1c): perhaps
Camillo is teasing Archidamus that
Sicilia's court plans to check up on
the Bohemians. Another meaning,
'punishment' or 'retribution' (*OED* 7,
8), prefigures Leontes' wish to punish
Polixenes.

8–9 **Wherein . . . loves** In whatever
ways the welcome and hospitality we
give is deficient, our love must make
amends for it; the reception you have
given us will put ours to shame,
but the love we show will settle the
account in our favour (cf. 1.2.3–9).
At 9 *justified* is a response to *justly*,
6 (Archidamus attempts to match
Camillo's exactness and propriety),
but it also meant acquitted, absolved.
Archidamus may intend a witty allusion to the doctrine of salvation by
faith and God's grace (see 1.2.80n.)
rather than good works, i.e. it will
be your mercy, not our efforts, that
redeem the 'sin' of our unworthy
hospitality.

TITLE WINTER'S] *(Winters)*   1.1] *(Actus Primus. Scæna Prima.)*   9 us,] *Theobald;* vs: *F*

CAMILLO Beseech you –   10

ARCHIDAMUS Verily, I speak it in the freedom of my
knowledge. We cannot with such magnificence – in so
rare – I know not what to say. We will give you sleepy
drinks, that your senses, unintelligent of our insuffi
cience, may, though they cannot praise us, as little   15
accuse us.

CAMILLO You pay a great deal too dear for what's given
freely.

ARCHIDAMUS Believe me, I speak as my understanding
instructs me, and as mine honesty puts it to utterance.   20

CAMILLO Sicilia cannot show himself over-kind to
Bohemia. They were trained together in their child-
hoods, and there rooted betwixt them then such an

10 please continue; I beg you (a polite
attempt to stem the effusiveness). F's
apostrophe before 'Beseech' marks
the omission of the nominative (see
Abbott, 399), as at 1.2.19; 2.1.112, 116;
3.2.149. The omission is not marked
like this at 1.2.262; 2.1.126; 2.3.145;
4.4.396, 452; 5.1.217; 5.2.1.

11–12 **Verily . . . knowledge** Truly, I
speak as my knowledge permits (gives
me *freedom*), from personal experience.

12 **magnificence** grandeur, lavishness
(of hospitality)

12–13 **so rare** such a marvellous (unfin-
ished phrase: he is running out of
exaggerations)

13–14 **sleepy drinks** a euphemism, 'get
you drunk and drowsy' (*OED* sleepy
3). Possibly meant as a compliment,
since Camillo, Polixenes' cupbearer,
would taste everything he drank
(1.2.310–16). Cf. 1.2.326–7 (see n.).

14, 28 **that** so that (Abbott, 283)

14–15 **unintelligent . . . insufficience**
unable to perceive our shortcomings
(as hosts)

15–16 **as . . . us** find as few faults in us
(as there are things to praise)

17 **a . . . dear** much too high a price;
i.e. you are thanking us too much
for hospitality we give not expecting
payment. Cf. 1.2.6–9 (see n.).

19–20 **my . . . utterance** my knowledge
informs me and my integrity obliges
me to (over-decorous speech)

21–2 **Sicilia . . . Bohemia** Leontes
could never show too much kindness
to, do enough for Polixenes (*OED* kind
a. 6). Gibbons (31) suggests other
meanings: (1) however strong the
expression, it can't exceed Leontes'
feelings of love; (2) Leontes tries but
fails to maintain the appearance of
love; (3) Leontes mustn't show that
his love for Polixenes goes too far.
The negative construction, Gibbons
says, touches on the 'maximum possible embarrassment' about a latent
homosexual love between the kings.

22 **trained** educated (punning on being
together in the same 'train' or king's
retinue). The metaphor is of vines or
trees grown alongside each other on
a trellis. In *Pandosto* the princes are
raised together, but their bonding isn't
emphasized; see 1.2.67n.

10 Beseech] ('Beseech)   17 too] *F2;* to *F*   19 Believe] ('Beleeue)

affection which cannot choose but branch now. Since
their more mature dignities and royal necessities made   25
separation of their society, their encounters – though
not personal – hath been royally attorneyed with
interchange of gifts, letters, loving embassies, that they
have seemed to be together, though absent; shook hands
as over a vast; and embraced as it were from the ends of   30
opposed winds. The heavens continue their loves.

24 **affection** a key word, with meanings
including deep fraternal love (as here),
overwhelming sexual desire, the power
of the mind, intense emotional longing, and disposition. See 1.2.137–46;
4.4.384, 485–6; 5.1.219; 5.2.36, 100;
and nn. See also *affects*, 4.4.425 and n.
and pp. 39–42.
branch put out shoots and branches;
flourish. The image of striplings at
22 is replaced by *affection* rooted in
or between the kings. Royal families
showed their lineages as genealogical
trees, with heraldic shields on branches, representing births and marriages
with other families (for other grafting,
see 1.2.244n., 4.4.92–5n.). Perhaps
Camillo contrasts *affection*, fraternal
love (fruit of Leontes' friendship with
Polixenes) with Mamillius (fruit of his
union with Hermione).
24–5 **Since . . . necessities** afterwards,
as adults, when their rank and the
demands on them as kings
26 **society** companionship
encounters contact with one other
27 **personal** in person
hath Third-person plural with *-th* was
common (Abbott, 334); see 1.2.1.
royally attorneyed conducted by
deputies in ways befitting kings (only
instance in *OED* of 'attorney' as verb,
but see *MM* 5.1.382)
28 **embassies** messages through ambassadors
29 **absent** separated
29–31 **shook . . . winds** Images of

growth at 23–4 are followed by an
emblem and a symbol from a map, the
first from a printer's device of hands
extended in friendship from opposite
clouds, the second from maps that
showed cherubs as the winds blowing
from each corner (cf. *Cym* 2.4.28).
The symbolic handshake, anticipating 1.2.443 (see n.), is parallel with
'handfasting', i.e. men and women
taking hands in betrothal: see 1.2.104n.
on *clap . . . love*, 4.4.353, 395 and nn.;
cf. Fig. 7.
30 **vast** huge expanse of sea or land; cf.
Per 3.1.1.
31 **The . . . continue** may the heavens
continue (subjunctive: Abbott, 365);
the heavens continue to further
(indicative)
heavens i.e. the gods, as at e.g.
3.2.143–4, 3.3.5, 4.4.535, 5.1.5. The
singular *heaven* is sometimes used
as an abstract, e.g. divine authority
(5.1.174), or as at 1.2.73 the Christian
God; elsewhere *heavens* and *heaven* are
used literally of the sky, e.g. 3.3.55,
4.4.376 (cf. *sky* and *skies*, 1.2.179,
3.3.3). In 1.2 the sky for Leontes
is a fantasy god-like vantage point,
from which to watch the adulterers
(178–9, 312–13). At 3.3.82–4, 87,
106–8, distinctions between sky and
sea, sea and earth are obliterated. At
5.1.131, Leontes, seeing Perdita and
Florizel, says he lost another couple
''twixt heaven and earth', which is full
of meaning (e.g. they were half-divine,

27 hath] have *F2*   30 vast] Vast Sea *F2*

ARCHIDAMUS   I think there is not in the world either malice or matter to alter it. You have an unspeakable comfort of your young prince, Mamillius. It is a gentleman of the greatest promise that ever came into 35 my note.

CAMILLO   I very well agree with you in the hopes of him. It is a gallant child; one that, indeed, physics the subject, makes old hearts fresh. They that went on crutches ere he was born desire yet their life to see him 40 a man.

ARCHIDAMUS   Would they else be content to die?

CAMILLO   Yes, if there were no other excuse why they should desire to live.

ARCHIDAMUS   If the king had no son they would desire 45 to live on crutches till he had one.   *Exeunt.*

---

half-human; or looked after by the gods and looked up to by people). At 5.1.202 *heaven* is the start of a metaphor for differences in rank (*stars, valleys*, 205).

33 **matter** cause

33–4 **unspeakable comfort** inexpressible source of succour (or consolation, or joy). The phrase is in 'Of Predestination and Election', *BCP*, Article 17, whence it passed into common use. Cf. *unspeakable estate*, 4.2.40 (see 39–40n.).

34, 38 **It** i.e. Mamillius (neuter pronoun, as at 5.2.33; possibly an endearment, i.e. it is *such* a wonderful child)

35 **gentleman** refers to quality, behaviour, not rank; probably an endearment, i.e. this lad, your prince, is the king's most promising servant (cf. *bawcock*, 1.2.121 and n.)

35–6 **into my note** to my attention; anticipating *note* at 1.2.2 (see n.)

37 **well** much

38 **gallant** polished, courtier-like (*OED* A *a.* 3); splendid, excellent (4a); brave,

daring (5a). Mamillius' dialogue at 2.1.3–15 suggests he is a fine young ladies' man too (B *n.* 3).

38–9 **physics the subject** acts as a tonic for, reinvigorates Sicily; *subject* is plural, all the king's subjects (only in Shakespeare according to *OED n.* I 1b); *physics* is a verb, medicates (cf. *Cym* 3.2.34). This is a key theme in the play, that youth renews life, giving older people, closer to death, a reason to live: but cf. 45–6 (see n.).

40 **crutches** i.e. because of age (crutches symbolize old age in *Cym* 4.2.198–201)

40–1 **desire . . . man** want to live to see him grown

43 **excuse** cause

45–6 probably qualifying Camillo's hyperbole that old people would be *content to die* but for the prospect of seeing Mamillius become king. Even without him, Archidamus says, they would struggle on, waiting for a male heir, i.e. the old use the young (even their children) as an *excuse* (43) for surviving.

1.2   *Enter* LEONTES, HERMIONE, MAMILLIUS,
POLIXENES [*and*] CAMILLO.

POLIXENES

Nine changes of the watery star hath been
The shepherd's note since we have left our throne
Without a burden. Time as long again
Would be filled up, my brother, with our thanks,
And yet we should for perpetuity   5
Go hence in debt. And therefore, like a cipher,

1.2 in open court, semi-public (receiving chamber: see 1.1n.), or in private: the playful explicitness between Hermione and Polixenes may indicate that servants weren't present (there are none in the SD in F, but F's SDs probably only listed major speaking roles; see 2.1.0.1n.).

0.1 Camillo exits at 1.1.46, and doesn't come forward until 208 (see n.), though he knows some of the conversation (211–31). On the modern stage he often remains or withdraws into the background as Leontes and the others enter. See 38n. In the Elizabethan theatre, trumpet fanfares sounded the arrival of royalty (Shirley, 18, 77).

1–2 Nine . . . note The shepherd has seen nine changes of the moon; i.e. nine months have passed. The moon, *watery* because it influences tides (cf. 422–3, *MND* 2.1.103), was associated with Diana and Lucina, goddesses of chastity and childbirth. Polixenes may have in mind Hermione's full-bellied pregnancy (2.1.16), but he doesn't connect the interval he has been with them to her condition. The appearance of upper-class Elizabethans when pregnant was celebrated rather than thought indelicate (Hearn, 39–40).

1 hath third-person singular, *note* as subject; third-person plural in *-th* with *changes* (Abbott, 334; see 1.1.27n.).

2 note punning on *note* as music, song

(shepherds piping and singing symbolized pastoral life), and account or bill to settle (3–9). Observing how time passes (*OED* note *n.*[2] 14b) is a major theme in *WT*: see pp. 78–81.

2–3 since . . . burden since I left my throne unoccupied, i.e. since I ruled in person. Polixenes begins with *we* and *our*, for 'I' and 'my' (plural pronouns used like this were exclusive to royalty), but switches to the more informal *I* at 7 (cf. 14). Cf. 83–6 (see 84n.). At 12–13, the plural may mean the Sicilians as a group.

3–6 Time . . . debt It would take me as long again (i.e. nine months) to thank you, brother, and even then I would depart forever in your debt.

4 brother Renaissance kings called each other 'brother' by convention (*OED* *n.* B 6), but Polixenes and Leontes are more fraternal (1.1.22–31), *twinned* (1.2.67). Also at 15, 148, 162; 4.2.23, 5.1.127, 140, 146; 5.3.5, 147 (see n.); cf. 5.1.116–17. Autolycus parodies brotherhood at 4.4.600–1; at 4.4.706 (see n.), 5.2.137–42, it becomes social fantasy.

6–9 And . . . it i.e. this final *thank you* is worth nothing (*cipher* = zero, the figure 0; cf. *KL* 1.4.183–5), but added (as 0) at the end of the sum of my earlier thanks it increases the amount by tenfold. Polixenes also flatters Leontes by declaring he is a nothing in

---

Yet standing in rich place, I multiply
With one 'we thank you' many thousands moe
That go before it.

LEONTES   Stay your thanks a while,
And pay them when you part.

POLIXENES   Sir, that's tomorrow.   10
I am questioned by my fears of what may chance
Or breed upon our absence, that may blow
No sneaping winds at home to make us say
This is put forth too truly. Besides, I have stayed
To tire your royalty.

LEONTES   We are tougher, brother,   15
Than you can put us to't.

POLIXENES   No longer stay.

LEONTES

One sev'night longer.

POLIXENES   Very sooth, tomorrow.

LEONTES

We'll part the time between's then; and in that

Sicilia's palace (*rich place*). Cf. 'He is a cipher among numbers' (Dent, C391); see Hulme, 79–80. The word *cipher* also suggests Hermione's pregnant roundness.

8 **moe** more; also at 4.4.273, 5.2.124
9 **Stay** delay
10 **part** depart
11–12 **I . . . absence** I am unsettled by fears about what might be happening because I am away; cf. *KL* 4.3.3–6.
12–14 **that . . . truly** that no nipping (*sneaping*) winds at home in time make me acknowledge (when I return) that my anxiety was well founded (*OED*'s second instance of 'sneaping'; first, *LLL* 1.1.100). He suspects that winds of change (perhaps conspiracies) may be blowing. 'This is put forth too truly' may mean he has trusted his subjects too much.

15 **tire your royalty** tire your majesty (*OED* royalty 1b); use up your magnificent wealth (2a); strain your generosity. To Leontes this might suggest 'wear out your wife sexually' (*tire*, tear at like a predator; cf. 2.3.73 and n., *Cym* 3.4.94).
15–16 **We . . . to't** I am more than equal, brother, to the most demanding test you can set me. Leontes takes *tire* (15) to mean tire out (possibly a reminder of boyhood trials of strength, i.e. you never exhausted me): 'to put someone to it' was to push him to the limit (*OED* put *v.* P2 b).
17 **sev'night** seven nights, week
Very sooth indeed (a mild oath)
18–19 **We'll . . . gainsaying** Then we'll split the difference in time between us (i.e. you'll stay three or four days), and I won't accept any contradiction.
18 **between's** between us. Other instances

17 sev'night] *(Seue'night)*

150

I'll no gainsaying.

POLIXENES   Press me not, beseech you, so.

There is no tongue that moves, none, none i'th' world   20
So soon as yours, could win me. So it should now,
Were there necessity in your request, although
'Twere needful I denied it. My affairs
Do even drag me homeward; which to hinder
Were, in your love, a whip to me; my stay,   25
To you a charge and trouble. To save both,
Farewell, our brother.

LEONTES   Tongue-tied, our queen? Speak you.

HERMIONE

I had thought, sir, to have held my peace until
You had drawn oaths from him not to stay. You, sir,
Charge him too coldly. Tell him you are sure   30

---

of *'s* for 'us' are at 77, 91, 94, 177, 205; 3.3.6, 68; 4.4.65; 5.3.138.

19 **Press . . . so** Don't insist, I beg you. Leontes may embrace Polixenes, as though to prevent him leaving, or even half-wrestle with him (see 15–16n.). *Press* could mean force into service (*OED v.*[2] 3), or put weights on a prisoner to obtain a guilty plea (cf. 2.3.38 and n.). Polixenes implores Leontes not to 'torture' him (cf. 24–5 and n.).

20 **There . . . moves** no one else's words; 'to move the tongue' was used of a dog's barking at its quarry (*OED* tongue *n.* 7a).

21–3 **So . . . it** It would do now too, if what you were asking were essential (*necessity*) to you, even though I had to refuse it.

21 **win** persuade

22 This line has 12 or 13 syllables: see pp. 126–7.

24–5 **which . . . me** to hinder which (my departure), even if you did it

out of love for me, would be a torture (*whip*). Ard[2] says *in your love* means 'if you will excuse me saying so'.

26 **charge and trouble** expense and inconvenience

27 **Tongue-tied** are you going to stay silent; are you too shy to speak. See Dent, T416, 'To be tongue-tied'. Cf. 2.2.32 (see n.).

29 **drawn . . . stay** extracted oaths from him that he wouldn't stay; Hermione has kept quiet (*held my peace*, 28), so that forcing Polixenes to retract his vows would be more pleasurably difficult.

29–30 **²You . . . coldly** *Charge* has several possible meanings here: (1) you're not attacking him forcefully enough (*OED v.* 22a) (cf. the banter in 15–16, 33: see nn.); (2) you're not ordering him with enough authority (14a); (3) you're not charging him enough for his stay (17) (cf. references to cost, 3–9, 26 and the likely pun on *satisfaction*, 31, i.e. full payment of debt, *OED* 1a).

19 beseech] (ʼbeseech)

All in Bohemia's well; this satisfaction
The bygone day proclaimed. Say this to him,
He's beat from his best ward.

LEONTES   Well said, Hermione.

HERMIONE
To tell he longs to see his son were strong;
But let him say so then, and let him go;   35
But let him swear so and he shall not stay,
We'll thwack him hence with distaffs.
[*to Polixenes*] Yet of your royal presence I'll adventure
The borrow of a week. When at Bohemia
You take my lord, I'll give him my commission   40
To let him there a month behind the gest
Prefixed for's parting: yet, good deed, Leontes,

31–2 **this . . . proclaimed** assurance of this was announced yesterday (*The bygone day*); i.e. the latest news from Bohemia is that everything is well there

31 **satisfaction** Cf. 230, 232 (see nn.).

32 **Say** if you say

33 **He's . . . ward** He's driven from his most fortified position or loses his strongest defence; i.e. you deprive him of his best excuse for leaving (*ward*, part of a fortress, or defensive posture in fencing: *OED n.*² 14, 8a).

34 **To tell** for him to say
were strong would be a compelling reason (for him to go home)

35, 36 **But** simply

36 **he . . . stay** we won't allow him to stay

37 i.e. my ladies and I will drive him away (*thwack*, beat vigorously with a stick, *OED v.* 1a). The line has seven syllables, stresses falling on *thwack* and *distaffs* (first syllable). Distaffs, rods used to spin flax, symbolized the female sphere, and were associated with chastity and modest behaviour among upper-class women (see *Luc* Argument 10–16; *KL* 4.2.17–18, where an unfaithful princess threatens to force a distaff into her weak husband's hands). Here, by contrast (and antici-

pating Paulina's knockabout scolding, 2.3.25–128), Hermione threatens to put them to a more unseemly use if Polixenes really means to go. Leontes thinks of flax-wenches (275) as sexually uncouth (see 274–6n.).

38 Schanzer has Leontes draw apart, and approach again at 86. It is not certain that the king hears what Hermione says to Polixenes, 38–86. He may draw aside at 44, observing the couple unseen. Cf. Camillo, not quite out of earshot (see 0.1n.).

38–9 **of . . . week** I'll risk borrowing your royal person for another week. At 39–42, the loan must be repaid four-fold, i.e. a month of Leontes for a week of Polixenes, hence the risk.

40 **take** charm, captivate (*OED v.* 10a); receive (*v.* 34)

40–2 **commission . . . parting** permission to stay a month longer than the date set for his departure

41 **behind** later than (*OED* B 4)
gest scheduled stopping-point on a progress, hence an arranged date; not, as *OED n.*⁴ b surmises, the time allotted for the stay

42 **for's** for his
good deed indeed

38 SD] *Oxf*   42 deed] heed *F2*

I love thee not a jar o'th' clock behind
What lady she her lord. You'll stay?

POLIXENES   No, madam.

HERMIONE
Nay, but you will.

POLIXENES   I may not, verily.   45

HERMIONE
Verily?
You put me off with limber vows. But I,
Though you would seek t'unsphere the stars with oaths,
Should yet say 'Sir, no going'. Verily
You shall not go. A lady's 'verily' is   50
As potent as a lord's. Will you go yet?
Force me to keep you as a prisoner,

---

43 **thee** First of over 160 instances of *thou, thee, thy*, i.e. archaic pronouns, now replaced by 'you', 'your'. At this date used in different, overlapping and sometimes apparently contradictory ways (Abbott, 231–5): to address friends, children, lovers, intimate servants, to show warmth, respect (cf. French *tu* and *vous*); to show anger or contempt; for superiors speaking to inferiors. See 209n., 212n.; 2.1.82n.; 2.2.3–4n.; 3.2.13–18n.; 4.3.54n., 4.4.423n.; 5.1.17n.; 5.2.147, 152n.

43–4 **not . . . lord** not a motion of the clock less than any lady, whoever she be, (loves) her husband, i.e. every second with him matters to her, so he must know how much she will be sacrificing to lose him for another month (40–2). Sherman (2) says people at this date described the pulse of clockwork not as a 'tick' but a *jar* (43), i.e. a 'harsh inharmonious' sound. At 44 *she* is probably for emphasis, but Blake (66) suggests that *What lady she* may mean 'whatever aristocratic woman'.

45 **verily** truly; a mild oath (cf. *Very sooth*, 17), associated with Jesus' sayings in the Gospels (Shaheen, 721)

47 **You . . . off** you're fobbing me off (Hermione is teasing him gently)
limber vows feeblest, most limp oaths; oaths you summon so easily, nimbly

48 even if you swore oaths so vehement they might (1) detach the stars (emblems of fixity) from their spheres; (2) shatter the heavens (in the Ptolemaic universe a set of concentric crystalline spheres, with planets and sun set in them, going round the earth); cf. 420–2 , 2.1.100–3 (see nn.). *OED*'s first citation of 'unsphere'.

50 **'verily'** F's apostrophe (see t.n.) indicates that the vowel *i* in *is* was to be elided. This is a scribal characteristic of Ralph Crane: see p. 356.

51 **potent** powerful. The latent meaning in 50–1 is connected to *limber* (47), i.e. women have the same sexual potency as men.
Will . . . yet? Are you still determined to go?

50 'verily' is] *(*Verely' is*)*; Verily's *Ard²*

Not like a guest: so you shall pay your fees
When you depart, and save your thanks. How say you?
My prisoner? Or my guest? By your dread 'verily'   55
One of them you shall be.

POLIXENES   Your guest then, madam.
To be your prisoner should import offending,
Which is for me less easy to commit
Than you to punish.

HERMIONE   Not your gaoler then,
But your kind hostess. Come, I'll question you   60
Of my lord's tricks and yours when you were boys.
You were pretty lordings then?

POLIXENES   We were, fair queen,
Two lads that thought there was no more behind
But such a day tomorrow as today,
And to be boy eternal.

HERMIONE   Was not my lord   65
The verier wag o'th' two?

53–4 **pay ... depart** On release from gaol, Elizabethan prisoners paid for their food and board. The exchanges at 52–60 prefigure Hermione's imprisonment in Act 2.

54 **save your thanks** i.e. if you're not a *guest* here (53), you won't have to pay the sum of thanks you calculated (at 3–9; see nn.)

55 **By your dread** I swear, using your own fearful oath. Cf. *dread*, 320; here used playfully, mocking the feebleness of *verily*.

57 **should import offending** would mean I had committed (and been imprisoned for) some crime. By refusing Hermione's request Polixenes would also risk offending her, which he would be loath to do: it would be easier for her to *punish* him (58–9).

61 **tricks** pranks, practical jokes; features (Hermione thinks they must have been *pretty*, 62); cf. 2.1.51–2, 4.4.646–7 and nn., and the *trick* of Leontes' face, 2.3.99.

62 **pretty lordings** handsome little fellows (an endearment)

63–4 **there ... today** that the future had no more to it than that tomorrow would be the same as today

63 **behind** beyond, hidden from view, to come

65 **boy eternal** boys for ever, i.e. always youthful and carefree; *eternal* is probably an adverb qualifying *be* but possibly an adjective with *boy* (Blake, 105).

66 **verier wag** more mischievous little devil; *wag* is an endearment for a baby boy (*OED n.*[2] 1).

65–6 Was ... two?] *one line Hanmer*

POLIXENES

We were as twinned lambs that did frisk i'th' sun
And bleat the one at th'other: what we changed
Was innocence for innocence; we knew not
The doctrine of ill-doing, nor dreamed   70
That any did. Had we pursued that life,
And our weak spirits ne'er been higher reared
With stronger blood, we should have answered heaven
Boldly, 'not guilty', the imposition cleared
Hereditary ours.

HERMIONE   By this we gather   75
You have tripped since.

---

67 **twinned lambs** lambs born together (biological twins, cf. *Tim* 4.3.3); totally alike and inseparable. F's 'twyn'd' suggests an image of them tangled in play (frisking), or entwined at birth.

68–9 **what . . . ²innocence** we exchanged innocent words or feelings; together we changed one innocent pastime for another. Lambs were proverbially chaste and gentle (Dent, L34 and L34.1).

69–70 **we . . . ill-doing** we had not learnt to do wrong or to teach others to; we had no notion of original sin (Christian doctrine, from Genesis, 3.1–24, Romans, 5.12, that everyone is born tainted by sin because Adam and Eve disobeyed God in Eden: see pp. 48–9). Cf. 2.2.28 (see n. on *innocent*).

70 This appears to be a syllable short, but it has five stresses; *doctrine* may be three syllables ('doc-ter-in'), but *OED* spellings at this date, 'doctryn(e)', 'doctrin', suggest it is two. Possibly a word was left out in the manuscript, or by the compositor. F2's arresting 'no, nor' for *nor* gives the line a convincing speech rhythm.

71–3 **Had . . . blood** had we been able to stay at that stage, and the weakness

of our animal *spirits* (puny because we were children) hadn't been fortified by more vigorous *blood* (adult passionate feelings). Throughout *WT* metaphors are mixed with Renaissance biological explanations of blood and humours (see 109n., 2.1.56n., 2.3.37n., 4.3.4n., 4.4.708n.). Here, growing sexual awareness affects the boys' hearts and minds (i.e. intangible *spirits*), but also bodies (spirits *higher reared* with *stronger blood* is the ability to have an erection: see 109n., 156n.). Mamillius is at this pre-pubertal stage: see pp. 34–5, 37.

74–5 **the . . . ours** having been cleared of what was imposed on us by inheritance, not our own actions. On the Day of Judgement, when God asks for an account of their lives, the boys, had they remained innocent, would have been exempt of all but original sin (see 69–70n.), able to answer *heaven* (73) with a not-guilty plea. This prefigures the trial in 3.2.

76 **tripped** fallen. Hermione refers to the boys behaving like lambs, but she also means they have stumbled figuratively since boyhood (i.e. they have lain down for sex and 'fallen', lost their innocence; see 74–5n.).

---

67 twinned] *(twyn'd)*   70 nor dreamed] no, nor dream'd *F2*

POLIXENES   O my most sacred lady,
Temptations have since then been born to's, for
In those unfledged days was my wife a girl;
Your precious self had then not crossed the eyes
Of my young playfellow.

HERMIONE   Grace to boot!   80
Of this make no conclusion, lest you say
Your queen and I are devils. Yet go on.
Th'offences we have made you do we'll answer,
If you first sinned with us, and that with us
You did continue fault, and that you slipped not   85
With any but with us.

LEONTES   Is he won yet?

HERMIONE
He'll stay, my lord.

LEONTES   At my request he would not.

sacred royal (but also, a teasing response, 'O pure divine one, unlike we men')

77 **born to's** F's spelling 'borne' may mean temptation wasn't innate (*to's*, in us), but from outside (*to* us).

78 **unfledged days** times of inexperience (when we were like young birds)

79 **precious** exquisite

79–80 **then . . . Of** i.e. not yet been seen by

80 **Grace to boot** May heaven give me its blessing; you are being courteous to us (your wife and me) into the bargain (*OED* boot *n.*[1] 1a). Different meanings of grace, gracious, graceful, overlap in *WT*: seemliness, as here (cf. *gracious*, 5.1.133 and n.); favour (3.2.46, 5.3.7n.); reputation, honour (see 2.1.121–2n.); highborn titles (1.2.262, 4.4.781–2n.); God's blessing, gift or salvation (as here) (105n., 5.2.108n., 5.3.122n.; cf. *blessing*, 2.3.188) or forgiveness, mercy (4.4.76n., 5.3.26–7n.); spiritual cleansing, purity (2.1.121–2n.); full of divine grace; virtuous (5.1.170n.).

81 **Of . . . conclusion** don't infer any-

thing; don't pursue that argument to its conclusion

82 **Your . . . devils** your wife and I, tempting you to sin, are why you *tripped* (76), perhaps with a quibble: *devils* had 'hell' in them, an Elizabethan word for 'vagina' (Williams, 660).

83 **answer** accept responsibility and punishment for

84 **If . . . [1]us** if the first time you sinned (i.e. had sex) was with us. Pronouns in 83–6 refer to Polixenes' relations with his wife and Hermione's with Leontes; but *sinned with us* could mean had sex with me (royal 'us': see 2–3n.), an ambiguity that might prompt Leontes' first words since 33.

84, 85 **that** if

85 **did continue fault** continued sinning **slipped not** didn't commit the offence (*OED* slip *v.*[1] 8c; cf. *MM* 5.1.469) – the sin may be venial not cardinal. Cf. *slippery*, 271 (see n.).

86 **Is . . . yet** Is he persuaded yet; (sarcastically) is his heart completely yours

87 **request** Cf. 5.1.220–1.

77 born] *(borne)*   80 Grace] Oh! Grace *Hanmer*   87 At . . . not] *as an aside Capell*

Hermione, my dearest, thou never spok'st
To better purpose.

HERMIONE   Never?

LEONTES   Never, but once.

HERMIONE

What? Have I twice said well? When was't before?   90
I prithee tell me; cram's with praise, and make's
As fat as tame things. One good deed, dying tongueless,
Slaughters a thousand waiting upon that.
Our praises are our wages. You may ride's
With one soft kiss a thousand furlongs ere   95
With spur we heat an acre. But to th' goal:
My last good deed was to entreat his stay.
What was my first? It has an elder sister,

---

88 **dearest** perhaps one syllable, as often with superlatives
91 **I prithee** I beg you
   cram's . . . make's contracted 'us' (also *ride's*, 94), i.e. we women
92 **tame things** pets; livestock fattened for slaughter. In *WT*, *things* is used of living beings, as here (see 3.3.110, 111n.; 5.1.177n.); matters, events, actions, opinions (139n., 234; 3.2.205; 4.1.13; 5.1.21); objects (4.3.62; 4.4.699n.).
92–3 **One . . . that** One unpraised good deed puts us off doing a thousand others that would have been inspired by that praise (because we think we won't get any for doing those either).
93 **waiting upon** depending on; waiting to see what happens; acting as a servant (*OED* wait *v*.[1] 14j); accompanying on one's way (14k), complementing the journey imagery, 94–6
94 **Our . . . wages** Praise is the reward we seek.
94–6 **You . . . acre** i.e. as with horses,

men handle women better by gentle encouragement than compulsion (literally, for one *kiss* you can get a *thousand furlongs* from us in less time than we can be made to cover a single furlong (see 95n.) by using a *spur*). For other references to and word-play on horses, riders, etc., see: 96n., 242n., 274, 284n., 286n., 292n.; 2.1.134–5n., 147n., 182n., 186–7n.; 2.3.50–1n.; 3.1n.; 4.3.64n.
95 **furlongs** A furlong was an eighth of a mile (201 metres).
96 **heat** race over swiftly (*OED v*. B 1c, only citation for this sense)
   acre plot of land a furlong square
   to th' goal to get to the point (punning on *goal* meaning 'finishing post'); see 94–6n.
97–9 touches playfully on contemporary Protestant debates about salvation through good works as opposed to faith alone and God's 'grace' or freely given gift (see 80n.).
97 **last** latest
98 **It** i.e. the earlier *good deed* (97)

92 deed] *F; omitted Cam*

Or I mistake you. O, would her name were Grace!
But once before I spoke to th' purpose? When? 100
Nay, let me have't – I long.
LEONTES   Why, that was when
Three crabbed months had soured themselves to death
Ere I could make thee open thy white hand
And clap thyself my love. Then didst thou utter,
'I am yours for ever.'
HERMIONE   'Tis grace indeed. 105
Why, lo you now, I have spoke to th' purpose twice.
The one for ever earned a royal husband;
Th'other for some while a friend.
    [*Gives her hand to Polixenes.*]
LEONTES [*aside*]   Too hot, too hot!

99 **mistake** have misunderstood
  would ... Grace Would (1) the *elder
  sister* (*deed*, 97) were called Grace;
  (2) the deed were gracious; (3) the
  deed might have heaven's grace in
  it. Hermione refers obliquely to the
  exchange at 76–82, where Polixenes
  almost implied that she and his wife
  were *devils*: let's hope, she says, my
  deed, imbued with God's saving grace,
  proves we are not. See 80n.
100 **But** only
101 **let me have't** tell me what it is
  I long said playfully: please, I'm
  desperate (cf. *LLL* 5.2.244)
102 **crabbed** crabbèd: (1) sour-tasting,
  like crab apples; (2) ill-tempered (cf.
  Tem 3.1.8); (3) perverse (like a crab's
  motion, his wooing went backwards
  or sideways, but not forward). Perhaps
  referring to summer: the sun enters
  the astrological sign Cancer, the crab,
  in June.
104 *And F's 'A' is probably the compositor's mistake (i.e. he set it instead of
  the ampersand in the manuscript).
  clap ... love by clasping my hand,
  pledge at once that you loved and

would marry me. To clap palms or
hands was to strike a bargain (*OED*
clap *v.*[1] 7a), or do something briskly
(15b); cf. *H5* 5.2.129–31. At 105, the
gesture and words show that this was
a handfasting (see 1.1.29–31n.). Cf.
4.4.395, 5.3.107 (see nn.), Fig. 7.
105 **'Tis grace indeed** I was right: my
  deed, 97 (agreeing to marry you, 104),
  did have heaven's blessing. Cf. 80 (see
  n.); Dent, M688, 'Marriages are made
  in heaven.'
106 **Why, lo you** well, just look at this
107 **royal husband** husband who is a
  king; magnificent, wonderful husband
108 **friend** This could mean a sexual
  lover (Williams, 553–4; *Cym* 1.4.68–9,
  where a husband is his wife's adorer
  not friend); cf. modern 'boyfriend'.
  Leontes fears this is what Polixenes is
  to Hermione (see 109nn.). Hermione's
  action in the added SD reminds
  Leontes how she first gave it him in
  marriage (see 104n.).
  hot i.e. they're behaving like lovers;
  hot could mean sexually aroused,
  lustful: cf. *Oth* 3.3.406, 'as hot as
  monkeys'.

104 And] F2; A F   108 SD Gives . . . Polixenes] Capell subst.   aside] Rowe

To mingle friendship far is mingling bloods.
I have *tremor cordis* on me. My heart dances,   110
But not for joy, not joy. This entertainment
May a free face put on, derive a liberty
From heartiness, from bounty, fertile bosom,
And well become the agent – 't may, I grant –
But to be paddling palms and pinching fingers,   115
As now they are, and making practised smiles
As in a looking-glass; and then to sigh, as 'twere
The mort o'th' deer – O, that is entertainment

109 **To ... far** to go further in intimacy with a friend (*mingle*, join in conversation or friendship, *OED v.* 2c). F's 'farre' is probably a comparative (as also at 216, 5.3.141).
   is mingling bloods i.e. shows you're having sex. In Renaissance physiology, bodily fluids were forms of blood. Red blood and white (i.e. semen) were the same: sperm was 'nothing else but Blood, made White' by the body's heat (cited in Babb, 129). Sexual intercourse was thus *mingling bloods*. See 71–3n., 2.1.57–8n., 4.3.4n.
110 **I ... me** My heart's racing, I'm shaking. The condition *tremor cordis* (Latin 'trembling of the heart', *OED* tremor *n.* 2a), was attributed to physical as well as mental causes (flatulence or emotions); symptoms included an irregular heartbeat.
110–11 **My ... ²joy** Cf. Dent, H333.1, 'To have one's heart dance [i.e. beat fast] for joy'. For its use in the Anglican Psalter, see Shaheen, 722–3.
111–12 **This ... on** This hospitality may look innocent; an innocent heart may offer hospitality like this. Leontes' linking *entertainment* to shame and love (109–19) is a distortion of what was said at 1.1.8–9.
112 **liberty** licence to act or freedom to speak; cf. *Oth* 3.4.36–46 (40).

113 **from** cordiality, generosity, warm feeling
114 **become the agent** be praiseworthy in the doer
115 **paddling ... fingers** stroking palms, gently squeezing fingers; Leontes associates this with sex (*OED* paddle *v.*¹ 2b). Citing *Oth* 2.1.252, Schanzer says a lady's paddling the palm of a gentleman could be either polite behaviour or a sign of lasciviousness.
116 **practised** carefully prepared, rehearsed (and concealing real desires)
117 an alexandrine (Abbott, 493–9) that doesn't need emendation, though the omission of *looking* has been proposed; see also 339, 441–2 and n.; 4.4.498 and n.
117–18 **sigh ... deer** sigh like a deer hunted to death (*mort*) breathing its last. Contemporary emblems showed a mortally wounded stag as a symbol of incurable love, while puns on 'deer' and 'dear' were common. Leontes also means the sigh at the end of a sexual 'chase', i.e. after intercourse (*O* at 118 is a vocative or expresses anger, or mimics a sexual groan). *OED*'s citation of these lines under mort *n.*¹ 3a, the note sounded on a horn when a deer is killed, is unconvincing, as is Schanzer's suggestion that the sigh is likened to the intake of breath needed to blow the horn (see pp. 131–3).

109 far] *(farre)*   114 't may] it may *F2*

My bosom likes not, nor my brows. – Mamillius,
Art thou my boy?

MAMILLIUS   Ay, my good lord.

LEONTES   I'fecks;   120

Why, that's my bawcock. What? Hast smutched thy
     nose?

They say it is a copy out of mine. Come, captain,

We must be neat – not neat, but cleanly, captain.

     [*Wipes Mamillius' face.*]

And yet the steer, the heifer and the calf

Are all called neat. – Still virginalling   125

Upon his palm? – How now, you wanton calf!

Art thou my calf?

MAMILLIUS   Yes, if you will, my lord.

LEONTES

Thou want'st a rough pash and the shoots that I have

---

119 **bosom** heart; feelings
     brows Husbands whose wives cuck-
     olded them were thought to sprout
     two small invisible horns on their
     foreheads (Williams, 158–60).
120 **Art . . . boy** As at 127 and 161,
     Leontes gently teases his son; there
     is also a more menacing question ('are
     you my child or someone else's?') or an
     indirect challenge ('are you on my side,
     my boy, or hers?').
     Ay F's 'I' means 'yes', or 'I (am)'.
     I'fecks truly (corruption of 'in faith');
     a mild oath, but perhaps signalling how
     anxious Leontes is. *I'fecks* sounded close
     to 'he fucks'; cf. *forked*, 185 (see n.).
121 **bawcock** fine lad; from French *beau
     coq*, an endearment, as with *captain*
     (122, 123; see n.), *calf* (126, 127), *sir*
     page (135), *villain* (136; see n.), *gentle-*
     man (160; see n.). Cf. *H5* 4.1.44–5.
     smutched dirtied; *OED*'s first cita-
     tion (smuch *v. a*)
122 **it . . . mine** you have your nose from
     me: it's exactly like mine. Leontes
     suspects that Hermione has 'dirtied' his

own nose: to have one's nose wiped
was proverbial for being cheated (Tilley,
N244), and the nose was often associated
bawdily with the penis (Williams, 954–6).
122, 123 **captain** my little soldier
123 **not neat** Leontes corrects himself,
     recalling that *neat* means clean and
     trim, but also horned cattle (see 124n.);
     he too is horned, a cuckold (see 119n.
     on *brows*).
124 **steer** young ox, especially a castrated
     one. Its horns, like those of the *heifer*
     (see n.), were emblems of placidity.
     heifer young cow that hasn't had a calf
125 **virginalling** moving her fingers
     (over his *palm*) as though playing the
     virginals (an early keyboard instru-
     ment): cf. *Son* 128; pretending to be a
     chaste (virginal) lady.
126 **wanton** frisky, frolicsome. The word
     was associated with children: 'As
     wanton as a calf' (Dent, W38.1); but
     also meant lascivious.
127 **will** command it, wish it so
128–9 **Thou . . . me** You lack my shaggy
     head (*pash*) and bull's horns (*shoots*),

---

120 Ay] *(1)*   121 Hast] *(has't)*   123 but] *omitted F2*   SD] *Hanmer subst.*

To be full like me. Yet they say we are
Almost as like as eggs – women say so,   130
That will say anything. But were they false
As o'erdyed blacks, as wind, as waters, false
As dice are to be wished by one that fixes
No bourn 'twixt his and mine, yet were it true
To say this boy were like me. Come, sir page,   135
Look on me with your welkin eye. Sweet villain,
Most dearest, my collop! Can thy dam? May't be
Affection? – Thy intention stabs the centre,
Thou dost make possible things not so held,
Communicat'st with dreams – how can this be? –   140

to be completely like me. Leontes
perhaps points to his hair and whiskers
(*shoots*), but he means he is a cuckold
(see 119n.). See Fig. 10.
128 **pash** head (dialect: *OED n.*²)
130 ¹**as . . . eggs** exactly alike; proverbial
(Dent, E66)
131 **they** women
132 **o'erdyed blacks** (1) fabrics weak-
ened by too frequent dyeing; (2)
wools dyed one colour over another to
produce a false black; (3) clothes dyed
black to conceal flaws. Leontes may
mean insincere widows who mourn
a succession of husbands and wear
black, or wives who hide their infidelity beneath false colours.
waters proverbially false and change-
able (Dent, W412, W86.1). Cf. *Oth*
5.2.132.
132–4 **false . . . mine** false as a cheat,
someone who accepts no boundary
(*bourn*) between his and mine, could
wish (loaded) dice to be (cf. 4.4.830–1
and n.), i.e. Polixenes is playing as
falsely as possible to cheat me of
Hermione; *his and mine* recalls the
Latin phrase for property, *meum et
tuum* (mine and yours).
136 **welkin** sky-blue or bright (the colour
of *welkin*, the sky)
villain little rogue, an endearment
137 **my collop** my own flesh and blood,
i.e. son; collop meant 'offspring' (*OED*

collop¹ 2b) and 'morsel of meat' (3b).
Cf. Dent, C517, 'It is a dear collop that
is cut out of the flesh'; and *1H6* 5.3.18.
Can thy dam Can your mother (really
be cheating me); do you know your
mother, can you tell who she is (*OED* can
*v.*¹ BI 1a); dam (from dame) was used
of animals, so Leontes probably means
heifer, mother of the *calf* (see 124n.).
137–46 **May't . . . brows** It is generally agreed that this passage turns
on the meaning of *Affection*, 138 (see
1.1.24n.). Leontes addresses it as
either (1) his (overwrought) mental
condition; or (2) his jealous feelings;
or (3) what he believes is Hermione's
lust. The glosses below are based on
(1). See pp. 39–42.
137–8 **May't be / Affection** Might what
I've thought be just a product of my
mental state (*OED* affection *n.* 2a).
138–9 **Thy . . . Thou**   addressing
Affection
138 **Thy . . . centre** i.e. my mental powers (*OED* intention *n.* 2) have got to
the heart of the matter
139 You make me know *things* (see 1.2.92n.)
everyone else thinks are impossible.
140 **Communicat'st with dreams**
(1) you put me in touch with what's
in her mind, what she keeps hidden
in *dreams*; (2) you're in contact with
dreams, and function in the way they
do. See 326–7n.

With what's unreal thou coactive art,
And fellow'st nothing. Then 'tis very credent
Thou mayst co-join with something, and thou dost,
And that beyond commission, and I find it,
And that to the infection of my brains   145
And hard'ning of my brows.

POLIXENES   What means Sicilia?

HERMIONE

He something seems unsettled.

POLIXENES   How? My lord?

LEONTES

What cheer? How is't with you, best brother?

HERMIONE   You look

As if you held a brow of much distraction.
Are you moved, my lord?

LEONTES   No, in good earnest.   150

How sometimes nature will betray its folly,

141–2 **With . . . nothing** You act together (*coactive art*) with the world of the
psyche (*what's unreal*), as partner to
non-existent or imaginary things.
142 **credent** credible (*OED* 2a, citing this
and *MM* 4.4.27)
143 **co-join** conjoin, act together
something something real (rather
than the imaginary *nothing* of 142); the
word is sexually charged but undefined
(penis? Hermione's infidelity?).
144 **commission** what can be allowed
and . . . it as I've discovered
145 **to . . . brains** to the extent of nearly
losing my mind
146 **hard'ning . . . brows** See 119n.
What means Sicilia What's on
your mind; why are you so distracted
(*Sicilia*, i.e. Leontes: see List of Roles,
0.1n.). Polixenes isn't supposed to
have heard 137–46, so he is not asking
'What do you mean?' See 38n.
147 **something seems** seems somewhat

unsettled Cf. 323.
148 **What . . . brother** How are you
doing, how are things with you, most
dear brother. Many editors reassign
this to Polixenes, interpreting *How
is't with you* as a question following
from *What means Sicilia?* at 146. But
Leontes, cunningly recovering his
poise, heads off questions at 146–7
with reassuring ones of his own. Cf.
Iago, *Oth* 4.2.112.
148–9 **You . . . distraction** From your
expression, you appear very upset.
Cf. *Ham* 2.2.490. Hermione refers
unintentionally to Leontes' forehead,
where he thinks cuckold's horns are
growing (see 119n.).
150 **moved** distressed, angry. Cf. *Oth*
3.3.221, 228.
in good earnest truthfully
151–3 **nature . . . bosoms** innate feeling (for one's child) will inadvertently reveal how doting it is, providing

---

141 unreal] vnreall: *F*   148 What . . . brother?] *assigned to Polixenes by Hanmer*   148–9 You . . .
distraction] *Theobald; one line F*   151–3 How . . . bosoms] *as an aside Capell*

Its tenderness, and make itself a pastime
To harder bosoms. Looking on the lines
Of my boy's face, methoughts I did recoil
Twenty-three years, and saw myself unbreeched,   155
In my green velvet coat; my dagger muzzled,
Lest it should bite its master, and so prove,
As ornaments oft does, too dangerous.
How like, methought, I then was to this kernel,
This squash, this gentleman. Mine honest friend,   160
Will you take eggs for money?

MAMILLIUS   No, my lord, I'll fight.

amusement (*pastime*) for less tender-hearted people

153–60 See pp. 34–5, 37.

153 **on the lines** at the features

154 **methoughts** variant of *methought* (159), probably coined, incorrectly, by analogy with 'methinks'; no instance in *OED* before Shakespeare
    recoil go back in memory (*OED v.*[1] 4d), punning on the recoil (rebound) of a gun when discharged (*OED n.* 3a; also used at 2.3.19), and so connected to *unbreeched*, 155 (i.e. a breech emptied at firing)

155 **Twenty-three years** i.e. to when he was Mamillius' age, seven: see List of Roles, 2n.
    unbreeched not wearing breeches (only instance in Shakespeare, *OED*'s first citation): see List of Roles, 2n., and Fig. 6; 1.2.154n. on *recoil*. Leontes might also mean 'not yet wounded ("breeched") by infidelity'; 'not sundered yet from false wife and friend'.

156 **coat** long petticoat (worn by both sexes until seven or eight)
    my dagger muzzled (1) with the blade of my little sword in its sheath (adults carried unguarded knives as weapons and to eat with); (2) with the point of my sword tipped (like a foil in fencing). The image is of an animal muzzled to stop it harming its

master. Leontes may also be recalling his limited sexual powers at that age, his little weapon a metaphor for the penis he couldn't yet use sexually: see 71–3n.

158 **ornaments** adornments
    does third-person singular with plural noun (Abbott, 335); cf. *hath*, 1.1.27 (see n.).

159 **kernel** pip, seed of a fleshy fruit, perhaps punning on 'colonel', little soldier (cf. *captain*, 122), though *OED* says early pronunciation of the words varied greatly

160 **squash** unripe pea pod (*OED n.*[1] 1a), an endearment; cf. *TN* 1.5.152–3, 'Not yet old enough for a man, nor young enough for a boy, as a squash is before 'tis a peascod'.
    gentleman an endearment (see 121n.), something like excellent, accomplished young companion (*OED* 3a); cf. 1.1.35 (see n.).
    honest honourable. Leontes may be reassuring himself that his son is legitimate (cf. 209).

161 **Will . . . money** Will you let yourself be fobbed off. Eggs were proverbially cheap. 'To take eggs for money' (Dent, E90) was to accept a trifle in exchange for something valuable; cf. *KL* 1.4.148–9. Leontes thinks he has lost out in an exchange over Hermione; see 173–4n., 246n.

158 ornaments oft does] ornament oft does *Capell;* ornaments oft do *Rowe*   161 my lord] *omitted Hanmer*

LEONTES

You will? Why, happy man be's dole! My brother,
Are you so fond of your young prince as we
Do seem to be of ours?

POLIXENES   If at home, sir,
He's all my exercise, my mirth, my matter;   165
Now my sworn friend, and then mine enemy;
My parasite, my soldier, statesman, all.
He makes a July's day short as December,
And with his varying childness cures in me
Thoughts that would thick my blood.

LEONTES   So stands this squire   170
Officed with me. We two will walk, my lord,
And leave you to your graver steps. Hermione,
How thou lov'st us show in our brother's welcome.
Let what is dear in Sicily be cheap.

---

162 **happy . . . dole** may your fortune
be that of a happy man. Proverbial
for 'good luck' (Dent, M158); cf. *MW*
3.4.62–3.

163 **Are . . . of** do you dote as much on
prince Florizel, almost exactly
Mamillius' age: see List of Roles, 2n.

164 **If at home** if I'm relaxing (*OED*
home *n.*[1] 11c); when I'm in private in
Bohemia

165 **exercise** habitual occupation (*OED*
n. 2)
mirth source of fun
my matter my only concern and
subject matter (in conversation and
thoughts)

166 **sworn** closest; sworn companions
at arms took a chivalric oath to share
their fates. Cf. 170–1 (see n.); 4.4.51,
601.

167 **parasite** court flatterer

168 **July** Jùly
December i.e. as a day in December

169 **varying childness** childish fluctua-
tions in mood (*OED*'s first citation of
'childness')

cures in me drives out of me (*OED*
cure *v.*[1] 5a)

170 **Thoughts . . . blood** i.e. mel-
ancholic and cruel thoughts. Blood
thickening was linked to despondency
(*OED* melancholy *n.*[1] 1); cf. 71–3, 109,
and see nn.

170–1 **So . . . me** Mamillius (*this squire*)
performs the same role in my household (a squire was a well-born youth
who attended a knight). Cf. 166 (see
n.).

171 **We two** Mamillius and I
my lord Polixenes

172 **graver steps** weightier, more serious
conversation as you walk; a contrast to
his light-hearted walk with Mamillius
(who takes smaller, less heavy steps)

173–4 By the welcome you give Polixenes,
show how you love me (*us*); let him
have what is valuable in Sicily for a
small price. Cf. Tilley, C257, 'Good
cheap is dear.' Leontes returns to
Polixenes' paying for his visit with
thanks (see 6–9 and n.), but with a
double meaning involving Hermione:

Next to thyself and my young rover, he's   175
Apparent to my heart.
HERMIONE   If you would seek us,
We are yours i'th' garden. Shall's attend you there?
LEONTES
To your own bents dispose you. You'll be found,
Be you beneath the sky. [*aside*] I am angling now,
Though you perceive me not how I give line.   180
Go to, go to!
How she holds up the neb, the bill to him,
And arms her with the boldness of a wife
To her allowing husband. [*Exeunt Polixenes and Hermione.*]
Gone already.

show how little you value me (by having sex with him), and make worthless
(*OED* cheap *a*. A 4a) what should be
precious (your chastity).
175 **rover** robber (*OED* rover² 2), another
endearment; little wanderer (cf. 'We
two will walk', 171)
176 **Apparent** heir apparent, i.e.
Polixenes is closest (next in line) to
Leontes' heart after his wife and son.
The word also suggests that Polixenes'
(supposed) treachery is now clear to
Leontes.
177 **yours** at your service
Shall's attend shall we wait for
178 **To . . . you** Do as you wish.
178–9 **You'll . . . sky** an allusion to
Adam and Eve in Eden unable to
conceal their sin from God (Genesis,
3.7–13; cf. 69–70, 74–5, and see nn.).
In *Pandosto*, the king becomes jealous
when his wife and friend walk in the
garden (p. 408).
179 **angling** scheming; both fish will be
caught with his bait. For imagery from
fish, angling, see 180, 194, 195; 2.3.7;
4.2.46; 4.4.275–81, 279–80; 5.2.81;
and nn.
180 **give line** feed out the line (cf. Dent,
L304.1, 'To give one line'). Letting

the hooked lovers swim around before
reeling them in continues the metaphor (see 179n.).
181 Come, come (this is disgraceful);
(said sarcastically) go on, enjoy yourselves; see 182n., 183–4n.
182 **neb** bird's beak (*bill*), which was associated with the nose, mouth and face; with
kissing, caressing (billing and cooing);
and with the penis (Williams, 106)
183–4 **arms . . . husband** (1) links arms
with him (*OED* arm *v*.² 2) with a
wife's assurance (*OED* boldness 3) (i.e.
Hermione behaves as though Polixenes
were her husband), knowing her husband won't object; (2) behaves like a
sexually demanding wife with a husband
who has no choice but give her what
she wants; (3) makes sexual advances
(to another man) like a wife sure her
husband won't object; (4) prepares to
defend herself (*OED* arm *v*.¹ 2e) (against
Leontes' suspicions), with the impudent
shamelessness (*OED* boldness 2) of a
wife abusing her husband's permission
(to welcome his friend, 173)
184 **allowing** probably spoken sarcastically (see 183-4n.)
Gone already (1) you couldn't get
away fast enough to be with him; (2)

178 You'll] *(you'le);* you'd *F3*   179 SD] *Ard²*   181 *(Goe too, goe too.)*   184 SD] *Rowe subst.,
after 183*

Inch-thick, knee-deep, o'er head and ears a forked one!   185
Go play, boy, play. Thy mother plays, and I
Play too; but so disgraced a part, whose issue
Will hiss me to my grave. Contempt and clamour
Will be my knell. Go play, boy, play. There have been,
Or I am much deceived, cuckolds ere now,   190
And many a man there is even at this present,

you're already lost (or dead) to me as a wife; (3) it's too late, you're a lost cause (sunk too deep in sin, see 185n.); (4) you've already gone too far (had sex) with him. The word 'gone' is used equivocally in *WT*, i.e. dead, done for, role ended, no longer present: see 2.3.7n., 128n., 3.2.142n., 3.3.57n., 4.4.826n., 5.1.35n.

185 Leontes means himself, a complete cuckold, or Hermione, an utter whore (see n. on *forked*). The imagery is of a person sinking, as if into quicksand or mire, i.e. *Inch-thick* one moment (but see also next n.), *knee-deep* the next. Thatcher (207–8) connects this immersion to *angling* (179–80) and the vocabulary of sex and infidelity: *sluiced* (see 193n.), *pond* (194), *slippery* (see 271n.).

Inch-thick beyond doubt. A standard wooden plank was an inch thick, hence a measure of solidity: cf. Tilley, I61, 'He will swear (look) through an inch board.' Thatcher (207) suggests that Leontes thinks of his cuckold's thick horns (see 119n. on *brows*).

knee-deep wholly; too deep in to get out

o'er . . . ears utterly; cf. Dent, H268, 'To be over head and ears in a thing', e.g. water, love, wickedness.

forked (1) his cuckold's horns make him look *forked* (*OED* 4b; see 119n.); (2) Hermione is an equivocator (*OED* 5), a fork-tongued serpent, or she-devil with horns; (3) she has divided herself between him and Polixenes; (4) she is just another two-legged thing (cf. *KL* 3.4.106, 'bare, forked animal'); (5) she has been fucked (close enough to *forked*, cf. *I'fecks*, 120 (see n.).

186–7 **play . . . play . . . plays . . . Play** The meanings range from the innocent 'amuse yourself, play a game' addressed to Mamillius (cf. *Tem* 5.1.185, the chess game), to Hermione's playing sexual games (while pretending to be a faithful wife), to Leontes' playing a role (as an actor).

187 **so . . . part** so shameful a role (as cuckold); *disgraced* may mean poorly received by audiences (not 'well graced'; cf. *R2* 5.2.24), unpopular, lacking social graces (Leontes may recall the puns on *grace* at 99, 105; see 80n.). The first of many allusions to the theatre, including: playing roles (see 255, 259; 3.2.34–41; 4.4.133; 5.1.1, 57–60; 5.2.93–4); addressing audiences, stage-managing (191 and n.; 4.1.19–20, 5.3.103–7); how scenes will be performed (4.4.552–9, 563–7), how spectators react (5.1.28–9, 5.3.85, 115–17), how well actors play parts (2.1.72, 121–2 and nn.); 5.3.152–4); narration and action (5.2.31 and n.).

187–8 **whose . . . grave** whose outcome will make me derided for the rest of my life. Leontes puns on *issue*, the 'bastard' she is carrying, and his being hissed off the stage.

188 **Contempt and clamour** contemptuous outcry, noisy jeering (the rhetorical device, hendiadys, of linking two words by a conjunction to express a single complex idea)

189 **Will . . . knell** will accompany my funeral (*knell*, solemn tolling bell at burials)

191 **this present** this very moment; present at this moment, i.e. among the audience watching me. For an

Now, while I speak this, holds his wife by th'arm,
That little thinks she has been sluiced in's absence,
And his pond fished by his next neighbour, by
Sir Smile, his neighbour. Nay, there's comfort in't,   195
Whiles other men have gates, and those gates opened,
As mine, against their will. Should all despair
That have revolted wives, the tenth of mankind
Would hang themselves. Physic for't there's none:
It is a bawdy planet, that will strike   200
Where 'tis predominant; and 'tis powerful, think it,
From east, west, north and south; be it concluded,
No barricado for a belly. Know't,
It will let in and out the enemy

instant Leontes *is* an actor, playing the
role on the stage, addressing husbands
and wives in the theatre (early audiences had women in them, especially
citizens' wives; see Gurr, *Playgoing*,
6–9, 19–20). See 187n.
193 **been sluiced** had sex. A sluice is
an adjustable gate in a dam, or pipe
through which water is let in or run off
(*OED n.* 1d); see 194n.
in's in his
194 **his pond fished** (1) The *wife* (192) is
imagined as a pond into which liquid
(semen) flows through a sluice (penis);
or out of whose sluice (vagina) sexual
fluids are drawn off illicitly. Williams
(1257) says Shakespeare confused the
images of penis as sluice with vagina
as fishpond. Cf. *Cym* 1.4.90, where
fowl (foul men) land on wives who
are ponds. (2) Fish (his wife) have
been poached from his pond. Leontes
resumes the metaphor from 179–80
(see 179n.), making Polixenes (his
neighbour) the angler.
next next-door
195 **Sir Smile** i.e. a hypocritical deceiver,
smiling as he cuckolds a man (cf.
practised smiles, 116); *Sir* is satirical,
derogatory. There may be a lewd pun

on 'smile' and 'smell' (the fishy smell
of penis and vagina; see 194n.).
195–7 **there's . . . will** Cf. Dent, C571,
'It is good to have company in misery.'
196 **gates** entrances, sluice-gates into
wives (see 193n., 194n.)
198 **revolted** rebellious, having cast off
allegiance (*OED* 1: first citation *R2*
2.2.57); unfaithful
199 **Physic . . . none** There's no cure for
it (female lust).
200–1 **It . . . predominant** Venus, the
planet (and goddess) of lust, will incite
people to lechery when in the ascendant. In astrology it was said that the
positions of planets (when *predominant*) gave them power over destiny;
cf. *Ham* 1.1.161, and see 360n., 422n.
201 **think it** believe it
202 **From . . . south** Cf. 1.1.30–1.
202–3 **be . . . belly** i.e. certainly there's
no way of blocking the passage to your
wife's vagina: nothing will stop men
(*the enemy*, 204) forcing a way into
her belly. Spanish *barricado* (street
barricade for obstructing an enemy)
reached England in the late 1590s.
203 **Know't** be sure of this
204 **It** female lust (see 199n., 200–1n.);
the *belly* (203)

    With bag and baggage. Many thousand on's   205
    Have the disease and feel't not. How now, boy?

MAMILLIUS

    I am like you, they say.

LEONTES   Why, that's some comfort.

    What, Camillo there!

CAMILLO [*Comes forward.*] Ay, my good lord.

LEONTES

    Go play, Mamillius; thou'rt an honest man.

                          [*Exit Mamillius.*]

    Camillo, this great sir will yet stay longer.   210

CAMILLO

    You had much ado to make his anchor hold;
    When you cast out, it still came home.

LEONTES   Didst note it?

CAMILLO

    He would not stay at your petitions, made
    His business more material.

LEONTES   Didst perceive it?

---

205 **bag and baggage** equipment carried by an *enemy* (204), here slang for scrotum and penis (see Williams, 57–9); *baggage* also meant whore, loose woman. H. Smith (*Romances*, 113) notes that the king in *Pandosto*, 'taking bag and baggage', escaped 'out of a postern gate' (pp. 411–12). Shakespeare borrowed 'postern' literally at 434 (see n.) and 2.1.52, but gave *bag and baggage* (and *gates*, 196) sexual meanings. See also 4.3.20n.; 4.4.615n., 616n.

    on's of us (Abbott, 182); we men

206 **Have . . . not** have the (cuckold's) sickness and don't know it or feel sick

    How now how are you

207 ***I . . . say** F2's 'they' supplies an omission in F. Mamillius echoes what

Leontes said at 129–30, perhaps to mollify him, after being sent away at 186–9.

208 **there** are you there? Schanzer adds the SD '*He comes forward*', i.e. Camillo has hovered back of stage, unable to hear all the dialogue; see 0.1n., 38n.

209 **thou'rt** thou art; see 43n.

    honest honourable; legitimate. Cf. 160 (see n.).

210 **this great sir** Polixenes

211–12 **You . . . home** You had a lot of difficulty making his anchor take hold on the seabed (i.e. persuading him to stay) – when you threw it out, it kept coming back.

212 **Didst** didst thou ('thou' because Camillo is a close servant: see 43n.)

214 **material** important

---

207 they] *F2; not in F*   208 SD] *Schanzer*   209 SD] *Rowe*

[*aside*] They're here with me already, whispering,
    rounding,   215
'Sicilia is a so-forth.' 'Tis far gone
When I shall gust it last. – How came't, Camillo,
That he did stay?

CAMILLO   At the good queen's entreaty.

LEONTES

'At the queen's' be't; 'good' should be pertinent,
But so it is, it is not. Was this taken   220
By any understanding pate but thine?
For thy conceit is soaking, will draw in
More than the common blocks. Not noted, is't,
But of the finer natures? By some severals
Of head-piece extraordinary? Lower messes   225
Perchance are to this business purblind? Say.

CAMILLO

Business, my lord? I think most understand
Bohemia stays here longer.

215 **They're . . . already** people have
  already caught on (see 216n.)
  rounding murmuring secretly (*OED*
  round *v.²* 2)
216 **Sicilia . . . so-forth** the king is such
  and such a thing (*OED*'s only instance
  of *so-forth*, but cf. *Ham* 2.1.59) –
  because the whisperers daren't say
  'cuckold'; or because he can't bear to
  say it. He may point to his forehead
  at 215, i.e. they have spotted horns
  growing *here*.
216–17 **'Tis . . . last** This must have
  been going on for a long time (or
  it, the adultery, must be well known
  already), since I'm the last to know
  it (*gust*, taste). Cf. Dent, C877, 'The
  cuckold is the last that knows of it.' F's
  'farre' at 216 is probably a comparative
  (as at 109, 5.3.141), i.e. their adultery
  has gone further.
217 **came't** did it come about

219 **pertinent** apposite
220 **so it is** as things are
  taken noted, observed
221 **pate** mind, brain
222–6 **For . . . blocks** Because your
  intelligence (*conceit*) readily absorbs
  things and will take in more than
  ordinary minds: a block was a wooden
  mould for shaping hats, thus lower-
  class people were blockheads. Cf. *MA*
  1.1.70–2.
224 **But . . . natures** except by superior
  (or acute, or sensitive) people
224–5 **some . . . extraordinary** by a few
  individuals with exceptional minds
225-6 **Lower. . . purblind** Perhaps the
  lower classes have no perception in this
  matter. A mess was a group of people
  of the same rank, usually four, who
  dined together; cf. 4.4.10–11 (see n.).
226 **purblind** (partially) blind, literally
  or figuratively

215 SD] *Hanmer*   216 far] *(*farre*)*

LEONTES	Ha?
CAMILLO	Stays here longer.

LEONTES
Ay, but why?

CAMILLO
To satisfy your highness, and the entreaties   230
Of our most gracious mistress.

LEONTES   Satisfy?
Th'entreaties of your mistress? Satisfy?
Let that suffice. I have trusted thee, Camillo,
With all the nearest things to my heart, as well
My chamber-counsels, wherein, priest-like, thou   235
Hast cleansed my bosom; I from thee departed
Thy penitent reformed. But we have been
Deceived in thy integrity, deceived
In that which seems so.

CAMILLO   Be it forbid, my lord.

LEONTES
To bide upon't: thou art not honest; or   240

228 **Ha?** What? His response to *most understand* (which he takes to mean most people know full well why).

230 **satisfy** comply with (*OED* satisfy 8) (your request); possibly discharge a debt, repay (*OED* 1a): cf. 3–9.

232 **Satisfy** Leontes takes Camillo to mean satisfy the queen sexually; cf. *Oth* 3.3.393–9, where Iago twists Othello's 'would I were satisfied' (if only I knew definitely Desdemona is unfaithful) until it means 'if only I could watch her having sex'. Leontes may have in mind Hermione's *satisfaction* (31) in persuading Polixenes to stay; at 2.1.189 *satisfied* (confident of the truth) probably has a similar sexual meaning (Partridge, 178).

233 **Let that suffice** I don't need to hear more.

234 **things** matters; see 92n.
    as well as well as

235 **chamber-counsels** affairs of state;

some editors think *chamber-counsels* are personal, even sexual secrets, ignoring the distinction *as well* at 234

235–6 **wherein . . . bosom** which you have listened to and absolved me like a priest taking confession. The emphasis is on Leontes' trust in Camillo as a confidential councillor (cf. 'of her bosom', *KL* 4.5.28), not on what has been said between them.

237 **Thy penitent reformed** repentant, made better by you
    we Leontes, standing on his dignity, switches to the royal pronoun (see 2–3n.).

238–9 **Deceived . . . so** Leontes plays on meanings of deceived: taken in by apparent integrity; mistaken about your integrity (*OED* deceive 2a, 2d).

239 **Be it forbid** heaven forbid

240 **bide upon't** insist on it (*OED* bide *v.* 2b)
    honest honourable

236 I] ay *Oxf (Furness)*

If thou inclin'st that way, thou art a coward,
Which hoxes honesty behind, restraining
From course required. Or else thou must be counted
A servant grafted in my serious trust,
And therein negligent; or else a fool, 245
That seest a game played home, the rich stake drawn,
And tak'st it all for jest.

CAMILLO   My gracious lord,
I may be negligent, foolish and fearful;
In every one of these no man is free,
But that his negligence, his folly, fear, 250
Among the infinite doings of the world
Sometime puts forth. In your affairs, my lord,
If ever I were wilful-negligent,
It was my folly; if industriously
I played the fool, it was my negligence, 255
Not weighing well the end; if ever fearful
To do a thing where I the issue doubted,
Whereof the execution did cry out

241 **If . . . way** if you have any inclination to be honourable
coward quibble on 'cowherd', the farmhand who tended and hoxed animals (see 242n.)
242 **Which . . . behind** who hamstrings the back legs of honour (*honesty*). Hoxing was laming animals by cutting their hamstring, or hobbling horses in a gallop *course*, 243 (*OED* course *n.* 1; see 284n., 94–6n.).
244 **grafted . . . trust** in whom my trust has been artificially implanted (and who has therefore been *negligent*, 245); for grafting, see also 1.1.24n. on *branch*; 4.4.92–5n.
246 **played . . . drawn** brought to its conclusion, the valuable prize won (the *stake*, Hermione, or sex with her). The meaning may be more explicit:

you know Hermione has been seduced by Polixenes (*game played*), with his penis (*stake*). Gambling was a favourite metaphor for an erection (Williams, 1302–3); cf. *MV* 3.2.213.
249, 262 **free** guiltless
251 **infinite . . . world** endless business everyone is engaged in
252 **Sometime puts forth** will show itself some time or other
253 **wilful-negligent** deliberately negligent
254–5 **if . . . fool** if I deliberately didn't take something seriously
256 **Not . . . end** not sufficiently considering the consequence (or the goal)
257 **issue** outcome
258–9 **Whereof . . . non-performance** even though the unperformed task was crying out to be done; where, when the

252 forth. In] *Theobald;* forth in *F*

171

Against the non-performance, 'twas a fear
Which oft infects the wisest. These, my lord,   260
Are such allowed infirmities that honesty
Is never free of. But beseech your grace
Be plainer with me, let me know my trespass
By its own visage. If I then deny it,
'Tis none of mine.

LEONTES   Ha' not you seen, Camillo –   265
But that's past doubt; you have, or your eye-glass
Is thicker than a cuckold's horn – or heard –
For, to a vision so apparent, rumour
Cannot be mute – or thought – for cogitation
Resides not in that man that does not think –   270
My wife is slippery? If thou wilt confess –
Or else be impudently negative
To have nor eyes, nor ears, nor thought – then say

task was subsequently performed, it
showed how wrong leaving it undone
would have been
260 **Which . . . wisest** that wisest men
are often guilty of
261 **allowed infirmities** weaknesses
tolerated (because unavoidable)
262 **beseech** I beg
grace See 80n.
263–4 **let . . . visage** show me what my
wrongdoing looks like (its *visage*, face)
265 **none of mine** Camillo means 'not
my responsibility', but the metaphor
is of an illegitimate child. This
anticipates Leontes' repudiating his
daughter, with the same words, at
2.3.91.
Ha' not haven't
266 **past** beyond
eye-glass the eye's vitreous humour;
cornea. *OED*'s only citation with this
sense (*n.* 1); eye-glasses to correct
sight aren't recorded before the 18th
century (*n.* 3a).
267 **thicker** more opaque, duller in
perception (*OED* thick *a.* 9a). In this

comparison with *a cuckold's horn*,
Leontes is probably referring to the
cataract, known as 'pin and web', the
pin a spot (or *horn*) like a pin's head
on the eyeball, the web a film: see 289
and n.
268–9 **For . . . mute** for gossip can't be
silent about something so obvious.
Leontes may mean *vision* sarcastically:
the queen's flagrant adultery is an
extraordinary sight people can scarcely
credit.
269–71 **cogitation . . . slippery** anyone
who does not believe Hermione is
slippery has no brains, is unthinking
271 **slippery** unfaithful (*OED* 5); also
'lubricious', because (1) she is greasy
or lecherous (the word was associated
with overusing the vagina in sex and
masturbation: Williams, 1255); (2) she
slips easily from virtue to infidelity.
See 85n. 2, 185n. 1.
confess admit it
272–3 **be . . . thought** shamelessly deny
you have eyes, ears or the capacity to
think

270 think] think't *Hanmer*

My wife's a hobby-horse, deserves a name
As rank as any flax-wench that puts to   275
Before her troth-plight. Say't, and justify't.

CAMILLO
I would not be a stander-by to hear
My sovereign mistress clouded so without
My present vengeance taken. 'Shrew my heart,
You never spoke what did become you less   280
Than this; which to reiterate were sin
As deep as that, though true.

LEONTES   Is whispering nothing?
Is leaning cheek to cheek? Is meeting noses?

---

274 *hobby-horse common whore, female ridden for pleasure. F's 'Holy-Horse' is a misprint or scribal error (see p. 365). The hobby-horse was a wickerwork figure worn in the morris dance by a performer imitating a skittish horse (Laroque, 120–30); see 94–6n. The term was used of foolish people, loose women and prostitutes (see Williams, 669–70; *Ham* 3.2.128; *Oth* 4.1.153; *OED* 3a, 3b). Also a toy horse, a stick with a horse's head which children pretended to ride. The meaning here is sexual but notions of performing in public and playing games are present too: see p. 64.

274–6 name . . . troth-plight reputation as gross as that of any common girl who goes at it (has sex) before she is engaged. A flax-wench was a lower-class woman who made clothes from flax. Women like this are so keen on sex, Leontes says, they can't wait for their *troth-plight*, i.e. the betrothal that allowed couples to have sex before their church wedding. See 104n., 1.1.29–31n., 4.4.395n.; Shaheen, 723; *H5* 2.1.18–20.

276 justify't prove it; give evidence of it

277 be a stander-by stand by (and do nothing) (*OED* stander 2a)

278 clouded defamed

279 My . . . taken taking immediate revenge. A gentleman would normally challenge anyone who insulted the queen; impossible here because the king is her detractor. Duelling protocol is parodied at 4.4.728–30 (see n.).
'Shrew beshrew, damn (moderate oath)

280 never spoke Cf. *never spok'st*, 88.
what . . . less anything less fitting for you; i.e. you have never said anything as low and indecorous as this

281–2 which . . . true i.e. repeating the accusation, even if it proved to be true, would be as sinful as the adultery itself (*that*). Shocked by 274–6, Camillo tries to silence the slander at once (if Leontes puts it about widely, it won't be easy to unsay it; cf. 2.1.96–100), so he exaggerates. A true accusation, strictly speaking, can't be a sin, and isn't commensurate with adultery.

282 though true even if it were true
whispering probably trisyllabic, in which case 282 is two half-lines of three feet

282–94 Is . . . nothing The rhetorical figure is apodiosis, the indignant rejection of an argument as impertinent or ridiculous. Nevo (111) says the appeal to items of evidence (parts

---

274 hobby-horse] *Rowe³;* Holy-Horse *F*

Kissing with inside lip? Stopping the career
Of laughter with a sigh? – A note infallible   285
Of breaking honesty. Horsing foot on foot?
Skulking in corners? Wishing clocks more swift?
Hours, minutes? Noon, midnight? And all eyes
Blind with the pin and web but theirs, theirs only,
That would unseen be wicked? Is this nothing?   290
Why then the world and all that's in't is nothing,
The covering sky is nothing, Bohemia nothing,
My wife is nothing, nor nothing have these nothings,
If this be nothing.

CAMILLO   Good my lord, be cured
Of this diseased opinion, and betimes,   295
For 'tis most dangerous.

LEONTES   Say it be, 'tis true.

---

of the body, clock, hidden signals) agitates Leontes' imagination, creating in words the sex he imagines watching. He does seem excited by his repeating *nothing*, which could mean the female genitalia. However, Colman (17) notes that of nine *nothing*s in this speech, not one definitely means 'vulva'.

284 **with inside lip** with the mouth open
   career course, a horse's gallop at full speed (*OED n.* 2a); see 94–6n. and cf. *LLL* 5.2.482.

285–6 ²**a . . . honesty** a sure sign of being unchaste; 'to break matrimony' was a common expression for adultery (*OED* break *v.* 15d).

286 **Horsing . . . foot** Oxf¹ glosses this 'mounted, but not on horseback' (cf. *OED* horse *v.* 6, to copulate), but Leontes means sexual foreplay: 'is it nothing they're playing footsy?', i.e. putting one foot over another (mounting, *OED* horse *v.* 2); see 94–6n.

287 **Skulking** sneaking about, hiding (*OED v.* 1, 2); only instance in Shakespeare

in corners A corner was a private place for sex, but also the vagina (Williams, 310–12).

288 **Hours . . . midnight** (wishing that) hours would pass like minutes, and noon be midnight (so they might be in bed together)

289 **pin and web** cataract (cause of opacity in the cornea, *OED* pin *n.*¹ 4a); cf. 266–7 (see 267n.), *KL* 3.4.113–14.

292 **covering sky** sky above, imagined as a sphere around the earth; see 48n., and cf. 179, 2.1.100–3 (see n.); 'covering heavens', *Cym* 5.5.351. The word *covering* had sexual connotations, being used of copulation, originally of horses (Williams, 324–5); see 94–6n., 284n., 286n.

Bohemia Polixenes; or the country (see List of Roles, 0.1n.)

293 **nor . . . nothings** and these nothings have nothing to them. Cf. Dent, N285; *Cym* 4.2.300; *KL* 1.1.90, 'nothing will come of nothing'.

295 **betimes** promptly

296 **Say it be** suppose it is (dangerous)

---

288 Noon] the Noone *F2*

CAMILLO

No, no, my lord.

LEONTES   It is – you lie, you lie!

I say thou liest, Camillo, and I hate thee,

Pronounce thee a gross lout, a mindless slave,

Or else a hovering temporizer, that   300

Canst with thine eyes at once see good and evil,

Inclining to them both. Were my wife's liver

Infected as her life, she would not live

The running of one glass.

CAMILLO   Who does infect her?

LEONTES

Why, he that wears her like her medal, hanging   305

About his neck, Bohemia – who, if I

Had servants true about me, that bare eyes

To see alike mine honour as their profits,

Their own particular thrifts, they would do that

Which should undo more doing. Ay, and thou   310

His cupbearer – whom I from meaner form

Have benched, and reared to worship, who mayst see

---

299 **gross lout** stupid bumpkin
300 **hovering temporizer** wavering time-server (*hovering*, uncertain, hesitating, *OED ppl. a.* b, first citation); punning on a scavenger bird *hovering* over two objects, *good and evil*, 301.
301 **at once** simultaneously
302 **Inclining to** favourably taken by (*OED* incline *v.* 9a)
302 **liver** thought to be the seat of the passions, including sexual desire
304 **running . . . glass** an hour, i.e. the time sand in an hour-glass takes to run out – anticipating Time's turning his hour-glass, when Hermione is supposed dead, 4.1.16 (see n.)
305 **her medal** the medal of herself that she gave him; her miniature portrait in a locket. Medals and miniatures were exchanged at Renaissance courts as

tokens of love and friendship (cf. *Ham* 3.4.51–2).
305–6 **hanging . . . neck** anticipating the embrace at 5.3.112
306 **who** to whom (*Bohemia*, i.e. Polixenes) they would *do that*, 309 (Abbott, 274)
307 **true** faithful
bare bore, i.e. possessed
308–9 **To . . . thrifts** to consider my honour as much as their personal advantage, their own private gains
309–10 **they . . . doing** they would do what would prevent any more sex (*doing*) with her (i.e. kill him); cf. *TC* 1.2.278.
311 **cupbearer** officer in the royal household whose duties included serving wine (see 1.1.13–14n.).
311–12 **whom . . . worship** to whom I've given a position above people of

Plainly as heaven sees earth and earth sees heaven,
How I am galled – mightst bespice a cup
To give mine enemy a lasting wink,   315
Which draught to me were cordial.

CAMILLO   Sir, my lord,
I could do this, and that with no rash potion,
But with a lingering dram that should not work
Maliciously, like poison. But I cannot
Believe this crack to be in my dread mistress,   320
So sovereignly being honourable.
I have loved thee –

LEONTES   Make that thy question, and go rot!
Dost think I am so muddy, so unsettled,

lower rank and raised to a place of honour. Camillo sits officially on the bench (like a magistrate), which marks his superiority over the lower sort (cf. 225) sitting on a *form* (a longer, lower bench). He is a gentleman and scholar (see 387–90n.) whom Leontes has elevated at court.

313 **heaven . . . heaven** as clearly as the gods can see the earth from the heavens, and one can see the sky from the earth. Leontes uses the rhetorical scheme antimetabole (i.e. the same words or phrases repeated in reversed order in successive clauses; see also 4.4.678–80) to remind Camillo that as king he is as high above him in rank (see 311–12 and n.) as the gods are above the earth.

314 **galled** sorely vexed

314–15 **bespice . . . wink** season (i.e. put poison in) a cup of wine to close my enemy's eyes for good (*lasting wink*; cf. *Tem* 2.1.286)

316 **Which . . . cordial** that drink (*draught*) would be a comfort (*cordial*) to my heart, or a medicine for my sickness (i.e. jealousy, or being a cuckold)

317 **rash** fast-acting

318 **lingering dram** slow-working small

dose (*OED* dram *n.*[1] 3b)

319 **Maliciously** virulently; i.e. not arousing suspicion

320 **crack** moral flaw (*OED n.* 8), often associated with infidelity (Williams, 326–9); cf. *Cym* 5.5.207, where Imogen's 'bond of chastity' is said to be 'quite crack'd'. Perhaps Camillo inadvertently introduces the sexual sense, i.e. vulva (the meaning Partridge, 88, says is used here for dramatic irony).
    dread revered

321 who is so supremely honourable

322 **I . . . thee** – Camillo is about to protest his loyalty, or threaten to withdraw his love, when he is interrupted. Addressing the king as *thee* is a breach of decorum (see 212n.), but Camillo is deeply moved. There is no need to emend (e.g. by assigning the half-line to Leontes or altering to 'T'have loved thee –').
    Make . . . question if you're going to question that (Hermione's infidelity, which Camillo doubts, 319–20)
    go rot a violent curse (cf. *Tit* 5.1.58, *Cym* 2.3.132)

323–4 [1]**so . . . vexation** so disturbed, deranged, that I would willingly bring

314 mightst] thou mightst *F2*   322 I . . . that] T'have . . . the – / *Leo.* Make that *Cam*[1]; *Leo.* I've . . . thee. Make't *Theobald*

To appoint myself in this vexation? Sully
The purity and whiteness of my sheets –   325
Which to preserve is sleep; which being spotted
Is goads, thorns, nettles, tails of wasps –
Give scandal to the blood o'th' prince, my son,
Who I do think is mine, and love as mine,
Without ripe moving to't? Would I do this?   330
Could man so blench?
CAMILLO   I must believe you, sir.
I do, and will fetch off Bohemia for't,
Provided that when he's removed your highness
Will take again your queen as yours at first,
Even for your son's sake, and thereby for sealing   335

this distress on myself; *appoint myself* has legal overtones, i.e. nominate myself for the office of cuckold (*OED* appoint *v.* 12a, 18).

324–5 **Sully . . . sheets** cited by *OED* to illustrate the literal meaning of sully (*v.* 1a), implying that the sheets on their marriage bed are soiled physically by the charge of infidelity. However, Leontes intends it as a metaphor for moral pollution (cf. 328, and the phrase 'sully one's reputation'). He does believe there are real stains, from the sex he is sure Hermione has had with Polixenes (cf. 'sweat of an enseamed bed', *Ham* 3.4.90).

326–7 Preserving the *purity* of my *sheets* (325) will mean I can sleep in peace, but their being stained would be like lying in a bed filled with things that torment and sting. Sleep usually isn't restorative in *WT*: there is either no sleep at all (2.3.1, 14–16, 38, 53), or troubled dreams, sluggishness and tears when waking (4.4.105–6), or sleep is brought on or sought simply for oblivion (1.1.13–14), getting from one moment in time to another (3.3.59–60, 4.3.30; cf. 4.1.16–17); see nn., and

see also 2.1.198n. The exception is Hermione's 'sleep', 5.3.19–20 (see n.); and see 5.3.94–5 and n. For dreams, see 1.2.140–2, 3.2.80, 82 (Leontes'); 3.3.17–18 (Antigonus'); 4.4.453–4 (Perdita's); and nn.

327 only eight syllables, five of them stressed: see p. 128.

328 **Give . . . prince** cast doubt, bring disgrace on the prince's legitimacy (*blood*, used figuratively for bloodline). Cf. 71–3, 109, 2.1.57–8 (see nn.); *Cym* 5.5.332).

330 **ripe moving to't** sound, fully thought-through reason for it

331 **man so blench** one go so astray; swerve from the truth

332 **fetch off** an equivocation: rescue (cf. *Cor* 1.4.62); kill (how Leontes understands it). Cf. 333, 343–4, 458 (see nn.).

for't because of it

333 **removed** like *fetch off*, 332 (see n.), an equivocation: disposed of, killed; left (the country)

334 **at first** (as she was) originally

335 **Even** merely

335–6 **thereby . . . tongues** by silencing this harmful talk. Some editors regard

The injury of tongues in courts and kingdoms
Known and allied to yours.

LEONTES   Thou dost advise me
Even so as I mine own course have set down.
I'll give no blemish to her honour, none.

CAMILLO   My lord,
Go then, and, with a countenance as clear   340
As friendship wears at feasts, keep with Bohemia
And with your queen. I am his cupbearer.
If from me he have wholesome beverage,
Account me not your servant.

LEONTES   This is all.
Do't, and thou hast the one half of my heart;   345
Do't not, thou splitt'st thine own.

CAMILLO   I'll do't, my lord.

LEONTES
I will seem friendly, as thou hast advised me.   *Exit.*

CAMILLO
O miserable lady. But for me,
What case stand I in? I must be the poisoner

thereby for sealing as too awkward for
Shakespeare, and emend to 'forestall-
ing' (or 'forsealing', i.e. by this 'tightly
sealing up'; *OED* has no record of
forsealing). The conjecture 'forefeel-
ing' is equally strained.

337 **Known . . . yours** As a diplomat
Camillo knows the slander would affect
Leontes' alliance with Hermione's
family, the imperial house of Russia
(see 3.2.117).

337–8 **Thou . . . down** Your advice
agrees exactly with what I had decided
to do. In *Pandosto*, the king from the
outset intended to poison the wife and
friend (p. 409).

339 **My lord** Lines 339 and 340 are
metrically complete without these
words, which are set on a separate
line in F. It is possible that the extra
syllables marked a pause (e.g. before
Camillo finally confirmed he would

kill Polixenes). As it stands, 339 is an
alexandrine; cf. 117 (see n.).
340 **clear** innocent
341 **keep with** continue to keep the
company of
343–4 another equivocation, i.e. I'll poison him to show my loyalty; I'd rather
no longer be your servant than poison
him. Cf. 332, 333 (see nn.).
344 **This is all** This is what the matter
comes to; this is all I want (that you
kill him).
346 **thou . . . own** you cut your own
(heart) in two; you'll be divided
between me and him; you'll have
shown you're half-hearted, a coward;
you'll have brought about your
own death, i.e. be stabbed in the
heart
348–9 **for . . . in** as for me, what is my
situation
349 **poisoner** two syllables ('pois-ner')

Of good Polixenes, and my ground to do't   350
Is the obedience to a master – one
Who in rebellion with himself will have
All that are his so too. To do this deed,
Promotion follows. If I could find example
Of thousands that had struck anointed kings   355
And flourished after, I'd not do't. But since
Nor brass, nor stone, nor parchment bears not one,
Let villainy itself forswear't. I must
Forsake the court. To do't or no is certain
To me a break-neck. Happy star reign now!   360

Enter POLIXENES.

Here comes Bohemia.
POLIXENES [*aside*]   This is strange. Methinks
My favour here begins to warp. Not speak?
– Good day, Camillo.
CAMILLO   Hail, most royal sir.
POLIXENES
What is the news i'th' court?

350 **ground to do't** reason for doing it
351–3 **one . . . too** a rebel who being at
war with his true self wants all his men
to be at war with themselves too
353–4 **To . . . follows** If I do this deed,
I'll be promoted (*To do*, infinitive as
gerundive: Abbott, 357).
354 **If** but even if
355 **struck** murdered
356–8 **since . . . forswear't** since neither memorials of brass or stone, nor
manuscripts record a single *example*
(354), villainy itself would promise
not to do it. Possibly alluding to
the assassination of the French king
in summer 1610, but it is standard
political doctrine: cf. the Tudor
'Homily against Disobedience and

Rebellion': 'reade the histories of all
Nations, looke ouer the Chronicles
of our owne countrey, call to
minde so many rebellions of old
time . . . yee shall not finde that
GOD euer prospered any rebellion
against their naturall and lawfull
Prince' (Shaheen, 724).
359–60 **To . . . break-neck** Whether I
do it or don't do it, the outcome will
certainly be my ruin.
360 **Happy star reign** May my star be
favourable; see 200–1n.
362 **My . . . warp** I am beginning to
feel less welcome here (*warp*, shrink,
shrivel, *OED* warp *v*. 15b).
Not speak i.e. Leontes didn't speak as
he went by

360.1] *after* Bohemia *361 F*   361 SD] *Oxf*

CAMILLO   None rare, my lord.
POLIXENES
    The king hath on him such a countenance   365
    As he had lost some province, and a region
    Loved as he loves himself. Even now I met him
    With customary compliment, when he,
    Wafting his eyes to th' contrary and falling
    A lip of much contempt, speeds from me, and   370
    So leaves me to consider what is breeding
    That changes thus his manners.
CAMILLO   I dare not know, my lord.
POLIXENES
    How, dare not? Do not? Do you know, and dare not?
    Be intelligent to me – 'tis thereabouts;
    For to yourself what you do know you must,   375
    And cannot say you dare not. Good Camillo,
    Your changed complexions are to me a mirror
    Which shows me mine changed too; for I must be
    A party in this alteration, finding
    Myself thus altered with't.
CAMILLO   There is a sickness   380
    Which puts some of us in distemper, but

---

364 **None rare** nothing special
366 **As** as if
367 **Even** just
368 **customary compliment** my usual greeting
369–70 **Wafting . . . contempt** averting his eyes and dropping his lip contemptuously
371 **breeding** going on; being nurtured
373–4 **How . . . me** What do you mean, *dare* not? Is it that you don't know? Or know but daren't say, or even think what you know? Be clear (*OED* intelligent *a*. 4, giving information). Cf. 4.4.457 (see n.).
374–6 **'tis . . . not** It's something like that, because you know what you know

and it's no good telling yourself you daren't know it.
377–80 **Your . . . too** i.e. seeing the changes in you is like looking in a mirror that shows me how (much) I've changed too
377 **complexions** facial expressions as well as character (*OED n.* 4a, 7a)
379 **A party in** a participant in, or in part the cause of
380 **altered with't** affected by it
    sickness jealousy
381 **puts . . . distemper** drives some men crazy; distemper indicated an imbalance of the four humours – blood, black bile, yellow bile, phlegm – in body and mind. Cf. 2.3.37 (see n.).

I cannot name the disease, and it is caught
Of you that yet are well.

POLIXENES   How caught of me?
Make me not sighted like the basilisk.
I have looked on thousands who have sped the better   385
By my regard, but killed none so. Camillo,
As you are certainly a gentleman, thereto
Clerk-like experienced, which no less adorns
Our gentry than our parents' noble names,
In whose success we are gentle; I beseech you,   390
If you know aught which does behove my knowledge
Thereof to be informed, imprison't not
In ignorant concealment.

CAMILLO   I may not answer.

POLIXENES

A sickness caught of me, and yet I well?
I must be answered. Dost thou hear, Camillo,   395
I conjure thee, by all the parts of man
Which honour does acknowledge, whereof the least
Is not this suit of mine, that thou declare
What incidency thou dost guess of harm

---

382 **cannot** dare not (see 373–4n.)
384 Don't make me out to have a basilisk's
gaze, i.e. that I can kill merely by looking at someone. The basilisk (or cockatrice) was a mythical serpent, hybrid
of cock and reptile, whose glance was
believed fatal (Dent, B99.1). In *Cym*
2.4.107–8 looking at a basilisk causes
death, not being looked at by it.
385 **sped** prospered
386 **By my regard** because of my glance
(*OED* regard *n.* 2a); because of my
attention and care (*OED* 6a, 8a)
By as a result of (Abbott, 146)
387–90 **gentleman . . . gentle** man of
good birth, as well as considerable
learning – learning that is no less
of an adornment to our place in life
than the noble names we inherit from

our parents, from whom we derive
our rank (*success*, succession). The
pronouns *we*, *our*, may be royal, or
refer to upper-class people in general: cultivation from learning, which
ought to be as important as rank, is a
common Renaissance theme.
391–3 **aught . . . concealment** anything
it's essential I should know about,
don't hold it back, concealing it (or
pretend you know nothing), so I'm left
in ignorance
396–8 **I . . . suit** I solemnly appeal to you
by all the obligations men of honour
recognize, not least of which is an
answer to my petition
399 what harm you suspect; *incidency*,
incident, something likely to happen
(*OED n.* 1, first citation)

    Is creeping toward me; how far off, how near,　　　　400
    Which way to be prevented, if to be;
    If not, how best to bear it.
CAMILLO　　　　　　　　　　　Sir, I will tell you,
    Since I am charged in honour, and by him
    That I think honourable. Therefore mark my counsel,
    Which must be ev'n as swiftly followed as　　　　405
    I mean to utter it, or both yourself and me
    Cry lost, and so good night!
POLIXENES　　　　　　　　　On, good Camillo.
CAMILLO
    I am appointed him to murder you.
POLIXENES
    By whom, Camillo?
CAMILLO　　　　　　　By the king.
POLIXENES　　　　　　　　　　For what?
CAMILLO
    He thinks – nay, with all confidence he swears,　　　410
    As he had seen't, or been an instrument
    To vice you to't – that you have touched his queen
    Forbiddenly.
POLIXENES　　　O, then my best blood turn
    To an infected jelly and my name
    Be yoked with his that did betray the best!　　　415

---

401 **if to be** if it's possible
403 **charged in honour** entreated according to my obligations (*OED* honour *n.* 9b)
   him i.e. Polixenes
406–7 **or . . . night** otherwise declare both of us done for, and kiss everything goodbye (cf. *Tem* 4.1.54)
408 **him** as the man who is; **by him**, Leontes (ethic dative: Abbott, 220)
411–12 **As . . . to't** as if he had seen it with his own eyes (i.e. you two having sex), or been a means to force you to it (*vice*, the action of a vice, clamping tight, metaphor for play-

ing a depraved part in arranging the adultery himself). Virtue and vice are repeatedly mentioned in *WT*, sometimes explicitly contrasted. For virtue, see 2.1.73–4, 4.2.26–8, 4.3.120–1, 4.4.391–2, 5.1.6–7, and nn.; for vice, 3.2.54–6 and n.; for virtue and vice, 4.3.87–92.
413 **Forbiddenly** i.e. had sex with her
413–14 **then . . . jelly** if that's true (*then*), may my blood, entirely healthy, become polluted and clotted (*OED* jelly *n.*[1] 4). Cf. 71–3, 109 (see nn.).
415 **that . . . best** i.e. Judas, who betrayed Jesus, best of men (Matthew, 10.4)

400 far] *(farre)*

Turn then my freshest reputation to
A savour that may strike the dullest nostril
Where I arrive, and my approach be shunned,
Nay hated too, worse than the great'st infection
That e'er was heard or read.

CAMILLO   Swear his thought over   420
By each particular star in heaven and
By all their influences, you may as well
Forbid the sea for to obey the moon
As or by oath remove or counsel shake
The fabric of his folly, whose foundation   425
Is piled upon his faith and will continue
The standing of his body.

POLIXENES   How should this grow?

CAMILLO

I know not, but I am sure 'tis safer to
Avoid what's grown than question how 'tis born.
If therefore you dare trust my honesty,   430
That lies enclosed in this trunk which you

---

416 **freshest** most pure and sweet-smelling
417–18 **savour . . . arrive** stench that may offend the least sensitive nose wherever I go; *savour* because it was believed that *infection* (see 419n.) could be contracted through smell (the reason flowers were used as prophylactics)
419 **infection** pestilence, plague (see Barroll, 70–98, 217–26)
420 **heard or read** heard of or read about
Swear . . . over you may deny with solemn oaths what he suspects. 'Swear over', otherwise unrecorded, may mean: over-swear (swear the opposite); swear again and again (he's wrong); try to win him over by swearing (cf. *MM* 5.1.241–4); swear down his suspicion, silence it (*OED* swear *v.* 20a).

421 **each particular** every single
422 **influences** ethereal fluids from the stars thought to shape destiny; cf. 200–1 (see n.).
423 **for to** to (used as infinitive: Abbott, 152)
424–7 **As . . . body** as either remove by a solemn oath or pull down by reasoning the structure (*OED* fabric *n.* 3a) of his delusion, the foundation of which rests on his settled belief and will last his lifetime. Cf. 2.1.100–3.
427 **How . . . grow?** How could this (delusion) have come about?
431–2 **this . . . impawned** Camillo asks to go with Polixenes: 'this body (*trunk*) of mine, which you'll take with you as a pledge of my good faith'; cf. 4.4.363 (see n.), and for quibbles on trunk and body see *Cym*

420 e'er] *(ere)*

183

Shall bear along impawned, away tonight!
Your followers I will whisper to the business,
And will by twos and threes at several posterns
Clear them o'th' city. For myself, I'll put   435
My fortunes to your service, which are here
By this discovery lost. Be not uncertain,
For, by the honour of my parents, I
Have uttered truth – which, if you seek to prove,
I dare not stand by; nor shall you be safer   440
Than one condemned by the king's own mouth,
Thereon his execution sworn.

POLIXENES   I do believe thee,
I saw his heart in's face. Give me thy hand.
Be pilot to me, and thy places shall
Still neighbour mine. My ships are ready, and   445
My people did expect my hence departure
Two days ago. This jealousy

1.7.209, 4.2.353–4). *OED*'s earliest
example of 'impawned', pledge as
security (impawn 1a), is *1H4* 4.3.108,
but the word also meant to risk someone's safety or reputation (*OED* 2;
H5 1.2.21).
433 **followers . . . to** men I will inform
secretly about
434 **several** various
   posterns small gates in a city's walls,
   normally locked, e.g. at night or in a
   curfew (see 205n.; 2.1.52–3).
435 **Clear them** get them out
436–7 **which . . . lost** i.e. his fortunes in
Sicily will be ruined by the disclosure
(of the plot)
437 **Be not uncertain** don't doubt
(me)
439 **prove** test whether it's true
440 **I . . . by** I must deny what I have
told you
441–2 **one . . . sworn** someone
the king has personally (from his
mouth) found guilty and sworn to

have executed. Camillo guesses that
Leontes will prosecute Hermione
in person and demand the death
penalty (3.2.88–9). F's 'condemn'd',
i.e. two syllables, leaves 441 with 9,
and 442 with 13. Some editors move
Thereon to the end of 441, to make
the line more regular, but a simpler
correction, suggested by F2, is to
leave it as it is and read 'condemnèd'.
Line 442 has 13 syllables, the final
one a feminine ending (not uncommon in *WT*: see pp. 125–7).
443 **his . . . face** proverbial: 'The face is
the index of the heart' (Dent, F1)
   Give . . . hand He pledges himself
   with a handshake: cf. 1.1.29–30 (see
   29–31n.), 4.4.367.
444–5 **Be . . . mine** Be my guide (*pilot*,
i.e. steer me out of this), and you'll
always enjoy high honours from
me.
446 **hence departure** departure from
here

441 condemned] *(condemn'd)*

Is for a precious creature. As she's rare,
Must it be great; and, as his person's mighty,
Must it be violent, and as he does conceive   450
He is dishonoured by a man which ever
Professed to him, why, his revenges must
In that be made more bitter. Fear o'ershades me.
Good expedition be my friend, and comfort
The gracious queen, part of his theme, but nothing   455
Of his ill-ta'en suspicion. Come, Camillo,
I will respect thee as a father if
Thou bear'st my life off. Hence! Let us avoid.

CAMILLO

It is in mine authority to command
The keys of all the posterns. Please your highness   460
To take the urgent hour. Come, sir, away.   *Exeunt.*

---

448 **precious creature** exquisite individual (as in *Tem* 3.1.25)
As she's rare because she's exceptional
451–2 **which . . . him** who always professed deep feeling for him (*which* for
who: Abbott, 265)
453 **In that** for that reason
o'ershades casts a shadow over
454–5 **Good . . . queen** May this
prompt departure assist me, and
(1) ease things for the virtuous
queen (by removing myself, who am
making Leontes jealous); (2) may
the virtuous queen be comforted
in her troubles. Neither meaning
puts Polixenes in a good light. His
sudden leaving can only worsen the
situation, by confirming Leontes'
suspicions. In (1) he sounds as if

he is deceiving himself; in (2) he is
wishing Hermione the best of luck
while making a quick getaway.
455–6 **part . . . suspicion** who (with me)
is part of his jealous fantasy, but is
innocent (*nothing* deserving) of his
ill-conceived suspicions
457 **respect** regard
458 **bear'st . . . off** save my life; cf. 332
(see n.).
*Hence . . . avoid Away! Let's be
gone. Cf. *Tem* 4.1.142. Some editors make F's 'off, hence: Let', less
emphatic by repunctuating it as 'off
hence. Let' (i.e. taking 'hence' as
belonging to *bear'st . . . off*).
459 **mine authority** my power
460 **posterns** See 434n.
Please may it please
461 **take . . . hour** act now, urgently

458 off. Hencc!] *(off, hence:); off hence Rowe*

2.1   *Enter* HERMIONE, MAMILLIUS, [*and*] Ladies.

HERMIONE
Take the boy to you. He so troubles me,
'Tis past enduring.

1 LADY   Come, my gracious lord,
Shall I be your playfellow?

MAMILLIUS   No, I'll none of you.

1 LADY
Why, my sweet lord?

MAMILLIUS
You'll kiss me hard, and speak to me as if   5
I were a baby still. [*to second Lady*] I love you better.

2 LADY
And why so, my lord?

MAMILLIUS   Not for because

2.1 The setting is private, perhaps the queen's bedchamber – a maternal space which the little boy Mamillius hasn't fully left behind yet, before progressing to the world of men and authority (the stateroom of 1.2). Leontes intrudes brutally at 32 SD, but his behaviour is so petulant and ridiculous that he is almost a figure of fun by the end of the scene (198–9). There are parallels between Mamillius' seeking attention in the exchanges at 1–15 and Leontes's insistence that he is the centre of things.

0.1 In F, SDs list all speaking roles for a scene in a 'massed entry', irrespective of when characters appear (see pp. 352–3 and Fig. 24; see also 1.2.0.1n., 3.2.0.1n.): Leontes, Antigonus and Lords actually enter at 32, but this is not marked in F. One of the Ladies is possibly Emilia (see List of Roles, 10n.).

1–32 Take ... ear one line in *Pandosto*: guards, sent to take the queen to prison, 'found her playing with her

young son' (p. 412).

1 troubles pesters

3 I'll ... you I'll have nothing to do with you.

5 kiss me hard smother me with kisses

7–15 Not ... eyebrows Mamillius' fascination with cosmetics – colours, pencilled-in eyebrows, painted eyelids (*eyebrows*, 13: see nn.) – points to what is implied at 4.4.101–3 about men only wanting sex with women when they are made up, their faces as beautiful masks (i.e. desiring art more than Nature), and to the statue's painted face at 5.3.63–8 (see 68n.), 81–3, mocking men with art. Cf. *mock* (14), putting on a *face* (1.2.112), wearing a *countenance* (1.2.340–1), *Masks for faces* (4.4.223: see n.). This contrast between real and false is connected to meanings of *colour* (4.4.560, 5.2.87–8, 5.3.47–8, and nn.), *colours* (2.3.104, 4.4.206), and *colouring* (2.2.19: see 18–19n.). See also 4.4.121–2n.

7 for because because (Abbott, 151). Cf. 1.2.423 (see n.).

2.1] *(Actus Secundus. Scena Prima.) F*   0.1] *Enter Hermione, Mamillius, Ladies: Leontes, Antigonus, Lords. F*   2+ SP] *Rowe subst.; Lady F*   6 SD] *Oxf*

Your brows are blacker – yet black brows they say
Become some women best, so that there be not
Too much hair there, but in a semicircle,   10
Or a half-moon made with a pen.

2 LADY   Who taught this?

MAMILLIUS

I learned it out of women's faces. Pray now,
What colour are your eyebrows?

1 LADY   Blue, my lord.

MAMILLIUS

Nay, that's a mock. I have seen a lady's nose
That has been blue, but not her eyebrows.

1 LADY   Hark ye,   15
The queen, your mother, rounds apace. We shall
Present our services to a fine new prince
One of these days, and then you'd wanton with us

8 **Your . . . blacker** probably cheeky: women with dark hair, eyebrows (*brows*) and skin were thought less beautiful than blondes (cf. *Son* 127, 130). Perhaps also intended to remind an audience of Leontes' *brow* (1.2.149; see 148–9n.), and of the horns in a cuckold's brows (see 1.2.119n.). To be black-browed was to scowl.

9–11 **so . . . pen** i.e. provided the eyebrow is trimmed, as was the fashion for ladies at court, in an arch (*semicircle*), or drawn in the same shape (*half-moon*) with a *pen*, a quill, brush or pencil (not the modern eyebrow pencil)

11 **half-moon** Cf. nine full moons, 1.2.1; *half-moon* mirrors Hermione's swelling (she *rounds apace*, 16).
  taught taught you; F's 'taught' indicates contraction for the metre (see p. 354, and cf. 2.3.146 and n.). The response may be a bit sharp (where did you pick up such low talk?): eyebrows were said to show how much pubic hair a woman had (Williams, 160).

12 **out of** from studying

Pray now now do please tell me

13 **eyebrows** eyelids. Cf. *brows*, 8 (see n.).
  Blue Blue eyelids (the veins, or from cosmetics) were alluring to upper-class men (cf. *Cym* 2.2.21–3). Blueness in the lid was taken as a sign of pregnancy (Williams, 454–5), so the First Lady may be expecting too.

14 **that's a mock** you're teasing me; *mock* is derisive.

15 **blue** (1) blue with cold; (2) disfigured by disease or age (with veins prominent); (3) that has been blown (a little boy's joke; F has 'blew').
  Hark ye you listen here

16 **rounds apace** is becoming round, filling out; the first explicit reference to her pregnancy

17 **Present our services** pay a formal call on (*OED* service *n.*[1] 9b); a conventional compliment, but she also means they will soon be servants to the new baby
  prince royal child of either sex

18 **wanton** play (without the sexual overtones of 1.2.126)

11 taught this] *(*taught 'this*); taught you this Rowe; taught't Alexander

If we would have you.

2 LADY   She is spread of late

Into a goodly bulk: good time encounter her!   20

HERMIONE

What wisdom stirs amongst you? Come, sir, now

I am for you again. Pray you sit by us,

And tell's a tale.

MAMILLIUS   Merry or sad shall't be?

HERMIONE

As merry as you will.

MAMILLIUS

A sad tale's best for winter. I have one   25

Of sprites and goblins.

HERMIONE   Let's have that, good sir.

Come on, sit down, come on, and do your best

To fright me with your sprites. You're powerful at it.

MAMILLIUS

There was a man –

HERMIONE   Nay, come sit down; then on.

MAMILLIUS

Dwelt by a churchyard – I will tell it softly,   30

20 **bulk** belly (*OED* bulk *n.*[1] 2a), as well as large size
good . . . her let's hope for an easy childbirth (literally, may the birth encounter her when she's most ready, at a *good time*; subjunctive, see Blake, 85); *good time* also suggests a favourable time astrologically (see 1.2.200–1n.); and generally (cf. 4.1.1–3, 29–32).

21 **What . . . you?** What weighty matters are you talking about?

22 **for you** ready to take you on, enjoy your company (Abbott, 155)

23 **tell's** tell us (ladies); to Mamillius she wouldn't use the royal 'us'.

23, 25 **sad** sorrowful, serious

24 **will** want it to be

25 **A . . . winter** another indication that

Acts 1–3 are in winter (see 1.1.5n.), when stories were part of entertainment. A 'tale for winter', or 'a winter's tale', was proverbial for a trivial pastime (Dent, W513.1); see p. 24.

26, 28 **sprites** ghosts

27 **Come . . . down** She tries to get the boy to settle down enough to begin his story (as at 29, 31).

27–8 **do . . . sprites** Schanzer notes the dramatic irony: Hermione plays at being frightened by a ghost story, unaware that seconds later she will be truly aghast at what Leontes has imagined.

28 **powerful at it** a master at it (frightening me)

30 **Dwelt . . . churchyard** The tale of ghosts and goblins starts with a man

22 Pray] (ʼPray)   25–6 A . . . goblins] *as Dyce; F lines* Winter: / Goblins. /

Yon crickets shall not hear it.

HERMIONE   Come on then,

And give't me in mine ear.

[*Enter* LEONTES, ANTIGONUS *and* Lords.]

LEONTES

Was he met there? His train? Camillo with him?

LORD

Behind the tuft of pines I met them. Never

Saw I men scour so on their way. I eyed them   35

Even to their ships.

LEONTES   How blest am I

In my just censure, in my true opinion!

Alack, for lesser knowledge – how accursed

In being so blest. There may be in the cup

A spider steeped, and one may drink, depart,   40

And yet partake no venom, for his knowledge

Is not infected; but if one present

Th'abhorred ingredient to his eye, make known

who lives beside a graveyard (or lives by working in it, i.e. a gravedigger; cf. *TN* 3.1.1–10). It is interrupted by Leontes, whose real-life story of mysterious deaths, lingering beside graves and reanimations, now begins.

31 **Yon crickets** i.e. those ladies (*Yon*, demonstrative pronoun), comparing the women's chattering to crickets chirping (cf. Dent, C825, 'merry as a cricket')

32 **give't . . . ear** whisper it to me secretly

32 SD See 0.1n.

33 **he** Polixenes
  train entourage

34 **tuft** clump of trees (*OED n.* 3a); an oddly specific location

35 **scour** scurry, run (*OED v.*¹ 1b)

35–6 **I . . . to** I watched them until the moment they reached

37 **true opinion** correct judgement

38 **Alack . . . knowledge** alas, if only I didn't know what I now do

39 **blest** blessed, i.e. with insight

40–5 **spider . . . hefts** Spiders were thought venomous; mixing them in food or drink made these poisonous too (cf. Dent, S749.1, 'To digest a spider'). Leontes varies this, saying the poison only works if the victim knows the spider is present. He may have in mind what he wanted put into Polixenes' drink (1.2.314).

40 **steeped** so saturated it has sunk to the bottom

41 **partake** imbibe

42 **infected** i.e. poisoned
  one present someone presents

43 **ingredient** literally 'something that enters', from Latin *ingredior*, 'I go in'. Cf. *Oth* 2.3.302–3, 'Every inordinate cup is unblest, and the ingredience is a devil.'

43–4 **make . . . hath** lets him know what he has

31 Yon] *(Yond)*   31–2 Come . . . ear] *as Capell; one line* F   32.1] F *subst. at* 0.1; *Enter Leontes.* F2

How he hath drunk, he cracks his gorge, his sides,
With violent hefts. I have drunk, and seen the spider.   45
Camillo was his help in this, his pander.
There is a plot against my life, my crown;
All's true that is mistrusted. That false villain
Whom I employed was pre-employed by him.
He has discovered my design, and I   50
Remain a pinched thing – yea, a very trick
For them to play at will. How came the posterns
So easily open?

LORD   By his great authority,
Which often hath no less prevailed than so
On your command.

LEONTES   I know't too well.   55
[*to Hermione*] Give me the boy. I am glad you did not
    nurse him.
Though he does bear some signs of me, yet you
Have too much blood in him.

44–5 ²**he . . . hefts** he splits his throat
(vomiting), makes his chest or guts
convulse in spasms of wretching (*hefts*,
violent heavings)

46 Camillo assisted Polixenes in this
(adultery with Hermione), as pimp or
go-between.

48 **All's . . . mistrusted** everything I
suspected (*mistrusted*) has proved to be
true; everything I think isn't true (that
Hermione is faithful) is true. Leontes
doesn't intend the second meaning.

50 **He . . . design** Camillo has revealed
my plot; Polixenes has found out what
I planned.

51 **pinched** squeezed (like a child's toy)
(*OED* pinch *v.* 1a); tortured (like a
prisoner on the rack) (*v.* 4); stung (cf.
Tem 1.2.330–2); distressed (*v.* 12a)

51–2 **very . . . will** mere plaything for
them to toy with as they choose (*trick*,

a reminder of *tricks*, 1.2.61; see n.)

52–3 **How . . . open** Why were the gates
opened so easily. For *posterns*, see
1.2.434n.

53 **his** i.e. Camillo's

54–5 **hath . . . command** has had as
much power to open the gates as your
own order would

56 **I . . . him** Personality and moral
outlook were thought to be shaped
by breast-milk, a refined form of
blood (cf. 1.2.71–3, 109, and see nn.).
Leontes is relieved Hermione didn't
suckle Mamillius (upper-class children
were often suckled by wet-nurses:
Mack, 9; Paster, 197–208). In prison
she does feed Perdita (3.2.97–8).

57–8 **yet . . . him** He already has too
much of your blood in him (i.e. not
through breast-milk, but blood-line,
as at 1.2.328).

56 SD] *Oxf*

HERMIONE   What is this? Sport?

LEONTES

Bear the boy hence: he shall not come about her.
Away with him, and let her sport herself   60
With that she's big with, [*to Hermione*] for 'tis
    Polixenes
Has made thee swell thus.   [*Mamillius is taken away.*]

HERMIONE   But I'd say he had not,
And I'll be sworn you would believe my saying,
Howe'er you lean to th' nayward.

LEONTES   You, my lords,
Look on her, mark her well. Be but about   65
To say she is a goodly lady, and
The justice of your hearts will thereto add
'Tis pity she's not honest, honourable.
Praise her but for this her without-door form –
Which on my faith deserves high speech – and straight   70
The shrug, the hum or ha, these petty brands
That calumny doth use – O, I am out!

58 **Sport?** Is this a game?
60 **sport herself** play; have sex (cf. *Oth*
    2.1.225, 4.3.100)
61 **that . . . with** the child she is
    carrying; Polixenes
62 **thee** See 82n.
    But I'd say Oxf¹ suggests that the
    conditional 'implies a hypothetical
    situation', i.e. one not yet taken seriously.
64 **lean . . . nayward** incline to the
    contrary view; *OED*'s only citation
    for 'to the nayward', meaning towards
    a denial. Hermione thinks she would
    only have to give him her word she
    was innocent.
66, 75 **goodly** beautiful, virtuous
67 **thereto** to that
68 **not honest, honourable** not faithful,
    nor worthy of her birth and rank

69 **without-door   form** outward
    appearance; manner in public: *form*
    could also mean 'beauty, comeliness'
    (*OED n.* 1e).
70 **on my faith** in truth
    high speech praise
70–2 **straight . . . use** immediately come
    the small gestures and expressions of
    reservation about her character, the
    little marks of disgrace (*brands*) that
    slander uses
71 **shrug** an expression of mild contempt
    hum or ha slight dissatisfaction and
    doubt
72 **I am out** I'm mistaken – correcting
    himself as if he had lost his place or
    muffed lines; cf. *Cor* 5.3.40–1, 'Like a
    dull actor now / I have forgot my part
    and I am out'. See 1.2.187n.

61 SD] *Oxf*   62 SD] *Capell subst.*

That mercy does, for calumny will sear
Virtue itself – these shrugs, these hums and ha's,
When you have said she's goodly, come between   75
Ere you can say she's honest. But be't known
From him that has most cause to grieve it should be,
She's an adulteress!

HERMIONE   Should a villain say so,
The most replenished villain in the world,
He were as much more villain – you, my lord,   80
Do but mistake.

LEONTES   You have mistook, my lady,
Polixenes for Leontes. O thou thing,
Which I'll not call a creature of thy place,
Lest barbarism, making me the precedent,
Should a like language use to all degrees,   85
And mannerly distinguishment leave out

---

73 **That mercy does** (I should have said the little marks) mercy uses, i.e. such small slurs show merciful treatment
73–4 **calumny . . . itself** Cf. Dent, E175, 'Calumny shoots at virtue'; *Ham* 3.1.135–6, 'be thou as chaste as ice, as pure as snow, thou shalt not escape calumny'; *MM* 3.2.178–80. See 1.2.411–12n.
73 **sear** continues the image begun with *brands*, 71
75–6 **come between / Ere** contradict before
76 **honest** chaste
77 **grieve . . . be** be sorry that it's so; be aggrieved as the injured party
78 **adulteress** The bluntness of this is a small shock after the involved clauses from 65. F's 'Adultresse' (as at 88 and 2.3.4) indicates three syllables.
79 **replenished** utter (cf. *R3* 4.3.18)
80 **as . . . villain** as much a villain again (i.e. merely calling me an adulteress would make him a villain). Cf. 1.2.281–2 (see n.).
81 **Do but mistake** are merely wrong
   You have mistook Cf. *Ham* 3.2.245, 'So you mistake your husbands', allud-

ing to the marriage ceremony in *BCP* ('Do you take this man . . .').
82–7 **O . . . beggar** Leontes means that Hermione should be spoken to with respect, despite her crime, because she is a queen; but his manner and accusations at 61–2, 65–78 are utterly disrespectful.
82 **thou** switching from *you* (81), shows anger (as at 62), intended to insult Hermione; see 1.2.43n.
   thing term of contempt, for someone not fit to be called human (*OED n.*[1] 10b). Williams (1380–1) says *thing* also meant vagina: perhaps Leontes nearly calls his wife a cunt, stopping just short in 83–7.
83 I shan't degrade you with the term I ought to use (because you've sunk so low); I won't address you by the title your rank deserves (you've forfeited this respect).
84 **barbarism** uncivilized rudeness (*OED n.* 2)
85 **all degrees** people of all ranks
86–7 **mannerly . . . Betwixt** distinguish between the proper ways of addressing

Betwixt the prince and beggar. I have said
She's an adulteress, I have said with whom.
More, she's a traitor, and Camillo is
A federary with her, and one that knows   90
What she should shame to know herself,
But with her most vile principal, that she's
A bed-swerver, even as bad as those
That vulgars give bold'st titles; ay, and privy
To this their late escape.

HERMIONE   No, by my life,   95
Privy to none of this. How will this grieve you
When you shall come to clearer knowledge, that
You thus have published me? Gentle my lord,
You scarce can right me throughly then to say
You did mistake.

---

90 **federary** accomplice, confederate.
Editors sometimes emend to 'fedarie'
or 'fedary', referring to F *MM* 2.4.122,
'fedarie'; F *Cym* 3.2.21, 'Fœdarie';
and claiming the shorter word better
fits the metre (*OED* fedarie cites only
these three). But 'Federarie' in F was
coined from Latin *foedus*, covenant,
league, and 'fedarie' isn't from *foedus*
at all, but from medieval Latin *feodum*,
tenant or retainer. Either Shakespeare
coined 'fedarie' from the wrong root,
or conflated the sense of 'confederate'
in *foedus* with 'dependant' in *feodum*.
There are no grounds for changing
the etymologically correct *federary*;
Shakespeare, mistaken in *MM* and
Cym, may have corrected it here.

91–2 **What . . . principal** What she
would be ashamed to know she has
become, if it weren't for her most
vile sexual partner; i.e. she's so besotted with Polixenes that she has no
shame. *OED n.* B. 2a defines principal
as 'chief actor or doer' or 'person
directly responsible for a crime'; here
it probably means whoremaster (cf. *Per*
4.5.80–91).

93 **bed-swerver** offender against her
marriage bed, i.e. adulteress
even just

94 **That . . . titles** to whom the common
people give the most immodest names
(ones he won't call her: see 82, 83 and
nn.)
bold'st either Hermione's behaviour
or the coarseness of lower-class people

94–5 **privy . . . escape** (1) Camillo knew
of (was *privy* to) their recent sexual
affair (*escape*, outrageous sexual transgression; cf. *Tit* 4.2.115); (2) Hermione
knew about their recent flight.

94 **privy** used of the genitals (Williams,
1100–1), perhaps revealing what is on
Leontes' mind

97 **clearer knowledge** fuller understanding

98 **published me** denounced me in
public (*OED* publish 4a)
Gentle my lord my noble lord

99 **You . . . me** you can scarcely rectify
the wrong you've done me; perhaps
'scarcely clear my name'
throughly thoroughly
then to say except by saying (*to say*,
infinitive as gerund: Abbott, 356)

---

90 federary] *(Federarie); Federaty Rowe;* feodary *Malone;* fedary *Dyce*

LEONTES   No. If I mistake   100
    In those foundations which I build upon,
    The centre is not big enough to bear
    A schoolboy's top. Away with her, to prison.
    He who shall speak for her is afar off guilty,
    But that he speaks!
HERMIONE   There's some ill planet reigns.   105
    I must be patient till the heavens look
    With an aspect more favourable. Good my lords,
    I am not prone to weeping, as our sex
    Commonly are, the want of which vain dew
    Perchance shall dry your pities; but I have   110
    That honourable grief lodged here which burns
    Worse than tears drown. Beseech you all, my lords,
    With thoughts so qualified as your charities

100–3 **If . . . top** If I'm wrong about
    the foundation (of evidence) for my
    allegations (what *I build upon*), then
    the earth itself isn't strong enough to
    carry a schoolboy's spinning top; i.e.
    if I'm mistaken about this, nothing
    can be trusted. Leontes pictures the
    earth as the centre of the universe
    around which the sun and planets
    move (see 1.2.48n.), adding the image
    of a top spinning with its point on the
    same centre. On the modern stage,
    Mamillius has been shown playing
    with a top here and at 1.2.189.
104 **afar off** at a distance, i.e. by associa-
    tion
105 **But . . . speaks** merely by speaking
    (on her behalf)
    There's . . . reigns Some malign
    planet is in the ascendant; cf. 1.2.200–1
    (see n.).
106–7 **till . . . favourable** until the
    heavens are (or seem) more favourably
    aligned (see 105n.); *aspect* (aspèct) was
    the term in astrology for the positions
    of planets and stars as seen from earth

(*OED n.* 4), but also 'face' or 'look'
    (*n.* 10), i.e. until the gods look on
    Hermione with kinder expressions.
107 **Good my lords** my good lords
109 **the . . . dew** the lack of which tears
    shed in vain (with a pun on *dew* as due)
110 **Perchance . . . pities** perhaps will
    cause your tears for my situation to dry
    up. For *pities* as plural (Shakespeare's
    only use), see *OED* pity *n.* 2b.
111 **honourable** seemly, dignified
    lodged here set within me; by *here*
    Hermione may mean her heart, per-
    haps gesturing to it.
111–12 **which . . . drown** which burns
    more agonizingly than tears do; i.e. no
    woman ever drowned in tears, but grief
    really can consume someone. The con-
    junction of dying by fire and drowning
    was common in Elizabethan writing (e.g.
    TGV 1.3.78–9, *RJ* 1.2.90–3; Sidney's
    New Arcadia, Book 1, ch. 1; the epigram
    'A Burnt Ship', Donne, 33).
112, 116, 126 **Beseech** I entreat
113–14 **With . . . me** Judge me (*OED*
    measure *v.* 13a) according to opinions

112, 116 Beseech] (ˊbeseech)

Shall best instruct you, measure me; and so
The king's will be performed.

LEONTES   Shall I be heard?   115

HERMIONE

Who is't that goes with me? Beseech your highness
My women may be with me, for you see
My plight requires it. Do not weep, good fools,
There is no cause. When you shall know your mistress
Has deserved prison, then abound in tears   120
As I come out; this action I now go on
Is for my better grace. Adieu, my lord.
I never wished to see you sorry; now
I trust I shall. My women, come, you have leave.

LEONTES

Go, do our bidding. Hence!   125

[Exit Hermione, as a prisoner, with Ladies.]

moderated with as much charity as you think proper.

115 **The ... performed** may what the king wishes be done (conventional phrase, cf. the Lord's Prayer, 'Thy will be done', Matthew, 6.10)
Shall ... heard Will no one listen to my command. The order to take Hermione to prison (103) has not been obeyed.

118 **plight** pregnant condition
good fools dear silly girls (uncritical endearment, *OED* fool *n.*[1] 1c)

119–21 **When ... out** If you ever learn I ought to be in prison (because I'm truly guilty), the proper time to cry will be when I'm released; i.e. then you should weep that a criminal is wrongly freed.

121–2 **this ... grace** i.e. imprisonment and trial as paths to spiritual cleansing, in essence the Christian commonplace (e.g. Dent, A53) that God sends undeserved afflictions for one's own good. Some editors take 'for my better grace'

to mean 'add to my honesty and credit' or 'redound to my honour', making Hermione hope for no more from her disgrace than an enhanced reputation. See 1.2.80n.

121 **this ... on** Different metaphors have been seen in this phrase: (1) legal indictment for which I'm now going to prison; (2) military campaign I'm now undertaking (fighting for my name); (3) role I now have to perform (like an actor: see 1.2.187n.). It may mean, more simply, this course of action I'm beginning.

122–4 **Adieu ... shall** Sanders (39) says Hermione is 'strong enough to wish upon her husband the misery to which his deeds have entitled him', and *trust* at 124 'is her trust in his better nature which reveals to her the necessity of his sorrow'. Even *Adieu* (final goodbye) is perhaps tinged with regret at irrevocable loss of trust (*OED* A *int.* 2).

124 **leave** permission (to go with me)
125 **Hence** Take her out of here.

125 SD] *Theobald subst.*

LORD

Beseech your highness, call the queen again.

ANTIGONUS

Be certain what you do, sir, lest your justice
Prove violence, in the which three great ones suffer:
Yourself, your queen, your son.

LORD   For her, my lord,
I dare my life lay down, and will do't, sir,   130
Please you t'accept it, that the queen is spotless
I'th' eyes of heaven and to you – I mean
In this which you accuse her.

ANTIGONUS   If it prove
She's otherwise, I'll keep my stables where
I lodge my wife; I'll go in couples with her;   135
Than when I feel and see her, no farther trust her;
For every inch of woman in the world,
Ay, every dram of woman's flesh, is false
If she be.

LEONTES   Hold your peaces.

126 **again** back
128 **Prove violence** turns out to be
  injurious
  in the which in which violence
  (Abbott, 270)
130 **my . . . down** surrender my life,
  pledge my life as surety
131 **Please** if it may please
  it my life
132 **to you** in relation to you
132–3 **I . . . her** The qualification
  avoids hyperbole: the Lord is sure
  of Hermione's fidelity and innocence
  (131), but he won't assert anything
  more.
133–6 **If . . . ²her** Some editors think
  this passage difficult, but the general meaning is plain. If Hermione is
  unchaste, no woman can be trusted,
  not even his wife: all women must be
  treated as animals, shut in stalls and

watched constantly.
134 **otherwise** i.e. not *spotless* (131)
134–5 **I'll . . . wife** I'll lock my wife in her
  rooms, as I do the mares in my stable,
  i.e. keep her apart from men the way
  I shut the mares away from stallions.
  Kermode's suggestion, that Antigonus
  'will keep his stallions locked up when
  his wife is near' (i.e. because she'd even
  have sex with horses), isn't persuasive.
  See 1.2.94–6n.
135 **I'll . . . her** I'll go everywhere with
  her tied to me; *in couples*, used of
  dogs leashed in pairs for a hunt (*OED*
  couple *n.* 1b).
136 Cf. Tilley, T557, 'I will trust you no
  farther than I can see you.'
138 **dram** tiny amount (eighth of an
  ounce, the smallest of measures)
139 **she** Hermione
  Hold your peaces All of you be silent.

136 Than] *(Then)*

LORD   Good my lord –

ANTIGONUS

It is for you we speak, not for ourselves.   140

You are abused, and by some putter-on

That will be damned for't. Would I knew the villain,

I would land-damn him. Be she honour-flawed,

I have three daughters – the eldest is eleven;

The second and the third, nine and some five.   145

If this prove true, they'll pay for't. By mine honour,

I'll geld 'em all. Fourteen they shall not see,

To bring false generations. They are co-heirs,

And I had rather glib myself than they

Should not produce fair issue.

LEONTES   Cease, no more!   150

You smell this business with a sense as cold

140 **you** your sake
141 **abused** deceived
   putter-on instigator (*OED* putter *n.*[1] C2), someone who has incited you; here a liar, like Iago in *Oth* or Jachimo in *Cym*
143 **land-damn** *OED*'s only citation, defined as 'To make a hell on earth for (a person)': Antigonus has just said the *putter-on* will be damned, but before then he will make him taste hell on earth. The word may be cognate with 'lambaste', slang for to thrash (*OED*), or the Cotswolds dialect 'landam', meaning abuse or revile throughout the land; or Shakespeare simply invented it.
   Be she honour-flawed if her chastity is corrupt
144–50 **I . . . issue** Cf. Lear, also without a son, who divides his estate between three daughters, wishing a barren womb on one of them for not honouring him (*KL* 1.4.267–73).
145 **some** about
146 **pay** suffer
147 **geld 'em** spay them, make them

barren. Williams (588) says it is unusual to apply *geld* to women, since it was used of castrating horses, but Antigonus often draws on the language of the stables (see List of Roles, 4n.; 2.1.133–6 and nn; 1.2.94–6n.).
147–8 **Fourteen . . . generations** I won't let them reach 14 to give birth to illegitimate children (not *fair issue*, 150: see n.); i.e. I'll castrate them before they reach child-bearing age. The contemporary age of consent for girls was 12.
148 **co-heirs** Under English law, with no primogeniture for females, three daughters would be joint heirs.
149 **glib** castrate (render himself incapable of fathering an heir or, more abstractly, deprive himself of posterity); *OED*'s first citation for this sense (*v.*[2])
150 **fair issue** legitimate offspring
151–2 **smell . . . nose** i.e. your understanding of this is useless. To 'smell a fault' in *KL* 1.1.15 means to perceive sexual misbehaviour (fathering a bastard); cf. Dent, S558.

143 land-damn] *(*Land-damne*)*; lant-dam *Hudson*

As is a dead man's nose. But I do see't and feel't
As you feel doing thus [*laying hold of Antigonus*] – and
  see withal
The instruments that feel.
ANTIGONUS   If it be so,
  We need no grave to bury honesty;   155
  There's not a grain of it the face to sweeten
  Of the whole dungy earth.
LEONTES   What! Lack I credit?
LORD
  I had rather you did lack than I, my lord,
  Upon this ground; and more it would content me
  To have her honour true than your suspicion,   160
  Be blamed for't how you might.
LEONTES   Why, what need we
  Commune with you of this, but rather follow
  Our forceful instigation? Our prerogative

153–4 **As . . . feel** with the same force
you feel when I grab you like this – and
moreover you see the fingers (*instruments*) that hurt you. F has no SD,
but Leontes appears to do something
to Antigonus as he says *doing thus*,
perhaps pulling his beard or tweaking
his nose to emphasize what he said at
151–2. 'As you feel doing thus' may
mean 'as one feels in doing this' (i.e.
you is impersonal), at which point
Leontes hits himself or something
close to him.
154 **If . . . so** if it's true (she's unfaithful)
155 **honesty** chastity (which has died as a
result of her infidelity)
156–7 **the . . . earth** to remove the stench
from the face of the whole dung-like
earth; *dungy earth* may derive from
'dung for the earth' in Psalms, 83.10
(Shaheen, 724). Cf. 'Our dungy earth',
AC 1.1.36, describing the baseness of
the world.

157 **Lack I credit?** Does no one believe
me? Are you showing me the reverence
(*credit*) I should have as king?
159 **Upon this ground** in this matter
(word-play on *ground* and *earth*, 157)
160 **than your suspicion** i.e. to have
your suspicion prove to be true
161 **Be . . . might** however much you
might be blamed for it
161–3 **what . . . instigation** What need
have I for your advice in this? I should
follow my own strong impulse instead
(for ellipsis in *but rather*, see Abbott,
385). Leontes uses the royal 'we'
throughout this speech.
163–5 **²Our . . . this** My royal authority
doesn't need your counsel – rather,
I have told you these things out of
the goodness of my nature. James I
asserted comparable prerogative and
authority over English Parliaments in
the years before and after the date
of *WT*.

153 SD] Hanmer subst.; *Striking him Rann*

Calls not your counsels, but our natural goodness
Imparts this; which if you, or stupefied   165
Or seeming so in skill, cannot or will not
Relish a truth like us, inform yourselves
We need no more of your advice. The matter,
The loss, the gain, the ordering on't, is all
Properly ours.

ANTIGONUS   And I wish, my liege,   170
You had only in your silent judgement tried it
Without more overture.

LEONTES   How could that be?
Either thou art most ignorant by age,
Or thou wert born a fool. Camillo's flight,
Added to their familiarity –   175
Which was as gross as ever touched conjecture
That lacked sight only, naught for approbation
But only seeing, all other circumstances
Made up to th' deed – doth push on this proceeding.
Yet for a greater confirmation –   180

165–6 **which . . . skill** as regards which, if you, either because you're too dull-witted to understand me or because you're pretending not to (for *which*, see Abbott, 249)
167 **Relish** comprehend
  inform yourselves you must understand that
168–70 **The . . . ours** The responsibility for handling the matter – whatever its losses and gains – as of right, belongs to me alone; *ordering* (F 'ord'ring') and *ours* are disyllabic.
170 **liege** sovereign
171 **tried** examined
172 **Without more overture** without this public disclosure (*OED* 3); without openly setting out a case against her. Overture also meant the formal opening of proceedings (*OED n.* 5).
173 **most . . . age** become completely

stupid through age; cf. the uselessness of the old at 4.4.402–7.
175 **familiarity** (sexual) intimacy
176 **gross** obvious; glaring, flagrant (*OED a* and *n.*⁴ 4)
  as . . . conjecture as (anything that) ever aroused suspicion
177–9 **That . . . deed** which lacked nothing by way of proof (to confirm it) but the evidence of one's eyes (seeing them have sex), and everything else amounting to proof they had done the deed. This is the 'ocular proof' of *Oth* 3.3.363.
179 **doth . . . proceeding** urges me to this course of action; 'proceeding' also meant an action in law (*OED n.* 2c): Leontes reveals his plan to try Hermione for treason.
180 **confirmation** five syllables, two in *-ion* (Abbott, 479)

169–70 The . . . ours] *as Theobald; F lines* on't, / ours. /   169 ordering] *(ord'ring)*

199

For in an act of this importance 'twere
Most piteous to be wild – I have dispatched in post
To sacred Delphos, to Apollo's temple,
Cleomenes and Dion, whom you know
Of stuffed sufficiency. Now from the oracle   185
They will bring all, whose spiritual counsel had,
Shall stop or spur me. Have I done well?

LORD

Well done, my lord.

LEONTES

Though I am satisfied, and need no more
Than what I know, yet shall the oracle   190
Give rest to th' minds of others; such as he
Whose ignorant credulity will not
Come up to th' truth. So have we thought it good
From our free person she should be confined,
Lest that the treachery of the two fled hence   195

181–2 **'twere . . . wild** it would be
utterly unmerciful to act rashly
182–7 **I . . . me** In *Pandosto* (p. 417) it
is the queen who requests Apollo's
judgement (see 183n.).
182 **in post** with all haste; literally,
riding post horses; see 1.2.94–6n. Cf.
posts, 2.3.191 (see n.).
183 **Delphos** Mediterranean Greek
island of Delos, in Shakespeare's day
known as Delphos, the site of a temple dedicated to Apollo, the sun god.
Apollo communicated prophecies and
judgements through his *oracle* (185) at
Delphos, as he did at the more famous
Delphi on the Greek mainland.
185 **of stuffed sufficiency** amply
qualified (to do this). Cf. *Oth* 1.3.225,
'allowed sufficiency'.
oracle Apollo's priestess in the temple at Delphos, through whom the
god was said to speak (see 183n.). At
3.1.18 (see n.) and 3.2.125 the *oracle*
is a scroll on which Apollo's spoken
message is written.

186–7 **all . . . me** the whole truth,
and when I have (Apollo's) divine
judgement, this will halt or spur me
on. The metaphor is of riding, so
Leontes may be thinking of horses
galloping towards Delphos (see
182n.). See 1.2.94–6n.
187 **Have . . . well** Have I done the
right thing (i.e. self-doubt); I've
done well, you must agree (self-
congratulation).
189 **satisfied** convinced (of her guilt):
cf. 1.2.230–2 (see nn.).
191 **he** Antigonus, or anyone who might
doubt the allegations
192 **ignorant** simple-minded (cf. 173)
193 **Come up to** face up to
we Leontes switches to the royal
pronoun to assert his right to
imprison Hermione.
194 **From** away from
free accessible (and vulnerable)
195 **treachery** the supposed plot to
murder him and steal his crown (cf.
47, 89)

Be left her to perform. Come, follow us,
We are to speak in public; for this business
Will raise us all.
ANTIGONUS [*aside*] To laughter, as I take it,
If the good truth were known.   *Exeunt.*

2.2   *Enter* PAULINA, *a Gentleman* [*and Attendants*].

PAULINA

The keeper of the prison, call to him.
Let him have knowledge who I am.   [*Exit Gentleman.*]
                                                 Good lady,
No court in Europe is too good for thee;
What dost thou then in prison?

            [*Enter the* GAOLER *and the Gentleman.*]

                                    Now, good sir,

You know me, do you not?
GAOLER   For a worthy lady,   5

And one who much I honour.
PAULINA   Pray you then,

196 **Be . . . perform** has been left for her
    to carry out
197 **speak in public** i.e. address the
    assembled court in the presence
    chamber (see 1.2n.), or in a place open
    to public access (*OED* public B *n*. 1a,
    citing this instance)
198 **raise us all** rouse everyone (from
    sleepiness about the conspiracy; see
    1.2.326–7n.); put us all on high alert
    (about danger to the state)
    laughter i.e. at the ridiculousness of
    the charges
2.2 Leontes has shut Hermione away
    and shut her up, but the word 'deliv-
    ered' (24) shows that this won't last
    long. He can't prevent the delivery

of the baby from the womb and from
the prison (58–62), any more than
he can stop Paulina's delivery of the
truth (30).
1   **keeper** See List of Roles, 11n.
    prison In Shakespeare's day, prisoners
    of Hermione's rank, however serious
    their crimes or the allegations against
    them, were confined in comfortable
    apartments in the Tower of London,
    where they could be visited.
    call to summon
2–4 **Good . . . prison** spoken as though
    addressing Hermione in person
3   **Europe** i.e. all the civilized world
3–4 **thee . . . thou** indicates respect and
    feeling; see 1.2.43n.

198 SD] *Hanmer*   **2.2**] (*Scena Secunda.*)   0.1] *Hanmer subst.; Enter Paulina, a Gentleman, Gaoler,
Emilia. F*   2 SD] *Rowe*   4 SD] *Rowe subst.*

Conduct me to the queen.

GAOLER   I may not, madam.

To the contrary I have express commandment.

PAULINA

Here's ado, to lock up honesty and honour from

Th'access of gentle visitors. Is't lawful, pray you,   10

To see her women? Any of them? Emilia?

GAOLER

So please you, madam,

To put apart these your attendants, I

Shall bring Emilia forth.

PAULINA   I pray now call her.

Withdraw yourselves.   *[Exeunt Gentleman and Attendants.]*

GAOLER   And, madam,   15

I must be present at your conference.

PAULINA

Well, be't so; prithee.   *[Exit Gaoler.]*

Here's such ado to make no stain a stain

As passes colouring.

[Enter the GAOLER *with* EMILIA.]

Dear gentlewoman,

How fares our gracious lady?   20

EMILIA

As well as one so great and so forlorn

---

8   **To the contrary** to do the opposite
9   **Here's ado** This is a fine state
    of affairs, a fuss about nothing; cf.
    18.
    honesty and honour virtue and high
    rank
10 **access** accèss
    gentle high-born; respectable; kind,
    harmless
    lawful permissible (*OED* 1b); cf.
    5.3.105, 111.
11 **women** attendants (cf. 2.1.117, 124)

12 **So please** if it pleases
13 **put apart** send away
16 **conference** meeting, conversation
17 **prithee** please (fetch her)
18–19 **make . . . colouring** make it seem
    that a spotless woman is indelibly
    stained with sin; cf. *Cym* 2.4.140.
    passes colouring is beyond excusing
    (*OED* colour *v.* 3a), i.e. the attempt
    to blemish her is unpardonable. Cf.
    1.2.131–2 (see 132 n.).
21 **great** eminent, royal

15 SD] *Theobald subst.*   17 SD] *Capell subst.*   19 SD] *Capell subst.; Enter Emilia F2*

May hold together. On her frights and griefs –
Which never tender lady hath borne greater –
She is, something before her time, delivered.

PAULINA

A boy?

EMILIA   A daughter, and a goodly babe,   25
Lusty, and like to live. The queen receives
Much comfort in't; says, 'My poor prisoner,
I am innocent as you.'

PAULINA   I dare be sworn.
These dangerous, unsafe lunes i'th' king, beshrew
them!
He must be told on't, and he shall. The office   30
Becomes a woman best; I'll take't upon me.
If I prove honey-mouthed, let my tongue blister
And never to my red-looked anger be

---

22 **hold together** hold herself together
On because of; in addition to
23 **Which** than which
tender lady lady in her delicate condition
24 she has given birth, earlier than expected
25 **goodly** beautiful
26 **Lusty . . . live** full of life, and likely to survive. In this period, high infant mortality particularly affected newly born babies.
27 **in't** from it (the baby)
28 **innocent** The innocence of babies was proverbial (Dent, B4), even though Christian doctrine insisted they inherited original sin (see 1.2.69–70n.).
   ^{2}**I . . . sworn** I'm absolutely sure of it (*OED* swear *v.* 10f); a common phrase, but the context for swearing to the truth of something is especially important here.
29 **lunes** fits of lunacy (from Latin *luna*, moon); *OED*'s first example (lune^2), but cf. *TC* 2.3.128.
   beshrew them curse them; a moderate oath
30 **on't** of it (the birth); about it (his

lunatic behaviour)
office responsibility
32 **honey-mouthed** a sweet-talking flatterer (not speaking bitter truths); cf. Dent, H547, 'He has honey in his mouth and the razor at his girdle.' Paulina is confirmed as anything but honey-mouthed at 2.3.170, 3.2.214–15, 5.1.18–19.
   tongue References to Paulina's tongue as uncontrollable are at 2.3.90, 108. Her willingness to speak contrasts with Hermione, who has so much self-control that Leontes asks if she is tongue-tied (1.2.27).
   blister It was proverbial that telling lies caused blisters on the tongue (Dent, R84).
33–4 **never . . . trumpet** never let (my tongue) give voice to my red-faced anger. On battlefields a *trumpet* (trumpeter) sounded the arrival of a herald in a red uniform bringing messages from an enemy camp; *red-looked* means dressed in red but also furious. Paulina's tongue announces harsh truths.

The trumpet any more. Pray you, Emilia,
Commend my best obedience to the queen.   35
If she dares trust me with her little babe,
I'll show't the king, and undertake to be
Her advocate to th' loudest. We do not know
How he may soften at the sight o'th' child.
The silence often of pure innocence   40
Persuades when speaking fails.

EMILIA   Most worthy madam,
Your honour and your goodness is so evident
That your free undertaking cannot miss
A thriving issue; there is no lady living
So meet for this great errand. Please your ladyship   45
To visit the next room, I'll presently
Acquaint the queen of your most noble offer,
Who but today hammered of this design,
But durst not tempt a minister of honour
Lest she should be denied.

PAULINA   Tell her, Emilia,   50
I'll use that tongue I have. If wit flow from't
As boldness from my bosom, let't not be doubted
I shall do good.

---

35 **Commend . . . obedience** present my most dutiful greetings (*OED* obedience 3)
38 **advocate . . . loudest** loudest, most vociferous advocate
40–1 The power of silence over words is returned to at 5.2.13–14: cf. *MM* 1.2.179–81.
40 **often** adverb qualifying *Persuades*; though according to Blake (107) it is probably an adjective, i.e. 'continual silence', since its position at 40 is unusual for an adverb
42 **honour** (impeccable) reputation
43–4 **free . . . issue** magnanimous enterprise cannot fail to have a successful outcome; punning on *issue* as offspring
45 **meet** suitable
46 **presently** immediately
48–50 **but . . . denied** just today was deliberating on a plan like this, but dared not ask someone of high rank, in case the request were refused (*OED* hammer *v.* 4a: cf. *R2* 5.5.5; *OED* tempt *v.* 1, test, put to the trial)
51 **that tongue** whatever eloquence
51–2 **If . . . bosom** if there's as much persuasiveness in my speaking as there's courage in my heart

52 let't] *F3;* le't *F*

EMILIA   Now be you blest for it!
I'll to the queen. Please you come something nearer.
GAOLER
Madam, if't please the queen to send the babe   55
I know not what I shall incur to pass it,
Having no warrant.
PAULINA   You need not fear it, sir.
This child was prisoner to the womb, and is
By law and process of great Nature thence
Freed and enfranchised, not a party to   60
The anger of the king, nor guilty of –
If any be – the trespass of the queen.
GAOLER   I do believe it.
PAULINA
Do not you fear. Upon mine honour, I
Will stand betwixt you and danger.   *Exeunt.*

2.3   *Enter* LEONTES.

LEONTES
Nor night nor day, no rest. It is but weakness
To bear the matter thus, mere weakness. If

---

54 **Please . . . nearer** repeating the request (45–6) that Paulina go into the next room
something somewhat
56 i.e. I don't know what penalty I'll incur for letting the baby out
57 **warrant** authorization
59 **law and process** legal process (hendiadys: see 1.2.188n.)
great Nature See 4.4.88n.
60 **Freed and enfranchised** liberated physically and given legal rights
a party to an object of
62 **any be** there be any
trespass offence
2.3 The setting is perhaps a private room (*chamber*, 120; see n.).

0.1 *Enter* LEONTES F's SD lists Paulina in the characters in the 'massed entry' (see pp. 352–3), but also marks her entry at 25. Leontes' speeches (1–9, 17–25) are either asides, with Antigonus and Lords onstage from the outset, perhaps at a distance, or soliloquies that end when Paulina carries in the baby (a stage property, hence not included in the SD), with Antigonus trying to stop her.
1 **Nor . . . rest** Cf. 15; see 14–16n.
Nor neither
2–3 **If . . . being** if the cause of the trouble didn't still exist. Cause also meant disease, sickness (*OED n.* 12); cf. 'malignant cause', *AW* 2.1.110.

64 betwixt] twixt *Pope*   **2.3**] *(Scæna Tertia.)*   0.1] *Capell subst.; Enter Leontes, Seruants, Paulina, Antigonus, and Lords. F*   2 weakness. If] *Collier;* weaknesse, if *F*

The cause were not in being – part o'th' cause,
She, th'adulteress; for the harlot king
Is quite beyond mine arm, out of the blank   5
And level of my brain, plot-proof; but she
I can hook to me – say that she were gone,
Given to the fire, a moiety of my rest
Might come to me again. Who's there?

[*Enter a* Servant.]

SERVANT   My lord.
LEONTES
How does the boy?
SERVANT   He took good rest tonight; 'tis hoped   10
His sickness is discharged.
LEONTES   To see his nobleness
Conceiving the dishonour of his mother!
He straight declined, drooped, took it deeply,
Fastened and fixed the shame on't in himself,

---

3   **part o'th' cause** Leontes interrupts himself: Polixenes is out of reach (5) so the only *part* in his power is Hermione.
4   **harlot** lewd (originally a term of abuse for both sexes)
5–6 **beyond . . . brain** beyond my arm's reach, beyond the target of my mind. The *blank* was the white bull's eye of a target (cf. *Oth* 3.4.129), the *level*, the action of taking aim or the mark aimed at (cf. 3.2.79, *Ham* 4.1.42, *AW* 2.1.155).
6   **plot-proof** invulnerable to any plot (of mine)
7   **hook to me** catch hold of; the metaphor is from grappling hooks in sea-fights and sieges (cf. *TGV* 3.1.117–19), or from angling (see 1.2.179n. and cf. *AC* 2.5.10–13).
    gone probably evasion, squeamishness about saying 'dead'; cf. 128 (see n.), and see 1.2.184n.
8   **Given . . . fire** burnt at the stake. Leontes considers Hermione guilty

of high treason against himself as king, and petty treason in planning to murder her husband (see 3.2.12–16): burning alive was the punishment.
    moiety small portion (*OED* 2a); half (*OED* 1), i.e. because one of the two 'adulterers' would be dead
9   **Who's there?** summoning a servant, not asking a question
9 SD See 25 SDn.
10 **tonight** last night, as at 30
11 **discharged** over
11–12 **his . . . mother** his noble spirit understanding the dishonourable things his mother has done. Leontes admits, unintentionally, 'he grew sick when I dishonoured his mother with my accusations'.
13 **straight** immediately
14 **Fastened and fixed** deliberate tautology, or doubling of words with similar meanings
    on't of it

---

9 Who's] *F3;* Whose *F*   9 SD] *Rowe subst.*   13 declined] declin'd, and *Hanmer*

Threw off his spirit, his appetite, his sleep,　　　　15
And downright languished. Leave me solely. Go,
See how he fares.　　　　　　　　　*[Exit Servant.]*
　　　　　Fie, fie, no thought of him.
The very thought of my revenges that way
Recoil upon me; in himself too mighty,
And in his parties, his alliance; let him be　　　　20
Until a time may serve. For present vengeance,
Take it on her. Camillo and Polixenes
Laugh at me, make their pastime at my sorrow.
They should not laugh if I could reach them, nor
Shall she, within my power.

Enter PAULINA *[carrying a baby, with* ANTIGONUS,
Lords *and the* Servant].

LORD　　　　　　　　　You must not enter.　　　　25
PAULINA

Nay rather, good my lords, be second to me.
Fear you his tyrannous passion more, alas,

14–16 **Fastened . . . languished** Shakespeare makes the boy's symptoms resemble Leontes' condition, i.e. sleeplessness (see 1.2.326–7n.), 'shame' at Hermione's dishonour, depression.

15 **Threw off** cast aside; the metaphor at 14–15 is of the child taking off one set of clothes and putting on another.

16 **solely** by myself

17 **Fie** an exclamation of disgust or reproach ('damn it')
no . . . him don't start thinking about him. Leontes checks himself as his thoughts move from Mamillius (*he*) to Polixenes (*him*).

18 **that way** i.e. towards Polixenes

19 **Recoil** metaphor from firing a gun (used at 1.2.154; see n.). The recoil

would hurt him if he shot at Polixenes (*OED v.*[1] 6b). For the plural verb with singular subject *thought*, 18 (confusion of proximity with *revenges*, 18), see Abbott, 412.

20 **his . . . alliance** his allies, his kin

20–1 **let . . . serve** leave him alone until the time is right

21 **present** immediate

23 **pastime at** amusement out of

25 SD **Servant** in attendance on Leontes (through the night, 30–1); probably different from the Servant tending Mamillius (10–11), who exits at 17. As Leontes' attendant, he either remains onstage until the king exits at 205, or leaves with Paulina at 128. He may be the Servant who enters at 191.

26 **be . . . me** support me

17 SD] *Theobald subst.*　25 SD *carrying . . .* Servant] *Oxf subst.*　25 SP] First Lord *Malone*

Than the queen's life? A gracious, innocent soul,
More free than he is jealous.

ANTIGONUS   That's enough.

SERVANT

Madam, he hath not slept tonight, commanded   30
None should come at him.

PAULINA   Not so hot, good sir.
I come to bring him sleep. 'Tis such as you,
That creep like shadows by him and do sigh
At each his needless heavings – such as you
Nourish the cause of his awaking. I   35
Do come with words as medicinal as true,
Honest as either, to purge him of that humour
That presses him from sleep.

LEONTES   What noise there, ho?

PAULINA

No noise, my lord, but needful conference
About some gossips for your highness.

LEONTES   How?   40
Away with that audacious lady! Antigonus,

---

28 **Than . . . life** than you are concerned
for the queen's survival
29 **free** innocent (*OED a.* 8); cf. *Ham*
2.2.499.
31 **at him** into his presence (*OED at prep.*
12b)
  hot heatedly; Paulina objects to the
Servant's manner and/or his manhandling her.
33 **shadows** spectres. In *Mac* 4.1.111 this
means apparitions (*OED n.* 7), but
here, 'insubstantial men', i.e. creeps
(*n.* 8a). Cf. *Pandosto*, the 'discourse of
Fortune so daunted them as they went
like shadows, not men' (p. 419).
34 **each . . . heavings** each of his unjustified groans
35 **cause . . . awaking** i.e. the wild fancies that keep him awake
36 **medicinal** restorative (three syllables,

mèd'cinal)
37 **Honest as either** i.e. words as well
intentioned as they are medicinal and
true
  humour disorder. Cf. 1.2.381 (see n.),
and see 1.2.71–3n.
38 **presses . . . sleep** weighs upon him,
stopping him from sleeping; cf. 1.2.19
(pressing to death: see n.), and see
1.2.326–7n.
  What . . . ho The commotion at 25–38
appears to happen out of Leontes'
hearing, or he tries to pretend he
hasn't heard (he knows what Paulina is
going to say, 42–3).
39 **needful conference** an essential
discussion
40 **gossips** godparents (i.e. for the
baptism of the new baby). Perdita
is apparently wrapped in the *bearing*

---

38 What] *F2;* Who *F*

208

I charged thee that she should not come about me.
I knew she would.

ANTIGONUS　　　　　　I told her so, my lord,
On your displeasure's peril and on mine,
She should not visit you.

LEONTES　　　　　　What, canst not rule her?　　　　45

PAULINA
From all dishonesty he can; in this –
Unless he take the course that you have done,
Commit me for committing honour – trust it,
He shall not rule me.

ANTIGONUS　　　　　　La you now, you hear,
When she will take the rein I let her run,　　　　50
But she'll not stumble.

PAULINA [*to Leontes*]　　Good my liege, I come –
And I beseech you hear me, who professes
Myself your loyal servant, your physician,
Your most obedient counsellor; yet that dares
Less appear so in comforting your evils　　　　55
Than such as most seem yours – I say, I come

---

cloth (3.3.112) or christening gown she
has on when abandoned (see 3.3.45
SD, 71–2 and nn.). The other sense of
'gossips', people talking about him, is
likely to inflame Leontes.
42 **charged** ordered
44 at the risk of incurring your displeasure and mine; my own peril, as well as
the peril of your displeasure
46 **dishonesty** dishonourable behaviour
48 **Commit . . . honour** imprison me
for acting honourably
49 **shall** according to Abbott (315–17),
probably 'must'
La . . . hear exclamation, equivalent
to 'you see what it's like when she
gets going'; perhaps with a gesture of
resignation

50–1 **When . . . stumble** when she wants
her own way, I let her have it, but she
won't make a wrong move (a metaphor
of a sure-footed horse; see 1.2.94–6n.).
51 **liege** sovereign
52 **professes** Third-person verb with
first-person noun or pronoun was
common, as with *dares*, 54 (Abbott,
247).
53 **physician** i.e. the person to cure
your sleeplessness (see 32–8). See
1.2.326–7n.
55 **so** i.e. *obedient*
comforting your evils countenanc-
ing the evil things you're doing
56 **Than . . . yours** than those (of your
servants) who seem most loyal to you
(because acquiescent)

51 SD] *Oxf*

From your good queen.

LEONTES   Good queen?

PAULINA

Good queen, my lord, good queen, I say good queen,
And would by combat make her good, so were I
A man, the worst about you.

LEONTES   Force her hence.   60

PAULINA

Let him that makes but trifles of his eyes
First hand me. On mine own accord, I'll off.
But first I'll do my errand. The good queen –
For she is good – hath brought you forth a daughter;
Here 'tis; [*laying the baby down*] commends it to your
    blessing.

LEONTES   Out!   65

A mankind witch! Hence with her, out o' door;
A most intelligencing bawd.

PAULINA   Not so.

I am as ignorant in that as you
In so entitling me, and no less honest

---

57 **Good queen?** said indignantly or
sarcastically; possibly, as Rubinstein
(5) suggests, punning on *queen* and
the homonym 'quean' or harlot (if so,
Good queen means 'yes, she's a whore,
and good at it')

59 **by** in trial by
  make her good prove her virtue;
  restore her name
  ***good, so** F has 'good so,' – i.e.
  (prove) she's as good as I say – which
  may be right. With the emendation,
  'so' means 'if'.

60 **worst** least valiant; lowest in rank
  about among

61–2 **Let . . . me** Let whoever values his
  eyes so little (he'll expose them to my
  nails) be the first man to lay hands on

me; *OED*'s earliest citation for 'hand',
grasp or touch (*v.* 1), with 4.4.353,
Tem 1.1.23.

62 **On . . . off** I'll leave of my own accord.

65 **commends** entrusts, commits; offers

66 **mankind** mannish, unwomanly (*OED*
  a.[1] 2); only instance in Shakespeare
  witch common term of abuse for
  women who were a threat to men,
  because they might overwhelm male
  authority with magic. Leontes also
  means Paulina is a repulsive old hag,
  as at 75, 106 (*OED* witch *sb.*[2] 3b(*b*)).

67 **intelligencing bawd** procuress, carrying information (for the adulterers)

69 **In . . . me** i.e. in calling me an *intelligencing bawd*, 67

69, 71 **honest** chaste

58] *as Capell; F lines* (my Lord) good Queene, / I say good Queene. /   59 good, so] *Theobald;* good
so, F   65 SD] *Rowe subst. after* blessing

Than you are mad, which is enough, I'll warrant,   70
As this world goes, to pass for honest.

LEONTES   Traitors!
Will you not push her out? [*to Antigonus*] Give her the
    bastard,
Thou dotard; thou art woman-tired, unroosted
By thy Dame Partlet here. Take up the bastard,
Take't up, I say; give't to thy crone.

PAULINA [*to Antigonus*]   For ever   75
Unvenerable be thy hands if thou
Tak'st up the princess by that forced baseness
Which he has put upon't.

LEONTES   He dreads his wife.

PAULINA
So I would you did. Then 'twere past all doubt
You'd call your children yours.

LEONTES   A nest of traitors!   80

ANTIGONUS
I am none, by this good light.

PAULINA   Nor I, nor any
But one that's here, and that's himself; for he
The sacred honour of himself, his queen's,
His hopeful son's, his babe's, betrays to slander,

---

71 **As . . . goes** Cf. the proverbial 'Thus
goes the world' (Dent, W884.1) and
Ham 2.2.175.
73 **dotard** old fool
    woman-tired henpecked, from 'tire',
    falconry term, to tear flesh with a beak
    (*OED v.*[2] 2a); cf. 1.2.15 and n.
    unroosted (a rooster) driven off
    your perch, i.e. your authority is
    usurped
74 **Dame Partlet** Partlet, the hen in
    stories of Reynard the Fox (Pertelotte
    in Chaucer's *Nun's Priest's Tale*), was
    a disrespectful term for a domineering
    woman. Cf. *Lady Margery*, 158 (see
    n.), *1H4* 3.3.51.

75 **crone** withered old woman (*OED n.*
    1); old ewe (*n.* 2). Leontes first likens
    Paulina to an angry clucking hen, then
    a bleating old sheep.
76 **Unvenerable** unblessed; *OED*'s first
    citation
77–8 **by . . . upon't** and by doing so
    accept the wrongful title of bastard he
    has forced on her
78 **dreads** is in awe of
81 **none** not one
    by . . . light a solemn oath, perhaps
    invoking the sun god, Apollo, to whom
    Leontes appealed at 2.1.180–7
84 **hopeful** from whom great things are
    expected

72 SD] *Rowe*   75 SD] *Oxf*

Whose sting is sharper than the sword's; and will not –   85
For, as the case now stands, it is a curse
He cannot be compelled to't – once remove
The root of his opinion, which is rotten
As ever oak or stone was sound.

LEONTES   A callat
Of boundless tongue, who late hath beat her husband,   90
And now baits me! This brat is none of mine.
It is the issue of Polixenes.
Hence with it, and together with the dam
Commit them to the fire.

PAULINA   It is yours,
And might we lay th'old proverb to your charge,   95
So like you, 'tis the worse. Behold, my lords,
Although the print be little, the whole matter
And copy of the father – eye, nose, lip,
The trick of's frown, his forehead, nay, the valley,
The pretty dimples of his chin and cheek, his smiles,   100
The very mould and frame of hand, nail, finger.

---

85 **Whose . . . sword's** Cf. Dent, S521.1, 'Slander is sharper than a sword'; *Cym* 3.4.32–3.

85–8 **will . . . opinion** the king will never for a moment change his mind (i.e. dig his opinion out at the *root*, 88) because, as things stand now, it's an evil (*curse*, 86) he can't be made to reconsider

89 **callat** scold; whore, lewd female companion of beggars (cf. 4.3.2, 11, and see nn.).

90 **Of boundless tongue** who speaks without restraint; see 2.2.32n.
late hath beat has recently beaten up; *beat*, pronounced 'bait', puns on *baits*, 91.

91 **baits** harasses
none of mine nothing to do with me; cf. 1.2.265 (see n.).

92 **is** The metre requires this to be stressed; Leontes is increasingly insistent, i.e. 'it *is* Polixenes' child'.

issue offspring

93–4 **Hence . . . fire** In *Pandosto*, when the king hears Bellaria has given birth to a 'fair and beautiful daughter', he decides immediately that she 'and the young infant should be burnt with fire' (p. 414).

93 **dam** mother (see 1.2.137n.)

95 **lay . . . charge** apply the old proverb to you (a child so like a parent as to be the worse for it: Dent, L290)

97–8 **Although . . . father** though the copy is a small one, the entire substance and image of the father (printing metaphor: *copy*, manuscript from which a book was printed, *OED n.* 9a). Cf. 5.1.124–5.

99 **trick of's frown** characteristic way he frowns. Cf. *AW* 1.1.97.
valley indentation in the upper lip or under the lower lip; cleft in the chin

101 **mould and frame** design and shape

212

And thou, good goddess Nature, which hast made it
So like to him that got it, if thou hast
The ordering of the mind too, 'mongst all colours,
No yellow in't, lest she suspect, as he does,   105
Her children not her husband's.

LEONTES   A gross hag!
[*to Antigonus*] And, lozel, thou art worthy to be hanged,
That wilt not stay her tongue.

ANTIGONUS   Hang all the husbands
That cannot do that feat, you'll leave yourself
Hardly one subject.

LEONTES   Once more, take her hence!   110

PAULINA

A most unworthy and unnatural lord
Can do no more.

LEONTES   I'll ha' thee burnt.

PAULINA   I care not.
It is an heretic that makes the fire,

---

102 **goddess Nature** Cf. *KL* 1.4.267,
Cym 4.2.170; and see pp. 53–8.
103 **got** begot, fathered
103–5 **if . . . in't** if you're responsible
for shaping the mind as well, don't let
there be jealousy in her; with a quibble
on *yellow*, the colour of jealousy (see
also 105–6n.), and *colours* meaning
characteristics
105–6 **lest . . . husband's** in case she
suspects, as her father does now, her
own children aren't her husband's, i.e.
it would be as preposterous for Perdita
to doubt her children's legitimacy as it
is for Leontes to doubt hers. Leontes'
wicked 'preposterousness' in Acts 1–3
is followed by a benevolent inversion
of order in Act 5 (see 5.2.145n.). The
expression 'all looks yellow to the
jaundiced eye' (Tilley, A160) may be
relevant. Kiessling (94–5) suggests an
allusion to the incubus which, while

disguised as their husbands, was said
to impregnate women, or to swap
changelings for newborn children
(3.3.115 (see n.), 4.4.691): i.e. if Perdita
inherited *yellow* from Leontes, it might
cause a fear, as irrational as his, that
her children had been fathered by a
sprite or were changelings.
106 **gross hag** rude and repulsive old
woman
107 **lozel** worthless fellow
108 **stay** stop
112 **no more** nothing worse
thee Leontes avoids speaking directly
to Paulina until now. He uses the
informal second-person pronoun to put
her down, addressing her, as he does
Antigonus, as if she were a contempt-
ible inferior. See 5.1.17n. and 1.2.43n.
113–14 **It . . . in't** Paulina twists
Leontes' threat to have her burnt for
treason (like Hermione at 8: see n.)

107 SD] *Oxf*

Not she which burns in't. I'll not call you tyrant;
But this most cruel usage of your queen,   115
Not able to produce more accusation
Than your own weak-hinged fancy, something savours
Of tyranny, and will ignoble make you,
Yea, scandalous to the world.

LEONTES   On your allegiance,
Out of the chamber with her! Were I a tyrant,   120
Where were her life? She durst not call me so
If she did know me one. Away with her!

PAULINA

I pray you do not push me, I'll be gone.
Look to your babe, my lord, 'tis yours – Jove send her
A better guiding spirit. What needs these hands?   125
You that are thus so tender o'er his follies
Will never do him good, not one of you.

---

to declare he is the heretic, not her.
He is making a fire to burn her, the
true believer in Hermione's innocence
(possibly comparing herself to religious martyrs). Her larger point is
that Leontes can execute her and the
queen, but punishment doesn't mean a
crime was committed.

114 **tyrant** In 2.3 this is the closest
Paulina comes to calling Leontes a
tyrant to his face, though she says it
later (3.2.172). To accuse a king of being
despotic was the gravest of insults, and
the charge preys on Leontes' mind (see
120–2, 3.2.4–6). Apollo confirms he is a
tyrant at 3.2.131.

117 **weak-hinged fancy** ill-supported
delusion (*hinged* as a door hangs; cf.
modern 'unhinged', mentally unsta-
ble).
fancy Cf. *Tem* 5.1.59.
something savours smacks somewhat

119 **Yea** indeed
scandalous dishonourable
to in the eyes of

On i.e. I command you on. Not to
obey after this would be treason.

120 **chamber** audience-chamber (see
1.1n.) or private apartment (*OED n.*
I 1a)

121 **Where . . . life** wouldn't I have had
her executed
durst dare

124–5 **Jove . . . spirit** May Jove send
someone better than you to look after
her. In classical mythology Jove, or
Jupiter, the thunder god ('Jupiter
Tonans'), was father of the gods
and ruler of the universe. Perhaps
Paulina thinks of him as protector
of vulnerable children (in *Cym*
5.4.39–40, Jupiter is father of orphans,
an attribute Shakespeare takes from
Psalms, 68.5, where God is 'father of
the fatherless'). Cf. 3.1.10.

125 **What . . . hands** Why are you grab-
bing me. The Lords try to bundle
her out.

126 **tender oe'r** soft about; the phrase
irks Leontes, who repeats it to
Antigonus at 131.

So, so; farewell, we are gone.   *Exit.*

LEONTES [*to Antigonus*]

    Thou, traitor, hast set on thy wife to this.

    My child? Away with't! Even thou, that hast   130

    A heart so tender o'er it, take it hence,

    And see it instantly consumed with fire.

    Even thou, and none but thou. Take it up straight.

    Within this hour bring me word 'tis done,

    And by good testimony, or I'll seize thy life,   135

    With what thou else call'st thine. If thou refuse,

    And wilt encounter with my wrath, say so;

    The bastard brains with these my proper hands

    Shall I dash out. Go, take it to the fire,

    For thou set'st on thy wife.

ANTIGONUS   I did not, sir.   140

    These lords, my noble fellows, if they please,

    Can clear me in't.

LORDS   We can. My royal liege,

    He is not guilty of her coming hither.

LEONTES

    You're liars all!

LORD

    Beseech your highness, give us better credit.   145

---

128 **So, so** very well (I'll leave); ah, I see how men push women about (see 125n.)

    we . . . gone often said onstage as the equivalent of 'I'm going' (cf. 123), but 'we' was exclusive to royalty. If *we* is an ordinary plural, Paulina may exit with a servant, or by it mean herself and the baby. Alternatively, she means 'we're all done for (he's mad)', probably prolepsis: see 1.2.184n.

132 **see . . . fire** make sure it's burnt to death at once

133 **Even thou** you yourself (Antigonus)
    straight at once

134 **hour** disyllabic

135 **by good testimony** with reliable evidence

135–6 **seize . . . thine** i.e. execute you as a traitor and appropriate your lands

137 **wilt encounter with** wish to stand up to

138 **proper** own

140 **set'st on** incited (contraction of 'settedst')

142 **in't** in it; i.e. of having incited my wife

145 **give . . . credit** think us more honourable (we're not *liars*, 144); you had better believe it.

129 SD] *Oxf*

We have always truly served you, and beseech
So to esteem of us; and on our knees we beg,
As recompense of our dear services
Past and to come, that you do change this purpose,
Which, being so horrible, so bloody, must   150
Lead on to some foul issue. We all kneel.

LEONTES
I am a feather for each wind that blows.
Shall I live on, to see this bastard kneel
And call me father? Better burn it now
Than curse it then. But be it; let it live.   155
It shall not neither. [*to Antigonus*] You, sir, come you
    hither,
You that have been so tenderly officious
With Lady Margery, your midwife there,
To save this bastard's life – for 'tis a bastard,
So sure as this beard's grey. What will you adventure   160
To save this brat's life?

ANTIGONUS   Anything, my lord,

146 *beseech F's apostrophe after 'beseech" indicates the omission of 'you'; cf. *taught*, 2.1.11 (see n.).

148 of for
dear valuable; loving

148–9 services . . . come Kurland (374) notes that this was a formula in letters patent.

151 foul issue terrible outcome

152 a . . . blows Cf. Dent, F162, 'like feathers in the wind' (of inconstancy).

155 be it let it be so; no matter

156 neither for all that; Leontes changes his mind, 'no, the child won't be spared'.

157 tenderly officious eager to do kind acts
tenderly Cf. 3.2.149 and *tender*, 2.3.126, 131.
officious attentive, but also meddle-some

158 Lady Margery In underworld slang a 'margery-prater' was a hen, hence Margery was a contemptuous term for women, especially unruly ones (cf. *Partlet*, 74; see n.); also a common name among midwives.
midwife Leontes mistakenly believes that Paulina helped deliver the baby, and therefore knows that Polixenes is the father (midwives were required to ascertain fathers of newborn children).

160 So as
this beard's grey Leontes is probably 30 at this point (see List of Roles, 2n.) whereas Antigonus is much older (see 164 and n.; 3.3.104–5.). He may gesture to, touch or pull Antigonus' beard.
adventure dare to do

161 brat's The term was often associated with beggary; cf. 3.2.85, *CE* 4.4.38–9.

146 beseech] *(beseech')*; beseech you *Rowe*   156 SD] *Oxf*

216

That my ability may undergo,
And nobleness impose – at least thus much:
I'll pawn the little blood which I have left
To save the innocent – anything possible.   165

LEONTES

It shall be possible. Swear by this sword
Thou wilt perform my bidding.

ANTIGONUS   I will, my lord.

LEONTES

Mark, and perform it, seest thou? For the fail
Of any point in't shall not only be
Death to thyself but to thy lewd-tongued wife,   170
Whom for this time we pardon. We enjoin thee,
As thou art liegeman to us, that thou carry
This female bastard hence, and that thou bear it
To some remote and desert place, quite out
Of our dominions; and that there thou leave it,   175
Without more mercy, to it own protection
And favour of the climate. As by strange fortune
It came to us, I do in justice charge thee,
On thy soul's peril and thy body's torture,

---

162 **undergo** undertake
163 **nobleness impose** a noble mind would order me to perform
164 It was believed that as people aged they had less blood in their bodies. Antigonus offers to *pawn* or risk what little he has left. See 160n., 1.2.71–3n.
165 **innocent** i.e. innocent child
166 **sword** Oaths were often sworn while touching a sword (because the hilt and blade formed a cross): cf. 3.2.122.
168 **Mark** pay attention
168–9 **the . . . in't** the failure to perform any detail of it; for *fail* as noun, cf. *H8* 1.2.145, 2.4.195.
170 **lewd-tongued** ill-mannered (*OED adj.* 4); foul-mouthed
171 **enjoin** order
172 **liegeman** a loyal servant
174 **desert** uninhabited

174–5 **quite out / Of** far beyond
176 **it** its (neuter genitive for possessive pronoun: Abbott, 228), as at 3.2.98
177 **favour . . . climate** whatever kindness the region (*OED* climate *n.*[1] 1a) may offer
177–81 **As . . . it** In *Pandosto* the king decides that because the child 'came by Fortune, so he would commit it to the charge of Fortune' (p. 415). The quibbles are on *strange fortune* (177), *strangely* (180) and *chance* (as Fortune), 181.
177–8 **As . . . us** since the child was fathered here by a foreigner (*strange*, alien); or arrived here by unusual chance
178 **in justice** i.e. because the child deserves banishment
179 **thy body's torture** i.e. on peril of being tormented in hell

217

    That thou commend it strangely to some place   180
    Where chance may nurse or end it. Take it up.

ANTIGONUS

    I swear to do this, though a present death
    Had been more merciful. [*Picks up the baby.*] Come on,
       poor babe,
    Some powerful spirit instruct the kites and ravens
    To be thy nurses. Wolves and bears, they say,   185
    Casting their savageness aside, have done
    Like offices of pity. [*to Leontes*] Sir, be prosperous
    In more than this deed does require; [*to the baby*] and
       blessing
    Against this cruelty, fight on thy side,
    Poor thing, condemned to loss.   *Exit* [*with the baby*].

LEONTES   No, I'll not rear   190
    Another's issue.

Enter a Servant.

SERVANT   Please your highness, posts

180–1 commend . . . ¹it take the child somewhere it is a stranger and where Fortune (*chance*) will either nurture it or let it die; cf. Dent, M874, 'Either mend or end.'

182–3 a . . . been (putting the child to) death straightaway would have been

184 Some may some
   kites and ravens i.e. birds of prey (cf. *Cor* 4.5.44–5); perhaps an allusion to 1 Kings, 17.4–6, where God sent ravens to feed Elijah (Shaheen, 725–6)

185 Wolves and bears In *Tim* 4.3.188, these animals are among the terrors wished on mankind, but there were famous stories of their looking after abandoned children. The orphan twins Romulus and Remus, legendary founders of Rome, were suckled by a she-wolf, and the huntress Atalanta, exposed in the wild by her father, survived by being suckled by a bear, then raised by shepherds.

187 Like . . . pity similar acts of kindness

187–8 be . . . require may you have better fortune than you deserve for this deed

188 blessing (may) divine grace; see 1.2.80n.

190 loss destruction

191 Another's issue another man's child

191 SD See 25 SDn.

191 *Please may it please. F's apostrophe after 'Please' may be in the wrong place (i.e. a mistake for ''Please''), or be a contraction for 'Please it' (i.e. may it please).
   posts messengers; cf. 2.1.182 (see n.).

183 SD] *Oxf¹*   187 SD] *Folger*   188 SD] *Oxf subst.*   190 SD *with the baby*] *Rowe subst.*   191 Please]
(*Please'*)

From those you sent to th'oracle are come
An hour since. Cleomenes and Dion,
Being well arrived from Delphos, are both landed,
Hasting to th' court.

LORD   So please you, sir, their speed   195
Hath been beyond account.

LEONTES   Twenty-three days
They have been absent; 'tis good speed, foretells
The great Apollo suddenly will have
The truth of this appear. Prepare you, lords,
Summon a session, that we may arraign   200
Our most disloyal lady; for, as she hath
Been publicly accused, so shall she have
A just and open trial. While she lives
My heart will be a burden to me. Leave me,   204
And think upon my bidding.   *Exeunt*.

3.1   *Enter* CLEOMENES *and* DION.

CLEOMENES
The climate's delicate, the air most sweet,

193 **since** ago
194 **well** safely
Delphos See 2.1.183n.
196 **beyond account** beyond explanation
(that they have returned so quickly),
rather than unprecedented
Twenty-three Shakespeare's invention. In *Pandosto* it takes three weeks
just to reach Delphos (pp. 417–18).
See List of Roles, 2n.
197 **good speed** remarkably quick (punning on 'a success')
foretells is a sign that
198 **suddenly** very speedily
200 **session** council of the Lords (to sit as
a judicial court)
arraign put on trial
203 **A . . . trial** Leontes has already
prejudged the outcome (he plans to

have Hermione executed), so the trial
cannot be *just*, however *open* or public
it is.
204 **a . . . me** weighed down
205 **think upon** take care to do
3.1 Still in Sicily, the action shifts to a
stopping-point (fresh horses are called
for at 21; see 1.2.94–6n. Back from
Delphos, Cleomenes and Dion are
hastening to court (2.3.191–5).
1–9 Spencer (201–2) shows that
Shakespeare probably borrowed details
of the 'isle' (2) from Virgil's *Aeneid*,
3.73–92: climate (1–2) from 73–8;
temple (2) from 84; dress and conduct
(4–6) from 80–1; 'ear-deafening voice
o'th' oracle' (9) from 90–2.
1 **delicate** temperate; delightful (*OED*
a. 1c)

3.1] *(Actus Tertius. Scena Prima.)*   0.1+ CLEOMENES] *(Cleomines)*

Fertile the isle, the temple much surpassing
The common praise it bears.

DION   I shall report,
For most it caught me, the celestial habits –
Methinks I so should term them – and the reverence   5
Of the grave wearers. O, the sacrifice,
How ceremonious, solemn and unearthly
It was i'th' offering!

CLEOMENES   But of all, the burst
And the ear-deafening voice o'th' oracle,
Kin to Jove's thunder, so surprised my sense   10
That I was nothing.

DION   If th'event o'th' journey
Prove as successful to the queen – O, be't so –
As it hath been to us rare, pleasant, speedy,
The time is worth the use on't.

CLEOMENES   Great Apollo
Turn all to th' best. These proclamations,   15

---

2 **Fertile** fèrtil
   isle Delphos. See 2.1.183n.
3 **common . . . bears** usual praise it
   receives
4–11 **For . . . nothing** Cf. the ecstatic
   reunion described at 5.2.10–19, 42–53,
   80–90, and wonder at 5.3.34–42,
   60–73, 109–11. See pp. 66, 68.
4 **most . . . me** what most caught my
   attention were
   celestial habits religious vestments;
   gorgeous clothes
6 **grave** dignified, sage (*wearers*, Apollo's
   priests)
   sacrifice In pagan rites, slaughtered
   animals were burnt as offerings to the
   gods (cf. *Cym* 5.5.477–9). However, in
   WT pagan and Christian elements are
   often mixed (e.g. at 14–15; see n.), so
   this sacrifice may be symbolic.
7 **unearthly** exalted (*OED*'s first citation)
8 **i'th' offering** i.e. as the sacrifice was
   made
10 **Kin to** like

Jove's thunder See 2.3.124–5n., *Cym*
5.4.114.
surprised overwhelmed
sense senses
11 **I was nothing** I realized how insignificant I was (compared to Apollo); it
   left me dumbfounded and emptied of
   feeling
   event outcome
12 **successful** fortunate; propitious
   (*OED* 3a)
   be't may it be
13 **rare** extraordinary (*OED a.*[1] 5a)
14 **The . . . on't** The time it has taken
   will have been well spent
   on't of it (Abbott, 182). Cf. *Tim*
   3.1.36–7.
14–15 **Apollo . . . best** pagan version of
   'God turn all to good' (Dent, G227.1)
15 **proclamations** (1) sheets posted up
   everywhere with the king's authority,
   accusing Hermione of treason and
   infidelity (see 3.2.99 and n., 4.4.187n.
   on *ballads*); (2) the king's public speaking against Hermione

So forcing faults upon Hermione,
I little like.

DION   The violent carriage of it
Will clear or end the business. When the oracle,
Thus by Apollo's great divine sealed up,
Shall the contents discover, something rare   20
Even then will rush to knowledge. Go. Fresh horses!
And gracious be the issue.   *Exeunt.*

3.2   *Enter* LEONTES, Lords *and* Officers.

LEONTES

This sessions, to our great grief we pronounce,
Even pushes 'gainst our heart; the party tried,
The daughter of a king, our wife, and one
Of us too much beloved. Let us be cleared
Of being tyrannous, since we so openly   5
Proceed in justice, which shall have due course

---

16 **forcing faults upon** (wrongly) attrib-
uting crimes to
17 **violent . . . it** unseemly haste with
which *it* (indictment and trial) has
been handled (*OED* carriage 10: conduct); (2) the breakneck pace to fetch
Apollo's judgement
18 **clear . . . business** settle the matter
one way or the other (proverbial: Dent,
M874); cf. 2.3.180–1 (see n.).
oracle Apollo's answer to the request
for *counsel* (2.1.186) is written on
a scroll, *sealed up* by the *divine*, or
high priest (19); this is sworn to at
3.2.122–8. In *Pandosto* the ambassadors are told to take the scroll they
'find behind the altar' (p. 418).
20 **discover** reveal
21 **rush to knowledge** be known at once
22 **gracious . . . issue** (may there) be a
happy outcome

3.2 See Fig. 11 for the trial setting.
0.1 The 'massed entry' in F (see 2.1.0.1n.)
omits Paulina and the Servant, the
only instance of an incomplete entry,
except for 2.3 which doesn't list the
baby (a stage property).
1–5 Leontes uses the royal 'we' as a
formal reminder of his authority; the
trial is to be conducted in his, the
monarch's, law court.
1 **sessions** trial, proceedings (collective
plural, as at 138)
2 **Even . . . heart** strikes at my very
heart; is the last thing I want to do
party tried defendant to be judged
(*tried*, probably past participle: Blake,
101).
3 **a king** the *Emperor of Russia*, 117 (see
n.); cf. 38.
5 **being tyrannous** See 2.3.114n.
6 **in justice** according to our laws

3.2] *(Scæna Secunda.)*   0.1] *Theobald subst.; Enter Leontes, Lords, Officers: Hermione (as to her Triall)*
Ladies: Cleomines, Dion. F

Even to the guilt or the purgation.
Produce the prisoner.

OFFICER
It is his highness' pleasure that the queen
Appear in person here in court.

[*Enter* HERMIONE *as a prisoner, with* PAULINA *and Ladies*.]

                              Silence.   10

LEONTES
Read the indictment.

OFFICER [*Reads*.]   *Hermione, queen to the worthy Leontes,*
King of Sicilia, thou art here accused and arraigned of
high treason in committing adultery with Polixenes, King
of Bohemia, and conspiring with Camillo to take away   15
the life of our sovereign lord the king, thy royal husband;
the pretence whereof being by circumstances partly laid
open, thou, Hermione, contrary to the faith and allegiance
of a true subject, didst counsel and aid them for their better
safety to fly away by night.   20

HERMIONE
Since what I am to say must be but that
Which contradicts my accusation, and
The testimony on my part no other

7   **purgation** acquittal
9   **pleasure** will
10   *****Silence** In F this is in the margin
     in italics, so it may be an SD. More
     likely it is a command by the Officer,
     announcing the entrance of the
     accused and calling the court to order
     (*H8* 2.4.2).
11–20 Travitsky (172–3) distinguishes
     between the *high treason* (14) for which
     Hermione is indicted because of adul-
     tery, and petty treason for conspiring
     to murder her husband. The charge

follows the wording in *Pandosto*: the
queen 'committed adultery with
Egistus and conspired with Franion
to poison Pandosto her husband, but,
their pretence being partly spied, she
counselled them to fly away by night
for their better safety' (p. 416).

13–18 *thou . . . thy . . . thou*   hostile,
     insulting pronouns (see 1.2.43n.)
13   *arraigned of* on trial for
17–18 *pretence . . . open* which plan hav-
     ing been in part exposed by events. Cf.
     'undivulged pretence', *Mac* 2.3.131.

10 SD] *Theobald subst.*   10 Silence] *Rowe; italicized F, as SD*   12 SD] *Capell*

But what comes from myself, it shall scarce boot me
To say 'Not guilty'. Mine integrity   25
Being counted falsehood shall, as I express it,
Be so received. But thus: if powers divine
Behold our human actions – as they do –
I doubt not then but innocence shall make
False accusation blush and tyranny   30
Tremble at patience. You, my lord, best know,
Whom least will seem to do so, my past life
Hath been as continent, as chaste, as true
As I am now unhappy; which is more
Than history can pattern, though devised   35
And played to take spectators. For behold me,
A fellow of the royal bed, which owe
A moiety of the throne; a great king's daughter,
The mother to a hopeful prince, here standing
To prate and talk for life and honour, 'fore   40
Who please to come and hear. For life, I prize it
As I weigh grief, which I would spare. For honour,

24 **scarce boot me** hardly be any advantage for me
26 **as ... it** even as I say it
27–31 **if ... patience** Cf. *Pandosto*: 'If the divine powers be privy to human actions (as no doubt they are), I hope my patience shall make Fortune blush, and my unspotted life shall stain spiteful discredit' (pp. 418–19).
29–30 **innocence ... blush** It was proverbial that a clear conscience wouldn't fear false accusations (Tilley, C597).
31 **Tremble at patience** be shaken by my unwavering trust in providence and the gods (27–8); be fearful as it beholds my resolution and forbearance (*OED* patience *n.*[1] 1b)
33 **continent** self-restrained, virtuous
34–6 **which ... spectators** which (unhappiness) exceeds anything any

story (*history*) can provide precedent for (*OED* pattern *v.* 3), even one turned into a play and performed to please audiences; *take* probably means charm, delight (*OED v.* 10) rather than capture.
37 **A ... bed** i.e. the king's wife, who shares his bed
37–8 **which ... moiety** who has a right to a part
38 **king's daughter** See 3n.
39 **hopeful** in whom the kingdom has great hopes; cf. 2.3.84.
40 **prate** plead in vain; cf. *Cor* 5.3.161.
for to save my
41–2 **For ... grief** as regards my life, I prize it as I value (*OED* weigh *v.*[1] 14b) grief; i.e. my life is only mourning **spare** willingly do without (*OED v.*[1] 8a)
42–4 **For ... for** As for honour, it's something my children inherit; the only reason I am defending myself.

32 Whom] Who *Rowe*   40 'fore] *(fore)*

'Tis a derivative from me to mine,
And only that I stand for. I appeal
To your own conscience, sir, before Polixenes   45
Came to your court how I was in your grace,
How merited to be so; since he came,
With what encounter so uncurrent I
Have strained t'appear thus. If one jot beyond
The bound of honour, or in act, or will   50
That way inclining, hardened be the hearts
Of all that hear me, and my nearest of kin
Cry fie upon my grave.

LEONTES   I ne'er heard yet
That any of these bolder vices wanted
Less impudence to gainsay what they did   55
Than to perform it first.

HERMIONE   That's true enough,
Though 'tis a saying, sir, not due to me.

LEONTES
You will not own it.

HERMIONE   More than mistress of

44–7 ²I . . . so Cf. *Pandosto*: 'How I have
led my life before Egistus' coming, I
appeal, Pandosto, to the gods and to
thy conscience' (p. 419).
46 **grace** favour (*OED n.* 6a). See 1.2.80n.
48–9 **With . . . thus** (tell me) with what
behaviour so unacceptable I have
transgressed that I should have to
appear (on trial) like this
48 **encounter** behaviour (*OED n.* 3)
  uncurrent unacceptable (*OED* 2)
49 **strained** transgressed (*OED* strain *v.*¹
  11b)
50 **bound** bounds, limits
  ¹**or . . . will** either in action or intention
52 **nearest of kin** closest relatives: her
  son and daughter, since her father is
  dead (118)
53 **fie** shame on you (exclamation of

disgust or reproach)
54 **bolder** more shameless
54–6 **wanted . . . first** were more lacking
  in effrontery to deny what they did
  than to do it in the first place (*wanted
  / Less* is a double negative, intensify-
  ing the negation: Abbott, 406); i.e. if
  you were shameless enough to do it
  in the first place, you'd certainly be
  shameless enough to deny you did. See
  1.2.411–12n.
57 **due** applicable
58 **You . . . it** possibly a question (Blake,
  128): you won't admit it?
58–60 **More . . . acknowledge** I utterly
  refuse to acknowledge faults I don't
  possess. Hermione accepts she has
  faults, but denies any of the *bolder
  vices* (54) she is charged with; 'in name
  of fault' may be more specific, mean-

Which comes to me in name of fault, I must not
At all acknowledge. For Polixenes,   60
With whom I am accused, I do confess
I loved him as in honour he required;
With such a kind of love as might become
A lady like me; with a love, even such,
So, and no other, as yourself commanded;   65
Which not to have done, I think, had been in me
Both disobedience and ingratitude
To you and toward your friend, whose love had spoke
Even since it could speak, from an infant, freely
That it was yours. Now, for conspiracy,   70
I know not how it tastes, though it be dished
For me to try how. All I know of it
Is that Camillo was an honest man;
And why he left your court the gods themselves,
Wotting no more than I, are ignorant.   75

LEONTES

You knew of his departure, as you know
What you have underta'en to do in's absence.

HERMIONE   Sir,

You speak a language that I understand not.

---

ing 'what you now term a fault', i.e.
the chaste love I showed Polixenes,
according to your command (64–5).

62 **as . . . required** as, given my reputation and his position (*OED* honour *n*.
3a, 4a), he was entitled to expect

64 **like me** i.e. of my rank and character

64–5 **even such / So** just such, and in the
same measure

67 **disobedience and ingratitude** i.e.
disobedience to him as her king and
husband, and ingratitude to Polixenes,
given his position and friendly love
towards her

70 **for** regarding

71–2 **though . . . how** even if it were

served up for me; Hermione means
that she is absolutely ignorant about
conspiracy, 70.

73 **honest** honourable, trustworthy

75 **Wotting** knowing

77 i.e. to murder me
underta'en pledged (*OED* undertake
v. 4c)
in's in his

78 **understand not** Hermione's response
to *underta'en* (77) may be a quibble on
understand and *stand*, 79; *underta'en*
could mean understand (*OED v*. 3;
though not recorded after *c*. 1510). Cf.
Oth 4.2.32–3, 'I understand a fury in
your words, / But not the words.'

69 Even] Ever *(Furness)*

225

My life stands in the level of your dreams,
Which I'll lay down.

LEONTES   Your actions are my dreams.   80
You had a bastard by Polixenes,
And I but dreamed it. As you were past all shame –
Those of your fact are so – so past all truth;
Which to deny concerns more than avails; for as
Thy brat hath been cast out, like to itself,   85
No father owning it – which is indeed
More criminal in thee than it – so thou
Shalt feel our justice, in whose easiest passage
Look for no less than death.

HERMIONE   Sir, spare your threats.
The bug which you would fright me with I seek.   90
To me can life be no commodity;
The crown and comfort of my life, your favour,
I do give lost, for I do feel it gone
But know not how it went. My second joy,

79–80 **My ... down** My life is the target (*level*: see 2.3.5–6n.) of your deluded fantasies, and I'll surrender it.

80 **Your ... dreams** (1) what you have done with Polixenes fills my dreams; (2) do you think I'm merely dreaming what you have actually done?; (3) the nightmares of your infidelity and plots haunt my dreams; (4) when I dream I learn what your actions really are; (5) it's your actions, rather than my imaginings, that trouble me. See 82n. and 1.2.326–7n.

82 **but dreamed it** This is precisely what Leontes has done, fallen into a gross reverie, imagining Hermione is pregnant by Polixenes.

82, 83 **past all** entirely without

83 **of your fact** guilty of your crime (*OED* fact *n.* 1c; cf. *Cym* 3.2.16)

84 **Which ... avails** your denial of which (*truth*, 83) is more important to you than any effect it is having (*OED*

avail *v.* 1a)
concerns Cf. *LLL* 4.2.140.

85 **brat** See 2.3.161n.

85–6 **like ... it** like the outcast it is, unacknowledged by its father

86–7 **which ... it** i.e. your giving birth to a *bastard* (81) is more criminal than its illegitimacy

88–9 **in ... death** i.e. the mildest form of justice you can hope for is death; a threat of torture

90 **bug** bugbear or hobgoblin (*OED n.* 1a), frightful thing: cf. Dent, B703, 'Bugbears to scare babes'. See pp. 133–4.

91 life for me is worthless (no *commodity*, of no advantage to me)

92 **crown and comfort** supreme joy
favour loving regard; *favour* may be used metaphorically as a love token (a glove or ribbon), which Hermione has lost, but doesn't know how (93–4).

93 **do give** consider; give up as

And first fruits of my body, from his presence   95
I am barred, like one infectious. My third comfort,
Starred most unluckily, is from my breast,
The innocent milk in it most innocent mouth,
Haled out to murder; myself on every post
Proclaimed a strumpet; with immodest hatred   100
The childbed privilege denied, which 'longs
To women of all fashion; lastly, hurried
Here, to this place, i'th' open air, before
I have got strength of limit. Now, my liege,
Tell me what blessings I have here alive,   105
That I should fear to die. Therefore proceed.
But yet hear this – mistake me not – no life,
I prize it not a straw, but for mine honour,
Which I would free – if I shall be condemned
Upon surmises, all proofs sleeping else   110
But what your jealousies awake, I tell you

95 **first . . . body** my first child (Mamillius); Shakespeare's only use of the phrase 'first fruits', associated with death and sacrifice (Shaheen, 726; I Corinthians, 15.20: 'But now is Christ risen from the dead, and was made the first fruits of them that slept')

96 **third comfort** i.e. Perdita, just born

97 **Starred most unluckily** born under a very unlucky star; cf. 2.1.106–7 (see n.).

97–8 **from . . . mouth** Perdita is breast-fed; see 2.1.56n.

98 **it** its; see 2.3.176n.

99 **Haled . . . murder** dragged away to be murdered
post i.e. proclamations fixed to posts; see 3.1.15n.

100 **immodest** excessive

101 **childbed privilege** the right of rest and seclusion after giving birth (Cressy, 83–4)

101–2 **'longs . . . fashion** is the right of (belongs to) every woman irrespective of rank

103 **open air** Fresh air was thought dangerous to invalids (cf. Tilley, A93, and *TN* 3.4.127–8) and women after childbirth. The court is either out of doors, or Hermione has been *hurried* (102) to the courtroom, not in a private carriage befitting her rank and condition, but in public view, on foot or in an open cart like a prostitute (*strumpet*, 100).

104 **got . . . limit** recovered my strength in the time allowed after childbirth (*limit*, prescribed period; cf. *MM* 3.1.214); recovered my strength, safe within the confines of my room; regained a limited degree of strength

105 **alive** while alive

107–9 **no . . . free** it's not my life (I'm defending), since I care nothing for it, it's my reputation. Cf. Dent, S917, 'Not to give a straw'.

110–11 **all . . . awake** all the evidence left unexamined except for what your suspicions have conjured up

101 'longs] *(longs)*   104 limit] limbs *F3*

'Tis rigour, and not law. Your honours all,
I do refer me to the oracle.
Apollo be my judge.

LORD   This your request
Is altogether just. Therefore bring forth,   115
And in Apollo's name, his oracle.   [*Exeunt certain Officers.*]

HERMIONE
The Emperor of Russia was my father.
O that he were alive, and here beholding
His daughter's trial; that he did but see
The flatness of my misery; yet with eyes   120
Of pity, not revenge.

[*Enter* Officers *with* CLEOMENES *and* DION.]

OFFICER
You here shall swear upon this sword of justice,
That you, Cleomenes and Dion, have
Been both at Delphos, and from thence have brought
This sealed-up oracle, by the hand delivered   125
Of great Apollo's priest; and that since then
You have not dared to break the holy seal,
Nor read the secrets in't.

CLEOMENES, DION   All this we swear.

LEONTES
Break up the seals and read.

---

112 **'Tis ... law** it's tyranny not justice.
A variation of 'rigour of the law' (*OED*
rigour 2b): cf. 'rigour of the statute',
MM 1.4.67.

112–13 **Your ... me** All my lords, I
appeal. Blake (106) suggests *all* is an
adverb qualifying *do refer me*, i.e. I
surrender myself entirely.

116 **his oracle** See 125n.

117 In *Pandosto*, the wife of the Polixenes

character is the Emperor of Russia's
daughter (p. 413).

120 **flatness** absoluteness (*OED* 5b, only
citation). Hermione may have in mind
a limitless expanse, e.g. the steppes of
Russia, her homeland.

122 **swear ... justice** The *sword*
symbolizes the court's authority. Cf.
2.3.166 (see n.).

125 **oracle** scroll (see 3.1.18n.)

116 SD] *Capell*   121.1] *Capell subst.*   128 SP] *(Cleo Dio.)*

OFFICER [*Reads.*]   *Hermione is chaste, Polixenes blameless,*   130
    Camillo a true subject, Leontes a jealous tyrant, his
    innocent babe truly begotten, and the king shall live
    without an heir if that which is lost be not found.

LORDS
    Now blessed be the great Apollo!

HERMIONE   Praised!

LEONTES
    Hast thou read truth?

OFFICER   Ay, my lord, even so   135
    As it is here set down.

LEONTES
    There is no truth at all i'th' oracle.
    The sessions shall proceed – this is mere falsehood.

[*Enter a* Servant.]

SERVANT
    My lord the king! The king!

LEONTES   What is the business?

SERVANT
    O sir, I shall be hated to report it.   140
    The prince your son, with mere conceit and fear
    Of the queen's speed, is gone.

LEONTES   How, 'gone'?

SERVANT   Is dead.

LEONTES
    Apollo's angry, and the heavens themselves

130–3 The wording in *Pandosto*: '*that which is lost*' (133) alludes to Perdita (see 3.3.32, List of Roles, 8n.).

135 **even so** exactly

137–8 In *Pandosto*, the king accepts Apollo's judgement at once, then hears his son has died (p. 419).

138 **mere** utter

141–2 **with . . . speed** from nothing more than the thought (*OED* conceit *n.* 11) and fear of the queen's fate (*OED* speed *n.* 3b)

142 **gone** See 1.2.184n., *KJ* 3.4.163.

143 **Apollo's angry** Apollo was the god of sudden death as well as prophecy.

---

130 SD] *Capell*   135–6 Ay . . . down] *as Capell; one line F*   138.1] *Rowe*

Do strike at my injustice. [*Hermione faints.*]
                              How now there?

PAULINA
This news is mortal to the queen. Look down   145
And see what death is doing.

LEONTES   Take her hence.
Her heart is but o'ercharged. She will recover.
I have too much believed mine own suspicion.
Beseech you, tenderly apply to her
Some remedies for life.

              [*Exeunt Paulina and Ladies, carrying Hermione,
                                        and Servant.*]

                            Apollo, pardon   150
My great profaneness 'gainst thine oracle.
I'll reconcile me to Polixenes,
New woo my queen, recall the good Camillo,
Whom I proclaim a man of truth, of mercy;
For being transported by my jealousies   155
To bloody thoughts and to revenge, I chose
Camillo for the minister to poison
My friend Polixenes, which had been done,
But that the good mind of Camillo tardied
My swift command. Though I with death and with   160
Reward did threaten and encourage him,
Not doing it and being done, he, most humane
And filled with honour, to my kingly guest

---

145 **Look down** i.e. look down, you gods;
  cf. *Tem* 5.1.201.
147 **o'ercharged** overburdened (by the
  strain)
149 **tenderly** Cf. 2.3.157 (see n.).
155 **transported** carried away (*OED v.*
  3)
157 **for the minister** as the instrument
158 **had** would have

159 **tardied** delayed; *OED*'s first citation
  (tardy *v.*)
160 **swift command** order to do it at
  once
160–2 ¹**with . . . done** I threatened him
  with death if he didn't do it, and
  promised him a reward if he did (*being
  done*, participle without noun: Abbott,
  378).

144 SD] *Rowe* 149 Beseech] ('Beseech) 150 SD *Exeunt . . . Hermione*] *Rowe, at 147* 150 SD
and Servant] *this edn*

Unclasped my practice, quit his fortunes here –
Which you knew great – and to the certain hazard   165
Of all incertainties himself commended,
No richer than his honour. How he glisters
Through my rust! And how his piety
Does my deeds make the blacker!

[*Enter* PAULINA.]

PAULINA   Woe the while!
O cut my lace, lest my heart, cracking it,   170
Break too.

LORD   What fit is this, good lady?

PAULINA

What studied torments, tyrant, hast for me?
What wheels, racks, fires? What flaying, boiling
In leads or oils? What old or newer torture
Must I receive, whose every word deserves   175

164 **Unclasped** revealed
   practice plot, trick; cf. *TN* 5.1.346.
   fortunes position and possessions
165–7 ***to ... honour** submitted (*commended*) himself to the definite peril
   (*OED* hazard *n.* 3) of every possible
   uncertain outcome (*incertainties*),
   leaving himself with nothing more
   (*No richer*) than his honour. In F
   there are only three stressed syllables
   in 165; *certain*, from F2, gives a
   Shakespearean balance to *incertainties*
   at 166.
167–8 **How ... rust** How he glitters
   through the layer of rust I tried to
   cast over his honour. The image is
   of bright armour Leontes failed to
   tarnish. If *Through* at 168 is monosyllabic, the line is metrically short (see
   pp. 127–8), but it might be emended
   to the disyllabic *Thorough*. F2's 'dark
   rust' is an unconvincing guess.
168 **piety** virtuous behaviour

169 **Woe the while** now grieve; literally,
   woe for the present time
170 **cut my lace** cut the laces of my
   bodice; i.e. help me to breathe, my
   heart is going to burst with grief. It
   was believed women might avoid faint-
   ing if the stays on their tight bodices
   were cut; cf. *AC* 1.3.72.
   cracking it bursting through the laces
171 **fit** madness
172 **studied** expertly devised
   tyrant Leontes is now openly called a
   tyrant; cf. 2.3.114 (see n.).
173 a syllable short, but with five stresses;
   F2's addition, 'Burning', is unnecessary
   (see p. 366).
173–4 **wheels ... oils** types of judicial
   torture: a prisoner's limbs were tied
   to a *wheel* and broken, or stretched on
   a *rack*; in *flaying*, a still-living victim's
   skin was stripped off (see 4.4.788);
   boiling involved putting a prisoner into
   molten lead or oil.

165 certain] *F2; not in F*   168 Through my] Thorough my *Ard²*; Through my dark *F2*   169 SD]
Rowe   173 boiling] boyling? Burning *F2*   174 newer] new *F2*

To taste of thy most worst? Thy tyranny,
Together working with thy jealousies –
Fancies too weak for boys, too green and idle
For girls of nine – O think what they have done,
And then run mad indeed, stark mad, for all   180
Thy bygone fooleries were but spices of it.
That thou betrayed'st Polixenes, 'twas nothing;
That did but show thee, of a fool, inconstant,
And damnable ingrateful. Nor was't much
Thou wouldst have poisoned good Camillo's honour,   185
To have him kill a king – poor trespasses,
More monstrous standing by; whereof I reckon
The casting forth to crows thy baby daughter
To be or none or little, though a devil
Would have shed water out of fire ere done't.   190
Nor is't directly laid to thee the death
Of the young prince, whose honourable thoughts –
Thoughts high for one so tender – cleft the heart
That could conceive a gross and foolish sire

176 **taste of** suffer
  most worst double superlative for emphasis (Abbott, 11)
178 **Fancies . . . boys** notions too foolish for even young boys to believe
  green and idle immature and silly
181 Your former absurdities (*bygone fooleries*) were just foretastes (*OED* spice *n.* 5b) of what you have done now.
183 **of** to be
185–6 **Thou . . . king** Paulina wasn't present when Leontes confessed this (156–60), so she could only know it from Camillo before his sudden departure. Inconsistencies like this and at 3.3.104–5 (see n.) usually go unnoticed in performance.
186–7 **poor . . . by** minor offences, compared with (*standing by*) your more monstrous ones; *poor trespasses* is a shocking understatement, given the

seriousness of regicide.
188 **crows** Cf. *kites and ravens*, 2.3.184 (see n.).
  thy of thy
189 **To . . . little** to be either nothing at all or the smallest of crimes
190 **water** i.e. tears
  out of fire while he burnt in hell-fire; out of his burning eyes. For the paradox of tears and fire together, cf. *H8* 2.4.71–2, *KL* 4.7.47–8 (tears 'like molten lead').
  ere done't sooner than do it
191 **laid** attributable; i.e. he is at least indirectly responsible: see pp. 37–8.
193 **Thoughts . . . tender** noble thoughts for someone so young
193–5 **cleft . . . dam** broke the heart which grasped that his stupid (*gross*) and foolish father had dishonoured his virtuous (*gracious*) mother

183 of] for *F2*

Blemished his gracious dam. This is not, no,   195
Laid to thy answer. But the last – O lords,
When I have said, cry woe! The queen, the queen,
The sweetest, dearest creature's dead, and vengeance
    for't
Not dropped down yet.

LORD   The higher powers forbid!

PAULINA

I say she's dead – I'll swear't. If word nor oath   200
Prevail not, go and see. If you can bring
Tincture or lustre in her lip, her eye,
Heat outwardly or breath within, I'll serve you
As I would do the gods. But O thou tyrant,
Do not repent these things, for they are heavier   205
Than all thy woes can stir. Therefore betake thee
To nothing but despair. A thousand knees,
Ten thousand years together, naked, fasting,
Upon a barren mountain, and still winter
In storm perpetual, could not move the gods   210
To look that way thou wert.

196 **Laid . . . answer** presented as a charge you have to answer
197 **said** finished speaking
198–9 **vengeance . . . yet** i.e. the gods have not yet sent down their punishment
199 **The . . . forbid** May the gods not let it happen (her death).
202 colour to her lip or lustre in her eye; anticipating 'ruddiness upon her lip', 5.3.81 (see n.)
203 **Heat . . . within** warmth in her body (*outwardly*) or breath within her
203–4 **serve . . . gods** i.e. because anyone who could restore Hermione to life must be a god
205 **things** actions; see 1.2.92n.
205–6 **heavier . . . stir** more wicked than all your grieving can make up for (or stir compassion to forgive)
206–7 **betake thee / To** prepare yourself for
207–11 **A . . . wert** The *knees* suggest

two meanings: (1) people kneeling in prayer (synecdoche: figure of speech where part of something is used to represent the whole), seeking forgiveness for Leontes, and after his death doing penance for his sins by going *naked* in storms and *fasting*. Perhaps alluding to the medieval chantries where masses were sung for the souls of the dead to deliver them from purgatory. Paulina means Leontes will be damned in hell for ever, without hope of salvation. (2) If he knelt a thousand times throughout ten thousand years, in never-ending wintry storms, the gods wouldn't feel a jot for him.
208 **together** consecutively
209 **still** always
211 **look . . . wert** turn towards you; i.e. all the prayers won't persuade the gods even to look at you, let alone be merciful

LEONTES   Go on, go on.
> Thou canst not speak too much. I have deserved
> All tongues to talk their bitterest.

LORD [*to Paulina*]   Say no more;
> Howe'er the business goes, you have made fault
> I'th' boldness of your speech.

PAULINA   I am sorry for't.   215
> All faults I make, when I shall come to know them,
> I do repent. Alas, I have showed too much
> The rashness of a woman. He is touched
> To th' noble heart. What's gone and what's past help
> Should be past grief. [*to Leontes*] Do not receive
>   affliction   220
> At my petition; I beseech you, rather
> Let me be punished, that have minded you
> Of what you should forget. Now, good my liege,
> Sir, royal sir, forgive a foolish woman.
> The love I bore your queen – lo, fool again!   225
> I'll speak of her no more, nor of your children.
> I'll not remember you of my own lord,
> Who is lost too. Take your patience to you,
> And I'll say nothing.

LEONTES   Thou didst speak but well
> When most the truth, which I receive much better   230
> Than to be pitied of thee. Prithee bring me

213 **All . . . bitterest** (to have) everyone say the most hurtful things they can
214–15 **made . . . speech** spoken too freely
219–20 **What's . . . grief** Cf. Dent, G453, 'Never grieve for that you cannot help'; C921, 'Past cure past care'; and *Mac* 3.2.11–12.
220–1 **Do . . . petition** Don't let my prayer (that you are beyond forgiveness) cause you pain.
222 **minded you** reminded you; put you in mind
225 **lo, fool again** there I go again, foolishly reminding you of her
227 **remember** remind
227–8 **my . . . too** Paulina is certain Antigonus won't come back.
228 **Take . . . you** arm yourself with patience (cf. Dent, H328.1, 'Take a man's heart to thee')
229–30 **Thou . . . truth** you only spoke properly when you were most truthful

213 SD] *Oxf*   220 SD] *Oxf*

254

To the dead bodies of my queen and son.
One grave shall be for both. Upon them shall
The causes of their death appear, unto
Our shame perpetual. Once a day I'll visit   235
The chapel where they lie, and tears shed there
Shall be my recreation. So long as nature
Will bear up with this exercise, so long
I daily vow to use it. Come, and lead me   239
To these sorrows.   *Exeunt.*

3.3   *Enter* ANTIGONUS, *[carrying the] baby,*
                          [with] a Mariner.

ANTIGONUS
    Thou art perfect, then, our ship hath touched upon
    The deserts of Bohemia?
MARINER   Ay, my lord, and fear
    We have landed in ill time. The skies look grimly
    And threaten present blusters. In my conscience,

233–5 **One . . . perpetual** In *Pandosto*,
the king has his wife 'embalmed and
wrapped in lead with her young son'
and erects a 'sepulchre wherein he
entombed them both'. The epitaph on
the tomb urges passers-by to curse him
for causing her death (p. 420).
235 **Our** a switch either to the royal
pronoun (he has brought shame on
himself but also on his sacred role as
king), or to the collective pronoun (he
has brought shame on all of Sicilia)
236 **chapel** at this date used of both
pagan and Christian places of worship
(*OED n.* 1–5, 6; *MA* 5.4.71, *Cym*
2.2.33); cf. the chapel in Paulina's
house, 5.3.86.
237 **recreation** diversion, pastime (meant
ironically: there will be no pleasure in
it). The word also means remaking,

re-creating (his penitent spirit).
237–8 **So . . . exercise** for as long as my
body can endure this habitual duty or
perform this ceremony (*OED* exercise
n. 2–4). Leontes vows to visit the tomb
every day for the rest of his life (*daily
vow*, 239).
240 **sorrows** i.e. the bodies of Hermione
and Mamillius
3.3 Set on the shore of Bohemia, this
is the first scene in the play entirely
invented by Shakespeare.
1 **perfect** certain
touched upon come to shore on. For
the imaginary coastline, see pp. 100–2.
2 **deserts** wild, uninhabited lands
4 **present blusters** imminent storms
In my conscience I truly believe
(*conscience* also meant sense of right
and wrong)

3.3] *(Scæna Tertia.)*   0.1] *Rowe subst.; Enter Antigonus, a Marriner, Babe, Sheepeheard, and Clowne.* F

The heavens with that we have in hand are angry,   5
And frown upon's.

ANTIGONUS
    Their sacred wills be done. Go get aboard;
    Look to thy barque; I'll not be long before
    I call upon thee.

MARINER   Make your best haste, and go not
    Too far i'th' land; 'tis like to be loud weather.   10
    Besides, this place is famous for the creatures
    Of prey that keep upon't.

ANTIGONUS   Go thou away;
    I'll follow instantly.

MARINER   I am glad at heart
    To be so rid o'th' business.   *Exit.*

ANTIGONUS   Come, poor babe.
    I have heard, but not believed, the spirits o'th' dead   15
    May walk again. If such thing be, thy mother
    Appeared to me last night, for ne'er was dream
    So like a waking. To me comes a creature,
    Sometimes her head on one side, some another;
    I never saw a vessel of like sorrow,   20
    So filled and so becoming. In pure white robes,

---

5 **heavens** i.e. gods
   that . . . hand what we're doing
6 **upon's** upon us
7 **Their . . . done** i.e. may it happen as
   the gods wish; an echo of the Lord's
   Prayer, Matthew, 6.10, 'Thy will be
   done' (Shaheen, 726)
8 **Look . . . barque** Look after your
   ship.
9 **your best haste** the greatest haste you
   can
10 **i'th' land** inland
   'tis . . . weather there's likely to be a
   storm
12 **keep upon't** live in it
15–40 **I . . . this** See pp. 5–7.
15 **spirits o'th' dead** Antigonus' scepti-
   cism (*not believed*) is in line with the

Protestant doctrine that ghosts did not
exist and were delusions produced by
the Devil.
16 **If . . . be** if this is the case; if such
   beings exist
18 **a waking** being awake; i.e. what happened wasn't like a dream, so the
   creature must have been a ghost. Cf.
   37–8, and see 1.2.326–7n.
19 **some another** sometimes on the
   other
20–1 **vessel . . . becoming** such a sorrowful person, so overflowing with
   grief (*filled*) and so beautiful. The
   metaphor of the body as a vessel
   derives from the Bible, e.g. 1 Peter,
   3.7, 'giving honour unto the woman,
   as unto the weaker vessel'.

Like very sanctity, she did approach
My cabin where I lay, thrice bowed before me,
And, gasping to begin some speech, her eyes
Became two spouts; the fury spent, anon   25
Did this break from her: 'Good Antigonus,
Since fate, against thy better disposition,
Hath made thy person for the thrower-out
Of my poor babe according to thine oath,
Places remote enough are in Bohemia;   30
There weep, and leave it crying; and for the babe
Is counted lost for ever, Perdita
I prithee call't. For this ungentle business
Put on thee by my lord, thou ne'er shalt see
Thy wife Paulina more.' And so, with shrieks,   35
She melted into air. Affrighted much,
I did in time collect myself, and thought
This was so and no slumber. Dreams are toys,
Yet for this once, yea superstitiously,
I will be squared by this. I do believe   40
Hermione hath suffered death, and that
Apollo would – this being indeed the issue
Of King Polixenes – it should here be laid,

22 **very sanctity** holiness itself
23 **cabin** berth (*OED n.* 5b)
25 **spouts** fountains of tears (cf. 5.2.54–5,
   an image of water gushing from a
   conduit; see n.)
   the fury spent her violent fit of
   weeping over
   anon immediately
28 **thrower-out** *OED*'s only citation
   before 1963; probably Shakespeare's
   invention
30 **Bohemia** This makes Antigonus
   believe the baby is Polixenes' (42–3).
31 **for** because
32 **Perdita** See 3.2.130–3n.
33 **For** on account of
   ungentle ignoble; unkind, violent
   (*OED* 3a); unfitting for someone of

high birth like you (*OED* 2c)
34 **Put** imposed
35 **more** again
   shrieks Cf. 5.1.65–6 (see n.).
38 **This . . . slumber** this happened and
   I hadn't been sleeping; cf. 18 (see n.).
   toys trivial things
39–40 **yea . . . this** even though I'm
   being superstitious, I'll be guided by
   what was said. Antigonus acknowledges Protestant teaching, that belief
   in ghosts is irreligious (see 15n.),
   but decides he has seen one. See
   p. 3.
40 **squared** guided (*OED v.* 4a; cf. *AW*
   2.1.149)
42 **would** desires that
   issue offspring

Either for life or death, upon the earth
Of its right father. Blossom, speed thee well!   45
   [*Lays the baby down in a mantle, with a box and letters.*]
There lie, and there thy character. There these,
Which may, if Fortune please, both breed thee, pretty,
And still rest thine.   [*Thunder*]
              The storm begins. Poor wretch,
That for thy mother's fault art thus exposed
To loss, and what may follow! Weep I cannot,   50

44 Either . . . death to live or die
upon the earth on the ground; in the
country
45 right rightful
   Blossom little flower; an endearment
   for a baby (cf. modern 'petal'); used of
   a promising child in *2H4* 2.2.90
   speed thee well may you enjoy good
   fortune; i.e. good luck (*thee* for thou,
   accusative for nominative: Abbott,
   212)
45 SD See 4.4.699n.
   mantle The mantle is Hermione's
   cloak or blanket (*OED n.* 1, 3), to
   which her jewel is attached (5.2.32–3);
   this is wrapped around the baby who is
   dressed in the christening gown (*bearing cloth*, 112; see n.) in which Paulina
   brought her to Leontes straight from
   the prison (see 2.2.36–41, 2.3.40n.).
   The baby in *Pandosto* is found in 'a
   mantle of scarlet, richly embroidered
   with gold' (p. 421).
   box of gold coins which the Clown
   opens at 117 and is brought onstage at
   4.4.686.1 (see n.)
   letters in his handwriting (see 46n.)
46 there thy character beside you a
   written account of who you are (the
   letters of Antigonus, 5.2.33–4). At this
   date character didn't mean personality
   but handwriting (*OED n.* 4c); see 45
   SDn. on *letters*, 5.2.35.
46–7 *There . . . pretty* There lie these
   (coins: see 45 SDn. on *box*) that may,
   if Fortune permits, be enough to pay

for your upbringing (*breed thee*), pretty
child.
47 pretty probably a noun (like *Blossom*,
   45), but Blake (107–8) says it may
   be an adverb, qualifying *breed*, i.e.
   'there's enough money to bring you up
   elegantly (prettily)'. F has parentheses,
   '(pretty)', but these aren't reliable
   indicators: see pp. 356–7.
48 And . . . thine and the remainder
   be yours to use. Antigonus probably
   means there is a large enough number
   of coins to spend on the child's
   upbringing without lessening the total
   very much.
48 SD, 55 SD Most thunder in
   Shakespeare has supernatural meanings. According to Shirley (109) only
   here and in *KL* and *Per* is there
   'purely natural thunder', but here
   it may indicate Apollo's displeasure
   (5–6), since he uses thunder to communicate with humans (3.1.9–10).
   The sound of thunder was imitated
   offstage by rolling cannon balls down
   a trough with an uneven inside
   (Shirley, 251).
50 loss ruin (as at 2.3.190); estrange-
   ment **what may follow** whatever else may
   happen to you. Antigonus avoids saying she is most likely to starve or be
   eaten by animals.
   Weep I cannot The spectre told
   Antigonus to weep (31), but he can't
   or won't, perhaps numb with guilt or
   thinking it would be unmanly.

45 SD *Lays . . . down*] Rowe subst.   *in . . . letters*] this edn   48 SD] Bevington

But my heart bleeds, and most accursed am I
To be by oath enjoined to this. Farewell.
The day frowns more and more. Thou'rt like to have
A lullaby too rough. I never saw
The heavens so dim by day.

[*Thunder, and the sounds of dogs barking and hunting horns*]

A savage clamour!   55

Well may I get aboard. This is the chase.
I am gone for ever!   *Exit, pursued by a bear.*

[*Enter* SHEPHERD.]

SHEPHERD   I would there were no age between ten and
three-and-twenty, or that youth would sleep out the
rest; for there is nothing in the between but getting   60
wenches with child, wronging the ancientry, stealing,

---

52 **enjoined to** required to do
53 **frowns** grows overcast and menacing
55–7 It is not clear what effects
Shakespeare was seeking. The storm,
begun at 48, continues, probably growing louder (54–5); there is a hunt in
progress (63–4), perhaps pursuing the
Bear that chases Antigonus offstage at
57 SD. How horrible, darkly comic or
bathetic the Bear's entry and pursuit
are supposed to be is as uncertain as
the meaning of Antigonus' final words
(see 57n.).
55 SD The sound of barking was imitated
offstage by actors or made by specially
trained dogs (Shirley, 10–11).
55 **A savage clamour** what a terrible
noise (i.e. from the storm and hunt);
what a savage roar (i.e. from the
Bear)
56 **Well . . . aboard** I'll be lucky to make
it back to the ship.
This . . . chase These are the sounds
of hunters; this is the hunt (and I'm
the prey). Cf. 5.1.188 (see n.).
57 **gone for ever** certain to die (see

1.2.184n.). In early productions perhaps this was also a remark from the
actor playing Antigonus, i.e. 'I won't
be seen in this role again' – appropriate
if the actor was well known and would
be playing other parts later in the play
(for early doubling of roles in *WT*, see
pp. 115–17).
57 SD See 4.4. 807n. and pp. 133–5.
58 Pope began a new scene here, on
the neoclassical principle that the
stage was cleared at 57, but this
interrupts the continuity of action.
The clowning that follows, in places
sending up the deaths of the sailors
and Antigonus (88–99), draws on the
audience's unsettled emotions after
the shock of the Bear's entry, however
it is staged.
59–60 **sleep . . . rest** spend the interval in sleep, i.e. between 10 and
23 (58–9). See List of Roles, 2n.;
1.2.326–7n.
61 **wenches with child** unmarried girls
pregnant
the ancientry their elders

55 SD] *Oxf*¹ *subst.*   57.1] *F2 (Enter a Shepherd)*

fighting – hark you now, would any but these boiled-
brains of nineteen and two-and-twenty hunt this
weather? They have scared away two of my best sheep,
which I fear the wolf will sooner find than the master.   65
If anywhere I have them, 'tis by the seaside, browsing
of ivy. Good luck, an't be thy will! [*Sees the baby.*]
What have we here? Mercy on's, a bairn! A very pretty
bairn. A boy or a child, I wonder? A pretty one, a
very pretty one – sure some scape; though I am not   70
bookish, yet I can read waiting-gentlewoman in the
scape. This has been some stair-work, some trunk-
work, some behind-door-work. They were warmer
that got this than the poor thing is here. I'll take it up

62 **hark you now** now listen to this
62–3 **boiled-brains** hotheads; addle-
brained youths. Cf. *Tem* 5.1.59–60.
64 **two . . . sheep** Heims (6) suggests the
lost sheep (just one in *Pandosto*: p. 421)
are meant to recall the *twinned lambs*,
Leontes and Polixenes (1.2.67–8, where
loss of boyhood is emphasized). Cf.
John, 10.1–16, for the parable of the
shepherd protecting his sheep from the
wolf because he owns them (cf. *master*,
65) and is not just a hired man.
66 **If . . . them** if I find them anywhere
66–7 **browsing of ivy** grazing on ivy
(seaweed or sea-holly, growing in sand
dunes). In *Pandosto*, the sheep feed on
'sea-ivy' (p. 421).
67 **Good . . . will** Send me good luck (to
find my sheep), if it is your will. The
Shepherd addresses a pagan god, but
uses the words in the Lord's Prayer, as
Antigonus does at 7 (see n.).
68 **Mercy on's** (God have) mercy on us
bairn child; bairn or barne is used in
Shakespeare by the uneducated (*AW*
1.3.25) or as a pun (*MA* 3.4.42–4). See
pp. 131, 372.
69 **child** probably dialect for 'girl', a
usage confined to the Midlands and
south-west of England. *OED* records

no other Standard English use of child
for girl before the late 1700s.
70 **sure some scape** certainly the result
of some sexual misconduct (*OED*
scape *n.*[1] 2)
71–2 **I . . . scape** I can tell some lady's
servant was involved in this misconduct (a *waiting-gentlewoman* attended a
lady in her chamber). The reference to
reading (*bookish*, 71) suggests *scape* as a
printing error in a book (*OED* 3). The
child's beauty and christening gown
(see 45 SDn.) convince him she is the
daughter of a superior lady.
72–3 **'some . . . behind-door-work**
'Work' was often associated with
intercourse (*Oth* 2.1.115); the stairs,
trunk and behind doors are places
where lovers might have casual sex
(tiptoeing up stairs; coupling in a
large clothes-trunk); they also refer
to sexual positions (going up a woman
in stages; one body or 'trunk' working
on another; entering the woman from
behind, i.e. by her rear); 'trunk' and
'behind-door' (backdoor) were probably euphemisms for the penis and
anus (Partridge, 65, 189, 206).
74 **that got this** i.e. the couple who were
making the baby (copulating)

67 SD] *Cam*[1] *subst.*

for pity; yet I'll tarry till my son come. He hallooed   75
but even now. Whoa-ho-hoa!

Enter CLOWN.

CLOWN   Hilloa, loa!

SHEPHERD   What, art so near? If thou'lt see a thing to talk
on when thou art dead and rotten, come hither. What
ail'st thou, man?   80

CLOWN   I have seen two such sights, by sea and by land!
But I am not to say it is a sea, for it is now the sky;
betwixt the firmament and it you cannot thrust a
bodkin's point.

SHEPHERD   Why, boy, how is it?   85

CLOWN   I would you did but see how it chafes, how it
rages, how it takes up the shore; but that's not to
the point. O, the most piteous cry of the poor souls!
Sometimes to see 'em, and not to see 'em; now the
ship boring the moon with her mainmast, and anon   90
swallowed with yeast and froth, as you'd thrust a cork

75–6 **He . . . now** He called out just a
moment ago.

76–7 **Whoa-ho-hoa . . . loa** exclama-
tions used to call out from a distance

76.1 CLOWN See List of Roles, 23n.

78–9 **If . . . rotten** if you want to see
something people will still be talking
about when you're long dead in your
grave (*rotten*); cf. Dent, D126.1, 'Dead
and rotten'.

79–80 **What ail'st thou** what's the matter with you

81 **such sights** extraordinary things
by on

82–96 **But . . . it** See pp. 29–30.

82 **But . . . sky** I can't really call it a sea,
since it's now the same as the sky. Cf.
Oth 2.1.39–40, where sea and sky are
just as indistinguishable.

83 **firmament** sky

84 **bodkin** small dagger; sharp-pointed
instrument for piercing holes in cloth;
lady's hairpin (*OED* 1, 2, 3a)

85 **how is it** how is that so

86 **chafes** rages (*OED* chafe *v.* 10c)

87 **takes up** swallows up; rebukes,
reproves (*OED* take *v.* 93o)

90 **boring** piercing. Cf. *Per* 3.1.45–6,
where the waves are so high they
appear to touch the moon.
anon immediately

91 **yeast** spume. Cf. *Tem* 1.2.12 for an
instance of the sea swallowing a ship.

91–2 **as . . . hogshead** i.e. the ship
went up and down just the way you
would plunge a cork in a large filled
cask (*hogshead*), and watch it bob
up again

into a hogshead. And then for the land-service, to see
how the bear tore out his shoulder-bone, how he cried
to me for help, and said his name was Antigonus, a
nobleman! But to make an end of the ship – to see how   95
the sea flapdragoned it! But first, how the poor souls
roared, and the sea mocked them, and how the poor
gentleman roared, and the bear mocked him, both
roaring louder than the sea or weather.

SHEPHERD   Name of mercy, when was this, boy?   100

CLOWN   Now, now. I have not winked since I saw these
sights. The men are not yet cold under water, nor the
bear half dined on the gentleman – he's at it now.

SHEPHERD   Would I had been by to have helped the old
man!   105

CLOWN   I would you had been by the ship side, to have
helped her; there your charity would have lacked
footing.

SHEPHERD   Heavy matters, heavy matters. But look thee
here, boy. Now bless thyself; thou met'st with things   110

---

92 **for the land-service** as regards
the action on land (cf. *AC* 2.6.95).
The Clown contrasts a land battle
between Antigonus and the Bear and
a naval action between ship and storm.
'Service' was also food served at a
meal (*OED n.*[1] 27b), i.e. the Bear ate
Antigonus while the sea gobbled the
ship.
93 **shoulder-bone** Cf. 4.3.73.
95 **make . . . ship** finish the story of the
shipwreck
96 **flapdragoned it** swallowed it like
a tiny morsel. In the party game,
snapdragon players had to snap up
raisins or plums (flap-dragons) in
their mouths from a bowl of burning
brandy: cf. *LLL* 5.1.40–1.
97, 98 **mocked** showed its scorn for;
imitated derisively (i.e. roared back).
Cf. 5.3.19, 20 (similar repetition), 68.
98 **both** i.e. Antigonus and the Bear
100 **Name of mercy** in the name of

(God's) mercy
101 **winked** blinked; i.e. it happened only
an instant before (or he's still wide-
eyed with wonder)
104 **by** nearby
104–5 **old man** The Shepherd is told
Antigonus' name and rank (94–5), but
not his age; cf. 3.2.185–6 (see n.).
106 **ship** ship's
107–8 **charity . . . footing** There is
a quibble on *footing* as a charitable
foundation and as a thing to stand on
(impossible in the sea). The Clown
teases the Shepherd: 'If you'd been
there, you bighead, I suppose you'd
have walked on water, saving both ship
and nobleman.'
109 **Heavy** sorrowful
110 **bless thyself** think yourself lucky
110–11 **thou . . . newborn** the turning-
point in *WT*: see pp. 17–18. Cf. 5.3.45
(see n.), and see 1.2.92n.
110, 111 **things** beings (see 1.2.92n.)

dying, I with things newborn. Here's a sight for thee.
Look thee, a bearing-cloth for a squire's child. [*Points
to the box.*] Look thee here, take up, take up, boy, open't.
So, let's see. It was told me I should be rich by the
fairies. This is some changeling; open't. What's within,   115
boy?

CLOWN [*Opens the box.*] You're a made old man. If the
sins of your youth are forgiven you, you're well to live.
Gold, all gold!

SHEPHERD   This is fairy gold, boy, and 'twill prove so.   120
Up with't, keep it close. Home, home, the next way.
We are lucky, boy, and to be so still requires nothing
but secrecy. Let my sheep go. Come, good boy, the next
way home.

CLOWN   Go you the next way with your findings. I'll go   125
see if the bear be gone from the gentleman, and how
much he hath eaten. They are never curst but when

112 **bearing-cloth** christening gown (see 45 SDn., 71–2n.)

113 SD *box* Some editors take this to be the '*bundle*' (or *fardel*, 721) brought on with a box at 4.4.686.1. A simpler explanation is that Antigonus leaves a box beside the baby, who is wrapped in a gown (see 112n.) and a cloak or blanket (see 45 SDn.).

113 **take up** pick it up

114–15 **It . . . fairies** It was foretold the fairies would make me rich.

115 **changeling** It was popularly believed that fairies stole beautiful children from the cradle, leaving ugly ones in exchange; a *changeling* was the fairy substitute or the abducted baby. The Shepherd thinks this beautiful but illegitimate child has been abandoned in favour of legitimate siblings. See 2.3.105–6n.

117 ***a . . . man** an old man whose prosperity is assured. Theobald's emendation of F's 'mad' is supported by *Pandosto*, where the shepherd declares

he and his wife are 'made for ever' by the gold (p. 422).

117–18 **If . . . you** Cf. Psalms, 25.7, 'Remember not the sins of my youth nor my rebellions' (Shaheen, 727).

118 **well to live** well off, wealthy; *to live*, infinitive used indefinitely (Abbott, 356), meaning 'as regards living'

120 **'twill prove so** i.e. the prophecy that the fairies will make him rich (114–15) will turn out to be true

121 **Up . . . close** Pick up the box, but keep it secret. Traditionally, gifts from fairies mustn't be spoken about or bad luck will follow (cf. 122–3); money from them (120) was believed to crumble away suddenly (*OED* fairy C 2).

121, 123–4, 125 **next way** nearest or shortest route

122 **to . . . still** to continue to be so

123 **Let . . . go** Let my (lost) sheep look after themselves.

125 **your findings** what you've found

127 **curst** savage, vicious (*OED* cursed 4b)

112–13 SD] *Oxf*   117 SD] *Oxf*   made] *Theobald*; mad *F*

they are hungry. If there be any of him left, I'll bury
it.

SHEPHERD   That's a good deed. If thou mayst discern   130
by that which is left of him what he is, fetch me to th'
sight of him.

CLOWN   Marry, will I; and you shall help to put him i'th'
ground.

SHEPHERD   'Tis a lucky day, boy, and we'll do good   135
deeds on't.   *Exeunt.*

4.1   *Enter* TIME, *the Chorus.*

TIME

I, that please some, try all; both joy and terror
Of good and bad, that makes and unfolds error,
Now take upon me, in the name of Time,
To use my wings. Impute it not a crime

131 **what he is** who he was
133 **Marry** indeed
135–6 **we'll . . . on't** Cf. Tilley, D60, 'The
better the day the better the deed.'
136 **on't** because of it
4.1 Time's speech is in 16 rhymed couplets – a couplet for each year that
has passed since the end of 3.3. These
are the only end-line rhymes in the
play, except for those in the songs in
4.3 and 4.4 (rhymes in the middle of
lines are discussed on pp. 123–5). This
difference in the form emphasizes that
Time is outside the action: see p. 81.
0.1 **Time** See pp. 76–81 and Fig. 15.
Chorus Classical plays in Renaissance
editions had an Argument that sum-
marized the story (see 27–9). The
Chorus, one person or several, com-
mented on and sometimes participated
in the action.
1 **try all** put everyone to the test. Cf.
Dent, T336, 'Time tries all things.'
Often shown as a judge, Time would
whip the guilty and the innocent;

cf. *Ham* 3.1.69 (see p. 79 and Chew,
Pilgrimage, 18–19). Compare Time's
attributes in 1–4 with *Luc* 936–59.
1–2 **both . . . bad** who am joy and terror
to everyone, good and bad; who brings
joy to good men and terrifies the bad
(isocolon, creating equality in rhythm
between different parts of a sentence,
also at 3.2.160–2). Cf. *Luc* 995, 'O
Time, thou tutor both to good and bad'.
2 **that . . . error** through whom mistakes are made but afterwards uncovered (or straightened out, creases
unfolded). Proverbially, 'Time reveals
all things' (Tilley, T333). For *I* with
makes and unfolds, see Abbott, 247.
3 **in . . . Time** with Time's authority
and rights; whose name is 'Time'
4 **use my wings** i.e. the action will
fly from the present (*wings* to show
time passes quickly). Cf. *Per* 4.0.5–50,
where the Chorus asks the audience to
pass by the interval between the birth
of the heroine and her reaching 16, i.e.
be told, not shown, what happened.

4.1] *(Actus Quartus. Scena Prima.)*

To me or my swift passage that I slide   5
O'er sixteen years, and leave the growth untried
Of that wide gap, since it is in my power
To o'erthrow law, and in one self-born hour
To plant and o'erwhelm custom. Let me pass
The same I am ere ancient'st order was,   10
Or what is now received. I witness to
The times that brought them in; so shall I do
To th' freshest things now reigning, and make stale
The glistering of this present as my tale
Now seems to it. Your patience this allowing,   15
I turn my glass, and give my scene such growing

5   **swift passage** Cf. Dent, T327, 'Time
    flees away without delay.'
    slide pass, slip (*OED v.* A 5c, which
    cites from 1620 'Time slides away like
    the running streame')
    sixteen years marked by 16 couplets
    in 1–32
6–7 **leave . . . gap** leave the events of
    that long interval unexamined (*untried*,
    perhaps 'undramatized, not shown to
    the audience')
7   **wide gap** Cf. 5.3.154, *AC* 1.5.5, *Cym*
    3.2.62–3.
8   **law** laws of Nature and the cosmos;
    laws made by men – including neo-
    Aristotelian rules that a play should
    have a single action, take place in a
    short period of time and be set in one
    place. None of these is kept in the
    play: see pp. 58–61.
8–9 **in . . . custom** in one and the same
    hour (*OED* self-born), i.e. in a single
    hour, Time can replace old ways
    with entirely new ones (*o'erwhelm*,
    overthrow). Another meaning is 'this
    hour is my offspring to do with what
    I want' (the Hours, Time's daughters,
    controlled the seasons). Also a pun on
    'born' and 'borne': Time is carried on
    his own wings.
9–10 **Let . . . was** Take me to be the
    same now as I was before civilization
    began (*ancient'st order*, most ancient
    societies; perhaps also alluding to the

Ancient Greek orders of architecture).
11 **what . . . received** current order of
    things; customary order
11–12 **I . . . in** i.e. I witnessed the ages
    that ushered in the earliest and most
    recent civilizations. Cf. *Luc* 939–41.
12–13 **so . . . reigning** I'll be the same
    to the most newly planted ones now
    holding sway.
13 **things** See 1.2.92n.
13–15 **make . . . it** making the lustre of
    present things seem as stale as my old
    story appears now
15 **Your . . . allowing** if you, an indul-
    gent audience, concede this (that I've
    seen all times and may do what I want
    with time); if you'll permit me this
    liberty (to indicate that 16 years have
    passed
16 **I . . . glass** Elizabethan plays were
    supposed to last two hours, but per-
    formances were often longer (Gurr,
    Playgoing, 33–4). Time turns his
    hourglass (*glass*) upside down, mid-way
    through the speech, showing that the
    first 'hour' or half the play is over.
    In the second half, everything will be
    turned upside down, like the hourglass
    (contemporary proverbs said that all
    things could be made topsy-turvy in an
    hour: Tilley, W903).
    growing advance, progress (*OED vbl.
    n.* 3b); cf. *Per* 4.0.6. The usage is
    metaphorical, as with *growth* (6), *plant*

As you had slept between. Leontes leaving –
Th'effects of his fond jealousies so grieving
That he shuts up himself – imagine me,
Gentle spectators, that I now may be   20
In fair Bohemia, and remember well
I mentioned a son o'th' king's, which Florizel
I now name to you; and with speed so pace
To speak of Perdita, now grown in grace
Equal with wondering. What of her ensues   25
I list not prophesy, but let Time's news
Be known when 'tis brought forth. A shepherd's
    daughter,
And what to her adheres, which follows after,
Is th'argument of Time. Of this allow,
If ever you have spent time worse ere now;   30
If never, yet that Time himself doth say
He wishes earnestly you never may.   *Exit.*

(9), *grown* (24), meaning developed naturally, i.e. without art; cf. the debate at 4.4.85–97.

16–17 **give . . . between** advance the action of my play so that you would think you had slept between now and 16 years hence

17 **slept** See.1.2.326–7n.

17–18 **Leontes . . . grieving** leaving Leontes, who grieves so much about the effects of his foolish (*fond*) jealousy

19 **imagine me** imagine, for my sake (*me*, ethic dative: Abbott, 220)

20 **Gentle** generous, not over-critical. Perhaps a compliment to the audience: they are all 'gentle', i.e. well born (anticipating 5.2.124–60).

22 **I mentioned** Time refers to 1.2.164–70, when Polixenes talked about his son, i.e. in time passed. There is no need to conclude that in some earlier version of the play Time appeared in person before 4.1, e.g. as a Prologue.

23 **with . . . pace** thus proceed promptly.

At *so* Time perhaps takes a step towards the audience.

24–5 **in . . . wondering** in beauty and charm fully equal to (or fully deserving) the wonder they inspire; *wondering* is disyllabic.

26 **list not prophesy** choose not to foretell. Cf. Gower as Chorus choosing to show rather than relate events in *Per* 2.0.39–40, 3.0.55–7.

26–7 **Time's . . . forth** Cf. Dent, T324, 'Time brings the truth to light': see pp. 79, 81.

27–8 **daughter . . . after** In Shakespeare's day a full rhyme. It is not clear whether the sounds were 'dafter' and 'after' (*f* sounded) or 'darter' and 'arter' (*f* silent): see Cercignani, 342.

28 **to her adheres** concerns her

29 **argument** subject-matter, theme (*OED* 6); see 0.1n. on *Chorus*.

29–32 **Of . . . may** i.e. if you have ever before spent your time worse than

4.2   *Enter* POLIXENES *and* CAMILLO.

POLIXENES   I pray thee, good Camillo, be no more
importunate. 'Tis a sickness denying thee anything, a
death to grant this.

CAMILLO   It is fifteen years since I saw my country.
Though I have for the most part been aired abroad,   5
I desire to lay my bones there. Besides, the penitent
king, my master, hath sent for me, to whose feeling
sorrows I might be some allay – or I o'erween to think
so – which is another spur to my departure.

POLIXENES   As thou lov'st me, Camillo, wipe not out the   10
rest of thy services by leaving me now. The need I
have of thee thine own goodness hath made. Better not
to have had thee than thus to want thee. Thou, having
made me businesses which none without thee can
sufficiently manage, must either stay to execute them   15
thyself, or take away with thee the very services thou
hast done; which if I have not enough considered –

in watching this play, grant me what
I've asked (letting 16 years go by,
and that the story now is of Perdita);
but if you have never spent your
time as badly as this before, at least
believe that Time himself hopes you
never will.

4.2 Set in Bohemia, probably at court,
4.2 reintroduces the theme in Acts 1–3
of male possessiveness and control.
Perhaps the scene is in prose because
Polixenes and Camillo (who elsewhere
speak to each other in verse) are in
private, and have known each other for
the past 16 years.

2–3 **'Tis . . . this** i.e. it sickens me to
refuse you anything, but would kill me
to give you my permission to (leave)

4 **fifteen** probably a mistake for
sixteen (see 4.1.6, 5.3.31, 50, and
p. 85), Shakespeare's or the scribe's;

or the compositor misread the Roman
numerals 'xvi' (or 'xvj') as 'xv'

5 **for . . . abroad** spent most of my life
abroad (i.e. away from Sicilia)
been aired abroad breathed foreign
air, i.e. lived abroad

7–8 **to . . . allay** whose deeply felt grief
I might alleviate to some extent (*OED*
allay *v.*[1] 11)

8 **or I o'erween** unless I'm being pre-
sumptuous

9 **spur** encouragement (as in spurring a
horse

10 **wipe not out** don't cancel out

13 **want** be without

13–16 **Thou . . . thyself** having started
projects that only you can handle
adequately, you must either stay and
see them through

17 **considered** rewarded; cf. 4.4.800
(see n.).

4.2] *(Scena Secunda.)*

as too much I cannot – to be more thankful to thee
shall be my study, and my profit therein the heaping
friendships. Of that fatal country Sicilia, prithee speak   20
no more, whose very naming punishes me with the
remembrance of that penitent – as thou call'st him –
and reconciled king my brother, whose loss of his most
precious queen and children are even now to be afresh
lamented. Say to me, when saw'st thou the Prince   25
Florizel, my son? Kings are no less unhappy, their issue
not being gracious, than they are in losing them when
they have approved their virtues.

CAMILLO   Sir, it is three days since I saw the prince.
What his happier affairs may be are to me unknown;   30
but I have missingly noted he is of late much retired
from court, and is less frequent to his princely exercises
than formerly he hath appeared.

POLIXENES   I have considered so much, Camillo, and
with some care, so far that I have eyes under my service   35
which look upon his removedness, from whom I have

19 **study** aim
19–20 **the heaping friendships** the
    growth of our friendship; your greater
    devotion to me
22 **call'st** describe. Polixenes either
    agrees that penitent is the correct
    word, or doubts whether Leontes
    could ever repent enough.
23 **reconciled** a rapprochement of some
    kind has occurred over the years, but it
    is probably very limited: see 5.1.133–7,
    146–50. Florizel's claims at 137–46
    may be wholly untrue (cf. 155–67).
24 **are** is: either confusion from proxim-
    ity of *queen and children* (Abbott, 412),
    or plural for singular (Abbott, 247)
24–5 **even . . . lamented** i.e. even after
    this length of time grieved for as
    though they had just died
    afresh lamented grieved for as
    though it had just happened
26–8 **Kings . . . virtues** i.e. kings are just
    as unhappy, if their heirs are disobedi-
    ent, as they would be if they lost virtu-

ous children. If *they* (28) means chil-
    dren not fathers, then it's the children
    who have proved their virtuousness.
    For Polixenes, his son's rebelliousness
    is a loss comparable to Mamillius' death
    (anticipating the tirade that begins at
    4.4.422. See 1.2.411–12n.)
30 **happier affairs** i.e. activities Florizel
    likes more than *princely exercises*, 32
    (see n.)
31 **missingly** with regret; *OED*'s only
    citation, defined as 'with a sense of
    loss'
31–2 **much . . . court** away from court
    a lot
32 **less frequent to** less wont to indulge
    in (*OED* frequent *a*. 5)
    princely exercises royal duties,
    including horsemanship and book
    learning
35–6 **so . . . removedness** to the extent
    that I have spies (i.e. men with *eyes*) at
    work for me looking into his absence
36 **whom** i.e. the spies

this intelligence: that he is seldom from the house of a most homely shepherd, a man, they say, that from very nothing, and beyond the imagination of his neighbours, is grown into an unspeakable estate.   40

CAMILLO   I have heard, sir, of such a man, who hath a daughter of most rare note. The report of her is extended more than can be thought to begin from such a cottage.

POLIXENES   That's likewise part of my intelligence; but,   45
I fear, the angle that plucks our son thither. Thou shalt accompany us to the place, where we will, not appearing what we are, have some question with the shepherd, from whose simplicity I think it not uneasy to get the cause of my son's resort thither. Prithee, be   50
my present partner in this business, and lay aside the thoughts of Sicilia.

CAMILLO   I willingly obey your command.

POLIXENES   My best Camillo! We must disguise ourselves.   54

Exeunt.

4.3   *Enter* AUTOLYCUS *singing.*

37 **from** away from
38 **homely** humble
38–40 **from . . . estate** from having no money, has become wealthy beyond his neighbours' wildest dreams
40 **unspeakable** Cf. 1.1.33–4 (see n.).
42 **most rare note** extraordinary distinction
42–4 **report . . . cottage** i.e. the estimate of her is so high that it's impossible to believe she has come from such humble origins
46 **the angle** (she is the bait on) the fish hook; see 1.2.179n. P. Parker (*Margins*, 144) detects a sexual sense in *angle*, i.e. a nook, hidden place men might enter (*OED n.*[2] 1a).
46 **plucks** associated with snatching or stealing (*OED v.* 4a)

47–8 **not . . . are** i.e. in disguise
48 **have . . . with** interrogate (*OED* question *n.* 4a)
49 **from whose simplicity** from whom, because he is such a simple man
uneasy difficult
51 **present partner** partner immediately
4.3 The scene is rural Bohemia, on a back road (see 28–9n.). Despite the reference to the early spring flowers (*daffodils*, 1), the scene isn't in March, but takes place immediately after sheep-shearing, i.e. June or July. See 1.1.5n.
0.1 AUTOLYCUS See List of Roles, 24n. *singing* The song that follows is the first in the play, and this SD is almost the first musical reference of any kind (see pp. 382–3).

50 Prithee] (ʾPrethe)   54 SD] *Rowe; Exit F*   **4.3**] (*Scena Tertia.*)   0.1 AUTOLYCUS] (*Autolicus*)

AUTOLYCUS

> When daffodils begin to peer,
> With heigh, the doxy over the dale,
> Why then comes in the sweet o'the year,
> For the red blood reigns in the winter's pale.
>
> The white sheet bleaching on the hedge,   5
> With heigh, the sweet birds, O how they sing!

1–12 The song alludes to the four seasons: spring *daffodils* mark the end of winter (1, 4), Autolycus and his girlfriends listen to *summer songs* (11) while having sex in autumn *hay* (12). Winter is over, and life, quickening again, hasn't been extinguished (see 4n.): sexual desire, and the itch to be stealing, drinking or just listening to birds, has survived.

1 **daffodils** signalling the return of spring; associated with jealousy (*OED* 3 cites Robert Greene in 1592 calling them flowers 'fit for jealous dotterels') and with dying early, because they were thought to perish before the sun reached its midsummer midday height **peer** appear (*OED v.*³ 1a); peep (above ground)

2, 6, 10 **heigh** exclamation or shout for joy. There are puns on *heigh* and 'hay' which reflect Autolycus' preoccupations. At 12 *hay* is mown, dried grass (*OED n.*¹ 1a), but it also meant a hedge or fence (*n.*² 1), a net for catching rabbits (*n.*³), a country dance (*n.*⁴ 1; see *LLL* 5.1.145), and a shout at a hit in fencing (*OED int.*).

2 **doxy . . . dale** *OED* says doxy was slang for a professional beggar's girlfriend, or loose woman accompanying rogues and thieves; *over the dale* means '(tramping with me) through valleys, common land and open fields' (*OED* dale¹ 1, dale² 1). Musgrove (5, n. 2) says dale is a variant of dell, which Thomas Harman described as a vagrant girl 'able for generation and not yet

known or broken' (cited in Kinney, 144). From this, 'doxy over the dale' would mean '(give me) an experienced woman rather than an untested girl, even if she's a virgin'.

3 **comes . . . year** the most pleasant time of the year arrives; i.e. springtime; see also 4n.

4 **reigns . . . pale** *reigns in* can mean: (1) is sovereign, all-powerful in; (2) reins in, controls; (3) rains in, pours in or through. The noun *pale* can mean: (1) paleness, pallor; (2) bounds, domain, (*OED n.*¹ 3–4), perhaps space of time; (3) pail or bucket. Line 4 explains 3 (the sweetest time is spring), so the most likely meanings are: (1) spring's red blood triumphs over winter's pale (anaemic) blood, i.e. spring comes alive as winter declines; (2) life-giving blood flows even in the grip of winter; (3) blood flows in veins even when wintry skin is pale. In this sense 3–4 mean: (1) spring returns because, however long winter is, male seed has the sovereign power of blood in it; (2) the capacity to give and return to life survives harsh challenges. See 1.1.5n.; 1.2.71–3n., 109n.

5 **sheet . . . hedge** Taking sheets off a hedge meant stealing openly (*OED* hedge *n.* 6a). The theft of sheets drying or whitening (*bleaching*) on hedges was common (cf. Tilley, H359, 'He has made many a white hedge black', and *1H4* 4.2.46–7). A hedge, a place for casual sex, was also a prostitute (Rubinstein, 332). See also 7n.

1 SP] *not in F*

Doth set my pugging tooth an edge,
For a quart of ale is a dish for a king.

The lark, that tirra-lirra chants,
With heigh, with heigh, the thrush and the jay,   10
Are summer songs for me and my aunts
While we lie tumbling in the hay.

I have served Prince Florizel, and in my time wore
three-pile, but now I am out of service.

But shall I go mourn for that, my dear?   15
The pale moon shines by night,

7 *OED*'s only citation for *pugging*, a
nonce word which Shakespeare probably coined from 'puggard', slang
for thief, but it may be a scribe's or
compositor's mistake for 'prigging',
stealing; cf. 26, 99 (see nn.). 'Tooth'
meant a taste for something, and 'to set
an edge upon', to stimulate, literally
sharpen (*OED* edge *n.* 2a): cf. Dent,
T431, 'To set one's teeth on edge';
1H4 3.1.129). Lines 5 and 7 therefore
mean 'the sight of a white sheet drying
on a hedge whets my appetite for
thieving'. If *tooth* is sexual desire (cf.
H8 1.3.48), and *pugging* is from 'pug'
or prostitute (*OED n.*[2] 1b), Autolycus
may mean 'the sight of clean linen
makes me long to be whoring'.
8 **quart** two pints (1.14 litres)
   a dish for fit for (proverbial: Dent,
   D363.1)
9 **tirra-lirra** *OED*'s first citation.
Cotgrave, who defines the French verb
tirelirer as to warble or sing like a lark,
and the noun *tirelire* as birdsong, adds
that *tirelire* can be a collecting-box,
used in France by friars and in England
by butlers and apprentices, so perhaps
Autolycus rattles a begging-box.
10 *****with heigh** F appears to omit a word
or two (possibly the name of another
bird), supplied in F2 by doubling

'*With heigh*'.
jay the songbird, but also slang for
'whore' (from Italian *putta*; cf. *Cym*
3.4.48)
11 **aunts** whores, mistresses (*OED* 3); cf.
doxy, 2 (see n.).
12 **lie tumbling** having sex (*OED* tumble
v. 9a)
13 **served** been a servant to; cheated,
swindled (*OED* serve *v.*[1] 47a), perhaps
why Autolycus was whipped out of
court (88)
13–14 **wore . . . service** I've worn plush
velvet livery but now I'm in not in
anybody's service (see 4.4.756–7n.).
'Three-pile', expensive velvet with a
pile of three layers, was also worn
by pimps and whores and associated
with sexual disease (cf. *MM* 1.2.31–5),
and to be in service was a euphemism
for being a prostitute, so perhaps
Autolycus means 'I've had the pox
from pimping and whoring, and no
longer offer these services.'
15–22 The song begins as if from an
abandoned but defiant lover: i.e. do
you think I'll mourn because you've
left me, my dear? But Autolycus'
defiance comes from someone living
on his wits, thieving by night (16–
18), tinker by day (19; see n.). See
p. 132.

10 With . . . ²heigh] *F2; With heigh F*

And when I wander here and there
I then do most go right.

If tinkers may have leave to live,
And bear the sow-skin budget,   20
Then my account I well may give,
And in the stocks avouch it.

My traffic is sheets – when the kite builds, look to
lesser linen. My father named me Autolycus, who
being, as I am, littered under Mercury, was likewise a   25
snapper-up of unconsidered trifles. With die and drab

---

17 **wander** perhaps from one woman to
another

18 **do . . . right** do what is best for me
(going wherever I choose); live most
true to my calling (a thief). Autolycus
acknowledges, possibly unwittingly,
the paradox that he does what's right
even when he is trying hardest to do
wrong. This is important at the end of
Act 4 when he dupes the rustics – for
his own gain he hopes, but with a
sense (one we share) that Fortune
and the gods may be directing him
(see 4.4.680–6, 715–16 and 834–40).
Cf. the subversive remark in *2H6*
4.2.178–9, 'But then are we in order
when we are most out of order.'

19 **tinkers** itinerant workmen selling and
mending pots and pans; like other
lower-class travellers they could be
arrested unless they had papers or
good reasons for moving around (see
21–2 and n.); 'tinker' was also slang for
'thief'; cf. 26 (see n.).
may . . . live are permitted to earn a
living

20 **bear** carry
sow-skin budget pigskin toolbag. A
budget, a pouch or bag (*OED n.* 1a), is
here slang for the scrotum. See 26n.;
1.2.205n.; 4.4.284n., 615n.

21–2 i.e. if I'm arrested and put in the
stocks, I can swear (*avouch*) I'm a tinker
not a vagabond (because of my toolbag)

23 **traffic** business; whore (*OED n.* 4c)
sheets bedsheets; broadside ballads
on single sheets of paper (part of
a pedlar's stock); in the sheets, i.e.
having sex, or pimping

23–4 **when . . . linen** i.e. just as when a
kite builds its nest, you need to watch
your smaller linen (the bird will steal it
for its nest), so you should mind your
sheets when I'm around; a kite was a
carrion bird, but also the name for a
predatory person.

25 **as . . . Mercury** born (*littered*), as I was
when the planet Mercury was in the
ascendant (see 1.2.200–1n.); born to take
Mercury (god of cheats, smooth talkers
and thieves) as my patron. In classical
mythology Mercury was Autolycus'
father; see List of Roles, 24n.

26 **snapper-up. . . trifles** a thief of
small-value items their owners don't
look after. 'Snapper-up', someone who
seizes something quickly, is probably
from rogue literature, e.g. Harman's
description of 'drunken Tinkers' or
'Prigs': if one of them sees an 'old
kettle, chafer, or pewter dish' lying
about, 'he quickly snappeth the same
up, and into the budget it goeth' (cited
in Kinney, 133); cf. 7, 19–20 (see nn.);
OED suggests a snapper (*n.* 1) was an
accomplice in cheating.

26–7 **With . . . caparison** It's through
(losing at) gambling (*die*, singular of

I purchased this caparison, and my revenue is the silly
cheat. Gallows and knock are too powerful on the
highway. Beating and hanging are terrors to me. For
the life to come, I sleep out the thought of it. A prize,   30
a prize!

Enter CLOWN.

CLOWN   Let me see. Every 'leven wether tods, every tod
yields pound and odd shilling. Fifteen hundred shorn,
what comes the wool to?

AUTOLYCUS [*aside*]   If the springe hold, the cock's mine.   35

CLOWN   I cannot do't without counters. Let me see, what

dice) and whoring (*drab*, prostitute)
that I got this fancy outfit (*OED*
caparison *n.* 2, used ironically since he
is in *rags*, 54).

27–8 **silly cheat** petty theft (or cheating ignorant people); cf. 119 (see n.).
Musgrove (5, n. 2) says *cheat* stands
for 'thing'; if so, *silly cheat* means
simply 'fool'.

28–9 **Gallows . . . highway** The possibility
of (being arrested and put to death on)
the gallows and being beaten make main
roads risky. Petty theft (27–8) was punishable by hanging, and vagrants could
be beaten, so Autolycus keeps to byways
(*footpath* 122) to avoid being caught.

29 **Beating and hanging** Cf. *Gallows
and knock*, 28.
For as for

30 **life to come** may mean future in
this life, as in *MM* 5.1.428, or life
in the hereafter, as in *Mac* 1.7.7 (see
next n.). According to Shaheen (727)
Shakespeare's source for *life to come*
was the phrase 'life of the world to
come' in the Nicene Creed in *BCP*.
sleep . . . it don't give it a thought.
Autolycus doesn't think beyond his
immediate fears, though *sleep out*,
i.e. be oblivious to (cf. *AC* 1.5.5),
may mean he doesn't believe there is

anything after death. See 1.2.326–7n.

30–1 **A . . . prize!** the cry pirates used
when sighting a ship to plunder; cf.
Per 4.1.89.

32–3 **Every . . . shilling** Every eleven
sheep (*wether*), when shorn, yield a
tod of wool, and every tod fetches one
pound one shilling (£1.05). A 'tod' was
a measure of weight in the wool trade,
i.e. 28lb (12.7 kilos). Sheep-shearing was
done quickly: clippers could shear 70 per
day, earning a shilling (Woodward, 22),
so the 24 clippers mentioned at 41 would
shear 1,500 or more sheep in a day.

34 **what . . . to?** Depending on the exact
number of tods (between 136 and 137),
the answer is probably £143 3s 7d
(£143.18), a huge amount at the date
of *WT*. Wool prices in Bohemia and
Shakespeare's Stratford are similar
(Hulme, 333–4).

35 If my snare works, I'll catch this woodcock. A springe was a trap for game,
especially birds; the cock or woodcock
was proverbially stupid and easily
caught (Dent, S788; cf. *Ham* 1.3.114).

36 **counters** flat disks of metal, used for
calculations

36–7 **what . . . buy** His *sister* (39), i.e.
Perdita, has given him a shopping-list
(*note*, 46) which he is able to read.

32 'leven wether tods] *Malone;* Leauen-weather toddes *F*   35 SD] *Rowe*

am I to buy for our sheep-shearing feast? Three pound
of sugar, five pound of currants, rice – what will this
sister of mine do with rice? But my father hath made
her mistress of the feast, and she lays it on. She hath   40
made me four-and-twenty nosegays for the shearers
– three-man songmen, all, and very good ones – but
they are most of them means and basses, but one
Puritan amongst them, and he sings psalms to hornpipes. I must have saffron to colour the warden pies;   45
mace; dates, none – that's out of my note; nutmegs,

37 **sheep-shearing feast** After the
shearing, wool-workers joined their
social betters at a feast (see 4.4.10–12
and nn.) paid for by the employer or a
local landowner.

37–8 **Three . . . sugar** Sugar was
extremely expensive, sold in small
twists of paper or cone-shaped loaves
of three or four pounds (1.5 kilos)
(Orton, 59). The Clown's buying a
whole loaf shows he has a great deal of
money on him.

38–9 **what . . . rice** Rice was used in
sweet puddings, with currants and
sugar: the Clown's question suggests
it was an unusual ingredient in the
country. Perdita is splashing out (see
40n.), but not in preparation for her
betrothal: corn, not rice, was thrown
at Elizabethan engagement parties and
wedding ceremonies.

40 **mistress** hostess; see 4.4.55–62.
    lays it on does it in style, lavishly (cf.
    Tem 3.2.152)

42 **three-man songmen** singers of
catches, lively part-songs for three
voices (as at 4.4.298–313)

43 **means** tenors (cf. *LLL* 5.2.327–8).
There is word-play on *means and
basses*, i.e. mean and base men, lower-
class types, who are nevertheless *very
good ones*, 42.
    but and only

44 **Puritan** Puritans in Shakespeare's
lifetime were Protestants who sought to
simplify and regulate forms of worship
in the Church of England. They urged a

strict moral code, sometimes saying that
pleasure (including pleasure in secular
music) was sinful. They were often
accused of sanctimoniousness, and
there was unease about their taking over
the government of towns (ultimately, in
the 1650s, they ruled the country). The
Puritan here is unobjectionable because
there is only one of him.

44–5 **psalms to hornpipes** (1) psalms
accompanied by the hornpipe, a wind
instrument (cf. *Oth* 3.1.3–6) used for
the rollicking dance-tunes hated by
Puritans; (2) in a high-pitched voice
like a hornpipe, unlike the other shearers (tenors and basses, 43). Puritans
were portrayed mockingly as singing in
high nasal tones. For the Clown's taste
in songs and music see 4.4.190–2n.

45–8 Most of the items on the Clown's
shopping list are *spices* (114) and dried
fruits. Spices were used with meat
and fish, but here for puddings and
pastries. Sweet dishes 'consisted of
stewed and spiced fruit, tarts and pies,
individual fruits in pastry cases and
stuffed dried fruits' (Orton, 72–3).

45 **saffron** Imported or home-grown saffron, used to colour and flavour pastry,
was very expensive (Orton, 58).
    warden pies pies made with warden
pears, a type of winter pear

46 **mace** spice from the dried outer coat-
ing of nutmeg
    out . . . note not on his shopping-list
or already bought and crossed off
    nutmegs used in cooking, and,

seven; a race or two of ginger – but that I may beg; four
pound of prunes, and as many of raisins o'th' sun.

AUTOLYCUS [*Grovels on the ground.*]   O, that ever I was
born!   50

CLOWN   I'th' name of me!

AUTOLYCUS   O help me, help me! Pluck but off these
rags, and then death, death!

CLOWN   Alack, poor soul, thou hast need of more rags to
lay on thee rather than have these off.   55

AUTOLYCUS   O sir, the loathsomeness of them offend me
more than the stripes I have received, which are mighty
ones and millions.

CLOWN   Alas, poor man, a million of beating may come to
a great matter.   60

AUTOLYCUS   I am robbed, sir, and beaten; my money and
apparel ta'en from me, and these detestable things put
upon me.

CLOWN   What, by a horseman, or a footman?

because they resembled the shape of
the brain, for treating mental ailments
(here probably a joke at the Clown's
expense: he needs nutmegs because
he's so dim)

47 **race** root

48 **raisins o'th' sun** sun-dried raisins

49–125 Autolycus has made money
out of Christ's parables before (see
94–5n.). Pretending to be wounded
and stripped by thieves, he is saved by
a Good Samaritan (Luke, 10.30–7).
Tricking the Clown and picking his
pocket are comic travesties of the parable which establish a holiday mood in
the play (Mahood, 157).

49–50 **O . . . born** proverbial: Dent,
B140.1, 'Alas that ever I was born'

51 **I'th . . . me** a mild oath (similar to *Out
upon him*, 99)

52–3 **Pluck . . . ²death** Just take these
rags off me, then let me die.

54 **thou** The Clown addresses Autolycus

as an inferior with *thou*, *thee* until he
hears about the well-off *kinsman*, 80.
He reverts to *thee* (112, 114) as a sign of
intimacy between equals. Autolycus uses
you throughout, flattering the Clown as
an equal or superior. See 1.2.43n.

56 **offend** offends (Abbott, 412)

57 **stripes** blows, cuts, perhaps from
whippings (29, 88)

58 **millions** very large numbers

59–60 **million . . . matter** The arith-
metically incompetent Clown is awed
at what a *million* must be. Possibly
a lurid joke about Autolycus' being
beaten like an egg (*OED* beat *v.*¹ 23)
and the purulent discharge from a
wound (*OED* matter *n.*¹ 19b).

60 **matter** amount (*OED n.*¹ 6a)

62 **things** clothes (see 1.2.92n.)

64 **horseman . . . footman** man on
horseback, or on foot. Men who could
afford horses wore better clothes (66–8)
than those on foot. See 1.2.94–6n.

49 SD] *Rowe*   56 offend] offends *F2*

AUTOLYCUS   A footman, sweet sir, a footman.   65

CLOWN   Indeed, he should be a footman, by the garments he has left with thee. If this be a horseman's
coat, it hath seen very hot service. Lend me thy
hand, I'll help thee. Come, lend me thy hand. [*Helps
Autolycus up.*]

AUTOLYCUS   O, good sir, tenderly. O!   70

CLOWN   Alas, poor soul!

AUTOLYCUS   O, good sir, softly, good sir! I fear, sir, my
shoulder-blade is out.

CLOWN   How now? Canst stand?

AUTOLYCUS   Softly, dear sir. Good sir, softly. [*Picks the*   75
Clown's pocket.] You ha' done me a charitable office.

CLOWN   Dost lack any money? I have a little money for
thee.

AUTOLYCUS   No, good sweet sir, no, I beseech you, sir.
I have a kinsman not past three-quarters of a mile   80
hence, unto whom I was going. I shall there have
money, or anything I want. Offer me no money, I pray
you – that kills my heart.

CLOWN   What manner of fellow was he that robbed you?

AUTOLYCUS   A fellow, sir, that I have known to go about   85
with troll-madams. I knew him once a servant of the

66 **should . . . footman** must certainly
have been a thief on foot, a quibble on
footman as a lowly servant who had to
tramp everywhere: see pp. 75–6.
by judging by
68 **very hot service** heavy use (in battles)
72, 75 **softly** be gentle; cf. *tenderly*, 70.
73 **shoulder-blade** Sixteen years earlier
the Bear tore out Antigonus' shoulder-
bone (3.3.93).
76 **charitable office** good deed, or
act of Christian love, like the Good
Samaritan's (*OED* charity 1, 2); see
49–125n. To do a charitable office also
meant 'give to the poor' (which the
Clown does unknowingly as Autolycus
picks his pocket).
80 **past** more than
82 **want** lack
83 **that . . . heart** your compassion
breaks my heart; the indignity of
accepting money would break my
heart. Cf. *AC* 4.6.33–5.
86 **troll-madams** Troll-madam was
an indoor game played by women in
which a ball was rolled through hoops
or into holes on a board. Autolycus
may have run one of these games for a

69 SD] *Rowe subst.*   75–6 SD] *Capell subst.*   86 troll-madams] *(*Troll-my-dames*)*

prince. I cannot tell, good sir, for which of his virtues
it was, but he was certainly whipped out of the court.

CLOWN　His vices, you would say – there's no virtue
whipped out of the court. They cherish it to make it　90
stay there, and yet it will no more but abide.

AUTOLYCUS　Vices, I would say, sir. I know this man
well. He hath been since an ape-bearer, then a process-
server – a bailiff – then he compassed a motion of the
Prodigal Son, and married a tinker's wife within a mile　95
where my land and living lies, and, having flown over
many knavish professions, he settled only in rogue.
Some call him Autolycus.

CLOWN　Out upon him! Prig, for my life, prig! He haunts
wakes, fairs and bear-baitings.　　100

living – one of his *knavish professions*,
97. It had smutty associations: troll-
madams were whores, and the game
was also called Nine Holes, Small
Trunks, The Hole (Willughby, 211,
273), which encouraged rude word-
play.

87–92 **virtues . . . vices . . . virtue
. . . Vices** See 1.2.411–12n.

88, 90 **whipped . . . court** thrust out of
the court, with a whipping

89, 92 **would** intended to

91 **no . . . abide** only remain there with
difficulty; only stay briefly. Hulme (51)
suggests that *abide* echoes the proverb
'Things well fitted abide' (Tilley,
T207), i.e. if virtue felt at home she
would remain at court. With the
qualification *no more but*, the Clown
gives *abide* a second, contrary sense,
'stay only for a moment'.

93 **ape-bearer** showman who charged
people to see a monkey perform tricks
(*OED* ape *n.* 8); cf. 5.2.97 (see n.).

93–4 **process-server** legal officer
who served summonses, the same
as *bailiff*, which Autolycus adds as
explanation, perhaps because the
Clown doesn't know the term (see
also 4.4.731–2n., 5.2.125n.). Process

also meant 'narrative', 'tale' (*OED
n.* 4a; cf. *Ham* 1.5.37, 'a forged process'), so Autolycus may be describing
himself slyly, i.e. someone who feeds
people stories.

94 **compassed** obtained; took on tour
(see Hulme, 308–9)
motion puppet-show

94–5 **the Prodigal Son** Christ's parable
(Luke, 15.11–31; see Shaheen, 727–8).

95 **tinker's wife** A tinker's travelling
wife or wench was another term for a
prostitute (Williams, 1429).

96 **land and living** landed estate (a brag
to impress the Clown)

96–7 **flown . . . professions** flitted
between many dishonest occupations

97 **only in** on being simply a

99 **Out upon him** Let him clear off
(very mild swearing).
Prig thief (*OED n.*[3] 2); thieves' jargon:
'to prig' meant to steal (see 7n., 26n.;
Kinney, 124)

99–100 **haunts wakes** frequents country
feasts. Pedlars sold their 'wares' at
'wakes, and wassails, meetings, markets, fairs' (*LLL* 5.2.317–18).

100 **bear-baitings** popular sport in
which a bear chained to a stake was
attacked by dogs

AUTOLYCUS Very true, sir. He, sir, he. That's the rogue
that put me into this apparel.

CLOWN Not a more cowardly rogue in all Bohemia. If you
had but looked big and spit at him, he'd have run.

AUTOLYCUS I must confess to you, sir, I am no fighter. I   105
am false of heart that way, and that he knew, I warrant
him.

CLOWN How do you now?

AUTOLYCUS Sweet sir, much better than I was. I can
stand and walk. I will even take my leave of you, and   110
pace softly towards my kinsman's.

CLOWN Shall I bring thee on the way?

AUTOLYCUS No, good-faced sir; no, sweet sir.

CLOWN Then fare thee well. I must go buy spices for our
sheep-shearing.   115

AUTOLYCUS Prosper you, sweet sir.   *Exit [Clown].*
Your purse is not hot enough to purchase your spice.
I'll be with you at your sheep-shearing, too. If I make
not this cheat bring out another and the shearers prove
sheep, let me be unrolled and my name put in the book   120
of virtue.

---

104 **but looked big** merely puffed out
your chest, looked brave
106 **false of heart** cowardly. Autolycus
may be testing the Clown's wits (cf.
virtues and *vices*, 87–92) by apparently
meaning to say '*faint* of heart', i.e.
lacking in courage, but substituting
false, deceitful.
106–7 **I warrant him** I'm sure
110 **even** just
111 **pace softly** walk gently (because of
his supposed injuries)
112 **bring** accompany
113 **good-faced** kindly faced; clean-
shaven; well-featured; stupid-looking
117 **not . . . spice** a quibble. An empty
purse was said to be cold (cf. *Tim*

3.4.14–16), whereas spice was 'hot'
(peppery, fiery). Autolycus has picked
the Clown's pocket, so his purse is too
cold to buy anything.
119 **cheat** trick (stealing from him); cf.
silly cheat, 27–8 (see n.).
   bring out lead to
119–20 **the . . . sheep** i.e. show the
shearers to be stupid, by being fleeced
(swindled)
120 **unrolled** removed from the roll; i.e.
struck off the register of villains
120–1 **put . . . virtue** be added to the list
of virtuous people; *book of virtue* recalls
the 'book of life' in Revelation, 3.5,
20.12, i.e. God's list of those promised
eternal life. See 1.2.411–12n.

116 SD] *Exit. F, opp. 115*

[*Sings.*] Jog on, jog on, the footpath way,
             And merrily hent the stile-a.
             A merry heart goes all the day,   124
             Your sad tires in a mile-a.   *Exit.*

4.4 *Enter* FLORIZEL, [*disguised as Doricles a countryman,*
         and] PERDITA [*as Queen of the Feast*].

FLORIZEL
These your unusual weeds to each part of you
Does give a life; no shepherdess, but Flora
Peering in April's front. This your sheep-shearing
Is as a meeting of the petty gods,
And you the queen on't.
PERDITA   Sir, my gracious lord,   5
To chide at your extremes it not becomes me –
O, pardon that I name them. Your high self,

122–5 Contemporary music and lyrics for this song have survived: see
  pp. 387–8.
123 **hent the stile-a** grab hold of the
  stile. For -*a* endings in rhymes, see
  TNK 3.5.61–7.
124–5 Someone who's jolly can keep
  going all day, but an unhappy person is
  worn out walking (just) a mile. Cf. *2H4*
  5.3.47; Dent, H320a, 'And a merry
  heart lives long-a.'
4.4 See pp. 72–3. The scene is set in the
  Shepherd's farm in rural Bohemia,
  close to the coast but far from
  highways (3.3.66, 4.3.28–9). The
  Shepherd has used Perdita's gold to
  buy land well above his station in life
  (3.3.117–19, 4.2.38–40). The action
  begins indoors (*at the door*, 183–4;
  come in, 356).
0.1 *Doricles* See List of Roles, 21n.
1   **unusual weeds** festive clothes (*weeds*),

over which Perdita wears garlands
of flowers (her holiday dress may be
from court: see pp. 74–5); everyday
garments, made *unusual* by flowers.
2   **Does** do (Abbott, 412)
    Flora The nymph Chloris, pursued
    by Zephyrus (the west wind), was
    turned into Flora, goddess of flowers
    and spring. In *Pandosto*, the Perdita
    character protects her face from the
    sun with a garland of flowers that
    'became her so gallantly as she seemed
    to be the goddess Flora herself'
    (p. 423).
3   **Peering . . . front** appearing at the
    start of April
4   **petty** lesser (minor Roman gods sub-
    ordinate to the 12 supreme divinities
    under Jupiter)
5   **on't** of it
6   **extremes** exaggerations (*OED*
    extreme C 5)

122 SD] Song. *F*   **4.4**] (*Scena Quarta.*)   0.1–2] *Oxf subst.; Enter Florizell, Perdita, Shepherd, Clowne,*
Polixenes, Camillo, Mopsa, Dorcas, Seruants, Autolicus. F   0.2 *as . . . Feast*] *this edn*   2 Does] (Do's)

259

The gracious mark o'th' land, you have obscured
With a swain's wearing, and me, poor lowly maid,
Most goddess-like pranked up. But that our feasts   10
In every mess have folly, and the feeders
Digest it with a custom, I should blush
To see you so attired; swoon, I think,
To show myself a glass.

FLORIZEL   I bless the time
When my good falcon made her flight across   15
Thy father's ground.

PERDITA   Now Jove afford you cause!
To me the difference forges dread; your greatness
Hath not been used to fear. Even now I tremble
To think your father by some accident
Should pass this way, as you did. O, the fates!   20
How would he look to see his work, so noble,

---

8   **mark o'th' land** object of everyone's attention (*OED* mark *n.*[1] 6); person everyone looks up to (cf. *2H4* 2.3.31–2, of Hotspur, the 'mark' that 'fashion'd others')

8–9   **obscured . . . wearing** degraded (or hidden) by shepherd's clothes. Florizel is probably wearing something more refined than ordinary working clothes: see p. 74.

10   **pranked up** decked out, dressed up (*OED* prank *v.*[4] 1a)

10–11   **But . . . folly** were it not that (1) our rural feasts always have some diners (*OED* mess *n.*[1] 5a: see 1.2.225–6n.) who behave foolishly; (2) in our feasts foolish antics accompany every course (*OED* mess *n.*[1] 1a: serving of food)

11–12   **feeders . . . custom** feasters swallow (foolishness) as customary, habitually put up with it

13–14   ***swoon . . . glass** faint if I saw myself in a mirror; swoon to recognize in your attire a reflection of mine. F's 'sworne', retained by some editors,

means 'intended, I think, to show me myself as in a mirror'.

15   **falcon** Hawking was a favourite sport of kings and noblemen (the Florizel character in *Pandosto* first sees the princess when hawking: p. 425).

16   **Jove . . . cause** may Jove give you good reason (to *bless the time*, 14); for Jove, see 2.3.124–5n.

17   **To . . . dread** the difference (in rank between us) makes me fearful

17–18   **greatness . . . fear** because of your rank you aren't used to feeling afraid

19   **accident** unusual chance

21–2   **How . . . up** How would he react to see his noble son (*work*) meanly dressed like this? The prince, who should be wearing velvet, looks like a valuable book bound in cheap covers (calf or sheepskin). Cf. the comparison reversed in *RJ* 3.2.83–4, i.e. a 'vile' book in a beautiful binding. Perdita also means that his father would think she had made him a prisoner (*bound*

12 it] *F2; not in F*   13 swoon] *Theobald;* sworne *F*

Vilely bound up? What would he say? Or how
Should I, in these my borrowed flaunts, behold
The sternness of his presence?

FLORIZEL   Apprehend
Nothing but jollity. The gods themselves,   25
Humbling their deities to love, have taken
The shapes of beasts upon them. Jupiter
Became a bull and bellowed; the green Neptune
A ram and bleated; and the fire-robed god,
Golden Apollo, a poor humble swain,   30
As I seem now. Their transformations
Were never for a piece of beauty rarer,
Nor in a way so chaste, since my desires
Run not before mine honour, nor my lusts
Burn hotter than my faith.

PERDITA   O, but sir,   35
Your resolution cannot hold when 'tis

---

up) with her rural charms: cf. 437–8
(see n.).

23 **borrowed flaunts** fancy clothes
(*OED* flaunt *n.* 2): see 1n.

24–5 **Apprehend . . . jollity** Don't think
about anything but having fun.

26 **Humbling . . . love** descending from
their divinity (1) to have sex with
humans; (2) compelled by love. The
list of gods, 27–30, is from *Pandosto*,
p. 431.

27–8 **Jupiter . . . bull** Jupiter turned
himself into a bull, carrying off
Europa (daughter of the King of
Phoenicia) to Crete where he returned
to his own form and mated with her
(a metamorphosis referred to in *MW*
5.5.3–6, *MA* 5.4.43–7).

28–9 **green . . . ram** Neptune, god of
the *green* ocean, assumed the form of
a ram and had sex with Theophane,
a princess of Thrace, whom he had
turned into a sheep.

29 **bleated** may be a comic touch; cf.

MA 5.4.48–51 (esp. *bleat*, 51). See
5.1.151–3n.

29–30 **fire-robed . . . swain** Apollo
served as a shepherd when banished
from heaven, where he was the sun-
god (*Phoebus*, 124), hence *fire-robed*,
Golden. See 2.1.183n.

31 **transformations** in Latin *metamorphoses*, hence possibly alluding to
Ovid's poem

32 **piece** person (*OED n.* 9b), woman,
girl (9a), both usages normally compli-
mentary at this date (e.g. *Tem* 1.2.56,
but cf. *Per* 4.2.41). Other meanings
in *WT* include 'work of art' (5.2.93;
see 93–4n.), 'masterpiece' or 'lady'
(5.3.38), 'something, bit' (4.4.682, 83),
'instance' or 'example' (4.4.427).

33 **way** manner; endeavour

33–4 **desires . . . honour** i.e. I don't
intend to have sex with you before
we're married

35 **faith** fidelity (to my promise to marry
you)

---

35 sir] deere sir *F2*

Opposed, as it must be, by th' power of the king.
One of these two must be necessities,
Which then will speak that you must change this purpose,
Or I my life.

FLORIZEL   Thou dearest Perdita,   40
With these forced thoughts I prithee darken not
The mirth o'th' feast – or I'll be thine, my fair,
Or not my father's. For I cannot be
Mine own, nor anything to any, if
I be not thine. To this I am most constant,   45
Though destiny say no. Be merry, gentle;
Strangle such thoughts as these with anything
That you behold the while. Your guests are coming.
Lift up your countenance as it were the day
Of celebration of that nuptial which   50
We two have sworn shall come.

PERDITA   O Lady Fortune,
Stand you auspicious!

FLORIZEL   See, your guests approach.
Address yourself to entertain them sprightly,
And let's be red with mirth.

Enter SHEPHERD, *[with]* POLIXENES *[and]* CAMILLO, *[both
disguised,]* CLOWN, MOPSA, DORCAS*[, Shepherds
and Shepherdesses]*.

38 One of two things (see 39–40n.) is inevitable.
39 **speak** declare
39–40 **you . . . life** you must change this plan (to marry me) or I must change my life; i.e. I shall be punished by your father when he finds out
41 **forced thoughts** strained, unnatural notions (*OED* thought[1] 4b, 4c); thoughts she is bound (*forced*) to have. They may stop her wanting to join the celebrations (see 135n.).
42–3 **or . . . Or** either . . . or

43–4 **For . . . any** because I shall be no good to myself or to anyone
46 **gentle** dear (girl)
48 **the while** in the meantime (before we marry)
50 **nuptial** marriage
51 **sworn** See 395n., 491.
52 **Stand you auspicious** may you favour us
53 **Address** prepare (*OED v.* 3a)
54 **red** red-faced, i.e. flushed
54.0.2 MOPSA, DORCAS See List of Roles, 27n., 28n.

54.1–3] *Rowe subst.; at 0.1–2 F; Enter All. F2*

SHEPHERD

Fie, daughter, when my old wife lived, upon   55
This day she was both pantler, butler, cook;
Both dame and servant, welcomed all, served all,
Would sing her song and dance her turn, now here
At upper end o'th' table, now i'th' middle;
On his shoulder and his, her face o'fire   60
With labour, and the thing she took to quench it
She would to each one sip. You are retired
As if you were a feasted one and not
The hostess of the meeting. Pray you, bid
These unknown friends to's welcome, for it is   65
A way to make us better friends, more known.
Come, quench your blushes and present yourself
That which you are, mistress o'th' feast. Come on,
And bid us welcome to your sheep-shearing,
As your good flock shall prosper.

PERDITA [*to Polixenes*]   Sir, welcome.   70
It is my father's will I should take on me
The hostess-ship o'th' day. [*to Camillo*] You're
          welcome, sir.
Give me those flowers there, Dorcas. Reverend sirs,

55 **Fie** exclamation, most likely said in mild annoyance (less vehement than at 2.3.17: see n.)
56 **pantler, butler** household servants in charge of food and drink, respectively
57 **dame** mistress (of the house)
59 Social distinctions were observed by seating lower-class men away from the head of the table (the diners appear to be men, 60).
60 **On . . . his** at one guest's shoulder (serving him), then another's
60–2 **o'fire . . . sip** flushed with exertion, and the alcohol (*thing*) she drank to put out the fire in her face, she would drink to each guest in turn (or give a *sip* to each)

62 **retired** reserved
63 **feasted one** guest at the feast
65 **unknown friends to's** friends who are unknown to us, i.e. Polixenes and Camillo (transposition of adjectival phrase: Abbott, 419a)
70 **As** so that
73–108 Perdita refers to many flowers and plants in Elizabethan gardens and fields. She presents evergreens (74), refers to early-autumn *carnations* (82), hands out midsummer herbs and flowers (104–5), speaks of spring flowers she wishes she had (118–26).
73 **Reverend** courteous reference to their dignity and age

70 SD] *Malone*   72 SD] *Malone*

For you there's rosemary and rue; these keep
Seeming and savour all the winter long.   75
Grace and remembrance be to you both,
And welcome to our shearing.

POLIXENES   Shepherdess,
A fair one are you. Well you fit our ages
With flowers of winter.

PERDITA   Sir, the year growing ancient,
Not yet on summer's death, nor on the birth   80
Of trembling winter, the fairest flowers o'th' season
Are our carnations and streaked gillyvors,
Which some call Nature's bastards; of that kind
Our rustic garden's barren, and I care not
To get slips of them.

POLIXENES   Wherefore, gentle maiden,   85
Do you neglect them?

PERDITA   For I have heard it said
There is an art which in their piedness shares
With great creating Nature.

74 **rosemary and rue** shrubs symbolizing faithfulness and remembrance, and sorrow and repentance respectively. Rosemary was believed to ward off plague, be good for the memory (hence an emblem of fidelity: cf. *Ham* 4.5.169), and was given at weddings. The bitter rue ('herb of grace' in *Ham* 4.5.174–5) was prescribed as an antidote to poison and a means of staying chaste (Beisley, 76–8).

75 **Seeming and savour** (their) appearance and scent

76 May you both obtain grace (God's forgiveness following repentance; see 1.2.80n.) and be remembered; see 74n.
remembrance probably four syllables.

79 **growing ancient** i.e. the first half of the year over (see 4.3n.)

82–3 **gillyvors . . . bastards** gillyflowers (pinks, also carnations), cultivated forms of dianthus. It was believed that streaked gillyflowers, cross-bred without assistance, were natural hybrids, even counterfeits (*OED* bastard *a*. 2a, 4); the other meaning of *bastards*, illegitimate children, is also present: see pp. 56–7. These were favourite flowers for flavouring wine and making garlands for celebrations (*carnation*, coronation, crowning).

83–4 **of . . . barren** our rural garden produces none of that variety (*gillyvors*)

85 **slips** cuttings (*OED n.*² 1a); see also 100.
Wherefore why

87 **piedness** variety of colour; for Perdita, the streaks confirm that gillyflowers are made by *art*, i.e. cross-fertilization, imitating the natural process; see 88n.

88 **great creating** powerful creator (*OED*'s first citation of 'creating' as *ppl. a.*): see pp. 50–8.

POLIXENES   Say there be,
Yet Nature is made better by no mean
But Nature makes that mean. So over that art,   90
Which you say adds to Nature, is an art
That Nature makes. You see, sweet maid, we marry
A gentler scion to the wildest stock,
And make conceive a bark of baser kind
By bud of nobler race. This is an art   95
Which does mend Nature – change it rather – but
The art itself is Nature.
PERDITA   So it is.
POLIXENES

Then make your garden rich in gillyvors,
And do not call them bastards.
PERDITA   I'll not put
The dibble in earth to set one slip of them;   100
No more than, were I painted, I would wish
This youth should say 'twere well, and only therefore
Desire to breed by me. Here's flowers for you:
Hot lavender, mints, savory, marjoram,

89–90 **Nature . . . mean** i.e. anything we do to improve Nature is still natural
89, 90 **mean** means
92–5 **marry . . . race** graft a carefully cultivated cutting (*gentler scion*) on the trunk of a tree (*stock*) growing entirely wild and (thus) fertilize a lower-grade bark with a bud from a higher-quality tree. The terms also refer to rank, marrying lower- to upper-class people. See 1.1.24n. on *branch*, 1.2.244n.
96 **mend** make up for a deficiency in
100 **dibble** dibber, a tool for making holes to plant (*set*) seeds and cuttings (slips)
101 **painted** wearing make-up
102 **This youth** i.e. Florizel
102–3 **'twere . . . me** i.e. only art (my wearing make-up) would kindle his

desire to do what Nature wills, to have sex and procreate
104 **Hot** The theory of humours held that plants, like humans, had four elements (hot, cold, dry, moist), that determined an organism. Elizabethans classified the herbs listed at 104–5 as hot, i.e. highly fragrant and aromatic. However, Perdita may be distinguishing between types of lavender: e.g. lavender spike (hot and dry) and French lavender (cold).
lavender emblematic of affection
mints i.e. different kinds of mint plant
savory common garden plant used in cooking
marjoram another herb used in cooking (now also called oregano)

98 your] *F2;* you *F*

The marigold, that goes to bed wi'th' sun,   105
And with him rises, weeping. These are flowers
Of middle summer, and I think they are given
To men of middle age. You're very welcome.
        [*Gives them flowers.*]

CAMILLO

I should leave grazing were I of your flock,
And only live by gazing.

PERDITA   Out, alas,   110
You'd be so lean that blasts of January
Would blow you through and through.
[*to Florizel*]   Now, my fair'st friend,
I would I had some flowers o'th' spring that might
Become your time of day; [*to Mopsa and Dorcas*] and
        yours, and yours,
That wear upon your virgin branches yet   115
Your maidenheads growing. O Proserpina,
For the flowers now that, frighted, thou let'st fall

105–6 **marigold . . . weeping** The garden marigold (*solsequium* or 'sun-follower' because its bright yellow flowers opened and closed with the sun rising and setting) is wet with morning dew (*weeping*). See 1.2.326–7n. The marigold *goes to bed* with the summer sun, i.e. sleeps when it does, but is also its lover (unlike spring *primroses* that *die unmarried*, 122–4; see n.).

108 **men . . . age** Cf. 78–9, where Polixenes implies that he and Camillo are men of old age. Perdita is apparently reassuring them that they don't look elderly. Florizel, Mopsa and Dorcas are clearly not yet middle aged (113–14).

109–10 [1]**I . . . gazing** courtly gallantry: (you're so beautiful that) were I one of your flock (of admirers) I wouldn't need to eat, I could live just by gazing at you.

110 **Out, alas** a mild exclamation; similar to modern 'come off it'

114 **Become . . . day** i.e. suit your age

115–16 **wear . . . growing** have your first blossoms (*OED* maidenhead *n.*[1] 2) still unplucked on your virgin branches. Mopsa and Dorcas, unmarried, are likened to young trees not yet ferti-lized (*virgin branches* also refers to the girls' hair, worn long to show they are unmarried).

116 **growing** perhaps one syllable; but see pp. 127, 129.

116–18 **Proserpina . . . wagon** In clas-sical mythology Proserpina ('pro-sèr-pin-a'), daughter of Ceres, goddess of agriculture, was abducted by Pluto (*Dis*), god of the dead, in his chariot (*wagon*) as she gathered spring flowers (including violets and lilies, 120, 126). See Fig. 8 and pp. 50–3.

117 **frighted** because you were frightened

105 wi'th'] *(with')*   108 SD] *Cam*[1]   112 SD] *Cam*[1]   114 SD] *Cam*[1] *subst.*

From Dis's wagon! Daffodils,
That come before the swallow dares, and take
The winds of March with beauty; violets, dim,   120
But sweeter than the lids of Juno's eyes
Or Cytherea's breath; pale primroses,
That die unmarried ere they can behold
Bright Phoebus in his strength – a malady
Most incident to maids; bold oxlips, and   125
The crown imperial; lilies of all kinds,
The flower-de-luce being one. O, these I lack

118 Four accented syllables, as here, are not unusual in Shakespeare (Abbott, 508–9). There is no need to regularize, e.g. by adding an adjective to *daffodils*: see p. 127.

119 **before . . . dares** The swallow's return from warmer lands was said to mark the start of summer.
take charm, captivate (cf. *Tem* 5.1.314)

120 **dim** homely (compared with bright daffodils); modest (heads of violets hang down, half-hidden)

121–2 **sweeter . . . breath** sweeter to *behold* than the lids of Juno's eyes, sweeter to *smell* than Cytherea's breath. Juno, queen of the gods, was renowned for beauty (her eyelids are praised in *Per* 5.1.101–2; see also 2.1.7–15n.). Cytherea was another name for Venus, goddess of love (born on the island of Cythera); cf. *Cym* 2.2.14. Violets, less attractive and prominent than daffodils (120), still surpass mythological goddesses in delicate beauty and fragrance.

122–4 **pale . . . strength** Primroses are early spring flowers that cease to bloom (*die unmarried*) or fail to produce seeds (Beisley, 81), before they *behold* the sun (*Phoebus*, the sun god) at its hottest in summer (*in his strength*). The sun has some flowers as lovers, e.g. marigolds, but not *primroses* (see 105–6n.).

124–5 **malady . . . maids** illness most likely to afflict young, unmarried girls.

This was known as green sickness, i.e. chlorosis, an anaemic condition, the chief symptom of which was a yellowish green complexion (colour of *pale primroses*, 122); according to folklore girls who died of it were turned into primroses.

125 **bold oxlips** The Elizabethan herbalist Gerard (635) claimed that the oxlip was a variety of cowslip. In fact it is a cross between cowslip and primrose (*OED* oxlip 1), *bold* because its stalk is bigger and stronger than the cowslip's, making it stand more upright.

126 **crown imperial** tall yellow fritillary, best-known species of liliaceous plants (first citation in *OED n.* 2). Gerard describes it as a recent import from Constantinople, its flowers growing at the top of the stalk, 'compassing it round about in form of an imperial crown' (153).

127 **flower-de-luce** fleur-de-lis, which herbalists correctly identified as a variety of iris (Gerard, 45–53, illustrates fifteen kinds of fleur-de-lis). Contemporary writers, e.g. Edmund Spenser and Ben Jonson, distinguished it from the white lily. However, the connection between the flowers (126–7) is here heraldic not botanical, the fleur-de-lis being the lily on the royal arms of France. Both crown imperial and flower-de-luce are referred to in *H5* (2.0.10, 5.2.208).

To make you garlands of, and my sweet friend
To strew him o'er and o'er.

FLORIZEL   What, like a corpse?

PERDITA
No, like a bank, for love to lie and play on,   130
Not like a corpse – or if, not to be buried,
But quick and in mine arms. Come, take your flowers.
Methinks I play as I have seen them do
In Whitsun pastorals; sure this robe of mine
Does change my disposition.

FLORIZEL   What you do   135
Still betters what is done. When you speak, sweet,
I'd have you do it ever; when you sing,
I'd have you buy and sell so, so give alms,
Pray so, and for the ordering your affairs,
To sing them too. When you do dance, I wish you   140
A wave o'th' sea, that you might ever do
Nothing but that, move still, still so,

129 **corpse** Wedding beds as well as graves were strewn with flowers (cf. *Ham* 5.1.234–5, *Per* 4.1.12–15). At 128–9 Perdita thinks of flowers to adorn her future husband, but Florizel asks, play-fully, whether she means ones for a grave (see 131–2n.). See 5.1.58n.

130 **bank** i.e. bank of flowers (or hedge-row)

to . . . on to have sex; to behave lovingly

131–2 **Not . . . quick** A corpse (Latin *corpus*, body), could mean a living or a dead body (*OED n.* 1). Perdita replies that he can only be like a corpse if he means a living body (*quick*, *OED* B *n.*[1] 1a).

133 **play** take a role. See 1.2.187n.

134 **Whitsun** White Sunday or Whitsuntide (English name for Pentecost, seventh Sunday after Easter), was the start of spring festivi-ties (*pastorals:* see p. 50) that included

plays, morris dancing and May games with a summer king and queen, whom Perdita may refer to at 133 (cf. the allusion to a Whitsun play in *TGV* 4.4.156–66).

sure certainly

135 **disposition** mood or inclination (see 41n.); tendency of mind, temperament (*OED* 6). By dressing and behaving as a superior, Perdita begins to feel she is one.

135–6 **What . . . done** Each of your actions outdoes the one before; your actions are always superior to anyone else's; everything you do is made special because you do it.

137–40 **when . . . too** i.e. sing while you do every ordinary and special thing: buying and selling, acts of charity (giving *alms* to the poor), praying and arranging personal matters

142 **move . . . so** i.e. always be in move-ment like that (dancing), exactly like

139 ordering] (ord'ring)

And own no other function. Each your doing,
So singular in each particular,
Crowns what you are doing in the present deeds,   145
That all your acts are queens.
PERDITA   O Doricles,
Your praises are too large. But that your youth
And the true blood which peeps fairly through't
Do plainly give you out an unstained shepherd,
With wisdom I might fear, my Doricles,   150
You wooed me the false way.
FLORIZEL   I think you have
As little skill to fear as I have purpose
To put you to't. But come, our dance, I pray;
Your hand, my Perdita – so turtles pair,
That never mean to part.
PERDITA   I'll swear for 'em.   155
POLIXENES [*to Camillo*]
This is the prettiest low-born lass that ever
Ran on the greensward. Nothing she does or seems
But smacks of something greater than herself,

that. Florizel pictures Perdita in movement, but frame by frame as it were,
hence the contradiction in *move still*.
Two of the four stresses in this line
fall on *still, still*, creating an impression
in sound of stillness, at the crest of
the wave (141), but also of successive
waves; cf. *so, so* (138), and see Abbott,
509, and pp. 47–8.
143 **own . . . function** do nothing else;
have no other being (but in dance)
143–6 **Each . . . queens** Everything you
do is so uniquely yours in every respect
that it brings perfection (*OED* crown
v.[1] 9) to whatever you're doing at the
moment, making all your actions superior (like a queen's). *Crowns* could also
mean 'brings to completion' (*OED* 10);
cf. *Mac* 4.1.149, 'crown my thoughts
with acts'.

146 **Doricles** See 0.1 and n.
146–51 **O . . . way** See 5.1.102n.
147 **But that** were it not that
148 **true . . . through't** virtuous passion (or noble birth), showing clearly
through his *youth*, 147
149 **give you out** show you to be
unstained pure
151 **the false way** i.e. with flattery
152 **skill** reason
152–3 **purpose . . . to't** i.e. intention to
frighten you
154 **turtles** turtle doves: symbols of
constancy, proverbially faithful (Dent,
T624, 'As true as a turtle to her mate').
Cf. 5.3.132.
155 **I'll . . . em** I'll swear they do.
157 **greensward** grassy turf
seems appears to be
158 **smacks of** hints at

148 fairly] so fairly *Capell*   156 SD] *Oxf*

Too noble for this place.
CAMILLO   He tells her something
    That makes her blood look out. Good sooth, she is   160
    The queen of curds and cream.
CLOWN   Come on, strike up!
DORCAS   Mopsa must be your mistress. Marry, garlic to
    mend her kissing with!
MOPSA   Now, in good time!   165
CLOWN   Not a word, a word, we stand upon our manners.
    Come, strike up!   [*Music*]
    Here a dance of Shepherds and Shepherdesses [*including*
    Florizel and Perdita]   [*Exeunt Shepherds and Shepherdesses.*]

---

160 ***makes . . . out** makes her blush.
Theobald's emendation, 'out' for F's
'on't', is plausible, despite the slight
difficulty about how the apostrophe got
there. One explanation is that the compositor misread an end-of-line comma
in the line above (159). Another is that
Crane, the scribe (see p. 352), formed
letters with a top curl, easily mistaken
for an apostrophe. Other instances of
'on't' where 'out' might be expected are
in *TN* 3.4.197, *Cym* 2.3.43.
  Good sooth in truth
161 **queen . . . cream** A shepherdess working outdoors ought to be
sunburnt, at this date a sign of low
rank, but Perdita's complexion is as
creamy as any court lady's (cf. the
red and white when she blushes,
160). She's also like a summer *queen*
(or whitepot queen, named after a
pudding made with cream or milk)
chosen to rule with a 'king' over the
May games.
162–7 In Shakespeare, lower-class characters as a rule speak in prose not
verse, and their superiors address them
in prose too. There are small anomalies
in 4.4 of *WT*, where this social rule

isn't observed and the speeches are
in fact in blank verse. This is the
case at 162–7, even though in F these
appear to be laid out as prose. There
are clearer instances of verse where
there should be prose at 632–3 and
749–51 (see nn.). All three passages are
arranged as prose in this edition.
162 **strike up** begin the music
163–4 **Marry . . . with** But get her to eat
some garlic to make her kisses sweeter;
i.e. her breath's so bad even garlic
would improve it. 'Garlic' was the
name of a popular jig (*OED* 2).
  Marry mild exclamation (from 'by the
Virgin Mary')
165 **in good time** that's rich (coming
from you)
166 **stand upon** pride ourselves on (*OED*
stand *v.* 78i); must be careful about
167 SD2 Perdita's participation (169)
suggests that the dance was more
sedate than the boisterous morris,
performed to pipes and drums (see
184–5), with dancers wearing bells on
their legs, waving sticks and handker-
chiefs. The morris was almost always
performed by men, even Maid Marian
being played by a man in drag.

160 out] *Theobald;* on't *F*   167 SD1] *Malone*   SD2 *including . . . Perdita*] *this edn*   SD3] *this edn*

POLIXENES

    Pray, good shepherd, what fair swain is this
    Which dances with your daughter?

SHEPHERD

    They call him Doricles, and boasts himself   170
    To have a worthy feeding; but I have it
    Upon his own report, and I believe it –
    He looks like sooth. He says he loves my daughter;
    I think so, too, for never gazed the moon
    Upon the water as he'll stand and read,   175
    As 'twere, my daughter's eyes; and, to be plain,
    I think there is not half a kiss to choose
    Who loves another best.

POLIXENES   She dances featly.

SHEPHERD

    So she does anything, though I report it
    That should be silent. If young Doricles   180
    Do light upon her, she shall bring him that
    Which he not dreams of.

Enter Servant.

SERVANT   O, master, if you did but hear the pedlar at the
    door, you would never dance again after a tabor and
    pipe. No, the bagpipe could not move you. He sings   185

170 **boasts himself** (he) brags, says of
himself (omitted nominative: Abbott,
399)
171 **To . . . feeding** that he owns extensive grazing lands
171–2 **I . . . report** I've only heard it
from him
173 **like sooth** truthful
175 **water** sea
    read read (like a book); guess the
meaning of
178 **Who . . . best** which of them loves
the other more
    featly elegantly
179–80 **though . . . silent** proverbial

(Dent, S114); cf. modern 'though I say
so myself'.
181 **light upon her** has the good luck
to marry her; suggesting discovery by
chance (*OED* light *v*.[1] 10d)
    that i.e. a huge dowry (cf. 3.3.118)
184–5 **after . . . pipe** to a small drum and
whistle-pipe (which could be played
together by one person, and were used
in the morris; see 167 SD2n.).
185 **bagpipe** popular musical instrument in
rural England. It had sexual connotations
(e.g. of male genitals: Williams, 59–60),
which the Servant doesn't acknowledge
or is unaware of (see 196–7n.).

271

several tunes faster than you'll tell money. He utters
them as he had eaten ballads, and all men's ears grew
to his tunes.

CLOWN He could never come better. He shall come in. I
love a ballad but even too well, if it be doleful matter   190
merrily set down, or a very pleasant thing indeed and
sung lamentably.

SERVANT He hath songs for man or woman of all sizes.
No milliner can so fit his customers with gloves. He has
the prettiest love songs for maids, so without bawdry,   195
which is strange, with such delicate burdens of dildos
and fadings, 'jump her and thump her'; and where
some stretch-mouthed rascal would, as it were, mean

186 **several** different
  tell count
187 **as . . . eaten** as if he had swallowed
  them whole or they were all he ate
  ballads songs on topical and romantic
  subjects, sung to well-known tunes.
  They also dealt with disasters, extraordinary events (cf. 5.2.23–5) and godly
  themes, e.g. repentance of sinners.
  Like proclamations (see 3.1.15n.), ballads were printed on one side of sheets
  of paper (broadsides).
187–8 **grew to** were stuck to; grew to be
  part of (*OED* grow *v.* 3b); i.e. people
  were so attracted to his *tunes* they
  couldn't stop listening. Cf. *stuck in
  ears*, 613–14 (see n.).
189 **come better** arrive at a better moment
190 **but even** only
190–2 **doleful . . . lamentably** The
  Clown's tastes in ballads (sad subjects
  set to jolly music and the reverse)
  are meant to appear unrefined, but
  only up to a point. In Shakespeare's
  day sacred subjects were set to old
  dance tunes, perhaps encouraging a
  pleasure in incongruity and contrast.
  See 4.3.44–5n.
193 **sizes** classes, kinds (*OED n.*[1] 12b)
194 **milliner** haberdasher; originally, a
  retailer selling clothes and fancy goods
  from Milan (*OED n.* 2a)

195 **without bawdry** free of indecent
  language, suitable for young girls
  (*maids*); ballads were often obscene, so
  the Servant says this is *strange* (196).
196 **delicate burdens** refined, exquisite
  refrains; possibly also an unintended
  reference to pregnancy (cf. 264 and
  see 196–7n.)
196–7 **dildos and fadings** Nonsense
  words like these appear as refrains
  in ballads without obvious sexual
  meanings; but they also had indecent
  connotations. By 1600 a dildo was
  an artificial penis (*OED* dildo[1]). It is
  less clear what a fading was, although
  there was a jig of that name, possibly a rude one (*OED*). Partridge
  (103) suggests it meant 'orgasm'
  (by association of 'amorous sighing
  and a steamy breath' with 'to fade',
  cognate with Latin *vapor*, exhala-
  tion), but it may have meant simply
  losing strength, i.e. detumescence.
  Thus *dildos and fadings* would be false
  penises and ineffectual ones; scarcely
  delicate burdens, 196.
197 **jump . . . thump** *jump* is in the
  refrains of contemporary songs: like
  the more brutal *thump*, it implies having vigorous sex.
198 **stretch-mouthed** loose-talking
  (Partridge, 201), i.e. foul-mouthed

mischief and break a foul gap into the matter, he makes
the maid to answer, 'Whoop, do me no harm, good   200
man'; puts him off, slights him, with 'Whoop, do me
no harm, good man!'

POLIXENES   This is a brave fellow.

CLOWN   Believe me, thou talkest of an admirable conceited
fellow. Has he any unbraided wares?   205

SERVANT   He hath ribbons of all the colours i'th' rainbow;
points more than all the lawyers in Bohemia can
learnedly handle, though they come to him by th' gross;
inkles, caddises, cambrics, lawns, why, he sings 'em
over as they were gods or goddesses. You would think a 210
smock were a she-angel, he so chants to the sleeve-hand

199 **break . . . matter** interject an
obscene remark into the song (to break
meant to speak). In the ballad, whenever the man is about to say something
rude, the maid cuts him short, with the
refrain in 200–2. Some earlier editors,
unhappy with *gap* (breach), emended it
to 'jape', a word rare at this date (*OED
n.* 2) and which Shakespeare doesn't
use elsewhere, or to 'jest' (dirty joke,
as in *MA* 5.1.181–2).
  he the pedlar (Autolycus)
200–1, 201–2 **Whoop . . . man** A contemporary tune with this title has survived,
but it has no lyrics.
201 **puts him off** interrupts him
  slights him dismisses him contemptuously
203 **brave** splendid (said ironically of the
Servant, the pedlar, or the *rascal* in the
ballad, 198)
204 **admirable conceited** wonderfully
clever
205 **unbraided wares** probably brand-
new goods, not shop-soiled. *OED* says
braided wares were goods that had
faded, defining 'unbraided' as untar-
nished (*OED* 1, only citation). Hulme
(298–300) argues that the Clown is
referring to songs, not haberdashery. If
he is, he may be asking whether there
are any ballads less filthy than the one
at 195–9; a 'braid' could be a subtle

trick (*OED n.* 3), so 'braided' lyrics
might be overly clever as well as rude
(see 204n.). Alternatively he is calling
for new songs, i.e. ones they haven't
heard lots of times (the girls have one
tune by heart; see 295n.).
206 **all . . . rainbow** proverbial (Dent,
C519)
207 **points** laces with metal tags on them,
to hold clothes together (with a pun on
points in a legal argument)
208 **gross** 12 dozen, i.e. in large quanti-
ties, wholesale (punning on to engross,
copy out a legal document)
209 **inkles** tape made of coarse linen thread
  caddises worsted tapes for garters
(*OED* caddis[1] 2c)
  cambrics, lawns types of high-qual-
ity linen (or cheaper cotton imitations
of them)
209–10 **sings . . . goddesses** i.e. sings
their praises (each in turn) as if they
were deities. A satirical hit at court
and city fashions and the praise they
attract, but Florizel's hyperbole (2–5)
may also be a target.
210 **over** from beginning to end (*OED
adv.* 14a)
211 **smock** petticoat (cf. *placket*, 243; see
n.); whore
  chants sings (in praise of)
  sleeve-hand wristband or cuff of a
sleeve (*OED* sleeve *n.* 8b)

and the work about the square on't.

CLOWN Prithee bring him in, and let him approach
singing.

PERDITA Forewarn him that he use no scurrilous words   215
in's tunes.   [*Exit Servant.*]

CLOWN You have of these pedlars that have more in them
than you'd think, sister.

PERDITA Ay, good brother, or go about to think.

Enter AUTOLYCUS, [*disguised, carrying his pack and*] *singing.*

AUTOLYCUS

Lawn as white as driven snow,   220
Cypress black as e'er was crow,
Gloves as sweet as damask roses,
Masks for faces and for noses;
Bugle-bracelet, necklace-amber,

---

212 **work . . . on't** embroidery on the
smock's *square*, the material covering
the bosom
216 **in's** in his
217 **You . . . pedlars** there are some of
these pedlars. For the construction
'You have of them', cf. *AW* 2.5.45, 'I
have kept of them tame'.
219 **go . . . think** have any intention
of thinking; *go about to*, 'intend to',
was common (repeated 704); cf. *Ham*
3.2.338.
220–31 The song belongs to the 'Cries
of London' genre, originally sung by
pedlars and street sellers: see pp. 388–9.
220 **Lawn** See 209n.
white . . . snow proverbial (Dent,
S591)
221 **Cypress** cypress lawn, a light, transparent material resembling crepe or
fine gauze, originally imported from
Cyprus; when black, used for mourning clothes (*OED* cypress[3] 1c)

black. . . . crow proverbial (Dent,
C844)
222 Gloves were commonly perfumed
(see 250 and cf. *MA* 3.4.56–7). Damask
roses, red or velvety pink, have a sweet
scent. Cf. Dent, R178, 'As sweet as
a rose'.
223 Silk masks, adornment or disguise
or to protect the face, were still novel
in Elizabethan England (*OED* mask
n.[3] 1a). Masks for the nose were small
black silk patches, worn by fashionable
women to hide a fault or to show off
their complexion (*OED* patch n.[1] 1c).
The joke is that country girls, outdoors
all year, without pale complexions to
preserve (see 161n.), might need such
masks. Early audiences probably associated masks for the nose with trying
to hide the effects of venereal disease.
224 **Bugle-bracelet** bracelet made of
small black glass beads (*OED* bugle
n.[3] 2)

---

216 SD] *Capell* 219.1] *at 0.2 F* 219.1+ AUTOLYCUS] *(Autolicus)* 219.1 *disguised . . . and*] *Oxf
subst.* 220 SP] *Schanzer; not in F*

Perfume for a lady's chamber; 225
Golden coifs and stomachers
For my lads to give their dears;
Pins and poking-sticks of steel,
What maids lack from head to heel –
Come buy of me, come, come buy, come buy, 230
Buy, lads, or else your lasses cry. Come buy!

CLOWN   If I were not in love with Mopsa, thou shouldst
take no money of me, but, being enthralled as I am, it
will also be the bondage of certain ribbons and gloves.

MOPSA   I was promised them against the feast, but they 235
come not too late now.

DORCAS   He hath promised you more than that, or there
be liars.

MOPSA   He hath paid you all he promised you. Maybe he
has paid you more, which will shame you to give him 240
again.

CLOWN   Is there no manners left among maids? Will they
wear their plackets where they should bear their faces?
Is there not milking-time, when you are going to bed,

225 **chamber** room, bedroom; probably
also vagina
226 **Golden coifs** women's gold-
coloured, close-fitting caps
stomachers decorative central parts
in women's bodices covering stomach
and chest
228 **poking-sticks** metal rods which,
when heated, were used to stiffen
starched ruffs; a joke about other
things *maids lack* (229), i.e. penises,
men to have sex with, is also intended.
229 **from . . . heel** proverbial (Dent,
T436)
233–4 **being . . . gloves** as I am tied to
her in love, certain of your ribbons
and gloves will also have to be tied in
a parcel
235 **against** in time for; before

239–41 **He . . . again** i.e. he has got you
pregnant, which will shame you when
you have to give back what he gave
you (a child)
242–3 **Will . . . faces** Do they intend
to show off (*OED* wear *v.*[1] 7) their
private parts in the way they bare
their faces (i.e. expose what should
stay hidden); do they have to speak
out of their placket-holes, i.e. bawdily, when they should talk normally
(Partridge, 161–2; *OED* where *adv.*
10b(*a*)).
243 **plackets** A placket was a petticoat,
but also a pocket or slit in a petticoat,
hence slang for the vagina; cf. 614
(see n.).
244–6 **Is . . . guests** i.e. must you speak
like this in public?

239 Maybe] (^May be)

275

or kiln-hole, to whistle of these secrets, but you must   245
be tittle-tattling before all our guests? 'Tis well they
are whispering. Clammer your tongues and not a word
more

MOPSA   I have done. Come, you promised me a tawdry-
lace and a pair of sweet gloves   250

CLOWN   Have I not told thee how I was cozened by the
way and lost all my money?

AUTOLYCUS   And indeed, sir, there are cozeners abroad,
therefore it behoves men to be wary.

CLOWN   Fear not thou, man, thou shalt lose nothing   255
here.

AUTOLYCUS   I hope so, sir, for I have about me many
parcels of charge.

CLOWN   What hast here? Ballads?

MOPSA   Pray now, buy some. I love a ballad in print,   260
a-life, for then we are sure they are true.

AUTOLYCUS   Here's one to a very doleful tune, how a
usurer's wife was brought to bed of twenty money-bags
at a burden, and how she longed to eat adders' heads
and toads carbonadoed.   265

245 **kiln-hole** large fireplace or oven in a
house (big enough to sit in and gossip);
probably also a bawdy reference to the
vagina. F's 'kill-hole' indicates original
pronunciation, as in F *MW* 4.2.54, the
only other instance in Shakespeare.
whistle whisper (*OED v.* 10); not used
elsewhere by Shakespeare with this
meaning
247 **Clammer your tongues** i.e. shut up,
stop making a din; 'to clamour', probably
a term from bell-ringing, from 'to clam',
make a harsh sound from ringing bells
wrongly (*OED v.²* 1a). Or it may refer
to deadening the sound by covering the
clapper with felt, or to the technique of
making a loud crescendo of peals followed immediately by silencing the bell
(*OED* clamour *v.²* 2, first citation). F's
spelling, 'Clammer', has been explained

as a misreading of 'charm 'a', or 'clam
'a' (your tongues), i.e. be quiet, as in *Oth*
5.2.180, 'charm your tongue'.
249–50 **tawdry-lace** brightly coloured
silk neckerchief
250 **sweet** See 222n.
251 **cozened . . . way** cheated on the
road
253 **abroad** about
258 **parcels of charge** valuable goods
261 **a-life** on my life (mild oath)
263 **was . . . of** gave birth to
264 **at a burden** in one birth
265 **carbonadoed** cut up, scored across,
broiled
262–5 Usury, lending money at exorbitant
rates, was legal but deplored. However
grotesquely absurd, a monstrous birth
of money-bags would have seemed
to Elizabethans a miraculous punish-

245 kiln-hole] *(*kill-hole*)*

MOPSA   Is it true, think you?

AUTOLYCUS   Very true, and but a month old.

DORCAS   Bless me from marrying a usurer!

AUTOLYCUS   Here's the midwife's name to't, one Mistress
Tale-Porter, and five or six honest wives' that were 270
present. Why should I carry lies abroad?

MOPSA [*to Clown*]   Pray you now, buy it.

CLOWN   Come on, lay it by, and let's first see moe ballads.
We'll buy the other things anon.

AUTOLYCUS   Here's another ballad, of a fish that 275
appeared upon the coast on Wednesday the fourscore
of April, forty thousand fathom above water, and sung
this ballad against the hard hearts of maids. It was
thought she was a woman and was turned into a cold
fish for she would not exchange flesh with one that 280
loved her. The ballad is very pitiful, and as true.

DORCAS   Is it true too, think you?

AUTOLYCUS   Five justices' hands at it, and witnesses

ment. The wife's desire to eat poisonous things may be God's judgement on
usury, or a craving for unusual food,
associated with pregnancy.
268 **Bless me** God keep me
269 **name to't** name (on the ballad),
attesting its truthfulness
270 **Tale-Porter** bearer of gossip, old
wives' tales (see 275–81n., 5.2.28 and
n.), with a pun on 'tale' as 'tail', penis:
she's a tail-porter, a whore who bears
the weight of pricks, or a doorkeeper
letting in tails or customers, i.e. a
bawd (something midwives were often
called).
  wives' i.e. wives' names
273 **lay it by** put it aside
  moe more
274 **anon** straightaway
275–81 Ballads like those about the fish
and the usurer's wife (262–5) dealt
with monstrosities and strange hap-

penings (cf. *Tem* 2.2.24–33, 3.2.27–8),
and with women punished for having
hard hearts (278) towards their suitors.
Ard² notes a 1604 ballad about a monstrous fish that was a woman from the
waist up. See 1.2.179n., 5.1.102n.
276 **fourscore** eightieth
277 **fathom** general measurement
of six feet (two metres), not just
for measuring depth. The fish was
supposedly flying 45 miles (72.4
kilometres) high.
279–80 **cold fish** sexually frigid girl
(Partridge, 81, 106); someone lacking
in feeling. See 1.2.179n.
280 **exchange flesh** have sex; cf. Dent,
F369, 'Young fish and old flesh are
best', connecting eating with sex.
283 **Five . . . it** It has the signed affidavits
of five justices of the peace (magis-
trates).
  witnesses testimonials (*OED n.* 2a)

269 Mistress] *(Mist.)*   272 SD] *Oxf*   Pray] *(*Pray)*

more than my pack will hold.

CLOWN   Lay it by, too. Another.   285

AUTOLYCUS   This is a merry ballad, but a very pretty
one.

MOPSA   Let's have some merry ones.

AUTOLYCUS   Why, this is a passing merry one, and goes
to the tune of 'Two Maids Wooing a Man'. There's   290
scarce a maid westward but she sings it. 'Tis in request,
I can tell you.

MOPSA   We can both sing it. If thou'lt bear a part thou
shalt hear; 'tis in three parts.

DORCAS   We had the tune on't a month ago.   295

AUTOLYCUS   I can bear my part, you must know 'tis my
occupation. Have at it with you.

    [*They sing.*]

AUTOLYCUS   Get you hence, for I must go
          Where it fits not you to know.

DORCAS   Whither?   300

MOPSA   O whither?

DORCAS   Whither?

MOPSA   It becomes thy oath full well,
          Thou to me thy secrets tell.

DORCAS   Me too. Let me go thither.   305

MOPSA   Or thou goest to th' grange or mill,

DORCAS   If to either, thou dost ill.

AUTOLYCUS   Neither.

---

284 **pack** large pedlar's bag; bigger than a
tinker's *budget* (see 4.3.20n.), allowing
Autolycus to hide one in the other
289 **passing** extremely
293, 296 **bear** sing; at 296, quibbling on
use (or 'bare', show you) my penis
295 The girls have learnt the tune of the
ballad (*on't*, of it) a month earlier; they
are literate enough to read and sing the
new lyrics straight off.
296–7 **'tis my occupation** it's my

job (I'm a singer); I'm a fornicator
(Partridge, 155)
297 **Have . . . you** Let's start; let's have a
go at it together (the song, but also sex).
298–313 Music and additional lyrics for
this song survive in manuscript: see
pp. 389–93, 399–400.
299 **it . . . to** you do not need to
300 **Whither** where (are you going) to
306 **Or . . . or** either . . . or
grange outlying farmhouse, large barn

297 SD] *Oxf*   298 SP] *Rowe;* Song *F (SP Aut. at 299)*

DORCAS	What neither?	
AUTOLYCUS	Neither.	310
DORCAS	Thou hast sworn my love to be.	
MOPSA	Thou hast sworn it more to me.	
	Then whither goest? Say, whither?	

CLOWN   We'll have this song out anon by ourselves. My
father and the gentlemen are in sad talk, and we'll not   315
trouble them. Come, bring away thy pack after me.
Wenches, I'll buy for you both. Pedlar, let's have the
first choice. Follow me, girls.

[Exit with Dorcas and Mopsa.]

AUTOLYCUS   And you shall pay well for 'em.

[Sings.]	Will you buy any tape,	320
	Or lace for your cape,	
	My dainty duck, my dear-a?	
	Any silk, any thread,	
	Any toys for your head,	
	Of the new'st and fin'st, fin'st wear-a?	325
	Come to the pedlar,	
	Money's a meddler,	
	That doth utter all men's ware-a.	*Exit.*

314 **out anon** in full straightaway
315 **gentlemen** F has 'Gent.', so it is possible that the Clown isn't referring to both of the gentlemen guests, just Polixenes.
sad serious
316 **pack** See 284n.
319 **pay well** i.e. the Clown will pay more than he knows because Autolycus will (if he can) have sex with his girlfriends, pick his pockets and charge him for the ballads and trinkets
320–8 unknown outside the play; the earliest setting is from the 18th century; see pp. 393, 401.
332 **duck** darling; cf. Dent, 630.1, 'Dainty as a duck'.
334 **toys . . . head** trinkets for your hair

(or perhaps caps, headdresses). Cf. Dent, T456.1, 'To have toys in one's head', i.e. indulge in idle fancies.
327–8 Money's a troublemaker that interferes, mixes up and puts on sale (*doth utter*) everything a man owns (*OED* meddler 2; utter *v.*¹ 1a). Autolycus means that the rustics will need money to buy wares (320–5), but also that money confuses ranks (would the Clown be chased by girls if he weren't rich?). The pun is on 'medlar', the brown fruit called 'open-arse' because of its gaping apex (associated with female genitalia, prostitutes: cf. *MM* 4.3.171). 'Money's a whore and bawd that can buy anything a man has', Autolycus sings, 'even his woman.'

315 gentlemen] *(Gent.)*   318 SD] *Rowe*   320 SD] *Staunton;* Song. *F*   320–1, 323–4, 326–7] *as Johnson; single lines F*

[*Enter the* Servant.]

SERVANT   Master, there is three carters, three shepherds,
three neatherds, three swineherds that have made   330
themselves all men of hair. They call themselves
saultiers, and they have a dance which the wenches
say is a gallimaufry of gambols, because they are not
in't. But they themselves are o'th' mind, if it be not
too rough for some that know little but bowling, it will   335
please plentifully.

SHEPHERD   Away! We'll none on't. Here has been too
much homely foolery already. [*to Polixenes*] I know, sir,
we weary you.

POLIXENES   You weary those that refresh us. Pray, let's see   340
these four threes of herdsmen.

SERVANT   One three of them, by their own report, sir,
hath danced before the king, and not the worst of the
three but jumps twelve foot and a half by th' square.

SHEPHERD   Leave your prating. Since these good men are   345
pleased, let them come in – but quickly, now.

SERVANT   Why, they stay at door, sir.

---

329 **carters** men who drive farm carts;
men of low breeding (*OED* carter[1]
2b)
330 **neatherds** cowherds
330–1 **made . . . hair** dressed in animal
skins, satyr costumes (see 343n.,
347.1)
332 **saultiers** tumblers, vaulters, from
the French *sauter*, to leap (*OED* sault
v.[2]). The Servant confuses *satyrs*
(347.1) with *saultiers* (pronounced
'sow-ti-airs'), an old word for acro-
bats.
333 **gallimaufry of gambols** confused
jumble of leaping and dancing
334 **are o'th' mind** believe that

335 **bowling** the game of bowls, i.e. a
sedate pastime
338 **homely** rough (*OED a.* 4a)
340 **weary** tire the patience (by keeping
them waiting)
refresh would refresh
343 **danced . . . king** i.e. before
Polixenes. Probably a reference to
the satyrs' dance in Jonson's masque
Oberon. See Fig. 13 and p. 70.
344 **by th' square** precisely (*OED n.*
1b); a square is a carpenter's tool for
measuring angles or accuracy (1a). Cf.
5.1.52, 81 (see nn.), *LLL* 5.2.474.
347 **at door** at the door (article omitted
after preposition: Abbott, 90)

328.1] *Rowe*   332 saultiers] *(Saltiers)*   338 SD] *Oxf*   344 square] *Rowe;* squire *F*

[*The Servant admits twelve rustic Dancers dressed as satyrs, who dance to music.*]

[*Exeunt Servant and Dancers.*]

POLIXENES [*to Shepherd*]

O, father, you'll know more of that hereafter.
[*to Camillo*] Is it not too far gone? 'Tis time to part
  them.
He's simple, and tells much. [*to Florizel*] How now, fair
  shepherd,   350
Your heart is full of something that does take
Your mind from feasting. Sooth, when I was young
And handed love as you do, I was wont
To load my she with knacks. I would have ransacked
The pedlar's silken treasury, and have poured it   355
To her acceptance. You have let him go,
And nothing marted with him. If your lass
Interpretation should abuse and call this
Your lack of love or bounty, you were straited
For a reply, at least if you make a care   360
Of happy holding her.

347.1–2 See List of Roles, 33n. For the dance, see 332n., 343n. and pp. 394–6, 402–4.
348 From the final words of the conversation it appears that the Shepherd (respectfully called *father*: OED *n.* 8a) has asked Polixenes who he is during the dance.
349 i.e. the romance between Florizel and Perdita is too serious
350 **simple** straightforward; dim; ignorant (about who their guests are). The Shepherd has revealed what he knows about the betrothal.
351 **take** distract
352 **Sooth** in truth
353 **handed** dealt with (cf. 2.3.61–2: see n.); also associated with taking hands

in betrothal, as Florizel does at 367: see 395n., 1.1.29–31n.
354 **she** girlfriend
  knacks trinkets
354–5 **ransacked . . . treasury** plundered the pedlar's rich store of silk; condescending hyperbole or ridicule, as pedlars sold cheap trashy finery
355–6 **poured . . . acceptance** presented it for her approval; splashed out to get her to accept me
357 **nothing marted with** done no business with, i.e. bought nothing from
358 **Interpretation should abuse** should choose to misunderstand
359 **were straited** would be stuck
360–1 **make . . . her** care about keeping her happy

347.1 *The . . . Dancers*] Oxf subst.   347.1–2] *dressed . . . music*] Hanmer subst., after 348; *Heere a Dance of twelue Satyres* F   347 SD] *Capell subst.*   348 SD] *Oxf*   349 SD] *Cam*   350 SD] *Cam¹*   360 reply, at least] *Dyce;* reply at least, *F*

FLORIZEL   Old sir, I know
She prizes not such trifles as these are.
The gifts she looks from me are packed and locked
Up in my heart, which I have given already,
But not delivered. [*to Perdita*] O, hear me breathe my
    life   365
Before this ancient sir, whom, it should seem,
Hath sometime loved. I take thy hand, this hand
As soft as dove's down and as white as it,
Or Ethiopian's tooth, or the fanned snow that's bolted
By th' northern blasts twice o'er.
POLIXENES   What follows this?   370
[*to Camillo*] How prettily th' young swain seems to
    wash
The hand was fair before! [*to Florizel*] I have put you
    out.

---

363 **looks** looks for
    packed and locked as if in a trunk
(or box for a trousseau). Said in an
explicitly non-sexual sense here (as
with *trunk*, 1.2.431: see 431–2n.), but
there are bawdy references involving
trunks at 3.3.72–3, 4.3.86 (see nn.).
364–5 **given ... delivered** promised
(my *heart*), but not yet delivered it
fully (in a betrothal); given (my *gifts*,
vows of love, 363) but not yet fulfilled
them (by marriage): see 395n.
365 **breathe my life** make vows for
life
366 **should seem** would appear
367 **Hath sometime loved** was once
in love
    I ... ¹hand See 395n.
368 Conventional praise (Dent, D576.1,
D573.2), but here surprising. A shepherdess's hands should be coarse and
dirty, but Perdita's are soft and white
(372), like her complexion (see 161n.).
369–70 'Ethiopian' was used for all black
African races. As well as the contrast

between black skin and white *tooth*,
there's a distinction between hot Africa
and cold Europe. Cf. 5.1.156 (see n.).
369 **fanned ... bolted** i.e. snow, blown
(*fanned*) by wintry winds (370) and
sifted (*bolted*), making it even more soft
and pure. Part of the image is proverbial: see Dent, S591, 'As white as the
driven snow'; *TNK* 5.1.139–40. But
Florizel could also be likening snow
blown by wintry winds to autumn's
winnowed grain, sieved twice (*twice
o-er*, 370) after grinding, to separate
bran from flour – a perhaps deliberately incongruous comparison.
371–2 **wash ... before** i.e. make her
hand, already beautifully white, still
whiter by his comparisons. If Florizel
is kissing her hand, however, Polixenes
means he is making a spotless hand
even cleaner. For the omission of
the relative pronoun before *was*, see
Abbott, 244.
372 **put you out** broken your concentration; annoyed you

---

365 SD] *Oxf*   366 whom] who *F2*   371 SD] *Oxf¹*   372 SD] *Oxf¹*

But to your protestation. Let me hear
What you profess.

FLORIZEL   Do, and be witness to't.

POLIXENES
And this my neighbour too?

FLORIZEL   And he, and more   375
Than he, and men, the earth, the heavens and all –
That were I crowned the most imperial monarch,
Thereof most worthy, were I the fairest youth
That ever made eye swerve, had force and knowledge
More than was ever man's, I would not prize them   380
Without her love, for her employ them all,
Commend them and condemn them to her service
Or to their own perdition.

POLIXENES   Fairly offered.

CAMILLO
This shows a sound affection.

SHEPHERD   But, my daughter,
Say you the like to him?

PERDITA   I cannot speak   385
So well, nothing so well, no, nor mean better.
By th' pattern of mine own thoughts I cut out
The purity of his.

SHEPHERD   Take hands, a bargain;
And, friends unknown, you shall bear witness to't.
I give my daughter to him, and will make   390

---

377 **imperial monarch** This is what
Florizel will become, ruling Sicily and
Bohemia, with Perdita, granddaughter
of the Emperor of Russia.
379 **eye swerve** people turn (and stare)
force and power as well as; power
of
381 **employ** I'd employ
382–3 **Commend . . . perdition** commit them (beauty, power, knowledge)
to her service or condemn them to
destruction; with word-play – every-

thing Florizel has must go to Perdita
or to perdition
384 **sound affection** solid, well-considered
love; see 1.1.24n.
387–8 **By. . . his** I judge the purity of his
intentions the same as mine; i.e. our
feelings are the same. The metaphor is
from cutting material to a *pattern*.
388 **Take . . . bargain** It's a deal, shake
hands on it (cf. Dent, H109.1, 'Clap
hands and a bargain'). Cf. 395 (see n.),
and see 1.1.29–31n.

    Her portion equal his.

FLORIZEL   O, that must be

    I'th' virtue of your daughter. One being dead,

    I shall have more than you can dream of yet,

    Enough then for your wonder. But come on,

    Contract us 'fore these witnesses.

SHEPHERD   Come, your hand;   395

    And, daughter, yours.

POLIXENES   Soft, swain, awhile, beseech you.

    Have you a father?

FLORIZEL   I have. But what of him?

POLIXENES

    Knows he of this?

FLORIZEL   He neither does nor shall.

POLIXENES

    Methinks a father

    Is at the nuptial of his son a guest   400

    That best becomes the table. Pray you once more,

    Is not your father grown incapable

    Of reasonable affairs? Is he not stupid

---

391 **portion** dowry
391–2 **that . . . daughter** i.e. your daughter's dowry is her virtue. See 1.2.411–12n.
392 **One being dead** i.e. when Polixenes dies, and Florizel succeeds him
393 **yet** at the moment
395 **Contract . . . witnesses** the culmination of the betrothal ritual of handfasting, a binding *de praesenti* contract when made before witnesses. In civil law, this united the couple, even if the marriage hadn't been solemnized in church, and thereby recognized in canon law (see 1.1.29–31n., 1.2.274–6n.). The ritual begins when Florizel takes Perdita's hand to make vows (365, 367). She

accepts (385–8) and they are about to *Contract*, by a formal holding of hands (388, 395), when Polixenes interrupts, rendering the betrothal incomplete (396–46). Their private *vow* or promise to marry (50–1, 491), unlike a *de praesenti* contract, might be annulled. Polixenes could divorce them (422), because of (apparent) disparity of rank. Simon Forman, who saw a performance in May 1611, says that the prince had married Perdita before 'they fled into Sicilia' (see p. 84). See 5.1.203; 5.3.150–1 and 150n.
396 **Soft, swain, awhile** hold on a moment, young man
403 **reasonable affairs** rational conduct

395 'fore] *(*fore*)*

With age and altering rheums? Can he speak? Hear?
Know man from man? Dispute his own estate?   405
Lies he not bed-rid? And again does nothing
But what he did being childish?

FLORIZEL   No, good sir.
He has his health and ampler strength indeed
Than most have of his age.

POLIXENES   By my white beard,
You offer him, if this be so, a wrong   410
Something unfilial. Reason my son
Should choose himself a wife, but as good reason
The father, all whose joy is nothing else
But fair posterity, should hold some counsel
In such a business.

FLORIZEL   I yield all this;   415
But for some other reasons, my grave sir,
Which 'tis not fit you know, I not acquaint
My father of this business.

POLIXENES   Let him know't.

FLORIZEL
He shall not.

POLIXENES   Prithee let him.

FLORIZEL   No, he must not.

---

404 **altering rheums** sicknesses
– catarrh, rheumatic illness – that
change (and weaken) him (affecting
his judgement)
altering changing (*OED*'s first citation, *ppl. a.* 1; as a medical term, *ppl. a.*
2, first instance 1605)
405 (Does he) know one man from
another? (Can he) discuss his own
condition?
407 **being childish** when a child
411 **Something** somewhat
unfilial *OED*'s first citation
Reason it is reasonable that (cf.

MW 1.1.196); there is a reason
that (cf. similar ellipsis in *KJ*
5.2.130)
my son either idiomatic for 'a son' (i.e.
sons in general), or a momentary lapse,
when Polixenes forgets the identity he
has assumed
414 **fair posterity** (having) proper (or
beautiful) descendants
hold some counsel have his opinion
sought
415 **yield** concede
417 ²**not** do not (Abbott, 305); see also
477.

411 my] the *(Cam¹)*

SHEPHERD

Let him, my son. He shall not need to grieve   420
At knowing of thy choice.

FLORIZEL   Come, come, he must not.
Mark our contract.

POLIXENES [*Removes his disguise.*]

Mark your divorce, young sir,
Whom son I dare not call. Thou art too base
To be acknowledged. Thou a sceptre's heir,
That thus affects a sheep-hook? [*to Shepherd*] Thou,
    old traitor,   425
I am sorry that by hanging thee I can
But shorten thy life one week. [*to Perdita*] And thou,
    fresh piece
Of excellent witchcraft, whom of force must know
The royal fool thou cop'st with –

SHEPHERD   O, my heart!

POLIXENES

I'll have thy beauty scratched with briars and made   430
More homely than thy state. [*to Florizel*] For thee,
    fond boy,

422 **Mark** observe, i.e. bear witness to
422–3 **contract . . . divorce** See 395n.
423 **Thou** From here to 446, Polixenes
    uses *thou, thee* (pronouns for children,
    inferiors and for showing anger: see
    1.2.43n.), with the exception of *you*
    at 439, when his fury lessens for a
    moment, probably when he sees how
    beautiful Perdita is.
    base ignoble, low
424 **sceptre's heir** i.e. the king's heir (a
    sceptre symbolized royal authority).
    Cf. 5.1.145–6.
425 **affects** is in love with; wants for
    his wife (second-person singular con-
    tracted from 'affect'st' for euphony:
    Abbott, 340). Cf. *affection*, 1.1.24 (see
    n.).

sheep-hook symbol of a shepherdess;
he also means the hook she has caught
Florizel with.
427–8 **fresh . . . witchcraft** young girl
    with such skill in bewitching men; i.e.
    Florizel has fallen for her because she
    has put a spell on him (*enchantment*,
    439). This is a metaphor, unlike *Oth*
    1.2.63–79, 1.3.61–5, *Per* 2.5.48–9,
    where the witchcraft is considered
    real.
427 **piece** girl; instance or example. See
    32n.
428 **of . . . know** must surely know
429 **cop'st** are dealing (*OED* cope *v.*² 5)
431 **More . . . state** more unattractive
    even than your low status
    fond foolish

422 SD] *Rowe subst.*   424 acknowledged] *F2;* acknowledge *F*   425 SD] *Oxf*   427 SD] *Oxf*
428 whom] who *F2*   431 SD] *Oxf*

If I may ever know thou dost but sigh
That thou no more shalt see this knack, as never
I mean thou shalt, we'll bar thee from succession,
Not hold thee of our blood, no, not our kin,   435
Far than Deucalion off. Mark thou my words.
Follow us to the court. [*to Shepherd*] Thou churl, for
    this time,
Though full of our displeasure, yet we free thee
From the dead blow of it. [*to Perdita*] And you,
    enchantment,
Worthy enough a herdsman – yea, him too,   440
That makes himself, but for our honour therein,
Unworthy thee – if ever henceforth thou
These rural latches to his entrance open,
Or hoop his body more with thy embraces,
I will devise a death as cruel for thee   445
As thou art tender to't.   *Exit.*

432–3 **If . . . knack** if I ever hear you so
much as sigh (in sadness) that you'll
never see this little plaything (*knack*)
again
433 **knack** toy; delicacy; deceitful thing
(*OED n.*[2] 3a, 3b, 1)
434 **we'll . . . succession** I'll disown you
as my heir to the throne; to assert his
full authority, Polixenes switches to
the royal pronoun at this point (cf.
Leontes' opening speech at the trial,
3.2.1–5).
436 **Far . . . off** (hold you) further (from
me) than Deucalion is in the distant
past (*far* is a comparative: Abbott,
478). Deucalion, the classical equivalent of Noah, survived a universal
deluge and repopulated the earth with
men transformed from stones.
437 **churl** peasant; a term of contempt,
i.e. boor or villain (*OED n.* 4, 5)
439 **dead** fatal (cf. *Ham* 1.1.64); full,

unrelieved (*OED a.* V). The Shepherd
isn't to be executed at once as suggested at 426.
enchantment beautiful witch (see
427–8n.)
440 **Worthy enough** entirely suitable for
440–2 **yea . . . thee** indeed, even worthy
of *him* (Florizel), who has behaved in
such a way that, if it weren't for our
royal blood (*honour*), he would have
made himself *Unworthy* of you
443 lift the latch on these humble doors
and let him in, i.e. let him have sex with
you. A latch was also a snare or trap
(*OED n.*[1] 1): he thinks she has been
enticing Florizel with her country ways.
444 i.e. put your arms round him (suggesting in *hoop* that she has been
constricting him)
446 **tender to't** sensitive to it; i.e. her
delicacy and susceptibility to pain will be
matched by as cruel a death as possible

---

433 see] *Rowe;* neuer see *F*   436 Far] *(Farre)*   437 SD] *Oxf*   439 SD] *Oxf*   444 hoop] *Pope;*
hope *F*

287

PERDITA   Even here undone.
I was not much afeard, for once or twice
I was about to speak and tell him plainly,
The selfsame sun that shines upon his court
Hides not his visage from our cottage, but   450
Looks on alike. [*to Florizel*] Will't please you, sir, be
    gone?
I told you what would come of this. Beseech you,
Of your own state take care. This dream of mine
Being now awake, I'll queen it no inch farther,
But milk my ewes and weep.

CAMILLO [*to Shepherd*]   Why, how now, father?   455
Speak ere thou diest.

SHEPHERD   I cannot speak, nor think,
Nor dare to know that which I know. [*to Florizel*] O sir,
You have undone a man of fourscore-three,
That thought to fill his grave in quiet, yea,
To die upon the bed my father died,   460
To lie close by his honest bones; but now
Some hangman must put on my shroud and lay me

Even here undone i.e. everything
destroyed in just this one moment
449–51 **selfsame . . . alike** Cf. Dent,
S985, and Ecclesiasticus, 42.16: 'The
sun that shineth, looketh upon all
things' (Shaheen, 728–9).
451 **alike** without social distinction
453 **state** well-being; social position
453–4 **This . . . farther** *OED*'s first citation of 'to queen it' (*v.* 1a; its second
is *H8* 2.3.37). Without punctuation
after *mine* (as in F), the lines mean:
'now being awake, I won't behave like
a queen in my own daydream any
longer'; if a dash is supplied (Ard²,
following Johnson), they mean: 'what
a dream I've been in – now I'm awake
I'll give up any thought of being a real
queen' (or 'I'll stop acting as queen of

this feast', perhaps removing her floral
garland). See 1.2.326–7n.
455 **milk my ewes** i.e. just be a shepherdess
456 **ere thou diest** before you die (from
shock, old age or the death sentence;
see 439n.)
457 **Nor . . . ²know** The Shepherd
daren't think about their plan to marry
or his inkling that Perdita is highborn.
Cf. 1.2.373–4 (see n.).
458 **fourscore-three** 83
460 **died** died on (see Abbott, 394, for
omitted prepositions)
462–3 **Some . . . dust** i.e. after he has
hanged me, the executioner will dress
me in my shroud, and bury me beside
the gallows, without a priest to cast
earth on my corpse. The setting is

451 SD] *Rowe*   455 SD] *Oxf*   457 SD] *Oxf*

Where no priest shovels in dust. [*to Perdita*] O cursed
    wretch,
That knewst this was the prince and wouldst adventure
To mingle faith with him. Undone, undone!   465
If I might die within this hour, I have lived
To die when I desire.   *Exit.*

FLORIZEL [*to Perdita*]   Why look you so upon me?
    I am but sorry, not afeard; delayed,
    But nothing altered. What I was, I am,
    More straining on for plucking back, not following   470
    My leash unwillingly.

CAMILLO   Gracious my lord,
    You know your father's temper. At this time
    He will allow no speech, which I do guess
    You do not purpose to him; and as hardly
    Will he endure your sight as yet, I fear;   475
    Then till the fury of his highness settle,
    Come not before him.

FLORIZEL   I not purpose it.
    I think Camillo?

CAMILLO   Even he, my lord.

PERDITA [*to Florizel*]
    How often have I told you 'twould be thus?
    How often said my dignity would last   480

pagan but the Shepherd wants a
Christian rite (which he can't have
because he is to die a felon). Shaheen
(729) notes that the stipulation that
a priest should cast earth on a body
being buried is from the First Prayer
Book of 1549 (i.e. *BCP*) rather than
the Second Prayer Book of 1552.
464–5 **adventure . . . faith** dare to
    exchange vows of love
470–1 **More . . . unwillingly** more eager
    than ever (to marry you) because of
    this, not dragged unwillingly. The
    image is of a dog straining at a leash,

plucked back, and chasing its quarry.
471 **Gracious my lord** This deference
    suggests that Florizel recognizes
    Camillo, who between here and 478
    takes off his disguise.
474 **purpose to him** i.e. you're not plan-
    ning to speak to him anyway
    as hardly with as much difficulty
476 **his highness** Polixenes' royal title;
    his majesty, greatness
477 **I . . . it** I don't propose to (omitted
    do: Abbott, 305)
480 **dignity** i.e. the honour of being
    betrothed to the prince

463 SD] *Oxf*   467 SD2] *Oxf*   472 your] *F2;* my *F*   475 sight as yet,] *(*sight, as yet*)*   479 SD] *Oxf*

But till 'twere known?

FLORIZEL   It cannot fail but by
The violation of my faith, and then
Let Nature crush the sides o'th' earth together,
And mar the seeds within. Lift up thy looks.
From my succession wipe me, father! I   485
Am heir to my affection.

CAMILLO   Be advised.

FLORIZEL

I am, and by my fancy; if my reason
Will thereto be obedient, I have reason.
If not, my senses, better pleased with madness,
Do bid it welcome.

CAMILLO   This is desperate, sir.   490

FLORIZEL

So call it; but it does fulfil my vow;
I needs must think it honesty. Camillo,
Not for Bohemia, nor the pomp that may

483–4 **Let . . . within** i.e. if I break my vow, may the world be destroyed and with it any chance of life starting again. Pagan and Christian thinkers said the earth had real seeds (e.g. semen, apple pips) as well as non-material essences inside matter, from which everything was born (cf. 'the seeds of time', *Mac* 1.3.58; and see Curry, 30–49). Florizel's vow, even allowing for intense feeling for Perdita, is uncomfortably close to the curses and conjurations in *KL* 3.2.8, 'Crack nature's moulds, all germens spill at once', and *Mac* 4.1.59, '[though] Nature's germens tumble all together'.

483 **sides o'th' earth** (1) earth's surfaces (*OED* side *n.*[1] 4c): cf. *AC* 1.2.199, *Cym* 3.1.51; (2) perhaps from Jeremiah, 6.22, referring to the limits of the earth (Shaheen, 729)

485–6 **I . . . affection** i.e. (1) I shall be the child of my love that has begotten

me anew; (2) my love shall be my only inheritance.

486 **affection** passionate love; cf. 1.1.24 (see n.).

Be advised Take some advice, i.e. change your mind.

487–90 **I . . . welcome** I am (indeed guided), by my love (*fancy*). If I can make my reason serve my love, I shall be sane (*have reason*); if not, my senses prefer and welcome madness. At this date 'fancy', associated with 'fantasy', meant the experience of love as well as the capacity to create mental images. Reason was a higher power than fancy, so Florizel is threatening to overturn the hierarchy of human understanding. His *fancy* parallels the destructive *affection* Leontes felt; see 1.2.137–46n.

491 **vow** See 50–1, 395n.

492 **honesty** honourable behaviour

493–4 **nor . . . gleaned** i.e. nor the splendour I might have as king of Bohemia

Be thereat gleaned; for all the sun sees, or
The close earth wombs, or the profound seas hides   495
In unknown fathoms, will I break my oath
To this my fair beloved. Therefore, I pray you,
As you have ever been my father's honoured friend,
When he shall miss me – as, in faith, I mean not
To see him any more – cast your good counsels   500
Upon his passion. Let myself and Fortune
Tug for the time to come. This you may know,
And so deliver: I am put to sea
With her who here I cannot hold on shore,
And, most opportune to our need, I have   505
A vessel rides fast by, but not prepared
For this design. What course I mean to hold
Shall nothing benefit your knowledge, nor
Concern me the reporting.

CAMILLO   O my lord!
I would your spirit were easier for advice.   510
Or stronger for your need.

FLORIZEL   Hark, Perdita –
    [*Takes Perdita aside.*]
    [*to Camillo*] I'll hear you by and by.

CAMILLO [*aside*]   He's irremovable,
    Resolved for flight. Now were I happy if

---

495 **wombs** noun as verb (Abbott, 290)
    hides For third-person plurals ending
    in *-s*, see Abbott, 333.
496 **fathoms** See 277n.
498 an alexandrine (not needing emenda-
    tion, e.g. by 'you've e'er'): see 1.2.117n.
499 **shall . . . me** finds I have left
500–1 **cast . . . passion** The emphasis
    may be on *his*: i.e. save your advice
    for my father in *his* passion of anger
    and pride.
501–2 **Let . . . come** Let me contend

with chance over what happens in
the future.
503 **deliver** report
505 **opportune** oppòrtune
506 **rides fast by** anchored nearby
507 **design** plan
508–9 **Shall . . . reporting** i.e. there is
    no need for you to know, or me to tell
510 **easier for** more receptive to
511 **stronger . . . need** steadier for what
    you need to do
512 **irremovable** unpersuadable

---

495 hides] hide *F2*   498 honoured] *omitted F2*   504 who] whom *F2*   505 our] *Theobald;* her *F*
511 SD] *Capell subst.*   512 SD1] *Theobald*   SD2] *Oxf*

His going I could frame to serve my turn,
Save him from danger, do him love and honour,   515
Purchase the sight again of dear Sicilia
And that unhappy king, my master, whom
I so much thirst to see.

FLORIZEL   Now, good Camillo,
I am so fraught with curious business that
I leave out ceremony.

CAMILLO   Sir, I think   520
You have heard of my poor services i'th' love
That I have borne your father?

FLORIZEL   Very nobly
Have you deserved. It is my father's music
To speak your deeds, not little of his care
To have them recompensed as thought on.

CAMILLO   Well, my lord,   525
If you may please to think I love the king,
And through him what's nearest to him, which is
Your gracious self, embrace but my direction,
If your more ponderous and settled project
May suffer alteration. On mine honour,   530
I'll point you where you shall have such receiving
As shall become your highness, where you may
Enjoy your mistress – from the whom I see

---

514 **frame . . . turn** turn to my purpose
516 **Purchase** obtain (*OED v.* 4a, 5a)
519–20 **so . . . ceremony** so occupied with anxious (or complex) matters (*OED* curious 1b, 10b) that I'm uncivil (an apology for breaking off to speak privately to Perdita at 512)
521–2 **poor. . . father** i.e. the few small things I've done out of love for Polixenes. Camillo is being modest.
523 **music** pleasure
524 **not . . . care** it's of great importance to him
525 **as thought on** immediately; as fully as possible
526 **may . . . think** are willing to believe.

Blake (92) says *may* is used to suggest something obvious to everyone, i.e. Camillo's love of Polixenes.
528–30 **embrace . . . alteration** merely accept my suggestion, if your settled plan, arrived at after serious consideration, may be changed. Camillo uses courtier's language to persuade, tactfully describing Florizel's plan as well thought out (529).
531–2 **receiving . . . highness** a reception fitting your majesty; *highness* also means greatness, grandeur (as at 476).
533–5 **Enjoy. . . ruin** have the pleasure of being with your lady, from whom I see you won't be separated without it

There's no disjunction to be made but by,
As heavens forfend, your ruin – marry her,   535
And with my best endeavours in your absence,
Your discontenting father strive to qualify,
And bring him up to liking.

FLORIZEL   How, Camillo,
May this, almost a miracle, be done?
That I may call thee something more than man,   540
And after that trust to thee.

CAMILLO   Have you thought on
A place whereto you'll go?

FLORIZEL   Not any yet.
But as th'unthought-on accident is guilty
To what we wildly do, so we profess
Ourselves to be the slaves of chance, and flies   545
Of every wind that blows.

CAMILLO   Then list to me.
This follows, if you will not change your purpose
But undergo this flight: make for Sicilia,
And there present yourself and your fair princess,
For so I see she must be, 'fore Leontes;   550
She shall be habited as it becomes

causing – may the gods forbid – your
ruin
537–8 **Your . . . liking** I'll do my best to
pacify (*OED* qualify 9a) your angry
father and bring him round. Some
editors think it is the prince who is to
calm Polixenes, taking *strive* (537) with
Enjoy (533) and *marry* (535). This is
unlikely. At 538–41 Florizel says that
only Camillo can appease his father.
540 **something . . . man** i.e. almost a
god
541 **after . . . thee** on account of that put
my trust in you
543–6 **But . . . blows** Because unex-

pected misfortune is responsible for
what we're doing now so haphazardly
(*wildly*), we see ourselves utterly in
the power of chance, like flies carried
along by every wind.
544 **wildly** without plan; cf. *Cor* 4.1.35,
'wild exposure to each chance'.
546 **list** listen
550 **For . . . be** i.e. since I accept you are
determined to marry her and make
her your princess; *she must be* may
hint that Perdita is a real princess
(see 457n.).
'fore before
551 **habited** dressed

293

The partner of your bed. Methinks I see
Leontes opening his free arms and weeping
His welcomes forth; asks thee there, 'Son, forgiveness!'
As 'twere i'th' father's person; kisses the hands   555
Of your fresh princess; o'er and o'er divides him
'Twixt his unkindness and his kindness. Th'one
He chides to hell, and bids the other grow
Faster than thought or time.

FLORIZEL   Worthy Camillo,
What colour for my visitation shall I   560
Hold up before him?

CAMILLO   Sent by the king your father
To greet him and to give him comforts. Sir,
The manner of your bearing towards him, with
What you, as from your father, shall deliver –
Things known betwixt us three – I'll write you down,   565
The which shall point you forth at every sitting
What you must say, that he shall not perceive
But that you have your father's bosom there
And speak his very heart.

---

553 **free** noble, generous (*OED a*. 3b)
554 **'Son, forgiveness!'** Alexander's repunctuation of F makes F3's emendation superfluous (see t.n.). Camillo imagines Leontes asking forgiveness from Polixenes' son, as proxy for his father (555), but also, through Florizel, from his *own* son. Oxf[1] says this oblique allusion to Mamillius' death is a sign of how deeply 'twinned' the childhood friends continue to be.
556 **fresh** young, blooming; newly created (*OED a.*[1] 2a)
556–7 **divides . . . kindness** i.e. alternates between speaking of his past inhumanity (to your father) and his present tender feelings (towards him and you)

558 **chides** consigns, curses with sorrow and anger
559 **Faster** firmer, more secure; more quickly; cf. Dent, T240, 'As swift as thought'.
560 **colour** pretext (*OED n.*[1] 12a)
visitation state visit; see also 1.1.6 and n.
562 **comforts** reassurances (of friendship)
565 **known . . . three** the three of us are familiar with; only the three of us know
566 **point . . . sitting** indicate at every audience with him
567 **that** so that
568–9 you are completely in your father's

554 thee there, 'Son] *Alexander;* thee there Sonne *F;* thee the Son *F3;* thee, the Son *Rowe*

FLORIZEL   I am bound to you.
There is some sap in this.

CAMILLO   A course more promising   570
Than a wild dedication of yourselves
To unpathed waters, undreamed shores; most certain
To miseries enough – no hope to help you,
But as you shake off one to take another;
Nothing so certain as your anchors, who   575
Do their best office if they can but stay you
Where you'll be loath to be. Besides, you know
Prosperity's the very bond of love,
Whose fresh complexion and whose heart together
Affliction alters.

PERDITA   One of these is true.   580
I think affliction may subdue the cheek,
But not take in the mind.

CAMILLO   Yea? Say you so?
There shall not at your father's house these seven years
Be born another such.

FLORIZEL   My good Camillo,
She's as forward of her breeding as   585

confidence (*bosom*, *OED* *n.* 6a) and
know his secret thoughts
569 **bound** obliged
570 **sap** life fluid; i.e. the plan may grow,
be a success
571 **wild dedication** rash, unplanned
committing; cf. 544 (see n.).
572 **unpathed** uncharted (*OED*'s first
citation)
undreamed undreamed-of, unimagi-
nable (*OED*'s first citation)
574 **one** one misery
575–7 **Nothing . . . be** (a *course*, 570) by
no means as secure as your anchors,
which do well if they just hold your
ship in a place you hate; i.e. anchors save
you from being wrecked, but keep you
where you don't want to be. At 575 *your*
may mean something that is commonly

known, i.e. 'anchors, as everyone knows'.
578–80 **Prosperity's . . . alters**   Cf.
Dent, T301, P611: 'Prosperity gets
friends, but adversity tries them.'
581 **subdue the cheek** drain the colour
from someone's face, i.e. wear them
out physically
582 **take . . . mind** capture the soul
(*OED* mind *n.*[1] 19a)
583–4 **There . . . such** i.e. you won't
see her like for a good while (*seven
years*, proverbially a long, indefinite
period: Dent, Y25). Perdita's wisdom
and resolution impress Camillo; he
may sense that she wasn't *born* in her
father's house (see 550n.).
585–6 **She's . . . birth** She's as much
above her upbringing as she is beneath
me in birth.

    She is i'th' rear our birth.

CAMILLO   I cannot say 'tis pity
    She lacks instructions, for she seems a mistress
    To most that teach.

PERDITA   Your pardon, sir; for this
    I'll blush you thanks.

FLORIZEL   My prettiest Perdita!
    But O, the thorns we stand upon! Camillo,   590
    Preserver of my father, now of me,
    The medicine of our house, how shall we do?
    We are not furnished like Bohemia's son,
    Nor shall appear in Sicilia –

CAMILLO   My lord,
    Fear none of this. I think you know my fortunes   595
    Do all lie there. It shall be so my care
    To have you royally appointed, as if
    The scene you play were mine. For instance, sir –
    That you may know you shall not want – one word.
    [*They speak apart.*]

Enter AUTOLYCUS.

AUTOLYCUS   Ha, ha! What a fool honesty is, and trust –   600
    his sworn brother – a very simple gentleman! I have
    sold all my trumpery; not a counterfeit stone, not a

586 **i'th' rear** lagging behind; cf. *Ham* 1.3.33.
587 **instructions** education
590 **thorns . . . upon** proverbial for impatient anxiety (Dent, T239)
592 **medicine** physician (*OED n.*²)
593 **furnished** dressed
594 **appear** appear as such
596 **so my care** my job, therefore
597 **royally appointed** equipped like a prince
597–8 **as . . . mine** as if he (Florizel)

acted in the scene, using Camillo's lines (cf. 565); with the same care he (Camillo) would take if he had to play the scene himself. For Florizel's ill-prepared arrival in Sicily, see 5.1.88–93.
600–23 borrowed from Greene, *Coney-Catching*, a pamphlet about thieving: see pp. 451–2.
600 **What . . . is** Cf. Dent, H539.1, 'Honesty is a fool.'
602 **trumpery** shoddy trash; cf. *Tem* 4.1.186. F's spelling (see t.n.) shows

586 rear our] *(*reare' our*)*   594 appear] appear so *Staunton*   599 SD] *Rowe subst.*   602 trumpery] *(*Tromperie*)*

ribbon, glass, pomander, brooch, table-book, ballad,
knife, tape, glove, shoe-tie, bracelet, horn-ring to keep
my pack from fasting. They throng who should buy   605
first, as if my trinkets had been hallowed and brought
a benediction to the buyer; by which means I saw
whose purse was best in picture; and what I saw, to
my good use I remembered. My clown, who wants but
something to be a reasonable man, grew so in love with   610
the wenches' song that he would not stir his pettitoes
till he had both tune and words, which so drew the
rest of the herd to me that all their other senses stuck
in ears. You might have pinched a placket, it was
senseless. 'Twas nothing to geld a codpiece of a purse.   615

the derivation from French *tromperie*,
i.e. lies, fraud, imposture: in England,
associated with practices and relics
of the Roman Catholic church (see
pp. 373–4).
counterfeit stone fake jewel
603 **glass** small mirror
  pomander ball of spices or perfume
  carried or worn to ward off infection
  table-book notebook
604 **shoe-tie** shoelace
  horn-ring Rings made of horn were
  said to be magical.
605 **fasting** going hungry, i.e. being
  empty
605–6 **throng . . . first** jostle (*OED*
  throng *v.* 4) to be first to buy
606–7 **trinkets . . . buyer** *trinkets* suggest
  the idolatrous and popish sale of religious relics, thought to confer blessings
608 **best in picture** most visible; the
  one with the most money in it that I
  could see
609–10 **wants . . . man** is only a bit
  short of being rational (*OED* reasonable *a.* 2), i.e. nearly witless; is just this
  side of being a ridiculous fool
611 **wenches' song** presumably the
  one sung with Mopsa and Dorcas at
  298–313
  pettitoes normally used of a pig's

trotters (*OED n.* 1a), but here perhaps
a diminutive for human toes (*n.* 2), or a
term of contempt (*n.* 1b)
612 **had** had learnt
613–14 **stuck in ears** probably a play on
  'to be all ears' (Tilley, E20), i.e. to pay
  complete attention. The rustics are so
  engrossed in the song that their senses,
  hearing and feeling, get 'stuck', can't
  function (which allows Autolycus to
  steal from them without their knowing, 614–18); the power of *tunes* is
  anticipated at 187–8 (see n.).
614–15 **pinched . . . senseless** stolen
  from a woman's pocket, or squeezed
  her vagina, it was (so) lacking in
  sensation (for the sexual meaning of
  placket, see 243n.); *it* may refer to
  the *herd* (613), rather than women
  so overwhelmed by the singing they
  wouldn't even feel a man fiddling with
  them.
615 **'Twas . . . purse** It would have been
  easy to cut a purse from a codpiece (the
  baggy appendage in breeches, for the
  penis and testicles, hence figuratively
  a man). Since purse also meant the
  scrotum, stealing a man's purse is like
  castrating him. Autolycus means 'you
  could have cut the balls off a man'. See
  616n., 4.3.20n.

605 fasting] fastning *F2*

297

I could have filed keys off that hung in chains. No
hearing, no feeling, but my sir's song, and admiring
the nothing of it. So that, in this time of lethargy, I
picked and cut most of their festival purses, and, had
not the old man come in with a hubbub against his   620
daughter and the king's son, and scared my choughs
from the chaff, I had not left a purse alive in the whole
army.

> [*Camillo, Florizel and Perdita come forward.*]

CAMILLO

Nay, but my letters, by this means being there
So soon as you arrive, shall clear that doubt.   625

FLORIZEL

And those that you'll procure from King Leontes?

CAMILLO

Shall satisfy your father.

PERDITA   Happy be you.
All that you speak shows fair.

CAMILLO [*Sees Autolycus.*]   Who have we here?
We'll make an instrument of this, omit

---

616 keys ... chains keys to a house or
cash box, attached to a chain round
the waist. But key also meant penis
(Williams, 759-60): Autolycus boasts
'I could have lopped off men's pricks'.
Cf. 4.3.20 (see n.).

617 my sir's i.e. the Clown's; used
contemptuously

617–18 admiring ... it (they were)
entranced by its triviality (with
a pun on *nothing* and 'noting', i.e.
musical notes and singing; cf. *MA*
2.3.52–5)

618 lethargy trance, stupor

619 picked and cut picked pockets and
cut purses; specialized tasks for the
'foist' or pickpocket, and the 'nip' or
cutpurse. See pp. 451–2.

festival i.e. full of money at holiday
time

621 choughs crows or jackdaws (birds easily attracted and caught, like the crowd);
rustics (*OED* chuff *n.*[1]). Pronounced
'chuffs', echoing *chaff*, 622.

622 chaff corn; worthless trash (*OED
n.*[1] 6a)

622–3 I ... army i.e. Autolycus would
have slit open every purse (cut all their
throats, as though they were soldiers
in an army)

624–5 i.e. the letters, having reached Sicily
by this means, will be there when Florizel
arrives, to resolve that problem (*doubt*).
The lines begin mid-conversation, leaving the *means* unexplained.

628 Who whom (Abbott, 274)

616 could] *Cam;* would *F*   filed] *(*fill'd*)*   623 SD] *Theobald*   628 SD] *Theobald*

Nothing may give us aid.   630

AUTOLYCUS [*aside*]
  If they have overheard me now – why, hanging!

CAMILLO   How now, good fellow? Why shakest thou so?
  Fear not, man. Here's no harm intended to thee.

AUTOLYCUS   I am a poor fellow, sir.

CAMILLO   Why, be so still. Here's nobody will steal that   635
  from thee. Yet, for the outside of thy poverty, we must
  make an exchange. Therefore discase thee instantly –
  thou must think there's a necessity in't – and change
  garments with this gentleman. Though the pennyworth on his side be the worst, yet hold thee, there's   640
  some boot. [*Gives him money.*]

AUTOLYCUS   I am a poor fellow, sir. [*aside*] I know ye well
  enough.

CAMILLO   Nay prithee, dispatch – the gentleman is half
  flayed already.   645

AUTOLYCUS   Are you in earnest, sir? [*aside*] I smell the
  trick on't.

FLORIZEL   Dispatch, I prithee.

---

631 Theft, even of minor kinds, was punishable by hanging.
632–3 Addressing someone lower-class, Camillo would use prose, as at 635–41; but 632–3 are blank verse in F; see 162–7n.
636 **outside . . . poverty** your poor clothing. Hulme (336) explains the unusual meaning of *outside*, i.e. 'outer garments'.
637 **discase** undress; only used here and in *Tem* 5.1.85 in this sense
638 **there's . . . in't** it's unavoidable; neither you nor he has a choice
639–40 **the . . . worst** he gets the worst of the bargain (*OED* pennyworth *n.* 3a)

641 **some boot** something extra (*OED* boot *n.*[1] 2)
642–3 [2]**I . . . enough** proverbial when recognizing villains (Dent, K171.1)
644 **dispatch** hurry up (as at 648)
645 **flayed** undressed; literally, skinned (see 788). F's 'fled' is probably just an obsolete spelling of 'flayed' (*OED* flay), but there may be a pun, i.e. Florizel is already half undressed and half fled (out of Bohemia).
646–7 **I . . . on't** I see the device in this, i.e. they want my clothes for a disguise (with a pun perhaps on *trick* as a way of dressing, *OED* *n.* 8a). Cf. Dent, S.558, 'I smell him out.'
647 **on't** of it (Abbott, 181)

---

631 SD] *Theobald*   632–3] *as Hanmer; F lines* Fellow) / man) / thee./   641 SD] *Dyce subst.*   642 SD] *Hanmer*   645 flayed] *Rowe subst.;* fled *F*   646 SD] *Hanmer*

AUTOLYCUS   Indeed, I have had earnest, but I cannot
with conscience take it.   650

CAMILLO   Unbuckle, unbuckle.

    [Florizel and Autolycus exchange clothes.]

    [to Perdita] Fortunate mistress – let my prophecy

Come home to ye! – you must retire yourself

Into some covert; take your sweetheart's hat

And pluck it o'er your brows, muffle your face,   655

Dismantle you and, as you can, disliken

The truth of your own seeming, that you may –

For I do fear eyes over – to shipboard

Get undescried.

PERDITA   I see the play so lies

That I must bear a part.

CAMILLO   No remedy.   660

– Have you done there?

FLORIZEL   Should I now meet my father,

He would not call me son.

CAMILLO   Nay, you shall have no hat.

    [Gives the hat to Perdita.]

Come, lady, come. Farewell, my friend.

---

649 **earnest** some money; advance payment, the *boot* of 641

652–3 **let . . . ye** may what I have predicted (by calling you *Fortunate*) prove true

654 **covert** hiding place

655 **pluck . . . brows** pull it down over your forehead

656 **Dismantle you** disrobe, i.e. remove these garments that show you as a queen (she may be wearing a court gown: see 1n. and pp. 74–5). *Dismantle* (to take off a mantle, *OED* 1) is a reminder of the queen's mantle which Perdita was wrapped in as baby (see 3.3.45 SDn.), which the Shepherd removed and hid.

as as much as

656–7 **disliken . . . seeming** make yourself unlike your true appearance (*OED*'s only instance of 'disliken'); perhaps with word-play, 'stop liking the fine clothes you're wearing'.

seeming at this point, only the audience understands the irony. Perdita's true identity is concealed beneath a gown in which she pretends she is a queen.

658 **eyes over** eyes watching over us, prying, i.e. the king's spies (see 4.2.35–6). Cf. *LLL* 4.3.77, '[I] fools' secrets heedfully o'er-eye'.

659–60 **I . . . part** I see our playacting requires me to (dress up and) play a role.

660 **No remedy** There's no alternative.

651 SD] *Capell subst.*   652 SD] *Oxf*   658 eyes over – to] *(eyes ouer) to); eyes – over to Ard¹ subst.*   662 SD] *Capell subst.*

AUTOLYCUS   Adieu, sir.

FLORIZEL

O Perdita, what have we twain forgot!

Pray you, a word.   [*They talk apart.*]   665

CAMILLO [*aside*]

What I do next shall be to tell the king

Of this escape, and whither they are bound;

Wherein my hope is I shall so prevail

To force him after, in whose company

I shall re-view Sicilia, for whose sight   670

I have a woman's longing.

FLORIZEL   Fortune speed us!

Thus we set on, Camillo, to th' seaside.

CAMILLO

The swifter speed the better.

                    Exeunt [*Florizel, Perdita and Camillo*].

AUTOLYCUS   I understand the business, I hear it. To have

an open ear, a quick eye and a nimble hand is necessary   675

for a cutpurse. A good nose is requisite also, to smell

out work for th'other senses. I see this is the time that

the unjust man doth thrive. What an exchange had

this been without boot! What a boot is here with this

exchange! Sure the gods do this year connive at us, and   680

---

664 **what . . . forgot** Florizel may chide
Perdita for doubting his constancy
(i.e. what, could we ever forget our
vows to each other?); then speak
privately (665). Or this may be a
real question (have we forgotten
something?), allowing Camillo to
address the audience while the
couple speak aside. What Florizel forgot isn't
specified (perhaps something he had
left in the clothes exchanged with
Autolycus).
669 **after** i.e. to follow them
671 **woman's longing** proverbial (Dent,
L421.1): a pregnant woman's cravings

(see 262–5n.), or her longing to give
birth
    speed favour
676 **cutpurse** thief who stole by cutting
purses; see 615n., 616n. and 619n.
678 **unjust** dishonest
678–80 **exchange . . . exchange** another
instance of antimetabole (see 1.2.313n.),
perhaps with a pun on the repeated
word *boot* (see 679n.)
679 **boot** extra payment (see 641n.,
649n.); possibly a joke about boots
exchanged with Florizel, 636–51
680 **this year connive** at the moment
look indulgently (*OED* connive 3)

---

665 Pray] (ʼPray*)* SD] *Capell subst.*   666 SD] *Oxf*   673 SD] *Rowe subst.; Exit. F*

we may do anything extempore. The prince himself is
about a piece of iniquity, stealing away from his father
with his clog at his heels. If I thought it were a piece of
honesty to acquaint the king withal, I would not do't. I
hold it the more knavery to conceal it, and therein am I   685
constant to my profession.

Enter CLOWN *and* SHEPHERD [*carrying a bundle and a box*].

Aside, aside! Here is more matter for a hot brain. Every
lane's end, every shop, church, session, hanging, yields
a careful man work.

CLOWN   See, see, what a man you are now! There is no   690
other way but to tell the king she's a changeling, and
none of your flesh and blood.

SHEPHERD   Nay, but hear me.

CLOWN   Nay, but hear me.

SHEPHERD   Go to, then.   695

CLOWN   She being none of your flesh and blood, your
flesh and blood has not offended the king, and so your
flesh and blood is not to be punished by him. Show

681 **extempore** without concern about
  what may happen; making things up
  as we go along, like actors in a play (cf.
  MND 1.2.65), watched by indulgent
  gods, 680
682 **about . . . iniquity** up to some
  wrongdoing. For *piece*, see 32n.
683 **clog** encumbrance, i.e. Perdita (cf.
  Dent, C426.1, 'To have a clog at one's
  heels'; *AW* 2.5.53)
  If even if
683–4 **piece of honesty** Cf. *piece of
  iniquity*, 682 (see n.).
684 **withal** with it
685 **more knavery** greater dishonesty
686 **profession** vocation (as a liar)
686.1 *bundle* the *fardel* (711, 721, 760),

comprising clothes (gown, cloak)
found with Perdita 16 years earlier (see
3.3.45 SDn.)
687 **Aside, aside** I'll just stand to one
  side (and listen)
  hot brain keen mind
688 **lane's end** where notices were
  posted and people stopped to read
  them (giving Autolycus the chance to
  pick their pockets)
  session session of the law courts
689 **careful** diligent
691 **changeling** foundling; child left by
  fairies (see 2.3.105–6n., 3.3.115n.).
692, 696–8 **flesh and blood** proverbial
  (Dent, F366)
695 **Go to** very well

686 SD *carrying . . . box*] *Oxf subst.*

those things you found about her, those secret things,
all but what she has with her. This being done, let the   700
law go whistle, I warrant you.

SHEPHERD   I will tell the king all, every word, yea, and his
son's pranks, too – who, I may say, is no honest man,
neither to his father nor to me, to go about to make me
the king's brother-in-law.   705

CLOWN   Indeed, brother-in-law was the farthest off you
could have been to him, and then your blood had been
the dearer by I know not how much an ounce.

AUTOLYCUS [*aside*]   Very wisely, puppies.

SHEPHERD   Well, let us to the king. There is that in this   710
fardel will make him scratch his beard.

AUTOLYCUS [*aside*]   I know not what impediment this
complaint may be to the flight of my master.

CLOWN   Pray heartily he be at palace.

AUTOLYCUS [*aside*]   Though I am not naturally honest,   715
I am so sometimes by chance. Let me pocket up my
pedlar's excrement. [*Removes his false beard.*] How
now, rustics, whither are you bound?

699 **secret things** i.e. clothes, box, letters left with Perdita (see 711, 3.3.45 SDn.). For *things*, see 1.2.92n.

700–1 **let . . . whistle** i.e. the law won't be able to touch you (proverbial: Dent, W313)

701 **warrant** assure

703 **pranks** mischievous tricks
   no honest not a respectable

704 **go about** propose

706 **brother-in-law**   The   Clown, confused over terms (see also 746n.; 5.2.125n., 145n.), thinks that Florizel's marrying Perdita makes the Shepherd the king's brother at least. See 1.2.4n.

708 **dearer . . . ounce** i.e. if you had become the king's brother-in-law, your blood would have been worth goodness knows how much more per

drop (*ounce*, twentieth of a pint, 28.4 millilitres). For literal and figurative blood, see 1.2.71–3n., 1.2.328n.

709 **puppies** little upstarts (*OED n.* 2a); cf. *Cym* 1.3.18.

711, 721, 760 **fardel** bundle. See 686.1n.

711 **make . . . beard** give him something to think about (*OED* scratch *v.* 2a)

713 **my master** i.e. Florizel. Autolycus seizes the chance to reinstate himself (see 839, 4.3.13–14n.).

714 **at** at the; omitted definite article (Abbott, 90), probably marked in F by the apostrophe after 'at'

717 **excrement** i.e. his false beard (from Latin *excrescere*, 'what grows out'; *OED* excrement[2]). Shakespeare uses it of hair, moustaches, beards (see *LLL* 5.1.96, *MV* 3.2.87).

708 know not] *Hanmer;* know *F*   709 SD] *Rowe*   712 SD] *Dyce*   714 Pray] ('Pray)   at palace] (at' Pallace)   715 SD] *Dyce*   717 SD] *Steevens subst.*

SHEPHERD   To th' palace, an it like your worship.

AUTOLYCUS   Your affairs there? What? With whom?   720
    The condition of that fardel? The place of your
    dwelling? Your names? Your ages? Of what having,
    breeding, and anything that is fitting to be known,
    discover!

CLOWN   We are but plain fellows, sir.   725

AUTOLYCUS   A lie – you are rough and hairy. Let me have
    no lying; it becomes none but tradesmen, and they
    often give us soldiers the lie, but we pay them for it with
    stamped coin, not stabbing steel, therefore they do not
    give us the lie.   730

CLOWN   Your worship had like to have given us one if you
    had not taken yourself with the manner.

SHEPHERD   Are you a courtier, an't like you, sir?

---

719 **an it like** if it please (as at 733, 745, 786–7)
    your worship respectful title for a superior
720–4 parody legal questioning, intended to intimidate the rustics who are frightened by the law (700–1)
721 **The condition** what's the nature
722 **having** wealth
724 **discover** reveal
725 **but plain fellows** only straightforward, humble men
726 **A lie** Calling the Clown a liar is the start of a joke about duelling protocol (see 728–30n.) that culminates in 5.2.126–32 (see 127–8n.). The joke is that neither Autolycus nor the Clown is sufficiently highborn to participate in a gentleman's duel.
    rough and hairy Autolycus, playing on another meaning of *plain* (725), i.e. smooth, free from roughness (*OED a.*[1] 3a), tells the rustics they are unshaven and shaggy-headed. Shaheen (730) detects an allusion to Genesis, 25.25, 27, where Esau was born first, his body covered with hair. His twin Jacob, smooth-skinned, cheated him of his

birthright. Autolycus suggests that the rustics can be similarly cheated.
727 **becomes none but** is only proper for
728–30 **give . . . lie** deceive us soldiers (by overcharging or giving short measure), but we pay them with genuine money, not sword thrusts (*steel*, a pun on steal, cheat): therefore they don't *give* us the lie, or a dishonest reckoning (they sell it us). To give the lie also meant to call a gentleman a liar, grounds for a duel or an immediate sword-thrust (see *Oth* 3.4.5–6). By pretending to be a courtier, Autolycus gets out of fighting the Clown, his 'inferior'.
731–2 **had . . . manner** would probably have lied to us if you hadn't caught your mistake in time; 'in the manner' was a legal phrase (Latin *a manu*, in the act), used of thieves caught red-handed (cf. Dent, M633; *LLL* 1.1.199–207). For other legal language see 4.3.93–4n., 5.2.125n. The Shaheen spots Autolycus' correcting himself: first he said tradesmen give soldiers the lie (728), then that they *don't* give it them (729–30).

AUTOLYCUS Whether it like me or no, I am a courtier.
Seest thou not the air of the court in these enfoldings?   735
Hath not my gait in it the measure of the court?
Receives not thy nose court-odour from me? Reflect
I not on thy baseness court-contempt? Think'st thou,
for that I insinuate to toze from thee thy business, I
am therefore no courtier? I am courtier cap-à-pie, and   740
one that will either push on or pluck back thy business
there. Whereupon I command thee to open thy affair.

SHEPHERD My business, sir, is to the king.

AUTOLYCUS What advocate hast thou to him?

SHEPHERD I know not, an't like you.   745

CLOWN [*aside to Shepherd*] Advocate's the court word for
a pheasant. Say you have none.

SHEPHERD None, sir. I have no pheasant, cock nor hen.

AUTOLYCUS How blessed are we that are not simple men!

735 **air . . . enfoldings** sweet scent (or
fashion) of the court in these garments
(the prince's, 651 SD), with a pun on
air and 'heir' (i.e. Florizel)

736 **gait** way of walking
measure style; literally, a stately
dance (*OED n.* 15a)

737 **court-odour** sweet fragrance of the
court

737–8 **Reflect . . . court-contempt**
Don't I shine down on your lowliness
with courtly disdain; *court-contempt*
may suggest the legal term 'contempt
of court'.

739 ***for . . . toze** because I'm seeking
to find out in a roundabout way. F's
'at' (see t.n.) may be an error for 'to'
(adopted by most editors, as here) or
for 'or' (as in F2).
toze tease out (*OED v.*¹ c)

740 **cap-à-pie** from head to foot, complete; proverbial: Dent, T436 ('*pe*' in
F, pronounced 'pea' or 'pay')

741 **that . . . business** i.e. important
enough to help or hinder you

742 **open thy affair** explain your business

744 **advocate** person to speak for you, as
at 2.2.38 and 5.1.220. See 746n.

746 **Advocate** The Clown misunder-
stands this as the technical word for
a bribe (of a pheasant, 747) taken by
judges in law courts (and by extension
courtiers around the king). Bribing
judges with game or poultry was
commonplace (cf. 'capon justice', i.e.
corrupt judgements bought with gifts
of capons (chickens), *OED* capon *n.* 5).
Cf. the Clown's misunderstanding of
gentlemen born, 5.2.125 (see n.).

749–51 Blank verse in F (see t.n.) but
relined as prose here (see 162–7 n.).
Ard² keeps them as verse on the
grounds that Autolycus is a 'temporary
gentleman', lording it over the rustics,
speaking above his rank. In 749 'men'
rhymes with 'hen' in 748, making 748–9
a simple, tinkling couplet.

749 **How . . . men** perhaps a comic
allusion to Jesus' parable of the Pharisee

739 to toze] *Capell;* at toaze *F;* or toaze *F2*   746 SD] *Capell subst.*   749–51] as *Ard¹; F* lines men?
/ are, / disdaine.

Yet Nature might have made me as these are. Therefore   750
I will not disdain.

CLOWN   This cannot be but a great courtier.

SHEPHERD   His garments are rich, but he wears them not
handsomely.

CLOWN   He seems to be the more noble in being fantas-   755
tical. A great man, I'll warrant. I know by the picking
on's teeth.

AUTOLYCUS   The fardel there, what's i'th' fardel?
Wherefore that box?

SHEPHERD   Sir, there lies such secrets in this fardel and   760
box which none must know but the king, and which he
shall know within this hour, if I may come to th' speech
of him.

AUTOLYCUS   Age, thou hast lost thy labour.

SHEPHERD   Why, sir?   765

AUTOLYCUS   The king is not at the palace; he is gone
aboard a new ship to purge melancholy and air himself;
for, if thou beest capable of things serious, thou must
know the king is full of grief.

and Publican, in Luke, 18.11, where the
Pharisee says 'O God, I thank thee that
I am not as other men, extortioners,
unjust, adulterers . . .' – all of these
Autolycus' offences

751 **disdain** regard (them) with contempt

754 **handsomely** properly, elegantly
(*OED* 2, 4a). For disguise conventions,
see pp. 72–4.

755–6 **fantastical** eccentric, whimsical
in attire (*OED a.* fantastic 4b)

756–7 **the . . . teeth** his picking his teeth.
Elizabethan courtiers used toothpicks,
often of gold or silver, to appear stylish.
By the date of *WT* this affectation was
going out of fashion (cf. *AW* 1.1.158–9),
perhaps showing how ignorant about
court Autolycus really is; see 4.3.13–14n.

757 **on's** of his

759 **Wherefore that box?** What's that
box for?

759, 761 **box** See 3.3.45 SDn.

760 **lies** quasi-singular verb before plural
subject (Abbott, 335)

762–3 **come . . . him** get to speak to him

764 Old man, your efforts have been
wasted; cf. Dent, L9, 'To lose your
labour'.

766–7 **he . . . ship** Autolycus lies to
prevent the rustics going to the palace
(it is Florizel, not Polixenes, who has
gone aboard) and begins his trick (see
801n.).

new newly fitted out, renovated

767 **purge melancholy** relieve his
depression (caused by *grief*, 769, about
Florizel)

768 **beest . . . serious** are able to understand important matters

SHEPHERD   So 'tis said, sir; about his son, that should have   770
married a shepherd's daughter.

AUTOLYCUS   If that shepherd be not in handfast, let him
fly; the curses he shall have, the tortures he shall feel,
will break the back of man, the heart of monster.

CLOWN   Think you so, sir?   775

AUTOLYCUS   Not he alone shall suffer what wit can
make heavy and vengeance bitter, but those that are
germane to him, though removed fifty times, shall all
come under the hangman, which, though it be great
pity, yet it is necessary. An old sheep-whistling rogue,   780
a ram-tender, to offer to have his daughter come
into grace! Some say he shall be stoned; but that
death is too soft for him, say I. Draw our throne into
a sheepcote? All deaths are too few, the sharpest too
easy.   785

CLOWN   Has the old man e'er a son, sir, do you hear, an't
like you, sir?

AUTOLYCUS   He has a son, who shall be flayed alive, then
'nointed over with honey, set on the head of a wasps'

770–1 **should have married** was going to marry (Blake, 96)
772 **in handfast** free but not permitted to depart (the legal term was 'mainprise', where pledges were given as security or bail); in custody. With *handfast* Autolycus reminds the Shepherd of Perdita's ruinous betrothal to Florizel (see 395n.).
774 **heart of monster** spirit of some unnatural creature (incapable of feeling pain)
776 **wit** ingenuity
777 **heavy** painful
778 **germane** related
779 **come . . . hangman** i.e. be executed
780 **sheep-whistling rogue** no-good shepherd
781 **ram-tender** keeper of sheep
offer presume
781–2 **come into grace** marry into royalty. See 1.2.80n.

783–4 **Draw . . . sheepcote** entice our prince into a hovel, i.e. degrade the royal family by marrying him to a shepherdess
784 **sheepcote** sheephouse
All . . . few There aren't enough kinds of death (appropriate for this crime); all the deaths he could die wouldn't be enough.
sharpest most excruciating; quickest
786 **Has . . . hear** Is it said the old man has a son at all, sir.
788–96 **flayed . . . death** Shakespeare took some of this from Boccaccio's *Decameron* (2.9), a source for *Cym*. The villain in Boccaccio is tied and impaled on a stake, his naked body is smeared with honey, and he is left to be devoured 'to the bare bones' by flies, wasps and hornets (Bullough, 8.62).
788 **flayed** skinned
789 **'nointed** anointed, smeared

307

nest, then stand till he be three-quarters-and-a-dram   790
dead, then recovered again with aqua vitae, or
some other hot infusion, then, raw as he is, and in
the hottest day prognostication proclaims, shall he
be set against a brick wall, the sun looking with a
southward eye upon him, where he is to behold him   795
with flies blown to death. But what talk we of these
traitorly rascals, whose miseries are to be smiled at,
their offences being so capital? Tell me – for you
seem to be honest plain men – what you have to the
king. Being something gently considered, I'll bring   800
you where he is aboard, tender your persons to his
presence, whisper him in your behalfs, and if it be
in man, besides the king, to effect your suits, here is
man shall do it.

CLOWN [*aside to Shepherd*] He seems to be of great   805
authority. Close with him, give him gold; and, though
authority be a stubborn bear, yet he is oft led by the

790 **a-dram** a tiny bit more; literally, one-eighth of a fluid ounce (see 708n.), 3.5 millilitres
791 **recovered again** brought round from unconsciousness
aqua vitae liquor
792 **hot infusion** pungent liquor (*OED* hot *a*. 4a)
793 **prognostication proclaims** predicted in the almanac (printed almanacs included weather forecasts for every day of the year)
794–5 **looking . . . eye** shining from the south, at its hottest
795 **he** the Shepherd (cf. 788); the sun
796 **with . . . death** die fly-blown, i.e. stung and swollen. Cf. *Tem* 3.1.63.
what why
797 **traitorly** treacherous
to . . . at i.e. amusing
798 **capital** notable; worthy of death
799 **what . . . to** what's your business with

800 **Being . . . considered** (if) I am somewhat civilly rewarded (a hint for a bribe, offered at 811–12); since I have influence because of my high rank
801 **aboard** Autolycus' lie (see 766–7n.) becomes a device to get the rustics on to Florizel's ship
801–2 **tender . . . presence** present you to him
802 **whisper him in** speak to him privately on
803 **in man** i.e. possible
besides the king (1) someone near to the king; (2) (for) anyone other than the king himself
effect your suits meet your request
804 **man** the man
806 **Close** make a deal, i.e. offer the bribe (see 800n.)
807 **stubborn** unmanageably obstinate; ferocious (*OED a.* 1a)
bear The action in Bohemia is framed by a savage bear offstage at the begin-

805 SD] *Capell subst.*

nose with gold. Show the inside of your purse to the outside of his hand, and no more ado. Remember, 'stoned', and 'flayed alive'. 810

SHEPHERD   An't please you, sir, to undertake the business for us, here is that gold I have. I'll make it as much more, and leave this young man in pawn till I bring it you.

AUTOLYCUS   After I have done what I promised? 815

SHEPHERD   Ay, sir.

AUTOLYCUS   Well, give me the moiety. [*to Clown*] Are you a party in this business?

CLOWN   In some sort, sir. But, though my case be a pitiful one, I hope I shall not be flayed out of it. 820

AUTOLYCUS   O, that's the case of the shepherd's son. Hang him, he'll be made an example.

CLOWN [*aside to Shepherd*]   Comfort, good comfort. We must to the king and show our strange sights. He must know 'tis none of your daughter, nor my sister. We are 825 gone else. – Sir, I will give you as much as this old man does when the business is performed, and remain, as he says, your pawn till it be brought you.

AUTOLYCUS   I will trust you. Walk before toward the

---

ning (3.3.57 SD), and the image of a tame bear led by the nose at the end.

807–8 **led . . . nose** i.e. made to follow tamely (proverbial: Dent, N233); cf. *Oth* 1.3.400–1.

808 **with gold** i.e. with the inducement (i.e. bribe) of gold

808–9 ²**the . . . hand** i.e. his palm

811 **An't** if it

813 **more** again (i.e. double it)
    in pawn as security

817 **moiety** first half

819, 821 **case** situation (as at 821), punning on *case* as skin: see pp. 637, 645,

788 and nn.

822 **Hang him** damn him; a common oath, but reminding the Clown of execution (see 788–96)
    made an example proverbial (Dent, E212.1)

823 **Comfort** have courage

824 **to** go to
    strange sights extraordinary things; things that aren't ours

825 **'tis none of** that she (Perdita) is not

826 **gone else** done for otherwise. See 1.2.184n.

829 **Walk before** go ahead of me

817 SD] *Oxf*   823 SD] *Capell subst.*

seaside; go on the right hand – I will but look upon the   830
hedge, and follow you.

CLOWN *[aside to Shepherd]*   We are blessed in this man, as
I may say, even blessed.

SHEPHERD   Let's before, as he bids us. He was provided to   834
do us good.   *[Exit with Clown.]*

AUTOLYCUS   If I had a mind to be honest, I see Fortune
would not suffer me – she drops booties in my mouth.
I am courted now with a double occasion: gold, and a
means to do the prince my master good, which who
knows how that may turn back to my advancement?   840
I will bring these two moles, these blind ones, aboard
him. If he think it fit to shore them again, and that the
complaint they have to the king concerns him nothing,
let him call me rogue for being so far officious; for I am
proof against that title and what shame else belongs   845
to't. To him will I present them. There may be matter
in it.   *Exit.*

5.1   *Enter* LEONTES, CLEOMENES, DION *[and]* PAULINA.

830–1 **I . . . hedge** I'll just take a leak.
Sending the rustics ahead allows them
to exit while he addresses the audience.
Urinating on the hedge emphasizes the
contempt he has for all boundaries set
by owners (hedges around property)
and for authority: cf. 4.3.5 (see n.) and
see 1.2.132–4n.

832 **blessed in** fortunate in (having)

833 **even blessed** entirely lucky; divinely
blessed even

834 **before** go ahead
  provided sent (by the gods)

837 **suffer me** allow me (to be so)
  booties gains (*OED* booty *n.* 3).
Waiting for things to drop into one's
mouth was proverbial for being lazy
(Tilley, M1261).

838 **courted . . . occasion** now presented with doubly good fortune, or
two opportunities in one

840 **turn back** turn out, redound

841 **moles . . . ones** Moles were proverbially blind (Dent, M1034).

841–2 **aboard him** on board his ship

842 **shore them** put them ashore

843 **concerns him nothing** isn't important to him

845 **proof . . . title** impervious to being
called that (*rogue*, 844)

846–7 **matter in it** something in it (I
can use)

5.1 The setting is Leontes' palace, probably the audience chamber (with a dais
or *stage*: see 58n.); cf. the setting for
1.2 (see n.).

832 SD] *Capell subst.*   835 SD] *Rowe subst.*   847 SD] *Rowe; Exeunt. F*   **5.1**] *(Actus Quintus. Scena
Prima.)*   0.1] *Enter Leontes, Cleomines, Dion, Paulina, Seruants: Florizel, Perdita. F*

CLEOMENES [*to Leontes*]
Sir, you have done enough, and have performed
A saint-like sorrow. No fault could you make
Which you have not redeemed; indeed, paid down
More penitence than done trespass. At the last
Do as the heavens have done, forget your evil;   5
With them, forgive yourself.

LEONTES   Whilst I remember
Her and her virtues, I cannot forget
My blemishes in them, and so still think of
The wrong I did myself, which was so much
That heirless it hath made my kingdom, and   10
Destroyed the sweet'st companion that e'er man
Bred his hopes out of. True?

1–4 Leontes vowed he would visit the chapel where Hermione and Mamillius were buried every day for the rest of his life (3.2.235–6). The concern in these lines, as in 1.2.3–10, is with paying a debt.

1–2 **performed . . . sorrow** undertaken a period of mourning worthy of a saint

1 **performed** completed, but also acted out, anticipating Leontes' remark that each person (actor) must answer for the part they played, 5.3.153–4 (see n.). Cf. 129 (see 128–9n.), 5.2.94 (see 93–4n.), and see 1.2.187n.

2–4 **No . . . trespass** There is no wrong you could commit that you have not already made amends for; indeed you have done more penance than your sin required.

4 **At the last** finally (*OED* last *a.* 10a)

5–6 **Do . . . yourself** proverbial: 'forgive and forget' (Dent, F597), derived from the prayer for the Visitation of the Sick, *BCP*, 'O most merciful God which . . . doest so put away the sins of those which truly repent, that thou remembrest them no more' (Shaheen, 731)

5 **heavens** gods

6 **With them** i.e. as the *heavens* have

6–7 **Whilst . . . virtues** for as long as I have Hermione and her goodness in my mind, i.e. as long as I live; see 1.2.411–12n.

6 **remember** commemorate (*OED* v.[1] 3b), remember in prayers (3d)

7 **virtues** The emphasis is on sexual chastity (*OED* n. 2c), the opposite of *vices* alleged at 3.2.54. See 1.2.411–12n.

8 **My . . . them** my defects in comparison with her virtues; my vices as I think about her virtues; the virtues in her I tried to make foul. A blemish is a moral defect or slur (*OED* n. 3). See Abbott, 162, for *in* meaning 'as regards'.
so still thus ever

9 **did myself** myself committed; did to myself

10 **heirless** punning on 'airless', stifling (as in *JC* 1.3.94, 'airless dungeon'), devoid of breath and life. Cf. 127, 5.3.78 (see nn.).

12 **Bred . . . of** had children (heirs) with (cf. 1.1.34–8); put his hopes of future happiness in
True? This is true, isn't it? F has 'of, true', so 'true' may mean truly or indeed. Some editors reassign the word to Paulina, making her speech begin 'True, too true'.

1 SD] *Oxf* 12 of . . . True] *Oxf;* of, true. / *Paul.* Too true F; of. / *Paul.* True, too true *Theobald*

PAULINA   Too true, my lord.
If one by one you wedded all the world,
Or from the all that are took something good
To make a perfect woman, she you killed   15
Would be unparalleled.

LEONTES   I think so. Killed?
She I killed? I did so. But thou strik'st me
Sorely, to say I did; it is as bitter
Upon thy tongue as in my thought. Now, good now,
Say so but seldom.

CLEOMENES   Not at all, good lady.   20
You might have spoken a thousand things that would
Have done the time more benefit and graced
Your kindness better.

PAULINA   You are one of those
Would have him wed again.

DION   If you would not so,
You pity not the state, nor the remembrance   25
Of his most sovereign name, consider little

---

13 if you married every woman in the world, one after another
14 the . . . are every living woman
15 perfect woman Cf. *AYL* 3.2.136–49, where Nature is said to have given Rosalind Helen of Troy's beauty, Cleopatra's majesty, Lucrece's modesty, and of 'many faces, eyes, and hearts' the 'touches dearest prized'. Miranda in *Tem* 3.1.46–8 is told 'O you, / So perfect and so peerless, are created / Of every creature's best.'
16 be still be
  unparalleled according to *OED*, in common use from *c.* 1610 (e.g. Cleopatra is 'a lass unparalleled', *AC* 5.2.315)
17–18 thou . . . say you hurt me greatly by saying
17 thou This pronoun could be used in very different ways (see 1.2.43n.). At 2.3.112 (see n.) Leontes uses it to show

contempt for Paulina, but throughout 5.1 it signifies respect for her, and the bond between them (e.g. 49–54). See 5.3.9n.
18 to say infinitive for gerund (Abbott, 356)
19 good now if you'll be so good now (i.e. 'I beg you', entreaty or expostulation); at this good moment
20 Not at all don't say it at all
21 things See 1.2.92n.
22–3 done . . . better been more helpful now and better suited your natural tenderness as a woman (said sarcastically)
24 Would . . . again who advise or wish him to remarry
25–6 pity . . . name neither pity the kingdom nor care about the perpetuation of the king's royal line. This is a zeugma, a rhetorical device for yoking together parts of speech.
26 consider little just think

312

What dangers, by his highness' fail of issue,
May drop upon his kingdom and devour
Incertain lookers-on. What were more holy
Than to rejoice the former queen is well?   30
What holier, than for royalty's repair,
For present comfort and for future good,
To bless the bed of majesty again
With a sweet fellow to't?

PAULINA   There is none worthy,
Respecting her that's gone. Besides, the gods   35
Will have fulfilled their secret purposes.
For has not the divine Apollo said?
Is't not the tenor of his oracle
That King Leontes shall not have an heir
Till his lost child be found? Which that it shall   40
Is all as monstrous to our human reason
As my Antigonus to break his grave
And come again to me; who, on my life,
Did perish with the infant. 'Tis your counsel
My lord should to the heavens be contrary,   45

---

27 **fail of issue** failure to have an heir
28–9 **devour . . . lookers-on** destroy the bystanders, i.e. the people of Sicily, who won't know what to do if Leontes dies without a secure succession. The metaphor at 27–9 is of *dangers* as birds of prey swooping down and gobbling victims (cf. 3.3.11–12).
29 **lookers-on** spectators (*OED* looker *n.* 1c, a)
   were more holy (action) would be more pious
30 **the . . . well** that the late queen is at rest. For 'well' used of the dead, free from care in heavenly bliss, see Dent, H347, 'He is well since he is in heaven'; *Mac* 4.3.179; *AC* 2.5.33.
31 **holier** more righteous
   for royalty's repair to restore the royal line (with an heir)
32 **For present comfort** i.e. to encour-

age the king and people now; cf. 1.1.34.
34 **sweet fellow** loving wife
35 **Respecting** in comparison with
   gone dead (equivocation if Hermione is alive, i.e. she is 'no longer present'); see 1.2.184n.
35–6 **Besides . . . purposes** Moreover the hidden will of the gods must be fulfilled.
37 **said** spoken (pronounced judgement)
40–2 **Which . . . grave** That this will happen must be as incredible to human understanding as it would be for my Antigonus to return from the dead.
40 **Till . . . found** The oracle used the word '*if*', not 'till' (3.2.133); perhaps Paulina thinks there is a chance Perdita is alive.
43 **on my life** I'll stake my life on it
45 **to . . . contrary** oppose the gods

313

Oppose against their wills. [*to Leontes*] Care not for
    issue;
The crown will find an heir. Great Alexander
Left his to th' worthiest, so his successor
Was like to be the best.

LEONTES   Good Paulina,
Who hast the memory of Hermione,   50
I know, in honour – O, that ever I
Had squared me to thy counsel! Then even now
I might have looked upon my queen's full eyes,
Have taken treasure from her lips.

PAULINA   And left them
More rich for what they yielded.

LEONTES   Thou speak'st truth.   55
No more such wives, therefore no wife. One worse,
And better used, would make her sainted spirit

---

46 **Oppose against** obstruct
   Care . . . issue don't worry about children
47–8 **Great . . . worthiest** Shakespeare probably took this from the Roman historian Curtius, who wrote a life of Alexander the Great. When Alexander died, there were rivals to succeed him as emperor. Curtius reported that on his deathbed Alexander told them 'When I shall depart, you shall find a king worthy for such men as you be.' They asked who his successor should be, to which he replied 'the worthiest' (Curtius, sigs 295ᵛ, 300ᵛ).
48 **worthiest** two syllables
   so in order that
   successor sùccessor
49 **like . . . best** likely to be the best choice
50–1 **Who . . . honour** I know you venerate the memory of Hermione
51–2 **that . . . counsel** if only I had always acted according to your advice
52 **squared me** been guided by (*OED*

square *v.* 4a). See 81n., 4.4.344n.
53 **full eyes** eyes, open and full of life (cf. the closed, dead eyes at 68)
54 **treasure** i.e. kisses
56 **No . . . wife** i.e. there can never be another wife like Hermione, so I won't marry again
56–9 *One . . . soul-vexed** to take a new wife, inferior to her (*worse*), and treat her better, would make Hermione's blessed spirit repossess her body, and on this very dais, were I now to offend by remarrying, she would present herself, in great distress. F's '(Where we Offendors now appeare) Soule-vext,' is often emended (see t.n.). It only means something as it stands if Leontes is saying 'everyone's a sinner' (in comparison with Hermione, or because of original sin; see 1.2.69–70n.). Rann's emendation, derived from Heath (219), is the most plausible, assuming that 'we ' in 59 is the royal pronoun.
57 **sainted** blessed, like a saint; cf. *Mac* 4.3.109.

46 SD] *Theobald subst.*

314

Again possess her corpse, and on this stage,
Were we offenders now, appear soul-vexed,
And begin, 'Why to me?'

PAULINA   Had she such power,   60
She had just cause.

LEONTES   She had, and would incense me
To murder her I married.

PAULINA   I should so.
Were I the ghost that walked, I'd bid you mark
Her eye, and tell me for what dull part in't
You chose her. Then I'd shriek that even your ears   65
Should rift to hear me, and the words that followed
Should be, 'Remember mine.'

58 **corpse** It was still believed that the soul after death might assume its former body. The figure Leontes imagines isn't spectral (unlike the spirit at 3.3.18); at 63 the *ghost* is a corpse (*OED* ghost *n*. 9) animated by Hermione's soul. Cf. 4.4.129 (see n.), and see Thomas (705–7, 715) for widowers haunted by dead wives for breaking vows not to marry again. See also pp. 5–6.

stage raised floor, dais. The actor playing Leontes also refers to the stage on which the play is being performed; see 1.2.191–2 and 191n. for another stepping out of part, addressing the audience.

60 **Why to me** Why are you doing this to me; possibly meaning 'Why did you mistreat me when I lived, and again after death?'

61 ***just** F's 'such' was probably a mistake by the compositor or Crane repeating the word from 'such power' in 60, the line above.

incense incite (*OED v.*[2] 4)

62 **murder her** i.e. so that she could resume her place as his wife – an extraordinary wish to attribute to Hermione, whom he calls *sainted* (57) and *tender* (5.3.26–7)

married perhaps three syllables, 'marrièd' ('marryed' in F). This would mean the line had 11 syllables, six stressed (/), with the final one unstressed (x), i.e. x / x / x / x / / / x. Such irregularities in the verse are common in *WT*: see pp. 125–7.

63 **ghost** See 58n.

mark pay attention to

64 **dull part in't** unattractive part of it

65–6 **that . . . me** so that your very ears would split on hearing me, i.e. my shriek would pierce your eardrums (cf. *shrieks*, 3.3.35)

66 **to hear** gerundive (Abbott, 356), like *to say*, 18

67 **mine** my eyes; everything properly mine, not to be given to another wife. Cf. the Ghost's 'remember me' in *Ham* 1.5.91, a common Elizabethan phrase.

59 Were . . . appear] *Rann;* (Where we Offendors now appeare) *F;* (Where we offend her now) appear *Theobald;* (Where we offenders now) appear *Knight subst.;* (Where we offenders move) appear *Ard¹ subst. (Delius);* Where we offend as now, appear *Sisson;* Where we offenders mourn, appear *Oxf* 61 just] *F3;* just such *F*

LEONTES   Stars, stars,
   And all eyes else, dead coals! Fear thou no wife;
   I'll have no wife, Paulina.
PAULINA   Will you swear
   Never to marry but by my free leave?   70
LEONTES
   Never, Paulina, so be blest my spirit.
PAULINA
   Then, good my lords, bear witness to his oath.
CLEOMENES
   You tempt him over-much.
PAULINA   Unless another
   As like Hermione as is her picture
   Affront his eye –
CLEOMENES   Good madam –
PAULINA   I have done.   75
   Yet if my lord will marry – if you will, sir,
   No remedy but you will – give me the office
   To choose you a queen. She shall not be so young
   As was your former, but she shall be such

67–8 **Stars . . . coals** i.e. Hermione's eyes were shining stars, all others are burnt-out cinders (cf. Song of Solomon, 8.6, quoted p. vi).
68 **Fear . . . wife** don't worry about my taking another wife
70 **but . . . leave** except with my unqualified, freely given permission
71 **so . . . spirit** as I hope my soul may be blest. At 72 Paulina treats this as a binding vow before witnesses.
73 **tempt . . . over-much** (1) push him too far (*OED* tempt *v.* 1a, test, make trial of); (2) pressurize him to make promises he shouldn't (*v.* 5, allure, invite; *v.* 4b, draw someone to a commitment); (3) presume on his good will (cf. Matthew, 4.7, 'thou shalt not tempt the Lord thy God').

74 **picture** statue, effigy on a monument (*OED n.* 1d); painting; 73–5, 78–84 may hint at a statue that comes to life.
75 **Affront** present herself to (*OED v.* 4), but also confront, even attack (*v.* 3a, b), implying an assault on the king's senses
   ***I have done** I have finished, i.e. I won't say any more. In F Cleomenes says this at 75, but it is more natural here. Cleomenes thinks that Paulina should shut up and stop making Leontes promise things he shouldn't; she insists on the final word (76–81).
76 ²**will** decide to
77 **No . . . will** i.e. it will have to happen if you (as king) wish it (*OED* remedy *n.* 2b)
   office task

75 CLEOMENES . . . done] *as Capell; Cleo.* Good Madame, I haue done *F; Cleo.* Good Madam, pray have done *Rowe*   78 you a] *F;* your *Hudson*

As, walked your first queen's ghost, it should take joy   80
To see her in your arms.

LEONTES   My true Paulina,
We shall not marry till thou bidd'st us.

PAULINA   That
Shall be when your first queen's again in breath.
Never till then.

Enter a [Gentleman].

GENTLEMAN
One that gives out himself Prince Florizel,   85
Son of Polixenes, with his princess – she
The fairest I have yet beheld – desires access
To your high presence.

LEONTES   What with him? He comes not
Like to his father's greatness. His approach,
So out of circumstance and sudden, tells us   90
'Tis not a visitation framed, but forced
By need and accident. What train?

GENTLEMAN   But few,

80 **As ... ghost** that, if the ghost of
your first queen were to walk again
(subjunctive: Abbott, 361–9)
take joy rejoice
81 **true** i.e. Paulina is a loyal subject and
friend to him, constant in her devotion
to Hermione's memory; the word suggests that Leontes is now *squared* by
(see 52 and n.) or measures his actions
according to her advice, because she
is as true, or accurate, as a carpenter's
square (cf. 4.4.344).
82 I shall not marry until you tell me to
(royal pronouns)
83 **in breath** breathing: cf. 5.3.78.
84 SD *Gentleman See List of Roles,
12n.
85 **gives out himself** announces he is;
claims to be
88 **presence** the monarch's ceremonial

space
What with him? (1) What company
attends him? As heir apparent to the
Bohemian throne, Florizel should have
an entourage of courtiers and servants
(cf. *What train?*, 92); (2) What can he
want? (Leontes tries to answer this at
89–92).
89 **Like to** in a manner appropriate to
90 **So ... circumstance** so lacking in
ceremony (*OED* circumstance *n.* 7a)
us royal pronoun
91–2 **not ... accident** not a planned
visit but one forced on him by necessity and mischance
91 **visitation** See 1.1.6n.
92 **What train?** What retinue has he with
him?
92–3 **But ... mean** Only a few, and
they are low in rank. Presumably

84.1 Gentleman] *Theobald; Seruant* F   85+ SP] *Theobald; Ser.* F

And those but mean.

LEONTES   His princess, say you, with him?

GENTLEMAN

Ay, the most peerless piece of earth, I think,
That e'er the sun shone bright on.

PAULINA   O, Hermione,   95
As every present time doth boast itself
Above a better, gone, so must thy grave
Give way to what's seen now. [*to the Gentleman*] Sir,
    you yourself
Have said and writ so; but your writing now
Is colder than that theme. She had not been   100
Nor was not to be equalled – thus your verse
Flowed with her beauty once; 'tis shrewdly ebbed
To say you have seen a better.

GENTLEMAN   Pardon, madam.
The one I have almost forgot – your pardon –

Camillo is still in his clothes for the feast, but without the disguise that made him unrecognizable (see 4.4.54.1–2, 471n.).

94 **peerless . . . earth** incomparable human being. Cf. Dent, P289.1, 'peerless piece'; P290.1, 'piece of earth'. See 4.4.32n.

95 **e'er . . . on** i.e. ever lived, also suggesting that the sun looks favourably on Perdita (*OED* shine *v.* 1d)

96–8 **As . . . now** just as every age boasts that it's better than a superior past, so you, now you're in your grave, must yield precedence to what is currently marvelled at. Cf. *Son* 59.

99 **writ so** written in these terms (i.e. 'She . . . equalled', 101–2; see n.)

99–100 **your . . . theme** your writing is colder than your former subject (i.e. Hermione, cold in her grave)

100–1 **She . . . equalled** Some editors put inverted commas round this, as if Paulina were quoting lines, but the tenses aren't right for direct speech

(which would be 'She *has* not been nor *is* not to be equalled').

102 **Flowed . . . once** i.e. once poured forth praise for her beauty

'tis shrewdly ebbed the flow of praise has drained away a great deal; it's an unkind lessening (of your earlier praise). Paulina may be using *shrewdly* ironically, even sarcastically, i.e. you've lessened your praise astutely now that Hermione can be compared with some new beauty. Exaggeration was a regular feature of panegyrics (cf. *Son* 17; satirized in *Tim* 1.1.43–51): parallels are intended here with the absurdities in ballads (see 4.4.275–81n.), and Perdita's unease about being over-praised, 4.4.146–51.

shrewdly severely (*OED adv.* 5); unkindly (*adv.* 2); astutely (*adv.* 7a)

103 **To say** for you to say (infinitive used indefinitely: Abbott, 356)

104–5 **one . . . other** i.e. Hermione and the stranger (Perdita)

98 SD] *Oxf*

The other, when she has obtained your eye,   105
Will have your tongue too. This is a creature,
Would she begin a sect, might quench the zeal
Of all professors else, make proselytes
Of who she but bid follow.

PAULINA   How? Not women!

GENTLEMAN
Women will love her, that she is a woman   110
More worth than any man; men, that she is
The rarest of all women.

LEONTES   Go, Cleomenes.
Yourself, assisted with your honoured friends,
Bring them to our embracement.

> *Exit* [*Cleomenes with Gentleman*].
>   Still 'tis strange
He thus should steal upon us.

PAULINA   Had our prince,   115
Jewel of children, seen this hour, he had paired
Well with this lord; there was not full a month

---

105 **obtained** prevailed over, taken captive (see *OED* 3b, 4a)
106 **tongue** i.e. praise
   creature probably accented 'creàture'
107–9 **Would . . . follow** who, were she to found a new religious sect, would dampen the fervour of members of all other faiths, and make converts of everyone she merely told to follow her
108 **professors** those who profess a religious faith; cf. *H8* 3.1.115.
109 **who** whom (Abbott, 274)
   bid follow may echo Jesus' command 'follow me' to his disciples (Mark, 10.21; Luke, 9.23)
   How? Not women! What? That surely wouldn't include women! Paulina says only men could worship a woman so much. F's question mark after *women* is the equivalent of a

modern exclamation mark.
110, 111 **that** because
111 **worth** deserving; valuable
112 **rarest** most wonderful
113–14 **Yourself . . . embracement** a formal command to welcome Florizel's party with all the courtesy due to visiting royalty
113 **assisted with** accompanied by
114 **to our embracement** so that I may embrace them (in friendship)
115 **steal upon us** arrive unannounced (perhaps suggesting that Florizel has approached furtively)
   our prince i.e. Mamillius
116 **Jewel** most precious
116–17 **had . . . with** would have made a fitting companion, brother for (like Polixenes and Leontes, 127; see 1.2.4n.)
117 **not full** less than

114 SD *Exit Cleomenes*] Rowe; *Exit. after* upon us *115 F   with Gentleman*] *this edn*

Between their births.

LEONTES　　　　　　　Prithee no more; cease. Thou knowest
He dies to me again when talked of. Sure,
When I shall see this gentleman, thy speeches　　　　　120
Will bring me to consider that which may
Unfurnish me of reason. They are come.

Enter FLORIZEL, PERDITA, CLEOMENES *and others.*

Your mother was most true to wedlock, prince,
For she did print your royal father off,
Conceiving you. Were I but twenty-one,　　　　　125
Your father's image is so hit in you,
His very air, that I should call you brother,
As I did him, and speak of something wildly
By us performed before. Most dearly welcome,
And your fair princess – goddess – O, alas,　　　　　130
I lost a couple that 'twixt heaven and earth

---

119 **dies . . . of** whenever he is spoken
about, it's as though I'm losing him
again. It was proverbial that talking
about grief renewed sorrow (Tilley,
R89).

120–2 **thy . . . reason** what you are saying will make me think about things
(i.e. why Mamillius died) that may
drive me mad

123 **most . . . wedlock** completely faithful in marriage

124–5 **For . . . you** for when she conceived you, she made a copy of your
royal father; i.e. you're the image of
Polixenes, and could be no one else's
child (123). Cf. the printing metaphor
Paulina used of Perdita, 2.3.97–8 (see
n.).

125 **twenty-one** not Florizel's exact age;
he is most probably 23. See List of
Roles, 2n.

126 **image . . . hit** looks are reproduced
so exactly

127 **very air** exact look; quibbling on
'true heir', legitimate son (see 10n.)
brother See 1.2.4n.

128–9 **speak . . . before** *wildly* qualifies
speak or *performed*: (1) gabble out-
rageously about something we did
together (when young); (2) speak of
something I did rashly in the past (*us*,
royal pronoun), i.e. my crimes 16 years
ago (the word *something* was in his
mind then: see 1.2.143n.)

129 **performed** done; acted on stage: cf.
1–2, 5.2.93–4 (see nn.), and see 1.2.187n.

130 **goddess** i.e. her beauty is heavenly

131 **couple** i.e. son and daughter
(Mamillius and Perdita)

131–2 **'twixt . . . wonder** might have
stood together like this, causing astonishment in everyone who beheld them,

---

118 Prithee] (*Prethee*)

Might thus have stood, begetting wonder, as
You, gracious couple, do; and then I lost –
All mine own folly – the society,
Amity too, of your brave father, whom,   135
Though bearing misery, I desire my life
Once more to look on him.

FLORIZEL   By his command
Have I here touched Sicilia, and from him
Give you all greetings that a king at friend
Can send his brother; and but infirmity,   140
Which waits upon worn times, hath something seized
His wished ability, he had himself
The lands and waters 'twixt your throne and his
Measured to look upon you, whom he loves –
He bade me say so – more than all the sceptres,   145
And those that bear them, living.

LEONTES   O, my brother!
Good gentleman, the wrongs I have done thee stir
Afresh within me, and these thy offices,

whether gods or men; 'heaven and earth' was used of all creation (*OED* heaven *n.* 3a), but Leontes may mean that the couple are mid-way between ('*twixt*) divine and human.

133 **gracious** a courtesy term; but also, 'full of grace', almost divine. See 1.2.80n.

135 **brave** noble, splendid

135–7 **whom . . . him** i.e. though I'm weighed down with grief, I want to live to see your father once more. For *whom* (135) with supplementary pronoun, where *him* (137) is redundant, see Abbott, 248–9.

138 **touched** landed upon Sicilia briefly (*OED* touch *v.* 11b): cf. 3.3.1 (see n.); greatly stirred the feelings of Sicilia's king (*v.* 24a)

139 **all greetings** every greeting (Abbott, 12)

at friend as a friend, i.e. by way of friendship (Abbott, 143)

140–2 **but . . . ability** were it not that sickness which comes with age has overwhelmed his desired ability (to travel)

142 **had** would have

144 **Measured . . . you** travelled to see you

145–6 **sceptres . . . them**   the Renaissance distinction between office and person, i.e. between Leontes as king and as man (who bears the burden of the sceptre, symbol of royal authority, as at 4.4.424)

146–50 **O . . . slackness** Leontes' apostrophe is addressed to the absent Polixenes.

147–8 **stir . . . me** are waking in me anew

148–50 **offices . . . slackness** greetings, so extraordinarily kind, serve to show

139 at] as *F2*

So rarely kind, are as interpreters
Of my behindhand slackness. Welcome hither,   150
As is the spring to th'earth! And hath he too
Exposed this paragon to th' fearful usage
At least ungentle – of the dreadful Neptune,
To greet a man not worth her pains, much less
Th'adventure of her person?

FLORIZEL   Good my lord,   155
She came from Libya.

LEONTES   Where the warlike Smalus,
That noble honoured lord, is feared and loved?

FLORIZEL

Most royal sir, from thence; from him whose daughter
His tears proclaimed his, parting with her. Thence,
A prosperous south wind friendly, we have crossed,   160
To execute the charge my father gave me

---

how negligent I've been in the attention overdue to you

150–1 **Welcome . . . earth** Cf. Dent,
F390, 'As welcome as flowers in May'.

151–3 **hath . . . Neptune** i.e. can he
(Polixenes) have risked her life on terrifying rough (*fearful . . . ungentle*) seas

152 **exposed** Sixteen years after Leontes
ordered Perdita to be exposed (see
2.3.173–7, 3.3.49–50), this is the word
he uses the moment he sees her.
paragon 'companion' as well as
'model of excellence'

153 **Neptune** See 4.4.28–9n.

154 **her pains** the trouble she takes (the
man is Leontes)

155 **Th'adventure . . . person** risking
her life for

156 **Libya** in Shakespeare's day not an
independent monarchy (suggested
at 156–7, 207), but under Ottoman
rule. Elizabethans expected Libyans
to have dark skins, like that of Othello
the Moor. When Perdita, with her

pale skin and her mother's Russian
features (see 4.4.161, 369–70 and nn.,
5.2.35–6), is said to be from Libya,
the racial joke may have brought the
house down.
Smalus Most likely borrowed from
Plutarch's life of Dion (see List of
Roles, 5–6n.), which mentions a voyage from Libya to a town in Sicily
governed by 'Synalus', a Carthaginian
captain (this life also contains
'Polyxenus' and 'Archidamus': see
List of Roles, 20n., 25n.; Lees, 161).
Smalus may be a misprint, or a mistake by the scribe Crane, misreading
the 'in' minims in 'Sinalus'.

158–9 2**from . . . her** from him (Smalus)
whose tears, as they parted, proclaimed
her to be his daughter

160 **A . . . friendly** a favourable south
wind assisting us (*friendly*, adjective
for participle: Abbott, 380)

161 **execute the charge** perform the
duty

158] *as Hanmer; F lines* Sir, / Daughter /   159 his, parting] *Hanmer;* his parting *F*

For visiting your highness. My best train
I have from your Sicilian shores dismissed;
Who for Bohemia bend, to signify
Not only my success in Libya, sir, 165
But my arrival and my wife's, in safety
Here where we are.

LEONTES   The blessed gods
Purge all infection from our air whilst you
Do climate here. You have a holy father,
A graceful gentleman, against whose person, 170
So sacred as it is, I have done sin,
For which the heavens, taking angry note,
Have left me issueless; and your father's blessed,
As he from heaven merits it, with you,
Worthy his goodness. What might I have been, 175
Might I a son and daughter now have looked on,
Such goodly things as you?

         Enter a Lord.

LORD   Most noble sir,
That which I shall report will bear no credit
Were not the proof so nigh. Please you, great sir,
Bohemia greets you from himself, by me; 180

---

162 **My best train** the chief members of my retinue
164 **bend** set their course
    signify announce
165 **success** good fortune (in marrying Smalus' daughter)
167 This line has only eight syllables: see pp. 127–8.
    The May the
169 **climate** reside (*OED v.*[1], only citation)
    holy of high and reverend excellence (*OED a.* 3c). Cf. *Tem* 5.1.62.
170 **graceful** full of divine grace; virtuous. See 1.2.80n.

171 **So . . . is** even though it is sacred (as God's deputy on earth, a king's *person*, 170, was *sacred*)
173 **issueless** childless
174 **merits it** deserves (the blessing), i.e. of having children
175 **Worthy** worthy of
176 **son and daughter** The words could mean, respectively, son-in-law and daughter-in-law; cf. 207–8.
177 **goodly things** beautiful beings; see 1.2.92n.
178 **will . . . credit** would never be believed
179 **proof so nigh** evidence so near

Desires you to attach his son, who has,
His dignity and duty both cast off,
Fled from his father, from his hopes, and with
A shepherd's daughter.

LEONTES   Where's Bohemia? Speak.

LORD

Here in your city. I now came from him.   185
I speak amazedly, and it becomes
My marvel and my message. To your court
Whiles he was hastening – in the chase, it seems,
Of this fair couple – meets he on the way
The father of this seeming lady and   190
Her brother, having both their country quitted
With this young prince.

FLORIZEL   Camillo has betrayed me,
Whose honour and whose honesty till now
Endured all weathers.

LORD   Lay't so to his charge.
He's with the king your father.

LEONTES   Who? Camillo?   195

LORD

Camillo, sir. I spake with him, who now
Has these poor men in question. Never saw I
Wretches so quake. They kneel, they kiss the earth,

---

181 **attach** arrest
182 thrown off both his princely rank and
filial duty
183 **hopes** prospects, i.e. inheritance;
what everyone hopes of (or for) him
(see 12n.)
186 **amazedly** in a confused way
186–7 **it . . . message** i.e. my confused
speaking matches the extraordinary
thing (or fits my sense of wonder, or
my utter bewilderment) I'm about to
relate
188 **the chase** pursuit; cf. 215–16, 3.3.56
(see n.)
190–1 **father . . . brother** i.e. the

Shepherd and Clown
190 **seeming** i.e. who looks like a highborn lady but isn't
194 **Endured all weathers** stood firm in
all circumstances
Lay't . . . charge Accuse him of it in
these terms yourself.
197 **in question** under interrogation
198 **quake** Lines 197–201 were probably meant to be half-comic: inferiors
ridiculed or frightened by superiors
were commonplace in comedies, e.g.
LLL 5.2.485–626, *MND* 5.1.108–256.
kneel . . . earth Cf. Dent, D651, 'To
kiss the ground'.

Forswear themselves as often as they speak.
Bohemia stops his ears, and threatens them   200
With divers deaths in death.

PERDITA   O, my poor father!
The heaven sets spies upon us, will not have
Our contract celebrated.

LEONTES   You are married?

FLORIZEL
We are not, sir, nor are we like to be.
The stars, I see, will kiss the valleys first;   205
The odds for high and low's alike.

LEONTES   My lord,
Is this the daughter of a king?

FLORIZEL   She is,
When once she is my wife.

LEONTES
That 'once', I see, by your good father's speed
Will come on very slowly. I am sorry,   210
Most sorry, you have broken from his liking,
Where you were tied in duty, and as sorry
Your choice is not so rich in worth as beauty,
That you might well enjoy her.

---

199 **Forswear themselves** deny everything under oath; curse themselves
200 **stops his ears** i.e. refuses to listen to
   their pleading
201 **divers ... death** different agonies
   as they are tortured to death
202 **The ... spies** the gods set inform-
   ers; cf. 'God's spies', *KL* 5.3.17.
203 **contract** See 4.4.395n.
204 **like** likely
206 Fortune (cf. 215) is the same for
   everyone, whether of *high* or *low* birth;
   there is as much chance of a prince
   marrying a shepherdess (*high and low*)
   as the *stars* have of kissing *the valleys*
   (205); loaded dice (*high and low*) are

used against everyone, i.e. the gods
   stack the *odds*.
207 **daughter** See 176n.
208 i.e. the moment she is married to me
209 **speed** i.e. because of your father's
   speed in arriving to stop you; punning
   on 'success'
211 **broken ... liking** acted against his
   will; displeased him
212 **tied in duty** bound to obey him
213 **so ... beauty** as superior in rank as
   in beauty
214 **well enjoy her** have her properly
   as your wife (cf. 4.4.533); 'enjoy' was
   often connected with sex, e.g. *Oth*
   4.2.217, *Cym* 2.4.43–4.

FLORIZEL [*to Perdita*]   Dear, look up.
Though Fortune, visible an enemy,   215
Should chase us with my father, power no jot
Hath she to change our loves. Beseech you, sir,
Remember since you owed no more to time
Than I do now. With thought of such affections,
Step forth mine advocate; at your request,   220
My father will grant precious things as trifles.

LEONTES
Would he do so, I'd beg your precious mistress,
Which he counts but a trifle.

PAULINA   Sir, my liege,
Your eye hath too much youth in't. Not a month
'Fore your queen died, she was more worth such gazes   225
Than what you look on now.

LEONTES   I thought of her
Even in these looks I made. [*to Florizel*] But your
    petition
Is yet unanswered. I will to your father.
Your honour not o'erthrown by your desires,
I am friend to them and you; upon which errand   230

look up keep your spirits up (Dent, L431.1)

215–17 **Though . . . she** even if Fortune, clearly opposed to us, joined my father in hunting us down, she hasn't the slightest power; 'chase us with my father' may mean 'use my father to hunt us'.

218–19 **Remember . . . now** recall when you were my age

219 **With . . . affections** i.e. remember the passions you felt; see 1.1.24n.

220 **Step . . . advocate** intercede for me; cf. *advocate*, 4.4.744, 746 (see nn.).
request a reminder of 1.2.87

221 **as trifles** as though of the smallest value

222 **I'd . . . mistress** the only trace of the king's incestuous desire in *Pandosto*

(pp. 439–40), rendered innocuous when Paulina tells Leontes he is too old to eye up this girl (224), and that Hermione was more beautiful than her, even when older, and nine months pregnant (*Not a month / 'Fore*, 224–5)

223 **my liege** Paulina addresses Leontes respectfully, but reproaches him.

225 **'Fore** before

226–7 **I . . . made** Leontes may mean he felt guilty about Hermione when looking at Perdita, or he may have half-recognized Hermione's features, sparking a moment of desire.

228 **to** go to

229–30 **Your . . . you** and speak on your behalf (*friend* to you) provided (1) your desires haven't led you to behave dishonourably (by having sex with

214 SD] *Oxf*   227 SD] *Theobald*

I now go toward him; therefore follow me,
And mark what way I make. Come, good my lord.   *Exeunt.*

5.2   *Enter* AUTOLYCUS *and a* Gentleman.

AUTOLYCUS   Beseech you, sir, were you present at this relation?

GENTLEMAN   I was by at the opening of the fardel, heard the old shepherd deliver the manner how he found it; whereupon, after a little amazedness, we were all com-   5
manded out of the chamber. Only this, methought I heard the shepherd say he found the child.

AUTOLYCUS   I would most gladly know the issue of it.

GENTLEMAN   I make a broken delivery of the business, but the changes I perceived in the king and Camillo   10
were very notes of admiration. They seemed almost, with staring on one another, to tear the cases of their eyes. There was speech in their dumbness, language in their very gesture. They looked as they had heard

Perdita): cf. *Tem* 4.1.14–22; (2) what you want is compatible with your rank
232 **mark . . . make** observe how far I succeed
5.2 set in the precincts of Leontes' palace, in a room or an area outside the audience chamber (where the first revelations were made and which the Gentleman and others were ordered out of, 3–7). The reunion of Leontes and Perdita – narrated piecemeal, not seen – is the culmination of many overturnings in the play of the pro-verbial 'seeing is believing' (Tilley, S212; cf. B267, B268). *Not* seeing yet still believing is what is asked of the audience (see 31n., and e.g. 3.3.81–99, 4.1.19–25), until 5.3, when they are to believe what they are shown. See p. 122.

1–2 **this relation** the telling of this story
3 **by** there
fardel bundle: see 3.3.45 SDn.
4 **deliver . . . how** recount the way
5 **after . . . amazedness** after everyone had got over their astonishment
6 **chamber** receiving chamber (see 1.2n.)
Only this I can add only one thing
8 **the . . . it** what the outcome is; with a pun on *issue*, i.e. whose child it was
9 **broken delivery** fragmentary report
10 **the king** i.e. Leontes
10–19, 42–53, 80–90 The ecstatic reac-tions recall the ceremony at Delphos; see 3.1.4–11n.
11 **very . . . admiration** true marks of wonder
12–13 **tear . . . eyes** i.e. their eyes were popping out of their heads
12 **cases** lids; cf. *Per* 3.2.97, 5.1.101–2.

5.2] *(Scæna Secunda.)*   0.1 AUTOLYCUS] *(Autolicus)*   3+ SP] *this edn; Gent.1. F*

of a world ransomed, or one destroyed. A notable   15
passion of wonder appeared in them, but the wisest
beholder, that knew no more but seeing, could not say if
th'importance were joy or sorrow; but in the extremity
of the one it must needs be.

Enter [ROGERO].

Here comes a gentleman that happily knows more. The   20
news, Rogero?

ROGERO Nothing but bonfires. The oracle is fulfilled,
the king's daughter is found. Such a deal of wonder is
broken out within this hour that ballad-makers cannot
be able to express it.   25

Enter [*the* Steward].

Here comes the Lady Paulina's steward; he can deliver
you more. How goes it now, sir? This news which is
called true is so like an old tale that the verity of it is in

---

15 **of ... destroyed** about a world
being saved or one dead and lost
(i.e. they were thinking either about
Perdita returned from the dead or
about Hermione and Mamillius lost
for ever). The word *ransomed* suggests ideas of sacrifice. Christ died to
redeem mankind, 'for the ransom of
many' (Mark, 10.45); Alcestis gave
her life for her husband but was
rescued from death by Hercules: see
pp. 13, 446–8. Cf. *2H6* 3.2.297, 'The
world shall not be ransom for thy
life'.
15–16 **notable ... appeared** extraordinary state of bewilderment was
evident. For *wonder* here and at 23, see
pp. 69–72.
17 **but seeing** than what he could see
17–19 **if ... be** whether joy or sorrow

were signified (by the *passion*, 16),
meant, only that it was certainly one
of these in extreme measure
20 **happily** perhaps
21 **Rogero** See List of Roles, 13n.
22 **bonfires** i.e. lit in celebration
oracle prophecy of the oracle
(3.2.130–3)
23–4 **Such ... hour** so many extraordinary things have happened in the
past hour
24 **ballad-makers ... it** See 4.4.187n.
24–5 **cannot be** will not be
25.1 **Steward** See List of Roles, 14n.
26 **deliver** tell
28 **like ... tale** i.e. quite unreliable:
cf. 60–1 (see n.), 5.3.117, and see
4.4.270n. See also pp. 24–5.
28–9 **verity ... suspicion** its truth is
very much in doubt

19.1 ROGERO] *Staunton; another Gentleman. F*   20 happily] haply *Collier*   22+ SP] *Gent.2. F*   25.1
the Steward] *Staunton subst.; another Gentleman. F*

strong suspicion. Has the king found his heir?

STEWARD   Most true, if ever truth were pregnant by   30
circumstance. That which you hear you'll swear you see;
there is such unity in the proofs. The mantle of Queen
Hermione's; her jewel about the neck of it; the letters
of Antigonus found with it, which they know to be his
character; the majesty of the creature, in resemblance   35
of the mother; the affection of nobleness which nature
shows above her breeding, and many other evidences
proclaim her with all certainty to be the king's daughter.
Did you see the meeting of the two kings?

ROGERO   No.   40

STEWARD   Then have you lost a sight which was to be
seen, cannot be spoken of. There might you have
beheld one joy crown another, so and in such manner
that it seemed sorrow wept to take leave of them,

---

30 **true** definitely
30–1 **pregnant by circumstance** made
    clear by circumstantial evidence (*preg-
    nant*, filled out)
31 **That . . . see** refers to the power of
    the theatre to persuade audiences to
    see what is narrated, as for example at
    4.1.19–25; conversely, the deficiency
    of description, compared with what is
    shown, is emphasized at 41–2, 56–7.
    See 1.2.187n.
32 **unity in** complete agreement between
    (i.e. between what the Shepherd and
    Clown say and the evidence at 32–8)
    mantle Hermione's cloak (or blanket);
    see 3.3.45 SDn. In *Cym* 5.5.360–3,
    a mantle made by his mother the
    queen identifies Arviragus, abducted
    as a child.
33 **neck of it** the baby's neck (neuter
    pronoun, as at 1.1.34, 38); the collar of
    the mantle
    letters See 3.3.45 SDn.

35 **character** handwriting; see 3.3.46n.
35–7 **majesty . . . breeding** the young
    woman's dignified bearing, like her
    mother's; her nobility, which her
    nature shows is above her humble
    upbringing
36 **affection** disposition (*OED n.*[1] 5); see
    1.1.24n.)
41–2 **lost . . . of** missed a sight that had
    to be seen, since it can't be described
43 **one . . . another** each joy add the
    finishing touch to the previous one
    (*OED* crown *v.*[1] 9)
44–5 **seemed . . . tears** it was as if
    sorrow itself (a personification) was
    weeping as it bid farewell to the kings
    who, as it were, waded knee-deep in
    their tears of joy. The Steward's figure
    of speech is affected and obscure (cf.
    the comparable instance of smiles and
    tears in an over-ingenious metaphor,
    KL 4.3.17–22 (1608 text), quoted
    above, p. 22).

30+ SP] *this edn; Gent.*3. F

for their joy waded in tears. There was casting up of   45
eyes, holding up of hands, with countenance of such
distraction that they were to be known by garment,
not by favour. Our king being ready to leap out of
himself for joy of his found daughter, as if that joy were
now become a loss, cries, 'O, thy mother, thy mother!',   50
then asks Bohemia forgiveness, then embraces his
son-in-law, then again worries he his daughter with
clipping her. Now he thanks the old shepherd, which
stands by like a weather-bitten conduit of many kings'
reigns. I never heard of such another encounter, which   55
lames report to follow it, and undoes description to
do it.

ROGERO   What, pray you, became of Antigonus, that
carried hence the child?

STEWARD   Like an old tale still, which will have matter to   60
rehearse though credit be asleep and not an ear open
– he was torn to pieces with a bear. This avouches the

45–6 **casting . . . hands** looking up to
heaven, holding their hands in prayer;
giving thanks to the gods. The gestures
and expressions at 45–7 suggest actors
in a theatre; see 31n.
46–8 **countenance . . . favour** with
features so contorted they were only
recognizable by their clothes, not their
faces
46 **countenance** an implied plural noun
(Abbott, 471)
47 **distraction** distortion; cf. *H8* 3.1.112.
48–9 **leap . . . joy** Cf. Dent, S507, 'To
leap out of his skin for joy'.
49 **of** about
52–3 **worries . . . her** hugs her vehemently (*OED v.* 3c)
53 **clipping** embracing (*OED* clip *v.*[1] 1a)
   which who (Abbott, 265)
54–5 **weather-bitten . . . reigns** cor-
roded water spout that has seen the
reigns of many kings, with a pun on
reigns and rains (*OED*'s first citation

of 'weather-bitten'). Spouts on buildings were often in the shape of an old
man's head or gargoyle (*OED* conduit
n. 2): the Shepherd's face is pouring
with tears (cf. 3.3.25; see n.). See
pp. 78–9.
55 **such another encounter** a meeting
like it
56–7 **lames . . . it** outstrips any account
of it, renders description incapable
of doing justice to it; i.e. no *report* can
keep up with (*follow*) what happened.
Cf. 41–2 (see n.); *AC* 2.2.208, where
Cleopatra 'beggared all description';
and *Cym* 5.5.162–4, where Imogen's
beauty lames, i.e. far exceeds, Venus'
statue in her shrine.
60–1 **Like . . . open** still like an old tale
(see 28n.), which carries on telling
its story even if it is impossible to
believe (*OED* credit *n.* 2a), and no one
is listening
62 **with** by (Abbott, 193)

54 weather-bitten] weather-beaten *F3*   58 pray] (ʌpray*)*

shepherd's son, who has not only his innocence, which
seems much, to justify him, but a handkerchief and
rings of his, that Paulina knows.   65
GENTLEMAN   What became of his barque and his
followers?
STEWARD   Wrecked the same instant of their master's
death, and in the view of the shepherd; so that all the
instruments which aided to expose the child were even   70
then lost when it was found. But O, the noble combat
that 'twixt joy and sorrow was fought in Paulina! She
had one eye declined for the loss of her husband,
another elevated that the oracle was fulfilled. She
lifted the princess from the earth, and so locks her in   75
embracing as if she would pin her to her heart, that she
might no more be in danger of losing.
GENTLEMAN   The dignity of this act was worth the
audience of kings and princes, for by such was it acted.
STEWARD   One of the prettiest touches of all, and that   80
which angled for mine eyes – caught the water, though
not the fish – was when at the relation of the queen's
death, with the manner how she came to't bravely

63–4 **innocence . . . him** guilelessness
(*OED* innocence 3), which appears
very considerable, to confirm what
he says
65 **of his** i.e. belonging to Antigonus
66 **barque** ship
67 **followers** attendants
70–1 **instruments . . . found** people
who helped cast out the child died at
the moment she was discovered
73–4 **one . . . elevated** Cf. Dent, E248,
'To cry with one eye and laugh with
the other', i.e. to have feelings of sorrow and joy mixed (*declined*, cast down;
elevated, raised). Cf. *Ham* 1.2.11.
74 **that** because
75 **earth** ground
75–6 **locks . . . embracing** clasps her in
her arms

76 **pin** fasten
77 **no . . . losing** never again be at risk of
being lost. F's 'loosing' may be a pun
on coming undone, following Paulina's
'fastening', 76.
78 **dignity . . . worth** grandeur of what
was done was worthy of; *this act* is
everything described at 41–77. The
metaphor at 78–9 is of kings and
princes acting a play (*OED* act *n.* 7a)
before a royal audience.
81 **angled . . . eyes** was fishing for my
eyes (i.e. to make me cry). See 1.2.179n.
caught the water i.e. brought tears to
my eyes
82 **relation** story, narration
83 **manner . . . to't** i.e. how (and why)
she died
bravely nobly

77 losing] *F2;* loosing *F*

confessed and lamented by the king, how attentiveness
wounded his daughter till from one sign of dolour to   85
another she did, with an 'Alas', I would fain say bleed
tears; for I am sure my heart wept blood. Who was
most marble there changed colour. Some swooned, all
sorrowed. If all the world could have seen't, the woe
had been universal.   90

GENTLEMAN   Are they returned to the court?

STEWARD   No. The princess, hearing of her mother's
statue, which is in the keeping of Paulina, a piece many
years in doing and now newly performed by that rare
Italian master Giulio Romano, who, had he himself   95
eternity and could put breath into his work, would
beguile Nature of her custom, so perfectly he is her ape.
He so near to Hermione hath done Hermione that they
say one would speak to her and stand in hope of answer.

84–5 **attentiveness . . . daughter** rapt
attention hurt his daughter; i.e. because
she was so caught up in the story
85–6 **from . . . another** after showing
one sign of grief (*dolour*) then another
86 **I . . . say** i.e. I can't describe it any
other way
86–7 **bleed tears . . . wept blood** 'The
heart bleeds' was a figure of speech
for experiencing great anguish (*OED*
bleed *v.* 1c).
87–8 **Who . . . colour** Even the most
hard-hearted (or perhaps, the ones
with the most self-control) went pale.
Cf. Dent, H311, 'Heart as hard as
marble'. There is a play on *marble*
and *marvel* (i.e. petrified in wonder
the onlookers were as motionless as
marble statues), anticipating 93–9 and
5.3.34–42, 57–8, 65–6.
89 **seen't** i.e. seen the princess's grief
92 **hearing** i.e. had heard (the sentence
'The princess . . . ape', 92–7, is
incomplete or elliptical)
93–4 **piece . . . performed** work of art

that took many years to make, and was
recently completed (see 4.4.32n.); *piece*
and *performed* are associated with the
theatre: see 5.1.1 and n.
94–5 **rare Italian master** marvellous
Italian artist (*OED* master *n.* 17a)
Romano See pp. 46, 57.
95–7 **had . . . custom** if he could make
his creations breathe and had endless
time to do it in, he would cheat Nature
of her business (*custom*, i.e. peopling
the earth). Cf. 5.3.19–20 (see n.) and
Cym 2.4.83–5, where a sculptor is
'another nature', excelling her but for
the movement and breath he can't give
his statues.
97 **ape** imitator (*OED* 3); sometimes used
contemptuously for a mimic (3a)
98 **He . . . ²Hermione** i.e. his statue of
Hermione is so lifelike
98–9 **they say** The reports of Romano,
the statue, and the people who have
seen it (92–9) are all Paulina's invention (unless there really is a statue:
see p. 72).

88 marble there] *F3 subst.*; Marble, there *F*

Thither with all greediness of affection are they gone,   100
   and there they intend to sup.

ROGERO   I thought she had some great matter there in
   hand, for she hath privately twice or thrice a day, ever
   since the death of Hermione, visited that removed
   house. Shall we thither, and with our company piece   105
   the rejoicing?

GENTLEMAN   Who would be thence, that has the benefit
   of access? Every wink of an eye some new grace will
   be born. Our absence makes us unthrifty to our
   knowledge. Let's along.   110

                Exeunt [Gentleman, Rogero and Steward].

AUTOLYCUS   Now, had I not the dash of my former life
   in me, would preferment drop on my head. I brought
   the old man and his son aboard the prince; told him I
   heard them talk of a fardel, and I know not what; but
   he at that time over-fond of the shepherd's daughter   115
   – so he then took her to be – who began to be much
   seasick and himself little better, extremity of weather
   continuing, this mystery remained undiscovered. But

---

100 **all . . . affection** full of eager desire
(to feast their eyes on the statue, hence
sup, 101: see n.); see 1.1.24n.

101 **sup** literally, 'have supper', metaphorically, 'feed (their emotions)'

102–3 **great . . . hand** big project on (in
her *house*, 105)

103 **privately** by herself

104–5 **that removed house** where
Romano has made the statue (or the
place Hermione has been hiding): the
setting for the final scene (see 5.3n.)

104 **removed** secluded

105 **thither** go there
   piece add to

107–8 **Who . . . access?** Who wouldn't
be there if they could get in?

108–9 **Every . . . born** Every instant it
takes to blink some new miracle will

happen

108 **grace** probably 'divine favour'; see
1.2.80n.

109–10 **Our . . . knowledge** If we are
not there, we'll lose the chance to know
more about it.

110 **Let's along** Let's go there.

111–12 **had . . . me** if it weren't for the
tinge (*OED* dash *n.*1 5b) of my former
life (as a scoundrel)

112 **preferment** promotion
   drop . . . head i.e. fall into my lap

113 **prince** prince's ship

114 **fardel** See 3.3.45 SDn.

115 **over-fond** being overwrought with
love

116 **so** as
   much very

118 **undiscovered** unrevealed

110 SD] *this edn; Exeunt / Rowe; Exit. F*

333

'tis all one to me, for had I been the finder-out of this
secret it would not have relished among my other   120
discredits.

Enter SHEPHERD *and* CLOWN [*dressed as gentlemen*].

Here come those I have done good to against my will,
and already appearing in the blossoms of their fortune.
SHEPHERD   Come, boy, I am past moe children, but thy
sons and daughters will be all gentlemen born.   125
CLOWN [*to Autolycus*]   You are well met, sir. You denied
to fight with me this other day because I was no
gentleman born. See you these clothes? Say you see
them not, and think me still no gentleman born. You
were best say these robes are not gentlemen born.   130
Give me the lie, do, and try whether I am not now a

---

119 **'tis all one** it's all the same
120–1 **would . . . discredits** would not
    have tasted right alongside my other
    disgraces; i.e. my misdeeds would have
    spoiled the effect of my revealing the
    secret
121.1 *gentlemen* Polixenes has given
    them this title to reward them (136–
    40). See 125n.
123 **in . . . fortune** blooming in their
    prosperity; i.e. in their new clothes
124 **past moe** too old to have any more
125 **gentlemen born** To be born a
    gentleman, according to Elizabethan
    rules, men had to descend from three
    degrees of gentry (see Dent, G58.1, 'It
    takes three generations to make a gen-
    tleman'). At 125–42 the Shepherd and
    Clown don't know what *gentlemen born*
    are; the phrase appeals because it is
    legal sounding (used correctly in *MW*
    1.1.7, 258). Cf. 4.3.93–4, 4.4.731–2
    (see nn.).
126 **You . . . met** a greeting; i.e. it's good
    to see you

126–8 **²You . . . born** Autolycus gave the
    Clown the lie but refused to fight
    him because he was an inferior (see
    4.4.728-30n.). See 131n.
126 **denied** refused
127 **this other day** i.e. not long ago
127–8 **because . . . born** Duelling was
    the prerogative of gentlemen. See
    121.1n., 125n., 130n.; 4.4.728–30n.
129–30 **You . . . say** you'd better say
    that (i.e. this is the most insulting
    way of contradicting me, to get our
    fight started; 131n.); you might as
    well say, i.e. it would be as ridiculous
    as denying that these robes are a
    gentleman's.
130 **robes** The outfits, probably high-
    quality gowns (*OED* robe *n.*¹ 2a) worn
    over ordinary clothes, indicate their
    new rank. Cf. *Cym* 4.2.81–3; Dent,
    A283, 'Clothes make the man'; and its
    opposite, S451, 'Fine clothes make not
    a gentleman.' See pp. 73–4.
131 **Give . . . lie** accuse me of lying. Cf.
    4.4.728–30 (see n.).

121.1 *dressed as gentlemen*] *Collier subst.*   124 moe] more *F2*   126 SD] *Oxf* gentleman born.

AUTOLYCUS   I know you are now, sir, a gentleman born.

CLOWN   Ay, and have been so any time these four hours.

SHEPHERD   And so have I, boy.   135

CLOWN   So you have; but I was a gentleman born before
my father, for the king's son took me by the hand and
called me brother, and then the two kings called my
father brother, and then the prince my brother and the
princess my sister called my father father, and so we   140
wept; and there was the first gentleman-like tears that
ever we shed.

SHEPHERD   We may live, son, to shed many more.

CLOWN   Ay, or else 'twere hard luck, being in so
preposterous estate as we are.   145

AUTOLYCUS   I humbly beseech you, sir, to pardon me all
the faults I have committed to your worship, and to give
me your good report to the prince my master.

SHEPHERD   Prithee, son, do; for we must be gentle now we
are gentlemen.   150

---

134 **any . . . hours** every moment during
the past few hours; four was used
indefinitely to mean several, as in *Ham*
2.2.157. Cf. *seven*, 4.4.583 and see
583–4n.
137 **took . . . hand** shook my hand; cf.
153 and see 1.1.29–31n.
141 **was . . . tears** plural subject *tears*
with quasi-singular verb (Abbott, 335)
143 We may shed more tears, son; so
long as we live, son, we'll weep, it's the
human condition. Cf. Lear, patiently,
'We came crying hither', *KL* 4.6.174.
144 **or . . . luck** i.e. I should hope so
145 **preposterous** A malapropism for
'prosperous', this literally means
inverted in order or position, thus
contrary to Nature, monstrous, perverse (the modern meaning, absurd,
ignores the Latin root *prae* + *poster-us*,
before + coming after). The phrase

preposterous estate sums up the benign
topsy-turviness of Act 5, in respect of
the rustics' new rank and the unbelievable miracles of reunion and the dead
restored to life. Through *preposterous*
Shakespeare explores the social and
psychological order of things and
'the world turned upside down': see
pp. 76–8, 100.
estate condition
147, 152 **your worship** honorific title,
equivalent to sir or master, used by
inferiors to superiors (*OED n.* 5a).
Now their social positions are reversed,
Autolycus addresses the Clown with
deferential pronouns, *you* and *your*
(133, 146–8, 152, while the Clown
replies, as a superior to an inferior,
with *thou* and *thy* (151, 153, 161–5,
168, 171). See 1.2.43n.
149 **be gentle** behave in a dignified way

149 Prithee] (*Prethee*)

CLOWN   Thou wilt amend thy life?

AUTOLYCUS   Ay, an it like your good worship.

CLOWN   Give me thy hand. I will swear to the prince thou
art as honest a true fellow as any is in Bohemia.

SHEPHERD   You may say it, but not swear it.   155

CLOWN   Not swear it, now I am a gentleman? Let boors
and franklins say it; I'll swear it.

SHEPHERD   How if it be false, son?

CLOWN   If it be ne'er so false, a true gentleman may swear
it in the behalf of his friend. [*to Autolycus*] And I'll   160
swear to the prince thou art a tall fellow of thy hands,
and that thou wilt not be drunk; but I know thou art no
tall fellow of thy hands, and that thou wilt be drunk;
but I'll swear it, and I would thou wouldst be a tall
fellow of thy hands.   165

AUTOLYCUS   I will prove so, sir, to my power.

CLOWN   Ay, by any means prove a tall fellow. If I do not
wonder how thou dar'st venture to be drunk, not being
a tall fellow, trust me not. [*Flourish sounded within.*]

---

151 **amend thy life** live a better life.
Cf. the Communion service in *BCP*,
'Amend your lives, and be in perfect
charity with all men' (Shaheen, 733).

152 **an it like** if it please

153 **Give . . . hand** Let's shake hands on
it (cf. 137).

154 **true fellow** man of good character

155 You may declare it to be true, but not
swear to it under oath. There may be
a quibble on swearing under oath and
swearing oaths (using bad language):
cf. *Cym* 2.1.11–12.

156–7 Upper-class men had the right to
attest the truth of something under
oath; *boors and franklins* (peasants and
yeomen) didn't.

159 **If . . . false** however false it is
ne'er abbreviation from 'never', here
perhaps a rural or provincial form

160 **in the** on

161, 164–5 **tall . . . hands** bold chap; tall
meant brave, dextrous (*OED* 3, 4). Cf.
Dent, M163, 'He is a tall man of his
hands' (said of a courageous fighter);
R3 1.4.148–51.

164 **would** wish

166 **to my power** to the best of my
ability. No doubt Autolycus means he
will use his dexterous *hands* (165) to
cut purses and pick pockets.

167 **by . . . fellow** become (*prove*) a
capable fellow any way you can

167–9 **If . . . not** It's beyond me, I assure
you, how you dare risk getting drunk,
since you're not a capable fellow; i.e.
when you're drunk you'll get into a
fight, which you're obviously no good
at. Cf. 'Never trust me if . . .' (Dent,
T558.1).

160 SD] *Oxf*   169 SD] *Collier subst.*

Hark, the kings and the princes, our kindred, are going   170
to see the queen's picture. Come, follow us. We'll be thy
good masters.   *Exeunt.*

5.3   *Enter* LEONTES, POLIXENES, FLORIZEL, PERDITA,
            CAMILLO, PAULINA, *Lords and others.*

LEONTES
O grave and good Paulina, the great comfort
That I have had of thee!
PAULINA   What, sovereign sir,
I did not well, I meant well. All my services
You have paid home, but that you have vouchsafed
With your crowned brother, and these your contracted   5
Heirs of your kingdoms, my poor house to visit,
It is a surplus of your grace which never
My life may last to answer.

---

170 **Hark** listen (a trumpet's sounding)
(*Flourish*, 169 SD); listen to me
the princes Florizel and Perdita; see
2.1.17n.
kindred relations (see 137–40)
171 **queen's picture** statue of the queen;
cf. 5.1.74 (see n.).
171–2 **thy good masters** true advocates
for you (promised at 153–4, 160–2);
another reversal of their roles at
4.4.800–17.
5.3 located in Paulina's secluded
house, which she has visited daily
since Hermione died (5.2.103–5: see
104–5n.). Paulina calls it her *poor
house* (6), perhaps because it is more
modest than the usual aristocratic
mansion. It has a *gallery*, however,
for *singularities* (see 10, 12 and nn.),
and a chapel to which Paulina brings
Leontes and the others (see 12–14,

86), where the statue stands by itself
(see 18n.) on a pedestal (or something
Hermione must *descend* from, 88, 99),
hidden behind a curtain (20 SD: see
n.).
1 **grave** worthy
4 **paid home** repaid in full; cf. Dent,
H535.1, 'To pay one home'.
vouchsafed deigned
5 **crowned brother** brother prince, i.e.
Polixenes. See 1.2.4n.
²**your** perhaps repeated from *your
crowned*, or caught from *your kingdoms*
contracted betrothed
6 **my poor house** See 5.3n.
7–8 **It . . . answer** (your visit) is an
overflowing of the honour you do me
(*your grace*), which I may never live
long enough to repay
7 **grace** favour; special honour to
Paulina (*OED n.* 6a, 8b). See 1.2.80n.

5.3] *(Scæna Tertia.)*   0.1–2] *Rowe subst.; Enter Leontes, Polixenes, Florizell, Perdita, Camillo, Paulina:
Hermione (like a Statue:) Lords, &c. F*   5 your contracted] *young contracted Oxf*

337

LEONTES   O Paulina,
We honour you with trouble. But we came
To see the statue of our queen. Your gallery   10
Have we passed through, not without much content
In many singularities, but we saw not
That which my daughter came to look upon,
The statue of her mother.

PAULINA   As she lived peerless,
So her dead likeness I do well believe   15
Excels whatever yet you looked upon,
Or hand of man hath done. Therefore I keep it
Lonely, apart. But here it is: prepare
To see the life as lively mocked as ever
Still sleep mocked death. Behold, and say 'tis well.   20

[*Draws a curtain and reveals the figure of Hermione,
standing like a statue.*]

---

9 **We . . . trouble** The 'honour' of our visit is really an imposition. Cf. *MA* 1.1.91–7.
you Leontes switches from *thee* (2), the pronoun he addressed Paulina with throughout 5.1 (see 5.1.17n.). He doesn't address her with it again until 136–42, perhaps because in the interval he uses the informal pronoun to show intense feeling (grief and love) for the statue of Hermione (25–6, 39–42).
10 **gallery** long, corridor-like room for exhibiting works of art (*OED n.* 5a, 6)
11 **content** pleasure
12 **singularities** curiosities, rare objects
14 **peerless** Cf. the descriptions of Perdita at 4.4.32, 5.1.94 (see nn.).
15 **dead** exact (*OED* dead *a.* 31c); lifelike but lifeless
18 ***Lonely** separate (*OED* 2). Hanmer's emendation of F's 'Louely' is compelling: Paulina keeps the statue *apart* (18) from her *singularities* (12) because it is *peerless* (14), as Hermione was.

19–20 **To . . . death** hints that Hermione's statue only looks dead, and that it is Nature who is doing the mocking (the queen is sleeping restfully, neither stone nor a dead body)
19 **lively mocked** convincingly counterfeited (*OED* mock *v.* 6b)
mocked Cf. 67–8, and see 5.2.97, where art is said to be Nature's ape (see n.).
20 **Still . . . death** Cf. Dent, S527, 'Sleep is the image of death'; *Cym* 2.2.31. See 1.2.326–7n.
Still calm
well well made
20 SD At the Globe, the curtain was probably hung across the tiring-house doorway, i.e. at the very back of the stage, with the statue in the space behind it hidden until Paulina drew the curtain. Modern productions have shown the statue seated, or even recumbent as if on a tomb, but in early performances it was most likely standing (*stands*, 36).

18 Lonely] *Hanmer*; Louely *F*   20 SD] *Rowe subst.*

I like your silence; it the more shows off
Your wonder. But yet speak – first you, my liege.
Comes it not something near?

LEONTES   Her natural posture.
Chide me, dear stone, that I may say indeed
Thou art Hermione – or, rather, thou art she   25
In thy not chiding; for she was as tender
As infancy and grace. But yet, Paulina,
Hermione was not so much wrinkled, nothing
So aged as this seems.

POLIXENES   O, not by much.

PAULINA
So much the more our carver's excellence,   30
Which lets go by some sixteen years and makes her
As she lived now.

LEONTES   As now she might have done,
So much to my good comfort as it is
Now piercing to my soul. O, thus she stood,
Even with such life of majesty – warm life,   35
As now it coldly stands – when first I wooed her.

21–2 **it . . . wonder** your speechlessness
shows how amazed you are
22 **yet speak** speak as well
23 **Comes . . . near?** Doesn't it look very
like her?
   Her natural posture exactly the way
   she used to hold herself in life; *posture*,
   pose, attitude
24–6 **Chide . . . chiding** i.e. he would
   believe the statue was Hermione if it
   were to rebuke him, as he believes she
   ought to; but the statue standing silent
   is truly like Hermione because it doesn't
25, 28 **Hermione** The name, which 'normally in the play has four syllables', is
   here 'reduced to three, the "o" being
   scarcely sounded' (Schanzer).
26–7 **tender . . . grace** gentle as a baby

and as divine mercy. See 1.2.80n.
28–9 **nothing / So** not nearly as
29 **aged** If Hermione is Leontes' age
   (see List of Roles, 2n.), she is in her
   mid-forties by 5.3, in Shakespeare's
   England almost an old woman.
   not by much (agreeing) not at all as
   old as this; (disagreeing) she doesn't
   look as old as all that
30 **carver's** sculptor's (*OED* carver[1] 2)
31 **lets go by** allows for the passage of
32 **As** as if
33–4 **So . . . soul** her presence would
   have been as great a joy to me as her
   absence (*it*) is now a torment to my
   soul; *it* could also mean (the sight of)
   the statue, as at 36.
36 **when . . . her** See 107n.

I am ashamed. Does not the stone rebuke me
For being more stone than it? O royal piece!
There's magic in thy majesty, which has
My evils conjured to remembrance, and   40
From thy admiring daughter took the spirits,
Standing like stone with thee.

PERDITA   And give me leave,
And do not say 'tis superstition, that
I kneel and then implore her blessing. Lady,
Dear queen, that ended when I but began,   45
Give me that hand of yours to kiss.

PAULINA   O patience!
The statue is but newly fixed; the colour's
Not dry.

CAMILLO [*to Leontes*]
My lord, your sorrow was too sore laid on,
Which sixteen winters cannot blow away,   50

---

38 **more stone** more stone-like, i.e.
harder, having less feeling; cf. Dent,
H310.1, H311, 'A heart of stone'. In
the 1590s, Donne writes of someone
dead, 'Here needs no marble tomb,
since he is gone, / He, and about him,
his, are turned to stone' ('Elegy 8',
Donne, 54).
piece work of art, masterpiece; lady.
See 4.4.32n.
39–42 **There's . . . thee** The metaphor
is from the magic of witchcraft, i.e.
supernatural powers of invocation, or
of rendering people powerless.
40 **My . . . remembrance** reminded me
of evil things I did
41 stunned your astonished (*admiring*)
daughter, taken her life force (*spirits*)
42 **like stone** motionless; cf. Dent,
S893.1, 'To turn to stone with wonder'.
43 **superstition** Kneeling and kissing
a parent's hand (44–6), indicated
filial love and obedience. However,
to do this to a statue would be, to

Protestant eyes, popish idolatry (*OED*
superstition 1a, 2b), in particular the
veneration of the Virgin Mary: see
pp. 46–7, 373–4.
45 **that . . . began** Cf. 3.3.110–11 (see n.).
47 **fixed** painted. The word could mean
fluids that had set or congealed (*OED*
fix *v.* 4b); by 1665 it was applied
specifically to colours made fast (*v.*
5a). It is possible it means 'set up in
its proper place' (*v.* 8a), but Paulina's
excuses (here and at 81–3) depend on
the paint still drying.
colour paint, pigment (*OED* colour *n.*[1]
8a). The Elizabethan convention was
to paint statues.
49–51 **your . . . dry** i.e. Leontes has wept
so many tears that not even 16 years of
winter winds and summer heat can dry
them. The image is probably from the
reference to the paint on the statue not
yet being dry (see 47n.).
49 **sore laid on** may mean thickly
applied, possibly another metaphor
from painting

49 SD] *Oxf*

So many summers dry. Scarce any joy
Did ever so long live; no sorrow
But killed itself much sooner.
POLIXENES [*to Leontes*]   Dear my brother,
  Let him that was the cause of this have power
  To take off so much grief from you as he   55
  Will piece up in himself.
PAULINA [*to Leontes*]   Indeed, my lord,
  If I had thought the sight of my poor image
  Would thus have wrought you – for the stone is mine –
  I'd not have showed it.   [*Makes to draw the curtain.*]
LEONTES   Do not draw the curtain.
PAULINA

No longer shall you gaze on't, lest your fancy   60
  May think anon it moves.
LEONTES   Let be, let be!
  Would I were dead but that methinks already –
  What was he that did make it? See, my lord,
  Would you not deem it breathed, and that those veins
  Did verily bear blood?
POLIXENES   Masterly done.   65

---

51 **So** nor as
52 The line is a syllable short. A word may have been lost (suggested emendations include 'sorrow sir' and 'sorrow ever'), or the compositor, who should have set *But* at the end of 52, put it at the beginning of 53.
53 **killed** extinguished
54–6 **Let . . . himself** Cf. *Son* 88.13–14, 'Such is my love, to thee I so belong, / That for thy right myself will bear all wrong.'
56 **Will . . . himself** can add to his own; *piece up* also indicates that the breach in their friendship is healed ('pieced up'); see 1.2.155n. on *unbreeched*.
57 **my poor image** Cf. *my poor house* (6),

and see 5.3n.
image statue
58 **wrought** agitated, though the statue was also wrought (made)
stone statue
61, 70 **anon** immediately; soon
61 **Let . . . be** i.e. don't worry about me, I *want* to see the statue move; leave it alone (*OED* let *v.*[1] 20a), i.e. don't touch the curtain (cf. 59, 68)
62 may I die if I don't think (it moves) already
63 **What** who
65 **verily** truly
*****Masterly** F's apostrophe (see t.n.) may indicate some kind of ellipsis or elision, e.g. It's or 'Tis.

53 SD] *Oxf*   56 SD] *Oxf*   59 SD] *Collier subst.*   65 Masterly] ('Masterly)

The very life seems warm upon her lip.

LEONTES

The fixure of her eye has motion in't,
As we are mocked with art.

PAULINA   I'll draw the curtain.
My lord's almost so far transported that
He'll think anon it lives.

LEONTES   O sweet Paulina,   70
Make me to think so twenty years together.
No settled senses of the world can match
The pleasure of that madness. Let't alone.

PAULINA

I am sorry, sir, I have thus far stirred you; but
I could afflict you farther.

LEONTES   Do, Paulina,   75
For this affliction has a taste as sweet
As any cordial comfort. Still methinks
There is an air comes from her. What fine chisel
Could ever yet cut breath? Let no man mock me,
For I will kiss her.

PAULINA   Good my lord, forbear;   80
The ruddiness upon her lip is wet.
You'll mar it if you kiss it, stain your own

---

66 the first explicit use of *her*, not *it*;
 echoed by Leontes at 67 (cf. 70)
67 **fixure** probably comes from 'fix'
 (see 47n.), but it also meant 'fixed-
 ness', 'fixed position', i.e. her eye is
 fixed but appears to move. Cf. *TC*
 1.3.101.
68 **As . . . art** so we are deluded by art
 (*OED* mock *v.* 1a); see 19n.
69 **transported** carried away
71, 84 **twenty** a long indefinite time; see
 5.2.134n.
71 **together** uninterrupted
72 **No . . . of** no calm mind in

73 **Let't alone** i.e. leave the curtain alone
 (cf. 61)
74 **thus . . . you** disturbed you like this,
 to this great extent
77 **cordial comfort** heart-warming
 restorative tonic. See pp. 19–20.
78 **an air** breath (*OED* air *n.*[1] 7a)
 fine sharp
79 **cut breath** sculpt (stone so it imitates)
 breath
80, 85 **forbear** desist (*OED v.* 5); restrain
 yourself (*v.* 7b)
81 **ruddiness** red colour; see 47n.,
 3.2.202n.

67 fixure] fixture *F4*

With oily painting. Shall I draw the curtain?

LEONTES

No, not these twenty years.

PERDITA   So long could I

Stand by, a looker-on.

PAULINA   Either forbear,   85

Quit presently the chapel, or resolve you

For more amazement. If you can behold it,

I'll make the statue move indeed, descend

And take you by the hand. But then you'll think –

Which I protest against – I am assisted   90

By wicked powers.

LEONTES   What you can make her do

I am content to look on; what to speak

I am content to hear; for 'tis as easy

To make her speak as move.

PAULINA   It is required

You do awake your faith. Then all stand still.   95

Or those that think it is unlawful business

I am about, let them depart.

LEONTES   Proceed.

No foot shall stir.

PAULINA   Music, awake her; strike!   [*Music*]

---

83 **painting** paint
84 **these** for the next
85 **forbear** withdraw
86 **presently** immediately
   chapel See 3.2.236n.
   resolve you prepare yourself
87 **behold** bear to look at
91 **wicked powers** arts of black magic
   (see 105, 111n.); evil spirits.
94–5 **It . . . faith** i.e. no miracle will
   happen unless your mind is fully open
95 **awake** See 1.2.326–7n.
96 ***Or those** Hanmer's emendation of
   F's 'On: those', is almost certainly
   right.

unlawful business i.e. irreligious and
illegal matters, witchcraft (see 105,
111n.)
98 **Music . . . strike** Cf. *Per* 3.2.90–4.
The power of music to restore life
is told most famously in the story of
Orpheus' attempt to rescue his dead
wife Eurydice from the underworld
by playing the harp for the gods: see
p. 10.
Music musicians; probably lutenists,
they are supposed to be in earshot
of the chapel, so they may have been
onstage in early performances.
strike strike up, begin playing

96 Or] *Hanmer;* On: *F*   98 SD] *Rowe*

[*to Hermione*] 'Tis time; descend; be stone no more;
  approach.
Strike all that look upon with marvel. Come,   100
I'll fill your grave up. Stir – nay, come away;
Bequeath to death your numbness, for from him
Dear life redeems you. You perceive she stirs
  [*Hermione steps down.*]
Start not. Her actions shall be holy as
You hear my spell is lawful. [*to Leontes*] Do not shun
  her   105
Until you see her die again, for then
You kill her double. Nay, present your hand.
When she was young, you wooed her; now in age,
Is she become the suitor?

LEONTES   O, she's warm!
If this be magic, let it be an art   110
Lawful as eating.

POLIXENES   She embraces him.

CAMILLO
  She hangs about his neck;

99 **'Tis time** The moment is here; punning on *time*, i.e. the music is being played in perfect time, everything is now in harmony for your return.
100 **Strike . . . marvel** Fill all these spectators with astonishment.
101 **I'll . . . up** I'll fill in your grave with earth (since it's no longer needed).
away towards me
102 **numbness** torpor, i.e. the coldness of death, but also lack of feeling
him i.e. death
104 **Start not** Don't move; don't be startled (*OED* start *v.* 5a).
holy as as free from sin as (*OED* holy 2); as pure as
105, 111 **lawful** permissible (*OED* 1b, as at 2.2.10). The distinction is between black magic (*wicked*, 91; *unlawful*, 96) and white or natural magic, permis-

sible if the *spell* (105) and *magic* (110) were benign.
105–7 **Do . . . double** i.e. never shun her again while she's alive, otherwise you'll kill her a second time (*double* as adverb) or kill this copy of her, the statue (*double* as noun)
107 **present your hand** offer her your hand (as you did, when you asked her to marry you, 1.2.103–5); cf. 144, 4.4.395 (see n.).
108 **When . . . her** For Leontes' recollection of wooing, see 1.2.101–4, 104n.
108–9 **in . . . suitor** when she is much older, does she have to do the wooing
110 **art** See pp. 53–4, 57–8.
112 **hangs about** Leontes may lift Hermione off the ground, her arms around his neck (cf. *Cym* 5.5.261–4).

99 SD] *Oxf*   103 SD] *Rowe subst.*   105 SD] *Ard²*

If she pertain to life, let her speak too!

POLIXENES

Ay, and make it manifest whcre she has lived,
Or how stolen from the dead.

PAULINA   That she is living,   115
Were it but told you, should be hooted at
Like an old tale. But it appears she lives,
Though yet she speak not. Mark a little while.
[*to Perdita*] Please you to interpose, fair madam.
   Kneel,
And pray your mother's blessing. [*to Hermione*] Turn,
   good lady,   120
Our Perdita is found.

HERMIONE   You gods, look down,
And from your sacred vials pour your graces
Upon my daughter's head! Tell me, mine own,
Where hast thou been preserved? Where lived? How
   found
Thy father's court? For thou shalt hear that I,   115   125
Knowing by Paulina that the oracle
Gave hope thou wast in being, have preserved
Myself to see the issue.

---

113 **pertain to life** i.e. is in the land of the living (*OED* pertain 1a, 1b)
115 **how ... dead** how she escaped death; how she has been brought back from the dead
116 **hooted** laughed
117 **old tale** See 5.2.28n.
   appears is evident
118 **Mark** observe
119 **interpose** intervene (*OED v.* 4b)
119–20 **Kneel ... blessing** See 43n.
120 **Turn** turn (towards your daughter); turn back from death

121 **Our ... found** The oracle is thus fulfilled (see 3.2.133).
122 **from ... graces** from your sacred vessels pour down your blessing (a metaphor from a rite of anointing, perhaps Christian baptism). See 1.2.80n.
124 **found** did you make your way to
126 **Knowing by Paulina** possibly a slip by Shakespeare. Hermione was present when the oracle was read (see 3.2.130–3).
127 **wast in being** were alive
128 **the issue** the outcome; my child

119 SD] *Ard²*   120 SD] *Ard²*

PAULINA   There's time enough for that,
        Lest they desire upon this push to trouble
        Your joys with like relation. Go together,   130
        You precious winners all; your exultation
        Partake to everyone. I, an old turtle,
        Will wing me to some withered bough, and there
        My mate, that's never to be found again,
        Lament till I am lost.
LEONTES   O peace, Paulina!   135
        Thou shouldst a husband take by my consent,
        As I by thine a wife. This is a match,
        And made between's by vows. Thou hast found mine,
        But how is to be questioned, for I saw her,
        As I thought, dead, and have in vain said many   140
        A prayer upon her grave. I'll not seek far –
        For him, I partly know his mind – to find thee
        An honourable husband. Come, Camillo,
        And take her by the hand, whose worth and honesty
        Is richly noted, and here justified   145
        By us, a pair of kings. Let's from this place.

129–30 *Lest ... relation* in case
  the people watching at this critical
  moment (*OED* push *n.*[2] 4a), should
  want to interrupt your joy by telling
  similar stories of their own. F's 'Least
  they desire' at 129 means 'the last
  thing they would wish'.
131 **You ... all** you who have all won
  something precious; all you wonderful
  people who have gained
132 **Partake to** share with (*OED* 3a)
  turtle turtle dove. See 4.4.154n.
134 **mate** husband, i.e. Antigonus
135 **Lament ... lost** mourn (for him)
  until I die. Perhaps word-play on *lost*:
  Perdita, our 'lost one', is found and
  now it is I who am abandoned (see List
  of Roles, 8n.).

peace don't say any more
136, 137 **by** with
137 **As ... wife** alludes to 5.1.69–71; see
  also 5.1.81–3.
  match punning on *mate*, 134 (husband)
138 **between's** between us
  vows with solemn promises
139 **But ... questioned** although the
  way it was done needs explanation
141 **not seek far** F's 'farre' is probably
  a comparative (as at 1.2.109), i.e. look
  no further.
142 **For** as for
144 **by the hand** i.e. in marriage; see 107n.
  whose refers either to Camillo or
  Paulina
145 **are** very well known, and here affirmed
146 **Let's from** let's leave

129 Lest] *F3;* Least *F*   141 far] *(farre)*

[*to Hermione*] What? Look upon my brother. Both your
   pardons,
That e'er I put between your holy looks
My ill suspicion. This your son-in-law,
And son unto the king, whom heavens directing,   150
Is troth-plight to your daughter. Good Paulina,
Lead us from hence, where we may leisurely
Each one demand and answer to his part
Performed in this wide gap of time since first   154
We were dissevered. Hastily lead away.   *Exeunt.*

147 **Look . . . brother** i.e. don't hesitate
to look at Polixenes. For *brother*, see
1.2.4n.
148–9 **That . . . suspicion** that I was so
wrongly suspicious of the pure (*holy*)
way you looked at each other
149 **son-in-law** proleptic: he isn't
Perdita's husband yet, though he soon
will be; see 4.4.395n.
150 **whom heavens directing** with the
gods guiding him

troth-plight engaged; see 1.2.274–6n.
153–4 **Each . . . Performed** ask and hear
from each person about the part they
played; cf. 5.1.1n. and see 1.2.187n.;
'answer to his part' is also a cue for the
actors to step forward in turn to take
the audience's applause.
154 **wide gap** Cf. 4.1.7 (see n.).
155 **dissevered** separated
Hastily lead away Lead us off
quickly.

147 SD] *Hanmer*

THE TEXT

Shakespeare wrote forty or so plays, about half of which appeared in print during his lifetime, published in quarto-format editions, a single play in each. These were printed from manuscripts of different kinds (either drafts, or 'playbooks', i.e. manuscripts used for staging). *The Winter's Tale* wasn't one of these quartos, nor was *The Tempest* or *Cymbeline*, the other plays of 1610–11 (see pp. 86–9). The only early substantive text of *The Winter's Tale* was published in 1623, in *Mr William Shakespeare's Comedies, Histories, and Tragedies*. This was a collection of thirty-six of the plays put together by members of the King's Men, and printed by William Jaggard. The book was financed by a publishing partnership of two booksellers, Edward Blount and Jaggard's son, Isaac. This edition, in folio format, is known as the First Folio, i.e. F (or F1). It was reprinted in 1632 with minor corrections and modernizations (the Second Folio, F2). Further reprints were published, with additional plays, in 1663–4 (F3) and 1685 (F4).

The textual history of *The Winter's Tale*, largely unwritten before the twentieth century, is now well understood. We know who copied the manuscript of the play used for F, how the play and manuscript were licensed, and how Jaggard's workmen printed the play. These findings are considered below, followed by a discussion of the text in this Arden edition.

RALPH CRANE AND THE MANUSCRIPT

Plays in F were printed from manuscripts, or from quarto editions of single plays, or from a mixture of the two. None of the manuscripts has survived, so everything about them must be inferred from the texts in F and the quartos, where these exist. One or two manuscripts may have been in Shakespeare's handwriting – *Antony and Cleopatra*, perhaps, which has what we take to be his idiosyncratic spellings and layout of text – but most were copies, or copies of copies, made by professional copyists ('scribes'), or people employed by the King's Men, such as the person in charge of the playbook. Some were copies of manuscripts used for performances; others had little or no connection with the theatre.

Five plays in F, and possibly two or three more, were printed from manuscripts copied by Ralph Crane, a legal scribe well known in Jacobean London. *The Winter's Tale* was one of these. Crane (?1560–1632) worked freelance as a copyist for the King's Men for five or six years, probably from around 1619; during this time he also copied plays by other dramatists. In later years he transcribed poems and other pieces for the nobility and gentry. At least sixteen of Crane's manuscripts have survived, transcripts of prose as well as poetry and plays, from which a good deal has been learnt about how he copied and prepared texts (Haas, 3–8). His regularizing of plays and his quirks as a copyist – heavy punctuation and a special way of listing characters in scene headings – are central to our understanding of the text of *The Winter's Tale*.

Eight of the surviving Crane transcripts are of public stage plays and other dramatic pieces, by Ben Jonson, Thomas Middleton and John Fletcher, all of whom had connections with the King's Men. The earliest manuscript is a copy of Jonson's court masque of 1618, *Pleasure Reconciled to Virtue*, which was probably prepared under the author's supervision. By imitating Jonson, Crane learnt how to set out a play in the manner of Renaissance editions of classical drama. Act and scene divisions were shown in Latin, and characters due to appear in a scene were all listed in its heading. Crane also picked up some of Jonson's distinctive punctuation, especially in unelided phrases, where vowels were retained graphically but not counted metrically (e.g. 'I'am' for 'I'm'). To these he added his own embellishments, including large numbers of hyphens, apostrophes, colons and parentheses.

Preparing the Jonson manuscript may have been Crane's big break. The polished appearance of the transcript and the clarity of his handwriting probably gave him an entrée with the theatre people Jonson knew (a page of his transcript of Middleton's *The Witch* is illustrated in *TxC*, 21). In the decade after *Pleasure Reconciled to Virtue*, Crane copied upwards of eighteen plays – for the King's Men, for patrons and for individual dramatists. Copies Crane made for F include *The Two Gentlemen of Verona*, *The Merry Wives of Windsor*, *Measure for Measure*, *The Tempest* and *The Winter's Tale*; also quite probably *Cymbeline*, and possibly *Othello* and *2 Henry IV* (Haas, 7–8; Honigmann, *Texts*, 165–8).

It is customary to speak of Crane as a scribe, but the surviving transcripts suggest that he acted more like an editor, or at least a copy-editor. With plays, his chief task was to transcribe the words, but he was expected (or permitted) to position the text in a standard way and to impose a system of punctuation. In some places Crane went further, adding words or deleting them (especially profanities and swearing, or where he thought the verse unmetrical); in others he elided or expanded contractions, or altered word forms (Howard-Hill, 'Crane', 120–2). Supplying punctuation and sorting out entries and speech prefixes (SPs) may have been important if he were copying Shakespeare. It is often said that three of the pages in the manuscript of the collaborative play *Sir Thomas More* are in Shakespeare's hand; if they are, it appears he didn't use much punctuation when drafting speeches, or mark SPs consistently (*TxC*, 463–7). Crane's job, copying from Shakespeare's handwriting – probably the case with *The Winter's Tale* – would be to provide these.

Compared with other tasks, copying an author's personal papers wouldn't have been very difficult for Crane. By contrast, his transcripts of *The Merry Wives of Windsor* and *Measure for Measure* were most likely from hard-to-read playbooks used for performances in the Globe (*TxC*, 340, 468). These would have been heavily annotated, possibly composite manuscripts, copied and added to several times over in more than one hand. Since *The Winter's Tale* has no trace of these or any other of the telltale signs of the theatre about it (e.g. detailed, practical directions for staging), most modern scholars think that Crane copied from Shakespeare's own manuscript – a working draft or neat transcript – or perhaps from a copy made for Shakespeare by another professional scribe (the possibility that Crane copied the play twice is considered below).

Looking at Crane's work as a whole, one thing is clear: the skills that made him an accomplished copyist – keeping to an ordered layout, standardizing SPs, sophisticating vocabulary and grammar – conceal from us the full character of the manuscripts he copied from. In effect he worked to a house style he perfected after transcribing Jonson's manuscript in 1618. Since one of his aims was to replace the irregular features of his sources, we can never be sure what kind of original he was working from – nor, rather alarmingly, what words (if any) he took out or elided.

Nevertheless Crane's copying shows through like fingerprints in F, as every page of *The Winter's Tale* confirms. Act and scene headings are in Latin ('*Actus Primus, Scœna Prima*') and, even more tellingly, thirteen of the play's fifteen scenes have Crane's 'massed entry' at their head, i.e. a list of characters for the whole scene irrespective of when they come onstage. The heading for 3.3 in F, for instance, is '*Enter Antigonus, a Marriner, Babe, Sheepeheard, and Clowne*' (see Fig. 24, p. 361), although the Shepherd and Clown don't appear until sixty lines into the scene. When the Shepherd does enter, at 3.3.58, there is no stage direction (SD), but there is for the Clown who comes on moments later (3.3.76.1). This is because in *The Winter's Tale*, as in other plays he transcribed, Crane mixed the English convention of dividing scenes with the neoclassical (or continental) one. In the former, scenes ended whenever the stage was completely cleared of characters, so it was necessary to mark when new characters entered or ones onstage exited. In the neoclassical system (used by Jonson), a new scene began when characters entered or left: the SD at the scene heading simply listed characters due to appear in the scene, and there was no need to use 'Enter' or 'Exit' (Bawcutt, 'Crane', 12).

Crane's lists in the scene headings are inconsistent, but he clearly intended to supply massed entries. Five of the lists name all the characters in the scene, who are onstage from the beginning (1.1, 1.2, 3.1, 4.1, 4.2). Two others miss out characters who enter during the scene (in 4.3 the Clown isn't named but enters at line 31.1; in 5.2, only one Gentleman is named, though two others enter, at 19.1 and 25.1, and all three exit at 110; the Shepherd and Clown, though not listed, enter at 121.1). In the other eight headings, all the speaking characters are named and enter in the sequence in which they are listed, whether they come on alone or in separate groups. The heading for 3.2, for example, reads '*Enter Leontes, Lords, Officers: Hermione (as to her Triall) Ladies: Cleomines, Dion*'. The first group, onstage when the scene begins, are joined by Hermione and Ladies, then by Cleomenes and Dion (perhaps coming forward from the back of the stage). Most non-speaking parts are omitted from the lists (e.g. shepherds, shepherdesses and satyrs in 4.4); the baby, presumably a stage property, is named in the heading for 3.3, but not for 2.3. The Bear in 3.3 isn't mentioned.

In addition to the massed entries there are forty-three SDs. Of these, twenty-six are simply '*Exit*' or '*Enter*', another fifteen an exit or entry with a named character or figure (e.g. '*Enter Polixenes*', 1.2.360.1; '*Exit pursued by a Beare*', 3.3.57), and two others that begin '*Heere a Da[u]nce*', for the dances of shepherds and satyrs at 4.4.167 and 347. It is possible that one SD in 3.3 was wrongly absorbed into the text (see 3.2.10n.). The brevity of the SDs is in marked contrast to those in *The Tempest*, printed from a Crane transcript, and also in *Cymbeline*, which may well be printed from one of his copies. Some scholars suspect that Crane added some of the elaborate 'literary' SDs in *The Tempest* (e.g. descriptions of the masque in 4.1), and they speculate that the phrases '*as to her Triall*' (3.2.10.1) and '*like a Statue*' (5.3.20) may be his too (Jowett, 114–15). But it is hard to believe that Crane, if he were indeed adding phrases to SDs in *The Winter's Tale*, would leave most of them as spare and uncommunicative as they are in F.

By contrast, the '*Names of the Actors*' (i.e. List of Roles) on the final page of the play looks very much like Crane's. Of the seven plays in F that have character lists, four are definitely printed from his transcripts (*The Two Gentlemen of Verona*, *Measure for Measure*, *The Tempest* and *The Winter's Tale*), and another two (*Othello* and *2 Henry IV*) may also be his. The only definite Crane transcript in F that doesn't have a character list is *The Merry Wives of Windsor*, which may be because this play ends close to the bottom of a page, leaving no space for a list. Outside F, there are character lists in Crane's manuscript of *The Witch* by Middleton, and in the 1623 edition of John Webster's *The Duchess of Malfi*, also printed from a Crane transcript. The character list was probably another neoclassical feature Crane imitated from Jonson, who provided such lists in the 1616 folio edition of his plays. It is not known for sure whether Crane copied the lists in F from manuscripts or simply invented them. The one for *The Winter's Tale* is seriously incomplete (no Mopsa, Dorcas, gaoler, mariner, shepherds, satyrs or Time), and it reads like a summation of the characters in the massed entries, for which Crane was definitely responsible, perhaps with one or two of his own touches (e.g. Autolycus is pointedly just '*A rogue*').

Evidence that Crane punctuated *The Winter's Tale* is compelling (Haas, 5–8, and Cam^2, 258–9, summarize what is known of his punctuation). At the beginning of 2.1, Mamillius tells the Ladies that women's eyebrows should be drawn in with a 'pen'. In F the exchange continues as shown in Fig. 23a.

Crane is everywhere here, in the vocative parenthesis '(my Lord.)', the brackets around 'your Mother', the hyphenated 'eye-browes', the colons (other Jacobeans might have used full stops), and the apostrophe in 'taught' this' (an elision, either for 'taught you this' or, more playfully, for 'taught it this', i.e. where 'it' is Mamillius).

Another example, in prose, is from the speech where Autolycus terrifies the Clown with fearful punishments (Fig. 23b).

2.*Lady*. Who taught 'this?

Mam. I learn'd it out of Womens faces: pray now,
What colour are your eye-browes?

Lady. Blew(my Lord.)

Mam. Nay,that's a mock:I haue feene a Ladies Nofe
That ha's beene blew,but not her eye-browes.

Lady. Harke ye,
The Queene(your Mother)rounds apace:we fhall
Prefent our feruices to a fine new Prince

23a   A verse passage from p. 281 (sig. Aa3ʳ) of the First Folio (2.1.11–17),
      showing the scribe Ralph Crane's distinctive punctuation

Aut. Hee ha's a Sonne : who fhall be flayd aliue, then
'noynted ouer with Honey, fet on the head of a Wafpes
Neft,then ftand till he be three quarters and a dram dead:
then recouer'd againe with Aquavite, or fome other hot
Infufion: then,raw as he is(and in the hoteft day Progno-
ftication proclaymes) fhall he be fet againft a Brick-wall,
(the Sunne looking with a South-ward eye vpon him;
where hee is to behold him,with Flyes blown to death.)
But what talke we of thefe Traitorly-Rafcals,whofe mi-
feries are to be fmil'd at,their offences being fo capitall?
                                                              Tel

23b   A prose passage from p. 297 (sig. Bb5ʳ) of the First Folio (4.4.788–98),
      showing further examples of Crane's distinctive use of colons, brackets
      and hyphens

This too has Crane's colons, in preference to commas or stops. There are 839 colons in *The Winter's Tale*, on average one every thirty-one words, a much higher ratio than in the five other 'Crane' comedies in F, but about the same as in the surviving Crane transcripts of plays (Cam², 258). This passage from 4.4 also has his brackets, non-vocative this time, as well as his hyphens, e.g. 'South-ward'.

Unusual and frequent hyphenation within and between words is a regular feature of Crane's copying (see further Table 3, pp. 379–81). With *The Winter's Tale*, he split words into discrete constituents (e.g. 'Mid-night', 1.2.288; 'out-side', 4.4.636, 809; 'Mary-gold' for 'marigold', 4.4.105; 'Gilly-vors', 4.4.82; 'Bon-fires', 5.2.22). The hyphens in compound phrases are less unusual, although profuse compared with modern usage (e.g. 'Traitorly Rascals', shown in Fig. 23b). Some compounds are distinctly Crane's ('push-on', 2.1.179, 4.4.741; 'big-with', 2.1.61), but others may be the compositor's (e.g. 'Me-thinkes', 4.4.399). There are also phrases where we might have expected hyphens but they aren't there. Most of these, interestingly, involve numbers, as with 'three quarters and a dram dead' (see Fig. 23b). At 1.2.155 and 2.3.196, F has 'Twentie three', and at 3.3.59 and 63 'three and twenty' and 'two and twenty' respectively. F has hyphens with numbers in some cases ('foure-threes', 4.4.341, and 'three-man', 4.3.42), but not many. It isn't clear whether these few hyphenated number phrases were special to Crane.

The hyphen for Crane was most likely a hybrid of punctuation mark and scribal procedure. Perhaps he broke words down ('Gilly-vors') or joined them up ('push-on') as a simple memory device to make sure he had understood and carried over the word(s) accurately when copying. This explanation doesn't work with another oddity, however, his frequent though not consistent writing of 'has' with a superfluous apostrophe, as 'ha's', as for example at 2.1.15 (see Fig. 23a), 2.3.78, 4.4.788 (Fig. 23b) and 5.3.114 (there is a counter-instance, 'heere has', at 4.4.337). In *The Winter's Tale* there is an apostrophe on average every twenty-six words (Cam[2], 259), which marks elisions (e.g. possessive 'it's', at 1.2.151, 152, 157, 264; 3.3.45), and 'notional' omitted words (e.g. ''Pray you' for 'I pray you', 2.1.22), or where a vowel is elided but the letter retained graphically ('Verely' is', 1.2.50). It appears that Crane's enthusiasm for the apostrophe just slipped over into his writing of 'has'.

Of slightly more concern, to an editor trying to interpret and then get rid of them (see pp. 374–6), are Crane's brackets. In *The Winter's Tale* there is a bracket on average every sixty-nine words, compared with an average of one every 923 in the sample of five 'Crane' comedies in F (Cam², 258). He uses them as alternatives to other punctuation (full stops, commas), and to mark characters addressing one another (e.g. '(my Lord.)', in Fig. 23a). There are seventy-six instances of brackets around single words, most but not all in direct address (e.g. '(Boy)', 1.2.186); seven of them are used, for no obvious reason, around words like 'missingly', 4.2.31 (Honigmann, *Texts*, 59–63, 162–3). In some of his play transcripts, but not it seems in *The Winter's Tale*, Crane uses brackets to mark asides.

Despite these inconsistencies, Crane's copying was good, and his work can't have come cheap: it took time to decipher handwriting, and to tidy up a play. The King's Men wouldn't pay him to make a new copy of *The Winter's Tale* unless it was unavoidable. Perhaps the printers couldn't work from the manuscript they had (because it was unreadable in places), or the actors couldn't find the company's playbook and were forced to have Crane make a copy from Shakespeare's posthumous papers (see p. 359). Neither explanation is decisive, though both may be relevant to the question of why the play was presented for relicensing in 1623.

LICENSING THE MANUSCRIPT

Public stage plays had to be read and licensed before actors were allowed to perform them. The person who examined plays, for seditious and blasphemous passages or remarks that might give offence, was the Master of the Revels. The actors paid this high-ranking official a fee for each play he read. Sir George Buc held the office between 1606 and 1622, and it was he who vetted *The Winter's Tale* for productions at the Globe and at court in 1611. Once Buc had approved it and been paid, the manuscript of the play, usually a copy prepared for theatre use, became an 'allowed book'. This licensed the King's Men to perform *The Winter's Tale* on subsequent occasions as well, which they did at court in

1613 and 1619, and no doubt at other times in the Globe and the Blackfriars theatre.

As Master of the Revels, Buc invented another duty for himself, which he was well paid for, of licensing stage plays for publication. When Buc lost his wits in 1622, his successor briefly was Sir John Astley, who sold the office to Sir Henry Herbert the following year. At first Herbert took the view that plays needed to be relicensed for new productions even if they had not been altered. On 19 August 1623, less than a month after he had taken over from Astley, Herbert relicensed two plays, one of them *The Winter's Tale*. The licence, he noted, was granted to 'the king's players', for

> An olde playe called Winter's Tale, formerly allowed
> of by Sir George Bucke, and likewyse by mee on Mr.
> Hemmings his worde that there was nothing profane
> added or reformed, thogh the allowed booke was
> missinge; and therefore I returned it without a fee.
>
> (Bawcutt, *Herbert*, 142)

The simplest explanation for this is that John Heminges, one of the King's Men, had sought a licence for a revival of *The Winter's Tale* that the company was planning for the Christmas season (in fact they played it at court in January 1624). The 'allowed book', the original manuscript Buc had licensed, was 'missing', but Heminges gave his word that the play was unchanged and nothing blasphemous had been added. Herbert didn't actually see a manuscript of any kind; in this reconstruction of events, the 'it' he returned was his written confirmation of the renewed licence, given without charging a fee.

A second explanation links the relicensing to the printing of *The Winter's Tale*. Jaggard's compositors began work on the first section of the First Folio, the Comedies, in spring 1622, but *The Winter's Tale*, the final play in this category, wasn't printed until December that year (Hinman, 1.363–4).

It appears that there was some delay in getting a manuscript of the play to the printer, and it has been suggested that the allowed book, the one used for staging, was already unavailable or 'missing' in 1622. The actors, so this argument goes, paid Crane to make a copy for the printer from the only manuscript they had, Shakespeare's own papers. Since they needed to replace the missing playbook too, they had Crane make a second copy for the theatre from the same source (Howard-Hill, 'Folio'). If this is true, the 'it' Herbert sent back 'without a fee' was one of these transcripts: i.e. the copy he had read and was returning wasn't the original allowed book, but he accepted that the King's Men had no intention of adding to or changing the version approved in 1611.

There is a third possibility, that the licence the King's Men were seeking was for the text of *The Winter's Tale* in F. Perhaps, like Buc before him, Herbert at first intended to vet plays before publication. A couple of weeks into his new office, he may have wanted to see the allowed book from which *The Winter's Tale* was to be printed. This manuscript was missing so Herbert was offered instead unbound pages of the play from F (printed late 1622), with Heminges's assurance that the performance version, authorized by Buc, was the same. If this is the case, the 'it' Herbert sent back to the actors was a sheaf of printed sheets.

These explanations assume that the King's Men acted in good faith. When Heminges told Herbert that the allowed book of *The Winter's Tale* was missing, he may have meant it was lost beyond hope of recovery (one guess, as suggested above, is that it went missing in the printing office in 1622); or simply that the company had misplaced it. When they found the manuscript again, after a fuller search, they intended to use it for the Christmas revival. But there were business reasons why this may not have been the full truth. The King's Men can't have relished the prospect of paying Herbert a new fee every time they revived an old play or sold one for printing. Surely the Master could only charge them if he actually read a manuscript. Why not tell him, before he established himself in the office, that the company wanted to stage a production of *The Winter's Tale* at court but couldn't just now lay their hands on the allowed book? If Herbert took Heminges's word that no changes had been made, perhaps (as happened) he would relicense it without a fee, and proceed like this in future with other plays.

TYPESETTING AND PRINTING THE FIRST FOLIO

Printing F was a big job that took most of two years, from early 1622 to late 1623 (Blayney, 5, 24). Like all books at this date, the text in it was set by hand, letter-by-letter. The thirty-six plays amounted to a million words: even when printed in double columns on tall pages, up to 130 lines per page (see Fig. 24), the book came out at more than 900 pages.

F was typeset and bound as a 'folio in sixes' (i.e. in gatherings of six leaves). Three large sheets of paper, taken together, were folded into a booklet or 'gathering' of six leaves (twelve pages). Once printed, the gatherings were assembled, copy by copy, and sewn together through the gutter of the folded sheets. Each copy of F was made up of seventy-seven gatherings. The text of *The Winter's Tale*, one of the longer plays, covers two gatherings and four pages of a third, i.e. twenty-eight pages in all, 277–304 (304 is unnumbered and blank). The printer as usual assigned letters at the foot of the first three leaves in each gathering, to help the binder put the book together in the right order: *The Winter's Tale* gatherings were signed Aa, Bb, and Cc (the latter consisting of only two leaves, i.e. a folded, single large sheet).

Before being folded as a gathering, the three sheets of paper were printed from two-page formes. This means that pages 1 and 12 of the gathering, set in type and locked alongside one another in a chase or metal frame (the forme comprised the

| 288 | *The Winters Tale.* |

The sweet'st, deer'st creature's dead:& vengeance for't
Not drop'd downe yet.
Lord. The higher powres forbid.
Pau. I say she's dead: Ile sweare't. If word,nor oath
Preuaile not, go and see : if you can bring
Tincture, or lustre in her lip, her eye
Heate outwardly, or breath within, Ile serue you
As I would do the Gods. But, O thou Tyrant,
Do not repent these things, for they are heauier
Then all thy woes can stirre : therefore betake thee
To nothing but dispaire. A thousand knees,
Ten thousand yeares together, naked, fasting,
Vpon a barren Mountaine, and still Winter
In storme perpetuall, could not moue the Gods
To looke that way thou wer't.
Leo. Go on, go on :
Thou canst not speake too much, I haue deseru'd
All tongues to talke their bittrest.
Lord. Say no more;
How ere the businesse goes, you haue made fault
I'th boldnesse of your speech.
Pau. I am sorry for't;
All faults I make, when I shall come to know them,
I do repent : Alas, I haue shew'd too much
The rashnesse of a woman : he is toucht
To th'Noble heart. What's gone, and what's past helpe
Should be past greefe : Do not receiue affliction
At my petitions; I beseech you, rather
Let me be punish'd, that haue minded you
Of what you should forget. Now (good my Liege)
Sir, Royall Sir, forgiue a foolish woman :
The loue I bore your Queene (Lo, foole againe)
Ile speake of her no more, nor of your Children :
Ile not remember you of my owne Lord,
(Who is lost too:) take your patience to you,
And Ile say nothing.
Leo. Thou didst speake but well,
When most the truth : which I receyue much better,
Then to be pittied of thee. Prethee bring me
To the dead bodies of my Queene, and Sonne,
One graue shall be for both : Vpon them shall
The causes of their death appeare (vnto
Our shame perpetuall) once a day, Ile visit
The Chappell where they lye, and teares shed there
Shall be my recreation. So long as Nature
Will beare vp with this exercise, so long
I dayly vow to vse it. Come, and leade me
To these sorrowes.   *Exeunt*

Scæna Tertia.

*Enter Antigonus, a Mariner, Babe, Shephe-
heard, and Clowne.*

Ant. Thou art perfect then, our ship hath toucht vpon
The Desarts of *Bohemia.*
Mar. I (my Lord) and feare
We haue Landed in ill time : the skies looke grimly,
And threaten present blusters. In my conscience
The heauens with that we haue in hand, are angry,
And frowne vpon's.
Ant. Their sacred wil's be done: go get a-boord,
Looke to thy barke, Ile not be long before

I call vpon thee.)
Mar. Make your best haste, and go not
Too-farre i'th Land : 'tis like to be lowd weather,
Besides this place is famous for the Creatures
Of prey, that keepe vpon't.
Antig. Go thou away,
Ile follow instantly.
Mar. I am glad at heart
To be so ridde o'th businesse.   *Exit*
Ant. Come, poore babe;
I haue heard (but not beleeu'd) the Spirits o'th'dead
May walke againe : if such thing be, thy Mother
Appear'd to me last night : for ne're was dreame
So like a waking. To me comes a creature,
Sometimes her head on one side, some another,
I neuer saw a vessell of like sorrow
So fill'd, and so becomming : in pure white Robes
Like very sanctity she did approach
My Cabine where I lay : thrice bow'd before me,
And (gasping to begin some speech) her eyes
Became two spouts ; the furie spent, anon
Did this breake from her. Good *Antigonus,*
Since Fate (against thy better disposition)
Hath made thy person for the Thower-out
Of my poore babe, according to thine oath,
Places remote enough are in *Bohemia,*
There weepe, and leaue it crying : and for the babe
Is counted lost for euer, *Perdita*
I prethee call't : For this vngentle businesse
Put on thee, by my Lord, thou ne're shalt see
Thy Wife *Paulina* more : and so, with shriekes
She melted into Ayre. Affrighted much,
I did in time collect my selfe, and thought
This was so, and no slumber : Dreames, are toyes,
Yet for this once, yea superstitiously,
I will be squar'd by this. I do beleeue
Hermione hath suffer'd death, and that
Apollo would (this being indeede the issue
Of King *Polixenes*) it should heere be laide
(Either for life, or death) vpon the earth
Of it's right Father. Blossome, speed thee well,
There lye, and there thy charracter : there these,
Which may if Fortune please, both breed thee (pretty)
And still rest thine. The storme beginnes, poore wretch,
That for thy mothers fault, art thus expos'd
To losse, and what may follow. Weepe I cannot,
But my heart bleedes : and most accurst am I
To be by oath enioyn'd to this. Farewell,
The day frownes more and more : thou'rt like to haue
A lullabie too rough : I neuer saw
The heauens so dim, by day. A sauage clamor?
Well may I get a-boord : This is the Chace,
I am gone for euer.   *Exit pursued by a Beare.*
Shep. I would there were no age betweene ten and
three and twenty, or that youth would sleep out the rest
for there is nothing (in the betweene) but getting wenches with childe, wronging the Auncientry, stealing,
fighting, hearke you now : would any but these boylde-
braines of nineteene, and two and twenty hunt this weather ? They haue scarr'd away two of my best Sheepe,
which I feare the Wolfe will sooner finde then the Master ; if any where I haue them, 'tis by the sea-side, broo-
zing of Iuy. Good-lucke (and't be thy will) what haue
we heere ? Mercy on's, a Barne ? A very pretty barne ; A
boy, or a Childe I wonder ? (A pretty one, a verie prettie
one) sure some Scape ; Though I am not bookish, yet I
can

24   Page 288 (sig. Aa6ᵛ) of the First Folio, which contains 3.2.198–3.3.71 of
The Winter's Tale. The page includes the most famous stage direction in
Shakespeare, '*Exit pursued by a Beare*' (3.3.57), and a 'massed entry' typical
of Crane

content of the locked-up chase), were printed simultaneously on one side of the first sheet; pages 2 and 11 were printed on the other side. The same was done with pages 3 and 10, and 4 and 9, on the second sheet, and pages 5 and 8, and 6 and 7, on the third. This pattern – conjugate pages, and verso (ᵛ) alongside recto (ʳ) – was repeated for all F's gatherings. In the case of *The Winter's Tale*, the first page of the play, 277, sig. Aa1ʳ (1.1.1 to 1.2.43) was conjugate with 288, Aa6ᵛ (3.2.198 to 3.3.71, reproduced in Fig. 24). Once the text in the forme had been printed, the type in the two pages was disassembled, and was redistributed for use in the next round of pages.

Working like this meant that the text had to be cast off, i.e. the typesetters or compositors had to plan beforehand how much text would fit on each page. A miscalculation would force them to expand or compress: a line of verse could be printed as two, or verse printed as prose; a line might even be omitted. Setting by formes also allowed compositors to work together, setting type for conjugate pages. Because spelling wasn't standardized in the Elizabethan period, modern scholars have identified the compositors who set different portions of F by the way they spelt particular words. It is thought that there were at least six compositors, now distinguished as A to F (Blayney, 10–11). Compositor B set half of the folio, Compositor A about a quarter of it. These two – experienced workmen who made relatively few mistakes – were responsible for *The Winter's Tale*.

The contents of F are arranged in the order Comedies, Histories and Tragedies, but not all of the book was printed in this sequence. *King John*, for instance, the first of the Histories, was printed before *Twelfth Night* and *The Winter's Tale*, the final two plays in the Comedies. Moreover, Compositor B, once he had finished *Twelfth Night*, didn't start work straightaway on *The Winter's Tale*. Instead, he and Compositor A set a portion of *Richard II*, the second play in the Histories. A and B then set *The Winter's Tale* together. This shifting between different parts of the book was probably due to two short delays in getting copy to the printer, first of *Twelfth Night*, then *The Winter's Tale*; when the manuscripts weren't available, the compositors did other work until they were (Hinman, 2.504, 521). The delay with *The Winter's Tale* may have been connected in some way with the King's Men not having the allowed book to hand in late summer 1623 (as discussed above), though by then the Comedies had already been printed. When at last they began *The Winter's Tale*, Compositors A and B shared the setting in the sequence shown in Table 1.

The press was stopped during the printing of F to make corrections or adjustments to the type, but only intermittently. In the Comedies as a whole, less than 10 per cent of pages have stop-press variants found in different copies of F. In *The Winter's Tale* there is only one: the page number on Aa3^r is 285 in one surviving copy, but all the other surviving copies have the correct page number 281 (Hinman, 1.264–5, 2.498, 502). More than thirty typographical errors weren't corrected, including spellings (e.g. 2.2.20, 'gtacious'), turned letters (3.2.144, 'r' upside down in 'strike'), and misplaced and omitted apostrophes (2.1.147, 'gell'd em' for 'gelld 'em'). Compositor B made a few more slips like these per page than A (Pafford, 177–8).

The compositors left out words and misread others. At 1.2.206, Leontes asks Mamillius 'How now, boy?', to which the reply in F, set by Compositor A, is 'I am like you say.' Editors generally agree that a pronoun is missing before 'say' and supply it from F2, which has 'they say', meaning 'everyone says' or '*women* say', i.e. the boy harks back to his father's words at 129–30, that 'women say' they are 'as like as eggs'. But it is equally possible that Shakespeare wrote 'I am like you, you say' (recalling Leontes at 134–5); this is perhaps more possible since the compositor's eye could easily skip over a second 'you'. Compositor B made a similar mistake over pronouns, at 4.4.472, setting 'my Fathers' instead of 'your Fathers' (another slip that F2 corrected: see pp. 366–7). At 4.4.505 he also set 'her neede' for 'our neede', eye-skip from, 'her, who heere' in the line above

Table 1 Compositors and order of setting of *The Winter's Tale* in F

The first column identifies the compositor, A or B

	Two-page forme	Page in F	TLN*	This edition
A	Aa3^v	282	623 754	2.1.29–142
B	Aa4^r	283	755–878	2.1.143–2.2.50
A	Aa3^r	281	497–622	1.2.385–2.1.28
B	Aa4^v	284	879–1004	2.2.50–2.3.82
A	Aa2^v	280	365–496	1.2.271–384
A	Aa5^r	285	1005–1136	2.3.83–198
A	Aa5^v	286	1137–1255	2.3.199–3.2.77
A	Aa2^r	279	233–364	1.2.154–270
A	Aa1^v	278	101–232	1.2.44–153
A	Aa6^r	287	1256–1387	3.2.77–197
A	Aa1^r	277	1–100	1.1.1–1.2.43
B	Aa6^v	288	1388–1513	3.2.198–3.3.71
B	Bb3^v	294	2147–2278	4.4.331–439
B	Bb4^r	295	2279–2410	4.4.440–550
B	Bb3^r	293	2016–2146	4.4.193–330
A	Bb4^v	296	2411–2542	4.4.551–664
B	Bb2^v	292	1884–2015	4.4.77–192
A	Bb5^r	297	2543–2674	4.4.665–798
B	Bb2^r	291	1759–1883	4.3.89–4.4.77
A	Bb5^v	298	2675–2800	4.4.798–5.1.62
B	Bb1^v	290	1635–1758	4.2.22–4.3.88
A	Bb6^r	299	2801–2932	5.1.62–170
B	Bb1^r	289	1514–1634	3.3.71–4.2.22
A	Bb6^v	300	2933–3058	5.1.171–5.2.48
A	Cc1^r	301	3059–3187	5.2.48–5.3.2
	Cc2^v	[304]	blank	
A	Cc1^v	302	3188–3319	5.3.2–110
B	Cc2^r	303	3320–3369	5.3.111–155

* TLN: Through line numbering in *The Norton Facsimile*

Source: Derived from *The Norton Facsimile: The First Folio of Shakespeare*, prepared by Charlton Hinman, 2nd edition with a new introduction by Peter W.M. Blayney (New York, 1996), xxxv (cf. the duplication of 'never' at 4.4.433, and the slip in 5.1.61, where Compositor A repeated 'such' from 'such power' in the line above: dittography that F3 put right in this case). Compositor B missed out words too, for example 'it' in 4.4.12.

Compositor B also made mistakes with single letters (at 4.4.160, he set 'on't' for 'out'), but A did this more frequently. In F, at 5.3.18, Paulina claims she keeps Hermione's likeness 'Louely, apart', but modern editors are sure that Shakespeare meant 'Lonely, apart'. Compositor A probably misread 'u' for 'n' in Crane's handwriting, though it may be a turned letter. On the same page, at 5.3.95, Paulina tells everyone to 'stand still', and then in F says 'On: those that thinke . . .'. This time editors believe that what Shakespeare meant was 'Or, those that think . . .', A's misreading of 'n' for 'r'. The most interesting of A's slips was on sig. Aa2^v, where he set 'Holy-Horse' instead of what was clearly intended, 'hobby-horse' (see 1.2.274n.). Perhaps Crane wrote 'Hoby-' or 'Hobby-' (he preferred doubled consonants) and A misread a looped 'b' for a letter 'l', or misread one 'b' and dropped the other.

Although the compositors made small mistakes, overall they produced a clean text from Crane's transcript. The fact that we can detect Crane's scene headings and punctuation so easily confirms that both compositors were pretty faithful to the manuscript in front of them. In a few cases they did miscalculate in casting off copy, but they put things right without much difficulty. Compositor A was left with too much text to fit on to page 277, for example, so he gained extra space by leaving out the standard spacing around the scene heading at 1.2 ('*Scœna Secunda*'; illustrated in Blayney, 13). Similarly, Compositor B saved space in the right-hand column on page 293, sig. Bb3^r, by displacing the heading 'Song' for the song 'Get you hence' to the position that should have been used for the first SP (4.4.298).

Something like this also happened in the same column, a few lines lower at the foot of page 293. There, Autolycus' retort 'And you shall pay . . .' isn't printed, as it ought to be, on a separate line, but on the same line as the final words spoken by the Clown in the preceding speech (4.4.318). Below that (as with 'Get you hence'), the word 'Song', which should be a heading, stands beside rather than above the first line of 'Will you buy' (320). It is tempting to attribute the squeezing and crowding on page 293 to something odd about the copy at this point. If one or both of the songs were supplied to the printer on separate sheets – and manuscript copies of 'Get you hence' were certainly in circulation in the 1620s and later (see pp. 389–90) – perhaps Compositor B didn't allow enough space for the lyrics in them when he was casting off the copy.

FROM THE FIRST FOLIO TO THIS EDITION

Shakespeare was corrected, added to and modernized from the moment he appeared in print – indeed even before print, given that (as discussed above) Crane probably changed words and word forms and certainly supplied punctuation and massed entries in the plays he transcribed for F. In the three seventeenth-century Folios derived from F, the text of *The Winter's Tale* changes very little. Scene headings are the same, and so too are most of the entries and exits and other SDs. In fact the changes in F2 (1632), F3 (1663–4) and F4 (1685) are either moderniza-tions of grammar and spelling or minor attempts to improve F's sense and metre, sometimes persuasively but often not. In F at 3.2.173–4, for instance, Paulina asks Leontes what 'studied torments' he has in mind for her:

> What Wheeles? Racks? Fires? What flaying? boyling?
> In Leads, or Oyles?

Line 173, a syllable short, has five stressed syllables (x / / / x / x / x), but the irregularity prompted F2 to add 'Burning?' at the end of the line to smooth it out (cf. 4.4.498 where F2 omitted 'honoured' because the line had twelve syllables in F). F2 also made changes in prose passages. Camillo, in the opening scene in F, says that the two kings, although separated, had seemed to shake hands as over 'a Vast' (1.1.30), which F2 alters to 'a Vast Sea'. This is either literal-mindedness or the earliest of several attempts to improve Shakespeare's geography (see pp. 100–2), i.e. if Bohemia has a coastline (3.3) there ought to be a vast sea between the kings.

F2 is generally sensible about F's slips (e.g. correcting 'What' for 'Who', 2.3.38; 'your' for 'my', 4.4.472; and 'losing' for 'loosing', 5.2.77), but it introduces errors of its own (e.g. 'common' for 'coming', 1.1.5), and it fiddles needlessly with plurals and tenses (e.g. 'derives' for F's 'derive', 1.2.112, and 'should' for 'would', 1.2.170). Indeed F2's modernizations and normalizing, made less than a decade after F, are an index of how quickly a sense of 'proper' English, especially grammatical concord, was developing in the seventeenth century (e.g. 'whom' for 'who', 4.4.504), and how small aspects of Shakespeare's language had already begun to puzzle readers. The selected F2 readings in the textual notes make this clear (e.g. F2's 'heed' for F's 'deed', 1.2.42).

F3, published nearly fifty years after Shakespeare's death, and F4, over twenty years later, move yet further from his language, and add new mistakes. Where Polixenes in F and F2 says, of his son back home, 'He's all' (1.2.165), F3 and F4 print 'Here's all'; and where in F and F2 Paulina recalls that there was not 'full a moneth' between the birth of Mamillius and Florizel (5.1.117), F3 and F4 give the phrase as 'a full month'. Spellings too began slowly to be modernized in the later Folios, especially in F3 and F4, but again there were errors. F4 for example modernized F's 'Heycfer' at 1.2.124 to 'Heifer', and F's 'moneth' to 'Month' at 1.2.41, 4.4.267 and elsewhere; but following F3, it also mistakenly replaced F's 'Gest' at 1.2.41 (referring to a fixed period) with 'guest'.

The editions of Shakespeare published in the eighteenth and nineteenth centuries continued the work of correcting, modernizing and standardizing, but they gave themselves two new functions: explaining and clarifying the text. They added entries and exits, reassigned speech prefixes, marked asides and described stage actions. In *The Winter's Tale*, eighteenth-century editors saw that at 2.1.152–4 Leontes probably struck or manhandled Antigonus, so they added the SDs '*Laying hold of his arm*' (Hanmer), or '*Striking him*' (Rann), or '*he tweaks his nose*' (Capell). Samuel Johnson thought that Leontes was more likely hitting himself, in desperation, and added the SD '*striking his brows*'. Editors began to supply notes to justify their emendations to the text, and to show why earlier editors had been mistaken. Illustrations of scenes were also added, along with fuller notes on the language of the plays and their historical contexts. Sometimes, however, it was an editor's erudition not his ignorance that misled him when altering the text. Because Hanmer knew that the real Bohemia had never had a coastline, he decided to correct this egregious 'error' by replacing Bohemia throughout with Bithynia, a region in Asia Minor long forgotten to all but those who, like Hanmer, had studied ancient history but didn't get the point of Shakespeare's simple, serious joke (see pp. 100–2).

Twentieth-century editors of Shakespeare were generally more cautious with the text than their predecessors. They had the new tools of the *Oxford English Dictionary* and Variorum editions, where they could see, in the record of emendations, plenty of Bithynia-like mistakes. With plays that had two or more early texts, modern editors certainly disputed which version to print (the Quarto or Folio of *King Lear*), and what names should be used for particular characters (Moth or Mote in *Love's Labour's Lost*, Imogen or Innogen in *Cymbeline*), but the temptation to alter words readily whenever a line in F wasn't metrically smooth enough, or the grammar seemed irregular, had long passed. Small cruxes remained, of course, and the meaning of certain words and phrases was still in doubt, as in

The Winter's Tale with F's 'for sealing' (1.2.335), 'Land-damne' (2.1.143) and 'fixure' (5.3.67) (see nn.).

At the end of the twentieth century, editors were still adding SDs, but by now they had got rid of most of F's spellings and capitals and much of its punctuation. The case for modernizing was pragmatic – that modern editions of Shakespeare are mainly for students, playgoers and the general reading public, who don't have the time, patience or experience of reading 'old-spelling' texts to get much benefit from them, indeed who might be misled by original spellings and punctuation. It was argued further that *thoroughgoing* modernization was needed, and that editions in modern spelling and punctuation shouldn't selectively preserve this or that particular word form to give a pseudo-historical 'flavour' of Shakespeare and his time (as the second series of the Arden Shakespeare had, for instance: see Wells, *Modernizing*, 3–5). The approach should be the same with punctuation: it should be neither lighter nor heavier than modern readers were accustomed to in, say, modern novels.

THE TEXT IN THIS EDITION

The above arguments were accepted for the third series of the Arden Shakespeare. The text in this edition of *The Winter's Tale* is therefore fully modernized in spelling and punctuation. Entries, exits and other SDs are added or modified where necessary, as are brackets, colons and semicolons. The advantages this modernization brings, of clarity, consistency and a text that is uncluttered, are evident if we compare an extract from F, where the Shepherd discovers Perdita, with the edited, modernized version. In F the text is as shown in Fig. 25 (from the right-hand bottom corner of sig. Aa6ᵛ, illustrated full-page in Fig. 24, p. 361).

In the modernized version, the semicolons and most of the capitals are eliminated, along with brackets and the letter 'e' at the end of words. Hyphens are removed in some places, and

> *Shep.* I would there were no age betweene ten and three and twenty, or that youth would sleep out the rest for there is nothing (in the betweene) but getting wenches with childe, wronging the Auncientry, stealing, fighting, hearke you now: would any but these boylde-braines of nineteene, and two and twenty hunt this weather ? They haue scarr'd away two of my best Sheepe, which I feare the Wolfe will sooner finde then the Maister; if any where I haue them, 'tis by the sea-side, brouzing of Iuy. Good-lucke (and't be thy will) what haue we heere? Mercy on's, a Barne? A very pretty barne; A boy, or a Childe I wonder? (A pretty one, a verie prettie one) sure some Scape; Though I am not bookish, yet I can

25   An extract from p. 288 (sig. Aa6ᵛ) of the First Folio (3.3.58–71)

added in others (e.g. in number phrases: see above, p. 356). The SP is expanded and an SD is introduced:

SHEPHERD   I would there were no age between ten and three-and-twenty, or that youth would sleep out the rest; for there is nothing in the between but getting wenches with child, wronging the ancientry, stealing, fighting – hark you now, would any but these boiled-brains of nineteen and two-and-twenty hunt this weather? They have scared away two of my best sheep, which I fear the wolf will sooner find than the master. If anywhere I have them, 'tis by the seaside, browsing of ivy. Good luck, an't be thy will! [*Sees the baby.*] What have we here? Mercy on's, a bairn! A very pretty bairn. A boy or a child, I wonder? A pretty one, a very pretty one – sure some scape; though I am not bookish, yet I . . .

(3.3.58–71)

Letter shapes and letters are also modernized. Long 's' ('thefe', 'fea-fide', 'fure') is replaced by square 's', and the ligatures ſt and ſh (in 'reſt' and 'bookiſh') are replaced by square 's' followed by the separate letter, 't' or 'h'. In early modern English, 'u' and 'v' weren't thought of as distinct letters but as different forms of the same letter – hence 'haue' and 'Iuy', which are here given the modern forms 'have' and 'ivy'. This is true of the letters 'i' and 'j' too, so F's 'Iealousie' at 1.2.447 and 'Maiestie' at 5.1.33 and elsewhere are modernized to 'jealousy' and 'majesty' respectively.

Some of the losses from modernizing this speech are small. Most of the brackets were probably Crane's (see pp. 356–7), but it is possible that a few were Shakespeare's, indications of how he wanted to characterize the Shepherd as an old man who would fall easily into self-musing and country wisdom. (There are other losses when F's brackets are removed: see Thompson, 77–9, 87.) Fully modernizing word forms and spellings brings other, small difficulties. In Shakespeare's day, the noun 'sea-side' meant, as it did from the thirteenth century, the margin or brink of the sea (*OED* 1a). The modern form 'seaside' has been used, since the late eighteenth century, of the coast as a place to go to for one's health or for pleasure, though the form 'sea-side' has been used to mean this too (*OED* 2). The problem is that 'sea-side' is now obsolete – there are no entries later than 1893 in the *OED* – so using it in a modern-spelling edition would be a deliberate archaism. Of course, the context in the play – this is where a ravenous bear appears – makes it certain that Bohemia's 'seaside' isn't a pleasure resort (such places didn't exist at all at the date of *The Winter's Tale*). In fact there isn't much risk that at this point we will think of deckchairs and seaside rock (*OED* 4), so the form 'seaside' is the one I have adopted in this edition.

Some of F's spellings may reflect contemporary pronunciation or non-standard forms. The first vowel (or possibly diphthong) in 'Mai-ſter' wasn't the same as in modern 'master', and this spelling, according to the *OED*, was non-standard in the early seventeenth century, i.e. it may have been the form a rustic would use, but not a courtier. However, the evidence isn't conclusive. Camillo uses 'Master' at 1.2.351, 4.2.7 and 4.4.517, as do Autolycus (4.4.713, 839; 5.2.148) and the Steward (5.2.68, 95). The Servant says 'Master' at 4.4.183 but 'Mayster' at 4.4.329; the Clown uses 'Masters' at 5.2.172. Once again I have adopted the modern form. Another touch disappears in the standardization of 'barne' to 'bairn', now the modern form but in Shakespeare's day a provincial or Scots spelling (*OED*). One risk in doing away with 'barne' is that we may not hear or spot its homonyms, which in this case would be unfortunate given the connections in sound it has, as others have argued, to the cluster of puns on 'bear' in *The Winter's Tale* (see p. 131; cf. Bevington, 'Modern spelling', 145–7, 149–50).

There are three contractions in the speech, ''tis' for 'it is', 'and't' for 'and it' and 'on's' for 'on us'. The first, ''tis', is used many times in *The Winter's Tale*, in prose and verse, by upper- as well as lower-class characters. The second, 'and't', is used here and three more times by the Shepherd (4.4.733, 745, 811), and once by the Clown (786). The Shepherd and Autolycus use the uncontracted form 'and it' once apiece. All these are in prose speeches, as part of deference phrases to superiors, for example 'and't like you' (4.4.733), which means 'if it pleases you' or 'may it please you' (where 'and' means 'if'). Presumably the examples in the *OED* under 'an' (*conj.* A2), from Marlowe, Shakespeare and Jonson, are what have prompted modern editors to choose 'an' over 'and', a decision I have followed in this edition, even though, strictly speaking, 'and' could be used.

When the Shepherd exclaims 'Mercy on's' he means 'may God have mercy upon us', i.e. the 's' is a contraction of 'us', as it is in several places in the play, for example 'cram's', 1.2.91. The 'on's' contraction can also stand for 'of his', as it does when the Clown speaks of Autolycus 'picking on's teeth', 4.4.756–7 (*OED* 'on' *prep.* 28). The contraction 'on't' (meaning e.g. 'of it', 2.1.169, and 'by it', 3.3.136) is used by upper- and lower-class characters, and this is true of 'on's' (of us) as well. Leontes, speaking of men who have been cuckolded but don't know it, says

> Many thousand on's
> Have the disease and feel't not.
>
> (1.2.205–6)

This is in verse, and the elisions 'on's' and 'feel't' are needed for the metre, but there may be something more to them. Leontes is addressing the men in the audience directly, in a vulgar way, so perhaps the contractions at this point show that his speech (189–206) has moved a couple of notches down the social scale. Elsewhere he is certainly conscious that the elite ought to speak properly (2.1.82–7).

We can't be sure, when the Shepherd uses 'on's' or on't (e.g. 4.4.337), how far such contractions are meant to reflect lower-class idiom – though this is more likely the case with 'and't'. For the most part in *The Winter's Tale* the vocabulary and word forms *aren't* socially layered – or not very much, so far as we can tell from the printed text in F. Words such as 'Clammer' may be non-standard (see 4.4.247n.), but they are the exceptions. What small trace there is of regional and non-elite speech is to be found in the patterns of clauses and punctuation.

Critics who don't want to lose the slightest echo of Shakespeare or the sounds he heard will protest that significant aural traces are always eliminated in modernizing, for instance when the older forms in F, 'murther' (1.2.408, 3.2.99, 5.1.62), 'vild' (2.1.92) and 'accompt' (2.3.196), are replaced by 'murder', 'vile' and 'account'. Beyond this general concern, there are cases in *The Winter's Tale* where a modern form may obscure something particularly important. In Act 4 in F, Autolycus says he has sold all his 'Tromperie', which in this edition appears as 'trumpery', i.e. trash (see 4.4.602n.). At the date of the play, 'Tromperie' did mean worthless stuff – Prospero calls it 'trumpery' (*Tem* 4.1.186) – but it was also associated with negative aspects of the

Roman Catholic faith, i.e. relics, idolatry and Popish superstition (*OED* 2c), relevant to the parochial backwater the festival is set in (and to the religious 'magic' of the statue in 5.3). F's spelling may have made this association clearer than the modern 'trumpery' which only means, more narrowly, cheap finery.

One solution to the problem of how to modernize words without losing too much is to draw attention to specific cases (such as 'Tromperie') in the commentary and elsewhere; another is to record selectively archaic and unusual spellings in F where sound or meaning may have been lost, including forms that suggest contraction (either for the metre or to characterize a speaker, e.g. 'deer'st', 4.4.40). These are the solutions I have adopted in this edition. Rather than clutter the textual notes set beneath the edited text, F's spellings and word forms are listed separately, in Tables 2a and 2b (pp. 377–8). In this, variations between F and modern usage are ignored unless it is clear what differences there might be in sound or sense (e.g. 'Sprindge', 4.3.35, but not 'daunces' and 'graunt', 1.2.110, 114, nor the form 'and't' for 'an't', discussed above).

The textual notes record places where F's words have been replaced or modified in this edition (about forty changes), and where SDs and SPs have been added or altered. The notes also include significant changes to the punctuation (discussed below) and lineation, and select alternative readings in F2 and subsequent editions.

The work of re-punctuating F for modern audiences isn't an exact science, and its appropriateness at every point has to be taken on trust. Recording all the punctuation marks altered in F (removed, lightened, added) isn't possible in an Arden edition. All editors can do, guided by what is known of Crane and F's compositors, is to hope that their judgement is right. The choices that need to be made can be illustrated by looking again at a section of the same passage from 3.3, but this time, as an experiment, with all of F's punctuation taken out, all the capitals except 'I' lowered, and the letter forms modernized:

> they have scarrd away two of my best sheepe which
> I feare the wolfe will sooner finde then the maister
> if any where I haue them tis by the sea side brouzing
> of iuy good lucke andt be thy will what haue we
> heere mercy ons a barne a very pretty barne a boy
> or a childe I wonder a pretty one a verie prettie one
> sure some scape though I am not bookish yet I . . .
>
> (3.3.64–71)

Even presented like this, clearly it would be perverse not to take from 'they' to 'maister' to be a complete sentence (and one must therefore change F's semicolon, 'maister;' to a full stop). From 'if' to 'iuy' looks just as complete, but after that the words fall more easily into slightly different groups. Should the editor for instance interpret what follows, from 'good' to 'heere', not as I have done in this edition (see p. 240), but instead as 'Good luck. An't be thy will, what have we here?' (i.e. wishing the sheep or himself good luck, followed by an exclamation at the discovery), then

> Mercy on's, a bairn, a very pretty bairn. A boy? Or
> a child I wonder? A pretty one? A very pretty one,
> sure. Some scape? Though I am not bookish, yet
> I . . .

This version has subtle differences from the text in this edition in the characterization of the Shepherd. In this he is more slow-witted, asking himself questions then answering them, just a bit ponderously. Also, in this case when he wonders if the baby is a girl ('a child'), the question that follows immediately is whether she is a 'pretty one', i.e. good looks are everything for a country girl who will eventually need a husband (a theme in 4.4). Of course, differences of emphasis like these are heard onstage in every production of *The Winter's Tale* – it is the reason actors and directors are applauded – but readers of printed texts, even F, largely punctuated by Crane, shouldn't think that any version in front of them is fixed and final. *Caveat lector.*

One last thing completely lost in modernizing is direct contact with the history of how F came into being. Crane's part in this, transcribing and editing, is outlined above, but the detailed study of his work as a copyist is still in progress. As yet there is no full printed text of all his transcripts, or a concordance that could be prepared from it. In F, *The Winter's Tale* is remarkable for a superabundance of colons and brackets, many if not all of them Crane's, but this is equally true for the hyphenated words and phrases. Eliminating these in a modernized text isn't an insupportable loss – readers will prefer 'handkerchief' to 'Hand-kerchief' (5.2.64) and 'shovels in' to 'shouels-in' (4.4.463) – but it does mean that Crane's unique way of copying is lost entirely. Table 3 (pp. 379–81) is intended to offset this, and to contribute to the continuing collection of data about this important scribe and his role in publishing Shakespeare. The table lists all of F's hyphens, except those used in printing, i.e. where the compositors split and hyphenated words to fit the text within the standard width of columns on the page (e.g. 'Progno-| stication', 4.4.793, illustrated in Fig. 23b, p. 355). In a few cases Crane's divided words and hyphens appear to coincide with the compositor's splitting the word for column width (e.g. 'tawdry-lace', 4.4.249–50); these are also included in Table 3.

Table 2a Archaic and unusual spellings and word forms in F (1)

The words are listed here in alphabetical order. For a listing in order of occurrence, see Table 2b. In both tables, words glossed in the commentary are marked with an asterisk.

accompt	2.3.196	knew'st	4.4.464
Adultresse	2.1.78, 88, 2.3.4	lingring	1.2.318
altring	4.4.404	loosing	4.2.27, *5.2.77
Aquavite	4.4.791	lowd'st	2.2.38
ballet	4.4.260	murther	1.2.408, 3.2.99,
Barne	3.3.68		5.1.62
barne	3.3.69	neer'st	3.2.52
Bases	4.3.43	Nosthrill	1.2.417
*bitten	5.2.54	Offring	3.1.8
bittrest	3.2.213	ord'ring	2.1.169, 4.4.139
Blew	2.1.13	Prewyns	4.3.48
*blew	2.1.15	raigne	1.2.360
borne	1.2.134	raignes	2.1.105
Bowget	4.3.20	*raigns	4.3.4
Burthen	1.2.3	requoyle	1.2.154
burthen	2.3.204, 4.4.264	Reysons	4.3.48
burthens	4.4.196	shak'st	4.4.632
Cap-a-pe	4.4.740	Sien	4.4.93
Chowghes	4.4.621	Sprindge	4.3.35
Coarse	4.4.129, 131	stolne	5.3.115
Compters	4.3.36	sweet'st	3.2.198, 5.1.11
Currence	4.3.38	swownded	5.2.88
deaff'ning	3.1.9	Tromperie	4.4.602
dear'st	1.2.137	vild	2.1.92
deer'st	3.2.198, 4.4.40	Vildely	4.4.22
enter-change	1.1.28	Viols	5.3.122
fadom	4.4.277	Watry	1.2.1
fadomes	4.4.496	Whilest	5.1.6
Farthell	4.4.711, 721, 758,	whilest	5.1.168
	760; 5.2.3, 114	whisp'ring	1.2.215
*fled	4.4.645	whispring	4.4.247
ghesse	1.2.399, 4.4.473	Whoo-bub	4.4.620
hallow'd	3.3.75	woe	3.2.153
hardned	3.2.51	wond'ring	4.1.25
hardning	1.2.146	Wrackt	5.2.68
hastning	5.1.188	Yond	2.1.31
Heycfer	1.2.124		
*kill-hole	4.4.245		

Table 2b Archaic and unusual spellings and word forms in F (2)

1.1.28	enter-change	4.3.38	Currence
1.2.1	Watry	4.3.43	Bases
1.2.3	Burthen	4.3.48	Prewyns, Reysons
1.2.124	Heycfer	4.4.22	Vildely
1.2.134	borne	4.4.40	deer'st
1.2.137	dear'st	4.4.93	Sien
1.2.146	hardning	4.4.129, 131	Coarse
1.2.154	requoyle	4.4.139	ord'ring
1.2.215	whisp'ring	4.4.196	burthens
1.2.318	lingring	4.4.245	*kill-hole
1.2.360	raigne	4.4.247	whispring
1.2.399	ghesse	4.4.260	ballet
1.2.408	murther	4.4.264	burthen
1.2.417	Nosthrill	4.4.277	fadom
2.1.13	Blew	4.4.404	altring
2.1.15	*blew	4.4.464	knew'st
2.1.31	Yond	4.4.473	ghesse
2.1.78, 88	Adultresse	4.4.496	fadomes
2.1.92	vild	4.4.602	Tromperie
2.1.105	raignes	4.4.620	Whoo-bub
2.1.169	ord'ring	4.4.621	Chowghes
2.2.38	lowd'st	4.4.632	shak'st
2.3.4	Adultresse	4.4.645	*fled
2.3.196	accompt	4.4.711, 721,	Farthell
2.3.204	burthen	758, 760	
3.1.8	Offring	4.4.740	Cap-a-pe
3.1.9	deaff'ning	4.4.791	Aquavite
3.2.51	hardned	5.1.6	Whilest
3.2.52	neer'st	5.1.11	sweet'st
3.2.99	murther	5.1.62	murther
3.2.153	woe	5.1.168	whilest
3.2.198	sweet'st, deer'st	5.1.188	hastning
3.2.213	bittrest	5.2.3, 114	Farthell
3.3.68	Barne	5.2.54	*bitten
3.3.69	barne	5.2.68	Wrackt
3.3.75	hallow'd	5.2.77	*loosing
4.1.25	wond'ring	5.2.88	swownded
4.2.27	loosing	5.3.115	stolne
4.3.4	*raigns	5.3.122	Viols
4.3.20	Bowget		
4.3.35	Sprindge		
4.3.36	Compters		

Table 3   Hyphenated words in F

This table excludes words split to fit the text within the standard width
of columns in F (illustrated in Fig. 24). The vertical bar (|) indicates
where a hyphenated word has been further split to fit the column width.

a–boord	3.3.7, 56	Cod–peece	4.4.615
a–crosse	4.4.15	co–heyres	2.1.148
a–do	2.2.9	co–ioyne	1.2.143
a–doe	2.2.18	Come–on	2.1.27, 4.4.273
a farre–off	2.1.104	come–on	2.1.27, 4.4.394,
a–fear'd	4.4.447		5.1.210
a–fresh	4.2.24	Court–Contempt	4.4.738
a–part	2.2.13	Court–Odour	4.4.737
Ape–bearer	4.3.93	Court–word	4.4.746
auouch–it	4.3.22	creating–Nature	4.4.88
a–while	4.4.396	Cup–bearer	1.2.311, 342
Baby–daughter	3.2.188	Cut–purse	4.4.676
Bag–pipe	4.4.185	dead–mans	2.1.152
Ballad–makers	5.2.24	deere–a	4.4.322
Bastard–braynes	2.3.138	dis–case	4.4.637
Beare–baitings	4.3.100	Dis–mantle	4.4.656
bearing–cloath	3.3.112	Doues–downe	4.4.368
bed–rid	4.4.406	down–right	2.3.16
Bed–swaruer	2.1.93	dungy–earth	2.1.157
behinde–doore	3.3.73	eare–deaff'ning	3.1.9
behind–hand	5.1.150	enter–change	1.1.28
be–spice	1.2.314	eye–browes	2.1.13, 15
big–with	2.1.61	eye–glasse	1.2.266
black–browes	2.1.8	finder–out	5.2.119
blind–ones	4.4.841	Fire–roab'd–God	4.4.29
Bon–fires	5.2.22	flap–	dragon'd	3.3.96
boylde–	braynes	3.3.62–3	Flax–Wench	1.2.275
breake–neck	1.2.360	Flowre–de–Luce	4.4.127
Brick–wall	4.4.794	foot–man	4.3.64
Bugle–bracelet	4.4.224	foot–path	4.3.122
by–gone	3.2.181	Fore–head	2.3.99
by–gone–day	1.2.32	fore–tells	2.3.197
Cap–a–pe	4.4.740	foure–threes	4.4.341
Chamber–Councels	1.2.235	gaine–say	3.2.55
Child–bed	3.2.101	gaine–saying	1.2.19
Child–hoods	1.1.22–3	gal–	ly–maufrey	4.4.333
child–nesse	1.2.169	Gentleman–like	5.2.141
Church–yard	2.1.30	Gilly–vors	4.4.82
Clerke–like	1.2.388	Goddess–like	4.4.10

Table 3 continued

goe-by	5.3.31	Mid-night	1.2.288
good-deed	1.2.42	Mid-wife	2.3.158
Good-lucke	3.3.67	Mile-a	4.3.125
greene-sord	4.4.157	milking-time	4.4.244
halfe-Moone	2.1.11	Nay-ward	2.1.64
hand-fast	4.4.772	Neat-herds	4.4.330
Hand-kerchief	5.2.64	Necke-lace	4.4.224
Hang-man	4.4.779	non-performance	1.2.259
harlot-King	2.3.4	Nose-gayes	4.3.41
Head-peece	1.2.225	old-man	4.4.620, 786
Heire-lesse	5.1.10	on-foot	1.1.3
Holy-Horse	1.2.274	o're-charg'd	3.2.147
home-ward	1.2.24	o're-dy'd	1.2.132
honor-flaw'd	2.1.143	ore-shades	1.2.453
hony-mouth'd	2.2.32	o're-throwne	5.1.229
horne-pipes	4.3.44–5	ore-whelme	4.1.9
Horne-Ring	4.4.604	ouer-fond	5.2.115
horse-man	4.3.64	ouer-heard	4.4.631
ill-doing	1.2.70	ouer-kind	1.1.21
ill-ta'ne	1.2.456	ouer-much	5.1.73
in-side	1.2.284, 4.4.808	out-side	4.4.636, 809
Iog-on, Iog-on	4.3.122	penny-worth	4.4.639–40
Issue-lesse	5.1.173	Petty-brands	2.1.71
Iump-her	4.4.197	Petty-toes	4.4.611
kill-hole	4.4.245	Play-fellow	1.2.80
knee-deepe	1.2.185	play-fellow	2.1.3
lay'd-on	5.3.49	plot-proofe	2.3.6
La-you	2.3.49	pluck-back	4.4.741
Land-damne	2.1.143	poaking-stickes	4.4.228
Land-seruice	3.3.92	pre-employ'd	2.1.49
Leauen-wether	4.3.32	Priest-like	1.2.235
lewd-tongu'd	2.3.170	Prime-roses	4.4.122
Liege-man	2.3.172	Process-server	4.3.93–4
looker-on	5.3.85	push-on	2.1.179, 4.4.741
Looking-Glasse	1.2.117	Ram-ten- | der	4.4.781
Loue-songs	4.4.195	re-view	4.4.670
Low-borne	4.4.156	Saint-like	5.1.2
lo-you	1.2.106	Schoole-Boyes	2.1.103
made-me	4.3.41	Sea-sick	5.2.117
Maiden-heads	4.4.116	Sea-side	4.4.672
Mary-gold	4.4.105	sea- | side	4.4.830
Me-thinkes	4.4.399	sea-side	3.3.66

Table 3 continued

self-same	4.4.449	Tale- | Porter	4.4.270
selfe-borne	4.1.8	talk'd-of	5.1.119
shee-Angell	4.4.211	tawdry- | lace	4.4.249–50
Sheep-Coat	4.4.784	three-man	4.3.42
sheepe-hooke	4.4.425	Threw-off	2.3.15
sheepe-shearing	4.3.115, 118;	Thrower-out	3.3.28
	4.4.3, 69	thump-her	4.4.197
Sheepe-shearing-Feast	4.3.37	tirra-Lyra	4.3.9
Sheepe-whistling	4.4.780	tittle-tatling	4.4.246
shewes-off	5.3.21	Tongue-ty'd	1.2.27
Ship-boord	4.4.658	Too-farre	3.3.10
Shooe-tye	4.4.604	Trades-men	4.4.727
shouels-in	4.4.463	Traitorly-Rascals	4.4.797
shoulder-blade	4.3.73	Troll-my-dames	4.3.86
shoulder-bone	3.3.93	troth-plight	1.2.276,
sleeue-hand	4.4.211		5.3.151
snapper-vp	4.3.26	Trunke-worke	3.3.72–3
so-forth	1.2.216	Virgin-branches	4.4.115
song-men	4.3.42	vn-answer'd	5.1.228
Son-in-law	5.3.149	vn-breech'd	1.2.155
Sonne-in-Law	5.2.52	vn-earthly	3.1.7
Soule-vext	5.1.59	vn-intelligent	1.1.14
South-ward	4.4.795	vnthought-on	4.4.543
South-wind	5.1.160	Waiting-Gentlewoman	3.3.71
Sow-skin	4.3.20	ware-a	4.4.328
staire-worke	3.3.72	Watry-Starre	1.2.1
Stand-by	5.3.85	weake-hindg'd	2.3.117
stander-by	1.2.277	weare-a	4.4.325
starke-mad	3.2.180	Weather-bitten	5.2.54
States-man	1.2.167	Whitson-Pastorals	4.4.134
Stile-a	4.3.123	Whoa-ho-hoa	3.3.76
stuff'd-sufficiency	2.1.185	Whoo-bub	4.4.620
sweet-hearts	4.4.654	wilfull-negligent	1.2.253
Swine-herds	4.4.330	With-draw	2.2.15
Table-booke	4.4.603	without-dore-Forme	2.1.69
take-in	4.4.582	woman-tyr'd	2.3.73
take-off	5.3.55	Ynch-thick	1.2.185

MUSIC

MUSIC AND SONG

Modern productions of *The Winter's Tale* often begin with music. Sometimes there is an incidental piece before the first speeches – a pavan perhaps, to remind audiences that the setting is a Renaissance court; other times the music is an integral part of the opening scene, jazz piano for a cabaret that Leontes and Hermione have put on for their guest, or music and magic tricks at a children's party for Mamillius. Directors often use these beginnings to announce musical motifs that will reappear throughout, aligned with some aspect of the action or a particular emotion; in his 1986 RSC production, for example, Terry Hands used a sequence of high notes sung at the outset by a boy soprano, which was repeated in subsequent scenes to signal grief or loss. Audiences are now so accustomed to musical soundtracks in films – preparing them for a shock, say, or soothing them after it – that in the theatre long stretches of unaccompanied spoken dialogue may seem emotionally bare.

Early performances probably had musical introductions and flourishes, marking for instance Leontes' entrances and exits. (Charlton, 266–7, reconstructs cues and timings for incidental music throughout the play.) Uniquely, no flourishes are indicated for *The Winter's Tale* in F. It is also possible that music was performed between the acts. This happened in the public theatres from 1610 onwards, according to Taylor and Jowett (6–7, 9), and there was music too in the indoor theatres between acts as the candles were being trimmed (Gurr, 'Blackfriar's', 93).

Once the play had begun, however, the action would have been noticeably without music. This is the way Shakespeare intended it, that the first three acts should have little or no music in them and, unusually for him when he writes about the court, very few references to music either. The only musical metaphor in the opening acts is a grubby one about 'virginalling' (1.2.125–6; see n.).

In these first three acts, songs and music are not simply missing but excluded. In Sicily, where Leontes screams abuse at his noblemen and tries to catch out his wife over this or that phrase, there is no place for musical harmonies (there is a deliberate contrast with the queen's name, 'Hermione', often associated with music and social harmony: see List of Roles, 7n.). The emphasis on speech alone continues into the fourth act, until 4.3, more than halfway into the action. Then suddenly, on a back road deep in the countryside in Bohemia, Autolycus enters singing. From then until the middle of 4.4 there are six songs, two separate full-scale dances to music, and many references to people singing, buying ballads, learning tunes by heart, dancing to the pipe and tabor or the bagpipes, and enjoying birdsong in spring and summer. All this happens in less than 500 lines, and then the music disappears again until 5.3 – a further 1000 lines on – when Paulina commands 'Music, awake her; strike!' and the statue of Hermione begins to move.

The concentration of music in 4.3 and 4.4 marks a holiday time when everyday rural work – sheep-shearing, milking, digging, planting, weaving and herding – gives way to an interval of rest and play. Everyone's mind is on their dinner and drinking, listening to songs and rude jokes, or hearing the latest ballad about hard-hearted girls and men who have deserted their lovers. Music at the feast celebrates temporary freedom and pleasure for the underclass, the time in the year when normal social rules are relaxed or suspended. Once the rules are reasserted, at the point that Polixenes decides that his son has consorted with a shepherdess for long enough (4.4.349), the music stops.

When it returns in the chapel in 5.3 the music on one level is 'real' and therapeutic, perhaps performed in full sight of the audience by Paulina's musician-servants, playing from a gallery above the stage. But the text also suggests that it is heavenly or supernatural, poured down in 'sacred vials' by the gods, so

Hermione says (5.3.121–3), in which case the musicians may have performed invisibly from beneath the stage. As in *Pericles*, 3.2.89, when Cerimon revives Thaisa, the pun on 'vials' (vessels) and 'viols' (stringed instruments) suggests that Paulina's music, whether it was performed above or below the action, was played on the viols – instruments emphatically more refined and sweeter than the drum and pipe or bagpipe that accompanied dances at rural feasts (see Fig. 3, p. 32).

There are six performed songs in the play, all sung by Autolycus (another of his songs, referred to but not performed, is 'Whoop, do me no harm, good man': see 4.4.200–1, 201–2n.). The first three songs are in 4.3, immediately before and after he encounters the Clown: 'When daffodils begin to peer' (1–12), 'But shall I go mourn for that, my dear?' (15–22) and 'Jog on, jog on, the footpath way' (122–5). The first two are probably Shakespeare's own, but the third, 'Jog on', is a refrain from a ballad that appears in seventeenth-century books and manuscripts of music. Versions of the lyrics were familiar in Tudor and Stuart settings.

The three other songs are in 4.4, at the feast: 'Lawn as white as driven snow' (220–31), 'Get you hence, for I must go' (298–13, sung as a trio with Mopsa and Dorcas), and 'Will you buy any tape' (320–8). 'Lawn as white' and 'Will you buy' are probably adaptations of existing street cries. The music and lyrics for the other song, 'Get you hence', were most likely written by Robert Johnson (1583–1633), a composer and musician at the court of James I who worked with the King's Men. A version longer than the song in the play has survived in manuscript, and is reproduced in edited form on p. 392.

Autolycus' songs mix things up – social ranks, the seasons, money and sex, mooning lovers and thieves working by night. More important, in the humble rural world away from the court, where singing is as natural as speaking, his ostensibly light and simple songs contain big truths about Nature and human nature: that 'the red blood reigns in the winter's pale', for instance (4.3.4; see n.), and that all men betray women (the girls sing, with Autolycus, 'Thou hast sworn my love to be. / Thou hast sworn it more to me', 4.4.311–12). It is important that an unpleasant side of Autolycus is exposed when he sneers at the effect of his singing. The crowd of rustics listening to him was so stupefied, he says, that you could have fiddled with people's genitals and not one of them would have noticed. 'No hearing, no feeling' in them, 'but my sir's song, and admiring the nothing of it' (4.4.616–18; see nn.). This is cynical and mean, and thereafter Autolycus has no contact with music or song.

LYRICS AND SETTINGS

Music for the songs that Autolycus sings appears in various seventeenth-century manuscripts and printed books. Some of the music is much older than *The Winter's Tale* itself, and is drawn from ballads and dance tunes. It is not certain that any of the seventeenth-century music was what audiences heard in early performances, though in one or two cases, 'Jog on' and 'Get you hence', there is a good chance that it was.

Just as the play's punctuation, spelling and word forms in F have been modernized in this edition, so the music for the songs has been edited with modern singers, musicians and audiences in mind (this holds too for the setting of 'The dance of satyrs' given on pp. 402–4). Three of the songs are presented here for voice and instrumental bass, another two for voice alone (see pp. 396–401). One of the songs isn't provided with music because there is no suitable contemporary setting for it (see pp. 388–9). In early productions, the way the songs were performed would have depended on the resources and conditions of the venue (an open-air theatre or a great hall in the palace). Most often they would have been sung as voice alone. Where instruments were to hand, a lute, cittern or viol would have accompanied. The bass parts given here provide sufficient indication for a harmonic 'realization'. The lyrics in the songs are from the text in this Arden edition, with slight alterations.

'When daffodils begin to peer' *(4.3.1–12)*

The tune for Autolycus' first song probably wasn't specially composed for the play. It is likely to have been adapted from an existing ballad tune, though we don't know which one. Musical scholars have suggested known ballads and settings they think would fit: 'Row well, ye mariners', for example, from Thomas Robinson's *School of Music* (1603), which recurs in all editions of *The English Dancing Master* from 1651 (Long, 72); or 'Lusty gallant', in William Ballet's Lute Book *c.* 1605 (Turner, 856). Duffin (440–1) opts for *Callino Casturame* because, of several ballad tunes, it seems to fit 'best of all'. He gives a version based on William Byrd's setting in the Fitzwilliam Virginal Book (before 1619), no. 158. It is in 6/4 and a fairly sophisticated tune.

Clement Robinson, in his *A Handful of Pleasant Delights* (1584), says that the tune accompanies the ballad 'Fain wold I have a pretie thing to give unto my Ladie' (Pattison, 169). This tune dates back to at least the early part of Elizabeth's reign, and it continued to be popular in the early seventeenth century. It appears in the 1566 Bodleian manuscript MS Ashmole 48, and was used in 1612 in connection with the London Lottery 'for the good of Virginia' (Simpson, 476, 478).

Simpson (477) gives a version of this setting in C minor. This, in conjunction with Ward (22), is the basis of the tune presented here – for voice and bass, suitable for an accompaniment.

'But shall I go mourn?' *(4.3.15–22)*

No original tune is known for this song but several contemporary ballad tunes have been suggested. Turner (857) chooses 'Who list to lead a soldier's life' (Simpson, no. 516) on the grounds that it 'aptly accommodates this lyric text' of eight lines alternating eight/six syllables (except for the extra syllable 'go' in the first line). The 'Soldier's life', however, is a version of Ophelia's song 'Tomorrow is St Valentine's Day' and is not particularly convincing in this context. Long (73), sets the text to a tune called 'The noble shrive' (Wooldridge, 1.126), whereas Duffin (84–5) argues for a version of 'Lusty gallant' because it 'seems to best match the literally parenthetical treatment of "my dear" in the first line'. In its 6/4 rhythm, as found in the Marsh Lute Book (*c.* 1595), this version represents the metrical form of the lyric fairly well. This is the version given here.

'Jog on, jog on, the footpath way' (4.3.122–5)

The lines Autolycus sings at the end of 4.3 are from a refrain in an Elizabethan song and country-dance tune. Words and music for 'Jog on' appeared in different versions, usually separately, in a number of manuscript and printed collections during the reigns of the Stuarts. The tune was included in all ten editions of John Playford's *English Dancing Master*, a collection of dances with tunes, published between 1651 and 1698. In the miscellany *An Antidote against Melancholy: Made up in Pills* (1661), the tune is found with two additional stanzas with a repeat of the first indicated at the end. This same arrangement is in Playford's *Catch That Catch Can or The Musical Companion* (1667) in a three-voice version by John Hilton, which is the setting given in Long, 74, and Oxf[1], 277.

The tune to 'Jog on' is from the late sixteenth century, when it was known as 'Hanskin', and associated with songs such 'Sir Francis Drake' and 'Eighty-eight' (about the Spanish Armada). In the Fitzwilliam Virginal Book (before 1619), a set of keyboard variations by Richard Farnaby (born *c.* 1594) uses the tune as its theme. It appears as 'Hansken' in the Dutch *Het Luitboek van Thysius*, no. 25 (*c.* 1620), clearly the same tune but in a different key.

Duffin (251–2) adapts the Farnaby setting. Farnaby's original is an art-music version of 'Hanskin' without the anacrusis (unstressed first note) and with a more sophisticated rhythmical line. The polyphonic texture of the keyboard arrangement and the cadential ornamentation mean that the tune is changed in several important details. Duffin expunges the ornamentation but keeps Farnaby's melodic outline. The simpler version in *Het Luitboek van Thysius* fits Autolycus' lyrics better and is used here. It is probably too high for an adult male to sing, even though Autolycus is supposed to be a professional ballad singer. It could easily be transposed down to match an actor's singing range and to relate to the pitches of the other songs.

'*Lawn as white as driven snow*' *(4.4.220–31)*

Shakespeare probably adapted 'Lawn as white' and 'Will you buy' (320–8), from existing songs or snatches of street cries, the shouts used by London hawkers to advertise what they were selling. In the sixteenth century the street cries became a musical subgenre when composers such as Orlando Gibbons and Thomas Weelkes gave them highly elaborate musical settings.

Most editors of *The Winter's Tale* print a version of 'Lawn as white' as it appears in John Wilson's 1660 *Cheerful Airs or Ballads*, perpetuating the theory that Wilson was merely providing his arrangement of the original tune by an earlier composer, perhaps Robert Johnson (see Turner, 863). In other words, Wilson (1595–1674) recollected a tune from fifty years earlier. As Seng points out, however, 'Wilson's version can hardly have been the original music for the song since he was only fifteen [actually sixteen] years old at the time of its first performance' (240). More importantly, the tune and its harmonization in Wilson's *Airs*, with its regular two-bar phrases and predictable cadences, represents the new 'baroque' style of mid-seventeenth-century England and not the late Renaissance musical style prevalent in England until the 1620s. Wilson's version is printed in Oxf[1], 278–9.

Duffin (251) prints an adaptation of the ballad tune 'In Crete' as appropriate for 'Lawn as white'. This tune is found in three lute manuscripts: the so-called Lodge Book (1559–*c.* 1575), the Mynshall Lute Book (1597–1600) and the Ballet Lute Book (*c.* 1590 and *c.* 1610). Duffin's argument is simply that the 'apparent six-line stanzas and rhyming couplets' of 'Lawn as white' seem to fit very well to 'In Crete' (252). In fact the 'second' stanza, which he doesn't underlay, is not a very good fit and the refrain 'Come buy' is decidedly awkward. What is needed is a pedlar's ballad tune to fit a ten-line stanza with a couplet refrain. No suitable tune has been identified, so no setting is included here.

'Get you hence' (4.4.298–313): music and extra lyrics

This is a prepared or 'formal' vocal song, and as a dialogue between Autolycus, Dorcas and Mopsa is more complicated than the other songs in the play. Differing kinds of ballads are discussed in the dialogue at 4.4.259–87. Mopsa asks for 'merry' ballads, and Autolycus says he has 'a passing merry one' which 'goes to the tune of "Two Maids Wooing a Man"' (288–90). There is a pun or allusion in 'passing': the ballad is unsurpassed in its merriness (*OED adv.* C a), but it also has a 'passing-measure' (*passamezzo*) bass, sometimes known in Elizabethan England as a 'quadran pavan' (e.g. in the Fitzwilliam Virginal Book, nos 31 and 133).

Settings and words for 'Get you hence' have survived in two seventeenth-century music manuscripts in the Drexel collection in the New York Public Library, Dx.4175 and Dx.4041. The manuscripts contain music and songs by different composers, some of whom can be identified. Manuscript Dx.4175 (hereafter A), was copied before 1630, Dx.4041 (hereafter B) about 1650.

The settings of 'Get you hence' in A (on fol. 23) and B (fols 127–9) are intrinsically the same but in a different key. In A the dialogue in the song is arranged for a single voice, with an accompaniment for the lyra viol which has been incorporated into the keyboard part. In B the music is incomplete, but it 'shows the original dialogue arrangement by using a base clef' for the man's part (Johnson, *Ayres*, 7). B's version of the song has additional lyrics not in A or the First Folio (F).

Manuscript A contains songs and music from the Jacobean theatre. Some of these were almost certainly by Robert Johnson, whose pieces for the King's Men included Ariel's song 'Where the bee sucks' in *The Tempest* (5.1.88–94). Johnson composed the music for the dance of the satyrs in Ben Jonson's 1611 masque *Oberon*, a dance that was probably repeated as the dance of the satyrs in *The Winter's Tale* (see pp. 394–5). All this leads scholars to conclude that 'Get you hence' was most likely by Johnson, an old ballad tune refurbished with settings and lyrics for three singers.

In both A and B 'Get you hence' contains vocal ornaments indicating that it was sung by a professional court and/or theatre singer. These ornaments, which differ between the manuscripts, have been taken out in the version given here, which is adapted from Manuscript B. An instrumental bass is provided, partly because an accompaniment would not be out of keeping in a formal song of this kind, and partly because of the pun or allusion to the passing-measures bass, noted above.

Manuscript B is a highly competent though often untidy source of songs, many connected with the early theatre. Although the music for 'Get you hence' in B is incomplete, ending at 'thou dost ill' in line 8, the song has additional lyrics. In F and both manuscripts the lyrics are the same, with minor differences, for the first twelve lines; in B they continue for another thirteen. The extra lines don't quite fit the existing music, probably because of mistakes in copying. The singers aren't named in A or B, but the extra lines continue to be distributed between a man and two women.

In the play, the Clown deliberately interrupts the singing of 'Get you hence', most likely to break up Autolycus' flirtation with Mopsa and Dorcas. He leads the girls offstage, saying he will buy ballads for both of them, beginning with the one about the usurer's wife – pointedly *not* the song about two young maids wooing a man. Up to the moment the Clown breaks in, the subject of 'Get you hence' is oblique. The man won't tell the maids where he is going, but they suspect it is to 'th' grange or mill' (306), something he ought not to be doing. The maids each claim he has sworn love to them (promises of marriage perhaps). Is he meeting yet another maid to have sex with her in a mill, or is she a woman with her own farm, whom he might mean to marry?

'Get you hence' in the play ends, tantalizingly, with the question 'whither?'. In Manuscript B the additional lines give an answer of a kind, though it too is obscure. The man will never again dance with girls at country feasts, perhaps because he will be married. The girls, 'Phil' and 'Friz', are aghast. He must 'recant' – renounce his vow to marry someone else? – or they will die of love. If he weren't there with them, in his best clothes, dancing on the village green, where would they ever be seen again? 'Sleeping' is his curt answer, because they wouldn't be bothered at all by his absence. No, the girls retort, they would be 'sitting sadly' or 'idly', or 'walking madly', in 'some dark, dark corner weeping'.

The shift of tone and content in the additional lines may explain why, if they were in Johnson's original version, they weren't used in the play. Perhaps the lines filled out too clearly the situation of country girls deserted by men – the subject of *A Lover's Complaint*, published in 1609 – or accused by their lovers of feeling nothing when in fact they suffered dejection, madness and tears. It is equally possible that the fuller version was performed at the Globe but abbreviated in the manuscript used to print F, or that someone other than Johnson added the lines, unconnected with the King's Men and *The Winter's Tale*.

The text of 'Get you hence' in B is reproduced on p. 392 in edited form, modernized and repaired in places from A and F, with some repeats filled out (following Cutts, 'Song', 88, who prints lines 24 and 25 with further repeats). The textual notes record where A varies from B or F from A and B, or where B is deficient or unclear. The reading that precedes the square bracket is in B unless otherwise indicated; notable original spellings in B, or different readings in A and/or F are given after the square bracket. Since neither A nor B provides SPs for

'Get you hence' with additional lyrics from Manuscript B

AUTOLYCUS	Get you hence, for I must go
	Where it fits not you to know.
DORCAS	Whither?
MOPSA	O whither?
DORCAS	Whither?
MOPSA	It becomes thy oath full well,
	Thou to me thy secrets tell.

5

DORCAS	And me too: let me go thither.
MOPSA	If thou goest to grange or mill,
	If to either, thou dost ill.
AUTOLYCUS	Neither.
MOPSA	What neither?
AUTOLYCUS	Neither.
DORCAS	Thou has sworn my love to be.

10

MOPSA	Thou has sworn it more to me.
	Then whither, whither goest thou? Whither?
AUTOLYCUS	Nevermore for lasses' sake
	Will I dance at fair or wake.
DORCAS	Ah me!
MOPSA	Ah, ah me!
DORCAS	Ah me!

15

MOPSA	Who shall then wear a raised shoe,
	Or what shall the bagpipe do?
DORCAS	Recant or else you slay me.
MOPSA	If thou leave our arbour green,
	Where shall Phil or Friz be seen?

20

AUTOLYCUS	Sleeping.
DORCAS	What, sleeping?
AUTOLYCUS	Sleeping.
MOPSA	No I'll warrant thee, sitting sadly,
	Or idly, walking madly.
DORCAS	In some dark
	In some dark, dark corner weeping.

25

3 **Whither?** Where are you going?

7 **grange** farmhouse, country house

14 **fair or wake** annual festivals, held on saints' days (see 4.3.99–100n.)

16 **raised** raisèd; i.e. the shoe had a raised heel

17 **what . . . do** i.e. without you, what's the point of music and dancing? The bagpipe was played at rural feasts;

because of its shape it was associated with the male genitals, so there may be a ribald meaning, 'how will you do without having sex with us?'

18 **Recant** take back what you've said

19 **arbour green** shaded place on the village green

20 **Phil or Friz** girls' names, short for Phillis and Frances; cf. *TNK* 3.5.26.

1 you] *altered from* ye; yee *A;* you *F* 3 O whither] *A and F; not in B, but there is a repeat mark at the end of the line* 4 becomes thy] befitts thine *A* 6 And] *not in F* 7 If] Or *F* to] to th' *F* 10 sworn . . . be] vow'de thy love to mee *A* 11 it . . . me] my love to bee *A* 12] *In B, written at the top of the page;* then whether *written at the bottom of the previous page, without musical notation, and repeated below that as a catchword* whither goest thou?] goest? Say, whither? *A and F* 13–25] *not in A or F* 15 Ah, ah] A Ah *possibly* O, Ah 19 arbour] Andorne *probably miscopied*

the singers (Phil and Friz at 20 are generic names), these have been supplied from F as Autolycus, Mopsa and Dorcas. It is not certain which female sings which verses from line 16 onwards.

'Will you buy any tape' *(4.4.320–8)*

This is Autolycus' second exit song. Duffin (471–2) argues that the song should be linked with 'Jog on' and he adapts the tune 'Hanskin' to it, without much conviction. The jaunty country-dance tune on a ground (bass) in Thomas Ravenscroft's 1609 *Pammelia* (no. 74) is much more suitable. It is reproduced in a harmonized version in Turner (868), which is rendered below for voice and bass; the last two bars have been altered to provide a more convincing ending with better word underlay.

TWO DANCES

'The dance of shepherds' *(4.4.167 SD)*

The first dance at the feast, at 4.4.167 SD, is of shepherds and shepherdesses, with Florizel and Perdita among them; the second, at 4.4.347.1–2, is of countrymen dressed as satyrs. The dances are separated by 190 lines, in which there are also three songs, so the playing time between shepherds and satyrs was at least seven or eight minutes, allowing the shepherd dancers to go offstage, change, and return as satyrs (see p. 117).

None of the original music for the shepherds' dance is known. In England by 1600 there were two styles of country dancing, each accompanied invariably by a single player on a pipe and tabor (a small drum). The older style, sometimes danced around a focus such as a tree, comprised 'rounds' or 'heys' (winding line dances concluding with a round). The new style was eclectic, borrowing from the old but also from the morris and from the sophisticated Italian dances newly fashionable at court. The emphasis in the new style, danced to different musical rhythms, was on complicated steps and choreography, couples exchanging partners decorously, curtsying and holding hands, palms upward. Given how unsophisticated the Shepherd's feasting is supposed to be, it seems likely that in *The Winter's Tale* the shepherds danced in the older style.

'The dance of satyrs' (4.4.347.1–2)

More is known about the dance of the countrymen as satyrs, because it was probably repeated in essentials from Ben Jonson's court masque *Oberon* performed on New Year's Day 1611. In *Oberon* the action began with ten satyrs howling and calling out as the moon rose over a dark rock. They sang and chattered until the rock split open to reveal a palace with transparent walls and battlements. Suddenly the satyrs began '*an antique dance, full of gesture, and swift motion, and continued it, till the crowing of the cock*' (Jonson, 7.351).

Music for the dance in *Oberon* has survived under the name 'The Satyrs' Masque' in a seventeenth-century manuscript collection of dance tunes performed at Jacobean court masques. The manuscript is now in the British Library, Add. MS 10444; the satyrs' dance tune is transcribed on fol. 31a (treble part) and fol. 82b (basses). The same tune appears in a book published in Hamburg in 1621, Thomas Simpson's *Taffel Consort*, where it is attributed to Robert Johnson, who probably wrote the song 'Get you hence' earlier in 4.4. Modern scholars accept that Johnson wrote the music for the satyrs' dance.

In *Oberon* the satyrs served as the 'antimasque', a term invented by Jonson to describe unruly figures brought to order or replaced by figures of rightful authority (in this case Prince Henry as Oberon). Sabol notes that the tune in 'The satyrs' masque' is longer than in most antimasque dances, composed of five strains of varying length and metre with a short coda. It is notable for the 'sustained notes of the second strain', suggesting that the dancers at court 'assumed stands, or poses, in the midst of the dance' (*Songs*, 2).

In all likelihood, the satyrs' antic dance in *Oberon* was repeated in *The Winter's Tale*, using the same professional dancers hired by the King's Men, who would also have danced as shepherds and shepherdesses. It is difficult to say whether the tune or dance steps would have been adapted for the play. Shakespeare's satyrs are said to be able to leap great distances, twelve feet and more (4.4.344), and in the play as in the masque, these jumps may have been done from the standing-still positions or 'poses' that Sabol speaks of – sudden, unexpected stops in the middle of exuberant swift motion followed by ballet-like leaps, imitating the nimbleness of goats (satyrs were half-men, half-goats: see Fig. 13, p. 71). But the satyrs in the play were supposed to be a troupe of country amateurs, so the professional dancers playing them may have pretended to be clownish and unskilled. Moreover if, as suggested above, one important function of Shakespeare's satyrs was to parody and thereby expel the gross sexual disorder in Leontes (see pp. 65–6), perhaps the dancers in their steps and acrobatics were more graphically explicit than they had been in *Oberon*.

The music for the dance is printed here, with minor alterations, from Cutts's realization of the British Library manuscript (Cutts, 'Musique', 294–5). Sabol also provides a modern score but he edits the music differently (*Songs*, 130–3). As Sternfeld

(398) notes, the pitches in the Cutts and Sabol realizations (with two detailed exceptions) are the same, but where 'in the absence of a time signature in the original' Sabol transcribes the fifth and sixth strains in 2/4, Cutts presents the fifth strain in 3/2 and the sixth strain in cut C (2/2). No relative speeds are given by Cutts or Sabol; these are suggested here. Individual strains, especially the last, probably were and can be repeated as necessary. In the court and professional theatre a consort of at least four instruments would have played; only treble and bass are given here, but alto and tenor parts could easily be added.

MUSICAL SCORES

'When daffodils begin to peer' (4.3.1–12)

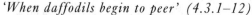

'But shall I go mourn?' (4.3.15–22)

'Jog on, jog on, the footpath way' (4.3.122–5)

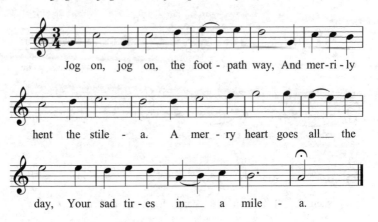

Jog on, jog on, the foot - path way, And mer-ri - ly hent the stile - a. A mer - ry heart goes all___ the day, Your sad tir - es in___ a mile - a.

'Get you hence' (4.4.298–313)

'*Will you buy any tape*' *(4.4.320–8)*

'The dance of satyrs' (4.4.347.1–2)

SOURCES

PANDOSTO

Robert Greene's *Pandosto* was first published in 1588 with two titles: *Pandosto: The Triumph of Time* on the title-page, and *The History of Dorastus and Fawnia* a few pages into the book. The edition was reprinted at least four times, in 1592, 1599, 1607 and 1609, before Shakespeare used it for *The Winter's Tale*. In the course of the reprints, minor differences appeared in the text, some of them corrections and sophistications, others printer's mistakes. One change was to the wording of the key phrase in the oracle, which in 1588 and early reprints reads 'The King shall live without an heir', the version in the play (3.2.132–3). In 1607 and subsequent reprints the phrase is altered to 'die without an heir', which may indicate that Shakespeare used an earlier edition.

The text below is from Bullough, 8.156–99, with minor corrections. Word forms, spelling and punctuation have been modernized, and annotation added. The notes record emendations and offer glosses and select parallels with the play, showing where Shakespeare followed, adapted or rejected Greene's plot and wording. The 1588 edition has survived in only one copy, in the British Library. It lacks several pages, about a sixth of the book, which Bullough supplies from a copy of the 1592 reprint in the Folger Shakespeare Library (the section marked at n. 8, p. 409, and n. 1, p. 416, below).

Greene or the publisher Thomas Cadman wrote the description given beneath the first title for the title-page of the 1588 edition. Greene dedicated the book to two contemporaries (the dedications are omitted here).

PANDOSTO
The Triumph of Time

Wherein is discovered by a pleasant history that although by the means of sinister[1] Fortune Truth may be concealed, yet by Time in spite of Fortune it is most manifestly revealed. Pleasant for age to avoid drowsy thoughts, profitable for youth to eschew other wanton[2] pastimes, and bringing to both a desired content. *Temporis filia veritas.*[3]

The History of Dorastus and Fawnia

Among all the passions wherewith human minds are perplexed, there is none that so galleth[4] with restless despite[5] as the infectious sore of jealousy. For all other griefs are either to be appeased with sensible persuasions,[6] to be cured with wholesome counsel,[7] to be relieved in want,[8] or by tract[9] of time to be worn out; jealousy only excepted, which is so sauced with suspicious doubts and pinching[10] mistrust that whoso seeks by friendly counsel to raze out[11] this hellish passion, it forthwith suspecteth that he giveth this advice to cover his own guiltiness. Yea, whoso is pained with this restless torment doubteth all, distrusteth himself, is always frozen with fear, and fired with suspicion, having that wherein consisteth all his joy to be the breeder of his misery. Yea, it is such a heavy enemy to that holy estate of matrimony, sowing between the married couples such deadly seeds of secret hatred as, love being once razed out by spiteful distrust, there oft ensueth bloody revenge, as this ensuing history manifestly proveth; wherein Pandosto, furiously incensed by causeless jealousy, procured the death of his most loving and loyal wife, and his own endless sorrow and misery.

In the country of Bohemia there reigned a king called Pandosto, whose fortunate success in wars against his foes, and bountiful courtesy towards his friends in peace, made him to be greatly feared and loved of all men. This Pandosto had to wife a lady called Bellaria, by birth royal, learned by education, fair by nature, by virtues famous, so that it was hard to judge whether her beauty, fortune or virtue won the greatest commendations. These two, linked together in perfect love, led their lives with such fortunate content that their subjects greatly rejoiced to see their quiet disposition. They had not been married long, but Fortune, willing to increase their happiness, lent them a son so adorned with the gifts of nature, as the perfection of the child[12] greatly augmented the love of the parents and the joys of their commons,[13] insomuch that the Bohemians, to show their inward joys by outward actions, made bonfires and triumphs[14] throughout all the kingdom, appointing jousts and tourneys[15] for the honour of their young prince; whither resorted not

---

1 adverse; malicious   2 frivolous; lascivious   3 'Truth is Time's daughter' (a proverb Greene used as his motto: see p. 81)   4 chafes   5 vexation   6 arguments   7 good advice   8 poverty   9 passage   10 tormenting (cf. Leontes, 'a pinched thing', 2.1.51)   11 erase   12 Cf. 1.1.33–6, 5.1.115–16.   13 people   14 celebrations (cf. 5.2.22)   15 tournaments

only his nobles, but also divers[1] kings and princes which were his neighbours, willing to show their friendship they ought to[2] Pandosto, and to win fame and glory by their prowess and valour. Pandosto, whose mind was fraught with[3] princely liberality,[4] entertained the kings, princes and noblemen with such submiss[5] courtesy and magnifical bounty[6] that they all saw how willing he was to gratify their good wills, making a general feast for his subjects, which continued by the space of twenty days; all which time the jousts and tourneys were kept, to the great content both of the lords and ladies there present. This solemn triumph being once ended, the assembly taking their leave of Pandosto and Bellaria, the young son, who was called Garinter, was nursed up in the house to the great joy and content of the parents.

Fortune, envious of such happy success, willing to show some sign of her inconstancy, turned her wheel and darkened their bright sun of prosperity with the misty clouds of mishap and misery. For it so happened that Egistus, King of Sicilia, who in his youth had been brought up with Pandosto, desirous to show that neither tract of time nor distance of place could diminish their former friendship,[7] provided a navy of ships and sailed into Bohemia to visit his old friend and companion; who, hearing of his arrival, went himself in person and his wife Bellaria, accompanied with a great train[8] of lords and ladies, to meet Egistus, and espying him, alighted from his horse, embraced him very lovingly, protesting that nothing in the world could have happened more acceptable to him than his coming, wishing his wife to welcome his old friend and acquaintance; who, to show how she liked him whom her husband loved, entertained him with such familiar courtesy as Egistus perceived himself to be very well welcome.[9] After they had thus saluted and embraced each other, they mounted again on horseback and rode toward the city, devising[10] and recounting how, being children, they had passed their youth in friendly pastimes; where, by the means of the citizens, Egistus was received with triumphs and shows in such sort, that he marvelled how on so small a warning they could make such preparation.

Passing the streets thus with such rare[11] sights they rode on to the palace, where Pandosto entertained Egistus and his Sicilians with such banqueting and sumptuous cheer, so royally, as they all had cause to commend his princely liberality. Yea, the very basest slave that was known to come from Sicilia was used with such courtesy, that Egistus might easily perceive how both he and his were honoured for his friend's sake. Bellaria, who in her time was the flower of courtesy, willing to show how unfeignedly she loved her husband by his friend's entertainment,[12] used him likewise so familiarly that her countenance bewrayed[13] how her mind was affected towards him, oftentimes coming herself

---

1 many   2 owed   3 full of   4 generosity   5 modest   6 generosity   7 Cf. 1.1.22–31.   8 following
9 Cf. 3.2.60–5.   10 discussing   11 superb   12 Cf. 1.1.8, 1.2.111.   13 revealed

into his bedchamber to see that nothing should be amiss to mislike[1] him. This honest familiarity increased daily more and more betwixt them, for Bellaria noting in Egistus a princely and bountiful mind, adorned with sundry and excellent qualities, and Egistus finding in her a virtuous and courteous disposition, there grew such a secret uniting of their affections that the one could not well be without the company of the other, insomuch that, when Pandosto was busied with such urgent affairs that he could not be present with his friend Egistus, Bellaria would walk with him into the garden,[2] where they two in private and pleasant devices[3] would pass away the time to both their contents. This custom still continuing betwixt them, a certain melancholy passion entering the mind of Pandosto drove him into sundry and doubtful[4] thoughts. First he called to mind the beauty of his wife Bellaria, the comeliness and bravery[5] of his friend Egistus, thinking that love was above all laws, and therefore to be stayed with[6] no law; that it was hard to put fire and flax together without burning; that their open[7] pleasures might breed his secret displeasures. He considered with himself that Egistus was a man and must needs love; that his wife was a woman and therefore subject unto love, and that where fancy forced, friendship was of no force.

These and suchlike doubtful thoughts, a long time smothering in his stomach,[8] began at last to kindle in his mind a secret mistrust which, increased by suspicion, grew at last to be a flaming jealousy that so tormented him as he could take no rest.[9] He then began to measure all their actions and to misconstrue of their too-private familiarity, judging that it was not for honest affection[10] but for disordinate fancy,[11] so that he began to watch them more narrowly[12] to see if he could get any true or certain proof to confirm his doubtful suspicion. While thus he noted their looks and gestures, and suspected their thoughts and meanings, they two, silly[13] souls who doubted[14] nothing of this his treacherous intent, frequented daily each other's company, which drove him into such a frantic passion that he began to bear a secret hate to Egistus, and a louring[15] countenance to Bellaria, who, marvelling at such unaccustomed frowns,[16] began to cast beyond the moon,[17] and to enter into a thousand sundry thoughts which way she should offend[18] her husband. But finding in herself a clear conscience, ceased to muse until such time as she might find fit opportunity to demand the cause of his dumps.[19] In the meantime, Pandosto's mind was so far charged[20] with jealousy that he did no longer doubt, but was assured (as he thought) that his friend Egistus had entered a wrong point in his tables,[21] and so had played him false play. Whereupon, desirous to revenge so great an injury, he thought

1 displease 2 Cf. 1.2.176–7. 3 pastimes 4 various dreadful 5 good looks and finery 6 prevented by 7 public 8 smouldering in him 9 Cf. 2.3.1. 10 Cf. 1.2.137–8 and see pp. 39–42. 11 improper love 12 closely 13 innocent 14 suspected 15 i.e. grimacing, disapproving 16 Cf. 1.2.148–9, 365–7. 17 i.e. rack her brains 18 might have offended 19 depressed state 20 filled 21 i.e. had cheated him ('point', a term in backgammon, perhaps double entendre for penis; cf. different play and games at 1.2.186–8, 246–7)

best to dissemble the grudge with a fair and friendly countenance,[1] and so, under the shape of a friend, to show him the trick of a foe. Devising[2] with himself a long time how he might best put away Egistus without suspicion of treacherous murder, he concluded at last to poison him;[3] which opinion pleasing his humour,[4] he became resolute in his determination and, the better to bring the matter to pass, he called unto him his cupbearer,[5] with whom in secret he broke the matter, promising to him for the performance thereof to give him a thousand crowns of yearly revenues. His cupbearer, either being of a good conscience or willing for fashion[6] sake to deny such a bloody request, began with great reasons to persuade Pandosto from his determinate[7] mischief, showing him what an offence murder was to the gods, how such unnatural actions did more displease the heavens than men,[8] and that causeless cruelty did seldom or never escape without revenge. He laid before his face that Egistus was his friend, a king, and one that was come into his kingdom to confirm a league of perpetual amity betwixt them; that he had and did show him a most friendly countenance; how Egistus was not only honoured of[9] his own people by obedience, but also loved of the Bohemians for his courtesy; and that if now he should without any just or manifest cause poison him, it would not only be a great dishonour to his majesty, and a means to sow perpetual enmity between the Sicilians and the Bohemians, but also his own subjects would repine at[10] such treacherous cruelty. These and suchlike persuasions of Franion (for so was his cupbearer called) could no whit[11] prevail to dissuade him from his devilish enterprise; but remaining resolute in his determination, his fury so fired with rage, as it could not be appeased with reason, he began with bitter taunts to take up[12] his man and to lay before him two baits, preferment and death; saying that if he would poison Egistus, he should advance him to high dignities; if he refused to do it of an obstinate mind, no torture should be too great to requite his disobedience.[13] Franion, seeing that to persuade Pandosto any more was but to strive against the stream, consented as soon as opportunity would give him leave to dispatch Egistus, wherewith Pandosto remained somewhat satisfied, hoping now he should be fully revenged of such mistrusted[14] injuries; intending also as soon as Egistus was dead, to give his wife a sop of the same sauce,[15] and so be rid of those which were the cause of his restless sorrow. While thus he lived in this hope, Franion, being secret in his chamber, began to meditate with himself in these terms:[16]

'Ah, Franion, treason is loved of many, but the traitor hated of all. Unjust offences may for a time escape without danger but never without revenge.

1 Cf. 1.2.340–2.   2 plotting   3 Cf. 1.2.314–16.   4 mood   5 Cf. 1.2.310–11, 342.   6 appearances   7 settled plan of   8 1592 from here to 'King who,', n. 1, p. 416 (see p. 405).   9 by   10 object vehemently to   11 in no way   12 rebuke; interrupt (cf. 1.2.322)   13 Cf. 1.2.345–6.   14 suspected (cf. 2.1.48)   15 i.e. poison her (a sop was bread dipped in gravy or drink)   16 His thoughts are altered and condensed at 1.2.348–60.

Thou art servant to a king and must obey at command; yet, Franion, against law and conscience it is not good to resist a tyrant with arms, nor to please an unjust king with obedience. What shalt thou do? Folly refuseth gold and frenzy preferment;[1] wisdom seeketh after dignity and counsel looketh for gain. Egistus is a stranger[2] to thee, and Pandosto thy sovereign; thou hast little cause to respect the one, and oughtest to have great care to obey the other. Think this, Franion, that a pound of gold is worth a ton of lead, great gifts are little gods, and preferment to a mean[3] man is a whetstone to[4] courage. There is nothing sweeter than promotion, nor lighter than report.[5] Care not then though most count thee a traitor, so all call thee rich. Dignity, Franion, advanceth thy posterity, and evil report can hurt but thyself. Know this: where eagles build, falcons may prey; where lions haunt,[6] foxes may steal. Kings are known to command, servants are blameless to consent. Fear not thou then to lift at[7] Egistus. Pandosto shall bear the burden.[8] Yea, but Franion, conscience is a worm[9] that ever biteth but never ceaseth. That which is rubbed with the stone galactites[10] will never be hot. Flesh dipped in the sea Aegeum[11] will never be sweet. The herb tragion[12] being once bit with an aspis[13] never groweth, and conscience once stained with innocent blood is always tied to a guilty remorse. Prefer thy content before riches and a clear mind before dignity; so, being poor, thou shalt have rich peace or else, rich, thou shalt enjoy disquiet.'

Franion, having muttered out these or suchlike words, seeing either he must die with a clear mind or live with a spotted[14] conscience, he was so cumbered with divers cogitations[15] that he could take no rest, until at last he determined to break the matter to Egistus. But fearing that the King should either suspect or hear of such matters, he concealed the device[16] till opportunity would permit him to reveal it.[17] Lingering thus in doubtful fear, in an evening he went to Egistus' lodging and, desirous to break with him of[18] certain affairs that touched[19] the King, after all were commanded out of the chamber, Franion made manifest the whole conspiracy which Pandosto had devised against him, desiring Egistus not to account him a traitor for bewraying his master's counsel, but to think that he did it for conscience; hoping that although his master, inflamed with rage or incensed by some sinister[20] reports or slanderous speeches, had imagined such causeless mischief, yet, when time should pacify his anger and try those talebearers but flattering parasites,[21] then he would count him as a faithful servant, that with such care had kept his master's credit.[22] Egistus had not fully heard Franion tell forth his tale, but a quaking fear possessed all his limbs,[23] thinking that there was

1 i.e. it would be madness to refuse promotion   2 foreigner   3 lower-class   4 sharpens (whetstones were used to sharpen knives and tools)   5 more flimsy than reputation   6 frequent a place   7 strike, kill   8 responsibility   9 snake   10 precious stones   11 Aegean sea   12 bitter, strong-smelling herb   13 by an asp   14 stained   15 weighed down with many thoughts   16 plot   17 There is no delay at 1.2.358–60.   18 reveal   19 concerned   20 malicious   21 i.e. show the gossips to be sycophants (cf. 'Tale-Porter', 4.4.270: see n.)   22 reputation   23 Cf. 1.2.453.

some treason wrought,[1] and that Franion did but shadow his craft[2] with these false colours. Wherefore he began to wax in choler,[3] and said that he doubted not Pandosto, sith[4] he was his friend and there had never as yet been any breach of amity.[5] He had not sought to invade his lands, to conspire with his enemies, to dissuade his subjects from their allegiance, but in word and thought he rested[6] his at all times. He knew not therefore any cause that should move Pandosto to seek his death, but suspected it to be a compacted knavery[7] of the Bohemians to bring the King and him at odds.

Franion, staying[8] him in the midst of his talk, told him that to dally[9] with princes was with[10] the swans to sing against their death,[11] and that if the Bohemians had intended any such secret mischief it might have been better brought to pass than by revealing the conspiracy. Therefore his majesty did ill to misconstrue of his good meaning, sith his intent was to hinder treason not to become a traitor; and to confirm his premises[12] if it please his majesty to flee into Sicilia for the safeguard of his life, he would go with him; and if then he found not such a practice to be pretended, let his imagined treachery be repaid with most monstrous torments.

Egistus, hearing the solemn protestation of Franion, began to consider that in love and kingdoms neither faith nor law is to be respected; doubting[13] that Pandosto thought by his death to destroy his men and with speedy war to invade Sicilia.[14] These and such doubts throughly[15] weighed, he gave great thanks to Franion, promising if he might with life return to Syracusa that he would create him a duke in Sicilia, craving his counsel how he might escape out of the country.[16] Franion, who having some small skill in navigation was well acquainted with the ports and havens and knew every danger in the sea, joining in counsel with the master of Egistus' navy, rigged all their ships, and setting them afloat let them lie at anchor, to be in the more readiness when time and wind should serve.[17]

Fortune, although blind,[18] yet by chance favouring this just cause, sent them within six days a good gale of wind, which Franion seeing fit for their purpose, to put Pandosto out of suspicion, the night before they should sail he went to him and promised that the next day he would put the device in practice, for he had got such a forcible[19] poison as the very smell thereof should procure sudden death. Pandosto was joyful to hear this good news, and thought every hour a day till he might be glutted with bloody revenge. But his suit had but ill success, for Egistus, fearing that delay might breed danger and willing that the grass should not be cut from under his feet, taking bag and baggage,[20] with the help of Franion conveyed himself and his

---

1 being prepared   2 conceal his cunning   3 grow angry   4 since   5 Polixenes is forewarned: 1.2.361–2, 365–72.   6 remained   7 conspiracy   8 interrupting   9 talk idly   10 like   11 i.e. show they would soon be dead (swans were said to sing before ('against') dying)   12 assertions ('premises' is perhaps a slip in 1592 for 'promises')   13 suspecting   14 Polixenes fears plotting against him back home, 1.2.11–14.   15 thoroughly   16 Cf. 1.2.443–5, 456–8.   17 Cf. 1.2.445–7.   18 Fortune was proverbially blind.   19 powerful (cf. 1.2.317–19)   20 See 1.2.205 and n.

men out of a postern gate[1] of the city so secretly and speedily that without any suspicion they got to the seashore, where, with many a bitter curse taking their leave of Bohemia, they went aboard. Weighing their anchors and hoisting sail, they passed as fast as wind and sea would permit towards Sicilia, Egistus being a joyful man that he had safely passed such treacherous perils.

But as they were quietly floating on the sea, so Pandosto and his citizens were in an uproar. For seeing that the Sicilians without taking their leave were fled away by night, the Bohemians feared some treason, and the King thought that without question his suspicion was true,[2] seeing his cupbearer had bewrayed the sum[3] of his secret pretence.[4] Whereupon he began to imagine that Franion and his wife Bellaria had conspired with Egistus,[5] and that the fervent affection she bore him was the only means of his secret departure, insomuch that, incensed with rage, he commanded that his wife should be carried to strait prison[6] until they heard further of his pleasure.[7]

The guard, unwilling to lay their hands on such a virtuous princess, and yet fearing the King's fury, went very sorrowfully to fulfil their charge.[8] Coming to the Queen's lodging, they found her playing with her young son Garinter.[9] Unto whom,[10] with tears doing the message, Bellaria astonished at such a hard censure[11] and finding her clear conscience a sure advocate to plead in her case, went to the prison most willingly,[12] where with sighs and tears[13] she passed away the time till she might come to her trial.

But Pandosto (whose reason was suppressed with rage and whose unbridled folly was incensed with fury), seeing Franion had bewrayed his secrets, and that Egistus might well be railed on but not revenged,[14] determined to wreak[15] all his wrath on poor Bellaria.[16] He therefore caused a general proclamation to be made through all his realm that the Queen and Egistus had, by the help of Franion, not only committed most incestuous adultery, but also had conspired the King's death. Whereupon the traitor Franion was fled away with Egistus, and Bellaria was most justly imprisoned.[17] This proclamation being once blazed through[18] the country, although the virtuous disposition of the Queen did half discredit the contents, yet the sudden and speedy passage of Egistus, and the secret departure of Franion, induced them, the circumstances throughly considered, to think that both the proclamation was true and the King greatly injured. Yet they pitied her case,[19] as sorrowful that so good a lady should be crossed with such adverse fortune.

But the King, whose restless rage would admit no pity, thought that, although he might sufficiently requite his wife's falsehood with the bitter plague of pinching[20] penury, yet his mind should never be glutted with

1 side gate (cf. 1.2.434–5, 460; 2.1.52–3)   2 Cf. 2.1.36–50.   3 revealed everything   4 plan   5 Cf. 2.1.87–95, 3.2.15–20.   6 i.e. very close confinement (cf. 2.2.7–16)   7 Cf. 2.1.103.   8 orders   9 Cf. 2.1.1–32.   10 i.e. with the guards   11 harsh judgement   12 Cf. 2.1.121–2.   13 Cf. 2.1.108–10, 118–21.   14 denounced but not paid back   15 inflict   16 Cf. 2.3.3–9.   17 Cf. 2.1.46–7, 3.2.12–20. 18 proclaimed throughout (cf. 3.1.15–16, 3.2.99–100)   19 Cf. 2.1.126–39.   20 See n. 10, p. 406.

revenge till he might have fit time and opportunity to repay the treachery of[1] Egistus with a fatal injury. But a curst cow hath oft times short horns, and a willing mind but a weak arm;[2] for Pandosto, although he felt that revenge was a spur to war, and that envy always proffereth steel,[3] yet he saw that Egistus was not only of great puissance[4] and prowess to withstand him, but had also many kings of his alliance[5] to aid him if need should serve, for he was[6] married to the Emperor's daughter of Russia.[7] These and the like considerations something daunted Pandosto his courage, so that he was content rather to put up[8] a manifest injury with peace than hunt after revenge with dishonour and loss; determining, since Egistus had escaped scot free, that Bellaria should pay for all[9] at an unreasonable price.

Remaining thus resolute in his determination, Bellaria, continuing still in prison, and hearing the contents of the proclamation, knowing that her mind was never touched with such affection,[10] nor that Egistus had ever offered her such discourtesy, would gladly have come to her answer,[11] that both she might have known her unjust accusers and cleared herself of that guiltless crime.

But Pandosto was so inflamed with rage and infected with jealousy as he would not vouchsafe to hear her nor admit any just excuse,[12] so that she was fain[13] to make a virtue of her need, and with patience to bear these heavy injuries. As thus she lay crossed with calamities (a great cause to increase her grief), she found herself quick with child;[14] which as soon as she felt stir in her body, she burst forth into bitter tears, exclaiming against fortune in these terms:

'Alas, Bellaria, how infortunate art thou, because fortunate! Better hadst thou been born a beggar than a prince. So shouldst thou have bridled Fortune with want,[15] where now she sporteth herself with thy plenty. Ah, happy life, where poor thoughts and mean desires live in secure content, not fearing Fortune because too low for Fortune! Thou seest now, Bellaria, that care is a companion to honour not to poverty, that high cedars are frushed with[16] tempests when low shrubs are not touched with the wind. Precious diamonds are cut with the file when despised pebbles lie safe in the sand. Delphos[17] is sought to by princes not beggars, and Fortune's altars smoke with kings' presents not with poor men's gifts. Happy are such, Bellaria, that curse Fortune for contempt not fear, and may wish they were, not sorrow they have been. Thou art a princess, Bellaria, and yet a prisoner, born to the one by descent, assigned to the other by despite,[18] accused without cause, and

---

1 'of' omitted 1592   2 i.e. no power to do what we want   3 draws a sword (i.e. seeks a fight)   4 military might   5 kinship by marriage (cf. 2.3.19–20)   6 'was' omitted 1592   7 Hermione is the Emperor's daughter (3.2.117).   8 put up with   9 Cf. 2.3.3–9.   10 Cf. 1.2.137–46 (see n.).   11 i.e. to a trial   12 i.e. to visit her (Leontes forbids Paulina to see Hermione or him, 2.2.7–8, 2.3.41–2)   13 obliged   14 pregnant   15 i.e. if she had been poor, Fortune would have had less power over her   16 smashed by   17 Mediterranean island with Apollo's oracle on it; see 2.1.183 and n.   18 evil feeling

therefore oughtest to die without care; for patience is a shield against Fortune and a guiltless mind yieldeth not to sorrow. Ah, but infamy galleth unto death,[1] and liveth after death. Report is plumed with Time's feathers,[2] and envy oftentimes soundeth Fame's trumpets. Thy suspected adultery shall fly in the air, and thy known virtues shall lie hid in the earth; one mole staineth a whole face, and what is once spotted with infamy can hardly be worn out with time. Die then, Bellaria, Bellaria, die! For if the gods should say thou art guiltless, yet envy would hear the gods but never believe the gods.[3] Ah, hapless wretch, cease these terms! Desperate thoughts are fit for them that fear shame, not for such as hope for credit. Pandosto hath darkened thy fame,[4] but shall never discredit thy virtues. Suspicion may enter a false action but proof shall never put in his plea. Care not then for envy, sith report hath a blister on her tongue;[5] and let sorrow bait[6] them which offend, not touch thee that are faultless. But alas, poor soul, how canst thou but sorrow? Thou art with child, and by him that instead of kind pity, pincheth[7] thee in cold prison.'

And with that, such gasping sighs so stopping her breath, that she could not utter moe[8] words but, wringing her hands and gushing forth streams of tears, she passed away the time with bitter complaints.[9] The gaoler, pitying these her heavy[10] passions, thinking that if the King knew she were with child he would somewhat appease his fury and release her from prison,[11] went in all haste and certified[12] Pandosto what the effect of Bellaria's complaint was; who no sooner heard the gaoler say she was with child but, as one possessed with a frenzy, he rose up in a rage, swearing that she and the bastard brat she was withal should die, if the gods themselves said no,[13] thinking assuredly by computation of time that Egistus and not he was father to the child.

This suspicious thought galled afresh this half-healed sore, insomuch as he could take no rest until he might mitigate his choler with a just revenge, which happened presently[14] after. For Bellaria was brought to bed of a fair and beautiful daughter, which no sooner Pandosto heard but he determined that both Bellaria and the young infant should be burnt with fire.[15]

His nobles, hearing of the King's cruel sentence, sought by persuasions to divert him from this bloody determination,[16] laying before his face the innocency of the child, and the virtuous disposition of his wife, how she had continually loved and honoured him so tenderly, that without due proof he could not nor ought not to appeach[17] her of that crime. And if she had faulted, yet it were more honourable to pardon with mercy than to punish

1 poisons one's life   2 i.e. reputations change over time   3 Cf. 3.2.137–8.   4 reputation   5 Cf. 2.2.32.   6 persecute (1592 has 'bite', a variant of 'bait')   7 torments   8 more   9 lamenting   10 sorrowful   11 Cf. Paulina's role, 2.2.36–41.   12 informed   13 Cf. 3.2.137–8.   14 immediately   15 Cf. 2.3.93–4, 131–2.   16 Cf. 2.3.145–51.   17 accuse

with extremity, and more kingly to be commended of[1]pity than accused of rigour.[2] And as for the child, if he should punish it for the mother's offence, it were to strive against nature and justice, and that unnatural actions do more offend the gods than men; how causeless cruelty nor innocent blood[3] never scapes[4] without revenge.

These and suchlike reasons could not appease his rage, but he rested resolute in this, that Bellaria being an adulteress, the child was a bastard, and he would not suffer[5] that such an infamous brat should call him father. Yet at last, seeing his noblemen were importunate upon him,[6] he was content to spare the child's life, and yet to put it to a worser death.[7] For he found out this device,[8] that seeing (as he thought) it came by Fortune, so he would commit it to the charge of Fortune; and therefore he caused a little cock-boat[9] to be provided, wherein he meant to put the babe and then send it to the mercy of the seas and the Destinies.[10]

From this his peers in no wise could persuade him, but that he sent presently two of his guard to fetch the child; who being come to the prison, and with weeping tears recounting their master's message, Bellaria no sooner heard the rigorous resolution of her merciless husband, but she fell down in a swound,[11] so that all thought she had been dead,[12] yet at last being come to herself, she cried and screeched out in this wise:

'Alas, sweet infortunate babe, scarce born before envied by Fortune. Would the day of thy birth had been the term of thy life, then shouldst thou have made an end to care, and prevented[13] thy father's rigour. Thy faults cannot yet deserve such hateful revenge, thy days are too short for so sharp a doom,[14] but thy untimely death must pay thy mother's debts, and her guiltless crime must be thy ghastly curse. And shalt thou, sweet babe, be committed to Fortune when thou art already spited by Fortune? Shall the seas be thy harbour, and the hard boat thy cradle? Shall thy tender mouth, instead of sweet kisses, be nipped with bitter storms? Shalt thou have the whistling winds for thy lullaby, and the salt sea foam instead of sweet milk?[15] Alas, what destinies would assign such hard hap?[16]

'What father would be so cruel? Or what gods will not revenge such rigour? Let me kiss thy lips, sweet infant, and wet thy tender cheeks with my tears, and put this chain about thy little neck, that, if Fortune save thee, it may help to succour thee. Thus, since thou must go to surge in the gastful[17] seas, with a sorrowful kiss I bid thee farewell, and I pray the gods thou mayst fare well.'

Such and so great was her grief that her vital spirits[18] being suppressed with sorrow, she fell down in a trance, having her senses so sotted[19] with care

1 for   2 unmerciful severity (cf. 3.2.109–12)   3 i.e. the shedding of innocent blood   4 escapes   5 allow   6 kept begging him   7 Cf. 2.3.155, 182–3.   8 devised this plan   9 rowing-boat   10 Cf. 2.3.172–81.   11 swoon   12 Cf. 3.2.145–6.   13 escaped   14 harsh a sentence   15 Cf. 3.3.53–4, 3.2.96–9.   16 fate   17 terrible   18 i.e. life force   19 overwhelmed

that, after she was revived, yet she lost her memory and lay for a great time without moving, as one in a trance. The guard left her in this perplexity and carried the child to the King who, quite[1] devoid of pity, commanded that without delay it should be put in the boat, having neither sail nor rudder to guide it, and so to be carried into the midst of the sea and there left to the wind and wave as the Destinies please to appoint. The very shipmen, seeing the sweet countenance of the young babe, began to accuse the King of rigour, and to pity the child's hard fortune, but fear constrained them to that which their nature did abhor, so that they placed it in one of the ends of the boat, and with a few green boughs made a homely[2] cabin to shroud it as they could from wind and weather. Having thus trimmed[3] the boat they tied it to a ship, and so haled[4] it into the main sea, and then cut in sunder the cord; which they had no sooner done but there arose a mighty tempest which tossed the little boat so vehemently in the waves that the shipmen thought it could not continue long without sinking, yea the storm grew so great that with much labour and peril they got to the shore.

But leaving the child to her fortunes, again to Pandosto who, not yet glutted with sufficient revenge, devised which way he should best increase his wife's calamity. But first assembling his nobles and counsellors, he called her for the more reproach into open court, where it was objected against her that she had committed adultery with Egistus and conspired with Franion to poison Pandosto her husband, but, their pretence being partly spied, she counselled them to fly away by night for their better safety.[5] Bellaria, who standing like a prisoner at the bar, feeling in herself a clear conscience to withstand her false accusers, seeing that no less than death could pacify her husband's wrath, waxed[6] bold and desired that she might have law and justice, for mercy she neither craved nor hoped for, and that those perjured wretches which had falsely accused her to the King might be brought before her face to give in evidence.

But Pandosto, whose rage and jealousy was such as no reason nor equity could appease, told her that, for her accusers, they were of such credit as their words were sufficient witness, and that the sudden and secret flight of Egistus and Franion confirmed that which they had confessed; and as for her, it was her part to deny such a monstrous crime and to be impudent in forswearing the fact,[7] since she had passed all shame in committing the fault;[8] but her stale[9] countenance should stand for no coin,[10] for as the bastard which she bore was served,[11] so she should with some cruel death be requited. Bellaria, no whit dismayed with this rough reply, told her husband Pandosto that he spake upon choler and not conscience; for her virtuous life had been ever such as no spot of suspicion could ever stain.[12] And if she had

---

1 1588 from here onwards (see n. 8, p. 409) 2 simple 3 fitted out 4 then dragged 5 Cf. 3.2.12–20. 6 grew 7 denying what she had done 8 Cf. 3.2.53–6. 9 deceitful (a stale was a decoy bird) 10 wouldn't dupe him (i.e. trying to pass off fake coins as real) 11 dealt with 12 Cf. 3.2.32–4.

borne a friendly countenance to Egistus, it was in respect he was his friend, and not for any lusting affection. Therefore, if she were condemned without any further proof, it was rigour and not law.[1]

The noblemen which sat in judgement said that Bellaria spake reason, and entreated the King that the accusers might be openly examined and sworn, and if then the evidence were such as the jury might find her guilty (for seeing she was a prince, she ought to be tried by her peers), then let her have such punishment as the extremity of the law will assign to such malefactors. The King presently made answer that in this case he might and would dispense with the law, and that, the jury being once panelled,[2] they should take his word for sufficient evidence, otherwise he would make the proudest of them repent it. The noblemen, seeing the King in choler, were all whist;[3] but Bellaria, whose life then hung in the balance, fearing more perpetual infamy than momentary death,[4] told the King, if his fury might stand for a law, that it were vain to have the jury yield their verdict, and therefore she fell down upon her knees and desired the King that for the love he bore to his young son Garinter, whom she brought into the world, that he would grant her a request, which was this: that it would please his majesty to send six of his noblemen whom he best trusted to the isle of Delphos, there to enquire of the oracle of Apollo[5] whether she had committed adultery with Egistus, or conspired to poison with Franion; and if the god Apollo, who by his divine essence knew all secrets, gave answer that she was guilty, she were content to suffer any torment, were it never so terrible. The request was so reasonable[6] that Pandosto could not for shame deny it, unless he would be counted of all his subjects more wilful than wise. He therefore agreed that with as much speed as might be, there should be certain ambassadors dispatched to the isle of Delphos; and in the mean season[7] he[8] commanded that his wife should be kept in close[9] prison.

Bellaria, having obtained this grant, was now more careful[10] for her little babe that floated on the seas than sorrowful for her own mishap. For of that she doubted; of herself she was assured, knowing if Apollo should give oracle according to the thoughts of the heart, yet the sentence should go on her side, such was the clearness of her mind in this case. But Pandosto, whose suspicious head still remained in one song, chose out six of his nobility, whom he knew were scarce indifferent men in the Queen's behalf, and, providing all things fit for their journey, sent them to Delphos. They, willing to fulfil the King's command and desirous to see the situation and custom of the island, dispatched their affairs with as much speed as might be, and embarked themselves to this voyage, which (the wind and weather serving fit for their purpose) was soon ended. For within three weeks they arrived at

---

1 Cf. 3.2.109–12.   2 sworn in   3 silent   4 Cf. 3.2.107–9.   5 It is Leontes' idea to send emissaries to Delphos (2.1.180–4).   6 Cf. 3.2.114–15.   7 meantime   8 'be' 1588   9 secret   10 anxious, troubled

Delphos,[1] where they were no sooner set on land but with great devotion they went to the temple of Apollo, and there offering sacrifice to the god and gifts to the priest, as the custom was, they humbly craved an answer of their demand. They had not long kneeled at the altar, but Apollo with a loud voice[2] said 'Bohemians, what you find behind the altar, take, and depart.' They forthwith obeying the oracle found a scroll of parchment,[3] wherein was written these words in letters of gold:

The Oracle

Suspicion is no proof; jealousy is an unequal judge; Bellaria is chaste; Egistus blameless; Franion a true subject; Pandosto treacherous; his babe an innocent; and the King shall live without an heir if that which is lost be not found.[4]

As soon as they had taken out this scroll, the priest of the god commanded them that they should not presume to read it before they came in the presence of Pandosto,[5] unless they would incur the displeasure of Apollo. The Bohemian lords carefully obeying his command, taking their leave of the priest, with great reverence departed out of the temple and went to their ships and, as soon as wind would permit them, sailed toward Bohemia; whither in short time they safely arrived and with great triumph issuing out of their ships went to the King's palace, whom they found in his chamber accompanied with other noblemen. Pandosto no sooner saw them but with a merry countenance he welcomed them home, asking what news. They told his majesty that they had received an answer of the god written in a scroll, but with this charge: that they should not read the contents before they came in the presence of the King, and with that they delivered him the parchment. But his noblemen entreated him that sith therein was contained either the safety of his wife's life and honesty, or her death and perpetual infamy, that he would have his nobles and commons assembled in the judgement hall, where the Queen, brought in as prisoner, should hear the contents. If she were found guilty by the oracle of the god, then all should have cause to think his rigour proceeded of due desert. If her grace were found faultless then she should be cleared before all, sith she had been accused openly.[6] This pleased the King so, that he appointed the day and assembled all his lords and commons, and caused the Queen to be brought in before the judgement seat,[7] commanding that the indictment should be read wherein she was accused of adultery with Egistus, and of conspiracy with Franion. Bellaria, hearing the contents, was no whit astonished,[8] but made this cheerful answer:[9]

'If the divine powers be privy to human actions (as no doubt they are), I hope my patience shall make Fortune blush, and my unspotted life shall stain

1 Cf. 2.3.196–7. 2 Cf. 3.1.8–10. 3 Cf. 3.1.125. 4 Cf. 3.2.130–3. 5 Cf. 3.1.18–21, 3.2.122–8. 6 publicly (cf. 2.1.96–100, 3.2.5–6) 7 judge's bench 8 not dismayed at all 9 Cf. Hermione's speech, 3.2.27–33, 44–7, 60–4, 72–5, 113.

spiteful[1] discredit. For although lying report hath sought to appeach mine honour, and suspicion hath intended to soil my credit with infamy, yet where virtue keepeth the fort, report and suspicion may assail but never sack.[2] How I have led my life before Egistus' coming, I appeal, Pandosto, to the gods and to thy conscience. What hath passed betwixt him and me the gods only know, and I hope will presently reveal. That I loved Egistus I cannot deny; that I honoured him I shame not to confess; to the one I was forced by his virtues, to the other for his dignities. But as touching lascivious lust, I say Egistus is honest, and hope myself to be found without spot. For Franion, I can neither accuse him nor excuse him, for I was not privy to his departure, and that this is true which I have here rehearsed, I refer myself to the divine oracle.'

Bellaria had no sooner said, but the King commanded that one of his dukes should read the contents of the scroll, which after the commons had heard, they gave a great shout, rejoicing and clapping their hands that the Queen was clear of that false accusation. But the King, whose conscience was a witness against him of his witless[3] fury and false suspected jealousy, was so ashamed of his rash folly[4] that he entreated his nobles to persuade Bellaria to forgive and forget these injuries; promising not only to show himself a loyal and loving husband, but also to reconcile himself to Egistus and Franion, revealing then before them all the cause of their secret flight, and how treacherously he thought to have practised his death, if the good mind of his cupbearer had not prevented his purpose.[5] As thus he was relating the whole matter, there was word brought him that his young son Garinter was suddenly dead, which news so soon as Bellaria heard, surcharged[6] before with extreme joy and now suppressed with heavy[7] sorrow, her vital spirits were so stopped that she fell down presently dead, and could be never revived.[8]

This sudden sight so appalled the King's senses that he sank from his seat in a swound so as he was fain to be[9] carried by his nobles to his palace, where he lay by the space of three days without speech. His commons were as men in despair, so diversely distressed. There was nothing but mourning and lamentation to be heard throughout all Bohemia: their young prince dead, their virtuous queen bereaved of her life, and their King and sovereign in great hazard. This tragical discourse of Fortune so daunted them as they went like shadows[10] not men. Yet somewhat to comfort their heavy hearts, they heard that Pandosto was come to himself and had recovered his speech, who as in a fury brayed[11] out these bitter speeches:

'O miserable Pandosto, what surer witness than conscience? What thoughts more sour than suspicion? What plague more bad than jealousy?

---

1 'spightfully' 1588   2 take and destroy   3 irrational   4 Cf. 3.2.135–8.   5 Cf. 3.2.152–67.   6 over-whelmed   7 grievous   8 Cf. 3.2.141–6.   9 in a swoon so that he had to be   10 ghosts   11 cried

Unnatural actions offend the gods more than men, and causeless cruelty never scapes without revenge. I have committed such a bloody fact,[1] as repent I may, but recall[2] I cannot. Ah jealousy, a hell to the mind, and a horror to the conscience, suppressing reason and inciting rage: a worse passion than frenzy, a greater plague than madness. Are the gods just? Then let them revenge such brutish cruelty. My innocent babe I have drowned in the seas; my loving wife I have slain with slanderous suspicion; my trusty friend I have sought to betray, and yet the gods are slack to plague such offences. Ah, unjust Apollo, Pandosto is the man that hath committed the fault, why should Garinter, silly[3] child, abide the pain? Well, sith the gods mean to prolong my days to increase my dolour,[4] I will offer my guilty blood a sacrifice to those sackless[5] souls whose lives are lost by my rigorous folly.'

And with that he reached at a rapier to have murdered himself, but his peers, being present, stayed him from such a bloody act, persuading him to think that the commonwealth consisted on his safety, and that those sheep could not but perish that wanted a shepherd; wishing that if he would not live for himself, yet he should have care of his subjects, and to put such fancies out of his mind, sith in sores past help, salves[6] do not heal but hurt, and in things past cure, care is a corrosive.[7] With these and suchlike persuasions the King was overcome, and began somewhat to quiet his mind, so that as soon as he could go abroad[8] he caused his wife to be embalmed and wrapped in lead with her young son Garinter, erecting a rich and famous sepulchre wherein he entombed them both, making such solemn obsequies[9] at her funeral as all Bohemia might perceive he did greatly repent him of his forepassed folly, causing this epitaph to be engraven on her tomb in letters of gold:[10]

THE EPITAPH
Here lies entombed Bellaria fair,
Falsely accused to be unchaste;
Cleared by Apollo's sacred doom,[11]
Yet slain by jealousy at last.
Whate'er thou be that passest by,
Curse him that caused this queen to die.

This epitaph being engraven, Pandosto would once a day repair[12] to the tomb, and there with watery plaints[13] bewail his misfortune,[14] coveting no other companion but sorrow, nor no other harmony but repentance. But leaving him to his dolorous passions, at last let us come to show the tragical discourse of the young infant.

Who, being tossed with wind and wave, floated two whole days without succour, ready at every puff to be drowned in the sea, till at last the tempest

1 deed 2 undo 3 innocent 4 grief 5 guiltless 6 ointments 7 damaging 8 i.e. was well enough to go out of doors 9 rites 10 Cf. 3.2.233–5. 11 judgement 12 go 13 tearful lamentations 14 Cf. 3.2.229–37.

ceased and the little boat was driven with the tide into the coast of Sicilia, where, sticking upon the sands, it rested. Fortune, minding to be wanton,[1] willing to show that as she hath wrinkles on her brows, so she hath dimples in her checks, thought after so many sour looks to lend a feigned smile, and after a puffing[2] storm to bring a pretty calm, she began thus to dally.[3] It fortuned[4] a poor mercenary shepherd that dwelled in Sicilia, who got his living by other men's flocks, missed one of his sheep and, thinking it had strayed into the covert[5] that was hard by, sought very diligently to find that which he could not see, fearing either that the wolves or eagles had undone him (for he was so poor as a sheep was half his substance), wandered down toward the sea cliffs to see if perchance the sheep was browsing on the sea-ivy,[6] whereon they greatly do feed; but not finding her there, as he was ready to return to his flock he heard a child cry; but knowing there was no house near, he thought he had mistaken the sound and that it was the bleating of his sheep. Wherefore, looking more narrowly,[7] as he cast his eye to the sea he spied a little boat from whence, as he attentively listened, he might hear the cry to come. Standing a good while in a maze[8] at last he went to the shore and, wading to the boat, as he looked in he saw the little babe lying all alone, ready to die for hunger and cold, wrapped in a mantle of scarlet, richly embroidered with gold, and having a chain about the neck.[9]

The shepherd (who before had never seen so fair a babe nor so rich jewels) thought assuredly that it was some little god, and began with great devotion to knock on[10] his breast. The babe, who writhed with the head to seek for the pap,[11] began again to cry afresh, whereby the poor man knew that it was a child which by some sinister means was driven thither by distress of[12]weather, marvelling how such a silly infant, which by the mantle and the chain could not be but born of noble parentage,[13] should be so hardly crossed[14] with deadly mishap. The poor shepherd, perplexed thus with divers thoughts, took pity of the child and determined with himself to carry it to the King, that there it might be brought up according to the worthiness of birth, for his ability[15] could not afford to foster it, though his good mind was willing to further it.

Taking therefore the child in his arms, as he folded the mantle together the better to defend it from cold there fell down at his foot a very fair and rich purse, wherein he found a great sum of gold;[16]which sight so revived the shepherd's spirits as he was greatly ravished[17] with joy and daunted with fear: joyful to see such a sum in his power and fearful, if it should be known, that it might breed his further danger.[18] Necessity wished him at the least to retain the gold, though he would not keep the child; the simplicity of his

---

1 capricious   2 blustering   3 play her game   4 happened that   5 thicket   6 seaweed; cf. 3.3.66–7 (see n.).   7 closely   8 in a state of bewilderment   9 Cf. 5.2.32–3.   10 beat   11 twisted her head about looking for her mother's breast   12 terrible   13 Cf. 3.3.112.   14 thwarted   15 means   16 Cf. 3.3.113–19.   17 carried away   18 Cf. 3.3.121–4.

conscience scared him from such a deceitful bribery. Thus was the poor man perplexed with a doubtful dilemma, until at last the covetousness of the coin[1] overcame him, for what will not the greedy desire of gold cause a man to do? So that he was resolved in himself to foster the child, and with the sum to relieve his want. Resting thus resolute in this point, he left seeking of his sheep and as covertly and secretly as he could went by a by-way to his house, lest any of his neighbours should perceive his carriage.[2] As soon as he was got home, entering in at the door, the child began to cry, which his wife hearing, and seeing her husband with a young babe in arms, began to be somewhat jealous, yet marvelling that her husband should be so wanton abroad[3] sith he was so quiet at home. But as women are naturally given to believe the worst, so his wife, thinking it was some bastard, began to crow against her goodman,[4] and taking up a cudgel (for the most master went breechless)[5] swore solemnly that she would make clubs trumps[6] if he brought any bastard brat within her doors. The goodman, seeing his wife in her majesty with her mace in her hand, thought it was time to bow for fear of blows, and desired her to be quiet, for there was none such matter; but if she could hold her peace, they were made for ever.[7] And with that he told her the whole matter: how he had found the child in a little boat, without any succour, wrapped in that costly mantle and having that rich chain about the neck. But at last, when he showed her the purse full of gold, she began to simper something sweetly and, taking her husband about the neck, kissed him after her homely fashion, saying that she hoped God had seen their want and now meant to relieve their poverty and, seeing they could get no[8] children, had sent them this little babe to be their heir. 'Take heed in any case,' quoth the shepherd, 'that you be secret[9] and blab it not out when you meet with your gossips,[10] for if you do, we are like not only to lose the gold and jewels but our other goods and lives.' 'Tush,' quoth his wife, 'profit is a good hatch before the door.[11] Fear not, I have other things to talk of than of this. But, I pray you, let us lay up the money surely,[12] and the jewels, lest by any mishap it be spied.'

After that they had set all things in order, the shepherd went to his sheep with a merry note,[13] and the good wife learned to sing lullaby at home with her young babe, wrapping it in a homely blanket instead of a rich mantle, nourishing it so cleanly[14] and carefully as it began to be a jolly girl, insomuch that they began both of them to be very fond of it, seeing, as it waxed in age,[15] so it increased in beauty. The shepherd every night at his coming home would sing and dance it on his knee and prattle, that in a short time it

1 desire for the money   2 behaviour   3 adulterous when not at home   4 shout at her husband 5 the master in their marriage was the one not wearing breeches (i.e. the wife)   6 i.e. she would win the day by beating him (alluding to trumps in cards)   7 Cf. 3.3.117 (see n.).   8 couldn't have   9 Cf. 3.3.120–3.   10 gossipy friends   11 i.e. incentive to keep quiet (a hatch was a gate) 12 securely   13 tune (cf. 1.2.2)   14 properly   15 grew older

began to speak and call him 'Dad,' and her 'Mam'. At last when it grew to ripe years, that it was about seven years old, the shepherd left keeping of other men's sheep and with the money he found in the purse he bought him the lease of a pretty[1] farm and got a small flock of sheep which, when Fawnia (for so they named the child) came to the age of ten years, he set her to keep, and she with such diligence performed her charge as the sheep prospered marvellously under her hand. Fawnia thought Porrus had been her father and Mopsa her mother (for so was the shepherd and his wife called), honoured and obeyed them with such reverence that all the neighbours praised the dutiful obedience of the child. Porrus grew in a short time to be a man of some wealth and credit;[2] for Fortune so favoured him in having no charge but Fawnia that he began to purchase land, intending after his death to give it to his daughter, so that divers rich farmers' sons came as wooers to his house; for Fawnia was something cleanly attired,[3] being of such singular beauty and excellent wit that whoso saw her would have thought she had been some heavenly nymph, and not a mortal creature. Insomuch that, when she came to the age of sixteen years,[4] she so increased with exquisite perfection both of body and mind as her natural disposition did bewray that she was born of some high parentage;[5] but the people, thinking she was daughter to the shepherd Porrus, rested only amazed at her beauty and wit. Yea, she won such favour and commendations in every man's eye as her beauty was not only praised in the country but also spoken of in the court.[6] Yet such was her submiss[7] modesty that, although her praise daily increased, her mind was no whit puffed up with pride but humbled herself as became a country maid and the daughter of a poor shepherd. Every day she went forth with her sheep to the field, keeping them with such care and diligence, as all men thought she was very painful,[8] defending her face from the heat of the sun with no other veil but with a garland made of boughs and flowers, which attire became her so gallantly[9] as she seemed to be the goddess Flora herself[10] for beauty.

Fortune, who all this while had showed a friendly face, began now to turn her back and to show a louring countenance,[11] intending as she had given Fawnia a slender check,[12] so she would give her a harder mate;[13] to bring which to pass, she laid her train on this wise.[14] Egistus had but one only son called Dorastus, about the age of twenty years, a prince so decked and adorned with the gifts of nature, so fraught with beauty and virtuous qualities, as not only his father joyed to have so good a son, and all his commons rejoiced that God had lent them such a noble prince to succeed in the kingdom.[15] Egistus, placing all his joy in the perfection of his son, seeing that he

---

1 substantial   2 Cf. 4.2.38–40.   3 neatly dressed   4 Cf. 4.1.6.   5 Cf. 4.4.156–9.   6 Cf. 4.2.41–4.
7 humble   8 took great pains   9 wonderfully   10 Roman goddess of flowers and Spring; cf.
4.4.1–3.   11 sour face   12 small setback (alluding to check in chess)   13 obstacle (checkmate)
14 set her trap like this   15 Cf. 4.4.7–8, and praise of Mamillius at 1.1.32–41.

was now marriageable, sent ambassadors to the King of Denmark to entreat a marriage between him and his daughter, who, willingly consenting, made answer that the next spring, if it please Egistus with his son to come into Denmark, he doubted not but they should agree upon reasonable conditions. Egistus, resting satisfied with this friendly answer, thought convenient in the meantime to break[1] with his son. Finding therefore on a day fit opportunity, he spake to him in these fatherly terms.

'Dorastus, thy youth warneth me to prevent the worst, and mine age to provide the best. Opportunities neglected are signs of folly; actions measured by time are seldom bitten with repentance. Thou art young, and I old. Age hath taught me that which thy youth cannot yet conceive. I therefore will counsel thee as a father, hoping thou wilt obey as a child. Thou seest my white hairs are blossoms for the grave, and thy fresh colour fruit for time and fortune, so that it behoveth me to think how to die, and for thee to care how to live. My crown I must leave by death, and thou enjoy my kingdom by succession, wherein I hope thy virtue and prowess shall be such as, though my subjects want my person, yet they shall see in thee my perfection. That nothing either may fail to satisfy thy mind or increase thy dignities; the only care I have is to see thee well married before I die and thou become old.'

Dorastus (who from his infancy, delighted rather to die with Mars in the field than to dally with Venus in the chamber),[2] fearing to displease his father, and yet not willing to be wed, made him this reverent answer:

'Sir, there is no greater bond than duty nor no straiter law than nature. Disobedience in youth is often galled with despite[3] in age. The command of the father ought to be a constraint to the child. So parents' wills are laws, so they pass not all laws. May it please your grace therefore to appoint whom I shall love, rather than by denial I should be appeached of disobedience. I rest content to love, though it be the only thing I hate.'

Egistus, hearing his son to fly so far from the mark, began to be somewhat choleric, and therefore made him his hasty answer:

'What, Dorastus, canst thou not love? Cometh this cynical passion of prone desires or peevish forwardness?[4] What, dost thou think thyself too good for all, or none good enough for thee? I tell thee, Dorastus, there is nothing sweeter than youth, nor swifter decreasing while it is increasing. Time passed with folly may be repented, but not recalled. If thou marry in age,[5] thy wife's fresh colours[6] will breed in thee dead thoughts and suspicion, and thy white hairs her loathsomeness and sorrow. For Venus' affections are not fed with kingdoms or treasures, but with youthful conceits[7] and sweet amours. Vulcan was allotted to shake the tree, but Mars allowed to reap the fruit.[8] Yield, Dorastus, to thy father's persuasions, which may prevent

1 speak about it   2 i.e. would rather fight than make love (Mars was god of war, Venus goddess of love)   3 becomes bitter contempt   4 from lack of desire or foolish obstinacy   5 when you are old   6 young looks   7 thoughts   8 Vulcan was Venus' husband but her lover was Mars.

thy perils. I have chosen thee a wife, fair by nature, royal by birth, by virtues famous, learned by education, and rich by possessions, so that it is hard to judge whether her bounty or fortune, her beauty or virtue, be of greater force. I mean, Dorastus, Euphania, daughter and heir to the King of Denmark.'

Egistus pausing here a while, looking when his son should make him answer, and seeing that he stood still as one in a trance, he shook him up thus sharply:

'Well, Dorastus, take heed; the tree alpya[1] wasteth not with fire, but withereth with the dew. That which love nourisheth not, perisheth with hate. If thou like Euphania, thou breedest my content, and in loving her thou shalt have my love; otherwise –.' And with that he flung from his son in a rage, leaving him a sorrowful man, in that he had by denial displeased his father, and half angry with himself that he could not yield to that passion whereto both reason and his father persuaded him. But see how Fortune is plumed with Time's feathers,[2] and how she can minister[3] strange causes to breed strange effects.

It happened not long after this that there was a meeting of all the farmers' daughters in Sicilia, whither Fawnia was also bidden as the mistress of the feast,[4] who having attired herself in her best garments[5] went among the rest of her companions to the merry meeting, there spending the day in such homely pastimes as shepherds use.[6] As the evening grew on and their sports ceased, each taking their leave at other, Fawnia, desiring one of her companions to bear her company, went home by the flock to see if they were well folded;[7] and as they returned, it fortuned that Dorastus (who all that day had been hawking,[8] and killed store of[9] game) encountered by the way these two maids, and casting his eye suddenly on Fawnia he was half afraid, fearing that with Actaeon he had seen Diana;[10] for he thought such exquisite perfection could not be found in any mortal creature. As thus he stood in a maze, one of his pages told him that the maid with the garland on her head was Fawnia, the fair shepherd whose beauty was so much talked of in the court.[11] Dorastus, desirous to see if nature had adorned her mind with any inward qualities as she had decked her body with outward shape, began to question with her whose daughter she was, of what age, and how she had been trained up;[12] who answered him with such modest reverence and sharpness of wit that Dorastus thought her outward beauty was but a counterfeit to darken her inward qualities, wondering how so courtly behaviour could be found in so simple a cottage,[13] and cursing Fortune that had shadowed wit and beauty with such hard fortune. As thus

1 not identified   2 i.e. uses Time to accomplish things   3 supply   4 Cf. 4.3.39–40, 4.4.68.
5 See pp. 74–5.   6 practice (cf. 4.4.10–12); are used to   7 enclosed in a sheepfold   8 Cf. 4.4.14–16.
9 a good deal of   10 The goddess Diana turned Actaeon into a stag when he saw her bathing
naked.   11 Cf. 4.2.41–4.   12 brought up   13 Cf. 4.4.583–4.

he held her a long while with chat, Beauty, seeing him at discovert,[1] thought not to lose the vantage,[2] but struck him so deeply with an envenomed shaft as he wholly lost his liberty and became a slave to love, which before contemned[3] love; glad now to gaze on a poor shepherd, who before refused the offer of a rich princess; for the perfection of Fawnia had so fired his fancy as he felt his mind greatly changed and his affections altered, cursing Love that had wrought such a change, and blaming the baseness of his mind that would make such a choice. But thinking these were but passionate toys that might be thrust out at pleasure,[4] to avoid the siren that enchanted him[5] he put spurs to his horse and bade this fair shepherd farewell.

Fawnia, who all this while had marked[6] the princely gesture of Dorastus, seeing his face so well featured and each limb so perfectly framed,[7] began greatly to praise his perfection, commending him so long till she found herself faulty, and perceived that if she waded but a little further she might slip over her shoes.[8] She therefore, seeking to quench that fire which never was put out, went home and feigning herself not well at ease, got her to bed, where, casting a thousand thoughts in her head, she could take no rest; for if she waked, she began to call to mind his beauty, and thinking to beguile such thoughts with sleep, she then dreamed of his perfection. Pestered thus with these unacquainted[9] passions, she passed the night as she could in short slumbers.

Dorastus, who all this while rode with a flea in his ear,[10] could not by any means forget the sweet favour of Fawnia, but rested[11] so bewitched with her wit and beauty as he could take no rest. He felt fancy to give the assault,[12] and his wounded mind ready to yield as vanquished. Yet he began with divers considerations to suppress this frantic affection, calling to mind that Fawnia was a shepherd, one not worthy to be looked at of a prince, much less to be loved of such a potentate; thinking what a discredit it were to himself and what a grief it would be to his father; blaming Fortune and accusing his own folly that should be so fond[13] as but once to cast a glance at such a country slut.[14] As thus he was raging against himself, Love (fearing if she dallied long to lose her champion)[15] stepped more nigh and gave him such a fresh wound as it pierced him at the heart, that he was fain to yield maugre his face,[16] and to forsake the company and get him to his chamber, where being solemnly set,[17] he burst into these passionate terms:

'Ah, Dorastus, art thou alone? No, not alone while thou art tried[18] with these unacquainted passions. Yield to fancy thou canst not by thy father's

---

1 off guard   2 advantage   3 scorned   4 silly feelings that he could rid himself of easily
5 Sirens lured sailors to their deaths by singing.   6 observed   7 formed   8 get in over her head
(cf. 1.2.185)   9 unfamiliar   10 i.e. was very troubled   11 remained   12 desire's onslaught
13 foolish   14 lower-class girl   15 i.e. if she delayed she might lose control over Dorastus
16 despite his boldness   17 sitting down unhappy   18 'tired' 1588

counsel, but in a frenzy thou art by just destinies. Thy father were content if thou couldst love, and thou therefore discontent because thou dost love. O, divine Love, feared of men because honoured of the gods; not to be suppressed by wisdom, because not to be comprehended by reason; without law, and therefore above all law. How now, Dorastus, why dost thou blaze[1] that with praises which thou hast cause to blaspheme with curses? Yet why should they curse love that are in love? Blush, Dorastus, at thy fortune, thy choice, thy love; thy thoughts cannot be uttered without shame, nor thy affections without discredit. Ah, Fawnia, sweet Fawnia, thy beauty, Fawnia! Shamest not thou, Dorastus, to name one unfit for thy birth, thy dignities, thy kingdoms? Die, Dorastus, Dorastus, die! Better hadst thou perish with high desires than live in base thoughts. Yea, but beauty must be obeyed because it is beauty; yet framed of the gods to feed the eye, not to fetter the heart. Ah, but he that striveth against Love shooteth with them of Scyrum against the wind,[2] and with the cockatrice[3] pecketh against the steel. I will therefore obey, because I must obey. Fawnia, yea Fawnia, shall be my fortune, in spite of Fortune. The gods above disdain not to love women beneath. Phoebus liked Sibylla, Jupiter Io,[4] and why not I then Fawnia? One something inferior to these in birth, but far superior to them in beauty; born to be a shepherd but worthy to be a goddess. Ah, Dorastus, wilt thou so forget thyself as to suffer affection to suppress wisdom and love to violate thine honour? How sour will thy choice be to thy father, sorrowful to thy subjects, to thy friends a grief, most gladsome to thy foes! Subdue then thy affections, and cease to love her whom thou couldst not love unless blinded with too much love. Tush, I talk to the wind, and in seeking to prevent the causes I further the effects. I will yet praise Fawnia, honour, yea, and love Fawnia, and at this day follow content, not counsel. Do, Dorastus, thou canst but repent.' And with that his page came into the chamber, whereupon he ceased from his complaints, hoping that time would wear out that which Fortune had wrought. As thus he was pained, so poor Fawnia was diversely perplexed; for the next morning, getting up very early, she went to her sheep, thinking with hard labours to pass away her new-conceived amours,[5] beginning very busily to drive them to the field and then to shift the folds.[6] At last, wearied with toil, she sat her down, where, poor soul, she was more tried with fond affections; for Love began to assault her insomuch that, as she sat upon the side of a hill, she began to accuse her own folly in these terms:

'Infortunate Fawnia, and therefore infortunate because Fawnia, thy shepherd's hook showeth thy poor state,[7] thy proud desires an aspiring mind. The one declareth thy want, the other thy pride. No bastard[8] hawk must soar so high as the hobby,[9] no fowl gaze against the sun but the eagle.

1 proclaim   2 i.e. pointlessly (the allusion to Scyrum is untraced)   3 legendary creature said to kill with a glance (cf. 'basilisk', 1.2.384: see n.)   4 Phoebus (Apollo) and Jupiter had sex with mortals   5 feelings of love   6 set up the sheepfolds   7 condition   8 common   9 kind of falcon

Actions wrought against nature reap despite,[1] and thoughts above Fortune, disdain. Fawnia, thou art a shepherd, daughter to poor Porrus. If thou rest content with this, thou art like to stand; if thou climb, thou art sure to fall. The herb aneta,[2] growing higher than six inches, becometh a weed. Nilus flowing more than twelve cubits procureth a dearth.[3] Daring affections that pass measure are cut short by time or Fortune. Suppress then, Fawnia, those thoughts which thou mayest shame to express. But ah, Fawnia, Love is a lord who will command by power and constrain by force. Dorastus, ah Dorastus is the man I love, the worse is thy hap, and the less cause hast thou to hope. Will eagles catch at flies, will cedars stoop to brambles, or mighty princes look at such homely trulls?[4] No, no, think this: Dorastus' disdain is greater than thy desire. He is a prince respecting his honour, thou a beggar's brat forgetting thy calling. Cease then not only to say, but to think to love Dorastus, and dissemble thy love, Fawnia; for better it were to die with grief than to live with shame. Yet in despite of love I will sigh, to see if I can sigh out love.'

Fawnia, somewhat appeasing her griefs with these pithy persuasions, began after her wonted[5] manner to walk about her sheep, and to keep them from straying into the corn, suppressing her affection with the due consideration of her base estate,[6] and with the impossibilities of her love, thinking it were frenzy not fancy to covet that which the very destinies did deny her to obtain.

But Dorastus was more impatient in his passions, for Love so fiercely assailed him that neither company nor music could mitigate his martyrdom, but did rather far the more increase his malady. Shame would not let him crave counsel in this case, nor fear of his father's displeasure reveal it to any secret friend, but he was fain to make a secretary[7] of himself, and to participate his thoughts with his own troubled mind. Lingering thus awhile in doubtful suspense, at last, stealing secretly from the court without either men or page, he went to see if he could espy Fawnia walking abroad in the field. But, as one having a great deal more skill to retrieve the partridge with his spaniels than to hunt after such a strange prey, he sought, but was little the better; which cross[8] luck drove him into a great choler, that he began both to accuse Love and Fortune. But as he was ready to retire, he saw Fawnia sitting all alone under the side of a hill, making a garland of such homely flowers as the fields did afford. This sight so revived his spirits that he drew nigh, with more judgement to take a view of her singular perfection, which he found to be such as in that country attire she stained[9] all the courtly dames of Sicilia. While thus he stood gazing with piercing looks on her surpassing beauty, Fawnia cast her eye aside and spied Dorastus, which[10]

1 arouse contempt 2 dill 3 i.e. a Nile flood 18 feet deep (a cubit was 18 inches, 45cm) would ruin the crop and cause a dearth 4 lowborn girls 5 usual 6 low birth 7 confidant 8 ill 9 put to shame, surpassed 10 'with' 1588

sudden sight made the poor girl to blush, and to dye her crystal cheeks with a vermilion red which gave her such a grace as she seemed far more beautiful. And with that she rose up, saluting the prince with such modest courtesies as he wondered how a country maid could afford such courtly behaviour. Dorastus, repaying her courtesy with a smiling countenance, began to parley with her on this manner:[1]

'Fair maid,' quoth he, 'either your want is great, or a shepherd's life very sweet, that your delight is in such country labours. I cannot conceive what pleasure you should take, unless you mean to imitate the nymphs, being yourself so like a nymph. To put me out of this doubt, show me what is to be commended in a shepherd's life, and what pleasures you have to countervail[2] these drudging labours.'

Fawnia with blushing face made him this ready answer: 'Sir, what richer state than content, or what sweeter life than quiet? We shepherds are not born to honour, nor beholding unto beauty, the less care we have to fear fame or fortune. We count our attire brave[3] enough if warm enough, and our food dainty, if to suffice nature. Our greatest enemy is the wolf, our only care in safe keeping our flock. Instead of courtly ditties, we spend the days with country songs. Our amorous conceits are homely thoughts, delighting as much to talk of Pan[4] and his country pranks as ladies to tell of Venus and her wanton toys. Our toil is in shifting the folds and looking to the lambs, easy labours; oft singing and telling tales, homely pleasures; our greatest wealth not to covet, our honour not to climb, our quiet not to care. Envy looketh not so low as shepherds; shepherds gaze not so high as ambition. We are rich in that we are poor with content, and proud only in this: that we have no cause to be proud.'

This witty answer of Fawnia so inflamed Dorastus' fancy as he commended himself for making so good a choice, thinking, if her birth were answerable to her wit and beauty, that she were a fit mate for the most famous prince in the world.[5] He therefore began to sift her more narrowly on this manner:[6]

'Fawnia, I see thou art content with country labours, because thou knowest not courtly pleasures. I commend thy wit and pity thy want; but wilt thou leave thy father's cottage, and serve a courtly mistress?'

'Sir,' quoth she, 'beggars ought not to strive against fortune, nor to gaze after honour, lest either their fall be greater, or they become blind. I am born to toil for the court, not in the court, my nature unfit for their nurture; better live then in mean degree[7] than in high disdain.'

'Well said, Fawnia,' quoth Dorastus, 'I guess at thy thoughts; thou art in love with some country shepherd.'

'No sir,' quoth she, 'shepherds cannot love that are so simple, and maids may not love that are so young.'

1 speak like this   2 relieve, compensate for   3 fine   4 god of Nature   5 Cf. 4.4.157–9, 583–8; 2.2.2–3 (of Hermione).   6 question her more closely like this   7 a humble life

'Nay, therefore,' quoth Dorastus, 'maids must love because they are young; for Cupid is a child, and Venus, though old, is painted with fresh colours.'

'I grant,' quoth she, 'age may be painted with new shadows,[1] and youth may have imperfect affections; but what art concealeth in one, ignorance revealeth in the other.'

Dorastus, seeing Fawnia held him so hard, thought it was vain so long to beat about the bush. Therefore he thought to have given her a fresh charge, but he was so prevented by certain of his men who, missing their master, came posting[2] to seek him, seeing that he was gone forth all alone; yet before they drew so nigh that they might hear their talk, he used these speeches:

'Why, Fawnia, perhaps I love thee, and then thou must needs yield; for thou knowest I can command and constrain.' 'Truth, sir,' quoth she, 'but not to love; for constrained love is force, not love. And know this, sir, mine honesty is such as I had rather die than be a concubine even to a king, and my birth is so base as I am unfit to be a wife to a poor farmer.' 'Why then,' quoth he, 'thou canst not love Dorastus?' 'Yes,' said Fawnia, 'when Dorastus becomes a shepherd,' – and with that the presence of his men broke off their parle,[3] so that he went with them to the palace, and left Fawnia sitting still on the hillside, who, seeing that the night drew on, shifted her folds and busied herself about other work to drive away such fond fancies as began to trouble her brain. But all this could not prevail, for the beauty of Dorastus had made such a deep impression in her heart as it could not be worn out without cracking,[4] so that she was forced to blame her own folly in this wise:

'Ah, Fawnia, why doest thou gaze against the sun, or catch at the wind? Stars are to be looked at with the eye, not reached at with the hand; thoughts are to be measured by fortunes, not by desires; falls come not by sitting low, but by climbing too high. What then, shall all fear to fall, because some hap to fall? No, luck cometh by lot,[5] and Fortune windeth those threads which the Destinies spin.[6] Thou art favoured, Fawnia, of a prince, and yet thou art so fond[7] to reject desired favours. Thou hast denial at thy tongue's end, and desire at thy heart's bottom; a woman's fault, to spurn at that with her foot which she greedily catcheth at with her hand. Thou lovest Dorastus, Fawnia, and yet seemest to lour. Take heed, if he retire, thou wilt repent; for unless he love, thou canst but die. Die then, Fawnia, for Dorastus doth but jest. The lion never preyeth on the mouse, nor falcons stoop not to dead stales.[8] Sit down then in sorrow, cease to love, and content thyself that Dorastus will vouchsafe to flatter Fawnia, though not to fancy Fawnia. Hey ho! Ah, fool, it were seemlier for thee to whistle as a shepherd than to sigh as

1 colours (i.e. make-up)   2 hurrying   3 talk   4 i.e. his image couldn't be erased without breaking her heart   5 chance   6 The Destinies determined people's fates by spinning and cutting the thread of life.   7 foolish   8 decoy birds

a lover.' And with that she ceased from these perplexed passions, folding her sheep, and hying[1] home to her poor cottage.

But such was the incessant sorrow of Dorastus to think on the wit and beauty of Fawnia, and to see how fond he was, being a prince, and how froward[2] she was being a beggar, then he began to lose his wonted[3] appetite, to look pale and wan; instead of mirth, to feed on melancholy; for courtly dances to use cold dumps;[4] insomuch that not only his own men but his father and all the court began to marvel at his sudden change, thinking that some lingering sickness had brought him into this state. Wherefore he caused physicians to come; but Dorastus neither would let them minister, nor so much as suffer them to see his urine,[5] but remained still so oppressed with these passions as he feared in himself a farther inconvenience. His honour wished him to cease from such folly, but love forced him to follow fancy. Yea, and in despite of honour, love won the conquest, so that his hot desires caused him to find new devices; for he presently made himself a shepherd's coat that he might go unknown, and with the less suspicion to prattle with Fawnia, and conveyed it secretly into a thick grove hard joining to the palace, whither, finding fit time and opportunity, he went all alone and, putting off his princely apparel, got on those shepherd's robes and taking a great hook in his hand, which he had also gotten, he went very anciently[6] to find out the mistress of his affection. But as he went by the way, seeing himself clad in such unseemly rags, he began to smile at his own folly, and to reprove his fondness in these terms:

'Well said, Dorastus, thou keepest a right decorum, base desires and homely attires! Thy thoughts are fit for none but a shepherd, and thy apparel such as only become a shepherd. A strange change from a prince to a peasant! What is it? Thy wretched fortune or thy wilful folly? Is it thy cursed destinies or thy crooked[7] desires that appointeth thee this penance? Ah, Dorastus, thou canst but love, and unless thou love, thou art like to perish for love. Yet, fond fool, choose flowers not weeds,[8] diamonds not pebbles; ladies which may honour thee, not shepherds which may disgrace thee. Venus is painted in silks, not in rags; and Cupid treadeth on disdain when he reacheth at dignity. And yet, Dorastus, shame not at thy shepherd's weed. The heavenly gods have sometime earthly thoughts: Neptune became a ram, Jupiter a bull, Apollo a shepherd;[9] they gods, and yet in love, and thou a man, appointed to love.'

Devising thus with himself, he drew nigh to the place where Fawnia was keeping her sheep, who, casting her eye aside and seeing such a mannerly shepherd perfectly limbed[10] and coming with so good a pace, she began half

1 hastening   2 wilful   3 customary   4 plaintive music   5 i.e. to diagnose his sickness   6 uncertainly (like an old man); in old fashioned (i.e. rustic) attire   7 perverse   8 punning on 'weeds' as clothes; cf. 4.4.1 (see n.).   9 gods that assumed mortal forms to have sex; cf. 4.4.25–31.   10 handsome (punning on 'limned', i.e. painted)

to forget Dorastus, and to favour this pretty shepherd whom she thought she might both love and obtain. But as she was in these thoughts, she perceived then it was the young prince Dorastus; wherefore she rose up and reverently saluted him. Dorastus, taking her by the hand, repaid her courtesy with a sweet kiss and, praying her to sit down by him, he began thus to lay the battery:[1]

'If thou marvel, Fawnia, at my strange attire, thou wouldst more muse at my unaccustomed thoughts. The one disgraceth but my outward shape, the other disturbeth my inward senses. I love Fawnia, and therefore what love liketh I cannot mislike. Fawnia, thou hast promised to love and I hope thou wilt perform no less. I have fulfilled thy request and now thou canst but grant my desire. Thou wert content to love Dorastus when he ceased to be a prince and chose[2] to become a shepherd, and see, I have made the change, and therefore hope[3] not to miss of my choice.'

'Truth,' quoth Fawnia, 'but all that wear cowls are not monks; painted eagles are pictures, not eagles; Zeuxis' grapes were like grapes, yet shadows.[4] Rich clothing make not princes, nor homely attire beggars. Shepherds are not called shepherds because they wear[5] hooks[6] and bags, but that they are born poor and live to keep sheep; so this attire hath not made Dorastus a shepherd, but to seem like a shepherd.'

'Well, Fawnia,' answered Dorastus, 'were I a shepherd I could not but like thee, and being a prince I am forced to love thee. Take heed, Fawnia, be not proud of beauty's painting, for it is a flower that fadeth in the blossom. Those which disdain in youth are despised in age. Beauty's shadows are tricked up[7] with Time's colours which, being set to dry in the sun, are stained with the sun, scarce pleasing the sight ere they begin not to be worth the sight, not much unlike the herb ephemeron[8] which flourisheth in the morning and is withered before the sun setting. If my desire were against law, thou mightest justly deny me by reason; but I love thee, Fawnia, not to misuse thee as a concubine but to use thee as my wife. I can promise no more, and mean to perform no less.'

Fawnia, hearing this solemn protestation of Dorastus, could no longer withstand the assault, but yielded up the fort in these friendly terms:

'Ah, Dorastus, I shame to express that thou forcest me with thy sugared speech to confess. My base birth causeth the one, and thy high dignities the other. Beggars' thoughts ought not to reach so far as kings, and yet my desires reach as high as princes. I dare not say "Dorastus, I love thee," because I am a shepherd; but the gods know I have honoured Dorastus (pardon if I say amiss), yea and loved Dorastus with such dutiful affection as

1 start the assault (to win her)   2 'chose' added this edn   3 'hope' added this edn
4 Zeuxis, ancient Greek painter famed for lifelike pictures ('shadows'), said to have painted grapes so realistic that birds mistook them for real grapes   5 i.e. carry ('were' 1588)   6 sheephooks
7 adorned   8 plant said to live for a single day

Fawnia can perform or Dorastus desire. I yield, not overcome with prayers but with love, resting Dorastus' handmaid, ready to obey his will, if no prejudice at all to his honour nor to my credit.'

Dorastus, hearing this friendly conclusion of Fawnia, embraced her in his arms, swearing that neither distance, time nor adverse fortune should diminish his affection, but that in despite of the Destinies he would remain loyal unto death.[1] Having thus plight their troth each to other, seeing they could not have the full fruition of their love in Sicilia for that Egistus' consent would never be granted to so mean a match,[2] Dorastus determined, as soon as time and opportunity would give them leave, to provide a great mass of money and many rich and costly jewels, for the easier carriage, and then to transport themselves and their treasure into Italy, where they should lead a contented life until such time as either he could be reconciled to his father, or else by succession come to the kingdom.[3] This device was greatly praised of Fawnia, for she feared, if the King his father should but hear of the contract, that his fury would be such as no less than death would stand for payment. She therefore told him that delay bred danger, that many mishaps did fall out between the cup and the lip, and that to avoid danger it were best with as much speed as might be to pass out of Sicilia, lest Fortune might prevent their pretence[4] with some new despite. Dorastus, whom love pricked[5] forward with desire, promised to dispatch his affairs with as great haste as either time or opportunity would give him leave; and so resting upon this point, after many embracings and sweet kisses they departed.[6]

Dorastus, having taken his leave of his best beloved Fawnia, went to the grove where he had his rich apparel, and there uncasing[7] himself as secretly as might be, hiding up his shepherd's attire till occasion should serve again to use it, he went to the palace, showing by his merry countenance that either the state of his body was amended or the case of his mind greatly redressed. Fawnia, poor soul, was no less joyful that, being a shepherd, Fortune had favoured her so as to reward her with the love of a prince, hoping in time to be advanced from the daughter of a poor farmer to be the wife of a rich king; so that she thought every hour a year till by their departure they might prevent danger, not ceasing still to go every day to her sheep, not so much for the care of her flock as for the desire she had to see her love and lord Dorastus, who oftentimes, when opportunity would serve, repaired thither to feed his fancy with the sweet content of Fawnia's presence. And although he never went to visit her but in his shepherd's rags, yet his oft repair[8] made him not only suspected but known to divers of their neighbours who, for the good will they bore to old Porrus, told him secretly of the matter, wishing him to keep his daughter at home lest she went so oft to the field that she brought him home a young son – for they feared that Fawnia being so

1 Cf. 4.4.42–6, 481–2, 493–7.   2 Cf. 4.4.17–22.   3 Cf. 4.4.499–507.   4 intention   5 urged   6 parted
7 changing clothes (cf. 'discase', 4.4.637)   8 frequent visits

beautiful, the young prince would allure her to folly. Porrus was stricken into a dump at these news, so that, thanking his neighbours for their good will, he hied him home to his wife, and, calling her aside, wringing his hands and shedding forth tears, he broke the matter to her in these terms:

'I am afraid, wife, that my daughter, Fawnia, hath made herself so fine that she will buy repentance too dear. I hear news which, if they be true, some will wish they had not proved true. It is told me by my neighbours that Dorastus, the King's son, begins to look at our daughter Fawnia, which if it be so, I will not give her a halfpenny for her honesty at the year's end. I tell thee, wife, nowadays beauty is a great stale[1] to trap young men, and fair words and sweet promises are two great enemies to a maiden's honesty, and thou knowest where poor men entreat and cannot obtain, there princes may command, and will obtain. Though kings' sons dance in nets,[2] they may not be seen; but poor men's faults are spied at a little hole. Well, it is a hard case where kings' lusts are laws, and that they should bind poor men to that which they themselves wilfully break.'

'Peace, husband,' quoth his wife, 'take heed what you say. Speak no more than you should, lest you hear what you would not. Great streams are to be stopped by sleight[3] not by force, and princes to be persuaded by submission not by rigour.[4] Do what you can, but no more than you may, lest in saving Fawnia's maidenhead you lose your own head. Take heed, I say, it is ill jesting with edged tools,[5] and bad sporting with kings. The wolf had his skin pulled over his ears for but looking into the lion's den. 'Tush, wife,' quoth he, 'thou speakest like a fool. If the King should know that Dorastus had begotten our daughter with child (as I fear it will fall out little better), the King's fury would be such as no doubt we should both lose our goods and lives. Necessity therefore hath no law, and I will prevent this mischief with a new device that is come in my head, which shall neither offend the King nor displease Dorastus. I mean to take the chain and the jewels that I found with Fawnia, and carry them to the King, letting him then to understand how she is none of my daughter, but that I found her beaten up with the water,[6] alone in a little boat wrapped in a rich mantle wherein was enclosed this treasure. By this means I hope the King will take Fawnia into his service, and we, whatsoever chanceth, shall be blameless.' This device pleased the good wife very well, so that they determined as soon as they might know the King at leisure to make him privy to this case.

In the meantime, Dorastus was not slack in his affairs, but applied his matters with such diligence that he provided all things fit for their journey. Treasure and jewels he had gotten great store, thinking there was no better friend than money in a strange[7] country; rich attire he had provided for

1 decoy-bird   2 i.e. what they do is seen by everybody   3 skill   4 by humility not anger   5 i.e. with a cutting edge (e.g. knives)   6 assailed by the waves; driven ashore by the sea   7 foreign

Fawnia and, because he could not bring the matter to pass without the help and advice of someone, he made an old servant of his called Capnio, who had served him from his childhood, privy to his affairs; who, seeing no persuasions could prevail to divert him from his settled determination, gave his consent, and dealt so secretly in the cause that within short space he had gotten a ship ready for their passage. The mariners, seeing a fit gale of wind for their purpose, wished Capnio to make no delays lest, if they pretermitted[1] this good weather, they might stay long ere they had such a fair wind. Capnio, fearing that his negligence should hinder the journey, in the night-time conveyed the trunks full of treasure into the ship, and by secret means let Fawnia understand that the next morning they meant to depart. She, upon this news, slept very little that night but got up very early and went to her sheep, looking every minute when she should see Dorastus, who tarried not long, for fear delay might breed danger, but came as fast as he could gallop, and without any great circumstance[2] took Fawnia up behind him and rode to the haven where the ship lay, which was not three-quarters of a mile distant from that place. He no sooner came there, but the mariners were ready with their cock-boat to set them aboard where, being couched[3] together in a cabin, they passed away the time in recounting their old loves till their man Capnio should come.

Porrus, who had heard that this morning the King would go abroad to take the air,[4] called in haste to his wife to bring him his holiday hose[5] and his best jacket that he might go like an honest, substantial man to tell his tale. His wife, a good cleanly wench, brought him all things fit and sponged[6] him up very handsomely, giving him the chains and jewels in a little box,[7] which Porrus (for the more safety) put in his bosom. Having thus all his trinkets in a readiness, taking his staff in his hand he bade his wife kiss him for good luck, and so he went towards the palace. But as he was going, Fortune, who meant to show him a little false play, prevented his purpose in this wise.

He met by chance in his way Capnio, who, trudging as fast as he could with a little coffer[8] under his arm to the ship, and spying Porrus (whom he knew to be Fawnia's father) going towards the palace, being a wily fellow began to doubt the worst, and therefore crossed him the way[9] and asked him whither he was going so early this morning.[10] Porrus (who knew by his face that he was one of the court), meaning simply, told him that the King's son, Dorastus, dealt hardly[11] with him; for he had but one daughter, who was a little beautiful, and that his neighbours told him the young prince had allured her to folly; he went therefore now to complain to the King how greatly he was abused.

Capnio (who straightway smelt the whole matter)[12] began to soothe him

1 didn't take advantage of   2 formality; ado   3 accommodated   4 Cf. 4.4.766–7.   5 breeches   6 smartened   7 Cf. 3.3.45 SD (see n.), 3.3.111–21.   8 treasure box   9 i.e. intercepted him   10 Cf. Autolycus at 4.4.717–24.   11 badly   12 Cf. 4.4.646–7.

in his talk, and said that Dorastus dealt not like a prince to spoil any poor man's daughter in that sort. He therefore would do the best for him he could, because he knew he was an honest man. 'But,' quoth Capnio, 'you lose your labour in going to the palace, for the King means this day to take the air of the sea, and to go aboard of a ship that lies in the haven.[1] I am going before, you see, to provide all things in readiness, and if you will follow my counsel, turn back with me to the haven, where I will set you in such a fit place as you may speak to the King at your pleasure.'[2] Porrus, giving credit to Capnio's smooth[3] tale, gave him a thousand thanks for his friendly advice and went with him to the haven, making all the way his complaints of Dorastus, yet concealing secretly the chain and the jewels. As soon as they were come to the seaside, the mariners, seeing Capnio came a-land with their cock-boat, who, still dissembling the matter, demanded of Porrus if he would go see the ship; who, unwilling and fearing the worst because he was not well acquainted with Capnio, made his excuse that he could not brook the sea, therefore would not trouble him.

Capnio, seeing that by fair means he could not get him aboard, commanded the mariners that by violence they should carry him into the ship, who, like sturdy knaves, hoisted the poor shepherd on their backs and bearing him to the boat launched from the land.

Porrus, seeing himself so cunningly betrayed, durst not cry out, for he saw it would not prevail, but began to entreat Capnio and the mariners to be good to him, and to pity his estate;[4] he was but a poor man that lived by his labour. They, laughing to see the shepherd so afraid, made as much haste as they could and set him aboard. Porrus was no sooner in the ship, but he saw Dorastus walking with Fawnia; yet he scarce knew her, for she had attired herself in rich apparel, which so increased her beauty that she resembled rather an angel than a mortal creature.[5]

Dorastus and Fawnia were half astonished to see the old shepherd, marvelling greatly what wind had brought him thither, till Capnio told them all the whole discourse; how Porrus was going to make his complaint to the King, if by policy he had not prevented him; and therefore now, sith he was aboard, for the avoiding of further danger it were best to carry him into Italy.

Dorastus praised greatly his man's device, and allowed of his counsel, but Fawnia (who still feared Porrus as her father) began to blush for shame that by her means he should either incur danger or displeasure.

The old shepherd, hearing this hard sentence, that he should on such a sudden be carried from his wife, his country and kinsfolk, into a foreign land amongst strangers, began with bitter tears to make his complaint, and on his knees to entreat Dorastus that, pardoning his unadvised folly, he would give

1 Cf. 4.4.766–7.   2 Cf. 4.4.800–2.   3 plausible   4 condition   5 Cf. 4.4.1–5 and 5.1.130.

him leave to go home; swearing that he would keep all things as secret as they could wish. But these protestations could not prevail, although Fawnia entreated Dorastus very earnestly, but the mariners hoisting their mainsails weighed anchors, and haled into the deep,[1] where we leave them to the favour of the wind and seas, and return to Egistus.

Who, having appointed this day to hunt in one of his forests, called for his son Dorastus to go sport[2] himself, because he saw that of late he began to lour.[3] But his men made answer that he was gone abroad none knew whither, except he were gone to the grove to walk all alone, as his custom was to do every day.

The King, willing to waken him out of his dumps, sent one of his men to go seek him; but in vain, for at last he returned but find him he could not, so that the King went himself to go see the sport, where passing away the day, returning at night from hunting he asked for his son, but he could not be heard of, which drove the King into a great choler. Whereupon most of his noblemen and other courtiers posted abroad to seek him, but they could not hear of him through all Sicilia, only they missed Capnio his man, which again made the King suspect that he was not gone far.

Two or three days being passed and no news heard of Dorastus, Egistus began to fear that he was devoured with[4] some wild beasts, and upon that made out a great troop of men to go seek him; who coasted[5] through all the country and searched in every dangerous and secret place, until at last they met with a fisherman that was sitting in a little covert[6] hard by the seaside mending his nets when Dorastus and Fawnia took shipping; who, being examined if he either knew or heard where the King's son was, without any secrecy at all revealed the whole matter: how he was sailed two days past, and had in his company his man Capnio, Porrus, and his fair daughter Fawnia. This heavy news was presently carried to the King who, half dead for sorrow, commanded Porrus' wife to be sent for. She, being come to the palace, after due examination confessed that her neighbours had oft told her that the King's son was too familiar with Fawnia, her daughter; whereupon her husband, fearing the worst, about two days past, hearing the King should go an-hunting, rose early in the morning and went to make his complaint; but since she neither heard of him nor saw him.

Egistus, perceiving the woman's unfeigned simplicity, let her depart without incurring further displeasure; concealing such secret grief for his son's reckless folly – that he had so forgotten his honour and parentage by so base a choice to dishonour his father and discredit himself – that with very care[7] and thought he fell into a quartan fever,[8] which was so unfit for his aged years and complexion that he became so weak as the physicians would grant him no life.

1 put to sea 2 enjoy 3 be despondent 4 by 5 went 6 sheltered place 7 sheer worry, intense concern 8 ague with feverish fits

But his son Dorastus little regarded either father, country or kingdom in respect of his lady Fawnia; for Fortune, smiling on this young novice,[1] lent him so lucky a gale of wind for the space of a day and a night that the mariners lay and slept upon the hatches. But on the next morning, about the break of the day, the air began to overcast, the winds to rise, the seas to swell; yea, presently there arose such a fearful tempest[2] as the ship was in danger to be swallowed up with every sea,[3] the mainmast with the violence of the wind was thrown overboard, the sails were torn, the tacklings went in sunder,[4] the storm raging still so furiously that poor Fawnia was almost dead for fear, but that she was greatly comforted with the presence of Dorastus. The tempest continued three days, all which time the mariners every minute looked for death, and the air was so darkened with clouds that the master could not tell by his compass in what coast they were. But upon the fourth day, about ten of the clock, the wind began to cease, the sea to wax calm and the sky to be clear, and the mariners descried the coast of Bohemia, shooting off their ordnance[5] for joy that they had escaped such a fearful tempest.

Dorastus, hearing that they were arrived at some harbour, sweetly kissed Fawnia, and bade her be of good cheer. When they told him that the port belonged unto the chief city of Bohemia, where Pandosto kept his court, Dorastus began to be sad, knowing that his father hated no man so much as Pandosto,[6] and that the King himself had sought secretly to betray Egistus. This considered, he was half afraid to go on land, but that Capnio counselled him to change his name and his country until such time as they could get some other barque to transport them into Italy. Dorastus, liking this device, made his case privy to the mariners, rewarding them bountifully for their pains and charging them to say that he was a gentleman of Trapalonia called Meleagrus.[7] The shipmen, willing to show what friendship they could to Dorastus, promised to be as secret as they could or he might wish, and upon this they landed in a little village a mile distant from the city; where after they had rested a day, thinking to make provision for their marriage, the fame of Fawnia's beauty[8] was spread throughout all the city so that it came to the ears of Pandosto who, then being about the age of fifty, had notwithstanding young and fresh affections;[9] so that he desired greatly to see Fawnia, and to bring this matter the better to pass, hearing they had but one man and how they rested at a very homely house, he caused them to be apprehended as spies and sent a dozen of his guard to take them who, being come to their lodging, told them the King's message. Dorastus, no whit dismayed, accompanied with Fawnia and Capnio, went to the court (for they left Porrus to keep the stuff), who being admitted to the King's presence, Dorastus and Fawnia with humble obeisance saluted his majesty.

1 new convert (to love)   2 Cf. 5.2.117–18, 3.3.82–99.   3 wave (cf. 'swallowed', 3.3.91)   4 were broken   5 cannon   6 Cf. 4.2.20–5.   7 the name of an Argonaut who sailed with the Greek hero Jason   8 Cf. 5.1.93–5.   9 sexual desires (cf. 5.1.222–4)

Pandosto, amazed at the singular perfection of Fawnia, stood half astonished viewing her beauty, so that he had almost forgot himself what he had
to do. At last with stern countenance he demanded their names, and of what
country they were, and what caused them to land in Bohemia. 'Sir,' quoth
Dorastus, 'know that my name is Meleagrus, a knight born and brought up
in Trapalonia, and this gentlewoman, whom I mean to take to my wife, is an
Italian born in Padua, from whence I have now brought her.[1] The cause I
have so small a train with me is for that her friends unwilling to consent, I
intended secretly to convey her into Trapalonia, whither as I was sailing by
distress of weather I was driven into these coasts. Thus have you heard my
name, my country and the cause of my voyage.' Pandosto, starting from his
seat as one in choler, made this rough reply:

'Meleagrus, I fear this smooth tale hath but small truth, and that thou
coverest a foul skin with fair paintings. No doubt this lady by her grace and
beauty is of her degree more meet[2] for a mighty prince than for a simple
knight, and thou, like a perjured traitor, hath[3] bereft her of her parents, to
their present grief and her ensuing sorrow. Till therefore I hear more of her
parentage, and of thy calling,[4] I will stay[5] you both here in Bohemia.'

Dorastus, in whom rested nothing but kingly valour, was not able to suffer
the reproaches of Pandosto, but that he made him this answer:

'It is not meet for a king without due proof to appeach any man of ill
behaviour, nor upon suspicion to infer belief. Strangers ought to be entertained with courtesy, not to be entreated with cruelty, lest, being forced by
want to put up[6] injuries, the gods revenge their cause with rigour.'

Pandosto, hearing Dorastus utter these words, commanded that he should
straight[7] be committed to prison until such time as they heard further of his
pleasure; but as for Fawnia, he charged that she should be entertained in the
court with such courtesy as belonged to a stranger and her calling. The rest
of the shipmen he put into the dungeon.

Having thus hardly handled the supposed Trapalonians, Pandosto, contrary to his aged years, began to be somewhat tickled with[8] the beauty of
Fawnia,[9] insomuch that he could take no rest but cast in his old head a thousand new devices.[10] At last he fell into these thoughts:

'How art thou pestered,[11] Pandosto, with fresh affections and unfit fancies, wishing to possess with an unwilling mind, and a hot desire troubled
with a cold disdain! Shall thy mind yield in age to that thou hast resisted in
youth? Peace, Pandosto, blab not out that which thou mayest be ashamed to
reveal to thyself. Ah, Fawnia is beautiful, and it is not for thine honour, fond
fool, to name her that is thy captive and another man's concubine. Alas, I
reach at that with my hand which my heart would fain refuse, playing like

---

1 Cf. 5.1.155–9.   2 by her rank more suitable   3 'hast' 1588   4 i.e. who and what you are
5 detain   6 endure   7 immediately   8 excited by   9 Cf. 5.1.222–4.   10 plans   11 troubled

the bird ibis[1] in Egypt, which hateth serpents yet feedeth on their eggs.

'Tush, hot desires turn oftentimes to cold disdain. Love is brittle where appetite, not reason, bears the sway.[2] Kings' thoughts ought not to climb so high as the heavens, but to look no lower than honour. Better it is to peck at the stars with the young eagles than to prey on dead carcasses with the vulture. 'Tis more honourable for Pandosto to die by concealing love than to enjoy such unfit love. Doth Pandosto then love? Yea. Whom? A maid unknown, yea, and perhaps immodest,[3] straggled[4] out of her own country; beautiful, but not therefore chaste; comely in body, but perhaps crooked in mind. Cease then, Pandosto, to look at Fawnia, much less to love her. Be not overtaken with a woman's beauty, whose eyes are framed by art to enamour, whose heart is framed by nature to enchant, whose false tears know their true times, and whose sweet words pierce deeper than sharp swords.'

Here Pandosto ceased from his talk, but not from his love; for although he sought by reason and wisdom to suppress this frantic affection, yet he could take no rest, the beauty of Fawnia had made such a deep impression in his heart. But on a day, walking abroad into a park which was hard adjoining to his house, he sent by one of his servants for Fawnia, unto whom he uttered these words:

'Fawnia, I commend thy beauty and wit, and now pity thy distress and want; but if thou wilt forsake Sir Meleagrus, whose poverty, though a knight, is not able to maintain an estate answerable to thy beauty, and yield thy consent to Pandosto, I will both increase thee with dignities and riches.' 'No, sir,' answered Fawnia, 'Meleagrus is a knight that hath won me by love, and none but he shall wear[5] me. His sinister[6] mischance shall not diminish my affection but rather increase my good will. Think not though your grace hath imprisoned him without cause that fear shall make me yield my consent. I had rather be Meleagrus' wife and a beggar than live in plenty and be Pandosto's concubine.'

Pandosto, hearing the assured answer of Fawnia, would notwithstanding prosecute his suit to the uttermost, seeking with fair words and great promises to scale the fort of her chastity, swearing that if she would grant to his desire, Meleagrus should not only be set at liberty but honoured in his court amongst his nobles. But these alluring baits could not entice her mind from the love of her new-betrothed mate,[7] Meleagrus; which Pandosto seeing, he left her alone for that time to consider more of the demand. Fawnia, being alone by herself, began to enter into these solitary meditations:

'Ah, infortunate Fawnia, thou seest to desire above fortune is to strive against the gods and Fortune. Who gazeth at the sun weakeneth his sight. They which stare at the sky fall oft into deep pits. Hadst thou rested content to have been a shepherd, thou needest not to have feared mischance. Better

1 sacred bird in ancient Egypt 2 takes control 3 unchaste 4 strayed 5 have (cf. 1.2.305)
6 unfortunate 7 fiancé

had it been for thee, by sitting low to have had quiet than by climbing high to have fallen into misery. But alas, I fear not mine own danger but Dorastus' displeasure. Ah, sweet Dorastus, thou art a prince but now a prisoner, by too much love procuring thine own loss. Hadst thou not loved Fawnia, thou hadst been fortunate. Shall I then be false to him that hath forsaken kingdoms for my cause? No, would my death might deliver him, so mine honour might be preserved.'

With that, fetching a deep sigh, she ceased from her complaints and went again to the palace, enjoying a liberty without content, and proffered pleasure with small joy. But poor Dorastus lay all this while in close prison, being pinched[1] with a hard restraint and pained with the burden of cold and heavy irons,[2] sorrowing sometimes that his fond[3] affection had procured him this mishap, that, by the disobedience of[4] his parents, he had wrought his own despite; another while cursing the gods and Fortune that they should cross him with such sinister chance; uttering at last his passions in these words:

'Ah, unfortunate wretch, born to mishap, now thy folly hath his desert. Art thou not worthy for thy base mind to have bad fortune? Could the Destinies favour thee which hast forgot thine honour and dignities? Will not the gods plague him with despite that paineth his father with disobedience? Oh gods, if any favour or justice be left, plague me, but favour poor Fawnia, and shroud her from the tyrannies of wretched Pandosto; but let my death free her from mishap and then, welcome death!' Dorastus, pained with these heavy passions, sorrowed and sighed, but in vain, for which he used the more patience.

But again to Pandosto who, broiling at the heat of unlawful lust, could take no rest, but still felt his mind disquieted with his new love, so that his nobles and subjects marvelled greatly at this sudden alteration, not being able to conjecture the cause of this his continued care. Pandosto, thinking every hour a year till he had talked once again with Fawnia, sent for her secretly into his chamber whither, though Fawnia unwillingly coming, Pandosto entertained her very courteously, using these familiar speeches, which Fawnia answered as shortly in this wise:

Pandosto

Fawnia, are you become less wilful and more wise, to prefer the love of a king before the liking of a poor knight? I think ere this you think it is better to be favoured of a king than of a subject.

Fawnia

Pandosto, the body is subject to victories, but the mind not to be subdued by conquest.[5] Honesty is to be preferred before honour, and a dram of faith weigheth down a ton of gold. I have promised Meleagrus to love, and will perform no less.

1 afflicted   2 leg-irons   3 foolish   4 by disobeying   5 Cf. 4.4.581–2.

Pandosto

Fawnia, I know thou art not so unwise in thy choice as to refuse the offer of a king nor so ingrateful as to despise a good turn. Thou art now in that place where I may command, and yet thou seest I entreat; my power is such as I may compel by force and yet I sue by prayers. Yield, Fawnia, thy love to him which burneth in thy love, Meleagrus shall be set free, thy countrymen discharged,[1] and thou both loved and honoured.

Fawnia

I see, Pandosto, where lust ruleth it is a miserable thing to be a virgin. But know this, that I will always prefer fame before life, and rather choose death than dishonour.

Pandosto, seeing that there was in Fawnia a determinate courage to love Meleagrus, and a resolution without fear to hate him, flung away from her in a rage, swearing if in short time she would not be won with reason, he would forget all courtesy and compel her to grant by rigour. But these threatening words no whit dismayed Fawnia[2] but that she still both despited[3] and despised Pandosto. While thus these two lovers strove, the one to win love, the other to live in hate, Egistus heard certain news by merchants of Bohemia that his son Dorastus was imprisoned by Pandosto, which made him fear greatly that his son should be but hardly entreated. Yet, considering that Bellaria and he was cleared by the oracle of Apollo from that crime wherewith Pandosto had unjustly charged them, he thought best to send with all speed to Pandosto, that he should set free his son Dorastus, and put to death Fawnia and her father Porrus. Finding this by the advice of counsel the speediest remedy to release his son, he caused presently two of his ships to be rigged, and thoroughly furnished[4] with provision of men and victuals, and sent divers of his nobles ambassadors[5] into Bohemia who, willing to obey their king and receive their young prince, made no delays for fear of danger but, with as much speed as might be, sailed towards Bohemia. The wind and seas favoured them greatly, which made them hope of some good hap,[6] for within three days they were landed; which Pandosto no sooner heard of their arrival but he in person went to meet them, entreating them with such sumptuous and familiar courtesy that they might well perceive how sorry he was for the former injuries he had offered to their king and how willing, if it might be, to make amends.[7]

As Pandosto made report to them, how one Meleagrus, a knight of Trapalonia, was lately arrived with a lady called Fawnia in his land (coming very suspiciously, accompanied only with one servant and an old shepherd), the ambassadors perceived by the half what the whole tale meant, and began to conjecture that it was Dorastus, who, for fear to be known, had changed

1 released 2 Cf. 4.4.447–51. 3 was contemptuous of 4 fully equipped 5 as ambassadors (Polixenes goes in person) 6 outcome 7 Cf. 4.4.552–5.

his name. But dissembling the matter they shortly arrived at the court, where, after they had been very solemnly and sumptuously feasted, the noblemen of Sicilia being gathered together, they made report of their embassage;[1] where they certified Pandosto that Meleagrus was son and heir to the King Egistus and that his name was Dorastus; how, contrary to the King's mind, he had privily[2] conveyed away that Fawnia, intending to marry her, being but daughter to that poor shepherd Porrus. Whereupon the King's request was that Capnio, Fawnia and Porrus might be murdered and put to death, and that his son Dorastus might be sent home in safety.[3]

Pandosto having attentively and with great marvel heard their embassage, willing to reconcile himself to Egistus and to show him how greatly he esteemed his favour,[4] although love and fancy forbade him to hurt Fawnia, yet in despite of love he determined to execute Egistus' will without mercy. And therefore he presently sent for Dorastus out of prison who, marvelling at this unlooked-for courtesy, found at his coming to the King's presence that which he least doubted of,[5] his father's ambassadors; who no sooner saw him but with great reverence they honoured him, and Pandosto, embracing Dorastus, set him by him very lovingly in a chair of estate.[6] Dorastus, ashamed that his folly was bewrayed, sat a long time as one in a muse, till Pandosto told him the sum of his father's embassage, which he had no sooner heard but he was touched at the quick[7] for the cruel sentence that was pronounced against Fawnia. But neither could his sorrow nor persuasions prevail, for Pandosto commanded that Fawnia, Porrus and Capnio should be brought to his presence; who were no sooner come, but Pandosto, having his former love turned to a disdainful hate, began to rage against Fawnia in these terms:

'Thou disdainful[8] vassal, thou currish kite,[9] assigned by the Destinies to base fortune and yet with an aspiring mind gazing after honour. How durst thou presume, being a beggar, to match with a prince; by thy alluring looks to enchant the son of a king[10] to leave his own country to fulfil thy disordinate[11] lusts? O despiteful mind! A proud heart in a beggar is not unlike to a great fire in a small cottage, which warmeth not the house but burneth it. Assure thyself thou shalt die; and thou, old doting fool, whose folly hath been such as to suffer thy daughter to reach above thy fortune, look for no other meed[12] but the like punishment.[13] But Capnio, thou which hast betrayed the King, and has consented to the unlawful lust of thy lord and master, I know not how justly I may plague thee. Death is too easy a punishment for thy falsehood, and to live, if not in extreme misery, were not to show thee equity. I therefore award[14] that thou shall have thine eyes put out, and continually while[15] thou diest grind in a mill like a brute beast.' The fear of

1 mission   2 secretly   3 Cf. 5.1.180–4.   4 'labour' 1588   5 expected   6 throne   7 deeply
8 contemptuous   9 disrespectful rogue (Autolycus is the kite, 4.3.23; see 23–4n.)   10 Cf. 4.4.427–9,
449–52.   11 inordinate   12 reward   13 Cf. 4.4.425–7, 437–9.   14 decree   15 until

death brought a sorrowful silence upon Fawnia and Capnio, but Porrus, seeing no hope of life, burst forth into these speeches:

'Pandosto, and ye noble ambassadors of Sicilia, seeing without cause I am condemned to die, I am yet glad I have opportunity to disburden my conscience before my death. I will tell you as much as I know, and yet no more than is true. Whereas I am accused that I have been a supporter of Fawnia's pride, and she disdained as a vile beggar, so it is that I am neither father unto her nor she daughter unto me. For so it happened that I, being a poor shepherd in Sicilia, living by keeping other men's flocks, one of my sheep straying down to the seaside, as I went to seek her I saw a little boat driven upon the shore, wherein I found a babe of six days old, wrapped in a mantle of scarlet, having about the neck this chain.[1] I, pitying the child, and desirous of the treasure, carried it home to my wife, who with great care nursed it up, and set it to keep sheep. Here is the chain and the jewels, and this Fawnia is the child whom I found in the boat. What she is, or of what parentage, I know not, but this I am assured, that she is none of mine.'

Pandosto would scarce suffer him to tell out his tale, but that he enquired the time of the year, the manner of the boat, and other circumstances which, when he found agreeing to his count,[2] he suddenly leapt from his seat and kissed Fawnia, wetting her tender cheeks with his tears,[3] and crying, 'My daughter Fawnia, ah sweet Fawnia! I am thy father, Fawnia!' This sudden passion of the King drove them all into a maze, especially Fawnia and Dorastus.[4] But when the King had breathed himself awhile in this new joy, he rehearsed before the ambassadors the whole matter, how he had entreated[5] his wife Bellaria for jealousy, and that this was the child whom he sent to float in the seas.

Fawnia was not more joyful that she had found such a father, than Dorastus was glad he should get such a wife. The ambassadors rejoiced that their young prince had made such a choice that those kingdoms which through enmity had long time been dissevered should now through perpetual amity be united and reconciled. The citizens and subjects of Bohemia (hearing that the King had found again his daughter which was supposed dead, joyful that there was an heir apparent to his kingdom) made bonfires and shows[6] throughout the city. The courtiers and knights appointed jousts and tourneys to signify their willing minds in gratifying the King's hap.[7]

Eighteen days being passed in these princely sports, Pandosto, willing to recompense old Porrus, of a shepherd made him a knight.[8] Which done, providing a sufficient navy to receive him and his retinue, accompanied with Dorastus, Fawnia and the Sicilian ambassadors, he sailed towards Sicilia, where he was most princely entertained by Egistus, who, hearing this comical

1 Cf. 5.2.32–3. 2 reckoning 3 Cf. 5.2.43–5. 4 Cf. 5.2.48–53. 5 accused 6 celebrations (cf. 5.2.22) 7 (good) fortune 8 Cf. 'gentlemen born', 5.2.124–35.

event,[1] rejoiced greatly at his son's good hap, and without delay (to the perpetual joy of the two young lovers), celebrated the marriage. Which was no sooner ended but Pandosto, calling to mind how first he betrayed his friend Egistus, how his jealousy was the cause of Bellaria's death, that, contrary to the law of nature, he had lusted after his own daughter, moved with these desperate thoughts, he fell into a melancholy fit and, to close up the comedy with a tragical stratagem,[2] he slew himself. Whose death being many days bewailed of Fawnia, Dorastus and his dear friend Egistus, Dorastus, taking his leave of his father, went with his wife and the dead corpse into Bohemia where, after they were sumptuously entombed,[3] Dorastus ended his days in contented quiet.

FINIS

1 happy outcome (i.e. the way comedies end)   2 plan   3 i.e. Pandosto was entombed with his wife and son

ALCESTIS

The Greek dramatist Euripides (480–406 BC) wrote *Alcestis* in 438 BC (see pp. 13 and 93–4 for an outline of the plot). Euripides' tragedies had appeared in print in the original Greek by 1500. The humanist scholar Erasmus translated several of the plays into Latin early in the sixteenth century, but not *Alcestis*. Another humanist, the Scot George Buchanan, translated *Alcestis* into Latin verse in the mid-1540s and published his version in Paris in 1556. It was reprinted many times. The extracts below are from Buchanan, 222 and 242–3 respectively.

In the first extract, lines 359–72, Admetus tells his wife Alcestis, as she is dying:

> quin et periti dextera artificis tua
> in lecto imago ficta collocabitur.   360
> amplectar illam manibus, illi procidens
> tuum vocabo nomen; ulnis coniugem
> caram tenere, non tenens, fingam tamen.
> est ea voluptas frigida, at molestiam
> animi levabit. umbra me per somnia   365
> utinam reversa oblectet; etiam lurida
> sub nocte amicos suave vultus cernere,
> quocumque sese in tempore offerent. mihi
> si lingua adesset Orphei et blandum melos,
> furvae canendo pectus ut Proserpinae   370
> duri vel Orci flecterem ac reducerem
> te, promptus irem . . .

Your likeness (*imago*), fashioned by the hand of a skilled craftsman, will be placed in my bed [360]. I will embrace it with my hands, falling down before it I will call your name; I will imagine that I hold my dear wife in my arms, though I am not really holding her (*non tenens*). This is a cold pleasure, but it will lighten the vexation of my soul [365]. Would that your ghost (*umbra*) might delight me, returning in my dreams; even in the ghastly night it is pleasant to look on friendly faces, at whatever time they show themselves [368]. If I had the tongue of Orpheus and his charming song, so that by singing I might change the heart (*pectus*) of gloomy Proserpina or stern Pluto,[1] and bring you back (from the land of the dead), I would readily go . . .

---

1 Proserpina and Pluto were gods of the dead and the underworld (see 4.4.116–18 and n., where Perdita refers to Pluto by his Greek name, Dis). Buchanan uses 'Orcus' at 371, another Latin name for Pluto.

In the second extract, lines 1194–1213, Hercules presents Alcestis to Admetus as a veiled stranger whom he must marry:

HER.   Protende promptus dexteram; tange hospitam.
ADM.   Protendo veluti Gorgonis sectum ad caput.   1195
HER.   Tenesne? *ADM.*   Sane teneo. *HER.*   Serva iam, et Iove
natum fatebere generosum olim hospitem.
ipsam intuere, similis uxori an tuae
sit, ac beatus luctuum iam desine.
ADM.   O di boni, o miraculum inopinum ac novum!   1200
oculis profecto coniugem intueor meam,
aut me deorum quispiam ludibrio
recreat, inani corda lactans gaudio.
HER.   Non ita, sed ipsam coniugem cernis tuam.
ADM.   Ne larva ab umbris missa sit, circumspice.   1205
HER.   Cave esse credas hospitem tuum magum.
ADM.   Sed quam sepelii coniugem intueor meam?
HER.   Sic. at fidem tu, et iure, sorti non habes.
ADM.   Tango adloquorque coniugem ut vivam meam?
HER.   Adloquere; votis quicquid optabas habes.   1210
ADM.   O corpus, ocule o coniugis carissimae!
spem praeter habeo te, videre postea
quam non putaram posse me?

Hercules   Hold out your right hand; touch the guest.[1]
Admetus   I hold it out, as if to the severed head of the Gorgon.   [1195]
Hercules   Are you holding her?
Admetus   I am indeed.
Hercules   Then keep her, and acknowledge hereafter that Jove's
son[2] was a generous guest. Look at her, see whether she resembles
your wife, and happily cease your mourning.
Admetus   O good gods, O unhoped for and unprecedented miracle!   [1200]
Do I really look on my wife with my eyes, or does some god revive
me with a trick, beguiling my heart with empty joy?
Hercules   Not so – you perceive your real wife.
Admetus   Beware, lest it be a spectre sent from the underworld.   [1205]
Hercules   Take care lest you think your guest a sorcerer.
Admetus   But do I look upon my wife whom I buried?
Hercules   Yes. But you, rightly, don't trust your fate.

1 At 1194 'hospitam' (accusative of 'hospes') could also mean 'friend' or 'hostess'.   2 Hercules is referring to himself.

Admetus   I can touch and speak to my wife as if she were alive?
Hercules   Speak to her; by your prayers you have what you
hoped for.   [1210]
Admetus   O body, O eye of my dearest wife! Do I have you,
whom I thought I would not be able to see again?

PYGMALION'S IMAGE

The Roman poet Ovid (43 BC–AD 17) finished *Metamorphoses*, a narrative poem in fifteen books describing the creation and history of the world, in AD 8. Arthur Golding published the first complete English translation of *Metamorphoses* in 1567. Shakespeare, who was familiar with *Metamorphoses* in the original Latin and in Golding's version, had used passages from Book 10 for his own poem of 1593, *Venus and Adonis*. The extract below, 10.265–324, is from the modernized text in Ovid, *Met.*, 302–4, with additional annotation supplied.

In Book 10, Orpheus tells stories about love and sexual obsession. One story is concerned with the sculptor Pygmalion, who hates the Propoetides, lascivious prostitutes whom the goddess Venus punishes for not honouring her by turning them to stone. Pygmalion, disgusted with all women, decides to live a single life, but in the meantime:

> by wondrous art an image he did grave[1]
> Of such proportion, shape and grace as nature never gave
> Nor can to any woman give. In this his work he took
> A certain love. The look of it was right a maiden's look,
> And such a one as that ye would believe had life and that
> Would movèd be, if womanhood and reverence letted not:[2]   270
> So artificial[3] was the work. He wond'reth at his art
> And of his counterfeited corse conceiveth love in heart.[4]
> He often touched it, feeling if the work that he had made
> Were very[5] flesh or ivory still. Yet could he not persuade
> Himself to think it ivory. For he oftentimes it kissed   275
> And thought it kissèd him again. He held it by the fist
> And talkèd to it. He believed his fingers made a dint
> Upon her flesh, and fearèd lest some black or bruisèd print
> Should come by touching overhard. Sometime with pleasant bourds[6]
> And wanton toys[7] he dallyingly doth cast forth amorous words.   280
> Sometime (the gifts wherein young maids are wonted to delight)
> He brought her ouches,[8] fine round stones and lilies fair and white
> And pretty singing birds and flowers of thousand sorts and hue,
> And painted balls and amber from the tree distillèd new.

1 sculpted a statue   2 didn't prevent it   3 skilfully made   4 he fell in love with the artificial body he had made   5 real   6 stories and jokes   7 playful tricks   8 brooches (or necklaces)

In gorgeous garments, furthermore, he did her also deck   285
And on her fingers put me[1] rings and chains about her neck.
Rich pearls were hanging at her ears and tablets at her breast.
All kind of things became her well. And when she was undressed
She seemèd not less beautiful. He laid her in a bed
The which with scarlet dyed in Tyre[2] was richly overspread   290
And, terming her his bedfellow, he couchèd down her head[3]
Upon a pillow soft, as though she could have felt the same.
The feast of Venus, hallowed through the isle of Cyprus, came;
And bullocks white with gilden horns were slain for sacrifice
And up to heaven of frankincense the smoky fume did rise   295
Whenas Pygmalion, having done his duty that same day,
Before the altar standing, thus with fearful heart did say:
'If that you gods can all things give, then let my wife, I pray' –
He durst not say 'be yon same wench of ivory', but – 'be like
My wench of ivory.' Venus, who was nought at all to seek[4]   300
What such a wish as that did mean, then present at her feast,
For handsel[5] of her friendly help did cause three times at least
The fire to kindle and to spire[6] thrice upward in the air.
As soon as he came home, straightway Pygmalion did repair
Unto the image of his wench and, leaning on the bed,   305
Did kiss her. In her body straight a warmness seemed to spread.
He put his mouth again to hers and on her breast did lay
His hand. The ivory waxèd soft and, putting quite away
All hardness, yielded underneath his fingers, as we see
A piece of wax made soft against the sun or drawn to be   310
In divers shapes by chafing it between one's hands and so
To serve to uses. He, amazed, stood wavering to and fro
'Tween joy and fear to be beguiled. Again he burnt in love,
Again with feeling he began his wishèd hope to prove.
He felt it very flesh indeed. By laying on his thumb   315
He felt her pulses beating. Then he stood no longer dumb
But thankèd Venus with his heart. And at the length he laid
His mouth to hers who was as then become a perfect maid.
She felt the kiss and blushed thereat and, lifting fearfully
Her eyelids up, her lover and the light at once did spy.   320
The marriage that herself had made the goddess blessèd so
That, when the moon with fulsome light nine times her course had go,[7]
This lady was delivered of a son that Paphos hight,[8]
Of whom the island takes that name.

1 i.e. put   2 purple-dyed textiles made in Tyre, worn by royalty   3 triple rhymes, 289–91, 296–8,
marked with a brace in the 1567 edn   4 i.e. knew full well   5 as a first sample   6 rise   7 i.e. when
nine months had passed   8 was called Paphos

CONEY-CATCHING

Robert Greene wrote pamphlets of different kinds, among them short fictional pieces, published in three parts, describing the 'art of coney-catching', i.e. methods that confidence tricksters and thieves used to steal from people (a 'coney' was a rabbit, hence the name for victims who could be preyed on easily). *The Third and Last Part of Coney-Catching* appeared in 1592. The extract below is from Bullough, 8.217–18, with word forms, spelling and punctuation modernized, and line numbers and annotation supplied.

In Greene's account, a London pickpocket tells how he and his gang used to operate outside the entrances to the public theatres and in markets and other open places. The pickpocket declares how,

> with outward simplicity on the one side and cunning close treachery
> on the other, divers honest citizens and day-labouring men that resort
> to such places as I am to speak of, only for recreation as opportunity
> serveth, have been of late sundry times deceived of their purses. This
> trade, or rather unsufferable loitering quality,[1] in singing of ballets[2]   5
> and songs at the doors of such houses where plays are used,[3] as also
> in open markets and other places of this city, where is most resort;[4]
> which is nothing else but a sly fetch[5] to draw many together who,
> listening unto an harmless ditty, afterward walk home to their houses
> with heavy hearts:[6] from such as are hereof true witnesses to their   10
> cost, do I deliver this example. A subtle fellow, belike emboldened by
> acquaintance with the former deceit, or else being but a beginner to
> practise the same, calling certain of his companions together, would
> try whether he could attain to be master of his art or no, by taking a
> great many of fools with one train.[7] But let his intent and what else   15
> beside remain to abide the censure after the matter is heard, and come
> to Gracious Street,[8] where this villainous prank was performed. A
> roguing mate and such another with him, were there got upon a stall
> singing of ballets which belike was some pretty toy,[9] for very many
> gathered about to hear it, and divers buying, as their affections   20
> served,[10] drew to their purses and paid the singers for them. The sly
> mate and his fellows, who were dispersed among them that stood to

1 intolerable practices that vagrants get up to 2 ballads: see 4.4.275–81n. 3 i.e. playhouses 4 i.e. the busiest places 5 dodge 6 i.e. because cheated or stolen from 7 trick 8 Gracechurch Street, which led to London Bridge 9 pleasing pastime 10 i.e. whatever they liked

hear the songs, well noted where every man that bought put up his purse again, and to such as would not buy, counterfeit[1] warning was sundry times given by the rogue and his associate, to beware of the cut purse, and look to their purses, which made them often feel where their purses were, either in sleeve, hose or at girdle,[2] to know whether they were safe or no. Thus the crafty copesmates[3] were acquainted with what they most desired, and as they were scattered, by shouldering, thrusting, feigning to let fall something and other wily tricks fit for their purpose: here one lost his purse, there another had his pocket picked, and to say all in brief, at one instant, upon the complaint of one or two that saw their purses were gone, eight more in the same company found themselves in like predicament. Some angry, others sorrowful, and all greatly discontented, looking about them knew not who to suspect or challenge, in that the villains themselves that had thus beguiled them made show that they had sustained like loss.

25

30

35

1 fake   2 belt, waistband   3 partners in crime

ABBREVIATIONS AND REFERENCES

Quotations and references to Shakespeare plays other than *The Winter's Tale* are from *The Arden Shakespeare Third Series*, where they exist; other quotations are from *The Arden Shakespeare Complete Works*, ed. Richard Proudfoot, Ann Thompson and David Scott Kastan, rev. edn (2001). Biblical quotations and references are from the Geneva Bible (1560), in modernized form. In all references, place of publication is London unless otherwise stated.

ABBREVIATIONS

ABBREVIATIONS USED IN NOTES

edn	edition
fol., fols	folio, folios
n., nn.	note, notes
n.s.	new series
opp.	opposite
SD	stage direction
sig., sigs	signature, signatures
SP	speech prefix
subst.	substantially
this edn	a reading adopted for the first time in this edition
t.n.	textual note
*	precedes commentary notes on readings which substantively emend F

WORKS BY AND PARTLY BY SHAKESPEARE

AC	*Antony and Cleopatra*
AW	*All's Well That Ends Well*
AYL	*As You Like It*
Car	*The History of Cardenio*
CE	*The Comedy of Errors*
Cor	*Coriolanus*
Cym	*Cymbeline*

DF	Double Falsehood
E3	Edward III
Ham	Hamlet
1H4	King Henry IV Part 1
2H4	King Henry IV Part 2
H5	King Henry V
1H6	King Henry VI Part 1
2H6	King Henry VI Part 2
3H6	King Henry VI Part 3
H8	King Henry VIII
JC	Julius Caesar
KJ	King John
KL	King Lear
LC	A Lover's Complaint
LLL	Love's Labour's Lost
Luc	The Rape of Lucrece
MA	Much Ado About Nothing
Mac	Macbeth
MM	Measure for Measure
MND	A Midsummer Night's Dream
MV	The Merchant of Venice
MW	The Merry Wives of Windsor
Oth	Othello
Per	Pericles
PP	The Passionate Pilgrim
PT	The Phoenix and Turtle
R2	King Richard II
R3	King Richard III
RJ	Romeo and Juliet
Son	Sonnets
STM	Sir Thomas More
TC	Troilus and Cressida
Tem	The Tempest
TGV	The Two Gentlemen of Verona
Tim	Timon of Athens
Tit	Titus Andronicus
TN	Twelfth Night
TNK	The Two Noble Kinsmen
TS	The Taming of the Shrew
VA	Venus and Adonis
WT	The Winter's Tale

REFERENCES

EDITIONS OF SHAKESPEARE COLLATED

Alexander	*Complete Works*, ed. Peter Alexander (1951)
Ard[1]	*The Winter's Tale*, ed. F.W. Moorman, Arden Shakespeare, 1st series (1912)
Ard[2]	*The Winter's Tale*, ed. J.H.P. Pafford, Arden Shakespeare, 2nd series (1963)
Bethell	*The Winter's Tale*, ed. S.L. Bethell, New Clarendon Shakespeare (Oxford, 1956)
Bevington	*Complete Works*, ed. David Bevington, 4th edn (New York, 1997)
Cam	*Works*, ed. W.G. Clark, J. Glover and W.A. Wright, 9 vols (Cambridge, 1863–6)
Cam[1]	*The Winter's Tale*, ed. Arthur Quiller-Couch and John Dover Wilson, New Cambridge Shakespeare, 1st series (Cambridge, 1931)
Cam[2]	*The Winter's Tale*, ed. Susan Snyder and Deborah T. Curren-Aquino, New Cambridge Shakespeare, 2nd series (Cambridge, 2007)
Capell	*Comedies, Histories, and Tragedies*, ed. Edward Capell, 10 vols (1767–8)
Collier	*Works*, ed. John Payne Collier, 8 vols (1842–4)
Delius	*Works* (*Werke*), ed. Nicholas Delius, 7 vols (Elberfeld, Germany, 1854–61)
Dyce	*Works*, ed. Alexander Dyce, 6 vols (1857)
F	*Comedies, Histories, and Tragedies*, The First Folio (1623)
F2	*Comedies, Histories, and Tragedies*, The Second Folio (1632)
F3	*Comedies, Histories, and Tragedies*, The Third Folio (1663–4)
F4	*Comedies, Histories, and Tragedies*, The Fourth Folio (1685)
Folger	*The Winter's Tale*, ed. Barbara A. Mowat and Paul Werstine, New Folger Library Shakespeare (New York, 1998)
Furness	*The Winter's Tale*, ed. Horace Howard Furness, New Variorum Shakespeare (Philadelphia, Penn., and London, 1898)
Hanmer	*Works*, ed. Sir Thomas Hanmer, 6 vols (Oxford, 1743–4)

References

Hudson | *Works*, ed. Henry N. Hudson, 20 vols (Boston and Cambridge, Mass., 1886)

Johnson | *Plays*, ed. Samuel Johnson, 8 vols (1765)

Kermode | *The Winter's Tale*, ed. Frank Kermode, revised edn (New York, 1988)

Knight | *Works*, ed. Charles Knight, 8 vols (1838–43)

Malone | *Works*, ed. Edmond Malone, 10 vols (1790)

Oxf | *Works*, ed. Stanley Wells, Gary Taylor, John Jowett and William Montgomery (Oxford, 1986)

Oxf[1] | *The Winter's Tale*, ed. Stephen Orgel, Oxford Shakespeare (Oxford, 1996)

Pope | *Works*, ed. Alexander Pope, 6 vols (1723–5)

Rann | *The Dramatic Works of Shakespeare*, ed. Joseph Rann, 6 vols (1786–91)

Rowe | *Works*, ed. Nicholas Rowe, 6 vols (1709)

Rowe[3] | *Works*, ed. Nicholas Rowe, 8 vols (1714)

Schanzer | *The Winter's Tale*, ed. Ernest Schanzer, New Penguin Shakespeare (Harmondsworth, England, 1966)

Sisson | *Works*, ed. Charles Jasper Sisson (1954)

Staunton | *Plays*, ed. Howard Staunton, 3 vols (1858–60)

Steevens | *Plays*, ed. Samuel Johnson and George Steevens, 10 vols (1773)

Theobald | *Works*, ed. Lewis Theobald, 7 vols (1733)

Turner | *The Winter's Tale*, ed. Robert Turner, Virginia Westling Haas et al., New Variorum Shakespeare (New York, 2005)

OTHER WORKS CITED

Abbott | E.A. Abbott, *A Shakespearian Grammar*, 2nd edn (1870)

AEB | *Analytical and Enumerative Bibliography*

Aeschylus, *Agamemnon* | Aeschylus, *Agamemnon*, in *Aeschylus: The Oresteia*, trans. Robert Fagles, ed. W.B. Stanford (Harmondsworth, England, 1979)

Altieri | Charles Altieri, 'Wonder in *The Winter's Tale*: a cautionary account of epistemic criticism', in John Gibson, Wolfgang Huemer and Luca Pocci (eds), *A Sense of the World: Essays on Fiction, Narrative, and Knowledge* (New York and London, 2007), 266–85

Archer | William Archer, review, 'The Winter's Tale', *Theatre*, 10 (1887), 214–19

Aristotle	Stephen Halliwell (trans. and ed.), *The Poetics of Aristotle* (1987)
Auerbach	Erich Auerbach, 'Figura', in *Scenes from the Drama of European Literature* (New York, 1959), 11–76
Babb	Lawrence Babb, *The Elizabethan Malady* (East Lansing, Mich., 1951)
Bacon	*Francis Bacon*, ed. Brian Vickers (Oxford, 1996)
Barkan	Leonard Barkan, '"Living sculptures": Ovid, Michelangelo, and *The Winter's Tale*', *ELH*, 48 (1981), 639–67
Barroll	Leeds Barroll, *Politics, Plague, and Shakespeare's Theater* (Ithaca, NY, 1991)
Bartholomeusz	Dennis Bartholomeusz, *'The Winter's Tale' in Performance in England and America 1611–1976* (Cambridge, 1982)
Bate, 'Islands'	Jonathan Bate, 'Shakespeare's Islands', in Tom Clayton, Susan Brock and Vicente Forés (eds), *Shakespeare and the Mediterranean* (Newark, NJ, 2004), 289–307
Bate, *Romantics*	Jonathan Bate (ed.), *The Romantics on Shakespeare* (Harmondsworth, England, 1992)
Bateson	F.W. Bateson, 'How old was Leontes?', *E&S*, 31 (1978), 65–74
Bawcutt, 'Crane'	N.W. Bawcutt (ed.), 'Ralph Crane's transcript of *A Game at Chess*, Bodleian Manuscript Malone 25', *Malone Society Collections Volume XV* (Oxford, 1993), 1–109
Bawcutt, *Herbert*	N.W. Bawcutt (ed.), *The Control and Censorship of Caroline Drama: The Records of Sir Henry Herbert, Master of the Revels 1623–73* (Oxford, 1996)
BCP	*Book of Common Prayer*
Beisley	Sidney Beisley, *Shakespeare's Garden* (1864)
Bevington, 'Modern spelling'	David Bevington, 'Modern spelling: the hard choices', in Lukas Erne and Margaret Jane Kidnie (eds), *Textual Performances* (Cambridge, 2004), 143–57
Bishop	T.G. Bishop, *Shakespeare and the Theatre of Wonder* (Cambridge, 1996)
Blake	N.F. Blake, *Shakespeare's Language: An Introduction* (London and Basingstoke, 1983)
Blayney	Peter W.M. Blayney, *The First Folio of Shakespeare* (Washington, DC, 1991)
Booth, 'Doubling'	Stephen Booth, 'Speculations on doubling in Shakespeare's plays', in Philip C. McGuire and David A Samuelson (eds), *Shakespeare: The Theatrical Dimension* (New York, 1979), 103–31

Booth, 'Exit'   Stephen Booth, 'Exit, pursued by a gentleman born',
                     in Wendell M. Aycock (ed.), *Shakespeare's Art from a*
                     Comparative Perspective (Lubbock, Tex., 1981), 51–66

Briggs   John C. Briggs, 'Catharsis in *The Tempest*', *Ben Jonson*
                     Journal, 5 (1998), 115–32

Buchanan   Euripides, *Alcestis*, trans. George Buchanan, in *George*
                     Buchanan Tragedies, ed. P. Sharrat and P.G. Walsh
                     (Edinburgh, 1983)

Bullough   Geoffrey Bullough, *The Narrative and Dramatic Sources*
                     of Shakespeare, 8 vols (1959–75)

Campbell   Thomas Campbell, *Life of Mrs. Siddons*, 2 vols (1834)

Cavell   Stanley Cavell, *Disowning Knowledge in Six Plays by*
                     Shakespeare (Cambridge, 1987)

Cercignani   Fausto Cercignani, *Shakespeare's Works and Elizabethan*
                     Pronunciation (Oxford, 1981)

Cerasano   S.P. Cerasano, 'Philip Henslowe, Simon Forman, and
                     the theatrical community of the 1590s', *SQ*, 44 (1993),
                     145–58

Chambers   E.K. Chambers, *William Shakespeare*, 2 vols (Oxford, 1930)

Charlton   Andrew Charlton, *Music in the Plays of Shakespeare: A*
                     Practicum (New York and London, 1991)

Chew, *Pilgrimage*   Samuel C. Chew, *The Pilgrimage of Life* (New Haven,
                     Conn., and London, 1962)

Chew, 'Time'   Samuel C. Chew, 'Time and Fortune', *ELH*, 6 (1939),
                     83–113

Colman   E.A.M. Colman, *The Dramatic Use of Bawdy in*
                     Shakespeare (1974)

Cooper   Thomas Cooper, *Thesaurus Linguae Romanae &*
                     Britannicae (1565)

Cotgrave   Randle Cotgrave, *A Dictionary of the French and English*
                     Tongues (1611)

Cressy   David Cressy, *Birth, Marriage, and Death* (Oxford, 1997)

Crider   Scott F. Crider, 'Weeping in the upper world: the Orphic
                     Frame in 5.3 of *The Winter's Tale* and the Archive of
                     Poetry', *Studies in the Literary Imagination*, 32 (1999),
                     153–72

Crosby   Alfred W. Crosby, *The Measure of Reality* (Cambridge,
                     1997)

Curry   Walter Clyde Curry, *Shakespeare's Philosophical Patterns*,
                     2nd edn (Baton Rouge, LA, 1959)

Curtius   *The Historie of Quintus Curtius*, trans. John Brende (1602)

Cutts, 'Musique'	John P. Cutts, 'Le rôle de la musique dans les masques de Ben Jonson', in Jean Jacquot (ed.), *Les Fêtes de la Renaissance* (Paris, 1956), 285–30
Cutts, 'Song'	John P. Cutts, 'An unpublished contemporary setting of a Shakespeare song', *SS 9* (1956), 86–9
da Vinci	*Leonardo da Vinci: Notebooks*, selected by Irma A. Richter, ed. Thereza Wells (Oxford, 2008)
de Grazia, 'Homonyms'	Margreta de Grazia, 'Homonyms before and after lexical standardization', *Jahrbuch* (1990), 143–56
de Grazia, 'Response'	Margreta de Grazia, 'Response to Manford Hanowell's response to "Homonyms before and after lexical standardization"', *Connotations*, 1 (1991), 299–301
Dent	R.W. Dent, *Shakespeare's Proverbial Language: An Index* (Berkeley, Calif., and London, 1981)
Dewar-Watson	Sarah Dewar-Watson, 'The *Alcestis* and the statue-scene in *The Winter's Tale*', *SQ*, 60 (2009), 73–80
Dolan	Frances E. Dolan, 'Hermione's ghost: Catholicism, the feminine, and the undead', in Dympna Callaghan (ed.), *The Impact of Feminism in English Renaissance Studies* (2007), 213–37
Donne	*John Donne: The Major Works*, ed. John Carey (Oxford, 1990)
Duffin	Ross W. Duffin, *Shakespeare's Songbook* (New York and London, 2004)
Duncan-Jones	E.E. Duncan-Jones, 'Hermione in Ovid and Shakespeare', *N&Q*, 211 (1966), 138–9
Eccles	Mark Eccles, 'Middleton's comedy *The Almanac*, or *No Wit, No Help Like a Woman's*', *N&Q*, 232 (1987), 296–7
ELH	*English Literary History*
Eliot, *Daniel Deronda*	George Eliot, *Daniel Deronda*, ed. Barbara Hardy (Harmondsworth, England, 1967)
E&S	*Essays and Studies*
Euripides, *Alcestis*	Euripides, *Alcestis*, in *Alcestis, Hippolytus, Iphigenia in Tauris*, trans. Philip Vellacott (Harmondsworth, England, 1974); see also Buchanan
Euripides, *Aulis*	Euripides, *Iphigenia in Aulis*, in *Orestes and Other Plays*, trans. Philip Vellacott (Harmondsworth, England, 1972)
Euripides, *Tauris*	Euripides, *Iphigenia in Tauris*, in *Alcestis, Hippolytus, Iphigenia in Tauris*, trans. Philip Vellacott (Harmondsworth, England, 1974)

Everett	Barbara Everett, 'Shakespeare's greening', *Times Literary Supplement*, 8 July 1994, 11–13
Fletcher	John Fletcher, *The Faithful Shepherdess*, ed. Florence Ada Kirk (New York and London, 1980)
Fowler	Alastair Fowler, 'Leontes' contrition and the repair of nature', *E&S*, 31 (1978), 36–64
Gasper & Williams	Julia Gasper and Carolyn Williams, 'The meaning of the name "Hermione"', *N&Q*, 231 (1986), 367
Gerard	John Gerard, *The Herbal or General History of Plants* (1597)
Gesner	Carol Gesner, *Shakespeare and the Greek Romance: A Study of Origins* (Lexington, Ky., 1970)
Gibbons	Brian Gibbons, 'Doubles and likenesses-with-difference: *The Comedy of Errors* and *The Winter's Tale*', *Connotations*, 6 (1996/7), 19–40
Gillies	John Gillies, *Shakespeare and the Geography of Difference* (Cambridge, 1994)
Greenblattt	Stephen Greenblatt, *Will in the World* (2004)
Greene, *Coney-Catching*	Robert Greene, *The Third and Last Part of Coney-Catching* (1592)
Greene, *Pandosto*	see *Pandosto*
Greene, T.	Thomas M. Greene, 'Ceremonial play and parody in the Renaissance', in Susan Zimmermann and Ronald F.E. Weissman (eds), *Urban Life in the Renaissance* (Newark, Del., London and Toronto, 1989), 281–93
Gurr, 'Blackfriars'	Andrew Gurr, '*The Tempest*'s Tempest at Blackfriars', *SS 41* (1989), 91–102
Gurr, *Playgoing*	Andrew Gurr, *Playgoing in Shakespeare's London* (Cambridge, 1987)
Haas	Virginia J. Haas, 'Ralph Crane: a status report', *AEB*, 3 (1989), 3–10
Hankins	John Erskine Hankins, *Backgrounds of Shakespeare's Thought* (Hassocks, England, 1978)
Hanowell	Manford Hanowell, 'A response to Margreta de Grazia, "Homonyms before and after lexical standardization"', *Connotations*, 1 (1991), 293–8
Hardman	C.B. Hardman, 'Theory, form, and meaning in Shakespeare's *The Winter's Tale*', *RES*, n.s. 36 (1985), 228–35

Hartwig	Joan Hartwig, 'Cloten, Autolycus, and Caliban: bearers of parodic burdens', in Carol McGinnis Kay and Henry E. Jacobs (eds), *Shakespeare's Romances Reconsidered* (Lincoln, Nebr., and London, 1978), 91–103
Hazlitt	William Hazlitt, *Characters of Shakespear's Plays* (1817)
Hearn	Karen Hearn, 'A fatal fertility? Elizabethan and Jacobean pregnancy portraits', *Costume*, 34 (2000), 39–43
Heath	Benjamin Heath, *A Revisal of Shakespear's Text* (1765)
Heims	Neil Heims, 'Shakespeare's *The Winter's Tale*', *Explicator*, 46 (1988), 6–7
Herbert	*The Autobiography of Edward, Lord Herbert of Cherbury*, ed. Sidney Lee, 2nd edn (1900)
Hinman	Charlton Hinman, *The Printing and Proof-reading of the First Folio of Shakespeare*, 2 vols (Oxford, 1963)
Homer, *Iliad*	Homer, *The Iliad*, trans. Robert Fagles, introduction by Bernard Knox (Harmondsworth, England, 1991)
Homer, *Odyssey*	Homer, *The Odyssey*, trans. Robert Fagles, introduction by Bernard Knox (Harmondsworth, England, 1996)
Honigmann, *Impact*	E.A.J. Honigmann, *Shakespeare's Impact on His Contemporaries* (1982)
Honigmann, *Texts*	E.A.J. Hongmann, *The Texts of 'Othello' and Shakespearian Revision* (1996)
Howard-Hill, 'Crane'	T.H. Howard-Hill, 'Shakespeare's earliest editor, Ralph Crane', *SS 44* (1992), 113–29
Howard-Hill, 'Folio'	T.H. Howard-Hill, 'Knight, Crane, and the copy for the Folio "Winter's Tale"', *N&Q*, 211 (1966), 139–40
Hulme	Hilda M. Hulme, *Explorations in Shakespeare's Language* (1962)
Jahrbuch	*Deutsche Shakespeare-Gesellschaft West: Jahrbuch*
Johnson, *Ayres*	*Robert Johnson: Ayres, Songs and Dialogues*, ed. Ian Spink, revised edn (1974)
Jones	John Jones, *Shakespeare at Work* (Oxford, 1995)
Jones & Stallybrass	Ann Rosalind Jones and Peter Stallybrass, *Renaissance Clothing and the Materials of Memory* (Cambridge, 2000)
Jones & Warren	Owen Jones with Henry Warren, *Scenes from the Winter's Tale* (1866)
Jonson	*Ben Jonson*, ed. C.H. Herford and Percy and Evelyn Simpson, 11 vols (Oxford, 1925–52)
Jowett	John Jowett, 'New created creatures: Ralph Crane and the stage directions in "The Tempest"', *SS 36* (1983), 107–20

Kennedy	Dennis Kennedy, *Granville Barker and the Dream of Theatre* (Cambridge, 1985)
Kerrigan	John Kerrigan, 'Revision, adaptation, and the Fool in *King Lear*', in Gary Taylor and Michael Warren (eds), *The Division of the Kingdoms*, revised pbk edn (Oxford, 1986), 195–245
Kiessling	Nicolas K. Kiessling, '*The Winter's Tale*, II.iii.103–7: an allusion to the hag-incubus', *SQ*, 28 (1977), 93–6
King	T.J. King, *Casting Shakespeare's Plays* (Cambridge, 1992)
Kinney	Arthur Kinney (ed.), *Rogues, Vagabonds and Sturdy Beggars* (Amherst, Mass., 1990)
Kökeritz	Helge Kökeritz, *Shakespeare's Pronunciation* (New Haven, Conn., 1953)
Kurland	Stuart M. Kurland, '"We need no more of your advice": political realism in *The Winter's Tale*', *Studies in English Literature*, 31 (1991), 365–86
Laroque	François Laroque, *Shakespeare's Festive World*, trans. Janet Lloyd, revised pbk edn (Cambridge, 1993)
Lees	Francis Noel Lees, 'Plutarch and *The Winter's Tale*', *N&Q*, 221 (1976), 161–2
Leimberg, 'Answer'	Inge Leimberg, 'An answer to Kenneth Muir', *Connotations*, 2 (1992), 290–4
Leimberg, 'Hermione'	Inge Leimberg, '"The image of Golden Aphrodite": some observations on the name "Hermione"', *Jahrbuch* (1988), 130–49
Leimberg, 'Names'	Inge Leimberg, '"Golden Apollo, a poor humble swain . . .": a study of names in *The Winter's Tale*', *Jahrbuch* (1991), 135–58
Levith	Murray J. Levith, *What's in Shakespeare's Names* (London and Sydney, 1978)
Long	John H. Long, *Shakespeare's Use of Music: The Final Comedies* (Gainesville, Fla., 1961)
MacIntyre	Jean MacIntyre, *Costumes and Scripts in the Elizabethan Theatres* (Edmonton, Canada, 1992)
Mack	Maynard Mack, *Rescuing Shakespeare* (Oxford, 1979)
Mahood	M.M. Mahood, *Shakespeare's Wordplay* (1957)
Maisano	Scott Maisano, 'Shakespeare's last act: The Starry Messenger and the Galilean book in *Cymbeline*', *Configurations*, 12 (2004), 401–34
Marcus	Leah Sinanoglou Marcus, *Childhood and Cultural Despair* (Pittsburgh, Penn., 1978)

Marvell	*Andrew Marvell: The Complete Poems*, ed. Elizabeth Story Donno (Harmondsworth, England, 1972)
Middleton	*Thomas Middleton: A Mad World, My Masters and other plays*, ed. Michael Taylor (Oxford, 1995)
Milton	*John Milton: The Major Works*, ed. Stephen Orgel and Jonathan Goldberg, revised pbk edn (Oxford, 2003)
Miola	Robert S. Miola, 'New comedy in *King Lear*', *Philological Quarterly*, 73 (1994), 329–46
'Mr Punch'	Anonymous reviews, 'Winter's Tale' and 'Mr. Kean's "Winter's Tale"', *Punch*, 30 (1856), 190, 198–9
Mucedorus	Anon., *Mucedorus* (*c.* 1590), in *The Shakespeare Apocrypha*, ed. C.F. Tucker Brooke (Oxford, 1908)
Muir, 'Naming'	Kenneth Muir, 'A comment on the naming of characters in *The Winter's Tale*', *Connotations*, 2 (1992), 287–90
Muir, 'Pentameter'	Kenneth Muir, 'Shakespeare and the metamorphosis of the pentameter', *SS 50* (1997), 147–50
Muir, 'Trick of style'	Kenneth Muir, 'A trick of style and some implications', *Shakespeare Studies*, 6 (1970), 305–10
Murphy	Arthur Murphy, *The Life of David Garrick*, 2 vols (1801)
Musgrove	S. Musgrove, 'Thieves' cant in *King Lear*', *English Studies*, 62 (1981), 5–13
N&Q	*Notes and Queries*
Nevo	Ruth Nevo, *Shakespeare's Other Language* (1987)
Newcombe	Lori Humphrey Newcombe, *Reading Popular Romance in Early Modern England* (New York, 2002)
Nicoll	Allardyce Nicoll, 'Shakespeare and the court masque', *SJ*, 94 (1958), 51–62
Nightingale	Benedict Nightingale, 'Leontes syndrome?', *New Statesman*, 23 May 1969, 745–6
OED	*Oxford English Dictionary* (*OED Online*, 2009) (http://dictionary.oed.com)
Orgel	*The Tempest*, ed. Stephen Orgel (Oxford, 1987)
Orton	Anne Orton, *Tudor Food and Cookery* (1985)
Ovid, *Met.*	*Ovid's Metamorphoses Translated by Arthur Golding*, ed. Madeleine Forey (2002)
Pafford	J.H.P. Pafford, '"The Winter's Tale": typographical peculiarities in the Folio text', *N&Q*, 206 (1961), 172–8

References

Pandosto	Robert Greene, *Pandosto: The Triumph of Time* and *The History of Dorastus and Fawnia* (1588); text reproduced, with missing pages taken from 1592 reprint, in Bullough, 8.156–99. Page references in the commentary are to the modernized text in this edition.
Panofsky	Erwin Panofsky, *Studies in Iconology* (New York, 1972)
Parker, F.	Fred Parker, 'Regression and romance in Shakespeare's late plays', *Cambridge Quarterly*, 24 (1995), 112–32
Parker, P., *Margins*	Patricia Parker, *Shakespeare from the Margins* (Chicago and London, 1996)
Parker, P., 'Polymorphic'	Patricia Parker, 'Sound government, polymorphic bears: *The Winter's Tale* and other metamorphoses of eye and ear', in Helen Reguerio Elam and Frances Ferguson (eds), *The Wordsworthian Enlightenment* (Baltimore, Md., 2005), 172–90
Partridge	Eric Partridge, *Shakespeare's Bawdy*, revised edn (1968)
Partridge, *Slang*	Eric Partridge, abridged by Jacqueline Simpson, *The Penguin Dictionary of Historical Slang* (Harmondsworth, England, 1972)
Paster	Gail Kern Paster, *The Body Embarrassed* (Ithaca, NY, 1993)
Pattison	Bruce Pattison, *Music and Poetry of the English Renaissance* (1948)
Pettie	George Pettie, *A Petite Pallace of Pettie His Pleasure*, ed. Herbert Hartman (1938)
Pitcher, 'Autolycus'	John Pitcher, 'Some call him Autolycus', in Ann Thompson and Gordon McMullan (eds), *In Arden: Editing Shakespeare* (2003), 252–68
Pitcher, 'Bear'	John Pitcher, '"Fronted with the sight of a bear": *Cox of Collumpton* and *The Winter's Tale*', *N&Q*, 239 (1994), 47–53
Pitcher, *Cymbeline*	John Pitcher (ed.), *Cymbeline*, Penguin Shakespeare (2005)
Plutarch	Plutarch, *The Lives of the Noble Grecians and Romans*, trans. Thomas North (1579)
Progresses	*The Progresses and Public Processions of Queen Elizabeth*, ed. John Nichols, 3 vols (1788–1805)
Randall	Dale B.J. Randall, '"This is the chase": or, the further pursuit of Shakespeare's bear', *SJ*, 121 (1985), 89–95

Ravelhofer	Barbara Ravelhofer, '"Beasts of recreacion": Henslowe's white bears', *English Literary Renaissance*, 32 (2002), 287–323
RES	*Review of English Studies*
Richardson, *Clarissa*	Samuel Richardson, *Clarissa* (Harmondsworth, England, 1985)
Roach	Joseph Roach, 'Makeup of memory in *The Winter's Tale*', *Modern Language Quarterly*, 70 (2009), 117–31
Roberts	Peter Roberts, review, 'Winter's Tale', *Plays and Players*, 16 (1969), 30–3
Rubinstein	Frankie Rubinstein, *A Dictionary of Shakespeare's Sexual Puns and their Significance*, 2nd edn (1989)
Sabol	Andrew J. Sabol, *Songs and Dances for the Stuart Masque* (Providence, RI, 1959)
Sanders	Wilbur Sanders, *The Winter's Tale* (Brighton, England, 1987)
Schanzer, '*Ages*'	Ernest Schanzer, 'Heywood's *Ages* and Shakespeare', *RES*, 11 (1960), 18–28
Schleiner	Louise Schleiner, 'Latinized Greek drama in Shakespeare's writing of *Hamlet*', *SQ*, 41 (1990), 29–48
Seng	Peter J. Seng, *The Vocal Songs in the Plays of Shakespeare* (Cambridge, Mass., 1967)
Shaheen	Naseeb Shaheen, *Biblical References in Shakespeare's Plays* (Newark, NJ, and London, 1999)
Sherman	Stuart Sherman, *Telling Time* (Chicago, Ill., and London, 1996)
Shirley	Frances Ann Shirley, *Shakespeare's Use of Off-stage Sounds* (Lincoln, Nebr., 1963)
Sidney, *Defence*	Sir Philip Sidney, *The Defence of Poesy*, in *Sir Philip Sidney: The Major Works*, ed. Katherine Duncan-Jones, revised edn (Oxford, 2002)
Sidney, *New Arcadia*	Sir Philip Sidney, *The Countess of Pembroke's Arcadia* (*The New Arcadia*, 1590), ed. Maurice Evans (Harmondsworth, England, 1977)
Simpson	Claude M. Simpson, *The British Broadside Ballad and Its Music* (New Brunswick, NJ, 1966)
SJ	*Shakespeare-Jahrbuch*
Smith, *Acoustic*	Bruce R. Smith, *The Acoustic World of Early Modern England* (Chicago and London, 1999)
Smith, H., '*Affectio*'	Hallett Smith, 'Leontes' *Affectio*', *SQ*, 14 (1963), 163–6

465

Smith, H., *Romances*	Hallett Smith, *Shakespeare's Romances* (San Marino, Calif., 1972)
Snyder	Susan Snyder, 'Mamillius and gender polarization in *The Winter's Tale*', *SQ*, 50 (1999), 1–8
Sophocles, *Oedipus*	Sophocles, *Oedipus the King*, in *The Three Theban Plays*, trans. Robert Fagles, ed. Bernard Knox (Harmondsworth, England, 1984)
Spencer	Terence Spencer, 'Shakespeare's Isle of Delphos', *Modern Language Review*, 47 (1952), 199–202
Spenser, *FQ*	Edmund Spenser, *The Faerie Queene*, ed. Thomas P. Roche, Jr, with the assistance of C. Patrick O'Donnell, Jr (Harmondsworth, England, 1978)
Sprague	Arthur Colby Sprague, *Shakespearian Players and Performances* (1954)
SQ	*Shakespeare Quarterly*
SS	*Shakespeare Survey*
Sternfeld	'F.W.S[ternfeld].', 'Masque', review of Sabol, *Songs*, *Music and Letters*, 40 (1959), 397–9
Tarlinskaja	Marina Tarlinskaja, *Shakespeare's Verse* (New York, 1987)
Tatspaugh	Patricia E. Tatspaugh, *The Winter's Tale* (2002)
Tayler	Edward William Tayler, *Nature and Art in Renaissance Literature* (New York and London, 1964)
Taylor	*All the Works of John Taylor the Water Poet* (1630)
Taylor, P.	Paul Taylor, review, 'She shines in a Tale wonderfully told', *Independent*, 7 January 1999
Taylor & Jowett	Gary Taylor and John Jowett, *Shakespeare Reshaped 1606–1623* (Oxford, 1993)
Thatcher	David Thatcher, '*The Winter's Tale*, I.ii.186', *Studia Neophilologica*, 59 (1987), 207–8
Thomas	Keith Thomas, *Religion and the Decline of Magic* (1973)
Thompson	Ann Thompson, 'Casting sense between the speech: parentheses in the Oxford Shakespeare', *AEB*, 4 (1990), 72–90
Tilley	Morris Palmer Tilley, *A Dictionary of the Proverbs in England in the Sixteenth and Seventeenth Centuries* (Ann Arbor, Mich., 1950)
Travitsky	Betty S. Travitsky, 'Husband-murder and petty treason in English Renaissance tragedy', *Renaissance Drama*, 21 (1990), 171–98

Tusser	Thomas Tusser, *A Hundred Good Points of Husbandry*, 1557
TxC	*William Shakespeare, A Textual Companion*, ed. Stanley Wells and Gary Taylor with John Jowett and William Montgomery (Oxford, 1987)
Venezky	Alice Venezky, 'Current Shakespearian productions in England and France', *SQ*, 2 (1951), 335–42
Virgil, *Aeneid*	Virgil, *The Aeneid*, in *Virgil*, trans. H. Rushton Fairclough, 2 vols, revised edn (Cambridge, Mass., and London, 1935)
Ward	John M. Ward, 'The Lute Books of Trinity College, Dublin II: MS. D.1.21 (the so-called Ballet Lute Book)', *Lute Society Journal*, 10 (1968), 14–32
Warren	*Cymbeline*, ed. Roger Warren (Oxford, 1998)
Weis	René Weis (ed.), *King Lear: A Parallel Text Edition* (London and New York, 1993)
Wells	Stanley Wells, *Modernizing Shakespeare's Spelling*, with Gary Taylor, *Three Studies in the Text of Henry V* (Oxford, 1979)
Williams	Gordon Williams, *A Dictionary of Sexual Language and Imagery in Shakespeare and Stuart Literature*, 3 vols (London and Atlantic Highlands, NJ, 1994)
Willughby	David Cram, Jeffrey L. Forgeng and Dorothy Johnston (eds), *Francis Willughby's Book of Games* (Aldershot, England, 2003)
Wilson	Douglas B. Wilson, 'Euripides' *Alcestis* and the ending of Shakespeare's *The Winter's Tale*', *Iowa State Journal of Research*, 58 (1984), 345–55
Woodward	Donald Woodward (ed.), *The Farming and Memorandum Books of Henry Best of Elmswell 1642* (1984)
Wooldridge	H. Ellis Wooldridge, *Old English Popular Music by William Chappell*, 2 vols (1893)
Wright	George T. Wright, *Shakespeare's Metrical Art* (Berkeley, Los Angeles and Oxford, 1988)

PRODUCTIONS CITED

Giffard, 1741	Covent Garden, London, directed by Henry Giffard
Morgan, 1754	Adapted as *The Sheep-Shearing: or, Florizel and Perdita*, Covent Garden, London, directed by Macnamara Morgan
Garrick, 1756	Adapted as *Florizel and Perdita*, Drury Lane, London, directed by David Garrick
Kemble, 1802	Drury Lane, London, directed by John Philip Kemble
Macready, 1823	Drury Lane, London, directed by William Charles Macready
Phelps, 1845	Sadler's Wells, London, directed by Samuel Phelps
Kean, 1856	Princess's Theatre, London, directed by Charles Kean
Anderson, 1887	Lyceum Theatre, London, and Palmer's Theatre, New York, directed by Mary Anderson
Beerbohm Tree, 1906	His Majesty's Theatre, London, directed by Herbert Beerbohm Tree
Granville-Barker, 1912	Savoy Theatre, London, directed by Harley Granville-Barker
Brook, 1951	Phoenix Theatre, London, directed by Peter Brook
Nunn, 1969	Royal Shakespeare Theatre, RSC, Stratford-upon-Avon, directed by Trevor Nunn
Hands, 1986	Royal Shakespeare Theatre, RSC, Stratford-upon-Avon, directed by Terry Hands
Arden, 1992	Lyric Theatre, Hammersmith, London, Théâtre de Complicité, directed by Annabel Arden
Donnellan, 1999	St Petersburg Maly Theatre, UK tour, directed by Declan Donnellan
Doran, 1999	Royal Shakespeare Theatre, RSC, Stratford-upon-Avon, 1999, directed by Gregory Doran

INDEX

Page numbers in italics refer to illustrations.

Index